River Thame

Bierton

Ivinghoe Beacon

Wheathampstead

Coldharbour
Farm Aylesbury

Aston Clinton

Welwyn Garden City

Berkhamstead

Beech Bottom Dyke
Verulamium

Pulpit Hill

Chinnor

River Chess

River Lea or Lee

Kingston Blount

tlington
ell Salome

on

River Wye

River Misbourne

Marlow

Newington

River Thames

Bisham

The Lee Denham

Colne Brook

Furze Platt

Uxbridge

oke

Taplow
Marsh Lane East
Lots Hole

Maidenhead

Cippenham Slough

Lower Bolney

Weir Bank
Stud Farm Bray

Lake End Road East

Prospect Park

Acton

River Thames

Stanwell

Perry Oaks/T5

Chertsey

Eton

Cranford Lane

Isleworth

Whitchurch

Lower Mill
Farm

Imperial Sports Ground

Brentford
Syon Park

Thames
Valley Park

River Loddon

Dorney
Eton Rowing
Course

Windsor Castle

Caesar's Camp

Marsh Lane
West

Old Windsor

Staines Moor

Mayfield Farm

Boveney Court

Horton

Hengrove Farm

Marshall Hills

Church Lammas

Ashford Prison
Littleton Reservoir

Vicarage Road
Sunbury

Teddington Lock

Reading
Buisness Park
and Green Park

Ashridge Wood

Petters Sports Field
Runnymede

Staines

Kingston

e Lea Park
ts Farm
d

Park Farm Binfield

Thorpe Leigh
Nurseries

Home Farm Laleham
Fairylands

Hurst Park
East Molesey

Sunningdale

St Ann's Hill

Shepperton

Riseley

Abbey Meads Chertsey

Oaklands Park
Walton-on-Thames

Carlshalton

Blackwater River

Addlestone

Weybridge

Yateley

Wey Manor Farm
Brooklands

River Hart

St George's Hill

River Mole

Tongham Nurseries

Runfold

Weston Wood Albury

Betchworth

River Wey

Farley Heath

Hambledon

CW00687592

The Thames through Time

The Archaeology of the Gravel Terraces of the Upper and Middle Thames

The Thames Valley in Late Prehistory: 1500 BC–AD 50

by George Lambrick with Mark Robinson

and with contributions by
Tim Allen

Illustrated by Magdalena Wachnik
with Peter Lorimer

Oxford Archaeology
Thames Valley Landscapes Monograph No. 29
2009

The preparation and publication of this volume has been funded by English Heritage from the Aggregates Levy Sustainability Fund

Published for Oxford Archaeology by Oxford University School of Archaeology as part of the Thames Valley Landscapes Monograph series

Designed by Oxford Archaeology Graphics Office

Edited by Lisa Brown
Thames Through Time series editor: Anne Dodd

This book is part of a series of monographs about the Thames Valley Landscapes, which can be bought from all good bookshops and internet bookshops
For more information visit www.thehumanjourney.net

ISBN: 9780-954962791

Typeset by Production Line, Oxford
Printed in Great Britain by Information Press, Eynsham, Oxford

Contents

CHAPTER 1 – INTRODUCTION: CHANGE AND SOCIETY IN LATE PREHISTORY *by George Lambrick*

CHAPTER 2 – SETTING THE SCENE: THE NATURAL ENVIRONMENT AND THE GEOGRAPHY OF SETTLEMENT *by Mark Robinson and George Lambrick*

CHAPTER 3 – DIVIDING UP THE COUNTRYSIDE *by George Lambrick*

CHAPTER 4 – SETTLEMENTS AND SETTLEMENT PATTERNS *by George Lambrick with contributions by Tim Allen*

CHAPTER 5 – HEARTH AND HOME: BUILDINGS AND DOMESTIC CULTURE *by George Lambrick*

CHAPTER 6 – MAKING A LIVING: PRODUCTION AND EXCHANGE *by George Lambrick with contributions by Mark Robinson*

CHAPTER 7 – LIVING OFF THE LAND: FARMING, WATER, STORAGE AND WASTE *by Mark Robinson and George Lambrick*

CHAPTER 10 – CONCLUSIONS: THE IMPACT OF CHANGE AND LEGACIES OF LATE PREHISTORIC SOCIETY *by George Lambrick*

Figures

Preface

In common with other volumes in the *Thames Through Time* series, this account of the Thames Valley in the millennium and a half before the Roman conquest seeks to examine change in human society from a thematic point of view. The geographical and chronological framework for this volume is established in Chapters 1 and 2, but thereafter we have tried to get away from the traditional, somewhat artificial pigeon-holes of 'periods' 'ages' 'eras' and 'phases' to look much harder at how change in human society actually works.

In a period when the 20th century has come to dominate secondary school history and much popular television, the notion that the first foundations of modern society can be traced back more than 3000 years may seem a rather surprising proposition. But some fundamental patterns of settlement and landuse, political boundaries, human impact on the environment, and even the specific use and form of a few places can be traced back to late prehistoric times despite millennia of subsequent change – even though otherwise we may now have very little in common with those remote ancestors. Exploring these issues on a thematic basis should help us to gain a better understanding of how human society evolves and also of how people have altered their natural environment, providing a better long term perspective on what we are doing to the planet.

Compiling this first major review of late pre-history for the whole of the non-tidal part of the Thames Valley has been both a challenge and a journey of exploration that could have taken much longer than the time available. I do not doubt that there are still errors, misunderstandings and omissions that deserve to be corrected, and some ideas that would have warranted more considered development; but I hope that any shortcomings that remain in these respects are at least partly offset by the relative freshness of much of the material that it has been possible to compile alongside older, more familiar results.

George Lambrick
July 2008

Acknowledgements

I would like to thank Mark Robinson and Tim Allen not only for their contributions to this book, but also for many fruitful discussions. I very much appreciate the major contribution of Magda Wachnik who has compiled all the illustrations with the sole exception of figure 5.8, for which I am grateful to Peter Lorimer.

I would like to thank Lisa Brown not only for many helpful comments and discussions, but also in particular for her support in editing the main text, compiling the picture essays and advising on illustrations. Ian Scott has been most helpful in obtaining copyright clearances. The French and German translations of the summary are by Magali Bailliot and Nathalie Haudecoeur-Wilks and Markus Dylewski respectively, and the index has been compiled by Paul Backhouse.

I am very grateful to Rob Poulton for his guidance on material relating to the Surrey and Middlesex part of the Middle Thames Valley, and for many other valuable comments and observations. I have also benefited from valued discussions, and in several instances comments on earlier drafts, from many other colleagues, including Alistair Barclay, Paul Booth, Richard Bradley, Gill Campbell, Chris Hayden, Gill Hey, Hugo Lamdin-Whymark, Gary Lock, John Moore, Fiona Roe, Kelly Powell, Alex Smith, Leo Webley, Chris Welch and Ken Welsh.

We are very grateful to the many colleagues and institutions who have provided us with images and allowed us use of the copyright material detailed in the list of picture credits at the start of this volume. An important element in compiling the book has been the opportunity to refer to numerous unpublished draft reports (as indicated in the bibliography) made available directly or indirectly by several individuals and organisations who have been working in the Thames Valley. In expressing my appreciation to their authors and contributors (with apologies for any misinterpretations), it is also important for the reader to appreciate that some of the conclusions reflected may be modified prior to final publication.

I would like to thank Anne Dodd for giving us the opportunity to contribute this volume to the Thames Through Time series, and for her support and that of Paul Backhouse in guiding it through to publication.

The volume has been funded by English Heritage with grants from the Aggregates Levy Sustainability Fund, and we are grateful to Buzz Busby and the Historic Environment Commissions team at English Heritage and the Project Officer, Helen Keeley, for their support and encouragement.

George Lambrick

Summary

The Thames Valley has been important for understanding late prehistory for 150 years. The landscape changed from being dominated by monuments and mobile patterns of residence to more organised forms of landuse and settlement. The dynamics of change were more subtle than is sometimes portrayed, but by the end of the period the impact of later prehistoric farming on the environment was altering the way that people used the landscape.

Around 800BC, the balance of economic development shifted from the Middle to the Upper Thames perhaps reflecting socio-economic disruption combined with differential population pressure. Agricultural surpluses were exchanged for prized products, and the region has produced evidence of the earliest specialist iron working in Britain.

Increasingly large defensive enclosures became the main communally built expressions of socio-political cohesion and rivalry. By the end of the period even larger communal works reflect the emergence of a new tribal politics prior to Roman annexation.

Traditions of how and where the dead were disposed of changed over the period but less radically than is often supposed. Deposition of metalwork, other objects and human body parts in the river and placing of burials in and around settlement areas were relatively constant features.

Zusammenfassung

Das Themsental ist seit 150 Jahren ein wichtiger Bestandteil des Verständnisses der späten Vorgeschichte. Es vollzog sich ein Wandel von einer durch Monumente und nicht sesshafte Strukturen geprägten Landschaft, hin zu einer weitaus organisierteren Form von Landnutzung und Siedlungen. Der Ablauf dieses Umbruchs war viel feiner als oftmals dargestellt, doch am Ende der Ära erzeugte der Einfluss, welchen der spätvorgeschichtliche Ackerbau auf die Umwelt hatte, einen Wandel in der Art und Weise wie der Mensch die Landschaft nutzte.

Um 800 v.Chr. verlagerte sich die wirtschaftliche Stärke vom mittleren zum oberen Tal der Themse, möglicherweise einhergehend mit sozialökonomischen Störungen und unterschiedlichem Bevölkerungsdruck. Landwirtschaftliche Überschüsse wurden gegen wertvolle Produkte eingetauscht und in der Region finden sich Hinweise auf die früheste Spezialisierung im Eisenhandwerk in Großbritannien.

Zunehmend größere, gemeinschaftlich angelegte, fortifikatorische Anlagen wurden zum Ausdruck sozialpolitischen Zusammenhalts und gleichsam zum Ausdruck von Rivalität. Gegen Ende dieser Periode reflektieren kommunale Großprojekte das Aufkommen einer neuen Stammespolitik im Vorfeld der römischen Annektierung.

Bestattungssitten, wo und wie die Toten beigesetzt wurden, veränderten sich durch die Generationen, jedoch nicht so drastisch wie oftmals angenommen. Deponierungen von Metallgegenständen und anderen Objekten sowie menschlichen Körperteilen in Flüssen und der Nähe von Siedlungen waren relativ beständige Merkmale.

Résumé

Les 150 dernières années nous ont permis d'arriver à une bien meilleure compréhension des dernières phases de la Préhistoire de la vallée de la Tamise.

Entre l'apparition de monuments et de divers types d'implantations saisonnières et celle d'une exploitation et d'une occupation plus structurées du sol, le paysage s'est modifié. Ce processus s'est opéré de façon bien plus subtile qu'on ne veut bien le croire habituellement. Toutefois, à la fin de la Préhistoire, l'impact de l'agriculture était tel qu'il a entraîné une exploitation de l'environnement différente.

Vers 800 av. J-C, l'équilibre économique se déplace du centre au bassin supérieur de la Tamise. Les surplus stockés étaient manifestement échangés contre les produits de valeur. La région se présente également comme un secteur de production de fer dont les gisements archéologiques sont à ce jour les plus précoces de Grande Bretagne.

Ces changements correspondent très certainement à des bouleversements socio-économiques supplées par une cohabitation – probablement conflictuelle - entre les différentes populations du territoire. En effet, à la même époque, on assiste à l'implantation progressive de vastes enclos défensifs qui, sans nul doute, traduisent les rapports de rivalité entre différents groupes ainsi qu'une cohésion socio-politique interne.

Juste avant la conquête romaine, de plus vastes édifices encore attestent de façon très nette l'émergence d'une nouvelle forme de politique qui devait alors structurer chaque tribu de la vallée de la Tamise.

Les modalités des rites funéraires ont évolué tout au long de la Préhistoire mais sans doute moins radicalement qu'on ne le suppose. Elles ne présentent pas de variations majeures, qu'il s'agisse du dépôt de mobilier (métallique etc...) et de dépouilles dans les cours d'eau ou de l'implantation des sépultures au sein ou aux environs des secteurs d'habitats.

Picture credits

Academic Press, (Dunning 1976 in Harding (ed) 1976, after p. 372, fig. 2) Fig. 5.9 (c, Salmonsbury)

© A. Lang and Bartlett-Clark Geophysical Consultants, (Lang 2009) Fig.4.21 (Rollright Heath magnetometer survey)

© Ashmolean Museum, University of Oxford, Fig. 1.6 (air photograph Cassington); 1.12 (c, & d, early and middle Iron Age pottery), 9.15 (air photograph Cherbury);

Ashmolean Museum, University of Oxford, and Council for British Archaeology, (Catling 1982, after fig.56) Fig. 9.1 (Standlake stone circle);

John Barrett, (Barrett 1973, Trans London Middlesex Archaeol Soc. 24, after p 123, fig. 7 with additions) Figs 8.7, (Barrett 1973, Trans London Middlesex Archaeol Soc. 24, after p 128, fig. 9) 8.9 (Sunningdale urnfield).

Berkshire Archaeological Committee (Richards 1978, fig. 11) Fig. 3.10

Berkshire Archaeological Society, Berkshire Archaeological Journal, (Johnston and Bowden 1985 vol 72 1983-85, after fig. 5) Fig. 5.10 (Pingewood)

Richard Bradley and Ann Ellison, (Bradley and Ellison 1975, fig. 2.21) Figs 5.11 (Rams Hill building), (Bradley and Ellison 1975, fig. 3.2) 7.1 (Rams Hill tool marks), (Bradley and Ellison 1975, after fig. 2.28) 7.12 (Rams Hill lynchets); (Bradley and Ellison 1975, after fig. 2.20) 9.9;

British Geological Survey, Figs 2.2 (topography), 2.3 (IPR/82-43C), background topography of Figs 2.4, 3.8, 4.20, 6.13 (2 maps), 9.19, 9.23 (3 maps), 9.24;

© Copyright the Trustees of The British Museum, Figs 5.17 (a, Weybridge bucket, b, Battersea cauldron), 5.20 (Aston Herts. mirror, Welwyn bronze human head), 5.21 (Crow Down hoard), 6.17 (bronze spoon, decorated spearhead, both R. Thames, Hounslow hoard boar figurines, Welwyn glass counters), 8.2 (Chertsey shield; Waterloo Bridge helmet);

© Copyright the Trustees of The British Museum, British Museum Press, (Needham 1991, after fig 51) Figs 5.10 (Runnymede rectilinear building), (Needham and Spence 1996, fig. 100, M24) 5.20 (Runnymede tweezers); (Needham and Spence 1996, fig. 101, B16) 6.8 (c, bone awls); (Needham and Spence 1996, plates 20-21) 6.9 (flint temper; bone burnishers), (Needham and Spence 1996, fig. 108) 7.18 (rubbish disposal), (Needham 2000, fig. 11.9) 7.18 (plan of the island midden site);

Copyright reserved (photography by Cambridge University Collection of Air Photographs), Figs 1.6 (air photographs Port Meadow, and Gravelly Guy), 3.11 (air photograph Frilford)

Cheltenham Museum and Art Gallery, Fig. 5.22 (Birdlip glass bead);

© Corinium Museum, Cotswold District Council, Fig. 6.17 (South Cerney harness mount);

The Master and Fellows of Corpus Christi College, Cambridge (CCC MS 313, f 99r) Fig. 1.1;

Courtesy and © Cotswold Archaeology (Hancock *et al.* 2003) 4.23 (Foxley Fields, Finmere), (Cotswold 2004) 5.10 (Radley); 6.17 (Phallic object, Taplow pipeline);

Philip Dixon, (after Dixon 1973, p. 11) Fig. 5.6 (Crickley Hill)

English Heritage, Fig. 9.13 (air photograph of middle Iron Age fort; magnetometer survey, Uffington);

Framework Archaeology, Figs 3.6; 3.13 (Perry Oaks); 4.14 (plan; reconstruction: Karen Nichols), 5.6 (Perry Oaks), 5.16 (e, wooden bowl), 5.17 ('feasting set'), 5.22 (finger ring, Perry Oaks), 6.5 (log ladder Perry Oaks); 6.6 (a and b, wooden axe hafts, Perry Oaks), 7.8 (Perry Oaks), 7.15 (waterhole; ramped well; wattle lining all Perry Oaks);

Gloucester City Museum & Art Gallery, Figs 5.22 (Birdlip necklace), 8.18 (Birdlip mirror burial group);

D W Harding (Harding 1972, pl. 77 H) Fig. 6.18 (Iron Age bridle bit from Hagbourne), (Harding 1972, pl. 76 D) 7.2 (c, Standlake knife with bone handle), (Harding 1972, pl 76 H) Fig. 7.11 (Frilford ard), (Harding 1972, pl. 34 b) 8.12 (Frilford bagged burial; roundhouse plan), (Harding 1972, after pl. 33) 9.4 (Frilford plan), (Harding 1972, pl 79 D) Fig. 9.7 (Little Wittenham chape);

George Lambrick, Fig. 1.5, 9.10, 9.16 (photographs);

Museum of London, Fig. 1.12 (a, middle Bronze Age urn), 5.17 (c, Brentford tankard), 5.20 (2 razors, from Thames at Old England; razors, Richmond and Syon Reach), 5.21 (gold earrings), 5.22 (phalera, 2 pins and ring headed pin, Syon Reach; ring headed pin, Hammersmith; glass beads, Richmond and Brentford; brooch, Heathrow and 2 brooches, Hammersmith), 6.6 (d, f-h), 6.8 (g, reconstructed Iron Age chisel), 6.17 (Brentford chariot hub), 7.2 (b, reconstructed late Bronze Age sickle; f, Kingston reaping hook), 7.11 (Bronze Age Ploughing: © Museum of London/Derek Lucas), 8.2 (Mortlake dagger); 9.8 (Fortified Enclosure (© Museum of London/Frank Gardiner);

Museum of London and Layton Collection, Fig. 8.2 (Mortlake sword);

The London Archaeologist (vol. 9, no. 11, p. 299, fig. 5) Fig. 3.12 (Imperial College Sports Ground)

National Monuments Record © Crown Copyright, NMR (air photographs), Figs 4.21 (NMR 15350/33 SP 3431/12 20 Jul 1995), 9.12 (US/7PH/GP/LOC93 frame 5032 2 Dec 1943), 9.13 (NMR 14967/27 SU

Eric Penser, Fig. 1.9 (photographs);

Images provided courtesy of the Portable Antiquities Scheme, (PAS ref: BERK-A46EE4) Figs 6.6 (e, chisel, Oxfordshire), (PAS ref: BERK-2C4F55) 6.18 (terret, Steventon), (PAS ref: BUC-033BD2) 9.7 (Henley spearhead)

Prehistoric Society, Proceedings (Collard, *et al.* 2006, vol 72, fig. 8) Fig. 4.19, (Collard, et al 2006, vol 72, fig. 5) 5.9 (Hartshill Copse), (Collard, *et al.* 2006, vol 72, fig. 5) 5.10 (Hartshill Copse), (Fulford and Creighton 1998, vol 64, fig. 3) 5.20 (Latchmere Green mirror), (Farley 1983, vol. 49, pl. 35) 5.20 (Dorton mirror), (Collard *et al.* 2006, vol 72, fig. 8) 6.16 (Hartshill Copse), (Grimes and Close-Brooks 1993, vol 59, p. 310, fig. 5) 9.3 (Heathrow Caesar's Camp), (Collard *et al.*, vol 72, fig. 18 and plate 1) 9.6 (Hartshill Copse plan);

Reading Museum, Fig. 5.21 (Moulsford torc), 8.2 (currency bars);

Dr Mark Robinson, Fig. 2.9 (photograph);

Royal Anthropological Institute, London, (J of the Ethnological Society, Vol 2:4 1870) Fig. 1.3 (plan of Dyke Hills);

SGI-UK Ltd for permission to reproduce photographs of the Taplow Court excavations Fig. 9.18.

Society for the Promotion of Roman Studies and Professor M Fulford (Fulford and Timby 2000, fig. 161, no. 81) 5.20 (Silchester razor handle); (Fulford and Timby 2000, fig.3) 9.25;

© Michael.G.Spiller Fig. 7.13 (modern coppice woodland)

© Hans Splitter, Fig. 6.16 (reconstructed furnace)

Society of Antiquaries, London Fig. 1.2;

© C Stanley Fig. 4.24 (air photograph);

Reproduced courtesy of the Surrey Archaeological Society, (O'Connell 1986, Research Volume 10, fig. 16 S1) Fig. 6.15 (section drawing), Hunt *et al.* 2002, Hidden Depths , p 121) 6.16 (interpretative plan, Brooklands);

Surrey County Council, (Surrey County Archaeological Unit/Giles Pattison) Figs. 3.12 (Hengrove Farm), 3.22 (Hengrove Farm); 4.15 (Lower Mill Farm, Stanwell), 5.7 (Home Farm, Laleham), 6.15 (Petters Sports Field simplified plan), 8.2 (Shepperton Ranges swords);

Surrey County Council, (Surrey County Archaeological Unit/Rob Poulton) 6.6 (c, axe Shepperton), Surrey County Council, (Surrey County Archaeological Unit) 5.5 (Home Farm, Laleham), 5.15 (b, Home Farm, Laleham), 7.15 (excavation of log ladder), 8.2 (dredging), 9.2 (Church Lamma);

Reproduced with permission of Thames Valley Archaeological Services (Ford, *et al.*, 2003, fig. 3.9) 3.22 (Cippenham), (Ford *et al.*, 2003, figs 6.2-6.3) 4.1, (Pine and Preston 2004, fig. 2.12) 4.17 (Horcott, Totterdown Lane);

Neil Thomas, 4.22 (air photograph, Preston);

Reproduced courtesy of the UK Detector Finds Database (UKDFD Ref. 4778) Fig. 6.17 (Aesica brooch)

© Vale of the White Horse District Council, Fig. 10.3 (White Horse logo; air photograph of White Horse Hill)

Reproduced with permission of Wessex Archaeology (Lobb and Rose 1996, figs 15-16) Figs 2.4, (Crockett 2001, p. 299, fig. 5) 3.12 (Imperial College Sports Ground), (Barnes, et al 1995, fig. 8) 3.13 (Weir Bank Stud Farm, Bray), (Andrews and Crockett 1996, fig. 62) 3.17, (Andrews 1996b, after fig. 35) 4.6, (Barnes *et al.*, 1995, after fig. 24) 4.9, (Barnes et al 1997, after fig. 19) 4.25, (Barnes *et al.* 1995, after fig. 35) 5.5, 5.7 (Dunston Park), (Butterworth and Lobb 1992, after fig 23-25) 8.10 (Shortheath Lane);

West Berkshire Council and Cotswold Archaeology, Fig. 9.6 (reconstruction painting: artist Steve Smith);

Wessex Archaeology and Wiltshire Archaeological and Natural History Society (Wiltshire Archaeological Magazine/Wiltshire Studies) (Gingell 1982, vol 76, 1982, p 37, fig. 3) 4.20 (Groundwell Farm), (Gingell 1982, vol 76, 1982, p.42, fig.6, House 2) 5.5 (Groundwell Farm);

Figures 1.7, 1.8, 1.10, 3.7, 3.8, 3.9, 3.13, 3.14, 4.1, 4.11, 4.21, 4.22, 9.13, 9.22, 9.26, reproduced from the Ordnance Survey on behalf of the controller of Her Majesty's Stationery Office, © Crown Copyright, AL10000556

Endpapers and figs 1.2, 2.3, 6.12, 6.13, 8.7 are reproduced under the licence IPR/117-40C British Geological Survey. © NERC 2009. NEXTMap Britain Elevation Data from Intermap Technologies. All rights reserved

Chapter 1 – Introduction: change and society in late prehistory

THE CHANGING SOCIAL, ECONOMIC AND POLITICAL BASIS OF LATE PREHISTORIC SOCIETY

There was an old joke still current in British archaeology in the 1970s that in the Bronze Age people died but never lived, whereas in the Iron Age they lived but never died. In fact the relative abundance of evidence for funerary monuments and settlements between the two periods, on which this sardonic observation was based, has changed radically in the last 30 years in the Thames Valley with the investigation of numerous Bronze Age settlements and field systems and a much clearer understanding of Iron Age burial practices.

Nevertheless, the millennium and a half we are dealing with here saw important changes in how land was used as the basis of human subsistence; how belief systems evolved; how traditions subsisted or began anew; and how power was exercised. There were associated developments in technology, agriculture and exchange that all had long-term ramifications. One of the results was an unprecedented impact on the environment, accelerating loss of tree cover with human interference for the first time inducing changes in the hydrology and sedimentation of the Thames basin on a scale that left a legacy which has affected people's use of the region ever since.

Trajectories of change

At the beginning of the period covered here we should probably envisage that much of the gravel terraces and possibly the floodplain along the floor of the valley had been cleared of trees – especially in areas around the confluences with other tributaries. These were the main focal points of complexes of ceremonial monuments and barrow cemeteries, which, by around 1500 cal BC were past the peak time of monument additions and refashioning, but were still revered and sometimes reused.

Serious expenditure of effort in the organisation of land for farming was only just beginning to shift from basic clearance coupled with mobile lifestyles to a much more sedentary existence with other forms of intensification of landuse through enclosure, artificial water supplies and more permanent settlement. As control of land became more important from the practical point of view of securing stable food supplies and creating wealth and status through highly valued domestic animals, so it seems likely that the source of social, economic and political influence also began to shift. Spiritual and social ties based on individual ancestry, familial connections and communal action may have been no less strong, but became more closely linked to control of land, territory and resources, and less in the creation of ceremonial gathering places and funerary monuments.

In an area with a fair climate and, more importantly, resilient soils, this intensification of landuse and settlement was supported by important technical innovations in tools and equipment and in land management arrangements that enabled settled communities to expand and flourish. Symbolically – and perhaps sometimes actually – territorial and social rivalries were expressed through the construction of massive defensive enclosures, most of which would have absorbed far more communal labour than the ceremonial and funerary monuments of most early prehistoric gathering places. At the same time, large amounts of labour were expended on land clearance and enclosure, probably both facilitated by and encouraging a substantial increase in population.

By the end of the period covered in this volume, we can detect a wide range of settlement types, evidence of specialisation in farming, a concentration of communal investment in a few major political earthworks, and the first emergence of a socio-economic system with coins and the beginnings of proto-urban communities onto which a fully-fledged Roman way of life could quite easily be grafted. The apparent ease and seeming lack of disruption caused by the Roman invasion (see Booth *et al.* 2007), bespeaks a degree of social and economic development that was already well-prepared for transformation over only a few more generations into a more fully urbanised society with a clear basis of property and land ownership, new social hierarchies and a fully fledged monetary economy and system of markets.

The legacy of later prehistory

Although at first sight we might seem to have little in common with our late prehistoric forebears, some of the basic foundations of society and landuse that they laid were permanent ones that in very broad terms are still recognizable today. The Thames Valley two thousand years ago would have been much more familiar to us than it would have been one and a half thousand years earlier. This proposition, that several of the most fundamental and familiar characteristics of the region today can be traced back to developments that took place in the last one and a half millennia BC, might seem a bit surprising, but can be considered within five very broad themes:

- The establishment of lasting broad patterns of settlement and landuse
- The emergence of sophisticated farming
- The emergence of communities living in permanent settlements
- The first inklings of urbanism
- The emergence of political and social control based on land and territory
- The intensification of human impact on the environment

Actual living survivals of what was created in later prehistory are rare, but they are not absent. The more tangible legacies that provide us with a direct living link with late prehistory include the White Horse of Uffington (Fig 1.1), communal grazing on Port Meadow, Oxford, and the River Thames as a political boundary (see Chapter 10). There are other aspects of late prehistoric life, however, which represented just as radical a change from earlier prehistory and survived into the first millennium AD, but then died out leaving little trace in today's world. Perhaps the most obvious of these is religion, wherein many of the practices of late prehistory would be abhorrent to present day European communities of any currently practised faith.

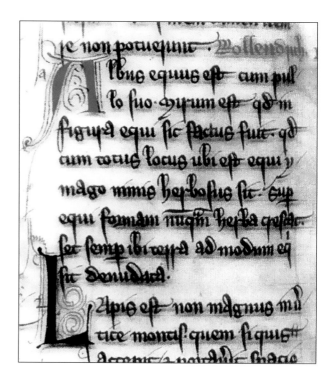

Fig. 1.1 Twelfth century manuscript 'De Mirabilibus Britanniae Abbreviationes Chronicorum' referring to the Uffington White Horse (Corpus Christi College, Cambridge)

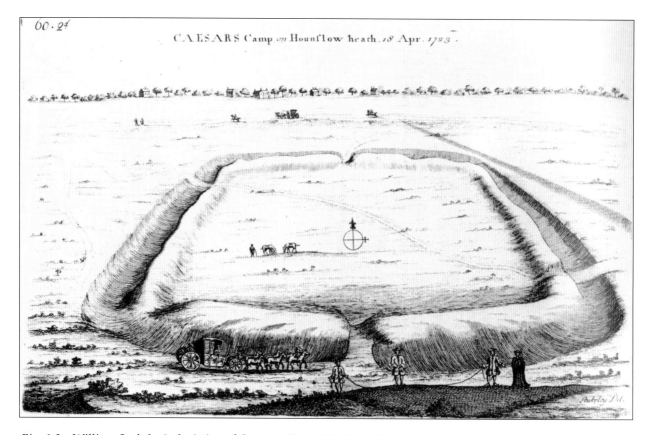

Fig. 1.2 William Stukeley's depiction of Caesar's Camp Heathrow (Soc. Antiq. London).

FRAMEWORKS FOR STUDYING LATE PREHISTORY IN THE THAMES VALLEY

Development of Fieldwork

Until the mid 19th century there was much uncertainty about the relative age of many of our monuments – the Stone, Bronze and Iron Ages of prehistory were invented only 150 years ago, and before then some impressive prehistoric monuments were often attributed to the Romans, Danes or Saxons. The earthwork known as Caesar's Camp at Heathrow was traditionally believed to be a Roman fortress (Fig. 1.2). By the time it was excavated by WF Grimes during construction of a World War II airfield, the earthworks had been ploughed almost flat.

Amongst the earliest excavations of late prehistoric sites in the Thames Valley were those by Stone (1857, 1858) of a ring ditch, middle Bronze Age occupation and Iron Age settlement at Standlake and Boyd Dawkins' work there and at Yarnton in 1854 (Boyd Dawkins 1862; 1864). These were followed by Rolleston in 1875-6, who also recovered material from Wytham (Rolleston 1884, 942-4). These were remarkable, both because they focussed on settlement sites rather than hillforts, and were very early examples of 'rescue' archaeology (in the context of gravel extraction and railway building respectively). Stone's work was particularly remarkable as one of the most scientific and well-recorded excavations of its time, and notable in having had a model made of the site as excavated.

To this important group of early excavations can be added Lane-Fox's excavation of a section through the earthworks at Dyke Hills, Dorchester-on-Thames in 1870 (Lane-Fox 1870). This was another 'rescue' project, this time in the face of destruction for intensive agriculture, and for his time Lane-Fox was also notably scientific in recording stratigraphy and the context of objects found (Fig. 1.3). This case became a *cause célèbre* in the campaign for the protection of ancient monuments that led to the passing of the first Ancient Monuments Act in 1882, under which Lane-Fox (by then General Pitt-Rivers) became the first Inspector of Ancient Monuments.

These early pieces of fieldwork were not in general followed up by much research in the succeeding decades, though there were occasional observations and records of finds. Indeed it was not until the 1920s and 1930s that a relatively coherent theoretical basis for research into late prehistory started to emerge. The nature and scale of archaeological excavation has changed radically over the last few decades and this has profoundly influenced the character, quality and quantity of evidence available. The response of archaeologists to the challenge of recording sites threatened with destruction by gravel extraction over very large areas has played a crucial role in the development of late prehistoric archaeology in Britain, and the Thames Valley has been at the forefront of such

developments. Apart from the work of W F Grimes on wartime airfields at Stanton Harcourt (Grimes 1940) and Heathrow (Grimes and Close-Brooks 1993) most work on gravel sites before the mid 1970s was relatively small scale, though one site in the region, Rough Ground Farm near Lechlade excavated by Margaret Jones from 1957 to 1965 (Allen *et al*. 1993), set a new standard in terms of the sheer extent of archaeology explored that did not become the norm till the 1980s and 1990s.

The distribution of fieldwork has also been very uneven, both geographically and chronologically, for a variety of reasons (*see endpaper distribution map of sites referred to in this volume*). In the 1940s to the mid 1970s a good deal of attention was paid to hillforts, with a pioneering campaign of investigations by the Oxford University Archaeological Society (OUAS) in the north-east Cotswolds and other sporadic work on the chalk. It is only recently, after a lull of about 30 years, that the approach of using geophysics and sample excavation pioneered by the OUAS in the 1950s and 1960s has been revived with all the benefits of more sophisticated magnetometers.

Patterns in the location of destruction have also led to a substantial bias in development-led archaeology towards the Thames gravels in general, but this too has varied along the valley according to the main foci of gravel digging and other development. Topographically the detailed pattern of work has changed in relation to different gravel terraces, with a greater concentration of gravel extraction on lower lying areas in recent years, responding to needs to maintain infrastructure where higher gravel terraces have already been quarried, and to avoid

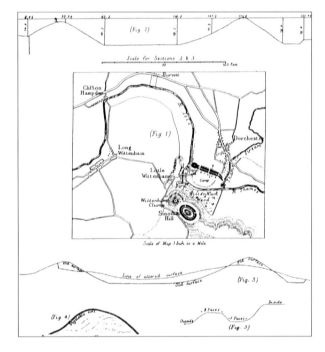

Fig. 1.3   Lane-Fox's 1870 excavations at Dyke Hills, Dorchester-on-Thames

better farmland and more visually exposed sites.

Biases have also arisen from the chronology of responses to development pressure: with the benefit of hindsight it is possible to identify areas where complexes of major interest and potential have been under recorded, their full potential having been only partly recovered through piecemeal salvage observations over several years by dedicated local archaeological societies like the Abingdon Area Archaeological and Historical Society's work at Thrupp (Everett and Eeles 2003; Mudd 1995; Ainslie 1992) or periodic visits and small scale interventions like those at Hatford on the Corallian Ridge near Faringdon (Bourn 2000; Booth and Simmonds 2004). Likewise, although the results of the salvage excavations carried out on the floodplain at Farmoor are very widely quoted (Lambrick and Robinson 1979), it is seldom appreciated how extremely limited they were. In the light of excavations at Yarnton, Eton and elsewhere, we can begin to appreciate how much more probably existed at Farmoor but was destroyed without record.

Chronological Frameworks

In thinking about how and why things changed in the past it is obvious that we need chronological frameworks that allow us to describe what happened when and in what sequence. But change happens in highly complex ways, and constructing chronological frameworks that facilitate rather than impede the study of change is not that simple. Prehistorians in particular work with huge imprecisions of absolute dating, and even to get within a span of several generations it is necessary to reconcile complex strands of evidence: stratigraphy and spatial relationships, pottery and other artefact typologies and a range of scientific dating techniques which for most of the first millennium BC are themselves intrinsically imprecise. As we know from our own experience, very different directions and trajectories of change apply to

different aspects of society within different spatial scales of physical geography and community or social networks. What is perhaps most important is to ensure that concepts that might have had some relevance to people at the time (eg their family, community, clan or tribal connections, and the geographical areas over which they interacted and sought to gain their livelihoods) are kept clearly distinguished from interpretative models imposed on data with the benefit of two or three thousand years' worth of hindsight.

Drivers of Change?

Although chronological, social and geographical frameworks of interpretation are vital tools, they are essentially techniques for describing change, not analysing it. Archaeologists have copious terminologies to define chronologies and other descriptive frameworks through which we explain what happened, but there is no equally well developed framework or language for explaining the character of change itself or the social, economic, environmental or other factors that act as drivers of change. Indeed, the language of periods and phases based on categorising time into chunks is so ingrained that it often does more to obscure than illuminate the dynamics of how past societies developed. The convenient traditional interpretative frameworks within which we pigeonhole the past too often do not do justice to the complexity and interest of how change really happened.

So although this study is still firmly rooted in well-established descriptive frameworks of periods and other categorisations, it does try to look beyond them to consider the dynamics of change from the perspective of some relatively universal factors that influence how human societies change and are relevant to late prehistoric societies in the Thames Valley between around 1500 cal BC and AD 50. Some of the dynamic factors that influence the nature, direction and pace of change in human society include:

Fig. 1.4   General view of excavations at Cassington

- The environment and natural resources (including how they change)
- Technology, ideas and inventiveness
- Communication and exchange
- Economics
- Population dynamics
- Family and community relations
- Rights and traditions
- Religion
- Politics

In considering the broad themes reflected in the chapters of this book we will explore and seek to define the main drivers and inhibitors of change for different aspects of life. We will look not only at how their interaction through people's individual or communal actions transformed the social, economic, political and environmental character of the Thames Valley by the eve of the Roman invasion, but also at how this shaped key characteristics of the Thames Valley landscape that represent a lasting legacy in the familiar surroundings of its present day inhabitants.

DISCOVERING LATE PREHISTORY IN THE THAMES VALLEY: SOURCES AND METHODS

The evidence from which we interpret the late prehistory of the Thames Valley has been acquired through a wide variety of means. It includes simple observation, and sometimes survey of upstanding earthworks, recording of subsoil features that generate crop- and soil-marks or geophysical signals, coring of geological deposits, the recovery of metalwork through metal-detecting or dredging, the recovery of other objects found accidentally or through systematic fieldwalking, and last but not least, various forms and scales of deliberate archaeological excavation (Fig. 1.4). Everything found and recorded has to be painstakingly analysed and reported to liberate the historical evidence that can be unlocked through a bewildering array of scientific and archaeological analyses.

Types of Evidence

Earthwork monuments

Late prehistoric earthworks are amongst the most impressive archaeological monuments of the Thames Valley. Most of them are either fortified enclosures or linear 'territorial' boundaries, which often rank, along with Roman towns and roads, as the largest civil engineering works to have been undertaken before the age of canals, railways and mechanical excavators. Although relatively few of these defensive enclosures and linear boundaries were built – or survive – on the Thames gravels, they include some important examples (Fig 1.5).

The prominent double banks of Dyke Hills, either side of a massive artificial moat linking up the Rivers Thames and Thame at Dorchester-on-Thames to protect a major Iron Age settlement, are still impressive where they survived the depredations of Victorian land improvers. The flattening of the western end of Dyke Hills was a *cause célèbre* in the campaign for legal protection of ancient monuments in the 1880s, and the contrast between those much diminished earthworks and the impressive eastern half of the Dyke Hills ramparts is a lasting memorial to the success of the campaign (despite a continuing problem with rabbit burrows). Other major earthworks on the Thames gravels, like the west end of the South Oxfordshire Grims Ditch, were major undertakings but do not survive as impressively. Ordinary settlements are seldom preserved as visible earthworks, and in this respect the middle Iron Age farmsteads on Port Meadow in Oxford are a very rare survival, largely due to the persistence of ancient grazing rights that could well date back to that time (Fig. 1.5; see Chapter 10, Fig. 10.2).

Aerial photography

Aerial photography and, more recently, other forms of imaging have been invaluable for revealing low earthworks and soil and crop marks of buried ditches and other features cut into the subsoil or disturbed within the topsoil. Many pioneering aerial discoveries were made in the Thames Valley where the tall growth and slower ripening of a crop over the moist, deep and often fertile soil of buried pits and ditches contrasts with lower growth and faster ripening of the crop where it is growing on thin soil over dry gravel (Fig. 1.6).

The Thames Valley was one of the areas where the discovery of archaeological sites through aerial photography was first developed, notably by Major G W Allen. From the 1920s onwards the rate of discovery was phenomenal, reflecting the interest of a series of exponents of aerial photography following Major Allen's pioneering example, such as Derrick Riley, Arnold Baker, J K St Joseph and members of the Royal Commission on the Historical Monuments of England, latterly English Heritage. Given the length and intensity of aerial survey over the last 75 years it is notable that new discoveries have continued to be made, still with little sign of abatement (Featherstone and Bewley 2000). Over the years often subtle changes in cropping patterns, weather flying conditions and developing technical expertise have all influenced the occurrence, clarity, location and recording of ephemeral differences of crop growth over buried archaeology. In some areas, especially the Surrey and West London gravels, there are multiple obstacles to aerial photography: unresponsive brickearth cover, extensive development and/or non-arable landuse and flying restrictions around Heathrow Airport.

Fig. 1.5   Late prehistoric earthworks on the Thames gravels: (above) *Dyke Hills, Dorchester-on-Thames;* (middle) *South Oxfordshire Grims Ditch prior to construction of Wallingford Bypass;* (below) *middle Iron Age settlement earthworks at Port Meadow, Oxford*

Cassington Big Ring

Port Meadow

Gravelly Guy

Sites revealed by aerial photography can belong to any era, so distinguishing those that belong to the late prehistoric period is a matter of interpretation based on the morphology of the marks as compared with known types of archaeological sites dated to the period. This is far from foolproof, especially with some classes of enclosure and field patterns, which may be either late prehistoric or Roman – or possibly other periods too. Nevertheless, there are many types of site revealed by aerial photography that are distinctively late prehistoric, such as pit alignments, banjo enclosures (oval or sub-circular with long funnel ditches extending from the entrance), distinctive forms of domestic pit clusters, and open settlements with penannular enclosures and house sites (similar to ploughed out barrows but generally less than 16 m across and with an entrance gap on one or both sides). Often these sites are discernible amongst many features of other periods.

Geophysics and Topographical survey

It is rare that late prehistoric sites are first discovered through detailed geophysical detection of subsoil magnetic or electrical variations that reveal buried features, or by measured topographical survey of earthworks, but these methods can be very valuable for elucidating aspects of the form and character of sites without involving physical intervention (Fig. 1.7). The use of geophysics coupled with sample excavation was pioneered by the OUAS in a campaign of hillfort investigations in the north-east Cotswolds in the 1950s and 1960s (Fowler 1960; Avery and Sutton 1967). Subsequently it has been used effectively on a series of enclosures and lesser sites (Lambrick 1988; Alex Lang pers. comm.). On the chalk research-led investigations of hillforts along the Ridgeway at Uffington and Segsbury have similarly coupled geophysics with sample excavation with considerable success (Miles *et al.* 2003; Lock *et al.* 2005). At Castle Hill, Little Wittenham a very detailed topographic survey carried out in the 1990s was followed by a major geophysical survey of areas covering about 30 ha both within and outside the hillfort, accompanied by sample excavations (Fig. 1.8; Allen *et al.* forthcoming a). With a few exceptions geophysics has tended not to be used as extensively on the gravels where it is usually supposed, almost certainly erroneously, that the technique does not offer much to add to what is known from air photography (cf Hey *et al.* forthcoming a and b).

Fieldwalking and Metal Detecting

Common artefacts such as pottery and worked flints that have been disturbed from subsoil

Fig. 1.6   Aerial photography and gravels archaeology: Iron Age enclosure ditch at Cassington; middle Iron Age settlement at Port Meadow; Iron Age settlement at Gravelly Guy

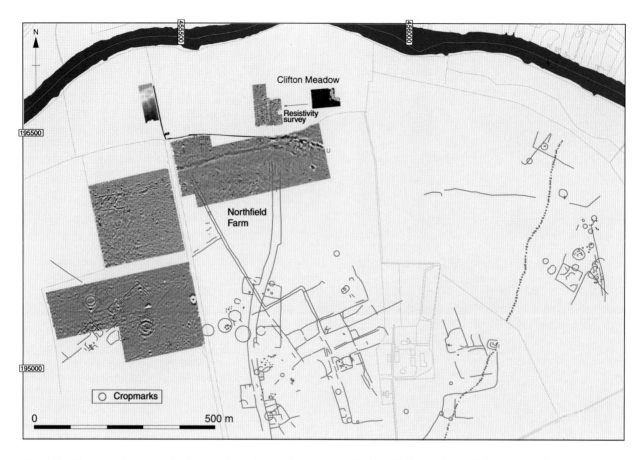

Fig. 1.7   Combined cropmark plots and geophysical survey at Northfield Farm, Long Wittenham, Oxon.

deposits by ploughing can be an indication of more substantial *in situ* remains beneath the surface, and collecting and plotting such surface finds can be an important mode of discovery of rural archaeological sites. This can also apply to metal objects found and reported by metal detectorists (Fig. 1.9). But how useful these are depends greatly on how common such material is in the original deposits from which they are derived, and how resilient they are to damage once they are included in the ploughsoil and subject to mechanical attrition, freeze-thaw and other agencies of damage.

For the period covered by this book some sites are discovered in these ways, but it is rare. Flint tools and waste became less common and less carefully fashioned, and so morphologically much less distinctive than in early periods, and from the end of the Bronze Age it is debatable whether flint tools were used at all. The decline of flint as a material for tools mirrors the increasing use of metal, but because any metal was a precious commodity that can readily be recycled, tools and other objects are relatively rare finds on settlement sites and are not accompanied by an equivalent of flint 'knapping waste.' Finds of late prehistoric metalwork thus tend to be rare (especially when compared with later periods) and are often hoards or casual losses of coins, rather than necessarily reflecting settlements or other focal points. The extent to which such

hoards and losses are associated with settlements or other activity is not very clear as they are rarely found by excavation like Petters Sports Field (O'Connell 1986), and it is only in recent years that hoard sites discovered by metal detecting have been investigated (Fig. 1.9; Miles *et al.* 2003). Such finds are nevertheless cumulatively an important source of evidence for late prehistoric society, reflecting aspects of economic and political relations.

Unlike flint tools, pottery becomes more abundant on late prehistoric settlement sites than in earlier prehistory, and as an inert material it can be an excellent indicator of the presence of subsoil deposits. Until 0 BC/AD, however, pottery was low-fired and, although it survives well in the subsoil, it is often not resistant to damage when it has been in the topsoil over some years. Finding scatters of late prehistoric pottery on the surface is therefore not a common means of discovering sites, and where they are seen it can be an indication that the *in situ* archaeology is being damaged by cultivation (Fig. 1.10).

Overall, although some significant limitations need to be recognised, surface finds can play a significant part in discovering and mapping settlements and fields where people lived and worked, and perhaps more particularly shedding light on social, economic and political issues through the cumulative evidence of more isolated material.

Fig. 1.8 Geophysical survey showing much late prehistoric activity in and around Castle Hill, Little Wittenham

Fig. 1.9   The Tower Hill hoard discovered by metal detecting: (above) *the excavation;* (below) *the hoard*

River dredging

An unusual but important way in which evidence for late prehistory in the Thames Valley has been acquired is the recovery of objects through the dredging and clearing of river channels. This took place mostly in a series of episodes over about 100 years between the 1860s and the 1960s. While objects and parts of human bodies, especially skulls, have been deposited in the river in both earlier and later periods, it seems to have been especially prevalent in late prehistory, and, for example, is our major source of evidence of later Bronze Age and Iron Age weaponry (York 2002) (see Chapter 8).

Careful, scientific excavation of old river channels has not been a traditional part of Thames Valley archaeology and an obvious shortcoming of material recovered by river dredging is the lack of stratigraphic context or close association between material found. In recent years, however, more serious efforts have been made to develop methods of investigating old river channels on a more systematic basis in the context of gravel digging and

other development (Allen and Welsh 1998; Allen *et al.* forthcoming b; Poulton forthcoming; Jones in prep.). But even modern efforts at more thorough investigation and recovery have posed substantial challenges in securing sufficient resources, on a largely speculative basis, for deep controlled excavation of complex deposits – especially over sufficiently extensive areas in the face of serious problems of water management. Much therefore still relies on salvage recording.

Excavations

Most evidence of human settlement in the Thames Valley comes from detailed excavations carried out in advance of sites under threat of destruction by gravel quarrying and other development (Fig. 1.11). This has been the case throughout the modern era.

The gravel industry is not unique in funding major investigations of threatened sites, and much of the work cited in this volume has been carried out on road schemes, pipelines, housing and

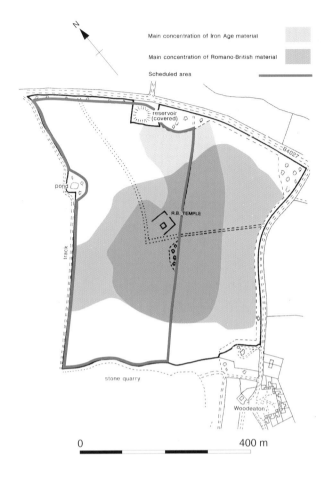

Main concentration of Iron Age material

Main concentration of Romano-British material

Scheduled area

Fig. 1.10   Fieldwalking survey: (above) *Iron Age and Roman finds scatters at the Woodeaton prehistoric midden and Roman Temple;* (below) *collecting surface finds at Woodeaton*

commercial developments, reservoirs, flood channels and a rowing lake. As has been the case on and off for the last 150 years, some evidence also comes from excavations of unthreatened sites carried out purely for purposes of research and education.

But while a vast number of sites threatened by development – and some that have not been – have been subjected to scientific excavation, these still

only form a tiny proportion of the sites and monuments in the Thames Valley known or likely to be late prehistoric, and often, even today, they are only a small proportion of the full extent of activity. The excavated evidence thus has to be interpreted within the much broader, but less detailed pattern of evidence available from the other ways of exploring the past outlined above. Nor is development the only agent of destruction: ongoing erosion through ploughing and drainage, animal poaching, scrub encroachment and burrowing have left few sites free from some damage.

USING THE EVIDENCE: FRAMEWORKS OF INTERPRETATION

How late prehistoric remains have been discovered, identified and mapped in the Thames Valley is thus related to what the remains consist of, their topographical location and the underlying geology and current and past landuse of the location. Both the subsurface geology and the methods of detection tend to bias what is known to the gravel terraces either side of the Thames, and this has had some influence on the key sites and areas that have been selected for intensive research. The way in which evidence is used is thus related to its means of discovery, but it also brings in other considerations that underpin much archaeological interpretation: spatial relationships, objects and biological remains, patterns from statistics and distributions, and the application of theory.

The Basis of Archaeological Chronologies

Interpreting and understanding patterns and processes of change, which is a fundamental theme of this volume, relies on establishing chronologies that are derived from three broad types of evidence: stratigraphic and spatial relationships within sites, artefact typologies (both within and between site assemblages) and independent scientific dating.

Stratigraphy

Most rural late prehistoric gravel sites, other than the few major earthworks, were never characterised by much vertical build-up of deposits, and what there was has very often been truncated by later ploughing. This applies particularly to the drier gravel terraces of the Thames Valley, which have often been in intensive arable landuse since at least the Middle Ages, and often before. But there are exceptions. Where they survive, later earthworks often bury relatively well preserved evidence of soils or settlement traces that would not survive elsewhere (Collins 1952/3; Miles *et al.* 2003; Lock *et al.* 2005; Cromarty *et al.* 2006, 157-200). Occasionally, as at Watkins Farm, deposits have been preserved beneath the headlands of medieval ridge-and-furrow (Allen 1993); or as at Gravelly Guy beneath accumulations of ploughwash (colluvium) spilling

Fig. 1.11   Excavations in progress at Gravelly Guy, Stanton Harcourt

over the edge of the higher gravel terraces (see Chapter 2, Fig. 2.10; Lambrick and Allen 2004, 32-4). A much commoner location of sites with surviving (if still very thin) vertical stratigraphy not truncated by later cultivation is the floodplain of the Thames (Lambrick and Robinson 1979; Allen and Robinson 1993). Here good preservation is much more frequently encountered, but, even so, medieval and particularly 20th century expansion of arable onto the slightly higher, better-drained areas of floodplain has taken its toll.

For most sites in the Thames Valley stratigraphic sequences rely on the relationships between deposits in truncated features dug into the subsoil. These relationships are fundamental in establishing the chronological sequences in which such features were created and used – especially where some vertical stratigraphy also occurs (albeit often only spanning short periods) within the fills of larger ditches, pits and waterholes. Sometimes intercutting ditches and other features can span very long periods, as in the case of Mount Farm, where one sequence stretched from the middle Bronze Age to the late Roman period (Lambrick forthcoming). But this depends on the nature of the evidence: even in the case of very dense intercutting pits and ditches such as at Gravelly Guy and Ashville, the length of sequences was actually quite limited (Lambrick 1984, fig. 11.6; Lambrick and Allen 2004, 103-6).

A third means of analysing physical relationships between features and deposits is to look at their spatial relationships. These lack the unambiguous logic of stratigraphic relationships and rely instead on inferences that can be derived from their layout, based on patterning that is unlikely to be coincidental. A very obvious example is the postholes of a circular roundhouse, but as we shall see, such relationships are usually much less clear-cut.

Artefact typologies and ceramic sequences

In very general terms objects that people make are subject to changes in fashion, technology and usage that influence their design and manufacture, allowing taxonomic types to be identified which can then be linked to other kinds of evidence – especially stratigraphic, associative (where found in conjunction with other material of known date) or scientific (especially if samples dated are directly related to the original manufacture of the object or more commonly its use and discard). Although, very occasionally, particular types of object (such as brooches) do occur within stratified sequences of deposits, this is rare, and most objects are dated through broader typological associations. Later Bronze Age metalwork has been a rich field of typological research, now much clarified by the application of scientific dating (Needham 1997).

Fig. 1.12 (opposite)   Examples of pottery styles from the Thames Valley: (a) middle Bronze Age;
(b) late Bronze Age; (c) early Iron Age; (d) middle Iron Age; (e) late Iron Age

a.

b.

c.

d.

e.

But metalwork finds are rare, and pottery by contrast has three key attributes that make it fundamentally important in determining chronology: being ceramic it generally survives well in most soils; it was very commonly used in the period, being almost ubiquitous in domestic rubbish and used for burials and other deliberate deposits; in terms of use and manufacture, it is durable but breakable and so needs replacing quite often, and in manufacture is a plastic medium and so choice of clay and tempering material, shapes of pots and their decoration are all readily alterable to meet current demand or fashion (Fig. 1.12). Hence pottery is both a common and chronologically and geographically distinctive basis for dating deposits. The main challenges in interpreting individual pottery assemblages in later prehistory are usually whether there are sufficient sherds (usually around 20 to 30 minimum) to be used for statistical analysis of fabrics, which help with dating; and whether a significant number of pieces have been redeposited from earlier periods of activity (Lambrick 1984; Needham and Spence 1996, 61-77).

Problems with pottery dating, despite the responsive plastic state of the medium, are first, that many pottery styles lasted a good deal longer than their main currency – some pots may have become heirlooms; and second, that pottery typologies are constructed from a complex web of associations that rarely involve long sequences of large stratified assemblages. Scientific dates associated with particular pottery styles in the later Bronze Age themselves have wide confidence margins, but could indicate significant overlaps. Even without the added potential complication of 'heirloom' pots used in burials, the evidence on which assumptions are made about relative contemporaneity and sequences of development based on pottery assemblages is often not as clear-cut as might be supposed (Cleal 1992; Morris 1995).

Scientific dating

Radiocarbon dating is the principal means of scientific dating used for this period, and for example an impressive programme of dating has been undertaken at Yarnton (Hey 1999). However, its use as a dating technique is not without its challenges. First, calibration problems affect much of the first millennium BC so that taking account of statistical probability (dates in this book are quoted at 95% probability) many samples give only very broad (and sometimes separated) date ranges that may be little better than broad pottery chronologies. In addition, results are always reliant on sample integrity and the exact nature of the samples analysed, including the intrinsic age of the sampled material (eg whether charcoal or timber samples are sapwood or old heartwood) and the reliability of the association between the material sampled and the context within which it was found. This latter problem can manifest itself in several different ways, including the presence of material accidentally redeposited from earlier

deposits or deliberately curated from earlier periods, a phenomenon that is of interest in its own right. The most secure dating is achieved by sampling the object that is of most direct interest itself, such as bones from a human burial.

Other scientific techniques have also been used such as luminescence dating of sediments at the White Horse, Taplow and Castle Hill (Miles *et al.* 2003, 75-7; Allen *et al.* forthcoming a, b), and magnetic dating of hearths at a few sites, but these again only give very broad ranges. Dendrochronology has the potential to provide highly accurate dates, but it is a characteristic of most waterlogged wood of the period that structural timbers and log ladders consisted almost entirely of fast-grown coppiced poles with too few rings to allow accurate dating (eg Cromarty *et al.* 2006, 19-25). Even where large oak timbers have been found, as at Eton Rowing course and Cassington West (Allen *et al.* forthcoming b; Hey *et al.* forthcoming a), the reference curves are not yet long enough to provide reliable dates.

Despite these limitations, however, there are many instances where scientific dating techniques would help. At present it remains a serious problem that in general far too little independent scientific dating has been done, especially on stratified sequences where analysis of results using Bayesian theory can substantially improve probabilistic accuracy, using multiple samples or high precision techniques to reduce the inherent statistical spread of date ranges of conventional dating. Although there are some important exceptions, such as Eynsham, Yarnton and to a lesser extent Green Park, there has not been a tradition of routinely using scientific dating for later prehistory, even for those periods when particular techniques do work well. There has been even less application of high precision techniques now available. Even at the most basic level, scientific dating is still often seen as a luxury in archaeological budgeting, not a routine cost.

Integrating dating evidence

The use of dating evidence to provide interpretations of chronology is strengthened when they are brought together. Absolute scientific dating can provide direct dating of some objects, biological specimens, sediments or structural materials, but to provide the evidence of dating on which whole sites or types of artefact can be based, it usually must be used in conjunction with artefact typologies and stratigraphy, as demonstrated by Needham's (1997) analysis of Bronze Age metalwork. Similarly, stratigraphic sequences are of rather limited use if they lack reasonably large assemblages of finds and/or environmental samples or, as commonly found on ploughed gravel sites, they provide only sequences of limited length. Virtually all dating, and other aspects of interpretation, is made considerably more complex if deposits are riddled with redeposited material, or there other problems with obtaining fully reliable samples (Lambrick 1984 a).

How did it get there? – models of deposition and human behaviour

The importance of taphonomy

The issue of whether the analysis of samples of excavated material provides reliable data raises the broader issue of understanding 'taphonomy' – that is to say the complex sequences of events and influential factors that determine how natural biological remains or sediments, manufactured objects and the waste products of human activity are created, used, moved around, deposited, possibly redeposited, disturbed and altered before they are recovered.

This is a complicated but important consideration in the detailed analysis and reporting of any archaeological data, and is a relevant consideration in its use in drawing wider conclusions or patterns. Understanding taphonomy is partly a precautionary exercise in not being misled by superficial appearances, but appreciating the nature of the evidence and how it can be used to draw valid conclusions. But it also offers a much more positive line of evidence because taphonomic analysis can help reveal how people behaved and lived, potentially allowing a wider variety of inferences to be drawn from the same body of data than might be supposed from first impressions.

A number of examples of taphonomic analysis have been carried out on material from late prehistoric sites in the Thames Valley that provide valuable insights into the interpretation of key groups of material that in many respects represent the backbone of archaeological data underpinning our subject. These include studies of pottery (eg Bradley *et al.* 1980; Lambrick 1984 a; Jennings *et al.* 2004, 171-6); bones (Wilson 1992; 1993; 1996); carbonised plant remains (Jones 1978; 1984; 1985; Stevens 1996; 2003; forthcoming); and beetles (Robinson 1983). For the major late Bronze Age site at Runnymede a very detailed multi-disciplinary study of taphonomic processes that affect a major midden deposit was carried out (Needham and Sørensen 1988; Needham and Spence 1996). Rather than summarise these studies here, it is perhaps more instructive to cite them where they have a particular bearing on how different lines of evidence are interpreted in the following chapters.

Ethnographic and socio-economic models

Understanding how the accumulated and piecemeal physical evidence of past societies can be disentangled to provide an idea of what physically existed and how it changed is a fundamental part of archaeology. However, interpreting this in terms of individual and communal behaviour and socio-economic and cultural customs, traditions and belief systems presents a further challenge. A very wide range of ethnographical studies and social and political theory has been brought to bear on British later prehistory, including Gerhard Bersu's (1940) ground breaking insights into the workings of Iron Age rural settlements. Other examples include Hingley (1984) on settlement patterns in the Upper Thames Valley; Needham (1993) and Hill (1995) on layout and depositional practices in settlements; Oswald (1997), Parker Pearson and Richards (1994) and Brück (1999) on the design and use of houses; Johnston (2001) on land tenure; Wait (1985), Brück (1995) and Carr (2002) on religion and burial practice; Bradley (1998), Needham (1990; 2001) on hoards and river deposition.

The strength of such models is that they provide potential explanations of otherwise opaque data that should certainly not be interpreted using the norms of 21st century western society; their danger is that the model takes over and other possibilities are shunned – or worse, that data is selectively chosen to fit the favoured model. Human life is highly structured through social and economic interrelationships and through religious and cosmological views of the world and pressures to conform to social norms, customs and traditions, and so particular ethnographical and socio-economic models provide invaluable insights. But human life is complex, even messy, and there are often different ways of explaining the same data. In moving on from the limitations of the 'processual' archaeology of the 1970s and 1980s, 'post-processual' approaches have sometimes swung too far towards interpreting everything in purely cosmological terms as if there was not a practical grind of daily living (Pope 2007). The strongest studies are those founded on solid data which allow for the complexities of depositional processes and recognise that human behaviour and interrelationships are influenced by a wide range of different practical and abstract factors whose significance may differ socially, geographically and over time.

In this book the intention is to present a review of the late prehistory of the Thames Valley in the light of both recent and older discoveries in a way that takes account of the valuable insights provided by ethnographical and socio-economic models, at the same time as building on the ideas that emerged from more 'processualist' approaches of earlier decades.

Chapter 2 – Setting the scene: the natural environment and the geography of settlement

The common physical characteristics of the floor of the Thames Valley and the contrasts within the wider catchment provide both a unifying thread and a varied backdrop for consideration of how late prehistoric people inhabited, exploited and shaped the environment to suit their changing needs. The influences of natural resources and social factors in shaping an important period of change in the development of human society and environment in the Thames Valley is a key theme, and this chapter explores the natural landforms, soils and drainage patterns of the Thames Valley and how its vegetation evolved through human interaction with the environment in later prehistory.

THE STUDY AREA (Figs. 2.1, 2.2)

This book is concerned mainly with the gravel terraces of the Upper and Middle Thames Valley, from the source of the Thames near Cricklade to the start of the present tidal zone at Teddington Lock, but this needs to be set within the river's wider catchment. This part of the Thames Basin represents a substantial area of central southern England. Topographically the area encompasses two main sub-sections referred to as the 'Upper' and 'Middle' Thames Valleys, located above and below the Goring Gap where the river cuts through the main Chalk escarpment. The 'Lower'

Thames Valley refers to its tidal reaches downstream of Teddington through London and out to the estuary.

The geology, geomorphology and soils of the regions (Fig. 2.3)

The Upper Thames drains part of a belt of Jurassic and Cretaceous sedimentary rocks which strike from Dorset north-east to the Wash and dip to the south-east. The Jurassic limestone hills of the Cotswolds comprise the watershed to the northwest. The Thames runs eastwards across a vale of Oxford Clay, collecting various tributaries from the Cotswolds, such as the Rivers Coln, Windrush and Evenlode, before turning south-east at Oxford towards the chalk escarpment of the Berkshire Downs and Chilterns. The River Cherwell, which drains the eastern end of the Cotswolds and the rolling hills of west Buckinghamshire, joins the Thames at Oxford. South of Oxford the river cuts through a second, lesser ridge of hills known as the Corallian Ridge and Oxford Heights, which are composed of Cretaceous sand and limestone and, like the Cotswolds, strike ENE with their dip slope to the SSE. As with its catchment above Oxford, the Thames south of the Corallian Ridge winds its way across a broad belt of clay, in this case composed of Gault and Kimmeridge beds, which are flanked to

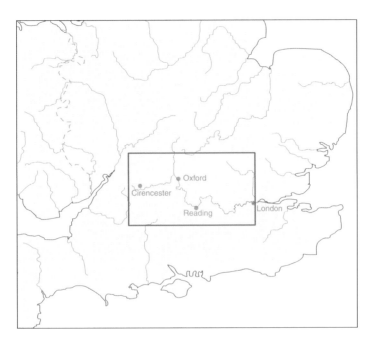

Fig. 2.1 The project area

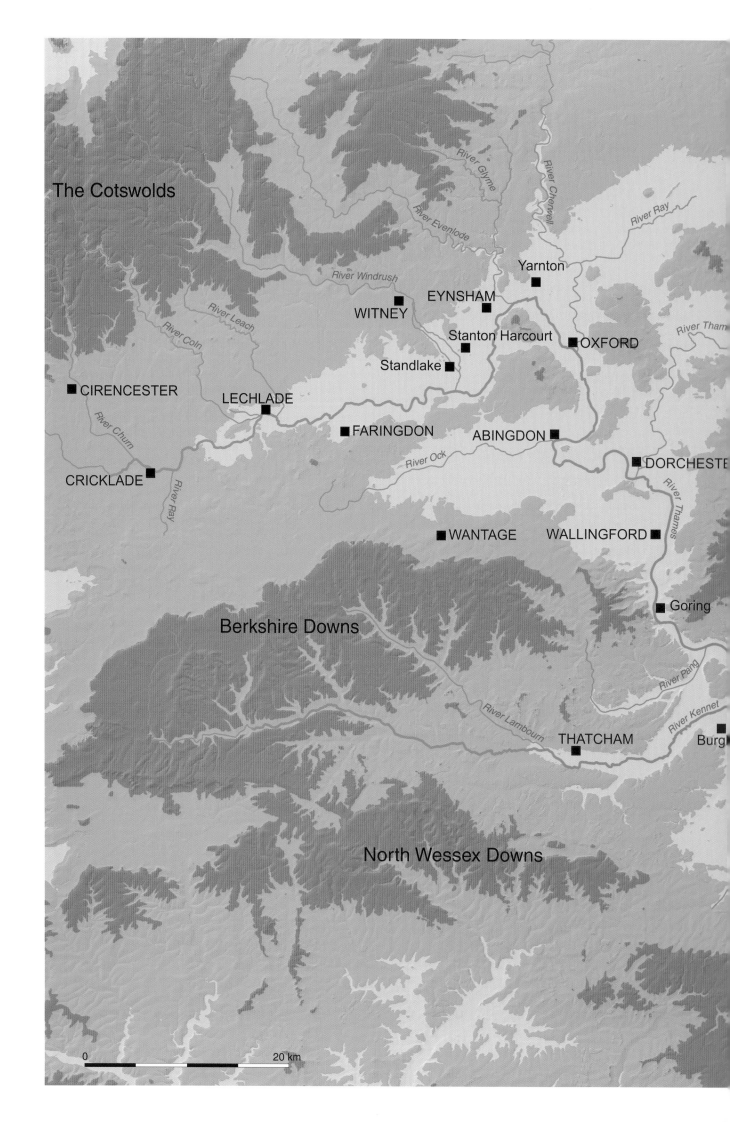

The Cotswolds

River Glyme

River Cherwell

River Evenlode

River Ray

River Windrush

Yarnton

River Leach

EYNSHAM

WITNEY

Stanton Harcourt

River Thame

River Coln

OXFORD

Standlake

CIRENCESTER

LECHLADE

FARINGDON

ABINGDON

River Churn

River Ock

DORCHESTER

CRICKLADE

River Ray

River Thames

WANTAGE

WALLINGFORD

Goring

Berkshire Downs

River Pang

River Lambourn

River Kennet

THATCHAM

Burg

North Wessex Downs

0   20 km

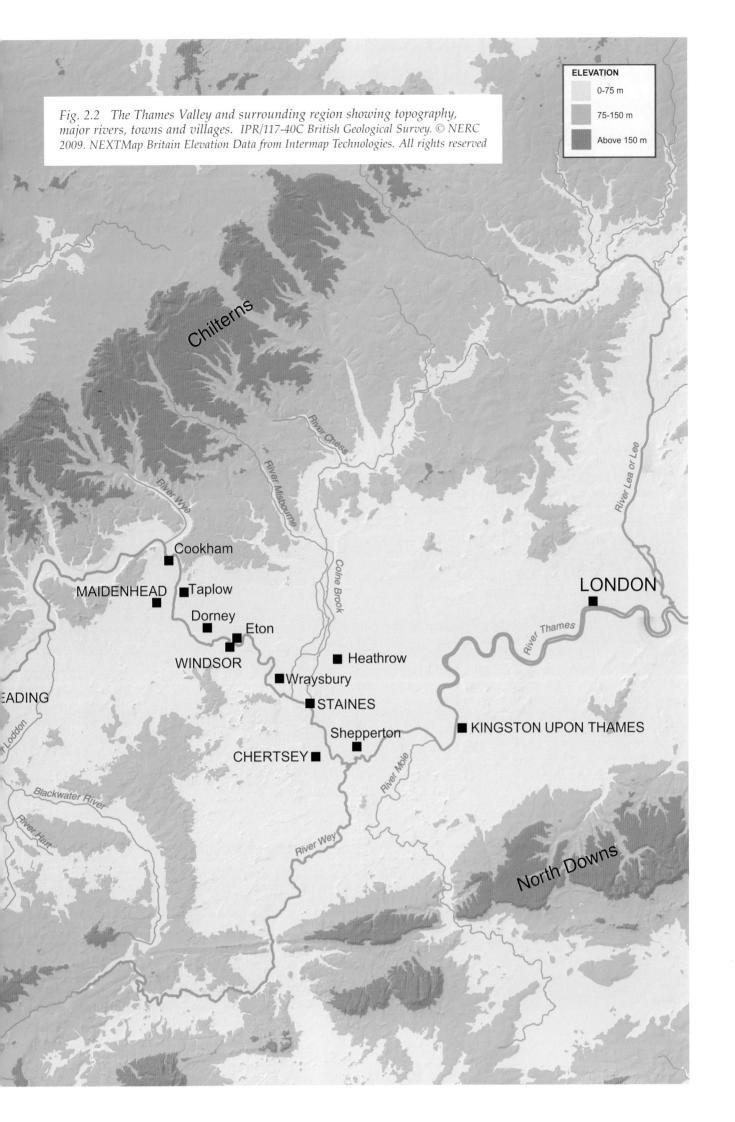

Fig. 2.2 The Thames Valley and surrounding region showing topography, major rivers, towns and villages. IPR/117-40C British Geological Survey. © NERC 2009. NEXTMap Britain Elevation Data from Intermap Technologies. All rights reserved

the south by the main Upper Greensand bench and Chalk escarpment of the Berkshire Downs and the Chilterns. To the west the Vale of the White Horse is drained by the Ock, which joins the Thames at Abingdon, while to the east the Vale of Aylesbury is drained by the Thame which flows into the Thames at Dorchester-on-Thames.

South of Dorchester the Thames follows a more direct course south to cut its way through the Chalk at the Goring Gap to emerge into the Middle Thames Valley which occupies the London Basin, a syncline in the Chalk filled with Tertiary sedimentary rocks of which London Clay is the most important. At Reading, the Thames is joined by the River Kennet, which runs eastwards along Tertiary deposits at the foot of the dip slope of the Berkshire Downs to the north and the escarpment of the Hampshire Chalk to the south. The dip slope of the Chilterns, drained into the Thames by the River Colne, rises to the north-west of the London Basin. The Chalk of the Weald anticline, including the North Downs, rises to the south of the London Basin and the Rivers Wey and Mole enter the Thames from the south. The Thames progresses eastwards from Reading across the London Basin to London and the estuary with first a northern loop, towards Marlow, and then a southern loop, towards Weybridge.

Both the Upper and Middle Thames are flanked by extensive gravel terraces, in places more than 3 km wide (Fig. 2.3). The prerequisites for the formation of such terraces are a supply of hard rock upstream or on the interfluves, and an area of very soft bedrock, which the river crosses with a shallow gradient. Terrace aggradation requires a period of high discharge and surface instability. The river forms a braided system of many minor migrating channels which work over the soft bedrock, depositing gravel on their beds and creating a level gravel floodplain. Cold climatic episodes facilitate high seasonal discharge from the melting of winter snow and also provide the erosive processes which result in fractured rock reaching the stream system. Periods of down-cutting can also occur, especially at times of very high spring and summer discharges from melting ice and snow at times of climatic ameliora-tion, resulting in the removal of much of a gravel terrace and its redeposition from a new base level. Such climatic fluctuations in successive cold and warm stages result in the series of terraces stepping down the valley side typified by the Thames Valley.

In the case of the Upper Thames Valley, the hard rock is provided by the limestone of the Cotswolds while the area of terrace aggradation is over the Oxford and Gault Clay vale. This creates terraces with a major component of oolitic limestone. In the Middle Thames Valley the main source of hard rock is flint from the Chalk of the Chilterns and Downs, with lesser quantities coming from some of the Tertiary beds, and the area of aggradation is over the London Clay. The greatest vertical range in the sequence of Thames terraces is seen at the Chilterns where the Thames has cut down over 300 m since

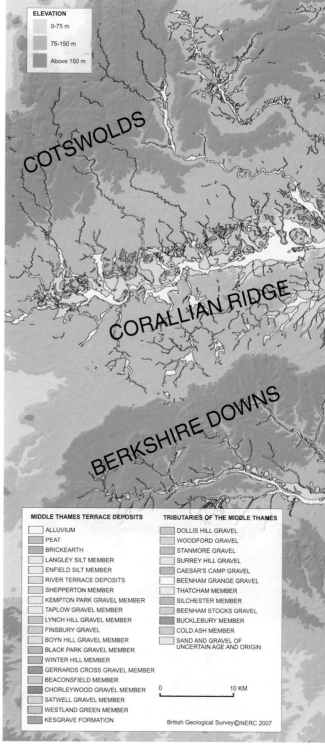

Fig. 2.3   The gravel terraces of the Upper and Middle Thames. IPR/117-40C British Geological Survey. © NERC 2009. NEXTMap Britain Elevation Data from Intermap Technologies. All rights reserved

the Late Tertiary. However, most of the highest, oldest terraces are of very limited extent.

The Upper Thames is isolated from the Middle Thames by the nick point of the Goring Gap. Its four major gravel terraces (Sandford 1924) were

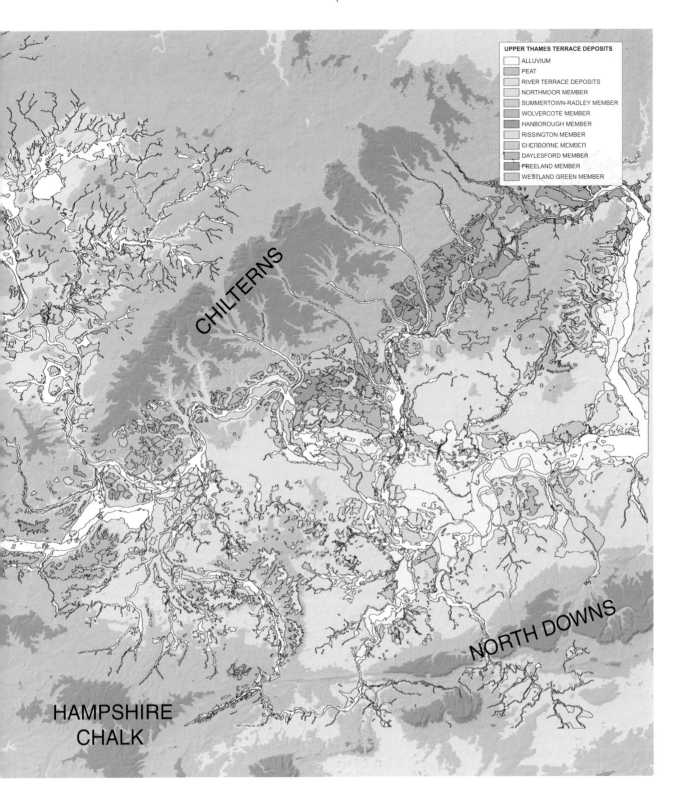

deposited during the cold periods of the Pleistocene, the lowest and youngest being of Devensian date. There are major Pleistocene gravel terraces in the Middle Thames, the lowest and youngest likewise being Devensian. The terraces range from 3-4 m to less than 1 m in thickness and the entire body of gravel comprising the lowest terrace in both regions is given the name floodplain terrace. All the terraces represent former floodplains but only the lowest part of the most recent flood-plain terrace, where its surface was lowered by erosion at the end of the last Ice Age, would ever have experienced flooding in the Holocene. This is evident in both the Upper and Middle Thames, where in each case parts of the lowest terrace were reworked and lowered during the very Late Glacial (the end of late Devensian Zone III) when erosive channel flow was becoming established in place of accretive braided flow. This area tends to have a covering of fine alluvial overbank sediments and in this book the term 'floodplain' (as opposed to 'floodplain terrace') is restricted to this area.

The channels of the Thames seem to have been incised to their greatest extent at the start of the Holocene. Thereafter the regime was one of channel silting and simplification from multiple to single channel systems (Robinson 1992, 47-8). Unlike some major rivers, such as the Trent (Salisbury 1992), there was little Holocene channel migration. In the Upper Thames, pedalogical processes predominated over alluvial accretion on the floodplain during the early and middle Holocene (Robinson and Lambrick 1984) and flooding was of limited extent. The present general covering of up to 2 m of alluvial clay was the result of sedimentation over the past 2000 years, though localised alluviation began earlier. In contrast, at least some parts of the floodplain of the Middle Thames began to experience fine overbank alluvial sedimentation in the early Holocene (Parker and Robinson 2003).

The Upper and Middle Thames have entirely lowland catchments and arable agriculture now extends to the watersheds. The soils of the Upper Thames Basin are mostly calcareous or circumneutral and in only a few areas of acid soils and plateau gravels are there serious problems of soil fertility. The limestone of the Cotswolds gives soils that are easily worked but they are often shallow and brashy, sometimes with problems of steep slopes. The Oxford Clay is relatively intractable and suffers from impeded drainage, but cultivation is possible and it is mostly ploughed. The light free-draining soils of the gravel terraces were originally stone-free argillic brown earths, but limestone gravel has been incorporated into them from at least the Iron Age onwards by cultivation and this has countered tendencies towards acidification. The gravel terraces are well suited to agriculture and those parts which have survived gravel extraction are under the plough. As has been mentioned, the alluvial clays of the floodplain were mostly deposited over the past 2000 years and seal thin soils over gravel. The floodplain is still regularly inundated where there is no flood protection, but modern drainage and river management have made cultivation possible, mostly of grass leys. There are extremely few areas of ancient grazed grassland of the kind that would have typified the late prehistoric valley floor, Port Meadow at Oxford being the only large example (Lambrick and Robinson 1988).

The soils of the Middle Thames Basin tend to be more acidic and less fertile than those of the Upper Thames Basin. Although the Chalk gives rise to light calcareous soils, much of the dip slope of the Chilterns is covered with acidic clay-with-flints where woodland is quite extensive. The London Clay produces soils more acidic than those of the Oxford Clay and light acidic soils are present on some of the other Tertiary and Cretaceous (Green-

sand) deposits in the region. The gravel terraces have light, free draining soils which, because the gravel is flint, are usually acidic. The floodplain has similar alluvial clay soils to the Upper Thames Valley. However, in the Lower Kennet Valley, there are extensive peat-filled backswamps beneath a thin layer of alluvial clay. Neither region has the chalky boulder clay which runs further north in Buckinghamshire because they were beyond the maximum extent of Pleistocene ice cover.

The modern River Thames has been substantially canalised by dredging, embanking and the insertion of locks and weirs for navigation. It has also experienced much natural silting, which has simplified a complex system of linked multiple channels (an anastomosing system) to a single channel. However, along part of its length, for example at Oxford, a complex channel system survives. The River Thames has a gradient of less than 1 m per kilometre and a non-flashy flow.

Preservation of the evidence

The topography of the gravel terraces and their suitability for agriculture means that ploughing has generally destroyed all traces of ancient soils and occupation spreads except where protected by earthworks. However, colluvial sediments derived from past cultivation have accumulated on terrace edges in a few localities and sequences of alluvial sediments occur on the floodplain sealing a non-alluvial palaeosol, and sometimes including interstratified archaeological deposits. Silted palaeochannels also occur on the floodplain.

Carbonised plant remains are usually present on settlement sites and the soils are often well suited to flotation processes of recovery. Bone preservation in the Upper Thames Valley is often satisfactory, especially from the Iron Age onwards, even if the soil is not calcareous, because the incorporation of limestone gravel into deposits buffers rainwater leaching. However, under the more acidic conditions on the terraces of the Middle Thames bone preservation is poorer. Shells of land and freshwater molluscs do not survive on gravel terrace sites in the Thames Valley except where there are locally calcareous conditions, often caused by human disturbance. However, since the waters of the River Thames are calcareous, palaeochannel sediments are usually calcareous and contain abundant shells. Overbank alluviation is sometimes decalcified but otherwise shells survive in it. Pollen is not preserved in non-waterlogged sediments on the gravels of the Upper Thames but some non-waterlogged sites on the terraces of the Middle Thames are sufficiently acidic for the preservation of pollen but results must be treated with caution because conditions are rarely sufficiently acidic to deter earthworm activity.

An important aspect of the environmental archaeology of the river gravels is that they present the opportunity to study relatively dry, fertile, well-settled agricultural landscapes from waterlogged remains. The nature of the formation of the gravel terraces means that, although the surface of the terrace is usually free draining, if there is underlying clay there is often a perched water table. In the Upper and Middle Thames Valley, especially on the lower terraces, the water table can be very close to the surface. Where this occurs ditches often extend below the water table, as do waterholes and wells. Organic sediments preserved at the bottom of these features contain pollen and waterlogged macroscopic plant remains, including seeds, leaves, twigs and wood, and insect remains. Palaeochannels containing waterlogged remains are frequently present on the floodplain and many appear to have experienced sedimentation in the later Bronze Age. Various categories of biological remains found in non-waterlogged deposits are also preserved in the waterlogged sediment, although the decay of organic material sometimes causes local acidification resulting in the loss of shells.

Thus a wide range of evidence is available from the Thames gravels and floodplain for the past environment. While the regions have neither the degree of organic survival of a wetland landscape with developing peat surfaces nor the extent of preservation of mollusc shells and palaeosols found in some Chalk landscapes, the many levels of evidence give a more balanced picture than from some other regions.

Population

Population dynamics are fundamental to the ways in which human societies develop. Although archaeological evidence does not provide a secure basis for establishing actual population levels, the effects of population change are detectable archaeologically. In setting the scene it is worth making some educated guesses about how the population of the Thames Valley might have changed in later prehistory which we can later test against various indicators (Chapter 10). Prehistorians have been interested in the topic of population for many decades and it provided much scope for debate for late prehistory in the late 1970s and 1980s (Brothwell 1972; Cunliffe 1978; Bradley 1978, 122-3; Fowler 1983, 32-6). Brothwell deduced a Bronze Age population of Britain at 20,000-100,000 people, and Iron Age from 50,000-500,000, which Cunliffe, making comparisons between Iron Age and medieval settlement density in Wessex, considered too low by a factor of two. Fowler considered Atkinson's Neolithic population estimate of 14,000, extrapolated from the number and distribution of long barrows, as reasonable and on the basis of likely populations of Roman towns and rural settlement and comparisons with Domesday, this would have risen to somewhere between two and four million by the first millennium AD. Based on this and further analysis of Bronze Age barrows by Atkinson, he suggested a maximum population of

about 100,000 by about 1600 cal BC. Bradley (1978, 105-6) cast some doubt on whether it was reasonable to assume a continuous exponential rise in population throughout the Neolithic and early Bronze Age, but accepted that there must have been a steady rise in population throughout later prehistory.

Much of the debate about actual population levels, however, was rather sterile because there was little chance of devising any means of making reliable estimates, and in the last 20 years the issue has rather faded from attention as the focus of prehistorians shifted towards individual actions and histories rather than larger scale patterns. This is unfortunate because population change does matter, both as a driver of change and as a result of change in human society. Because alterations in birth and death rates tend to result in exponential changes in the size of population, the effects over the kind of time scales we are dealing with can be dramatic. Changes in settlement pattern, landuse and much else may reflect whether the population of the area was growing fast or slowly, stable, in decline or collapsing. Moreover the dynamics of population in conjunction with the environmental, social and political capacity of an area can be cyclical. If rapid growth outstrips capacity stagnation or collapse can be triggered.

Thus we can only consider how the population of the Thames Valley may have changed in later prehistory when we have looked at other aspects of human society for which we have much more direct evidence. These may provide more useful insights into how the broadly assumed growth in population was sustained, how it may have both driven and responded to social and economic change and how growth, stagnation and decline may have varied chronologically and geographically (see Chapter 10). For the moment we will simply note that for the millennium and a half covered by this book there is a strong likelihood that the population of the Thames Valley grew significantly, from quite low levels of earlier prehistoric periods to a much higher level by the time that Britain was seen as a valuable target for Roman expansion.

THE GEOGRAPHY OF LATE PREHISTORIC SETTLEMENT AND LANDUSE IN THE THAMES VALLEY

River valleys are often seen as a natural focus of human settlement. They can provide good cultivable soils, a ready supply of water and other natural resources, shelter from climatic extremes, good corridors of communication and defensible sites and territories using water as a natural barrier or boundary. All this applies in the case of the Thames Valley, and in a sense the River Thames itself can be seen as the unifying thread. However, the geography of settlement patterns in lowland river basins can be as much about the role of high ground and the interfluves between river catchments as the valleys that they divide. The mere existence of a geographically benign river valley does not explain anything very fundamental about how it was settled, especially if soils in the rest of the catchment are no less fertile and resilient to agricultural exploitation, as is the case of at least the Upper Thames Valley.

The legacy of monuments, settlement patterns and landuse from earlier prehistory

As we shall see, the manner in which such ways of life evolve can be influenced as much by tradition and the legacy of past customs and rights as by innovation, deliberate planning or forced reaction to changed circumstances. A key starting point is therefore to have some appreciation of where existing earlier prehistoric populations of the area are likely to have been concentrated and, even if they may not have lived much in permanent settlements, where their principal landuse activities were based.

By the end of the early Bronze Age the Upper Thames Valley was characterised by a series of major ceremonial and funerary complexes spread along the valley floor, especially at the river confluences, where almost every one had such a centre (Barclay *et al.* 1996; 1995; 1999; 2003; Whittle *et al.* 1992). These centres of communal activity were established in areas that were substantially, though not entirely, cleared of trees and scrub. Beyond such centres where the most spectacular communal ceremonial monuments and most extensive funerary complexes were created there was an extremely widespread occurrence of lesser funerary and other monuments. This latter pattern was much more the general character of the Middle Thames terraces, where the earlier prehistoric causewayed enclosures and cursuses of the Thames gravel terraces do not seem to have been succeeded by major henge monuments or especially large, rich barrow cemeteries.

In all these areas, from major complexes to lesser ones, from sites with single monuments to some with no obvious ceremonial or funerary connections at all, a broadly similar pattern of domestic activity seems to have prevailed, reflected in surface finds scatters and clusters of small pits containing domestic debris that may have been deliberately selected. Although the density of such features and of surface finds generally seems to have been higher in the vicinity of monuments than in the wider countryside, this is not always the case, and there seems to have been considerable variability in the patterns of activity represented by such features.

The easily worked calcareous and neutral soils of the flat well-drained gravel terraces of the Thames Valley were at least as attractive in this respect as those of the chalk and limestone hills that define the Thames catchment area. The valley floor had the added advantage of offering a linear ribbon of easy

waterborne communication as well as terrestrial routes that in many ways were no less advantageous than the hilltop ridges. In the absence of identifiable farmsteads it is widely thought that in the early Bronze Age these favoured areas were focal points within a wider pattern of clearance and farming believed to have been based on a pattern of mobile settlement (Barrett 1994, 136-46; Bruck 2000, 281-5). This would have created and maintained some extensive, permanently cleared places, while in less favoured areas there may still have been a more varied cycle of clearance and regeneration, as suggested by the pollen sequence at Sidlings Copse (Day 1991).

The major late Neolithic and early Bronze Age monument complexes do not generally seem to have been a prime focus for later prehistoric settlement, and there are very few cases where earlier monuments were not respected in the middle to late Bronze Age. The main exceptions are cursus monuments. Those at Lechlade, Dorchester and Stanwell had major middle to late Bronze Age or early Iron Age field systems or boundaries laid out across them (followed by early Iron Age settlement within the cursus at Lechlade). Despite these exceptions, it generally seems that for a few hundred years in the middle to late Bronze Age some care was taken not to impinge inappropriately on ancient sacred places, but that cursuses were not recognised as such. As the relationship of the Perry Oaks/T5 field system to the Stanwell cursus shows (Framework Archaeology 2006, 98-101), they were recognisable earthworks, but must have been as much of an enigma to the archaeological instincts and folk memories of inhabitants of the Thames Valley 3000 years ago as to more recent antiquaries and archaeologists.

Later in the Iron Age such concern for earlier monuments seems to have been less clear-cut. In some places, like Stanton Harcourt, this kind of respect had established a pattern of landuse and settlement that lasted well into the Roman period. In others, where landuse and/or settlement patterns were abandoned, shifted location, or were reorganised more radically in the Iron Age, such connections with the past seem to have been lost more quickly. But there are enough cases of early prehistoric ceremonial complexes untouched by Iron Age and early Roman land divisions and settlements to indicate that some degree of respect remained ingrained for centuries or even millennia, if only through inertia and survival of traditional rights, as suggested for Stanton Harcourt (Lambrick 1992; Lambrick and Allen 2004, 482-3).

This evidence for continuation of respect for previously important areas raises questions about how and why changes towards more organised use of land and permanent settlement came about. Were major land divisions and field systems laid out as new intakes of land, or within areas of established, seasonal, landuse and settlement? Did more permanent settlements evolve simply from more continuous use of pre-existing landuse patterns? How far did respect for earlier monuments reflect a survival of earlier community groupings and spiritual values? How far did the physical enclosure of land reflect pre-existing rights? Was it a purely practical matter or a deliberate symbol of a settled existence and communal or political control of territory? What was the interplay between social and environmental factors in determining the character of later prehistoric society in the Thames Valley?

The Upper Thames Valley and Tributaries

The principal foci of earlier prehistoric activity in terms of communal monuments and funerary complexes were river confluences, notably those of the Leach, Windrush, Ock and Thame, and to a lesser extent the Evenlode and Cherwell. These and other parts of the gravel terraces became the main locations of later prehistoric occupation, though seldom within the specific areas of earlier ceremonial and funerary complexes. The Upper Thames floodplain was not subject to extensive flooding in the Bronze Age and had a lower watertable, which did not inhibit its use, as demonstrated at Yarnton (Hey *et al.* forthcoming b). Although some old channels and low-lying areas were beginning to silt up in the Iron Age (Hey *et al.* forthcoming a; Ainslie 1999; 2002), in most areas the build-up of clayey alluvial soil did not occur until towards the end of the Iron Age (Robinson 1992b; Lambrick 1992).

Most later Bronze Age settlements in the Upper Thames Valley have been discovered on the gravels, corresponding to the densest distribution of Iron Age settlements. From the middle Bronze Age onwards a recognised variety of broad settlement forms include both ephemeral traces of domestic activity and more intensive occupation, sometimes associated with enclosures or extensive field systems, the latter mainly south of the Corallian Ridge. Most display a low density of features and little domestic debris, though this increases in the later Bronze Age. Areas of more extensive occupation have been examined at Shorncote/Cotswold Community on the Gloucestershire/Wiltshire border, and in the Yarnton/Cassington area north-west of Oxford. Most middle to late Bronze Age settlements seem to be based on pastoralism with some crop growing, but in the absence of larger groups of occupation debris, this is not easy to establish.

Whereas there are many Iron Age sites with little or no sign of later Bronze Age activity, there are few examples of later Bronze Age settlements that do not also display Iron Age occupation activity either in the same area or close by. Excavations at Yarnton showed how such settlements shifted location from the floodplain to the drier gravel terrace a few hundred metres away, so even in the few cases where later Bronze Age occupation areas do not obviously also produce evidence of Iron Age settlement, the absence may be due more to the limited extent of investigations than a true negative.

It must also be noted that later Bronze Age settlements can be relatively invisible to most reconnaissance techniques (notably aerial photography and surface collection survey) other than excavation because they consist of sparse subsoil features and pottery, and are not easily distinguishable from Iron Age ones. Since excavation in the past was biased towards earlier prehistoric monuments or Iron Age sites more readily recognised from aerial photographs, there is substantial uncertainty about the true extent of later Bronze Age activity. However, through recent work in the Middle and Lower Thames Valley, coupled with the greater use of systematic evaluation of areas affected by large-scale gravel extraction, patterns are beginning to emerge.

A general attribute of settlement sites in the central part of the Upper Thames from the early Iron Age onwards, and more generally from the middle Iron Age, is that they are mostly much more compact and characterised by a greater density of features and finds, suggesting a significant increase in the intensity, duration and/or permanence of occupation. Most early Iron Age settlements appear to have practised mixed farming, and clusters of pits usually considered to be subsoil seed grain stores become key features of at least some of these, though not as universally characteristic of the area as might appear from the few frequently cited well-known sites. Both enclosed and open settlement are known, but this distinction, based largely on aerial photographic evidence, disguises a considerable variety of forms within these categories. It is also increasingly apparent that the unenclosed/enclosed status of settlements may evolve over time on long-lived sites, blurring the distinctions that seem obvious from aerial survey.

Most settlements with early Iron Age origins continued to be occupied into the middle Iron Age, usually, though not always in the same place. By the middle Iron Age a greater diversity of settlement forms appears – or at least distinctions in form and agricultural purpose become clearer. There is more evidence of economic specialisation (as between mainly pastoral and mixed farms), which also relates to topographical location (as between second gravel terrace, first terrace and floodplain). A significant number of excavated settlements of this period are on sites not occupied in the earlier Iron Age. In particular, there was more settlement on the lower (first) gravel terrace and some specialised re-occupation of the floodplain on a seasonal basis.

The pattern for the late Iron Age is less clear-cut. Although in many respects the broad pattern of settlement and cultural and economic activity remained largely unchanged, there were many detailed changes. For example, there is less evidence of specialised low-lying grazing settlements; some but by no means all middle Iron Age settlements continued to be occupied, and some new sites were settled. Even where there was continuity of occupation a marked relocation of settlement focus has been observed. Many settlements of the later Iron Age display characteristics of change from earlier practices, with fewer pits and greater emphasis on ditched paddocks or enclosures apparently within a renewed impetus to enclosing land. It is difficult to identify the form of houses of this period, and the practice of underground storage of grain began to decline around this time. Nearly all early Roman settlements originated before the Conquest, and for several decades this political change had so little impact on local activity that it is very difficult to discern in most settlements of the period.

Distribution of Farming Settlements across the Upper Thames

Lambrick (1992) showed that Iron Age settlements on the different terraces of the Thames gravels exhibited different trajectories of change. Most long-lived settlements on the higher, drier terraces engaged in mixed farming, and the lower lying parts of the valley floor were occupied in the middle Iron Age with farmsteads often of more short-lived character thought to be more engaged with pastoralism, including the extreme case of short lived summer grazing farmsteads at Farmoor (Lambrick and Robinson 1979). Work over the last 15 years has generally filled in and expanded this picture without superseding it, but has added more detail and a greater variety of elements. In particular, there is more evidence of the later Bronze Age antecedents of the Iron Age pattern, showing a somewhat different pattern of activity, most settlements being more dispersed in character and favouring the lower ground which at that stage was not as wet as it later became.

Based largely on aerial photographic evidence Hingley (1984) argued that Iron Age settlement on the valley floor was much denser on the gravels than the Cotswolds and was characterised mainly by open settlements, whereas on the Cotswolds and Chalk the sparser settlement pattern was represented mainly by enclosed settlements. Since then there has been a remapping of the cropmark evidence along the Thames Valley (RCHME 1995) and a substantial increase in the number of enclosed sites now known on the dip slope of the Cotswolds and the Berkshire Downs (Featherstone and Bewley 2000; Winton 2003). These appear to reinforce the general pattern, and to some extent the picture is being explored through an increasing number of investigations off the gravels. These include sites on the dip slope of the Cotswolds along the major A419/A417 Swindon to Gloucester road scheme and elsewhere; around Bicester; on the Corallian Ridge and Oxford Heights; in the Vale of White Horse south-west of Abingdon; in the Vale of Aylesbury; and on the chalk escarpment of the Berkshire Downs and outlying hills.

To some extent, the late prehistoric pattern of settlement builds on the broad distribution of earlier prehistoric activity as revealed by the varying density of round barrows, with the overall size of barrow clusters or cemeteries and density of barrows greater on the floor of the valley (especially the gravel terraces) than in the surrounding areas (Lambrick 1988, 124-9).

It has long been thought that the picture off the gravels was probably more complex in detail than Hingley's broad-brush model suggests (Haselgrove 1984; Lambrick 1988, 125-9). This has been reinforced by new research by Moore (2006) and Lang (pers. comm.). For example, a greater variety of settlement forms is apparent in the north-east Cotswolds, such as a large open settlement adjacent to Madmarston Hill, another open settlement near Tadmarton and a variety of enclosure forms that call into question traditional morphological typologies (Allen 2000; Featherstone and Bewley 2000; Alex Lang pers. comm.). Small and large scale excavation has shown both the presence (Saville 1979; Lambrick 1988; Marshall 1990; 1991; 1995) and virtual absence (Mudd *et al.* 1999) of settlement associated with some enclosures on the Cotswolds, and glimpses of a few other settlements with complex sequences of development (eg Cropper and Hardy 1997) suggest that they do not fit into simplistic categories.

On the Berkshire Downs and outlying chalk hills the nature of settlement has been clarified by various research projects over the last 10 years though these have also raised major questions. They involved the examination of a late Bronze Age open settlement at Tower Hill (Miles *et al.* 2003), Helen Winton's (2003) work identifying a relatively discrete cluster of banjo enclosures, and new insights into the character of defensive enclosures, including the multi-period defended enclosure with a major external open settlement and midden at Castle Hill, Little Wittenham (Miles *et al.* 2003; Lock *et al.* 2005; Gosden and Lock 2001; 2002; Allen *et al.* forthcoming a).

Several pipeline and evaluation projects have provided insights into settlement in the clay vales, suggesting that they were much more comprehensively occupied than once supposed (Farley *et al.* 1984; Catherall *et al.* 1984; Wilson and Cater 2005; Hearne 2000).

Reconnaissance, academic research and development-led excavations in areas off the gravels are increasingly changing the context in which the archaeology of the valley floor is seen. Ultimately it cannot be properly understood without having a much clearer idea of what was happening in the surrounding areas with which its inhabitants interacted. It is inevitable that new work off the gravels has revealed great complexity, and there remain clear distinctions in the patterns of settlement in different parts of the Upper Thames Valley which offer fruitful avenues of research, but require more excavation if the overall picture is to be understood (Moore 2006; Alex Lang pers. comm.).

Middle Thames Valley and Tributaries

Since the late 1970s a series of late Bronze Age settlements and field systems have been investigated in the lower Kennet valley around Burghfield, west of Reading and Thames Valley Park to the east; between Maidenhead and Slough at Taplow, Dorney, Cippenham, Eton Rowing Course; and on the west London and Surrey gravels around Staines and Egham, including Runnymede, Petters Sportsfield and the very extensive Perry Oaks/T5 excavations at Heathrow. Additionally a significant number of small Iron Age enclosures and open settlements have been excavated, though these are mostly more ephemeral than their Upper Thames counterparts.

For a long time it has been recognised that both the background and the sequence of development of the Upper and Middle Thames areas have seemed quite different, with more impressive early prehistoric monuments and Iron Age development in the Upper Thames area contrasting with rather less impressive monument complexes but more evidence of later Bronze Age field systems and settlement in the Middle Thames (Barrett and Bradley 1980). Although this pattern still holds good to a reasonable extent, there has also been more convergence between the two parts of the valley with parts of the sequence being filled out, suggesting that we now need more refined explanations of differences in the development of the two areas.

The settlement pattern of the lower Kennet valley was surveyed by Wessex Archaeology in the 1970s and 1980s (Fig. 2.4; Lobb and Rose 1996) and the Loddon valley by Thames Valley Archaeological Services at much the same period (Ford 1994-7). These surveys combined desk studies with field walking, aerial photography and limited trenching or trial pitting and some review of excavated sites. The background they provide has subsequently been filled in with more detail through excavations in advance of gravel extraction and other development.

In the Burghfield area several middle to late Bronze Age ring ditches, fields systems and settlements have been investigated. Some settlements were associated with fields, others not; some represented more intensive areas of activity than others, but few revealed direct survival into and through the Iron Age (Moore and Jennings 1992; Bradley *et al.* 1980). Recently discovered evidence of very early iron working firmly in the late Bronze Age, together with a subsequent early Iron Age enclosed settlement on the higher gravels north of the Kennet at Hartshill Copse is of considerable interest. Evidence of other early and middle Iron Age settlement is patchy, usually occurring in different localities from the late Bronze Age sites, and with little evidence of long-lived settlements developing through the Iron Age. A middle Iron Age enclosure close to the Thames north-east of Reading at Thames Valley Park hints at more Iron Age activity waiting to be discovered in the main river valley, while further south at Risely a sequence of middle to late Iron Age settlement also associated with iron working has been investigated (Lobb and Morris 1991-3).

This variable pattern of settlement also applies to the area between Maidenhead and Slough, where very extensive work on the Thames Flood Channel and the Eton Rowing Course, together with smaller scale gravel quarries mostly south of the river and building development around Slough, have provided opportunities to investigate the development of settlement and landuse. This has revealed a broadly similar pattern of areas of later Bronze Age fields and small settlements, little evidence of early Iron Age activity but some small middle to late Iron Age enclosures. The sequence at Eton Rowing Lake provides evidence of the dispersal of different elements of the pattern over a large area of the valley floor interspersed with palaeochannels.

The pattern of later prehistoric settlement further off the gravels in this part of the valley, on the wooded dip slope of the Chilterns and the clay and sand Tertiary beds below the scarp of the Hampshire chalk is as yet relatively poorly understood (eg Kidd 2007).

East of Slough a major focus during the middle and late Bronze Ages would have been important settlements sampled at Runnymede Bridge (Longley 1980; Needham 1991; Needham and Spence 1996) and Petters Sports Field (O'Connell 1986), an ill-defined area of possibly high status multi-period settlement at Brentford (eg Bell 1996) and the somewhat enigmatic site at Mayfield Farm south-east of Heathrow (Merriman 1990). Elsewhere, middle to late Bronze Age occupation sites are very common (Cotton 1991; 2000; Cotton *et al.* 1986; Needham 1987), and it is increasingly clear that many were associated with broadly contemporary field systems (O'Conell 1990; Hayman 1991b; 2002b; forthcoming c and d; Crockett 2001; Framework Archaeology 2006).

Some of these settlements seem to have continued, perhaps with little change, into the early Iron Age within the old fields and enclosures that were not renewed, or in other cases were largely abandoned as settlements or shifted location. In the middle to late Iron Age small open settlements become more visible archaeologically amongst the earlier field systems, partly respecting, partly superseding the earlier layout. In cases like Thorpe Lea Nurseries a rather longer sequence of Iron Age occupation seems to be in evidence (Hayman 1998; forthcoming a), as was the case of the Iron Age settlement associated with the iron working site at Brooklands (Hanworth and Tomalin 1977; Hayman 1991c).

The pattern of Iron Age settlement development off the gravels south of the river is rather different, with less evidence of late Bronze Age fields and settlements. But an increasing number of middle to late Iron Age enclosed settlements, with relatively minor traces of earlier Iron Age activity have been

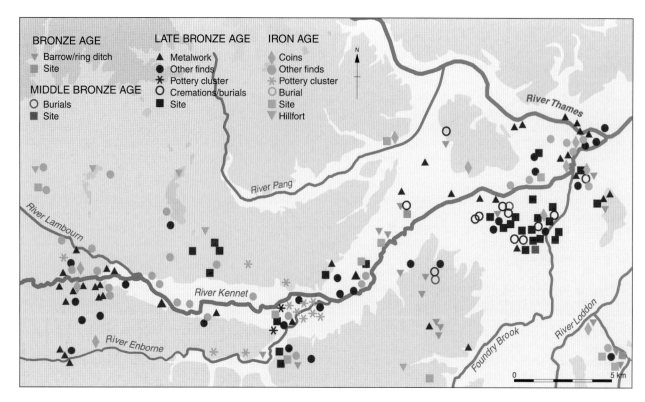

Fig. 2.4   Later prehistoric activity in the lower Kennet Valley from the lower Kennet survey

discovered in the last 15 years, as exemplified by the substantially investigated enclosed settlements at Runfold Farm and Tongham Nurseries near Farnham in the Blackwater valley, and perhaps Pirbright on the Surrey Heaths (Poulton 2004, 58-60; Hayman 2002a). There is also some evidence of Iron Age activity on the London Clay though this is still limited (Poulton 2004).

Communal enclosures and late Iron Age developments

Throughout later prehistory there were major communal earthworks, notably hilltop enclosures and forts that were part of the overall pattern of settlement. In the late Bronze Age to early Iron Age these were mainly established in prominent places on the hills surrounding the valley, in some cases immediately overlooking the river. But there are also examples of such sites on the valley floor.

In the late Iron Age the general pattern of settlement established through the first millennium BC continued on the gravels, but a consolidation of the political ambitions of tribal leaders saw the development of important new centres, both away from the gravels and within the valley. In the Middle Thames Valley this trend was especially strong on the dip slope of the Chilterns around the major Catuvellaunian centre at Verlamion (Roman Verulamium and modern St Albans) and south of the river around the Atrebates' oppidum at *Calleva* (Silchester). In the Upper Thames Valley upstream of the Corallian Ridge the Dobunnic centres of

Bagendon and Salmonsbury were established on the dip slope of the Cotswolds, while between the Corallian and Chalk ridges late Iron Age centres were established beside the river at Abingdon and Dorchester. In a sense, these centres were development of the settlement patterns already established. At a lower level of settlement, as we have seen, there was often a fair degree of continuity from middle Iron Age settlements, but detailed chronologies are too ill-defined to be sure of relative patterns of change, and the fortunes of one area would no doubt have differed from others, depending on local political and socio-economic circumstances.

Overview

Having briefly introduced some of the broad patterns, it is worth noting that the character of late prehistoric settlements and the ways that they changed through time differ quite markedly from one part of the Thames Valley to another. The reasons are complicated and as we shall see, relate to different trajectories of social, cultural and economic change. The patterns also relate, however, to interaction between human farming settlements and the natural environment, which both influenced and was modified by human exploitation of the valley. The next sections review how the environment of the Thames Valley changed through later prehistory, beginning with the river and its floodplain and wider catchment before considering broad changes in vegetation and habitats.

THE PALAEOHYDROLOGY OF THE THAMES AND ITS FLOODPLAIN

The Middle and Late Bronze Age

Palaeochannels, soils and sedimentation patterns on the floor of the Thames Valley in the late second millennium BC have been studied in detail in both parts of the valley but hydrological conditions on the general surface of the floodplain are better known from the Upper Thames than the Middle Thames Valley. Evidence is derived from a combination of sediment and soils, biological remains of plants, beetles and snails, together with dating evidence based mainly on stratigraphic relationships and sequences and radiocarbon dating of preserved organic remains. The alluvium of the Thames floodplain has not proved very amenable to magnetic dating, perhaps because seasonal drying causes deep cracking of the clay. However, successful results were obtained from the alluvial sediments partly filling the ditch of a Neolithic cursus at Drayton, where Dr A Clark was able to show that alluviation was underway by 50 BC (Barclay *et al* 2003, 185-6, 172 Fig 7.3).

The Upper Thames Valley

Soil formation processes predominated over alluvial accretion on the floodplain of the Upper Thames for much of the Holocene. The water table was at least seasonally low and large areas of the floodplain had a thin covering of a brown earth soil without evidence for waterlogging above the Late Devensian gravels of the Floodplain Terrace. Such soils survive beneath the alluvial clays which now cover the floodplain but are best studied where they are sealed beneath prehistoric earthworks. One such example was found beneath the bank of the Drayton Cursus where it crossed a low area of

floodplain (Barclay *et al* 2003). Similar palaeosols are also present beneath Bronze Age barrows on the floodplain, for example at King's Weir (Bowler and Robinson 1980). Evidence for a seasonally low water table is provided by sites with Neolithic or early Bronze Age pits or ditches which extend below the permanent water table but have ungleyed fills, whereas later archaeological features on those sites of a similar depth have gleyed fills, sometimes with preserved organic remains at the base. For example, at Port Meadow, Oxford the fills of Bronze Age ring ditches were found to be non-gleyed but waterlogged macroscopic plant remains were present in Iron Age enclosure ditches at the same depth (Robinson and Lambrick 1984).

The earliest evidence that the water table was rising in the Upper Thames Valley during the Bronze Age comes from Yarnton (Fig. 2.5). A pair of middle Bronze Age ceremonial ditches ran across a low area of the floodplain towards a palaeochannel. The preservation of organic remains was very poor in the initial cuts of these ditches (Robinson in Hey *et al.* forthcoming b), but well-preserved remains were found in recuts of the ditches. Six radiocarbon dates were obtained from the bases of the recuts, ranging from 1630-1320 cal BC to 1420-1210 cal BC. The palaeochannel was dry during the mid Holocene. Trees grew even on the lowest part of the channel bed and a Neolithic flint scatter extended well into the channel. However, by the late Bronze Age, there was sufficient water in the channel to result in the preservation of a timber and brushwood platform. A radiocarbon date of 920-520 cal BC was obtained on an oak stake from the structure. The occurrence of shells of flowing water molluscs in the sediment trapped by the platform suggested that there was at least a seasonal flow of water from the main river along the channel.

Fig. 2.5 Investigating a buried river channel at Yarnton

At Oxford, a very broad shallow palaeochannel or particularly low-lying area of the floodplain in the St Aldates area, which had probably been dry for much of the Holocene, became drowned in the late Bronze Age or early Iron Age (Robinson 2003, 77). This created an area of shallow water extending several hundred metres from the edge of the Second Gravel Terrace southwards to a deeper channel of the river. A radiocarbon date of 1010-400 cal BC was obtained on seeds from plants of seasonally exposed mud such as redshank (*Polygonum persicaria*) and golden dock (*Rumex maritimus*) from the base of the deposit.

There is also clear evidence for a rising water table in the headwaters of the Thames. A minor palaeochannel at Latton near Cricklade had tree throw holes on the bed (Robinson 1999a, 497-500). A radiocarbon date of 1376-929 cal BC was obtained on waterlogged seeds from the bottom of organic sediments which covered the tree throw holes.

There is no evidence of channel migration in the Upper Thames Valley during the Bronze Age; indeed the river regime was rather one of channel sedimentation. At Whitecross Farm, Wallingford sediments from a channel bed of the Thames were analysed, showing that sedimentation began during the late Bronze Age when flow was obstructed by a timber jetty or bridge, such that the channel ceased to be active before the start of the Iron Age (Cromarty *et al.* 2006). The aquatic insects and molluscs comprised a rich fauna of a well-oxygenated mesotrophic lowland river in all its aspects. These ranged from open water in the centre of a channel to densely vegetated marginal reedswamp. The aquatic Coleoptera included some species from the family Elmidae. These are now of restricted distribution in the Thames or are entirely absent from the drainage basin as they require clean, well-oxygenated moving water. They are well-adapted to a strong current of water, clinging to stones and aquatic plants. The smaller species, including *Esolus parallelopipedis* and *Oulimnius* sp., are now confined to weir outflows and faster flowing tributaries of the Thames. One larger beetle, *Stenelmis canaliculata*, is so fastidious in its need for large bodies of clean water that it is now found only in a couple of river systems and a single lake in Britain. Such fauna probably occurred throughout much of the length of the Thames while it remained in an unpolluted, unmanaged state and its waters carried a low level of silt.

The molluscan assemblages from the Wallingford Bypass palaeochannel comprised typical clean water riverine faunas, with many specimens of *Theodoxus fluviatilis*, *Valvata piscinalis*, *Bithynia tentaculata*, *B. leachii* and *Gyraulus albus*. There were also examples of *G. acronicus*, which is restricted in Britain to part of the Thames drainage system. Variation within the habitats of the river is exemplified by the occurrence of both *Sphaerium corneum*, a bivalve which lives in a silt bed below clean water, and *Ancylus fluviatilis* a freshwater limpet that attaches to stones in quick-moving water where the turbulence of the current is sufficient to keep the stones clean.

The Middle Thames Valley

The middle to late Bronze Age hydrology of the Middle Thames Valley is less straightforward. Holocene sediments overlying the Late Devensian gravels of the Shepperton Terrace are classified as the Staines Alluvial Deposit (Gibbard 1985). The sediments of this stratigraphic unit include coarse organic deposits from the active phase of palaeochannels and silty clay of overbank alluvium (Branch and Green 2004, 8-9). The Staines Alluvial Deposit has been recorded from Pangbourne downstream to the Lower Thames and it ranges from a maximum thickness of about 3 m to absence where the Shepperton Gravels outcrop. Most of the dates obtained on this deposit belong to the early Holocene but it has produced some Bronze Age material. The variations in thickness have been interpreted as a reflection of the pattern of channels and intervening bars forming the surface of the underlying gravel.

Most of the investigations of the Staines Alluvial Deposit have been by borehole survey or the inspection of narrow trenches. However, the construction of a rowing course by Eton College at Dorney provided an opportunity to study a block of floodplain in the Middle Thames Valley about 0.75 km wide and running about 2 km alongside the present channel of the Thames (Parker and Robinson 2003). It comprised an undulating surface of Shepperton Terrace gravels dissected by Holocene palaeochannels filled with fine organic sediments and large low-lying areas where overbank clay alluvium covered the gravels. There were several islands where the gravel terrace rose above the surrounding floodplain. In the early Holocene, low-lying areas that had originated in the Late Devensian became backswamps where fine alluvial sediments accumulated. Much of this alluviation had already occurred by 5230-4940 cal BC but it is possible that seasonal overbank flooding and alluviation was occurring on these areas during the middle and late Bronze Age.

From the Neolithic until the middle Bronze Age, the channel activity was one of episodes of bank erosion followed by periods of sedimentation within a relatively narrow zone. There was no large-scale channel migration. The sediments which accumulated during this period in the palaeochannels mostly comprised calcareous organic silts and sands with abundant broken shell and calcium carbonate encrustations. In the middle Bronze Age, a substantial timber bridge was built across one of the palaeochannels with a double row of oak piles which produced radiocarbon dates of 1530-1310 cal BC and 1420-1210 cal BC. The wooden structure undoubtedly influenced local sedimentation patterns in the channel, although the absence of piles from the central part of the bridge suggested that episodes of peak flow along the channel were capable of carrying away obstructions. There was, however, a change in sedimentation from the time of the bridge onwards. Finely broken shell and fragments of calcium carbonate encrustation were no longer major components and there was no further channel migration.

The excavation of a complex sequence of Holocene palaeochannels and alluvial bars at Runnymede Bridge showed channel activity over the period from 6000 to 2000 cal BC to have been a series of erosion and deposition cycles (Needham 1992, 256-7). However, although there was channel migration, this occurred within a restricted zone and there were no major meander developments across the floodplain. After 2000 BC, channels became more confined and there was widespread overbank alluviation within the palaeochannel zone. During the late Bronze Age, substantial oak piles of waterfront structures were inserted into the edge of one of the palaeochannels which was beginning to silt up. The aquatic insect assemblages from these sediments, which were deposited between about 1000 and 850 cal BC, included the same species of elmid beetles which require very clean flowing water that were found in the Upper Thames at Whitecross Farm, Wallingford Bypass (Robinson 1991, 322).

There are several examples elsewhere in the Middle Thames Valley of palaeochannels which were experiencing sedimentation during the Bronze Age (Branch and Green 2004). This was all part of the process of channel simplification from a multiple to a single channel system which had been occurring during the Holocene. The lower part of the Kennet Valley, which is characterised by early Holocene peat development and alluviation in backswamps on the floodplain, shows some similarity to the Middle Thames Valley although it is possible that Holocene channel migration occurred over a greater proportion of the floodplain. At Anslow's Cottages on the Kennet floodplain, fine sedimentation was occurring in a palaeochannel during the late Bronze Age. The molluscs showed evidence of a transition from permanent well-oxygenated flowing water through seasonal mudflats to marshy grassland (Evans 1992).

The Iron Age

The Upper Thames Valley

The rising water table in the Upper Thames Valley continued from the late Bronze Age into the Iron Age. The drowning of the floodplain of the St Aldates area of Oxford had created what was in effect a large shallow lake during the late Bronze Age perhaps 0.5 km or more wide (see above). Such an area of water, which was probably less than 0.5 m deep for much of the year, could not be expected to remain open for long given the mesotrophic conditions of the Thames water, which provide adequate levels of dissolved nutrients for plant growth; indeed rhizomes of common reed (*Phragmites australis*) were found to have grown into organic sediments on its bed (Robinson 2003, 73-8). A radiocarbon date of 760-50 cal BC was given by reedswamp peat above the organic silt on the bed. Once the river began to carry a heavy sediment load, silting is likely to have been very rapid amongst the reeds, probably raising much of the area above summer water level well before the end of the Iron Age.

By the middle Iron Age, seasonal inundation was occurring on the lower-lying areas of the floodplain. This process has been studied in detail at Yarnton (Robinson in Hey *et al.* forthcoming a). A stone causeway and gravel paths had been constructed in the middle to late Iron Age across one of the above-mentioned palaeochannels which had been re-activated during the Bronze Age, extending onto adjacent areas of low-lying floodplain. One of the paths sealed a brown-earth soil which contained shells of snails such as *Vallonia costata*, indicating at least seasonally dry conditions, whereas shells of marsh and aquatic molluscs were absent. Various alignments of small pits and slots had been cut into the floodplain soil at the edge of the palaeochannel during the later Bronze Age, apparently for ceremonial purposes. The primary fills of some of these features contained shells of the amphibious snail *Lymnaea truncatula*, which was likely to have been living in temporary pools of water in them. However, there were also shells of the flowing water mollusc *Bithynia* sp. This water snail is able to live in the clean flowing well-oxygenated water of the Thames but would not have been able to thrive in stagnant water or temporary pools. Its occurrence showed that at least some of these features were open to receive floodwaters with little suspended sediment.

The character of the floodwaters changed in the middle Iron Age and they began to contain a significant sediment load. Alluviation filled the tops of the small pits and slots and sealed the palaeosol on this part of the floodplain. The rising water table resulted in the preservation of organic remains in the alluvium. Radiocarbon dates of 440-170 cal BC and 100 cal BC – AD 120 were obtained on seeds of non-aquatic plants from this sediment.

Evidence of a similar sequence on the floodplain of the Upper Thames was found at Farmoor (Lambrick and Robinson 1979, 111). Here, a middle Iron Age settlement on a low-lying part of the floodplain adjacent to a former channel experienced flooding which deposited molluscs of flowing water, such as *Bithynia tentaculata*, both on the ground surface and in ditches dated to 229 cal BC to 80 AD. However, little sedimentation was taking place. At one of the lowest-lying farmsteads on the inner edge of a broad sweeping palaeochannel defining the edge of the floodplain, the thin pre-alluvial soil overlying the gravel had been stripped off and a narrow causeway built on the exposed gravel surface. Subsequently at least 0.8 m of alluvium was deposited over this area and most of the floodplain experienced alluvial deposition, at least some of which was Roman, with further alluviation likely to be medieval.

At Mingies Ditch, on the floodplain of the Lower Windrush, there was evidence for a rise in the water table between the late Bronze Age and the middle Iron Age when the site was occupied (Allen and Robinson 1993, 108; Robinson and Lambrick 1984). The settlement was above any flooding, but its enclosure ditches extended below the water table when they had first been dug. Initially, waterlogged sediments accumulated in them but soon sedimentation reached the top of the water table and mineral sediments accumulated until the ditch sides stabilised. The renewed onset of peat growth above the mineral sediments suggested that the water table had subsequently risen to at least this level. This 'recurrence surface' for peat preservation post-dated the abandonment of the site and was possibly late Iron Age. Alluviation gradually became more extensive in the Upper Thames Valley during the Roman period but at Mingies Ditch it was not until the late Roman period that regular seasonal flooding was occurring over almost all the flood-plain, and alluviation did not occur over the settle-ment area until the late Saxon or medieval period. Some of the minor palaeochannels reactivated in the late Bronze Age were filled in by Roman alluviation, which greatly changed floodplain topography by levelling it up.

One response to the increasing wetness of the floodplain of the Upper Thames Valley during the Iron Age was the construction of narrow cause-ways, usually of gravel, across the lower lying areas and newly re-activated minor palaeochannels. One such causeway was constructed at Farmoor after the onset of flooding but before significant alluvial deposition began (Lambrick and Robinson 1979, 25). At Yarnton at least six causeways of middle Iron Age, or presumed middle Iron Age, date were constructed across the minor channels, which were becoming active from the late Bronze Age onwards. One causeway, which was originally of stone, was heightened using gravel, presumably in response to rising water levels. It is likely that the causeways would have prevented any flow of water along the channels during the summer, reducing them to pools of stagnant water (Robinson in Hey *et al.* forthcoming a). At Thrupp two causeways have been identified crossing former channels, resting on up to 0.3 m of alluvial or peaty soil overlying the natural gravel, and covered by up to 1.3 m of later alluvium (Ainslie 1998; 2002). Many of the minor channels in the multiple channel system of the Upper Thames were not necessarily active throughout the year.

Although the extent of flooding increased progressively during the middle Iron Age, some areas of the floodplain remained dry. The erosive action of the Late Devensian braided channels migrating back and forth across parts of the flood-plain at times of high meltwater had left an undulating surface. The lower areas now became covered in fine alluvium but in places gravel islands project through the clay. Middle Iron Age farmsteads at Port Meadow were situated on islands above contemporaneous flood levels (Lambrick and Robinson 1988). Larger areas of floodplain which experienced Roman or later flooding were also above Iron Age flood levels.

The Middle Thames Valley

It is likely that the water table of the floodplain of the Middle Thames was also rising during the Iron Age and there was an increase in the area vulner-able to flooding. Nevertheless, some areas of flood-plain which experienced alluviation in the Roman or medieval period were above flood levels throughout the Bronze Age and Iron Age, as at Reading Business Park on the floodplain of the Kennet near its junction with the Thames (Robinson 1992, 5).

At Marsh Lane East, on the Maidenhead Windsor and Eton flood-relief channel, middle Bronze Age ditches which cut humified early Flandrian peat in a palaeochannel were sealed by alluvial clay but the date of alluviation is unknown (Robinson unpub-lished). Not far away at Dorney the low-lying areas of floodplain had experienced at least limited alluviation for much of the Holocene and it is possible that there was some Iron Age overbank alluviation although this could not be confirmed (Parker and Robinson 2003). The Bronze Age bridge at Dorney was replaced in the Iron Age by one dated to 770-400 cal BC (BM-3023) and 770-390 cal BC (BM-3021) from its oak piles (Parker and Robinson 2003). A further four bridges were constructed across the channel during the Iron Age, as were various hurdle structures, some of which were probably related to ceremonial activities in the channel. These structures probably encouraged sedimentation (evident in a narrowing of the width of water that needed to be bridged) though the channel remained active into the Roman period and had a water beetle fauna which included species of Elmidae, characteristic of very clean flowing water, also noted from Bronze Age palaeochannels.

There is no evidence from the Middle Thames for channel migration. Indeed, the process of channel silting and sedimentation seems to have continued from the Bronze Age. The Dorney palaeochannel continued to show a broad and shallow profile that seems to have been typical of later prehistoric channels of the Thames.

Discussion

The floodplains of the Upper and Middle Thames Valleys had different Holocene hydrological histo-ries prior to the middle Bronze Age. In the Upper Thames Valley, even the low areas were above flood levels and the beds of some of the minor Late

Devensian channels were dry. The floodplain had much in common with the First Gravel Terrace. In contrast, the lower areas of the floodplain of the Middle Thames Valley developed into backswamps early in the Holocene and received a covering of alluvial clay. This would have made them very distinct from the higher areas of the Shepperton Terrace. The active channels of the Thames in both regions showed episodes of erosion and sedimentation but there was no large-scale migration of channels across the floodplain. Both the relatively dry nature of the floodplain and the scale of environmental archaeology done in the Upper Thames Valley has meant that it has been possible to detect the rising floodplain water table in the middle Bronze Age and the re-activation of minor palaeochannels in the late Bronze Age. It is possible that there was also a rising water table on the floodplain of the Middle Thames Valley during the later Bronze Age but that it has been harder to detect on a floodplain which was already wet.

Likewise, it has also been easier to detect the onset of the period of clean-water flooding in the middle Iron Age in the Upper Thames Valley, while also showing that large areas of the floodplain of the Upper Thames Valley which eventually experienced alluviation remained above flood levels throughout the Iron Age. In the Middle Thames flooding with at least limited sedimentation could have been a feature of the low-lying areas throughout the Holocene, though at least some areas of the Middle Thames floodplain also stayed above flood levels during the Iron Age.

In addition to eroded soil being deposited as overbank alluvium, much of it probably accumulated in channels which were falling out of use. The change in sediments in the Dorney palaeochannel perhaps reflected an increased input of mineral material from beyond the banks of the river. The Neolithic sediment had a major component of broken mollusc shell and calcium carbonate fragments which had their origin from within the channel. These components were greatly reduced in the Iron Age sediments.

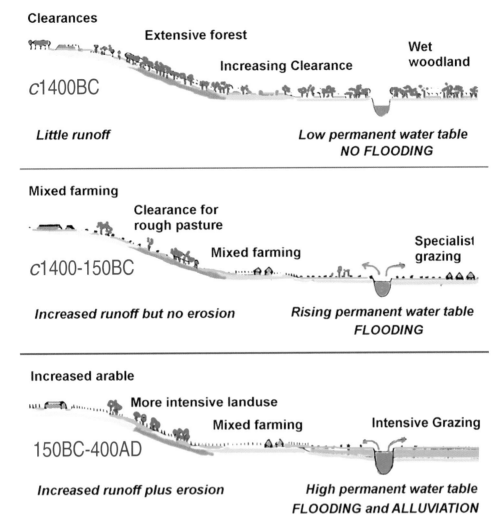

Fig. 2.6   Diagram illustrating the effects of expanding human exploitation on the palaeohydrology of the Upper Thames Valley

It has been argued that the rising water table and the onset of clean water flooding in the Upper Thames Valley were the result of extensive tree clearance in the catchment to create grazing land (Robinson and Lambrick 1984). The removal of trees would have reduced the loss of water from the system by transpiration (trees absorb water through both roots and leaves and release some back into the atmosphere, so if they are removed more water remains in the ground to emerge through springs and streams). Their removal would also have reduced the rate of interception of rainwater (trees slow down the rate at which rain enters the ground resulting in less surface water flow). The result of clearance would thus have been increased surface run-off and stream flow. Without the buffering and slowing down effect of trees on surface water runoff and groundwater levels, flow rates tend to become uneven, increasing the likelihood of flooding.

It is possible that the initial rise in water table was the result of clearance on the gravel terraces themselves. During the Iron Age clearance became widespread on the Cotswold slopes. If grassland is converted to arable, slope erosion is greatly increased. The later onset of general alluviation in the Upper Thames Valley, especially from about 50 BC onwards is interpreted as the result of increased cultivation on the slopes of the region, exposing ploughed soil which was no longer being held together by roots to surface rainwater flow (Fig. 2.6). It is not clear to what extent this might be related to increased cultivation of clay slopes around the periphery of the gravels, or of higher ground, or perhaps both.

The extent to which climate change might also have contributed to these changes is uncertain. The first millennium BC was a period when the climate of the British Isles was becoming cooler and wetter, and increased rainfall could also have contributed to these developments. However, the rise in water table began in the middle Bronze Age, before the onset of climatic deterioration, and the extent of flooding was greater in the Roman period, when the climate is regarded as having ameliorated, than in the Iron Age. On this basis it seems likely that if climate did play a part it may only have had the effect of accelerating change that was mainly triggered by the environmental impact of expanding clearance and cultivation by people exploiting the region's rich natural resources. This is explored in detail below, and we shall return to the issue in drawing strands together in Chapter 10.

THE VEGETATION AND ENVIRONMENT OF THE THAMES TERRACES AND FLOODPLAIN

The Middle Bronze Age Environment of the Upper Thames Valley

Evidence for the general environment of the Upper Thames gravels in the middle Bronze Age is provided partly by pollen, insects and plant remains from palaeochannels, fen deposits and some large monuments, and partly by a growing number of waterlogged deposits from waterholes associated with settlements and fields. In some cases the waterholes associated with middle Bronze Age fields and settlement activity were more pond-like than well-like as was demonstrated by the range of aquatic plants which lived in them; for example, the seeds from the middle Bronze Age waterhole at Eight Acre Field included water crowfoot (*Ranunculus* S. *Batrachium* sp.), water plantain (*Alisma* sp.) and yellow flag (*Iris pseuda-corus*) which are all typical of ponds (Robinson 1995). As a result, open waterholes such as these provide a more useful insight into the surrounding vegetation than is generally the case with narrow shafted wells.

Extent of Clearance and Surviving Woodland

The degree of clearance on the gravel terraces of the Upper Thames Valley around 1500 cal BC remains uncertain, not least because evidence tends to be biased to areas that may have seen the most extensive clearance. There is certainly strong evidence for the continuity of open conditions around major monument complexes into the middle Bronze Age and beyond. The molluscan sequence from the ditch of the Devil's Quoits henge, on the Second Terrace at Stanton Harcourt, showed an open environment throughout the silting of the ditch (Evans 1995). Evidence from soils and of the continuity of land usage at Gravelly Guy and other nearby sites further suggests that a large block of land on the Second Terrace around the Devil's Quoits monument complex remained grassland from before the middle Bronze Age until the end of the middle Iron Age (Lambrick 1992, 90-1; Lambrick and Allen 2004, 407-12 and 417-20).

Close to the Barrow Hills Neolithic and Bronze Age monument complex near Radley two pollen analyses provide useful evidence of the general environment around the beginning of the middle Bronze Age. At Daisy Banks, a fen in a narrow stream valley crossing the Second Gravel Terrace immediately west of the barrow cemetery the uppermost radiocarbon date obtained on the prehistoric part of a core analysed by Adrian Parker was 2500-1750 cal BC and deposition ceased at around the middle of the second millennium cal BC (Parker 1999). 1.2 km to the east, 600 m from the other end of the barrow cemetery, pollen has been analysed from a waterhole at Eight Acre Field dated to 1680-1420 cal BC (Parker 1995). Values for tree pollen at Daisy Banks were low and there appears to have been no more than a background presence of mixed oak, lime and hazel woodland in the catchment. However, a small quantity of *Crataegus* sp. (hawthorn) pollen hinted at areas of thorn scrub. This shrub is insect-pollinated so tends to be greatly under-represented in pollen assemblages. Trees and shrubs accounted for about 9% of the Eight Acre

Field pollen (3.2% being trees) mostly low levels of oak and hazel. This is similar to the results from the Daisy Banks Fen and together they suggest a relatively extensively cleared area centred on the Barrow Hills complex, with rather few trees perhaps reflecting only the last vestiges of the former woodland of the gravel terrace, or possibly more distant woodland.

Further evidence of the general environment of the Upper Thames gravels in the middle Bronze Age is provided by a growing number of water-logged deposits from other waterholes associated with settlements and fields, including Latton Lands on First Terrace gravels towards the head of the valley, dated 1440 to 1210 and 1440 to 1130 cal BC (Huckerby in Stansbie and Laws 2004 135-8); Yarnton on a relatively high area of floodplain (Robinson, unpublished); Appleford Sidings on the First Terrace (Robinson, unpublished); Bradford's Brook on Second Gravel Terrace south of Walling-ford, dated to 1740 to 1410 and 1440 to 1120 cal BC (Robinson in Cromarty *et al.* 2006, 216-22); and Mount Farm near Dorchester on a patch of Second Terrace gravel at some distance from the river, dated to 1508 to 931 and 1310 to 820 cal BC (Robinson 1992; Lambrick forthcoming).

Wood and tree-dependent Coleoptera were entirely absent at Bradford's Brook and averaged only 2-3% of the Coleoptera from the waterholes at Yarnton, Radley, Appleford and Mount Farm, confirming the pollen evidence. The more host-specific of the tree and shrub-dependent beetles were mostly species of scrub and hedgerow rather than beetles that feed on major woodland trees. The bark beetle *Scolytus rugulosus*, which tends to be associ-ated with *Prunus* spp. (sloe etc) and the weevil *Acalles turbatus*, which bores into dead twigs, especially in hedges, were present in several of the waterholes.

The evidence of a very open landscape at Mount Farm is of interest, being on a site with a long, though probably very sporadic sequence of Neolithic and early Bronze Age activity including funerary monuments and a post circle, situated between and about 1km from the ceremonial complexes associated with the cursus monuments at Dorchester and Drayton St Leonard. Like Radley, it suggests that by the middle Bronze Age and perhaps much earlier, there were extensive cleared areas in the vicinity of major ceremonial complexes.

At Yarnton additional evidence for floodplain vegetation on the floodplain of the Upper Thames during the middle Bronze Age comes from water-logged macroscopic plant and insect remains associ-ated with a pair of ceremonial ditches which led down towards a palaeochannel which was not necessarily active at the time (Robinson in Hey *et al.* forthcoming). Six radiocarbon dates were obtained on the remains ranging from 1630-1320 cal BC to 1420-1210 cal BC. There were few wood and tree dependent Coleoptera but a few seeds of alder (*Alnus glutinosa*) and leaf fragments of oak (*Quercus* sp.) showed that trees were not entirely absent.

Further up the river a somewhat different picture emerges. At Latton Lands there is again evidence of earlier prehistoric funerary monuments, but no major ceremonial complex. Here the trees and shrubs accounted for 10-20% of the pollen, the main tree being alder (*Alnus* sp.) with only very low levels of oak and other species, and the main shrub being hazel (*Corylus*). The rather higher level of trees and shrubs at Latton compared with the Radley evidence is consistent with a somewhat later pollen sequence from a peat deposit about 1.5 km away at Latton Roman Pond where there seems to have been a much stronger presence of woodland, with trees and shrubs roughly equally contributing to about 40% of the pollen, including a significant proportion of lime (Scaife 1999). At Shorncote Quarry, Somerford Keynes on the First Terrace there is evidence of oak, lime and hazel woodland persisting through the Middle Bronze Age, and there are some indications that it had experienced relatively little disturbance (Robinson 2002).

The Latton and Shorncote areas thus seem to have supported a mixture of grassland, scrub and some woodland, and even if the gravel terraces of the main valley of the Upper Thames Valley downstream of Lechlade had been almost completely cleared by 1500 cal BC, it is likely that there was still much woodland on at least the lower-lying terraces and floodplain of the higher reaches of the valley. This may also apply to some tributary valleys. Alder woodland was not cleared from part of the floodplain of the Lower Windrush until the late Bronze Age (see below Allen and Robinson 1993). It is also assumed that the clay slopes of the valley-side largely remained wooded, but evidence is very sparse.

The Upper Thames Valley thus probably presented a picture of a wide open corridor or a string of large stretches of extensively cleared land winding thorough a rather more wooded landscape. There is rather little evidence from the valley sides, but at Sidlings Copse north-east of Oxford, the pre-clearance levels of tree and shrub pollen were around 90%, dropping 10% in the early Bronze Age before reverting to (and staying) around 20% through the later Bronze Age and Iron Age (Day 1991).

Grassland

The many early Bronze Age ring ditches on the river gravels usually contain a layer of fine soil above their primary silting and any deposits related to remodel-ling during their main period of use. These fine, stone-free soils contrast with the gravelly ploughsoil of Iron Age, Roman or later date which often fills the top of these features and they indicate that there was a long stable phase which is assumed to have been grassland (Robinson 1992, 53). Such deposits were typical of the ring ditches at Barrow Hills and grass-land was the major component of the open landscape reflected in the Daisy Banks fen just west of the cemetery, with high values for pollen of ribwort plantain (*Plantago lanceolata*) and grass (Gramineae).

At Mount Farm, such a deposit was cut by the large middle to late Bronze Age waterhole, with clear evidence of an open grassy environment before the remaining depression left by the ring ditch and waterhole was filled with an early Iron Age gravelly ploughsoil with associated ardmarks (Lambrick forthcoming; below Chapter 7).

Tubers of the grass onion couch (*Arrhenatherum elatius* var. *bulbosus*) seem to be particularly characteristic of Bronze Age cremations (Robinson 1988, 102), including those associated with the ring ditches, as at Barrow Hills (Moffett 1999). This grass is characteristic of ungrazed or very lightly grazed grassland but it does not withstand heavy grazing. It is an early colonist of cleared land and abandoned arable and its tuberous roots are believed to make it particularly well-adapted to survive disturbance by ploughing, but it may also have flourished in the disturbed ground created by the construction and refurbishment of ring ditches and barrows before they went out of use. Perhaps the ring ditches were set amidst lightly grazed grassland from which tussocks of onion couch growing in disturbed soil around them were collected for the funeral pyres.

On the floodplain at Yarnton scarabaeoid beetles particularly *Phyllopertha horticola* and elaterid beetles which have larvae that feed on the roots of grassland plants were well represented, comprising over 6% of the terrestrial Coleoptera. One of the elaterids, *Agrypnus murinus*, favours permanent grassland on well-aerated soil and was probably reflecting conditions over much of the floodplain before the water table became sufficiently high to cause soil waterlogging. Scarabaeoid dung beetles, such as species of *Aphodius*, comprised 8% of the terrestrial Coleoptera, showing that the grassland was being grazed, although the concentration of domestic animals need not have been particularly high. The seeds gave an indication of the composition of the grassland flora. They suggested well-drained mesotrophic grassland akin to a grazed variant of the damp flowery meadows MG5 and MG6 of the National Vegetation Classification (Rodwell 1992, 22). Seeds from plants of such vegetation included *Ranunculus* cf. *acris* (meadow buttercup), *R.* cf. *bulbosus* (bulbous buttercup), *Cerastium* cf. *fontanum* (mouse-ear chickweed), *Potentilla reptans* (creeping cinquefoil), *Prunella vulgaris* (self heal) and *Leontodon* sp. (hawkbit).

Pasture of this sort was probably widespread on the better-drained areas of the floodplain. There were also seeds from plants of marshy grassland which perhaps grew on wetter ground alongside the palaeochannel and might have been similar to rush pasture MG10 (Rodwell 1992, 24). Seeds from plants of this community included *Ranunculus* cf. *repens* (creeping buttercup), *Potentilla anserina* (silverweed), *Rumex conglomeratus* (sharp dock), *Mentha* cf. *aquatica* (water mint), *Juncus effusus* gp. (tussock rush) and *Carex* sp. (sedge).

The vast majority of pollen from the middle Bronze Age waterholes at Eight Acre Field, Latton and the middle to late Bronze Age one at Mount Farm came from grassland plants including Gramineae (grasses), *Plantago lanceolata* (ribwort plantain) and Compositae-Liguliflorae (hawkbit etc). The Coleoptera from the waterholes at Yarnton, Radley, Appleford and Mount Farm had also largely been derived from grassy landscapes. Indeed a well-drained sunny aspect to some of the grassland at Appleford Sidings is suggested by the occurrence of *Brachinus crepitans* (bombardier beetle) in one of the waterholes. Scarabaeoid dung beetles showed that domestic animals were being grazed in the area. Waterlogged macroscopic remains of plants of open habitats are not entirely absent from these sites. There were a few seed of herbaceous plants of disturbed ground and grassland.

While the insect evidence from the Yarnton, Radley and Appleford waterholes and the pollen from Radley suggest largely unwooded landscapes, the macroscopic plant remains from them were dominated by remains from species of mixed scrub which were also common at Mount Farm. The woody species represented included *Rhamnus catharticus* (purging buckthorn); *Rubus fruticosus* agg. (blackberry), *Rosa* sp. (rose), *Prunus spinosa* (blackthorn), *Crataegus* cf. *monogyna* (hawthorn), *Cornus sanguinea* (dogwood), *Salix* sp. (sallow, willow) and *Sambucus nigra* (elder).

There were also seeds of herbaceous plants likely to have grown in shaded conditions amongst the bushes, such as *Moehringia trinervia* (three-nerved sandwort), *Chaerophyllum temulentum* (rough chervil) and *Urtica dioica* (stinging nettle).

The apparent discrepancy between the evidence from macroscopic plant remains as compared with the pollen and insects is probably due to the different sizes of the catchments from which they had been derived. Unless human transport is involved macroscopic plant remains tend to have a very local origin whereas pollen grains and insects usually come from a wider radius. Thus it is likely that the general landscape around these waterholes was probably open and mostly grassland, but there were patches of scrub in their immediate vicinity. Such vegetation is typical of the scrub which develops on the gravels of the Upper Thames Valley when some grazing is occurring but not enough to eliminate the thorny species. It is also characteristic of old hedges and hedges which have been created by selective clearance or mixed planting. It seems likely that once the waterholes began to fall out of use and fill with organic sediment, scrub was allowed to become established around them, perhaps colonising from nearby hedges. However, there was no evidence at these sites of general abandonment of the grassland to scrub regeneration. It is possible that there were superstitions, social rituals or religious reasons why abandoned waterholes were not kept clear of scrub and incorporated into the surrounding pastureland (as may be suggested by possible deliberate deposits in their backfill (see Chapter 8), but natural scrubbing over of abandoned ponds is quite familiar in today's countryside.

Fields, Arable and Human Habitation

The middle Bronze Age agricultural economy of the Upper Thames Valley is described in detail below but some aspects are of relevance to this general consideration of the environment. The middle Bronze Age was the period when the landscape began to be divided for territorial and agricultural purposes, including areas of fields (see Chapter 3). Between the fields there may have been rough grassland which only experienced light grazing, probably with some thorn scrub. The field boundaries themselves may have been marked by mixed hedges including the same thorny species as the remains of woody plants in the waterhole deposits.

Wheat and barley, the major cereals of prehistoric Britain, are self-pollinated and their pollen tends to remain associated with the bracts and grain rather than being scattered to the wind (Robinson and Hubbard 1977). Cereal pollen, therefore, tends to be under-represented in pollen assemblages in relation to the proportion of the catchment under these crops. Cereal pollen was present at around 1% of the dry land pollen sum in the sequence at Daisy Banks west of Barrow Hills, and also occurs at similarly low levels at Eight Acre Field Radley, and Latton Lands. At Mount Farm, on a relatively dry patch of the higher Second Terrace cereal pollen was a more definite presence, accounting for 2% to 6% of total pollen, and there was a relatively high proportion of weeds of disturbed ground. At Bradford's Brook, there was also good representation of weeds of dry disturbed ground and some charred cereals.

It is likely that there was at least limited cereal cultivation on the gravel terraces adjacent to the Barrow Hills cemetery, and this is probably common for most of the Upper Thames gravels where there was middle Bronze Age activity, especially on the higher terraces a little further away from major ceremonial complexes as at Mount Farm and Bradford's Brook.

In terms of their environmental footprint, the 'scale of human occupation' of middle Bronze Age settlements associated with the waterholes at Yarnton, Radley, Appleford and Mount Farm was slight, though at least at Radley and Yarnton there is good archaeological evidence of nearby occupation. Although some of the seeds from weeds of disturbed ground and beetles of decaying organic material were from habitats related to the occupation on these sites, there was only a very slight presence of woodworm beetle (*Anobium punctatum*), which flourishes in timber structures. At Bradford's Brook there was much more distinct evidence of nearby occupation with more evidence of decaying organic material and woodworm beetles.

Climate

One insect assemblage in the Upper Thames Valley, from a well on a relatively high area of floodplain at Yarnton, stands apart from all the other middle Bronze Age assemblages from the region and has implications for the climate (Robinson in Hey *et al*. forthcoming). Radiocarbon determinations of 1740-1410 cal BC and 1530-1220 cal BC were made on charred plant remains from the context. The macroscopic plant remains of scrub species which were abundant in some of the other waterhole assemblages described above were absent, and the insects also suggested entirely open conditions. Almost all the insects, mostly beetles, were species associated with grass-land habitats. They included *Crepidodera ferruginea*, which feeds on grasses, *Sitona hispidulus*, which mostly feeds on red clover (*Trifolium pratense*) and *Mecinus pyraster*, which feeds on plantains (*Plantago lanceolata* and *P. media*), as well as the elaterid *Agrypnus murinus*. Scarabaeoid dung beetles which feed on the droppings of domestic animals on pasture provided overwhelming evidence for a high concentration of domestic animals on the site. They comprised 55% of the terrestrial Coleoptera. The composition of the scarabaeoid beetle assemblage was unusual. Whereas the number of individuals from the genus *Aphodius* greatly exceeds that of individuals of the genus *Onthophagus* in modern faunas from Britain, the proportions were reversed in the Yarnton well, and four of the species of dung beetle are now extinct or very rare in Britain: *Copris lunaris*, *Onthophagus fracticornis*, *O. nutans* and *O. taurus*.

Not all the Scarabaeoidea were species which are now extinct. Indeed the most numerous individuals were *Onthophagus ovatus*, now the only common member of the genus in Britain, followed by *Aphodius* cf. *sphacelatus*, which is now common in the region.

While it is clear that there was heavy grazing in the vicinity of the well, it is difficult to establish which species of domestic animal were involved. None of the dung beetles is specific to the droppings of any particular mammal. However, taking into consideration the ecology of modern dung faunas in France, where all these species of beetles are still common, the Yarnton assemblage is reminiscent of the fauna of cattle droppings. While there are other sites in the Upper and Middle Thames Valley, particularly of Neolithic and Bronze Age date, where some of the extinct or rare species have been found, it is only the Yarnton well which has had both the range of species and the high proportion of individuals from the genus *Onthophagus*. The one beetle assemblage from Britain which shows a close similarity to Yarnton in these aspects is from the middle Bronze Age Wilsford Shaft on the Wiltshire Chalk near Stonehenge (Osborne 1969, 1989), which is more or less contemprorary, the combined radiocarbon dates for the Yarnton well being 1610-1390 cal BC while those for the Wilsford Shaft are 1520-1390 cal BC.

The ratio of *Onthophagus* to *Aphodius* on these sites would now be more appropriate to mid-France and populations of these beetles would be expected to respond very rapidly to any climatic change. In the absence of any obvious ecological reasons as to the abundance of the *Onthophagus* spp., it is tentatively suggested that there could have been a brief warm episode that might have lasted only a few decades in the middle Bronze Age, when summer temperatures in Southern England were as warm as those in mid-France today.

The Middle Bronze Age Environment of the Middle Thames Valley

Extent of Clearance and Surviving Woodland

There are several pollen diagrams from palaeochannels of the Middle Thames which span the middle Bronze Age although this part of the sequence is not closely dated. In general, they suggest a landscape which had largely been cleared. There is a long pollen record from the Late Devensian to the present day from a palaeochannel of the Thames at Thames Valley Park, on the floodplain downstream from Reading (Keith-Lucas 1997). The pollen zone interpreted as running from the earlier Bronze Age to the Bronze Age/Iron Age boundary, TVP-7, gave low values for tree and shrub pollen, with oak (*Quercus*) pollen frequencies below 5%, alder (*Alnus glutinosa*) below 2.2% and hazel (*Corylus avellana*) below 15%. Grass pollen rose to more than 18% and there was a significant presence of cereal pollen. The results were interpreted as reflecting a period of intensive agricultural activity, both arable and pastoral. However, a high level of spores of *Pteridium aquilinum* (bracken) suggested more acidic soil on the gravel than on the terraces of the Upper Thames Valley, and compared with later samples with much lower levels of bracken, may indicate relatively non-intensive rough grazing.

Another Thames palaeochannel sequence, again poorly dated but probably spanning much of the Holocene, from Meadlake Place near Staines, was analysed for pollen by Branch and Green (2004). It likewise showed a decline in woodland during the Bronze Age and there was a continuous record of cereal pollen for this period.

Organic palaeochannel sediments of middle Bronze Age date were largely absent from both Runnymede and Dorney, where detailed palaeoenvironmental investigations have been undertaken on palaeochannels of the Thames. By the late Bronze Age the pollen and insect evidence suggested little woodland survived at Runnymede and Dorney (Greig 1991; Robinson 1991; Parker and Robinson 2003, 56), although bankside alders persisted at Dorney. It is possible, however, that the tributary valleys, for example the Lower Kennet, retained more woodland.

As in the Upper Thames Valley, there have been several recent investigations of organic remains from waterholes on middle Bronze Age settlements on the gravels of the Middle Thames Valley such as one at Dorney, dated to 1410-1120 cal BC. They have largely given similar evidence: waterlogged macroscopic plant remains suggest a localised presence of mixed scrub while the insect evidence suggests more open conditions including grassland.

The radiocarbon dates so far available from the waterholes at Perry Oaks/T5 centre on 1325 cal BC. The wood and tree-dependent Coleoptera suggested no more than a background presence of woodland although, for example, the bark beetle *Scolytus intricatus* showed the presence of oak (*Quercus* sp.) and the very rare beetle *Lytta vesicatoria* had perhaps been attracted to a tree of ash (*Fraxinus excelsior*). At Green Park and Moores Farm pollen sequences have been examined from two middle Bronze Age and one late Bronze Age waterhole (Scaife 2004; forthcoming; Huckerby forthcoming). Low values for tree and shrub pollen occurring in all three deposits suggest that woodland had probably been cleared from around the settlement by the middle Bronze Age when the waterhole fills were accumulating, and the area remained fairly open. Among the trees and shrubs that were present there was some variation in the proportion of alder and oak pollen alongside hazel.

Grassland

At Perry Oaks/T5 all the middle Bronze Age insect assemblages gave strong evidence for grassland. Scarabaeoid dung beetles ranged from 9% to over 19% of the terrestrial Coleoptera, suggesting domestic animals were concentrated on the site. Terrestrial species of well-drained warm open habitats predominated amongst insect assemblages including, for example, *Brachinus crepitans* (bombardier beetle), which was also found at Dorney (Robinson unpublished).

Most of the insects from the middle Bronze Age waterhole at Dorney were from species characteristic of grassland habitats (Robinson, unpublished). Grass-feeding insects included the leaf beetle *Crepidodera ferruginea* and the homopteran bug *Aphrodes bicinctus*. Insects that feed on grassland herbs included *Ceuthorhynchidius troglodytes*, which develops on *Plantago lanceolata* (ribwort plantain) and *Alophus triguttatus*, which shows a strong preference for *P. lanceolata*. Scarabaeoid dung beetles which feed on the dung of herbivores comprised almost 13% of the terrestrial Coleoptera. Most numerous were *Aphodius* cf. *sphacelatus* and *Onthophagus ovatus* but two species which are now extinct in Britain, *Caccobius schreberi* and *Onthophagus taurus*, were also present. The abundance of dung beetles suggested pastureland grazed by domestic animals was a major part of the landscape. Like the waterholes in the Upper Thames Valley, in contrast to the insects, by far the most numerous waterlogged macroscopic plant remains at Dorney represent mixed scrub. The concentration of prickles and seeds of blackberry (*Rubus fruticosus* agg.) was particularly high but there were also seeds of species such as purging buckthorn (*Rhamnus catharticus*) and sloe (*Prunus spinosa*).

In the two middle Bronze Age deposits at Green Park Phase 3 and at Moores Farm the major components of the pollen sum are grasses (Poaceae), ribwort plantain (*Plantago lanceolata*), dandelion-type (Lactuceae) and bracken (*Pteridium*), with only low values of cereal-type pollen and arable weeds such as corn spurrey (*Spergula*-type). However, the late Bronze Age waterhole at Green Park Phase 2 produced rather higher percentages of cereal-type pollen and arable weeds, suggesting that cultivation may have become more important in that area though there is a possibility that pollen from arable weeds and cereals may have been introduced into the deposits indirectly as a result of crop processing (Scaife 2004).

Fields, Arable, and Human Habitation

Middle Bronze Age waterholes on the very broad expanse of gravel terrace at Perry Oaks/T5 were set amidst small ditched fields. The majority of the insects of woody plants were species which tend to be associated with scrub and hedgerow bushes. They included *Acalles turbatus*, a weevil which bores into dead twigs, especially of *Crataegus* sp. (hawthorn) in hedges and numerous examples of the bug *Dolycoris baccarum*, which feeds on sloe. In most of the samples, the relative abundance of these species would be consistent with a landscape divided by thorn hedges but a higher percentage in one of the waterholes was probably the result of local scrub regeneration after it had fallen out of use.

Coleoptera are very good at demonstrating the importance, species composition and use of grassland within the vicinity of a waterlogged deposit but are less effective at indicating the presence of arable (Robinson 1983). However, possible evidence of cultivation at Perry Oaks/T5 was given by carabid (ground) beetles of weedy disturbed or bare ground, including *Agonum dorsale*, *Harpalus rufipes* and *Amara apricaria*. Crop remains were present in some of the waterholes (Carruthers, pers. comm.).

Several of the waterholes from Perry Oaks/T5 contained insects which feed on plants of waste-ground habitats. An indication of nettle-covered areas was given by the beetles *Apion urticarium* and *Cidnorhinus quadrimaculatus* and the bug *Heterogaster urticae*. Several of the samples contained beetles which feed on members of the Malvaceae, particularly *Malva sylvestris* (common mallow), such as *Podagrica fuscicornis* and *Apion aeneum*. The Malvaceae are very vulnerable to grazing and are most likely to have grown in areas from which stock were excluded, such as waste ground within the settlement. Many of the insects from the waterholes feed on a wide range of foul organic material. While it is possible that some would have been from refuse

on the settlement, they were no more abundant than might be expected given the occurrence of pasture grazed by domestic animals. However, the insects from two intercutting waterholes gave good evidence for the presence of timber buildings and other aspects of a settlement. Woodworm beetles, mostly *Anobium punctatum* but also *Lyctus linearis*, comprised up to 3.6% of the Coleoptera in the samples from these deposits. They are rare members of the British woodland insect fauna under natural conditions because their habitat of dry dead wood is uncommon but they thrive in timber structures. More general synanthropic beetles, represented by *Ptinus fur*, were also present in these samples. *P. fur* naturally feeds on debris in birds' and rodents' nests but flourishes in much larger numbers inside buildings amongst relatively dry waste, from food preparation, in neglected corners. The synanthropic beetles from the samples provide the earliest evidence from the Thames Valley for the insect fauna of timber buildings and indoor habitats.

Although there were few seeds of weeds of open disturbed habitats at Dorney, it is possible that there were also small cultivated fields in the vicinity of the waterhole. Interestingly, there were seeds of three species of poppy, field poppy (*Papaver rhoeas* tp.), long prickly-headed poppy (*P. argemone*) and opium poppy (*P. somniferum*). They could all have been growing on disturbed ground on the settlement or as weeds in cereal fields, but it is also possible that field and long prickly-headed poppies were part of the specialised weed community of a cultivated plot of opium poppy.

Climate

The radiocarbon dates of the Dorney waterhole and some of the waterholes at Perry Oaks/T5 overlap with the date of the middle Bronze Age well at Yarnton. Some of the species of scarabaeoid dung beetle now extinct in Britain which were found at Yarnton were also present in these waterholes. The proportion of beetles from the genus *Onthophagus*, although higher than in late Bronze Age and Iron Age assemblages, was not as high as at Yarnton. However, these results give further support to the idea that there was a brief warm climatic episode in the middle Bronze Age.

Overview

The middle Bronze Age around 1500 cal BC saw the beginning of major changes to the landscape of the Thames Valley. Much, probably most, of the gravel terraces and floodplain of the main valley had been cleared by this date. Cereals were certainly being cultivated in both the Upper and Middle Thames Valley before this date although on a very small-scale basis. Likewise, domestic animals were being raised and perhaps grazed extensively but the pressure of grazing was light. The organisation of the open landscape seems to have been related as much to earlier ceremonial monuments as to agricultural production. After this date, more intensive agricultural intensification began in some areas within the small, probably hedged, fields which were laid out around an increasing number of settlements. The main use of the fields seems to have been pasture but cereal and other crops were also being cultivated. The areas between the settlements were perhaps lightly grazed rough pasture on which limited thorn scrub was presumably present. Even by the end of the middle Bronze Age, there was certainly some woodland remaining on the gravels at the top of the Upper Thames Valley, in the tributary valleys and perhaps in some of the gaps between settlements. The hinterland to the Thames Valley, particularly the clay slopes of the Upper Thames Valley and the various acid geologies of the Middle Thames Valley, probably retained much woodland.

With settlements beginning to be characterised by more structures and perhaps more permanent occupation, even if only on a seasonal basis, distinctive faunas and floras developed which were adapted to nutrient-rich disturbed ground and indoor habitats. One noticeable aspect of the settlement environment seems to be that when waterholes fell out of use, scrub was allowed to become established around them even though the general environment remained open. This is perhaps not unlike many abandoned ponds in the present day countryside.

The Late Bronze Age Environment in the Upper Thames Valley

Extent of Clearance and Surviving Woodland

The late Bronze Age saw a continuation of the processes which began in the middle Bronze Age of a gradual agricultural intensification and progressive clearance. In the Upper Thames Valley, around Latton 'Roman Pond', near Cricklade, oak-lime-hazel woodland was being cleared at about 1376-929 cal BC although initially, some oak-hazel-alder woodland remained (Robinson 1999a; Scaife 1999). There was also evidence for persistence of some woodland in the late Bronze Age at Shorncote Quarry on the First Gravel Terrace (Robinson 2002). A well dated to 1110-811 cal BC in a Bronze Age settlement became overgrown by trees of field maple (*Acer campestre*) following its abandonment although insect evidence suggested some grazed grassland as well as mixed woodland in the wider catchment. Despite its English name, field maple is a woodland tree which is not a usual early colonist of scrub and its occurrence implies that there were at least remnants of woodland nearby from which it could become established.

Clearance in the tributary valleys included the removal of woodland from the floodplain of the Windrush at Mingies Ditch. A combined radiocarbon date of 1190-840 cal BC was given by a spread of charcoal of ash (*Fraxinus excelsior*) and oak (*Quercus* sp.) in a palaeosol beneath an Iron Age bank, and a partly burnt-out stump of alder (*Alnus glutinosa*) in a tree pit (Allen and Robinson 1993, 140).

Further down the Windrush Valley at Gravelly Guy, pollen, seed and insect evidence from two features close to the floodplain edge at the base of the Second Gravel Terrace showed that by 920-780 cal BC clearance had been substantial, not only on the gravel terrace (as would be expected in the vicinity of the major ceremonial complex round the Devil's Quoits henge circle) but also on the adjacent floodplain (Scaife 2004; Robinson 2004). Alder had so declined that compared with a high level in the later Neolithic around 2340-2020 cal BC, its pollen was substantially outnumbered by that of grass and there were only a very few seeds of alder.

Grassland

At Gravelly Guy there were relatively high pollen values for other grassland herbs including *Plantago lanceolata* (ribwort plantain) and Liguliflorae (dandelions, hawkbits etc). One curious aspect of these results was the relatively high value for spores of bracken (*Pteridium aquilinum*), which reached a value of 12% of total pollen and spores in one sample. *P. aquilinum* is a plant of both open woodland and fully open habitats which is particularly favoured by episodes of clearance because it is able to spread before other plants of open habitats have managed to colonise. However, bracken is a plant of acid soils and is no longer a member of the flora of the gravel terraces, so its presence at Gravelly Guy is surprising because although adult bracken plants can tolerate calcareous conditions, sporelings are unable to colonise. There is evidence for bracken being brought to Iron Age settlements, probably for use as animal bedding but this is not a satisfactory explanation here. It may be that sufficiently acidic conditions for bracken colonisation developed at least locally in the soil surface in patches of peat or under woodland on the floodplain but that the soil disturbance of clearance itself incorporated gravel into the soil, making it more calcareous. Bracken may have briefly flourished following clearance but was unable to sustain itself.

The evidence from late Bronze Age waterholes on sites in the Upper Thames Valley gives a somewhat similar environmental picture to that from the middle Bronze Age waterholes, though as we have seen with the examples at Mount Farm and Bradford's Brook spanning the middle to late Bronze Age there are some differences suggesting more indication of cultivation and/or settlement activity.

A second waterhole at Eight Acre Field, Radley, with a late Bronze Age radiocarbon date of 1020-800 cal BC for a log ladder found at the bottom provided strong evidence for grassland, but no evidence for the local presence of mixed thorn scrub (Parker 1995; Robinson 1995).

Fields, Arable, and Human Habitation

The overall picture for fields arable cultivation and human habitation in the late Bronze Age of the Upper Thames Valley is similarly meagre although crop remains were also present. At Gravelly Guy cultivation on the gravel terrace was suggested by pollen of some annual weeds and limited cereal type pollen.

The Late Bronze Age Environment of the Middle Thames Valley

Extent of Clearance and Surviving Woodland

Detailed palaeoenvironmental studies have been undertaken on two late Bronze Age waterfront sites, Runnymede Bridge in the Middle Thames Valley (Greig 1991; Robinson 1991; Robinson 2000a; Scaife 2000) and Whitecross Farm Wallingford in the Upper Thames Valley (Thomas *et al.* 1986; Robinson 2006a). Sediment columns were analysed for pollen, macroscopic plant remains and insects, the sequence from Runnymede dating from about 850 to 775 cal BC, the organic sediments from Whitecross Farm probably contemporary with the timber structure dated to around 1000 to 800 cal BC.

Wood and tree-dependent Coleoptera from both sites comprised around 2% of the total terrestrial Coleoptera. Many of the more host-specific of these were species which feed on rosaceous scrub or hedgerow shrubs such as hawthorn or sloe rather than the major trees of primary woodland. This picture was confirmed by the pollen. For example pollen from dry-land trees, mostly oak, comprised less than 10% of dry-land pollen from Runnymede column WF1B (Greig 1991, 250). Only a few water-side alder trees remained from the dense alder woodland which once flanked the Thames. The oak woodland which remained had perhaps been substantially modified by management. The piles of the waterfront structure at Whitecross Farm were 30-35 years old at felling and had an average annual ring width of 2.8 mm. This would suggest rapid growth under well-illuminated conditions as occurs when trees regenerate after felling and grazing animals are excluded. Cut hazel rods in the Whitecross Farm palaeochannel had perhaps been derived from coppice woodland, which may also apply to the oak (Taylor *et al.* 2006).

Pollen was analysed from a waterhole on an adjacent late Bronze Age settlement on the First Gravel Terrace at Green Park (Scaife 2004). The editors of the excavation report regrettably omitted any pollen diagram or table of results. However, it is stated that the pollen was from a diverse range of herbaceous plants with little pollen from trees and shrubs. Pollen from grassland predominated but pollen from crops and weeds of cultivation was also present.

Waterlogged macroscopic plant remains and insects have been analysed from two other late Bronze Age settlements in the lower Kennet valley,

Knight's Farm (Bradley *et al.* 1980) and Anslows Cottages (Carruthers 1992; Robinson 1992c). Pollen analysis was also undertaken at Anslows Cottages (Thompson and Allen 1992). The results suggested that alder carr persisted on areas of peat on the floodplain whereas oak-hazel woodland had largely been removed from the drier ground. Pasture and some arable predominated on the open areas.

Grassland

The background landscape which comprised the catchment for the waterlogged plant and invertebrate remains at Runnymede and Whitecross Farm in the late Bronze Age was mostly grassland. Chafer and elaterid beetles with larvae that feed on roots in grassland were well-represented. The strong presence of *Agrypnus murinus* suggests that the soils were well aerated rather than gleyed. The water-logged seeds of potential grassland plants included *Ranunculus* cf. *acris* (meadow buttercup), *R.* cf. *repens* (creeping buttercup), *R.* cf. *bulbosus* (bulbous buttercup), *Stellaria graminea* (stitchwort), *Linum catharticum* (fairy flax), *Sanguisorba minor* (salad burnet), *Rumex conglomeratus* (sharp dock), *Scabiosa columbaria* (small scabious), *Leucanthemum vulgare* (ox-eye daisy) and *Leontodon* sp. (hawkbit).

Taken together, they would make up a community of relatively well-drained calcareous soil. The range of flowers which were able to set seed suggests that grazing was relatively light and that the grassland had an appearance somewhat similar to hay meadow. These aspects contrast with the evidence described below from middle and late Bronze Age settlement sites. The explanation probably lies in the catchment from which the seeds were derived. At both Runnymede and Whitecross Farm, the majority of the seeds would have been from a relatively narrow strip either side of the river extending several kilometres upstream. The soils alongside the river were probably less decalcified than on the main bodies of the floodplain and the gravel terraces, enabling calcicolous plants such as *S. columbaria* to thrive. The evidence of scarabaeoid dung beetles from both sites showed that the grass-land was indeed being grazed but it is possible that many of the seeds were from the large areas of less heavily grazed grassland between the settlements.

Waterlogged macroscopic plant and insect remains were analysed from late Bronze Age pits and a pond at Reading Business Park on the first terrace of the Kennet (Campbell 1992; Robinson 1992d). They suggested the settlement was set amidst rough grassland although there was a background presence of woodland and scrub. It is possible that the scrub took the form of thorny hedges adjacent to the settlement with any woodland more distant. Interestingly, leaves of *Ilex aquifolium* (holly) were found in one of the samples. It is uncertain whether this shrub was a chance survivor from more extensive woodland or whether the leaves represented a placed deposit. The presence of scarabaeoid dung beetles suggested that grassland was being grazed. Although there were two examples of scarabaeoid dung beetles which are now extinct or very rare in Britain, *Copris lunaris* and *Onthophagus taurus*, the assemblages were dominated by species of *Aphodius* as is usual for assemblages of late Bronze Age and more recent date.

Fields, Arable, and Human Habitation

By the late Bronze Age some of the small middle Bronze Age settlements dispersed amongst the field system at Perry Oaks/T5 were abandoned and the field ditches were not necessarily being maintained, but in some areas settlement activity continued and the field boundaries seem still to have been hedged; it is also quite possible that the field system was being extended or subdivided in the late Bronze Age. The main use of the fields probably continued as pasture but some cereal cultivation was also occurring (Framework Archaeology 2006, 133).

In the Kennet Valley crop remains and seeds of annual weeds of cultivation raised the possibility that there was also arable activity nearby. One weed of cultivation, *Camelina* sp. (gold of pleasure), which was represented by pod fragments, is generally associated with flax.

As island sites involving middens it is not surprising that there was evidence from Runnymede and Whitecross Farm for nutrient-rich disturbed ground within their confines supporting such vegetation as *Chenopodium album* (fat hen) and *Urtica dioica* (stinging nettle) as well as a few plants of *Hyoscyamus niger* (henbane). There were seeds of *Conium maculatum* (hemlock), another member of this community, from both sites. Curiously, hemlock has not been found from other Bronze Age or Iron Age settlements in the Thames Valley whereas its seeds are often very common on Roman settlements. This was possibly a reflection of the scale or character of waste-ground type habitats and the amount of organic refuse which had been dumped on them. Some midden material at Runnymede had spilt into the palaeochannel, resulting in the preservation of insect remains. The most numerous beetles of decaying organic material were *Cercyon analis*, *Oxytelus sculptus*, *Leptacinus pusillus* and *Gyrohypnus fracticornis*.

This community is associated with foul rotting matter including dung. There were also many puparia of *Musca domestica* (house fly), which breeds in a wide range of decaying plant and animal remains. Puparia of *Stomoxys calcitrans* (stable fly or biting house fly) were also present. This fly is more fastidious and usually lays eggs on old straw or hay which has been enriched with urine and faeces. The adult of *S. calcitrans* bites both humans and domestic animals. It can be a considerable nuisance when present in numbers. The presence of a few puparia resembling *Scopeuma stercorarium* (yellow dung fly), whose larvae live in fresh dung, suggested dung to have been a constituent of the midden but the plant material from the midden included frond fragments of *Pteridium aquilinum* (bracken), leaves of *Sphagnum* sp. (bog moss) and capsules of *Linum usitatissimum* (flax). It is likely that the midden contained a mixture of refuse including dung, animal bedding and crop processing remains. Synanthropic insects which occur in indoor habitats were not particularly abundant at either Runnymede or Whitecross Farm. However, an example of *Stegobium paniceum* (bread beetle) was found at Runnymede. It develops in various farinaceous materials and can be a minor pest in granaries or bakeries. It can also infest a great variety of other stored plant and animal products such as spices. *S. paniceum* is the only grain pest to have been identified from pre-Roman sites in Britain and this is the only prehistoric record for the Middle or Upper Thames Valley. This was perhaps both a reflection of the scale of storage of vulnerable commodities at Runnymede and the opportunities for the dispersal of pests presented by trade along the river.

Climate

Unlike the middle Bronze Age sites in the regions, those from the late Bronze Age provide no evidence from insects to suggest that climatic conditions were much different from those of the late 20th century. Some extinct and very rare species were present but they were not abundant. Numbers of beetles from the genus *Aphodius* greatly exceeded numbers from the genus *Onthophagus*. For example, 174 individuals of *Aphodius* (and *Colobopterus*) were identified from the late Bronze Age WF1b sequence at Runnymede whereas there were only 23 individuals of *Onthophagus*.

Overview

By the end of the late Bronze Age, the landscape of the Thames Valley was more open than it had been a few centuries previously and larger areas of the gravel terraces were under cultivation. However, the gravel terraces were not being managed intensively over their entire area. There were lightly grazed areas of grassland between the settlements and the enclosed fields which surrounded them.

The status of the hinterland to the gravel terraces is largely unknown. While it is likely that some areas still supported much woodland, others may have been quite extensively cleared. For example, the pollen sequence at Sydlings Copse in the Upper Thames Valley shows that clearance during the early Bronze Age around 2496 to 1977 cal BC had reduced the proportion of trees and shrubs from *c* 90% to a low point of about 15% before reverting to around 20-25%. The clearance was accompanied by much higher levels of grasses, herbs, and especially bracken, suggesting clearance for rough grazing that lasted throughout the Iron Age (Day 1991).

The Early to Middle Iron Age Environment of the Upper Thames Valley

Extent of Clearance and Surviving Woodland

In the Upper Thames there is a shortage of much waterlogged environmental data for the early Iron Age, which is partly because waterholes in which organic sediments are preserved are less common on the gravel terraces than in the late Bronze Age, and partly because there is little evidence of early Iron Age activity on the floodplain and other low-lying areas. An intriguing exception to this was noted at Yarnton, where an area of late Bronze Age or early Iron Age coppicing debris dated to *c* 800-600 cal BC was discovered on the south side of a river channel. A period of ponding and silting followed, which appears to be early Iron Age on the basis of radiocarbon results from roundwood debris deposited in the sediments.

By the middle Iron Age, the Upper Thames gravel terraces were part of an organised agricultural landscape. Conditions were mostly very open. Pollen evidence has so far only been obtained from floodplain sites but conditions seem to have been very open with, for example, only 1.9% tree and shrub pollen from middle Iron Age deposits at Port Meadow, Oxford analysed by JRA Greig (Lambrick and Robinson 1988, 65-8).

In very general terms, the Iron Age exploitation of the Upper Thames Valley followed what might be expected given the potential of the various soils. Charred cereal-processing remains tend to be abundant on middle Iron Age settlements on the higher gravel terraces. Sheep bones generally outnumber cattle bones on the higher terrace sites such as Ashville, Abingdon, where the well-drained conditions would have been particularly suitable for the raising of sheep (Grant 1992; Wilson 1978). Cattle and horse bones tend to be better represented on some of the sites in the valley bottom which would have been rather too wet for sheep, for example Farmoor, where the snail *Lymnaea truncatula*, which is the intermediate host of the sheep liver fluke, was living on the Iron Age floodplain (Lambrick and Robinson 1979, 126; Grant 1992).

Not all the middle Iron Age settlements on the First Gravel Terraces and floodplain were set amidst fully cleared agricultural landscapes. For example, Mingies Ditch, on the floodplain of the Lower

Fig. 2.7   Artist's impression of the vegetational environment of the middle Iron Age enclosed settlement at Watkins Farm

Windrush, was an enclosed settlement which seems to have been primarily related to pastoralism in a less managed landscape which retained more scrub (Allen and Robinson 1993, 149-50). Tree and shrub pollen, particularly willow and sallow (*Salix* sp.), hazel (*Corylus avellana*) and oak (*Quercus* sp.) comprised 18% of the total pollen. Macroscopic plant remains preserved by waterlogging in the enclosure ditches around the settlement suggested that they ran alongside hedges which had been created either by selective clearance of established scrub or mixed planting from a woodland source. The very diverse range of woody species included field maple (*Acer campestre*), purging buckthorn (*Rhamnus catharticus*), sloe (*Prunus spinosa*), hawthorn (*Crataegus* cf. *monogyna*), hazel (*Corylus avellana*), dogwood (*Cornus sanguinea*) and guelder rose (*Viburnum opulus*). It is not clear if such sites were restricted to the tributary valleys or significant parts of the main floodplain, but somewhat similar results were obtained from a settlement at Watkins Farm, Northmoor, on the First Terrace in the main valley of the Thames downstream of its confluence with the Windrush (Figs. 2.7 and 2.8; Robinson 1990b).

The identification of charcoal from middle Iron Age settlements on the gravel terraces usually gives a much narrower range of taxa than those identified by waterlogging at Mingies Ditch. Much of it tends to be of rosaceous taxa, particularly hawthorn etc (Pomoideae) but sloe (*Prunus* cf. *spinosa*) is also often abundant. This suggests that thorn scrub or hedgerows were an important source exploited for fuel. However, oak (*Quercus* sp.) is usually well represented, along with smaller quantities of hazel (*Corylus avellana*). They are more likely to have been derived from woodland. Sloe or plum and oak predominated at Gravelly Guy (Gale 2004). It is possible that the Oxford and Gault Clay hinterland to the gravel terraces and perhaps parts of the limestone still retained much woodland. The clay slopes between terraces could also have supported scrub although it is assumed that, with the exception of some of the tributary valleys, the terraces themselves were largely devoid of woodland or scrub. At Sidlings Copse the area remained cleared but with very high levels of bracken throughout the Iron Age (Day 1991). At Woodham in the Vale of Aylesbury pollen from a humic horizon dated to *c* 545 to 111 cal BC containing middle Iron Age pottery beneath alluvial or colluvial clay sediments produced evidence of a very open landscape (Farley *et al.* 1984).

Iron Age evidence for the wild vertebrate fauna of the Upper Thames Valley is limited, in part perhaps because there was a general reluctance to eat wild animals. Both red and roe deer have been recorded amongst bone assemblages on settlements but they are even rarer than in the early Iron Age, probably because there was little, if any, woodland on the gravels. Beaver survived in the more remote parts of the valley and was identified from Mingies Ditch in

the Windrush Valley (Wilson 1993). Hare and fox were probably common while possible wild cat, pine marten and hedgehog occur occasionally (Robinson and Wilson 1987, 48). Small rodents have been recorded from several sites and, interestingly, they often include water vole (*Arvicola terrestris*). It is possible that water vole occurred in a greater range of grassland habitats until restricted to wetlands by competition with the rabbit from the medieval period onwards. Few wild bird remains have been found but they include widgeon and raven.

Grassland

There is rather little direct evidence of the distribution and character of grassland in the Upper Thames Valley during the early Iron Age, principally due to a shortage of well-dated deposits. As noted below, the region saw a significant increase in arable agriculture, especially on the higher terraces during the early Iron Age, and the damper, circumneutral brown-earth, silty to silty-clay clay loams which comprised the original soils of the floodplain would have been better suited to grass, although cultivation was certainly possible, though the increasing wetness of the lower areas and, in places, the shallowness of the soil, would have imposed some limitations. However, it is not until the middle Iron Age that there is sufficient evidence to confirm the preponderance of grassland in the valley bottom.

It is also likely that the picture was more complex than might be expected from a simple ecological model of dry ground being suitable for arable and damp ground for pasture. Traces of early Iron Age occupation on the first gravel terrace are slight and virtually absent on the floodplain, so although these areas may well have been grazed, it is far from clear that they were intensively managed or were principal grazing grounds. There is also evidence that grazing was a key part of the mixed farming regime on the higher terraces. At Gravelly Guy there was soil and settlement evidence to suggest that the arable fields reflected in the colluvium on the adjacent floodplain only formed a 200 m wide band along the outer margin of the gravel terrace. The central core of the terrace, dominated by the Neolithic and Bronze Age ceremonial complex around the Devil's Quoits, seems to have remained grazed grassland long after the monuments had fallen out of use, throughout the Iron Age and well into the Roman period. It was calculated that this 'core' grazing area may have covered *c* 500 ha, and is likely to have provided more than enough grazing to serve the basic subsistence requirements of the surrounding settlements like Gravelly Guy (Lambrick and Allen 2004, 485-6).

Middle Iron Age settlements on the First Gravel Terrace and the floodplain tend to have lower concentrations of cereal remains. The waterlogged macroscopic plant remains and insects from floodplain sites, for example Farmoor and Port Meadow, suggest that grazed grassland predominated on the floodplain (Lambrick and Robinson 1979; 1988).

The changing hydrological conditions of the floodplain were altering the grassland flora. Pollen, seeds and insects were identified from a middle Iron Age ditch on a higher area of the floodplain at Yarnton which was probably above any contemporaneous flood levels (Robinson in Hey *et al.* forthcoming a). Conditions were very open, with no evidence for local scrub or even boundary hedges. The seeds suggested a diverse flora including creeping buttercup (*Ranunculus* cf. *repens*), self-heal (*Prunella vulgaris*), ribwort plantain (*Plantago lanceolata*) and hawkbit (*Leontodon* sp.). Scarabaeoid dung beetles, especially *Aphodius* spp., showed that grazing by domestic animals was occurring. However, the range of grassland insects, such as the plantain-feeding weevils *Ceuthorhynchidius troglodytes* and *Mecinus pyraster*, vetch and clover-feeding weevils from the genera *Apion* and *Sitona*, and the grass-feeding leaf beetle *Crepidodera ferruginea*, all suggested that the grassland was not being closely grazed. Dry, well-drained conditions were suggested by some of the ground beetles, for example *Lebia chlorocephala*, and snails such as *Vallonia costata*.

It is likely that such grassland was widespread both on those areas of the floodplain above flood levels and on the gravel terraces. In modern botanical terms, it is perhaps best seen as a grazed variant of a species-rich type of unimproved grassland

classified as *Cynosurus cristatus* – *Centaurea nigra* MG5 in the national vegetation classification (Rodwell 1992, 60-6). This kind of grassland is now almost entirely known from traditionally managed hay meadows, although it does occur as pasture on the highest area of Port Meadow, Oxford (A McDonald, pers. comm.). Elsewhere on the gravel terraces almost all the modern pasture has been subject to cultivation and re-seeding, along with applications of fertiliser and herbicide. The damper areas of the floodplain which were not being broken up by overgrazing seem to have supported a range of damp to wet permanent pastures (perhaps comparable with mesotrophic grasslands of the national vegetation survey such as *Lolium perenne* – *Cynosurus cristatus* MG6 on the areas above flood levels, through *Lolium perenne* – *Plantago major* MG7 pasture on the occasionally-flooded areas, to perhaps *Festuca rubra* – *Agrostis stolonifera* – *Potentilla anserina* MG11 inundation grassland on the most frequently flooded but non-waterlogged areas of the floodplain). There was evidence of such grassland from the waterlogged enclosure of Mingies Ditch and Farmoor Floodplain Enclosures 1 and 2 (Lambrick and Robinson 1988, 63-71).

All these sites gave coleopteran evidence that they were set amidst land grazed by domestic animals. The waterlogged seeds suggested plants such as creeping buttercup (*Ranunculus* cf. *repens*),

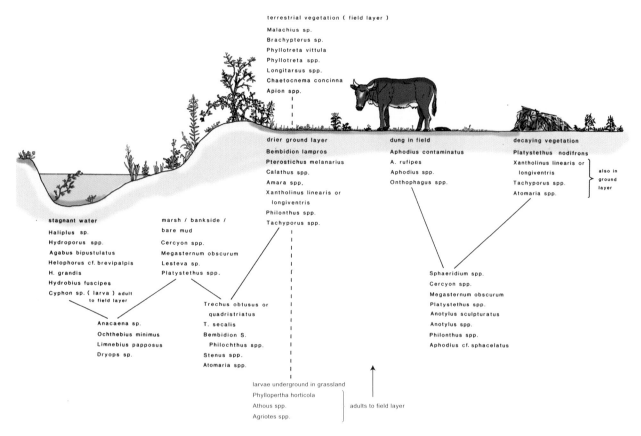

Fig. 2.8 Diagram illustrating insect and vegetational environment of the middle Iron Age enclosed settlement at Mingies Ditch

creeping cinquefoil (*Potentilla reptans*) and silver-weed (*P. anserina*) grew in the pasture. Seeds of spike rush (*Eleocharis palustris* or *uniglumis*) were quite well represented. Both species are grazing-tolerant and require a high water table in the spring but can tolerate dry conditions for the remainder of the year. Spikerush is often a member of modern inundation communities in the Thames Valley (in contrast to its absence from modern arable fields) although it is frequently overlooked by botanists. Some samples contained many seeds of great plantain (*Plantago major*) which would have been favoured in MG6 grassland by heavy grazing and trampling.

Several middle Iron Age settlements on the floodplain of the Upper Thames Valley have given evidence of overgrazing and soil damage on lower areas of the floodplain resulting in the development of rush pasture (*Holcus lanatus – Juncus effusus* MG10). For example, samples from the Port Meadow Iron Age enclosures and Enclosure 3 at Farmoor contained very high proportions of scarabaeoid dung beetles, such as *Aphodius granarius* and *A.* cf. *sphacelatus*, comprising over 25% of the terrestrial Coleoptera (Lambrick and Robinson 1988, 65-71; Fig. 2.9). The very wet conditions of the ground on which the domestic animals which produced the dung were grazing was suggested by the presence of ground beetles (Carabidae) such as *Elaphrus cupreus, Agonum marginatum* and *Chlaenius vestitus*, which occur in marshy grassland and on mud at the edge of pools. The trampling of cattle combined with the beginning of alluviation probably created permanently waterlogged soil. The most numerous seeds were from the tussock-forming rushes (*Juncus effusus, J. inflexus* and *J. conglomeratus*). Other seeds from plants conspicuous in rush pasture included ragged robin (*Lychnis flos-cuculi*) and sharp dock (*Rumex conglomeratus*).

The pasture in the vicinity of these enclosures seems to have become very broken up from the trampling of stock, being churned into mud enriched with dung. It supported a flora of annual weeds which would now be considered very unusual. Seeds of red goosefoot (*Chenopodium rubrum*), golden dock (*Rumex maritimus*) and toad rush (*Juncus bufonius* gp.) were particularly numerous.

The seeds found in both the Iron Age overbank alluvium and the palaeochannel sediments at Yarnton give an indication of the aquatic vegetation of the Thames. The more slowly-moving lengths of the river appear to have been very densely vegetated with a deeper water floating leaved flora which included yellow water lily (*Nuphar lutea*) and, interestingly, fringed water lily (*Nymphoides peltata*), which is a plant of local distribution that was common in the Upper Thames during the early 20th century, then almost completely disappeared, but is now returning. The deeper-water reedswamp flora included bulrush (*Schoenoplectus lacustris*) and arrowhead (*Sagittaria sagittifolia*). Shallow-water, submerged to floating plants included various pondweeds (both *Potamogeton* spp. and *Zannichellia palustris*) and water crowfoot (*Ranunculus* S. *Batrachium* sp.). Grazing pressure perhaps reduced some of the reedswamp species along the river margins, enabling lower growing plants, such as water plantain (*Alisma* sp.) and water mint (*Mentha aquatica*), to grow alongside sedges (*Carex* sp.).

Dung beetle (*Aphodius granarius)* (right)
modern specimen (left),
Port Meadow

Head of worker honey bee (*Apis mellifera*).
Mingies Ditch

Fig. 2.9   Middle Iron Age insect evidence

Fields, Arable, and Human Habitation

The abundant evidence from charred crop processing remains and occurrence of many early Iron Age pits potentially used for grain storage at some settlements (see below for discussion of this function) is a distinct feature of some settlements on the higher gravel terraces such as Ashville, Abingdon (Jones 1978), Gravelly Guy, Stanton Harcourt (Moffett 2004) and Yarnton (Pelling and Stevens in Hey *et al.* forthcoming a). The silty to sandy or sandy-clay loams of the gravel terraces would have been well suited to cultivation. The flat topography of the terraces would have minimised any problem with erosion, and the modern soils derived from them, the Sutton Series, are relatively fertile (Jarvis 1973). It is possible that the rising water table on the floodplain was beginning to have an influence on settlement patterns and land usage. For example, late Bronze Age settlements on the floodplain at Yarnton and Cassington were replaced in the early Iron Age by settlements on the second gravel terrace, but later on settlements like the enclosures at Mingies Ditch and Watkins Farm and open settlements like Claydon Pike, Port Meadow and Farmoor seem to have been established primarily as pastoral farms.

It is likely that cultivated fields became a more significant part of the Upper Thames landscape, especially on the drier terraces. Evidence for cultivation is also given by the occurrence of ploughsoil filling the upper part of some early Bronze Age ring ditches (Robinson 1992, 53), which can only occasionally be demonstrated to be Iron Age but in the case of Mount Farm included ploughmarks under a ploughsoil that was cut by a middle Iron Age gully (see below Chapter 7). At Gravelly Guy, Stanton Harcourt colluvial sediment spilt by cultivation over the edge of the terrace was found interstratified with alluvium on the Windrush floodplain at the edge of the second gravel terrace (Fig. 2.10; Lambrick and Allen 2004 2005, 32-4). The colluvium began to be deposited in the late Bronze Age or early Iron Age, at much the same time as significant amounts of charred cereal remains are found in settlement deposits.

The greater abundance of charred remains of crop plants and the proliferation of probable storage pits on some settlements might be taken to suggest that arable fields came to dominate some parts of the higher terraces. But even where crop husbandry became much more significant, this does not mean that arable fields dominated the landscape. This is clearest at Stanton Harcourt, where, as we have seen, the arable fields probably occupied only a narrow strip around a large central core of grassland, and it is pertinent to note that this remained sufficient into the early Roman period. The absence of any pattern of Celtic fields is unsurprising given the flat topography.

Unless stock were tethered or very closely watched over, the boundaries between arable and pasture would have had to be effective hedges or fences to prevent animals from raiding the crops. There is little biological evidence for the division of the higher gravel terraces into field systems, though there are examples of fence lines on some of the sites at Stanton Harcourt. On the lower terraces, especially in the upper reaches of the valley at places like Shorncote and Latton, it is very difficult to distinguish early Iron Age from late Bronze Age activity and non-intensive pastoralism with small scale crop-growing probably continued largely unchanged through the earlier Iron Age and beyond. Charred crop remains occur only at very low levels in both early and middle Iron Age settlements at Latton Lands, Shorncote, Horcott Totterdown Lane and Claydon Pike and Thornhill Farm.

Many of the lower lying middle Iron Age settlements of the Upper Thames Valley had developed characteristic faunas and floras reflecting human habitation. The nutrient-rich disturbed habitats within them were colonised by annual weeds of disturbed ground, particularly members of the Chenopodietalia, such as fat hen (*Chenopodium album*), chickweed (*Stellaria media* gp.), redshank (*Polygonum persicaria*) and small nettle (*Urtica urens*). In some instances, such as the settlement on the floodplain at Farmoor, they were of such short duration that perennial weeds of waste ground habitats did not become established (Lambrick and Robinson 1979). More usually, however, seeds of perennial weeds such as stinging nettle (*Urtica dioica*) were also very abundant. The vegetation of the settlements included some weeds which no longer commonly occur in the region (Robinson 1981). One of them, henbane (*Hyoscyamus niger*),

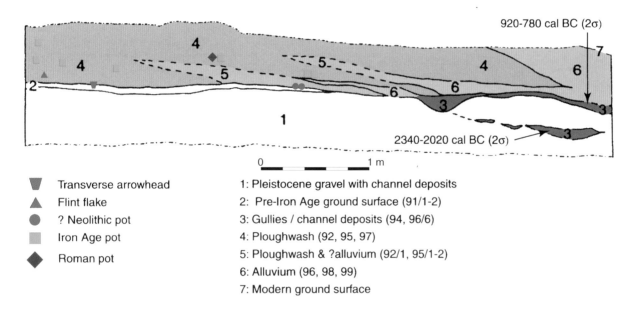

Fig. 2.10 Colluvial ploughwash deposits interstratified with alluvium at Gravelly Guy

was a common plant of middens and farmyards until the early post-medieval period. Two other plants, scotch thistle (*Onopordum acanthium*) and bur chervil (*Anthriscus caucalis*) have rarely been recorded living in the region although they are more common in Eastern England. Curiously, there was an 'outbreak' of scotch thistle in the 1990s growing along the side of a newly constructed road in Abingdon, but it rapidly declined.

Organic refuse does not seem to have been a major habitat on the settlements but the structural timbers of the Iron Age houses provided a home for woodworm beetle (*Anobium punctatum*). The only other synanthropic insect was the beetle *Ptinus fur*, recorded from Watkins Farm (Robinson 1990) and Mingies Ditch (Allen and Robinson 1993). There was no evidence of serious insect pests of stored grain from any of the Iron Age settlements.

Overview

The overall impression of the Upper Thames Valley at the end of the middle Iron Age is of a productive agricultural landscape. Any large areas of scrub with rough grazing or waste were probably restricted to tributary valleys, clay slopes between terraces and geologies beyond the gravel terraces, as seems to be reflected in the pollen sequence from Sidlings Copse.

The main arable areas were probably on the higher terraces but some very extensive areas of grassland were also present on them, and this was probably the predominant landuse. The lower terraces are likely to have been mainly pasture but with at least some crop growing. The floodplain was probably very largely grassland, the lower areas experiencing seasonal flooding and any crop growing probably restricted to small plots on slightly higher drier areas that did not flood. As the floods became more extensive, so the pasture experienced damage from overgrazing while wet.

The Early to Middle Iron Age Environment of the Middle Thames Valley

With the exception of some palaeochannel sequences, there is little useful early Iron Age information from the Middle Thames Valley, though at least some early Iron Age waterholes at Perry Oaks/T5 and a few other sites suggest a continuation of late Bronze Age conditions. While in the Upper Thames the lack of evidence seems to be due to changes in the location and pattern of settlement and farming activity resulting in less suitable deposits for sampling despite farming becoming if anything more intensive, in the Middle Thames Valley it is possible that there was a real decline in the number of settlements compared with late Bronze Age activity – certainly far fewer are known.

Extent of Clearance and Surviving Woodland

A useful palaeochannel sequence spanning the Iron Age has been analysed for pollen, insects and macroscopic plant remains at Dorney (Parker and Robinson 2003). Both pollen and insect evidence from that part of the sequence dated to 770-400 cal BC suggested the general landscape to have been as open as that at Runnymede Bridge in the late Bronze Age, although there seem to have been more alders in wet areas along the riverbank. Interestingly, seeds of yew (*Taxus baccata*), a tree which no longer commonly occurs in the Thames Valley, were found in these samples. The seeds of terrestrial herbs included a strong pastureland element with, for example, creeping buttercup (*Ranunculus* cf. *repens*) and silverweed (*Potentilla anserina*). Scarabaeoid dung beetles rose to almost 15% of the terrestrial Coleoptera, showing a strong presence of domestic animals nearby.

In contrast, what was estimated to be the early Iron Age part of a pollen sequence from a palaeochannel at Thames Valley Park, Reading, gave evidence for a relaxation of grazing on the floodplain (Keith-Lucas 1997). There was an increase in the pollen of alder and the spores of ferns which probably reflected the spread of damp woodland. Another undated pollen diagram, from Staines Moor, at the confluence of the Colne with the Thames, suggested open conditions by the early Iron Age and showed no evidence for any episodes of woodland regeneration (Keith-Lucas 2000).

Grassland

Evidence for the early Iron Age environment from settlement sites in the Middle Thames Valley is generally very limited, with few sites on low-lying ground and not as many waterholes to act as local traps of pollen and insects. The scale of settlement at Perry Oaks/T5 declined and if anything a greater emphasis seems to have been placed on pastoral agriculture (Framework Archaeology 2006, 166). Some of the hedged fields, however, appear to have been maintained.

Fields Arable, and Human Habitation

In general, concentrations of charred cereal processing remains are lower on early Iron Age settlements in the Middle Thames Valley than on Upper Thames Valley sites, and are seldom accompanied by storage pits. The early Iron Age house at Dunstan Park and a pit at Wickhams Field each produced samples rich in chaff with some grain, but very few weed seeds, but charred cereal remains were noticeably scarce or absent from other features – possibly indicative of the settlements having access to relatively clean stored grain that needed final processing, but not much engaged with arable farming. The virtual absence of charred cereals at Moores Farm and their sparseness at Brooklands (Hayman 1991c) and Perry Oaks/T5 is also noticeable.

Whereas the Upper Thames Valley was becoming a more intensively managed agricultural landscape in the early Iron Age this trend does not seem to have been as strong in the Middle Thames Valley. Indeed it is possible that there were some areas of agricultural decline. Soils on the higher gravel terraces of the Upper Thames Valley retained their fertility because the underlying limestone gravel prevented complete decalcification, but the soils overlying the flint gravel on the higher gravel terraces of the Middle Thames Valley were more vulnerable to acidification and consequent nutrient loss. In the Upper Thames, rainwater leaching did not progress beyond the formation of argillic brown-earth soils and most of the Iron Age soils were circumneutral. But on some sites in the Middle Thames podsolisation occurred. It is not clear when this process of soil deterioration began, and indeed it need not have been synchronous through the valley, but in some areas it may have been well established by the early Iron Age, as appears to have been the case at Perry Oaks/T5 where heathland plants became more common in the later Bronze Age samples (Wiltshire in Framework Archaeology 2006). The complete absence of charred cereal remains from Perry Oaks/T5, despite the occurrence of some cereal pollen in waterholes is particularly striking, and waterlogged cereal remains became less common than they had been in the Bronze Age (Carruthers in Framework Archaeology 2006). Charred cereal remains were also very sparse in Iron Age samples at Thorpe Lea Nurseries (Robinson unpublished).

As we have seen, there were probably fewer middle Iron Age settlements in the Middle Thames Valley than in the Upper Thames, and they tend to be different in character, with few much engaged in significant arable production and storage. This may again be due to soil acidification and consequent nutrient loss. Podsolisation occurred on some sites, including for example, Larkwhistle Farm, Brimpton, where there was charcoal of ling or heather (*Calluna* or *Erica* sp.) (Robinson 1999b).

Overview

Overall, the early to middle Iron Age landscape of the Middle Thames probably showed some similarities to that of the Upper Thames in being extensively cleared and dominated by grazed grassland, but it was probably not being farmed as intensively. Old fields, first established in the Bronze Age may have survived as significant features. There was possibly some heathland which had been created by earlier occupation, and rough grassland and scrub may have been more common between the more organised landscapes around settlements. Arable agriculture was probably much less extensive in many parts of the Middle Thames Valley than in the Upper Thames.

The Late Iron Age and Early Roman Environment of the Upper Thames Valley (AD1-AD100)

It is difficult to attribute much of the palaeoenvironmental evidence specifically to the late Iron Age. Environmental changes were occurring in the late Iron Age or at the start of the Roman period.

Extent of Clearance, Grassland and Surviving Woodland

In the Upper Thames Valley, the period from about AD25 until AD150 was one of agricultural intensification. As we have seen, the valley floor had already become very open by the middle Iron Age, and there continued to be no evidence of reversion to woodland, although patches of scrub and woods may well have survived nearby. Rather more woodland may have survived (or regenerated) on the surrounding hills. For example, in the Duntisbourne area near Bagendon on the dip slope of the Cotswolds west of the River Churn in the upper reaches of the valley, there are indications that a relatively high level of woodland may have survived into the middle to late Iron Age (Mudd *et al.* 1999, 77-97).

Grassland

Conditions of overgrazed, ill-drained pasture with rush tussocks, similar to those already noted for Thornhill Farm and Port Meadow, developed around a settlement on an island of First Terrace at Claydon Pike which was occupied from *c* AD 25-125 (Robinson in Miles *et al.* 2007). Scarabaeoid dung beetles, such as *Aphodius granarius*, were particularly abundant and as on the other two sites, the pasture in the vicinity of the settlement had been churned into mud enriched with dung, supporting weeds such as *Chenopodium rubrum* (red goosefoot).

One new category of vegetation to make its appearance in the Upper Thames Valley in the early Roman period was hay meadow. It is very likely that areas of grassland were sometimes left ungrazed in the region during the Iron Age. However, a very distinctive type of species-rich grassland results if grazing animals are excluded in the spring, a crop of hay is taken in the summer and grazing of the late summer and early autumn regrowth follows. The first evidence for hay meadow in the region is from the early 2nd century AD at Claydon Pike (Robinson in Miles *et al.* 2007). A waterlogged deposit of what is now recognised as cut hay was found in a 2nd century pit on the First Gravel Terrace at Farmoor (Lambrick and Robinson 1988, 60). Although there is as yet no botanical evidence of late Iron Age hay-making, the discovery of a scythe-like implement at Dorney makes an earlier, pre-Roman origin possible (Allen *et al.* 2001).

Fields, Arable, and Human Habitation

Late Iron Age and early Roman rural settlements in the Upper Thames Valley tended to have more extensive ditched enclosure systems associated with them than their Iron Age predecessors. These often took the form of rectilinear fields or paddocks adjoining ditched trackways which linked the settlements (see Chapters 3 and 4). Waterlogged remains from these ditches often include thorny twigs and stones of hawthorn (*Crataegus* sp.) and sloe (*Prunus* cf. *spinosa*) suggesting the presence of thorn hedges alongside the ditches.

As well as an intensification of grazing on the wetter areas of the floodplain, cultivated fields were being extended onto the high parts of the floodplain. Early Roman arable fields were laid out on the floodplain at Yarnton (Hey *et al.* forthcoming a) and Drayton (Barclay *et al.* 2003). It is possible that grassland was also being ploughed up quite extensively on the gravel terraces as part of an intensification of cereal production. At Gravelly Guy and probably other settlements in the Stanton Harcourt complex, Roman cultivation extended over the area of the Iron Age settlement and settlement expanded into the central area of grassland on the Second Terrace, though it was not until the second century AD that the organisation that had grown up in the late Bronze Age and early Iron Age was abandoned (Lambrick and Allen 2004).

The extent to which arable formed an important part of the landscape away from the gravel terraces is more doubtful. Only low levels of charred cereal remains were found on a series of middle to late Iron Age sites along the A417/A419 road scheme and at the late Iron Age enclosed settlement at Field Farm Bicester (Pelling in Mudd *et al.* 1999, 473-5; Pelling in Cromarty *et al.* 1999, 222-3), but at Watchfield there was an increase in cereal remains from the early to middle Iron Age through the late Iron Age and into the Roman period (Hinton in Birbeck 2001, 280-3).

The main cultivated fields on the gravel terraces probably continued to be large blocks of land without archaeologically evident sub-divisions. Weed seeds from amongst charred cereal-processing assemblages showed slight changes to the arable weed flora at the end of the Iron Age and start of the Roman period (see Chapter 7). Some additions to the flora were the result of the introduction of Southern European species through increasing trade with the Continent. Charred seeds of corn cockle (*Agrostemma githago*) were found in a late Iron Age context at Barton Court Farm, Abingdon (Jones 1986). Corn cockle reached Yarnton by the early Roman period (Pelling in Hey *et al.* forthcoming). Shepherd's needle (*Scandix pecten-veneris*) also arrived very early in the Roman period (Giorgi and Robinson 1984). These weeds are annual plants adapted to a climatic regime in which summer drought creates bare ground for colonisation by the next generation. Under British conditions, they are dependent upon cultivation to create the open conditions needed for their seedlings to escape competition from other plants and, in the case of corn cockle and shepherd's needle, their seeds being inadvertently harvested and sown with the crop. These two species persisted as weeds in Britain until improved seed cleaning techniques in the 19th century began their decline and they have now almost been eliminated by the use of herbicides.

Another annual weed which makes its appearance in the region in the early Roman period is stinking mayweed (*Anthemis cotula*). Unlike the species mentioned above, it has a more versatile ecology under British conditions and also became established on nutrient-rich disturbed ground in settlements and so is therefore commonly found in waterlogged deposits on occupation sites.

The nutrient-rich, disturbed and neglected ground habitats of the late Iron Age/early Roman settlements of the Upper Thames Valley supported the same range of vegetation already noted for the middle Iron Age settlements. Elder (*Sambucus nigra*) seems to have had a greater presence with the addition of hemlock (*Conium maculatum*). *C. maculatum* made a very early Roman appearance at Alchester, with seeds being present in the annex ditch of the conquest fort (Robinson 2000b) and thereafter it became common on many early Roman sites in the region.

Late Iron Age and early Roman rural settlements in the Upper Thames Valley have produced insect evidence which suggest a much greater intensity of occupation than on their Iron Age predecessors. At Claydon Pike the abundance of woodworm beetle (*Anobium punctatum*) rose from about 0.3% of the terrestrial Coleoptera in the 1st century AD 'native' phase to over 1.4% in the 'Romanised' phase which began in the early 2nd century (Robinson in Miles *et al.* 2007). The various synanthropic beetles such as *Ptinus fur*, which occur in indoor habitats and in accumulations of organic material such as old straw and haystacks, were absent from the 1st century phase but comprised 1.5% of the Coleoptera from the 2nd century phase. It is likely that the abundance of woodworm and other synanthropic beetles reached very much higher levels in the developing Roman towns of the Thames Valley.

The synanthropic beetles found in the early Roman settlements included occasional examples of bread beetle (*Stegobium paniceum*) which does occur in grain residues but is not seen as a serious pest of stored grain. While the pit storage of grain which was practised in the Iron Age would not have been conducive to grain beetles, because of the build up of carbon dioxide which keeps the grain dormant, the above-ground storage of grain in granaries, as practised by the Romans, would have provided ideal conditions in which these pests could flourish. Several exotic species of grain beetle were introduced to Britain in the early Roman period and there is certainly evidence of very severe infestations elsewhere in Britain in the early Roman period, for example York (Kenward and Williams 1979). One of these beetles, *Sitophilus granarius* (grain weevil), was in the region at the start of the Roman period, an example being identified from the early sediments in the ditches of the conquest fortress annex at Alchester (Robinson, unpublished). It had presumably been introduced in the grain supply for the army from the Continent. This pest was then spread by the advancing Roman army, reaching the legionary fortresses at Exeter (Straker *et al.* 1984), York (Kenward and Williams 1979) and Carlisle (Robinson unpublished) before the end of the 1st century AD.

Overview

The changes brought to the environment of the Upper Thames Valley in the late Iron Age and at the start of the Roman period were primarily those related to alluviation becoming widespread on the floodplain, and to more general agricultural intensification and horticulture. This led to floodplain grassland being ploughed up just as it was becoming wetter. Grassland was also ploughed up on the gravel terraces. It is quite possible that this was occurring alongside clearance for pasture on the clay hinterland. The linking of settlements by ditched trackways possibly brought about more division of the landscape with hedges. Around the settlements, the proliferation of small ditched enclosures not only created the environments of the horticultural plots themselves, but may also have introduced more hedges. Beetle evidence suggests a much greater intensification of occupation of the settlements – more accumulations of various categories of decomposing organic material and more buildings. Various weed species introduced as a result of increased contact with Continental Europe around the time of the Roman conquest became established as part of the flora of the arable fields of the Upper Thames Valley.

The Late Iron Age Environment of the Middle Thames Valley

As with the middle Iron Age, there is much less evidence for the Middle Thames Valley, but with the exception of the hydrological changes, most of the changes described above probably also occurred in this region. The increase in the number of early Roman settlements in the Middle Thames and lower Kennet valleys, for example, was probably also a reflection of agricultural intensification. Only limited evidence is available for the Middle Thames Valley.

The pollen, insect and waterlogged macroscopic plant remains from the Dorney palaeochannel sequence suggest that very open conditions persisted (Parker and Robinson 2003). In the late Iron Age to early Roman period at Perry Oaks/T5 results from insect analysis (Robinson, 2006) suggest a continuation of the open conditions with both arable and pastureland activity.

A rise in cereal pollen and the presence of waterlogged glumes of *Triticum spelta* and a seed of *Agrostemma githago* (corn cockle) in a sample from the Dorney channel dated to 110 cal BC-cal AD80, pointed to an increase in cereal cultivation. This was consistent with the evidence from charred cereal remains from nearby settlements which suggested that large-scale cereal processing only began in the Roman period.

Chapter 3 – Dividing up the countryside

In this chapter we look more closely at how the countryside was organised, divided up and enclosed. This begins with a general account of broad kinds of landuse division, and then explores what we know of the physical form of boundaries and their practical use in demarcating or enclosing areas of land, first in terms of boundaries related to land division and then in terms of field systems and patterns of small paddocks and enclosures.

The distinction between land division and land enclosure is worth making because demarcating areas of different landuse or tenure does not automatically require or imply the enclosure of fields or paddocks as a means of managing the land. Nor need the existence of fields and paddocks reflect how larger scale divisions of land worked.

In looking at the development of land division and enclosure it is important to recognise that the physical evidence that is archaeologically most visible may not equate to what the most important characteristics of boundaries were. Subsoil features may be only the physical expression of land divisions that were already well established and recognised by other means. Likewise, although sequences of development (and apparent abandonment) can often be identified from intersections and recuts of ditches defining field systems, these may have little or nothing to do with how the hedges or other barriers that they represent were first established and developed, or how they may have survived long after their subsoil manifestations had filled up.

How fields and paddocks were used in terms of crop-growing and animal husbandry is discussed in more detail in Chapter 7 along with other aspects of agricultural practice, but it is important to bear in mind here that while these practical uses may well have influenced the size, shape, form and layout of field patterns and enclosures, it is probably also reasonable to suppose that their use for animals and crops may have varied, whether or not there was any deliberate pattern of rotation.

ORGANISING THE COUNTRYSIDE: WOODLAND, OPEN LAND, FIELDS AND ENCLOSURES

Woodland and Forest

Because of the overall emphasis on the sedentary agricultural lifestyle of late prehistoric society, there is a tendency to ignore what an important part woods and forest must have played in the management of land. Even though woodland may have become quite scarce in the more intensively used

areas of the Thames gravel terraces and floodplain, it may well have been more extensive elsewhere.

The insights to be gained on this from pollen and beetles in waterlogged peat, channel and ditch or waterhole deposits are, unfortunately, patchy. Carbonised plant remains and bones from the middle to late Bronze Age onwards lack the characteristic emphasis of earlier deposits on gathered wild plants, deer and domestic animals that are at home in woodland. But while this might suggest less reliance on woodland food resources, it could also represent a change of tradition associated with the character of such deposits, for example, from a relatively ritualised and symbolic deposition of debris that emphasised a connection with wild resources, to practices that emphasised domesticity and farming.

Clearance

Today, ancient woodland is virtually absent on the Thames gravel terraces and floodplain. As indicated above, biological evidence and changing hydrological and sedimentation conditions suggest that the process of clearance, already well advanced for many parts of the valley floor in earlier prehistory, was consolidated, extended and probably largely completed during the late prehistoric period. However, it is also clear that this varied geographically and chronologically, and patterns of clearance on the valley floor probably differed from the rest of the catchment. For example there is possible evidence of at least localised woodland regeneration after the later Bronze Age phases at Castle Hill and Rams Hill (Allen *et al.* forthcoming a; Bradley and Ellison 1975).

How clearance was organised and achieved is a poorly understood aspect of British prehistory, though arguably our open landscape of mixed farming is its greatest enduring legacy. It is certainly a phenomenon deserving much more attention than it has received to date. There are fundamentally five ways of killing and clearing trees and shrubs from land to create areas for grazing or cultivation: toppling, cutting, ring-barking, burning, and grazing. These have very different characteristics, and involve substantially different levels of human effort to be effective. Nor are they mutually exclusive, and are likely to have been most effective when used in conjunction with each other, so it seems likely that all of them played a role.

There tends to be a largely unwritten assumption that throughout prehistory people cleared forest by chopping down trees with axes – first stone, then bronze and eventually iron. Although there is good

a.

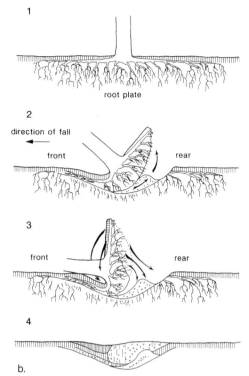

1

root plate

2

direction of fall

front   rear

3

front   rear

4

b.

c.

Yarnton

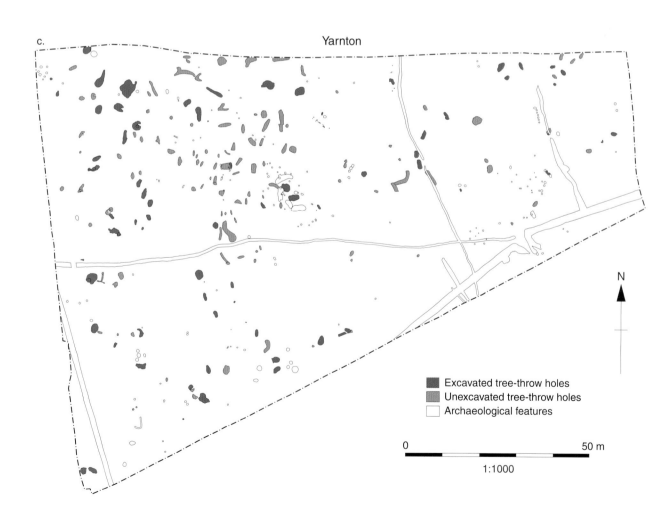

N

■ Excavated tree-throw holes
▨ Unexcavated tree-throw holes
□ Archaeological features

0   50 m

1:1000

evidence that even large trees like the central upturned tree trunk at the centre of Seahenge could be cut through using axes, detailed analysis suggests that the Seahenge tree was cut up on site having been dragged there after it was toppled (Brennand and Taylor 2003, 62). It is thus far from clear whether felling was the normal method of clearance, rather than obtaining timber for building structures. Although the development of metal axes would have improved efficiency in cutting wood, it may not have been very important in facilitating clearance, and certainly would not have directly led to increased removal of forest cover.

Toppling trees by pulling them over might at first sight seem an unlikely method of clearance, but the forces required to pull a tree over, especially in full leaf giving extra top heavy leverage, are quite feasible for a relatively small group of people (eg using a 'Spanish windlass' and progressively cutting through exposed roots), and is a historically recognised method (Maisie Taylor pers. comm.). The characteristic 'tree throw' holes left by trees being toppled by natural windthrow or deliberate human agency have occasionally been investigated archaeologically, though there are significant problems interpreting dating evidence from contexts that inherently involve redeposition of surface soils (Fig. 3.1). It is very difficult to establish clearly whether such features reflect deliberate clearance rather than removal of natural wind-throws. On the floodplain site of the Neolithic cursus at Drayton, 30% of the pre-alluvial ground surface consisted of tree throw holes, and flints, pottery and scorching in them were all consistent with carbon dates on root charcoal ranging between 3960-3530 cal BC and 2580-2140 cal BC, both before and after the construction of the cursus (Barclay *et al.* 2003, 60-7).

At Perry Oaks/T5 it is assumed that the very straight course of the Stanwell cursus must have been cleared prior to construction and a few tree throw holes produced possible evidence of Neolithic middening, but pollen from a pit cutting the cursus produced clear evidence for woodland cover (Framework Archaeology 2006, 61-3). Although it is clear from pollen and insect evidence that by the middle Bronze Age there was a largely open environment at Perry Oaks/T5, there is not enough stratigraphic or other evidence from the several hundred other tree throw holes to establish how and when clearance might have occurred, or whether these features had anything to do with it.

At the late Bronze Age site at Reading Business Park (Moore and Jennings 1992, 13) 72 tree throw holes were recognised, of which two thirds contained scorched material, but only six were excavated. Amongst the 32 cases where the direction of fall was discernible there was no preferred

orientation, but it cannot be concluded that this apparent lack of correlation with prevailing winds is a significant indicator of human intervention. In a third of the cases of scorching, it was restricted to the area of disturbed topsoil, suggesting that it resulted from burning at the base of the trunk, but it is not clear if this was directly related to clearance. The only dating evidence was that four tree throw holes were cut by a late Bronze Age ditch, and one of them cut three pre-existing but undated pits. The only finds recovered were a few flints and one sherd of Late Bronze Age pottery, but this is not inconsistent with the trees having fallen at a much later date. It is worth noting that toppling trees has decided advantages where stumps need to be removed prior to cultivation, but there is no direct evidence of such a link.

The use of axes to ring-bark trees, could also have contributed to clearance. Ring barking does not in itself remove a tree completely (though it will eventually fall), but it very substantially reduces a tree's shading effects in the growing season. Cutting, burning and grazing are all effective means of preventing regrowth from the base. To date, however, there have been no observations of axe marks, bark chips or other possible indications that ring barking was used. Ring-barking does have drawbacks however: once a tree is dead, it is very much more difficult to cut up than when it is green, especially in the case of oak which is impossible to cut effectively with stone or bronze axes once it is seasoned (Maisie Taylor pers. comm.). Waiting for a ring-barked tree to fall, or trying to pull it over without the extra leverage provided by a full crown of leaves provides next to no advantage. Burning standing dead wood is a great deal more difficult than a heap of wood on the ground.

Clearing deciduous forests by burning live trees is not really practicable in the damp British climate, but whatever methods were used for felling or toppling trees, fire is likely to have been important in clearing branches, bushes, and perhaps smaller tree trunks that had already been felled or toppled, possibly also taking the opportunity to light fires on top of tree stumps or around the base of dead standing trees to prevent regrowth. General evidence that burning played a significant part in clearance comes with the common occurrence of microscopic charcoal associated with sharp declines of tree species represented in pollen sequences that reflect clearance episodes (eg Day 1991).

Although the means by which much remaining forest cover was cleared in late prehistory are still very unclear, there is little doubt that clearance probably accelerated considerably on the hills surrounding the Upper Thames gravels and both on and off the Middle Thames terraces, and would have consumed significant effort. However, once

Fig. 3.1 (opposite) Tree throws and clearance: (a) a toppled tree and (inset) *excavation of a tree throw hole; (b) creation of a tree throw hole; (c) distribution of tree throw holes at Yarnton*

trees were cleared a combination of grazing and natural processes of rotting would accelerate the processes of making the ground open and unimpeded enough for grazing and cultivation. The need to keep cleared ground open would have become an increasingly important reason, when pastoral landuse started to be intensified, for cleared areas to be managed through intensive grazing, rather than allowing natural regeneration to scrubby rough grazing, dense scrub, or woodland, which would otherwise rapidly take hold in a few years. In effect this may have resulted in a process by which increasing grazing pressure with animals encroaching into woodland and beginning to thin undergrowth defined the need and areas of further gradual clearance.

Overall, the evidence for methods of clearance is tantalisingly inconclusive, and the scarcity of good artefactual or environmental evidence and problems of interpretation seem to have persuaded archaeologists that, although clearance is an important issue, it is not worth risking time and energy recovering potentially inconclusive results from contexts like tree throw holes. Ironically, it may be necessary to accumulate a significant body of such evidence (eg through extensive sampling of tree throw holes on numerous sites) to enable clearer patterns to emerge.

Open land and pasture

The way in which cleared land is kept clear by grazing pressure is inextricably bound up with the natural annual cyclical variation in the growth rate of vegetation between the dormant winter period and spring, summer and autumn growing season. This means that the effects of grazing pressure would vary through the year, such that for a given herd of animals much more land is needed to feed them in winter than in summer, or given a limited area of land, measures must be taken to slaughter a proportion of animals in the autumn and/or supplement their food with collected fodder (which might be leaf fodder, straw or grain – and ultimately hay). Where land shortage is not a problem, winter grazing of foggage (grass that has been allowed to grow tall through undergrazing in summer) is the least labour-intensive option. In a mobile pastoral system and a low population, there need have been no automatic ecological differentiation between summer and winter grazing grounds, though there might well have been social ones.

The widespread incidence of scrubby grassland (perhaps sometimes half cleared, or half-reverting to woodland or a form of wood pasture), and the common incidence of bracken in pollen sequences and as possible bedding material, are all consistent with a scenario of gradual clearance consolidated through high winter grazing pressure that slackened off in spring and summer.

Throughout later prehistory it seems likely that in between areas of managed and largely unman-aged woodland on the one hand, and relatively small areas of fully enclosed land on the other, there would have been a very extensive mosaic of intensively grazed open land, rough pasture and scrubby grassland or wood pasture.

Land division and enclosure

Division of land to demarcate areas of control or management is rather different from enclosure, designed to improve management of pastoral or arable resources. Although in some other parts of Britain and Ireland enclosure and subdivision of land into fields and paddocks began in the Neolithic, this has not yet been demonstrated in the Thames Valley, though there are quite frequent instances of odd lengths of ditch containing Neolithic material that may or may not be redeposited (Boyle *et al.* 1995, 205). The possible emergence of ditched land division and fields in the early Bronze Age is more plausible but not yet fully proven (see below).

There is a tendency to assume that the advent of permanent settlement goes hand in hand with the division and enclosure of land for more intensive agricultural production or vice-versa, but this does not entirely follow. While an expansion of arable farming typically demands a more sedentary existence to spend longer cultivating the soil, sowing seeds, tending crops and harvesting them, this may have become a major influence only at the time when arable crops began to provide a substantial (or even principal) source of nutrition, especially if yields were enhanced by introduction of husbandry practices such as autumn sowing, thereby requiring year-round management of arable land. But for most of the Thames Valley, increased production from arable agriculture seems to have developed gradually and in many cases does not seem to have happened on a substantial scale until the late Bronze Age or Iron Age (see below, Chapter 7), often long after the establishment of extensive networks of enclosed fields in the middle to late Bronze Age. Initially such fields may have been associated with pastoral landuse, even though arable cultivation was also practised.

THE PHYSICAL FORM OF LAND DIVISION, FIELDS AND OTHER BOUNDARIES

Open boundaries and tethering

The possible existence of well-understood boundaries recognisable by reference to lines between visible landmarks (trees, earlier prehistoric monuments, confluences and bends in streams and rivers, or other readily recognisable features) may have been fundamental in the earliest steps taken to agree who had the right to use different areas of land for particular purposes. Apart from demarcating territorial rights to, or ownership of land, which may have included wider social and political

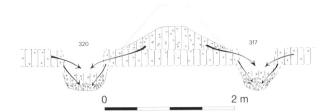

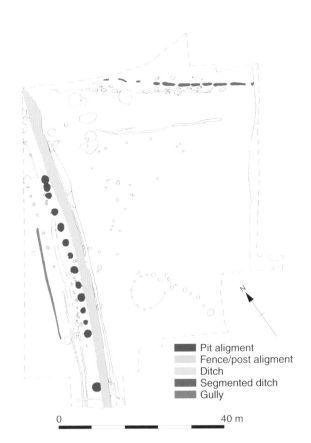

Pit aligment
Fence/post aligment
Ditch
Segmented ditch
Gully

division as well as more local and personal rights, the principal practical reason for investing the labour needed to create visible boundaries would have been either to demarcate ownership or other rights to land or territory, or to control stock from entering or leaving particular areas. There may also have been a social impetus to demonstrate this in an overt manner, but the extent to which control of animals using physical linear barriers was necessary would also have depended partly on what other means of control were available. This could have included tethering, stinting, and simple herding and shepherding, with or without dogs, which would have been a fundamental part of pastoral management, allowing significant control of landuse and both inside and outside enclosed areas. Landuse division and management could often have been achieved without recourse to physical boundaries and barriers.

Physical manifestations of land division

Most evidence of the physical form of early boundaries comes from subsoil ditches, gullies, pits and postholes. A wide variety of such features may reflect different stages in the maintenance or redefinition of a long-lived boundary, as at Butler's Field Lechlade (Fig. 3.2; Boyle *et al.* 1998, 13-8, figs 2.3-2.6). But direct evidence rarely survives of above-ground boundaries such as banks, fence posts, hedge trimmings or other plant remains or invertebrates caught in waterlogged ditches. Yet the above-ground character of boundaries is fundamental to any understanding of how field systems and enclosures functioned and developed through time, and is also important in proposing interpretations for some rather curious subsoil manifestations of linear boundaries, such as pit alignments. It is also likely that the above-ground manifestation of some 'types' of boundary were actually more similar than the subsoil traces might suggest at first sight. Furthermore, some hedged or fenced boundaries may have left no subsoil trace.

Ditches and gullies with banks, hedges and fences

Ditches and gullies are the commonest archaeological manifestation of land boundaries and would have had associated banks that seldom survive on the Thames gravels. To be stock-proof they would also have had to be accompanied by a hedge or fence, which could have been maintained, altered or repaired independently of accompanying ditches. An example of this is the suggested development of middle and later Iron Age paddocks and fields at Mount Farm, Dorchester (Lambrick 1979; forth-

Fig. 3.2 Physical manifestations of land boundaries: (above) *Bronze Age double ditched boundary at Mount Farm;* (below) *complex boundary at Butler's Field Lechlade*

coming), where the presumed existence of adjacent banks and/or hedges was used to explain various detailed changes of layout such as the position of ditches appearing to change from one side of a hedge to the other, breaks in alignment, gaps and other spatial characteristics that could not easily be explained by other means. In one case a shallow gully with an uneven pitted base was interpreted as the bedding trench for a hedge. At Ashford Prison an apparently asymmetrical layout of ditches may reflect a much more regular alignment of hedges. Both there and at Perry Oaks/T5 and other sites, the location of later features respecting the alignment of probable hedges or fences alongside long-since infilled ditches strongly suggests the continued existence of above-ground elements of these boundaries, in some cases long after the dating available from the ditches themselves. Many kilometres of ditch that were dug across drier gravel terraces would have been of little or no use for drainage, but some ditches on lower lying or less well-drained areas ended in small sumps designed to allow water to soak away rapidly into porous gravel, as at Blackditch Stanton Harcourt (Lambrick and Allen 2004, 157-9, fig. 3.23).

Hedge banks

A distinctive form of boundary, which in the Thames Valley appears to be of middle or late Bronze Age origin, is characterised by pairs of small parallel ditches spaced *c* 2 m apart. These differ from wider-spaced parallel ditches characteristic of ditched trackways. Examples of this kind of boundary are known from Mount Farm (Lambrick forthcoming), Eight Acre Field, Radley (Mudd 1995, fig. 3), Northfield Farm Long Wittenham (Gray 1977; Thomas 1980), probably Dorchester on Thames (Bradley and Chambers 1988, fig. 3), Crowmarsh (Ford *et al.* forthcoming), Eton Rowing Course (Allen *et al.* in prep b) and Perry Oaks/T5 (Framework Archaeology 2006, 104-14). While it is possible that some boundaries of this form might be early Bronze Age (eg Mount Farm, Crowmarsh, Perry Oaks/T5), this is not definite. Almost all formed parts of middle to late Bronze Age field systems and tend to be part of distinct rectilinear enclosure patterns. A few further examples may be detectable from aerial photography, as at Datchett (Gates 1975), but unless there is a very clear rectilinear pattern of double ditched boundaries (as at Long Wittenham) there are dangers in trying to interpret these types of boundary as automatically indicating middle to late Bronze Age enclosures.

Such features are sometimes interpreted as narrow tracks or paths, especially where there is no evidence of similar double-ditched boundaries extending at right-angles to the main alignment

(Pryor 1996; Framework Archaeology 2006, 104-14; Ford *et al.* forthcoming). In other cases, as suggested by Lambrick (1992; forthcoming), for example at Mount Farm Dorchester, they are interpreted as hedge banks with the spoil from the ditches piled up in a bank between them, creating a double or treble thickness of topsoil for the hedge to grow in. An extensive pattern of such features forming small fields and trackways is known at Fengate near Peterborough (Pryor 2001) which shows the existence of parallel pairs of such double-ditched boundaries either side of a trackway with the ditches stopping at entrances from the trackway into adjacent fields, indicating that they were not themselves track- or pathways.

While in many cases this type of boundary may have been created as an entity, there are also less convincing examples where the parallel second ditch only exists in limited places. Some of these may represent the coincidence of ditches being dug either side of a hedge or other linear feature at different times. This appears to be the case at Mount Farm where analysis of the stratigraphic development of the fields and paddocks from the middle Iron Age into the Roman period suggests instances of redefinition of boundaries of this sort (Lambrick forthcoming), and may also be suspected for other cases where a sequence of boundary rearrangements and additions has been discerned, as at Reading Business Park (Moore and Jennings 1992, 31, fig. 18). This fortuitous creation of what at first sight might look like a double ditched boundary may also be suspected in other cases where closely spaced double ditches are not very similar or not quite parallel, as at Knight's Farm (Bradley *et al.* 1980, 259, fig. 28), or simply where there is a proliferation of parallel ditches marking the same alignment, as at Uxbridge (Barclay *et al.* 1997) or Cotswold Community (Oxford Archaeology 2004a) and the north-south alignment at Butler's Field Lechlade (Boyle *et al.* 1998, 15-8, figs 2.5, 2.6).

There are also examples of closely spaced double-ditched boundaries following long sweeping curves with few if any boundaries abutting or joining them, that appear to be of late Iron Age, Roman or later origin, as at Shorncote/Cotswold Community (Barclay and Glass 1995, 25 fig. 2), Stonehenge Farm, Northmoor (Benson and Miles 1974) and Yarnton (Hey *et al.* forthcoming).

Segmented Ditches

There are numerous instances of segmented ditches (linear rows of short lengths of ditch or gully) often either parallel to or acting as a continuation of ditches or gullies (Fig. 3.3). These vary considerably in date, from middle Bronze Age, as at Eton Rowing

Fig. 3.3 (opposite) Segmented ditches and pit alignments at (top left and right) *Shorncote/Cotswold Community and* (below left) *Langford Downs, Lechlade*

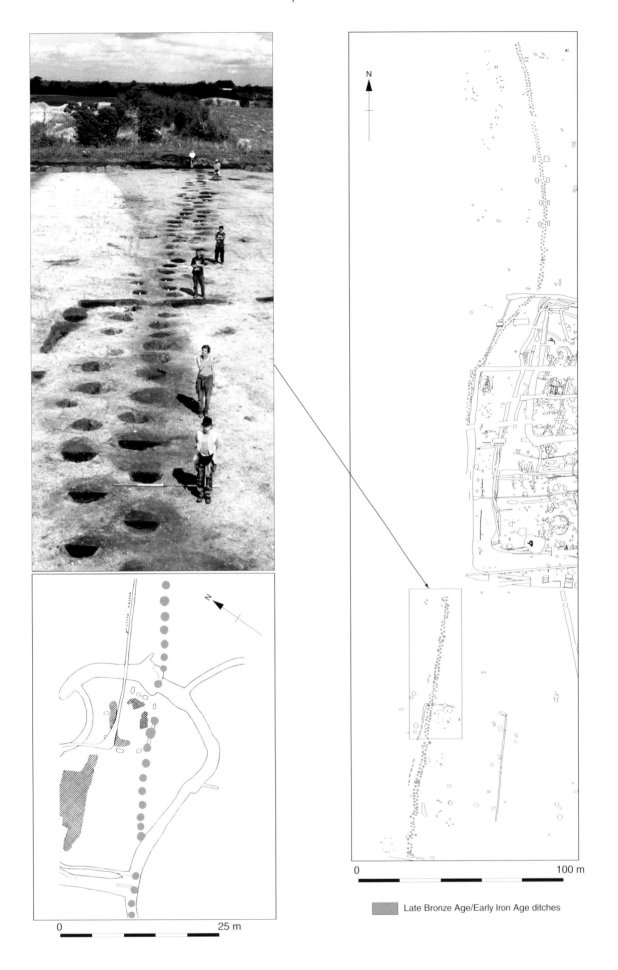

Late Bronze Age/Early Iron Age ditches

Course and Perry Oaks/T5 to middle or late Iron Age, as at St Augustine's Farm, Butler's Field and Roughground Farm (Allen *et al.* in prep a; Framework Archaeology 2006; Mudd *et al.* 1999; Boyle *et al.* 1998, 13-5, fig. 2.4; Allen *et al.* 1993). In some cases such features are produced when the undulating base of a very shallow ditch has been truncated by ploughing. More often they have terminals that suggest they were dug as short lengths of ditch, suggesting either that they were never completed as a continuous ditch or that they were small quarries to make a continuous bank (eg on which to plant a hedge). Some are much more regular than others and it is far from clear in any instance that creating a segmented ditch (or ditch and bank) was the principal objective of digging these features.

Pit alignments and linear palisades

Pit alignments are another, more distinctive form of boundary represented by rows of holes dug in the ground. They are not as common in the Thames Valley as in some other parts of England (eg Kidd 1999, 5-6) but nevertheless the Thames Valley can be seen as one of the areas where this form of boundary is relatively common (Bradley and Yates 2007) and they come in various forms. Most of the known examples, both from excavation and aerial photography, are in the Upper Thames catchment, but some are well documented for the Middle Thames Valley (eg at Datchett and Staines Road Farm) and the distribution may be biased because of greater constraints on aerial photography in the Middle Thames.

In some instances double or even occasionally triple pit alignments are found, the latter seldom maintained along the complete length of the alignment. Most excavated examples are in the Lechlade/Fairford area, and where dated or where probable dates have been suggested, most are late Bronze Age or early Iron Age, as at Shorncote/Cotswold Community (Fig. 3.3; Oxford Archaeology 2004a) Roughground Farm (Allen *et al.* 1993, 36 fig. 78), Butler's Field (Boyle *et al.* 1998, 16-18, fig. 19, J, K and L) and Little London, Lechlade (Allen pers. comm.). At Langford Downs, Lechlade, however, several pits of a typical single alignment were cut into the infilled ditches of a late Iron Age farmstead enclosure, indicating a late Iron Age or even Roman date, though the pits themselves produced no direct dating evidence (Fig. 3.3; Williams 1946).

Langford Downs was one of the earliest excavations of a pit alignment and Williams' careful observation of the pit fills led her to conclude that they had never held posts, although in line with the then prevailing assumption that pit alignments did hold posts she suggested that they had been dug to take a palisade that was never actually built (Williams 1946, 54-5). Since then it has become generally evident that pit alignments do not represent palisades or rows of posts. They are generally too

shallow to have held large posts and unnecessarily wide for small ones, and no evidence of packing or 'post-pipes' has ever been observed.

The pits in such alignments are generally reasonably circular or sometimes oval or subrectangular, usually less than 1 m in diameter and dug up to 0.5 m into the ground, spaced typically at intervals of 0.75 to 1.5 times their own diameter. At Butler's Field an alignment of pits averaging 1.68 m diameter by 0.88 m deep were thought to be a pit alignment rather than simply a row of storage or refuse pits dug adjacent to the boundary to which they may have been related (Boyle *et al.* 1998, 18 fig. 2.6 J).

The filling of pits is typically with moderately clean topsoil, sometimes, as Williams (1946, 54-5) observed, with no sign of deliberate backfilling. Pits seldom contain finds, making dating problematic, though stratigraphic relationships with earlier and later features can be helpful. Spatial relationships are more problematic as an indication of their origin, since pit alignments can remain visible as earthworks long after their original function has been abandoned, and indeed there are a few cases where alignments are still visible as low earthworks. This in itself is of interest in showing how they may have acted as long term boundary markers (Rylatt and Bevan 2007).

The regularity in the shape of the component pits, their spacing and other characteristics

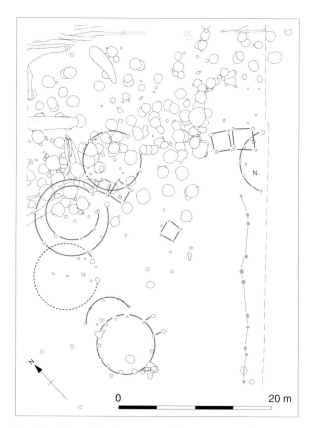

Fig. 3.4 Fenceline, houses and four posters at Gravelly Guy

suggest a much greater sense of deliberate intent in creating pit alignments as the subsoil manifestation of a finished form of boundary than is apparent in segmented ditches, which seem more likely to be incomplete ditches or the by-product of creating a bank. While other interpretations, such as being planting holes for hedges, have been put forward, it is considered most likely that the pits were left open more as a symbolic boundary than a physical barrier, eventually being infilled by natural erosion leaving visible small hollows and low banks either side. In some cases pit alignments were clay lined suggesting that standing water enhanced their visibility (Rylatt and Bevan 2007, 221-223), but this has not been noted in the Thames Valley.

At Yarnton a unique collection of several late Bronze Age or early Iron Age rows of parallel slots and holes represented by shallow, elongated and circular pits was found in an area of late Neolithic and early to middle Bronze Age activity either side of and partly within a former palaeochannel later crossed by a middle Iron Age raised path. Whether these were open pit alignments or the remains of timber trackways is a matter of debate, but many aspects of their form, general character and spatial associations suggests that these features were not simple boundary markers. They are further described and discussed in Chapter 9.

Linear fences and hurdles

Apart from palisades and other structures associated with defensive and ceremonial enclosures and other sites (see Chapter 9) evidence of fences and

the use of hurdles is relatively sparse. Ordinary post and stakeholes are too small to be detectable through aerial photography and have in any case often been truncated by centuries of ploughing. But it would be surprising if fences and hurdles had not been extensively utilised for controlling animals, both in relatively permanent enclosures and temporary pens *etc*. There are instances where rows of postholes suggesting a fence have been noted alongside ditches, as at Radley Eight Acre Field (Mudd 1995, 33 fig. 3), Butler's Field, Lechlade (Boyle *et al.* 1998 18, fig 2.6) and Field Farm Burghfield (Butterworth and Lobb 1992, 17). Alignments of fence posts that may have been channel revetments or designed for controlling animals' access to water were found at the Eton Rowing Course along the edge of a palaeochannel of the Thames (Allen forthcoming b), at Anslows Cottages alongside a channel of the Kennet (Butterworth and Lobb 1992), and at Lower Bolney (Campbell 1992). At Yarnton various fence lines were found within a palaeochannel of the Thames (Hey *et al.* forthcoming a). In many other cases there are simple lines of postholes indicating fences which occasionally also relate to other indications of spatial patterning, for example the occurrence of other features respecting the same alignment or the general layout of settlement (Fig. 3.4; Lambrick and Allen 2004, 146-7, fig. 1.22, 3.2). Because of the variable survival of rows of postholes it is seldom that coherent layouts (eg even turning a corner) can be discerned. Dating is also highly problematical because of the small size of postholes, lack of associated domestic activity and likelihood of material from earlier activity being redeposited when the

Fig. 3.5   Preserved waterlogged hurdle at Eton Rowing Course

postholes are filled in. Broadly speaking, fence lines have been found on sites of every period of later prehistory.

The spacing of fence posts seems to have varied. Widely spaced fences may have been of post-and-rail construction or posts to which hurdles were attached; closer spaced posts may have been interwoven with rods, and some very close-spaced postholes may represent palisades. Some close-spaced or palisade-type fences seem to have had special uses. At Hartshill Copse two diagonally intersecting timber screens, represented by extensive alignments of closely spaced posts appear to have been part of a wider ceremonial space (Collard *et al.* 2006; see Chapters 6 and 9). At Field Farm the ditch and almost parallel fence of small, closely set postholes about 1 m from its edge were thought to divide the funerary area from domestic activity (Butterworth and Lobb 1992, 17). At Horcott Pit, Gloucestershire an early Iron Age stockade enclosure was formed from a palisade of closely set posts (Lamdin-Whymark *et al.* forthcoming).

The use of hurdles was probably very common, certainly much more so than is usually evident archaeologically. There are a few examples of waterlogged hurdling, as at Eton Rowing Course where sections of waterlogged hurdling were found both as complete hurdles *c* 1.5 m long and 1.2 m high and as sections of hurdle fencing linking lines of uprights over distances of up to 4 m or so (Fig. 3.5).

There is also possible indirect evidence for the use of hurdles or fences. At the middle Iron Age floodplain farmsteads at Farmoor it was concluded that the clear absence of botanical or invertebrate evidence of hedges implied the use of fences or hurdles to supplement the small gullies that demarcated animal or working enclosures that formed part of each site. It is generally assumed that small pens and enclosures such as these that are defined by gullies cut only just into the subsoil would have needed to be defined by some aboveground barrier such as a fence or hurdling. At Mount Farm Lambrick (forthcoming) has tentatively suggested that the dimensions of the entrances and gaps between a group of such enclosures might indicate a layout designed for the use of fairly standard width hurdles to close off or open up entrances and gaps to facilitate the sorting of animals into different groups (see Chapter 7).

Palaeoenvironmental evidence for hedges

A number of sites have produced some botanical evidence of hedges (Robinson and Allen 1993), though it is not always easy to distinguish these from more general scrub. Suggestions that it is possible to infer the age of hedges from waterlogged remains (Wiltshire in Framework Archaeology 2006) are questionable.

Possible evidence for the active management of hedges comes from a small number of finds from waterlogged contexts of curiously shaped pieces of roundwood that have grown in bent positions as a result of being bound or woven into other branches, as is still done with laid hedges. Examples that have grown into right-angled kinks have been recovered from Green Park and Whitecross Farm, and a forked stick from Whitecross Farm may be from a hedge with wear marks suggesting contact with other branches (Taylor forthcoming; Cromarty *et al.* 2006, 152 wood no. 26 and 150, fig. 4.10 wood no 89).

Streams and channels as boundaries

Apart from the obvious case of the River Thames and its main tributaries, many local streams and minor river channels are likely to have acted as boundaries between areas of landuse and/or communities, or simply were built into other boundary arrangements. One such instance is the middle Iron Age settlement at Mingies Ditch, where the layout of the enclosed settlement was deliberately intended to incorporate a sharp meander in a small channel of the Windrush to provide access to a water supply (see Chapter 7).

Banks of river channels were reinforced or revetted in relatively minor ways at Boveney Court, Anslows Cottages and more substantially in connection with specialised settlement sites at Runnymede and Wallingford (see Chapter 9). At Port Meadow, Claydon Pike, Thornhill Farm Mingies Ditch and Tongham Nurseries stream and river channels formed parts of the boundaries of fields and paddocks associated with middle Iron Age pastoral farmsteads (see Chapter 4). Stream and river channels were important parts of the strategic siting of defensive sites at Burroway, Cherbury, Salmonsbury, Dyke Hills, Abingdon and Cassington Big Ring (see below, Chapter 9). At Abingdon and Dyke Hills, and possibly some other defensive sites, ditches were dug to create artificial moats or channels of flowing water.

Relict stream channels are more complex. At Yarnton, Reading Business Park/Green Park and Perry Oaks/T5 (Hey *et al.* forthcoming a; Brossler *et al.* 2004, fig. 3.1; Framework Archaeology 2006, 123-4, figs 3.1, 3.20) palaeochannels had middle to late BronzeAge ditches crossing them, and where they were close to settlement areas, wetter ones were used for activities that involved the accumulation of very large quantities of burnt stone, as at Yarnton and Green Park. At Yarnton the waterlogged remains of a series of *in situ* post structures and fences probably of early to middle Iron Age date were found aligned both along and across a relict river channel amongst a mass of other discarded wood, some of which may represent the remains of other disturbed structures.

Large- and medium-scale land division

The need for large-scale divisions of land, ie those that relate to a community or larger group, may be marked by boundaries that run for more than 1 – 2 km, and are likely to reflect areas of political or social and economic control. These may include landuse rights and/or practical divisions of landuse, for example between enclosed and unenclosed or in-field and out-field areas. While the largest, longest boundaries are those least likely to be related purely to organisation of landuse and most likely to be politically motivated on a grand scale, it is equally the case that more localised division of the countryside at a strategic level may also reflect local political control of territory or community organisation of landuse, making it difficult to disentangle the landuse issues from a more political rationale for such boundaries. In either case it seems likely that they were important in defining land and territory from a community point of view.

Valley floor land division: cross-terrace ditched boundaries and meander cut-offs

In the middle Thames Valley substantial ditched boundaries appear to be amongst the first signs of land division and enclosure. At Perry Oaks/T5 six major north-south double-ditched boundaries or tracks of possible earlier Bronze Age origin (Framework Archaeology 2006, 102-12; see below) have been traced over 380 m and may have extended at least twice as far (Fig. 3.6). One of these partly respected the Stanwell cursus and another earlier prehistoric monument and one of the others respected a ring ditch. They became the defining framework for an extensive coaxial field system, which cut across the cursus. To the south, in another part of the Stanwell complex a more substantial, rather irregular steep sided ditch dateable to the middle Bronze Age, oriented east-west cutting

across the cursus, was traced from cropmarks for at least 120 m (O'Connell 1990). It was shown by excavation to have been crossed at right-angles by one of two curving trackways that formed the basis for another extensive coaxial field system which respected both the original boundary ditch, perhaps defined by above-ground hedges, and the trackways. At Thorpe Lea Nurseries (Hayman 1998; forthcoming a) a somewhat similar major boundary at least 200 m long was defined by two main lengths of substantial ditch, which in one place produced a significant quantity of middle Bronze Age occupation debris. Other smaller ditches showed that it too became, or originated as, part of a rectilinear field system. At the Eton Rowing Course a boundary ditch at least 600 m long ran between the Thames and the Cress Brook channel and formed the basis of the middle Bronze Age enclosed fields. Although it was not a very substantial boundary it could have been intended to demarcate a large area of land between the Thames and the Cress Brook.

A number of boundaries of significant lengths dividing up areas of gravel terrace or other suitable land may also have formed the framework for various field systems of the middle to late Bronze Age in the Upper Thames Valley, and in some cases seem to have been used to divide up large areas of gravel terrace. At Northfield Farm, Long Wittenham the boundary against which an area of small double ditched fields and paddocks was laid out has now been traced for c 600 m, though this has still not been firmly dated (Baker 2002; Tim Allen pers. comm.).

It has been suggested (Boyle et al. 1998, 33, fig. 2.10) that the Northfield Farm alignment and another 500 m long boundary ditch at Fullamoor

Fig. 3.6   Middle to late Bronze Age land division in the Middle Thames Valley: Perry Oaks/T5

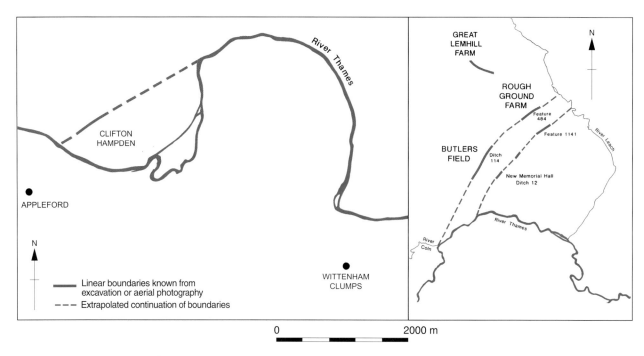

Fig. 3.7   Late Bronze Age/early Iron Age 'meander cut-off' land divisions in the Upper Thames Valley at (left) *Clifton Hampden and* (right) *Lechlade*

Farm, which is known from cropmarks and very limited excavation (Boyle *et al.* 1998), might be examples of a form of late prehistoric land division referred to as 'meander cut-offs'. These are identifiable where large areas of land surrounded on three sides by river channels (either a large meander or the confluence of two rivers) were enclosed in the later Bronze Age or early Iron Age by digging one or more boundary ditches across the fourth side (Fig. 3.7). The existence of such major boundaries was mooted in the report on excavations at Roughground Farm (Allen *et al.* 1993, 46) and Hingley (1996) noted examples at Wasperton and elsewhere in Warwickshire. Further work in the Lechlade area has enhanced the evidence for a major early Iron Age land division enclosing an area of about 250 ha between the Thames and its tributary the Leach. Yates (1997, 1999) has identified suitable locations for land divisions of this type in the Middle Thames Valley at Datchett and Cookham, but in neither case have actual boundaries been found.

Valley floor pit alignments

Pit alignments represent another form of land boundary dividing up areas of gravel terrace of varying size, though it is inherently difficult in most cases to be sure of either the full length or definite terminals of these boundaries, and in some instances, such as Butler's Field they seem to have been components of more complex ditched boundaries.

The sinuous late Bronze Age or early Iron Age double pit alignment at Shorncote/Cotswold Community is unusual in that both ends have been

defined by excavation (Hearne and Adam 1999, fig. 2; Oxford Archaeology 2004a) showing that it stretched over 410 m, with no apparent off-shoots. It cut a Bronze Age pit and stopped just short of another. Although it was impinged upon by gullies defining one side of a middle to late Iron Age and Roman settlement enclosure extending back from the terrace edge boundary, its southern terminal was crossed by an undated, possibly Roman ditch running at right-angles to it. Either side of the terminal of the pit alignment adjacent to the later ditch were two Roman inhumation burials. It is difficult to see that the relationship of these features to the terminal of the pit alignment could be coincidental, implying that the alignment had survived either as a visible earthwork or as a hedged boundary for several hundred years. This would be consistent with other aspects of land division at Shorncote/ Cotswold Community since the pit alignment was more or less parallel to a complex ditched boundary stretching along the edge of the gravel terrace and floodplain about 100 m to 140 m to the east. This seems to have originated in the late Bronze Age to early Iron Age as a fragmentary alignment of ditched segments and pits, but became a long-standing boundary with multiple recuts and adjustments lasting into the Roman period and beyond.

The late Iron Age pit alignment at Langford Downs which intersected a small settlement enclosure extended for several kilometres, crossing an area of gravel terrace next to the River Leach (Williams 1946-7). Of the undated examples known from cropmarks, the most impressive are two at Northfield Farm, Long Wittenham, one 950 m long, crossing an area of gravel terrace oriented at right-angles to the river, the other 150 m long at some distance away on a converging alignment (Fig. 3.8). Topographically it appears that at least the longer one was intended to subdivide a large area of land enclosed in a loop of the Thames. Neither has been dated, although Baker (2002, 11-12) suggests they may be early to middle Iron Age, possibly intersecting a part of a middle to late Bronze Age field system and putatively predating a late Iron Age and Roman trackway and network of fields and paddocks. None of this has been tested by excavation.

At Binsey, just west of Oxford an alignment *c* 400 m long with a shorter, almost parallel section is discernible from cropmarks running up the middle of an elongated patch of gravel terrace roughly parallel with the river (Benson and Miles 1974). The most convincing, but unexcavated example of a pit alignment in the Middle Thames is at Datchett (Gates 1975, map 30, pl 14) where the alignment intersects a possible Bronze Age ditched field system, but coincides with one side of a possible Iron Age or Roman settlement enclosure in a manner similar to the excavated example at Shorncote/Cotswold Community. Like most of the others, the Datchett alignment bisects a patch of gravel terrace.

A similar use of pit alignments to divide up the gravel terraces and delineate river bends has been noted both in the upper Severn (Wigley 2007) and in the Avon Valley (Hingley 1996) and has been recognised from cropmarks elsewhere (Webster and Hobley 1964). Moore (2006, 80-2) observes that the Thames Valley evidence suggests that linear land divisions were sometimes formed by ditches on higher ground and pit alignments in low lying areas, but he nevertheless notes unexcavated pit alignments high on the Cotswolds at Condicote (RCHME 1976, 39) and on the Corallian Ridge at Groundwell West (Walker *et al.* 2001).

In the Midlands some pit alignments seem to have been used to differentiate topographical zones, perhaps demarcating areas of different landuse or

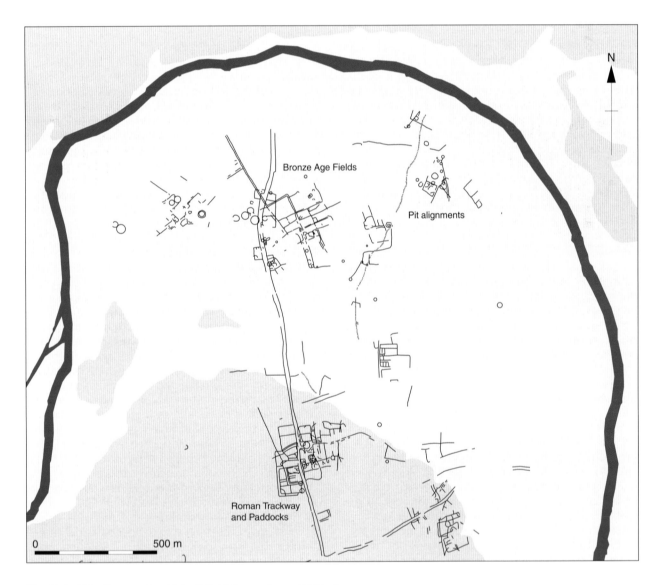

Fig. 3.8   Pit alignments at Northfield Farm, Long Wittenham

access (Rylatt and Bevan 2007, 231) rather than dividing them up in the way that clearly seems to predominate in the Thames Valley.

Although pit alignments are often seen as a very odd and mysterious kind of boundary, this may be because too much attention is paid to their detailed form rather than the type of boundary they may have represented. There are innumerable extant examples in the present day landscape of boundaries demarcating changes of ownership, management or landuse rights that are physically apparent but permeable to grazing animals or other access. Some of these have ancient origins, especially where they relate to common land. For example, just outside Oxford the shallow Shirelake Ditch divides the open common pasture of Port Meadow from Wolvercote Common where the Freemen of Oxford and the commoners of Wolvercote have intercommoning rights, their animals being free to graze as they wish across both areas (VCH 1990). Far from demarcating different topographical or landuse zones this ditch and others like it in the Thames Valley act as permeable boundaries marking different land rights and communal ownership between two areas of seamless topography and landuse, not a physical barrier to control access or usage. This sort of scenario may be the best model to explain the character and role of most pit alignments in the Thames Valley, though this does not preclude their having had other roles of the kind that Rylatt and Bevan suggest. The likelihood that they remained visible features for very long periods is borne out by the Shorncote/Cotswold Community case, where the southern terminal was respected by Roman inhumation graves and by a later boundary ditch that passed at right-angles to it.

Iron Age ditched land divisions

At a location similar to Shorncote/Cotswold Community, on low-lying alluvial sand and gravels in the valley of the Thame at Coldharbour Farm, Aylesbury, an early Iron Age ditch consisting of two end-to-end sections separated by a gap of 2 m, was traced for at least 330 m in a straight line broadly parallel with a former course of the Southcourt Brook, just south of its confluence with the Bear Brook (Parkhouse and Bonner 1997). The southern terminal of the southern section was located with no indication whether it was abutted by another section, and the northern section continued beyond the limit of excavation. There was no sign of ditches extending out from the boundary to create field subdivisions, though the ditch appears to have enclosed a long narrow area over a hectare in extent at the edge of lower-lying ground adjacent to the stream. There was no clearly definable area of domestic structures, but two groups of innumerable intercutting pits and some discrete ones lay between the ditch and the stream, broadly contemporary with early Iron Age domestic debris that was found in the upper fills of the ditch.

The straight early Iron Age boundary ditch was later crossed on a slightly different alignment by smaller ditches apparently forming a droveway, again parallel to the Southcourt Brook but a bit further away and with more evidence that it was a part of a field or paddock system, but still enclosing a similarly large area adjacent to the stream. Features attributable to this stage of development included a cluster of four posters in much the same area as the southern pit cluster and a number of penannular gullies and pens in the vicinity of the northern group. Although attributed to the 'early' Iron Age, the pottery lacks obvious angular forms and early decoration and probably belongs to the early/middle Iron Age transition

There are several other examples of mainly middle Iron Age ditches used to divide up areas of limestone or gravel terrace, or to create boundaries along their edges. At St Augustine's Farm east of Cirencester (Fig. 3.9) two lengths of segmented and composite ditches formed parts of a discontinuous middle Iron Age boundary that may have marked a pre-existing division between two communities suggested by groups of ring ditches which it passed between (Mudd *et al.* 1999 Vol 1, 35-40; Moore 2006). At Latton Lands a sinuous middle Iron Age ditch reflecting a pre-existing linear settlement extended over 460 m (Powell *et al.* 2007), while at Thornhill Farm a middle to late Iron Age ditch was traced from excavation and cropmarks in a great curving loop 850 m long enclosing an area of low lying first gravel terrace adjacent to a palaeochannel (Jennings *et al.* 2004, figs 3.1, 3.5). It was probably only one of several such boundaries dividing up the gravel terraces in that area. At Bicester Slade Farm (Fig. 3.9) an early to middle Iron Age boundary, apparently associated with animal pens and pastoral management either side of it, was traced over 470 m (Ellis *et al.* 2000, figs 2 4 and 22).

A 1.9 m wide boundary ditch was traced over 305 m across a very extensive area of floodplain between Yarnton and Cassington. It had been recut at least twice and waterlogged seeds from the base of the first recut were dated to 370 to 110 cal BC. One small ditch set out at right-angles to it was observed, but no other signs of an associated field system. It is possible that this NNW-SSE ditch, roughly equidistant between the main concentrations of Iron Age activity about 1 km away on the higher gravel terraces at Cassington to the west and Yarnton to the east, could have been established as a demarcation of land associated with these settlement groups (Hey *et al.* forthcoming a).

At Blackditch, Stanton Harcourt, just north of a banjo enclosure known from aerial photographs (Fig. 3.9), a small ditch was traced for 240 m along the line of a bypass (Lambrick and Allen 2004, 155-9). Each end of the ditch was deepened as if to act as a sump, the northern one with a shallower gully leading to it from the east. There were no intermediate side ditches, but about a third of the way along the ditch from the southern end there were

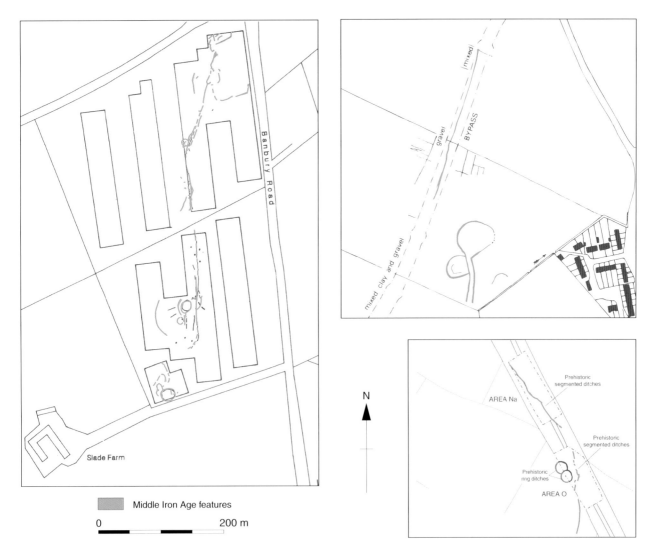

Fig. 3.9   Middle Iron Age land division ditches: (left) Slade Farm, Bicester; (upper right) Blackditch; (lower right) St. Augustine's Farm, Cirencester

two kinks in the alignment 20 m apart, as if it had changed course where it crossed or was met by transverse boundaries not marked by ditches, a feature also evident in the early Iron Age boundaries at Roughground Farm (Allen *et al.* 1993, 36, fig. 7). A sherd of Iron Age pottery and some burnt stone and bone were found in the southern end of the ditch. It appeared to follow a band of very thin and patchy gravel over clay, possibly the interface between second and third gravel terraces, and waterlogged remains suggested that the southern end was in an area of hazel woodland or a large old hedge with hazel trees and remains of a woodland flora set within an open, grazed grassland environment. The purpose of the ditch is not entirely clear. It was not big enough to be a major land division, but may have defined the edge of an area of managed grazing next to a banjo enclosure.

In the Middle Thames Valley, the middle Bronze Age field system at Eton Rowing Course was transected by two middle Iron Age ditches, one of which diverged and ran alongside one of the Bronze

Age enclosure ditches, suggesting that these were still defined above ground by hedges, although their ditches had filled long before. The larger middle Iron Age ditch was traced in excavation for 400 m and as a cropmark for another 200 m. It met another ditch at right-angles, traced for 350 m with a four-post structure alongside it.

Landuse divisions defined by settlement location

A noticeable feature of settlement and landuse patterns particularly evident in the Iron Age in the Thames Valley is the location of settlements along topographical or landuse boundaries, whether or not they were also defined by ditches or other subsoil features. At Stanton Harcourt the main concentration of earlier prehistoric monuments occupied a large central core of the extensive area of second gravel terrace, focussed on the Devil's Quoits henge-circle. There is no evidence for boundaries or landuse divisions within the earlier prehistoric landscape, and the palaeo-environmental evidence at Gravelly Guy suggests that for much of this period the area was predominantly grassland with scrub or woodland margins (Lambrick and Allen 2004). As usual, crop remains were sparse compared with the later prehistoric and Roman settlement, and domestic activity was apparently ephemeral. A sequence of ploughwash and alluvial soils on the adjacent Windrush floodplain showed that an increase in arable landuse may have begun by the late Bronze Age. In the Iron Age cultivation was taking place between the main settlement and the edge of the gravel terrace prior to the onset of alluviation in the late Iron Age or Roman period and continued into the Roman period when ploughsoils became inter-stratified with alluvium (Lambrick 1992; Lambrick and Allen 2004/5). The layout of the settlement and later soils indicated that arable fields were located towards the edge of the gravel terrace with extensive pasture in the area of the former barrow cemetery towards the centre of the gravel terrace. Although probably originating before the settlement was established at the end of the late Bronze Age or early in the Iron Age, there was no ditched boundary to mark this landuse division until the late Iron Age. The settlement seems to have been located on the arable side of the line in the early to middle or late Iron Age and was relocated to the pasture side during the late Iron Age/early Roman period.

Several other Iron Age settlements at Stanton Harcourt share a similar layout to Gravelly Guy, both in terms of date range and features and in the repeated establishment of late Iron Age and Roman paddocks and fields encroaching onto the central core of the gravel terrace. It is notable that all these settlements were situated roughly on a line that can be drawn round the main cluster of earlier prehistoric monuments. It was concluded that they were all established along a common landuse division, each with its own fields on one side around the edge of the gravel terrace, while on the other they shared a large area of pasture defined by the older monument complex (Lambrick 1992b; Lambrick and Allen 2004).

A number of other cases of linear pit clusters may indicate similar arrangements. At Standlake areas of Iron Age settlement appear to have been located largely around the periphery of an earlier prehistoric barrow cemetery (Riley 1946/7, figs 6 and 9). At City Farm Hanborough the 'west' settlement was a linear cluster of pits that lay at right-angles to a local stream with another cluster of pits, the 'east' settlement, equidistant from a linear group of round barrows between them (Case *et al.* 1964/5, fig. 2). An L-shaped pit scatter settlement at Cresswell Field Yarnton may have demarcated the corner of an area of different landuse and the same may apply to other cases less easy to demonstrate.

There are several other settlements associated with ditches and/or topographical boundaries which may similarly have marked differences in landuse or tenure. At Thorpe Lea Nurseries a significant amount of middle Bronze Age domestic occupation debris was found in an otherwise rather amorphous occupation area adjacent to a long linear boundary. At Latton Lands (Powell *et al.* forthcoming) a long sinuous middle to late Iron Age boundary ditch with a gated entrance overlay an early to middle Iron Age settlement spread out on a similar alignment (Fig. 4.12). The ditch, which had many minor recuts and segments, appears to have formalised and rationalised a pre-existing division in landuse marked by the location of the earlier settlement. At the northern end of this boundary was a rectilinear field system on one side and an apparently open area to the south contained an earlier prehistoric oval ditched enclosure. The gateway through the boundary gave access to a settlement area on the east side characterised by penannular gullies and sub-circular enclosures which continued to develop as a settlement into the late Iron Age and early Roman period before being superseded by one of the major roads to Cirencester and a new field system. Pending full analysis it is not yet clear how land use was organised in relation to the boundary, but the oval enclosure may have been situated in open pasture with the gateway providing access to and from the settlement area, while the fields further north might have been used for more intensive grazing or arable.

Following the highly dispersed late Bronze Age and early Iron Age settlement, a middle Iron Age settlement was established at Shorncote/Cotswold Community alongside a long-lived boundary marking a topographical edge of gravel terrace and flood plain (Oxford Archaeology 2004). A similar sequence is in evidence at Horcott Pit, at the junction between first and second terrace gravels (Pine and Preston 2004; Whymark *et al.* 2007). At Bicester Slade Farm a small early to middle Iron Age settlement seems to have been associated with a linear boundary along the boundary between an area of clay and limestone (Ellis *et al.* 2000), and a series of small middle Iron Age settlements occupying terrace edge sites are recorded in the Upper Thames Valley, as at Farmoor (Lambrick and Robinson 1979), Thrupp (Everett and Eeles 1999) and Thornhill Farm (Jennings *et al.* 2004).

'Ranch' boundaries and land division on the chalk

A well-established type of late prehistoric land divisions on the Wessex chalk are the so-called ranch boundaries. These often divide areas of arable and pasture or enclose very large areas of pasture, and have been examined especially in the area around Danebury and Quarley Hill in Hampshire (Cunliffe and Poole 2000). Within the Thames basin a few similar types of boundary can be seen on the Berkshire Downs and to a lesser extent other chalkland areas, though few have been excavated and both their date and purpose are debatable, as is their relationship to linear territorial boundaries like the Berkshire and Chilterns Grims Ditches (see Chapter 9).

From the relatively diminutive size of the Berkshire Grims Ditch, Ford (1982) concluded that it was not defensive, but probably a territorial boundary of late Bronze Age origin. He argued that its topographical position, mainly following the escarpment along the junction of two soil types, might also indicate a division between two different landuse areas, perhaps between open pasture land and more intensively farmed land.

Further west along the chalk scarp of the Berkshire Downs from the Berkshire Grims Ditch, there are a number of long linear ditches set out at right-angles to the scarp, as if dividing the Downs into major land units. The western end of the Grims Ditch is not clear, but one possibility is that it turned south-west to run down the dip slope of the Downs instead of following the scarp. This would fit well with the predominant alignment of major ditches

Fig. 3.10   Major land divisions on the Berkshire Downs (the field systems may be Roman)

further west from Segsbury to Uffington, which are aligned mainly north-south up and down the dipslope spurs with only occasional sections parallel to the ridge (Fig. 3.10). At Whitehorse Hill, Uffington one of these boundaries was sampled on a small scale as part of the White Horse Hill project (Miles *et al.* 2003, 127-31). The results were somewhat ambiguous: although there were small pieces of Roman pottery in the primary fill, suggesting either a much later origin, the possibility of the ditch having been maintained over a much longer period, or the part excavated representing only an extension of an earlier ditch on the same line were also suggested. At Wayland's Smithy to the west another north-south linear ditch containing early Iron Age pottery cut the silted up quarry ditch of an early Neolithic chambered tomb (Whittle 1991, 84, 87, 99, figs 6 and 12). Further west again, in the vicinity of Alfred's Castle, a series of late Bronze Age linear ditches were sampled, providing some evidence that they were aligned on earlier barrows. Rather than following the natural ridges and spurs they appear to have cut across the topography defining large irregular areas. The substantial early Iron Age settlement enclosure of Alfred's Castle was inserted into the southern end of one of these areas.

The relationship between the Grims Ditch, other major linear boundaries, enclosures and field systems on the Berkshire Downs is only gradually becoming clear, and it is apparent from multiple ditches found in the Alfred's Castle area that their history is a good deal more complicated than superficial indications might suggest. Overall, these major linear ditches give the impression that the Berkshire Downs, like the Hampshire and Wiltshire chalk, was subject to large-scale land division in the later Bronze Age or early Iron Age, perhaps mainly in connection with grazing, since it appears that at least some if not most of the very extensive 'celtic' fields on the Downs may be of Roman origin (Bowden *et al.* 1991-3). In the absence of more comprehensive excavation and the good stratigraphic evidence of plough lynchets sealed by the Iron Age ramparts at Rams Hill (Bradley and Ellison 1975), all this is still far from certain, and from the point of view of understanding major landuse and land division in the Thames Valley generally, this is most unfortunate. The potential agricultural production of the area could have had a major bearing on the rest of the region, and the amount of labour required to create the linear boundaries would have been substantial.

At first sight, the Chilterns with their extensive areas of clay-with-flints and beech woods present a very different picture, but despite the basic geological differences a comparison with the Berkshire Downs is not inappropriate. A linear ditch in a broadly similar topographical position to the Berkshire Grims Ditch follows the Chiltern escarpment further east, and limited excavations at various points along it produced late Bronze Age or early Iron Age pottery, suggesting that it may be of broadly similar date and function (Kidd 2007).

Late Iron Age linear dykes

A number of larger linear dykes such as the South Oxfordshire Grims Ditch and Aves Ditch created in the late Iron Age and/or the early Roman period seem more overtly political in character. Like the two Grims Ditches dating is notoriously difficult but recent excavations have shed some light on them. Their construction is generally considered to reflect broad political control of territory at the end of the Iron Age and in the early Roman period (see Chapter 9). It is not clear how far this related to pre-existing land divisions, but it is worth noting that the western end of the South Oxfordshire Grims Ditch, which extends across the southern end of the Chilterns between Wallingford and Henley, overlay ploughed fields (Cromarty *et al.* 2006, 163-72). Although this does not mean that the whole of it was laid out as a new barrier across farmland, it does reflect how strategic land division often overrides local landuse arrangements. Other dyke systems were associated with territorial oppida (see Chapter 9).

Middle Bronze Age and later L-shaped Enclosure Ditches (Fig. 3.11)

Four examples of ditches set at right-angles, apparently to define an area of occupation or other activity, have been observed in the Upper Thames Valley, at Latton Lands (Stansbie and Laws 2003, 106-43), Shorncote/Cotswold Community (Oxford Archaeology 2004), Eynsham (Barclay *et al.* 2001) and Frilford (Lock *et al.* 2002). All probably date to the middle Bronze Age.

The L-shaped ditch at Shorncote/Cotswold Community ran 62 m N-S and 50 m E-W. The eastern terminal contained sherds of bucket urn, worked flint and animal bone and respected a cluster of earlier segmented ditches and a waterhole. Two pits containing middle Bronze Age pottery were located within the area defined by the ditch, one containing mould fragments of a socketed axe. An undated fence line of postholes and a gully ran obliquely across the 'enclosure', turning northwards to respect the western arm of the ditch. About 300 m south of the L-shaped ditch was an L-shaped fence line forming a south-east corner with an east facing entrance. A waterhole containing Bronze Age or early Iron Age pottery lay within the angle of the fence and two post-ring buildings just beyond the fence terminals.

At Latton Lands (Stansbie and Laws 2004) two ditches 65 m and 55 m long converged leaving a 20 m gap on one side of the apex for a large waterhole with a space around it. The ditches produced middle Bronze Age pottery and other domestic debris, concentrated at the terminals, and the waterhole contained a pottery assemblage of similar date, including bucket urn sherds, flints an antler and fragments of a wooden bowl. A post-built roundhouse lay close to one of the ditches, and another further away.

At Frilford aerial photography and geophysical survey have defined two L-shaped ditches set out in close proximity (Harding 1987 cover and frontispiece; Lock *et al.* 2002, fig. 14). During excavation (Lock *et al.* 2002, 76-9, figs 18, 9, 21, 22) sherds of a near complete bucket urn were found on the base of the V-shaped ditch of the northernmost enclosure, which was cut by early Iron Age pits and a small sub-rectangular Iron Age enclosure. The L-shaped ditch was subsequently recut in the Roman period, demonstrating that it was still visible as an earthwork at that time. The other L-shaped enclosure ditch was morphologically similar, but undated, though a fragment of coarse Bronze Age urn was found in a hollow to the east. Excavation of a small part of the 'interior' corner of this enclosure revealed nothing.

Another possible L-shaped ditch was found on the site of Eynsham Abbey (Barclay *et al.* 2001). The ditch and interior were highly disturbed by later features, but an area of relatively undisturbed topsoil survived in parts of the interior. The excavations were too limited to demonstrate the full extent of the ditches but the corner can be inferred as north-east, lying just outside the excavation. The dating of the ditch is uncertain, but an episode of mid to late Bronze Age activity is evident from the undisturbed soils, small pits, and a possible small roundhouse in the interior and from similar material from the middle and upper fill of the ditch. These deposits provided grouped radiocarbon dates of 1270 to 1080 and 1220 to 1040 cal BC, but by this stage the ditch had silted to a stable profile. Beaker and early Bronze Age sherds and flints together with exotic stone objects (mace head, axe fragment and pendant) and a large broken fragment of a limestone boulder from the site were unstratified but could indicate an earlier origin for the enclosure, comparable to other Neolithic and Bronze Age ceremonial sites. This interpretation was preferred in the excavation report, but in the light of the middle Bronze Age L-shaped ditches referred to above, all from sites with earlier prehistoric ceremonial or funerary monuments nearby, it seems appropriate to consider the possibility that the Eynsham enclosure was an example of this type of monument.

In the Middle Thames Valley a less convincing example of an L-shaped enclosure ditch was identified at Bankside Close, Isleworth (Hull 1998). The feature was excavated in trial trenches and it was not established whether there were return ditches creating an enclosure with an eastern entrance, or whether this was part of a more extensive field system, the preferred interpretation of the excavators. Finds of pottery concentrated near the excavated terminal included a number of smashed vessel bases, together with flints and a possible

quern fragment. Of the 176 sherds recovered most were thought to come from only five vessels.

At Home Farm Laleham (Hayman forthcoming c) a substantial Bronze Age ditch formed a right-angled corner. The terminals of the ditch were not identified in either direction so the possibility remains that, as at Isleworth, this was a fully enclosed site. The deeper north-south length of ditch contained a concentration of late Bronze Age pottery, and a large number of perforated clay slabs lay in the top fill of the ditch length running close to a large roundhouse, but the date of the original cutting of the ditches was not established. The ditch was significantly different in character from the relatively barren gullies of middle to late Bronze Age rectilinear fields on different orientations recorded over a large area to the south.

Another possible example much more obviously associated with a middle Bronze Age field system is a shallower, U-profile L-shaped ditch (enclosure 918) with arms only about 15 m long recorded at Weir Bank Stud Farm, Bray. The more substantial ditches of enclosure 926 could represent another L-shaped ditch complex, but could equally be part of a complete enclosure relating to a complex of other ditches situated on the edge of the excavated area. Other ditches belonged to a rectilinear field system with areas of domestic occupation, which raises the possibility that some L-shaped ditches were formative elements in the emergence of rectilinear field systems, or were sometimes created within them. This is not obviously evident in rectilinear field systems at Green Park, Appleford, Eton, Dorney, Hengrove, Ashford Prison or Perry Oaks/T5, but remains a possibility worth further consideration.

Whether L-shaped ditches had more than a prosaic domestic or agricultural use is doubtful. Of examples unrelated to fully-fledged field systems, the smashed bucket urn on the base of the Frilford ditch, a fine nail-headed bronze pin from Eynsham, the mould fragments from a pit at Shorncote/Cotswold Community, the objects from the waterhole at Latton Lands, and pottery from the terminal at Isleworth are all vaguely suggestive of 'special' deposits but nothing that cannot be paralleled on ordinary settlement sites. At Latton Lands and Shorncote/Cotswold Community there was good evidence for contemporary domestic activity, which is also evident at Weir Bank Stud Farm and Home Farm Laleham. In terms of agricultural functions, the ditches were more substantial than most field ditches, and their wide, often V-shaped profiles would have deterred animals from crossing or entering them. The Latton Lands and Frilford examples, with gaps at their angles and the presence of waterholes at Latton and the Shorncote/Cotswold Community L-shaped fence may indicate a possible use for funneling and/or corralling animals. The possibility that L-shaped ditches of this type were either formative elements or later additions in the development of early field systems might be a further reason to assume a

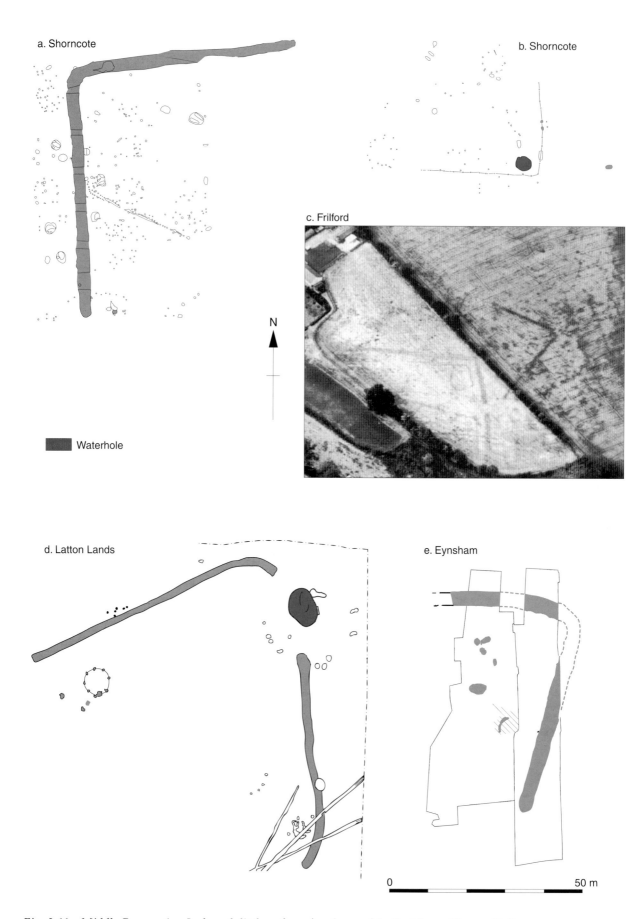

a. Shorncote

b. Shorncote

c. Frilford

N

Waterhole

d. Latton Lands

e. Eynsham

0   50 m

Fig. 3.11   Middle Bronze Age L-shaped ditch or fence 'enclosures' in the Upper Thames Valley

connection with agricultural uses: if they were used for corralling animals, it would not be surprising if some became a focus for domestic activity.

L-shaped enclosures of this type have been recognised on several sites in Wessex, (Stone 1941, 115; Rahtz 1962; Barrett *et al.* 1991, 183-214) and seem to have been established in the corners of 'celtic fields', but they have not previously been seen as a particular feature of the Thames Valley. Discussing the possibility that the Isleworth ditch might be an example of an L-shaped enclosure, Ford and Hull concluded, in the absence of domestic activity, that it was not comparable to the Wessex ones (Hull 1998, 9-10). But Cleal considered that, while the quantity of material from Bray and the settlement morphology was not like the Wessex sites in their fully developed form, there were quite strong general similarities, especially with the earlier stages of some of the Wessex sites (Barnes and Cleal 1995, 48-51). The most convincing examples of free-standing L-shaped ditches identified so far are in the Upper Thames Valley, but these might be cases where more extensive rectilinear fields and enclosures did not develop, and the similar elements within the rectilinear field system at Weir Bank Stud may indicate that others were pre-cursor elements or later developments within elaborate rectilinear ditched field systems.

FIELD SYSTEMS AND ENCLOSURES

Later Bronze Age and Iron Age co-axial and rectilinear field systems

Co-axial field systems are characterised by groups of widely spaced long parallel ditches, on a straight or gently curving alignment, the spaces between them subdivided by ditches set at right-angles and generally confined between the parallel alignments. The combination of regular and irregular spacing of the transverse boundaries creates recognisable blocks of fields and enclosures exhibiting a varied pattern of rectangular fields. Such field systems on Dartmoor and elsewhere are later Bronze Age in origin (Fleming 1978; 1983) but the extensive areas of field systems on the Berkshire Downs appear to be mostly Roman in date (Bowden *et al.* 1991-3).

Not all such field systems are based on a strictly co-axial alignment, and some appear to have been more irregular in layout despite retaining a strict rectangularity. However, in many cases rectilinear fields of this period have not been examined on a large enough scale to establish whether or not a co-axial layout is present.

Several middle and late Bronze Age rectilinear field systems have been investigated in the Thames Valley on a reasonable scale, resulting in a growing understanding of their layout and characteristics. The overall pattern is seldom revealed by crop-marks and even around Heathrow and Staines, where some of the most extensive excavations have been carried out, only a small proportion of the co-

axial field systems known to have existed in the area has been investigated. Even this is still a relatively limited area compared with the hundreds of square kilometeres of such fields that have been traced on Dartmoor and elsewhere.

Amongst the earliest and the most thoroughly explored late prehistoric fields in the Thames Valley is the co-axial field system at Perry Oaks/T5, where over 80 ha has been examined archaeologically (see Fig. 3.6). The fields were set out from a series of broadly parallel double ditched boundaries or trackways extending north-south for at least 350m across the gravel terrace, spaced at intervals of about 130 m, 100 m and 145m. Some of these main co-axial spine boundaries appear to have been aligned on and/or respected earlier, still visible earthwork monuments, notably the Stanwell cursus and its associated subsidiary cursuses, and various ring ditches and enclosures. These distinctive 'spine' boundaries showed evidence of recuts and redefinition and are thought to represent principal divisions of seven 'landholdings' represented by blocks of fields, some differing markedly from the others in the overall character of their layout despite displaying internally regular arrangements of fields (Framework Archaeology 2006, Chapter 3).

These main boundaries may have long predated the subdivision of the linear strips into co-axial fields. However this is partly based on the ecological evidence of mixed flowery scrub, interpreted as old hedges, and in one or two cases the main coaxial 'spines' cut the ends of cross ditches. Based on evidence from waterholes interstratified with ditches of the field system with earliest radiocarbon determinations consistently dated to *c* 1610-1390 cal BC. The suggestion, based purely on this ecological evidence, that the origin of the hedged boundaries was probably closer to *c* 1700 cal BC (despite a notable lack of much earlier Bronze Age flintwork or ceramics) seems very speculative. Another question is whether these main coaxial boundaries were trackways, as suggested by the excavators (Framework Archaeology 2006, 108-112), or hedgebanks, or a bit of both. Either interpretation would make sense, and the issue is perhaps more pertinent to the detail of how people moved through the landscape than its overall development.

Whatever their origin and function, the main coaxial 'spines' seem to have provided the basis for defining at least seven blocks of fields at Heathrow, each with its own distinctive layout. Taking account of subtle variations, there may have been at least 12 such units, perhaps representing the holdings of different families or groups. It is not clear what the totality of any single 'landholding' may have been because they appear to have been established as long north-south strips while the main excavation area covers a very substantial east-west band that crosses several of these units but has not definitively identified the northern or southern limits of any. From what can be inferred, some of the most coherent blocks of fields within the 'landholdings' cover at least 4.5 ha but probably much more.

Four, possibly six such strips lay to the east of what the excavators interpret as having started as an open area east of a D-shaped enclosure, and two other strips extended north and south of the enclosure. Another strip with one side respecting or reusing part of the eastern ditch of the Stanwell Cursus, adjoined the west side of D-shaped enclosure. To the west of this, there was another tapering strip of land straddling the still extant bank and ditches of the Stanwell cursus, its western side following the course of a palaeochannel, which appears not to have been divided longitudinally but by a series of fairly regularly spaced cross ditches. Further west and to the south of this block there were other, apparently less regular blocks of fields and paddocks. The putative 'open area' between the D-shaped enclosure and the blocks of strip fields in the eastern part of the complex was also divided up transversely rather than longitudinally.

The paucity of detailed stratigraphic relationships and dating evidence and the practice of ditch maintenance and recutting make it difficult to establish a definitive interpretation of how the complex developed, including whether differences of layout in the main 'landholding' blocks reflect chronological, social or agricultural differences. It is possible to suggest that changes may have taken place within the landholdings – for example the landholdings in the eastern half of the complex seem to have been sub-divided longitudinally into half strips and in some cases quarter strips, suggesting stages of subdivision of the landholdings through inheritance or other acquisition of rights. It would not be surprising if regular subdivisions of coaxial strips and enclosure and subdivision of other areas reflect quite complex arrangements of tenure and inheritance over several generations. Other modifications may have been made as different areas were enclosed, for example in addition to a track round the inside of the southeastern sector of the D-shaped enclosure, another track may have been added round the outside of its north-east corner allowing passage between the enclosure and one of the large fields carved out of the former open area.

It is reasonable to imagine that the field system complex at Heathrow developed in a piecemeal way. The subsidiary ditches that divided the major strips into fields cut across the cursus monuments but appear to have been more ephemeral features in terms of the key structural components of the layout, being less prone to recutting and realignment, the hedges or fences alongside them being the most important functional manifestation of these boundaries. Nevertheless their spacing and generally strict rectilinearity is a fundamental characteristic of the pattern and they define a wide range of field sizes. Some of the larger areas apparently lack subdivisions, but may have been divided by fences, hedges or gullies that have left little or no trace.

Waterholes were dug in numerous places within these fields often at corners or at the sides and in gaps in boundaries, occasionally in the middle of fields. Environmental evidence suggests that the landscape was primarily pastoral, and the waterholes and wells may have been intended as water sources within the fields, thereby avoiding the need to collect water or take animals to drink at the nearest natural water sources up to a few kilometres away. The silting up, re-modelling of old waterholes and excavation of new ones, together with general scatter of domestic debris in some areas provide the principal evidence for the continued use and development of the field system through the late Bronze Age and into the Iron Age. Environmental evidence suggests that crop growing if anything reduced in this period, though in some parts of the field system where waterholes were not renewed, this may not apply.

Evidence of domestic activity was more concentrated in some parts of the field system than others but it is doubtful if any of these rather amorphous areas of occupation represent permanent year-round settlement. As the land filled with small fields it became desirable to maintain routeways through it, some following pre-existing paths along the main axes, to allow passage across the gravel terrace between the floodplain to the south and higher ground to the north.

In summary, although it is not possible to demonstrate in detail how the complex developed, it is likely that its layout may have emerged from a pre-existing framework of recognised divisions in the landscape that reflected older monuments, habitual routeways and natural topography. It developed and was in use from at least the middle Bronze Age through to the early Iron Age and was probably extant in the middle Iron Age. There appeared to be clear landholding blocks and it is likely that these were occupied and developed by several family or community groups engaged principally in stock-raising but with some crop-growing.

To the south of Heathrow T5 further parts of the same or an adjacent field system were investigated on a smaller scale at Stanwell (O'Connell 1990), where a major middle Bronze Age boundary was cut at right-angles by one of two curving 'trackways'. The ditches formed a rectilinear arrangement with one plot occupying 12 ha. The numerous gullies on these alignments were not easily distinguished from medieval features. Whereas at Perry Oaks/T5 the initial Bronze Age ditches respected the Stanwell cursus, both the main middle Bronze Age ditch and the trackways at Stanwell cut across the cursus. Four waterholes all cut or were adjacent to field system boundaries. Late Bronze Age occupation consisted of two post-built roundhouses, one with an off-centre pit/hearth.

Part of a middle Bronze Age field system about 2.5 km north-east of Perry Oaks/T5 was investigated at Imperial Sports Ground (Fig. 3.12). It consisted of nine fields defined by regularly spaced parallel coaxial boundaries, some of them double-ditched, on a NNE-SSW alignment (Crockett 2001). Some boundaries were aligned on a Neolithic mortuary enclosure while a double ring ditch and a middle Bronze Age penannular cemetery lay at the centre of a double width field with one ditch aligned to respect the south side of the double ring ditch. Another penannular enclosure lay in the centre of a field to the north. There was virtually no recutting or realignment of ditches after they were established. Dating of the fields is uncertain, including whether the middle Bronze Age cemetery groups were established or continued in use within the fields or were pre-existing burial places respected but no longer in use. Several waterholes were identified, most at the corners of fields, one containing a log ladder and another a bucket base. Other large pits may have been multiple recut waterholes comparable with examples at Perry Oaks/T5 and Hengrove. Some of the enclosed areas appear to have been settlements where significantly more domestic debris was found, these occurring at 250 m to 320 m intervals. One of the possible settlement enclosures on a different alignment may have pre- or post-dated the main layout.

More fragmentary evidence of middle and late Bronze Age field systems has been found at sites north of Heathrow, including Prospect Park, Nobel Drive and Cranford Lane (Andrews 1996 c, 48-9 fig. 11; Elsden 1996; 1997; Yates 2001).

A similar pattern of extensive field systems has been emerging over several years on the Surrey gravels. A multi-period site at Hengrove Farm includes a broadly coaxial field system exposed by excavations and monitoring over the last 5 years of gravel extraction in an area of about 14.5 ha (Fig. 3.12; Hayman forthcoming d). They resemble the Perry Oaks/T5 field system in terms of regular spacing of boundaries, numerous wells and waterholes and concentrations of domestic activities in particular areas – in certain fields or paddocks and around waterholes which accumulated domestic debris in their upper fills when they were abandoned. Nearby at Ashford Prison another system of later Bronze Age coaxial fields on a slightly different alignment had long, relatively straight ditches, respecting a NE-SW orientation established by earlier ditches aligned on a Neolithic hengiform enclosure (Carew *et al.* 2006). The layout indicates that the fields were more extensive to the north-west, probably linking up with the Hengrove area, which may have been part of the same field system on a slightly different alignment. It is possible that the excavated area happens to coincide with the south-west limit of the fields, or an open area within the field system later occupied by a middle Iron Age settlement. The sparseness of finds and absence of waterholes and wells contrasts with Hengrove, suggesting that the area excavated was peripheral to the main area of domestic activity.

As is common with later Bronze Age field systems, the ditches and gullies at Ashford were not continuous, varied in size and did not generally intersect at junctions. At one intersection of four fields an arrangement of gaps in the ditches would have allowed access between them and was maintained in a later modification. The position of hedges or banks can be inferred from the detailed layout, suggesting that it was the hedges, not the ditches that were aligned on each other. The sequence of development indicated by the intersecting and recut ditches and gullies that make up the field system can be interpreted in different ways, but it appears that the cross ditches were sometimes realigned whereas the main coaxial elements retained their alignment. Although a few small pits were found, there were no contemporary waterholes or significant traces of settlement within the area excavated.

At Home Farm, Laleham parts of another extensive field system had several different alignments, and in places a fairly coherent rectilinear plan (Hayman forthcoming c). The corner of a separate enclosure, possibly L-shaped, was defined by a more substantial ditch forming a right-angle and extending beyond the excavated area in both directions. It appears to have been associated with a clear concentration of late Bronze Age domestic debris, including the concentration of perforated clay slabs (see above), while a late Bronze Age post-built roundhouse with a significant concentration of occupation material was found nearby. The sparse distribution of finds in the smaller ditches makes dating the detail of the field system difficult, but there was evidence of earlier Bronze Age activity, though the main fields were probably middle to late Bronze Age in origin. Since a number of the sampled areas revealed rectilinear patterns of ditches on different orientations, it seems likely that they were not all laid out at the same time, or may reflect different land holdings.

At Thorpe Lea Nurseries the long straight boundary ditch referred to in the context of land division (see above) was revealed over a distance of about 200 m, including one area with a concentration of middle Bronze Age pottery, but there were only two recognisable ditches set at right-angles to it attributable to this period. This does not amount to much of a field system, but other shallow gullies and ditches may have left no trace and it is interesting to note that some small gully fragments attributable to the Iron Age and Roman periods on the site appear to share the original Bronze Age alignment. Possible explanations might be either that the Bronze Age gullies survived as earthworks finally filled in only when the site was more intensively used in later periods; that the gullies were dug or cleaned out alongside extant hedges surviving from the Bronze Age layout; or that the alignment of these later gullies was purely coincidental. Given the re-orientation of other Iron Age and Roman ditches, the last is perhaps least likely.

Further up river in the Bray-Maidenhead area of the Middle Thames several sites have produced

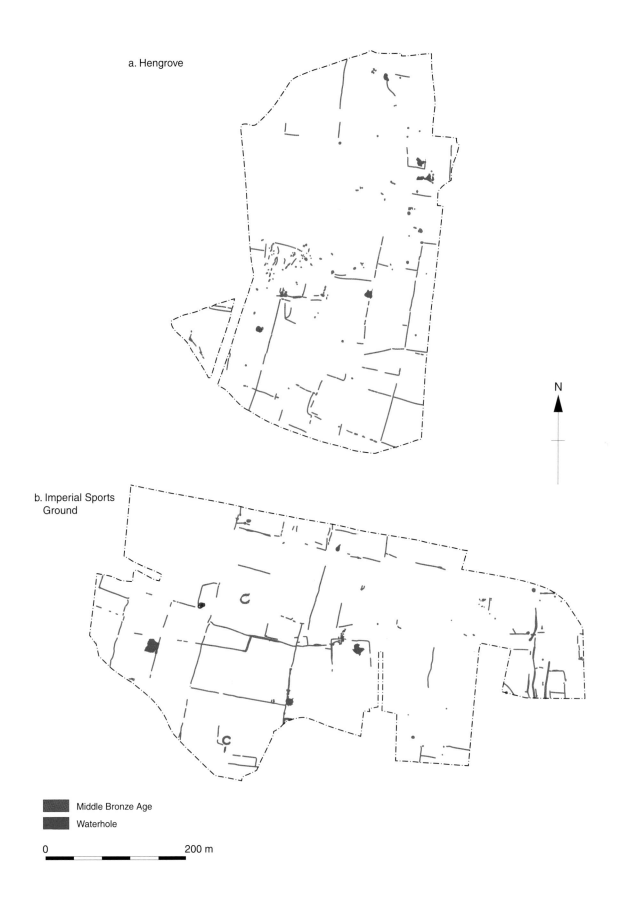

a. Hengrove

b. Imperial Sports
Ground

N

Middle Bronze Age

Waterhole

0   200 m

Fig. 3.12   Middle Bronze Age field systems on the Surrey gravels at Hengrove and Imperial Sports Ground

evidence of fields. Two areas of Bronze Age enclosures and fields are known from cropmarks at the Eton Rowing Course, the larger subject to substantial excavation. The baseline boundary from which the field system was laid out was a straight ditch traced for 600 m running north-east across a peninsula of gravel from the river Thames to the Cress Brook, formerly a major channel of the river. Next to the Thames the ditch formed the west side of a square enclosure surrounding an unexcavated, triple-ditched barrow or henge, the date of which could be hinted at by late Neolithic and early Bronze Age pits found nearby. North of this enclosure the baseline formed one side of two mirror-image pairs of small enclosures either side of a five-sided field. The primary small enclosure of each pair had a waterhole in one corner, the northern one dated to 1430-1260 cal BC, and the large pentagonal field was subdivided by another pair of mirror-image ditches. East of the pentagonal field two further parallel ditches ran at right-angles to the baseline, forming the limits of at least four rhomboid-shaped fields.

There were more unexcavated cropmark enclosures alongside the baseline to the north-east. North-west of the baseline was another field or enclosure next to the more northerly of the small pair of enclosures, and cropmarks suggest that there was another to the south next to the Thames. Finds were few, but were concentrated in the primary small enclosures, and included a saddle quern and charred spelt wheat grains dated to 1409-1262 cal BC as well as the bones of cattle, sheep, pigs and dogs. A group of four cremation burials, three of them urned, lay within the larger of the southern pair of enclosures, and a crouched inhumation burial in the smaller primary enclosure. Small pits and pottery suggesting small domestic foci were also found south and east of the rhomboidal fields.

The second set of Bronze Age enclosures is known largely from cropmarks east of the first across a small contemporary channel, and limited excavation has recovered middle Bronze Age pottery. It consisted of a central ditch co-axial with the baseline of the first set of enclosures, with two ditches crossing it at right-angles. Ditches parallel to the central ditch formed rectangular fields or enclosures on both sides, south of which the central ditch changed alignment and became a double-ditched trackway running across a low-lying area towards a former channel of the Thames. A sandbank in the river at this point contained human bones and was flanked by upright wooden stakes. South of the main rectangular enclosures was a third sinuous ditch aligned at right-angles to the central ditch with a small D-shaped enclosure attached to it.

The enclosures and fields at the Eton Rowing Course together cover about 40 ha. The symmetrical, but not fully rectilinear mirror-image layout of two pairs of enclosures and their associated fields is unusual, though they were later modified in different ways. The enclosures at the Rowing Course were only one element of the varied exploitation of this landscape, with groups of other waterholes and pits and animal burials in a largely unenclosed grazing area on the opposite side of the former Thames channel and flint knapping scatters and burnt areas indicating temporary encampments on the floodplain.

In the hinterland of the Rowing Course site, further boundary ditches have been found on the Maidenhead-Windsor Flood Alleviation Channel at Marsh Lane West, where a ditch terminal produced a dump of occupation material, and scattered cremation burials were found alongside the ditches in various places.

Across the river at Weir Bank Stud Farm, Bray (Barnes *et al.* 1995), another area of middle Bronze Age fields or enclosures was found (Fig 3.13). Two small sub-square enclosures were completely revealed, and in the late Bronze Age a roundhouse was erected outside one of these, where the partially preserved ground surface contained a large quantity of pottery and other domestic debris.

At Horton parts of a middle Bronze Age field system and farmland boundaries were examined, with pits and waterholes containing evidence of domestic activity apparently used to mark land divisions. It is suggested that by the late Bronze Age there was a change in farming practices, with many fields abandoned because they could no longer be farmed effectively, either because the land had been over-farmed or because the area had become much wetter, forcing people to live further away in higher, drier locations.

Parts of several field systems have been investigated in the Lower Kennet valley around Reading. At Reading Business Park/Green Park and Moores Farm middle to late Bronze Age field systems have been investigated (Moore and Jennings 1992; Brossler *et al.* 2004). These field systems are not co-axial, and although they are basically rectilinear, each block had a slightly different orientation. The best-preserved area was at Reading Business Park/Green Park. Here, unlike many other sites, ditches tended to intersect rather than stopping short at junctions and it was possible to discern a sequence of development that suggests the field system grew incrementally, fields being added one at a time apparently with relatively little cleaning out of earlier ditches, though some had secondary gullies which might have been additions. A tiny ring-ditch was clearly respected by one corner of the earliest field, reminiscent of other field systems respecting pre-existing burial mounds (see above Perry Oaks/T5 and Eton), but it produced no remains of any description and its original date and function are unknown.

The other areas of field system that developed in the Reading Business Park/Green Park area have either not survived as well or were not extensively explored, but taken together they help define a clearer overall picture (Fig. 3.14). Each of the areas,

Fig. 3.13 Bronze Age field systems at (above) *Weir Bank Stud Farm* (below) *Perry Oaks/T5*

including those at Moores Farm, is associated with broadly contemporary waterholes but rather little indication of substantial domestic occupation until the late Bronze Age, when at least at Reading Business Park/Green Park there was a significant settlement (Moore and Jennings 1992; Brossler *et al.* 2004). The full limits of the fields were not defined in any direction, and it is not clear if any of the blocks of fields extended over more than 5-6 ha.

At Green Park features associated with the late Bronze Age domestic settlement impinged on ditches of the field system, suggesting to the excavators that the fields were abandoned. However, it is also clear that the layout of the domestic settlement reflects boundaries of the field system and an alternative interpretation would be that hedged boundaries still existed and the settlement only modified one part of the field system, other parts remaining in use. At Moores Farm it appears that the middle Bronze Age field boundaries were respected and in some cases recut, probably as late as the early Iron Age.

In the Upper Thames Valley areas of possible middle Bronze Age rectilinear fields have been identified around Didcot (Fig. 3.15). Most recently extensive middle to late Bronze Age rectilinear co-

axial fields were investigated prior to gravel extraction at Appleford Sidings. The site resembles Hengrove on the Surrey gravels in having a Roman rectilinear field system sharing the same alignment, in places possibly respecting surviving hedges. In the absence of much dating evidence it is difficult to distinguish to which period the various ditches belong. Not far to the south two other field systems have been investigated. At Didcot Power Station the corner of a field was revealed as an L-shaped ditch, part of which had been recut several times by short lengths of ditch or elongated pits. The only dating evidence was two sherds of Neolithic pottery and some flints from the recuts, probably redeposited from earlier activity indicated by a Grooved Ware pit found in the angle formed by the ditches. A similar problem applies to more extensive but still fragmentary rectilinear ditched enclosures found at Wallingford Road Didcot, where earlier Bronze Age occupation debris was found in ditches considered to belong to a middle Bronze Age field system (Ruben and Ford 1992, 26, figs 3, 8-10). Further west, in a similar topographical situation at the foot of the Upper Greensand bench between Steventon and East Hanney, south-west of Abingdon, a coaxial field system incorporating two boundaries

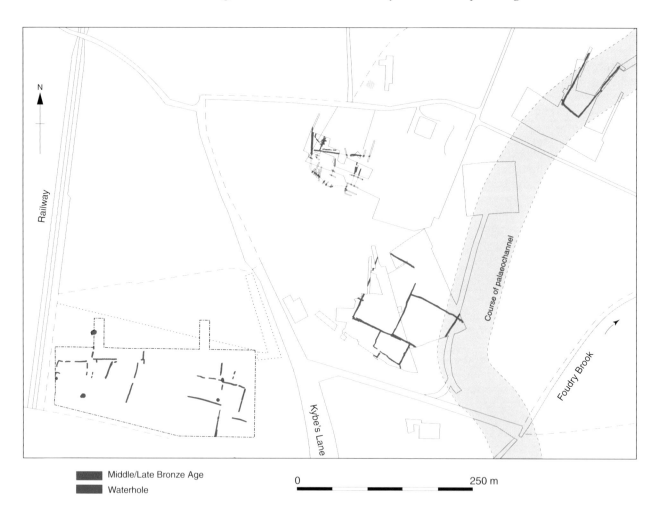

Middle/Late Bronze Age

Waterhole

0   250 m

Fig. 3.14 Middle to late Bronze Age field systems at Reading Business Park/Green Park

extending over 400 m was identified during an evaluation (Hearne 2001). Rectilinear subdivisions were exposed along with a large sub-rectangular enclosure adjoining one of the main axial boundaries, thought to be a main focus of settlement. Another field system and a settlement were identified in two other locations within an area about 2 km square located at the southern end of the evaluation area, which occupies slightly higher ground equivalent to the second and third gravel terraces at the eastern end of the Vale of White Horse Vale.

Bronze Age fields have also been identified on the gravels around Dorchester-on-Thames and Abingdon. At Northfield Farm, Long Wittenham there is a well-defined area of generally small rectangular fields, some with double-ditched boundaries (perhaps hedge banks) of typologically middle to late Bronze Age date (Gray 1977, 13; Thomas *et al.* 1986). The aerial photographic evidence suggests that the most coherent part of the field system extended over an area of *c* 7 ha with another, less obvious area to the west covering a similar area, while an associated element to the south-east covers about 3-4 ha (Baker 2002, fig. 4). This small field system was apparently not coaxial and so resembles the Green Park complex.

The corner of another such system formed by double ditched boundaries aligned on an early to middle Bronze Age barrow was excavated at Mount Farm near Dorchester (Fig. 3.16; Lambrick 1979, 1981; forthcoming), and a possibly co-axial double ditched field system overlying the Dorchester cursus was sampled by Atkinson before it was destroyed by quarrying (Whittle *et al.* 1992, 153, 159, figs 4, 7 and 26). The ditches at Site IX, sometimes paired sometimes triple, were aligned on the entrances of the Big Rings henge monument, but cut across the Neolithic long enclosure and the cursus, and one ditch cut the bank of the henge. A similar pair of ditches 1.2 km to the east cut a D-shaped enclose at the east end of the cursus.

Part of a field system at Eight Acre Field, Radley, east of Abingdon, incorporated boundary features including single, segmented and double ditches and a fence (Fig. 3.16; Mudd 1995 23-33, figs 2, 3). The boundaries involved both a rectilinear layout and oblique alignments. The main NNE-SSW axis, which both alignments respected, was marked by a double ditched boundary forming the acute corner of a field to the west. A single ditched boundary comprising several elements parallel to it respected a waterhole dated to 1680-1420 cal BC, which occupied most of a gap in the boundary. A penannular gully, perhaps representing a house, was located immediately adjacent to the waterhole within a small paddock defined by a sequence of segmented ditches either modifying or predating the main layout. The second waterhole, dated to 1020-800 cal BC, was located the other side of the NNE-SSW boundary, just south of the gap occupied by the earlier one which had by then filled in.

The likelihood that the complex developed in several stages is indicated by intersections and realignments of different elements, especially in the area around the house, radiocarbon dates of two waterholes and middle Bronze Age to early Iron Age pottery. Two other intriguing features of the complex are that the outer corner of the double ditched enclosure coincided with a tree throw hole, while the northern end of the other main NNE-SSW boundary coincided with a complex of two pits and an earlier tree throw hole which contained Neolithic material.

Above Oxford in the Upper Thames Valley north of the Corallian Ridge there is much less evidence of later Bronze Age co-axial or rectilinear field systems. At Yarnton and Cassington very extensive areas of earlier and later prehistoric activity have been investigated and a number of ditched boundaries located, but these do not obviously represent field systems. For example two middle Bronze Age parallel ditches 60 m apart, radiocarbon dated to *c* 1500 cal BC, crossed a palaeochannel, but they seem more likely to have had ceremonial rather than agricultural origins, though they were dug at a time of rapid intensification of landuse evident from pollen and other waterlogged remains. Elsewhere at Yarnton and Cassington there are middle and late Bronze Age boundary ditches and occasional fence lines, but these have not to date been shown to form a coherent field system.

A fragment of a possible double-ditched boundary on the floodplain at Farmoor (Lambrick and Robinson 1979) could be part of a later Bronze Age field system, and on the Cotswolds a later Bronze Age trackway and field system of uncertain form was identified at Rollright (Lambrick 1988).

Yates (2000) discusses other possible examples of middle to later Bronze Age coaxial or rectilinear field systems discerned from aerial photographs, such as those at Datchett (Gates 1975). A degree of caution is needed, however, since these are based partly on the RCHME *morph* database which assigns groups of features sharing broadly similar characteristics to generalised morphological types that do not seek to analyse more subtle distinctions of form or relationship to other features. Most are undated and some could be Roman or later, and other examples with very straight alignments could be modern.

Iron Age fields and land enclosure

While field systems are very much a part of the middle to late Bronze Age landscape, their creation and use in the early Iron Age is less obvious. However, it is possible that in the upper reaches of the Thames Valley coaxial fields continued to be constructed into the Iron Age. An extensive evaluation at Lady Lamb Farm on the Gloucestershire/Wiltshire border near Fairford revealed a series of parallel ditches set at regular 30 m or 60 m intervals. These may be a remnant coaxial or other field system, although cross ditches to form fields or

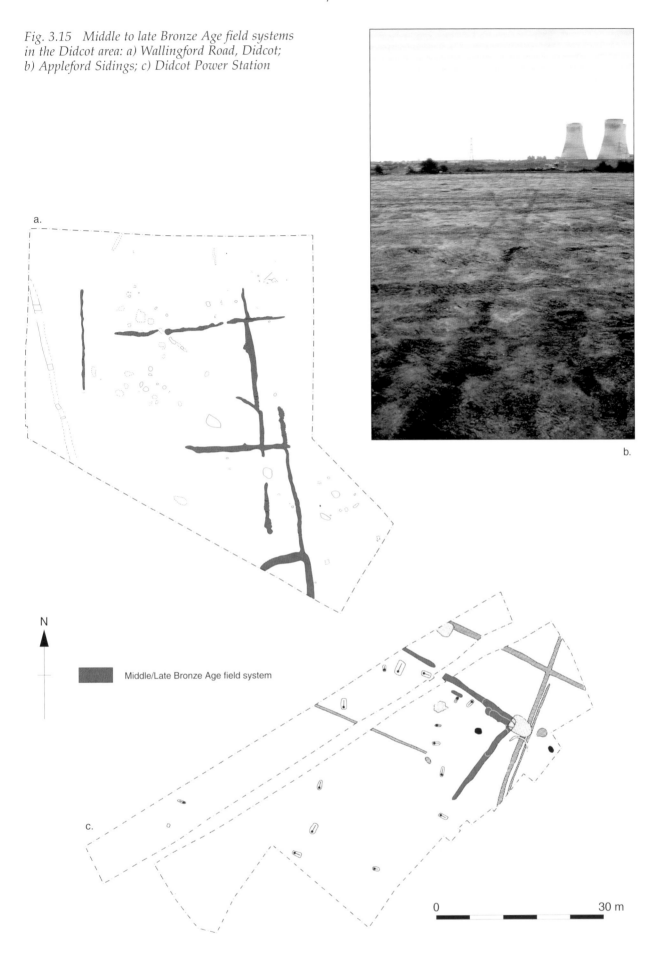

Fig. 3.15   Middle to late Bronze Age field systems
in the Didcot area: a) Wallingford Road, Didcot;
b) Appleford Sidings; c) Didcot Power Station

a.

b.

N

Middle/Late Bronze Age field system

c.

0   30 m

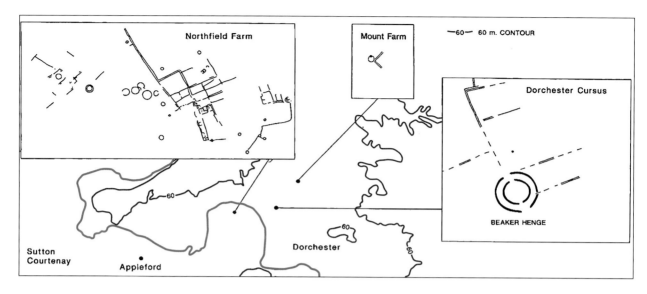

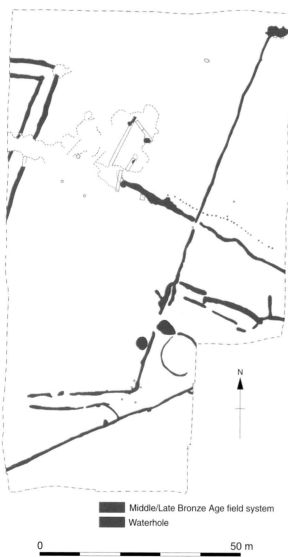

Middle/Late Bronze Age field system

Waterhole

0   50 m

Fig. 3.16 Middle to late Bronze Age field systems (above) *around Dorchester and* (below) *at Eight Acre Field, Radley*

paddocks were not evident. Probable domestic activity was indicated by pits and postholes. Dating is uncertain, but the most of the pottery was in shelly fabrics and shouldered and angular forms suggest an early Iron Age rather than late Bronze Age date (Roberts 1993). Burials, early Bronze Age ring ditches and middle Bronze Age pottery, including sherds from a pit alignment, suggest long-lived activity at the site. At Latton Lands a corner of a possible middle Iron Age coaxial field system was recorded, with two parallel curving ditches about 50 m apart (Powell *et al.* forthcoming). Alternatively, however, this could be the end of a large rectilinear field or paddock like the undated example that forms part of a middle Iron Age farmstead at Port Meadow (see below).

In some places pre-existing coaxial and other field systems established in the middle or late Bronze Age seem to have survived in use into the Iron Age and possibly beyond, their ditches having been neither extended nor maintained. Perry Oaks/T5 is a case in point, where traces of early Iron Age occupation were found in and around middle to late Bronze Age fields. Here new wells and waterholes continued to be dug in locations that respected the Bronze Age field pattern before a cluster of small middle Iron Age enclosures and waterholes were established. These respected the pre-existing layout to some degree, but on a different alignment later reinforced by new enclosures and eventually superseded by a late Iron Age and Roman field system reflecting the new alignment (Framework Archaeology 2006, 176). Even so, in the western part of the T5 complex Bronze Age field boundaries appear to have been respected by Saxon and medieval fields. Although tenuous, this supports the claim that extensive areas of pre-Roman co-axial field alignments are still detectable in the present day landscape in parts of eastern England (Rodwell 1978; Williamson 1987) though this has been challenged, and defended, more recently (Hinton 1997; Williamson 1998).

The survival of above-ground hedged bound-aries has been observed on the West London and Surrey gravels at Hengrove Farm and Ashford Prison. Compared with the Perry Oaks/T5 complex, there was a similar lack of maintenance or recutting of ditches, but also much less evidence of early Iron Age occupation or waterholes, especially compared with the relatively dense middle Bronze Age activity. On the other hand, there is similar evidence that small middle and late Iron Age settle-ments were established in parts of the field system and particularly that Bronze Age alignments were respected by the subsequent Roman layout. At Thorpe Lea Nurseries there is evidence for the survival and maintenance of ditches. Here a number of straight shallow ditches of the same alignment and character as the Bronze Age ditches were assigned to the Iron Age and Roman periods, suggesting partial maintenance of existing bound-aries, although by then new ditch complexes had also been dug, suggesting more radical alteration of the Bronze Age layout.

At other sites in the Middle Thames Valley traces of late Bronze Age occupation and fields similarly appear to have been abandoned in the early Iron Age, on the basis that they produced scant evidence of early Iron Age domestic activity or modification of the fields. However, maintenance of above-ground hedges and use of the fields may have continued, while the focus of domestic activity and the management of water supplies changed, leaving little archaeological trace of activity within that area. This applies to Eton Rowing Course, where middle Iron Age boundaries partly cut across a pre-existing

middle Bronze Age field system but also respected it, although the ditches had long since silted up.

At Green Park activity shifted in the early Iron Age away from the focus of middle to late Bronze Age fields and domestic occupation around Small Mead Farm to an area about 1 km to the south near Moores Farm. Here there were traces of middle and later Bronze Age fields and occupation tentatively datable to the early Iron Age, which included ditches and a concentration of pits and other traces of domestic activity. At Brimpton, long sinuous early to middle Iron Age linear boundaries were located close to the Silchester-Cirencester Roman Road (Lobb 1977-8 39, 43 fig. 2).

At Wickham Fields to the west an early Iron Age trackway ran along the edge of the Reading Beds with a rectilinear field system respecting it on one side (Fig. 3.17). Two areas of broadly contemporary occupation, one about 150 m away on the other side of the trackway and the other at its northern end, later became a focus for Roman occupation, suggesting that the trackway and fields survived long after their initial creation (Crockett 1996, fig. 66).

There is thus evidence of continuity of use, but seldom much modification or refurbishment of existing field systems laid out in the middle to late Bronze Age. Although there is less evidence for the establishment of new field systems in the early Iron Age, the example at Wickhams Field is significant, and abandonment or shifts in the location of settle-ment, as at Green Park, do not necessarily mean the complete abandonment of fields, as has sometimes been suggested. The possible early Iron Age fields at Lake End Road West on the Maidenhead Flood Relief Channel were respected by late Iron Age or Roman fields, with little sign of change (Fig. 3.18; OA forthcoming a) and results emerging from Perry Oaks/T5 indicate a subtle evolution in the relation-ship between the use of fields and settlements that needs more cautious analysis than is allowed for in current interpretations of widespread abandonment (Yates 2000).

In the Upper Thames Valley, where it was once thought that a very different pattern applies compared with the Middle Thames (Barrett and Bradley 1980), there are many similarities in terms of what happened to the later Bronze Age field systems known in the area. At Eight Acre Field, like Perry Oaks/T5, an early Iron Age waterhole within the field system was the only evidence for continuing use of the fields, but early Iron Age settlement is well attested nearby (Mudd 1995). There is even less evidence of significant early Iron Age occupation, maintenance or modification of Bronze Age fields at Appleford Sidings, Didcot or the Dorchester Cursus site, but there are known areas of late Bronze Age or early Iron Age occupation close by at both Appleford (Hinchliffe and Thomas 1980) and at Allen's Pit Dorchester (Bradford 1942), so the possi-bility that these fields continued in use cannot be ruled out. As in the Middle Thames Valley, these field systems appear to have been finally super-

0   100 m   Early Iron Age field system

Fig. 3.17   Early Iron Age fields in the Middle Thames Valley at Wickhams Field

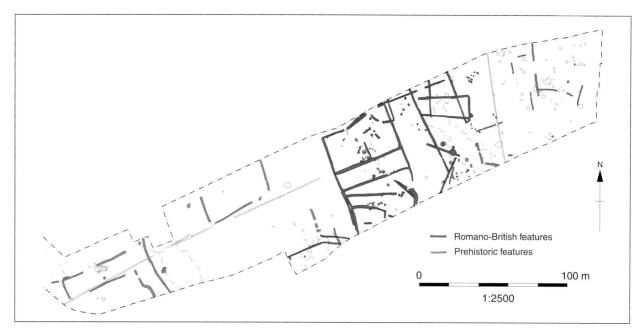

Fig. 3.18   Late prehistoric and Roman fields at Lake End Road West

seded only by Roman (or in a few cases middle to late Iron Age) enclosures and fields, which in the case of Appleford Sidings clearly perpetuated the Bronze Age alignment.

On the other hand, there is evidence at Mount Farm that early Iron Age cultivation outside the Bronze Age double ditched boundary was on a different alignment, and the middle to late Iron Age and Roman fields there were established on a different alignment again (Lambrick forthcoming). Less certainly it has been argued that the Northfield Farm fields were superseded by Iron Age land division on a different alignment, and certainly the later Roman droveway and paddocks ignored the Bronze Age alignment (Baker 2002, 1-28).

As in the Middle Thames Valley, there are few cases in the Upper Thames of entirely new ditched field systems established in the early Iron Age. We have already noted the possible coaxial system at Lady Lamb Farm, but otherwise the fragmentary evidence of coherent early Iron Age ditched fields is no more impressive than those at Wickhams Field or Moores Farm and equally difficult to date. Nor are they in the most obvious areas of dense early Iron Age settlement in the heart of the Upper Thames, and in some cases are not on the Thames gravels at all.

As noted above, at Mount Farm, cultivation marks preserved under a ploughsoil cut by a middle Iron Age gully and overlying the middle Bronze Age upper fill of a ring ditch were on a different alignment to the Bronze Age double-ditched boundary that respected the ring ditch (Lambrick forthcoming). Further east a line of

postholes roughly parallel to the ploughmarks might have been a field boundary on a different alignment to the double-ditched Bronze Age field system and the ditched fields and paddocks that developed from the middle Iron Age onwards.

The possibility that two widely separated early Iron Age meander cut-off boundaries proposed at Lechlade might have been part of a co-axial field system was raised in the Rough Ground Farm excavation report, but at 300 m apart and with no known intervening parallel ditches or definite cross-linking boundaries to create fields, this was considered at best equivocal. However, the presence at Rough Ground Farm of a parallel ditch south-east of the southern of the two major ditches with fragments of ditches and gullies set at right-angles suggests some sort of rectilinear field system (Fig. 3.19; Allen *et al.* 1993, 36, figs 7 and 26). Further evidence for these boundaries has since been found at Butler's Field (Boyle *et al.* 1998).

At Watchfield, on the Corallian sands and limestone at the head of the Ock valley, a complex funnel type entrance developed during the early to middle Iron Age, apparently as part of a larger, possibly rectilinear field system (Fig. 3.19; Birbeck 2001, 228-32, fig. 3). A small area of early to middle Iron Age rectilinear fields was located on similar bedrock at Blackbird Leys, Oxford (Booth and Edgeley-Long 2003, 208-11, fig. 3).

There is virtually no evidence of ditched field systems in areas of more intensive early Iron Age settlement, but there is some evidence of fenced fields. At Gravelly Guy, Beard Mill and the Aerodrome site at Stanton Harcourt (Lambrick and

Fig. 3.19 (opposite)   Early to middle Iron Age fields in the Upper Thames Valley:
(above) Roughground Farm; (below) Watchfield

BK Beaker

BA Bronze Age

Early Iron Age

BK Beaker
BA Bronze Age

Natural hollows

CR Cremation

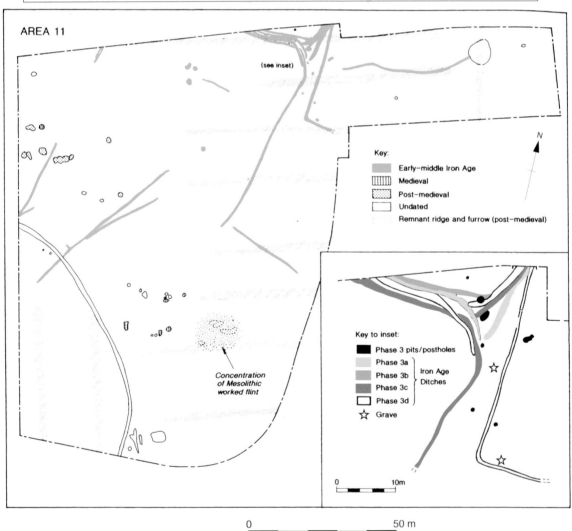

AREA 11

(see inset)

Key:

Early-middle Iron Age
Medieval
Post-medieval
Undated
Remnant ridge and furrow (post-medieval)

Concentration
of Mesolithic
worked flint

Key to inset:

Phase 3 pits/postholes
Phase 3a
Phase 3b
Phase 3c
Phase 3d
Grave

Iron Age
Ditches

0   10m

0   50 m

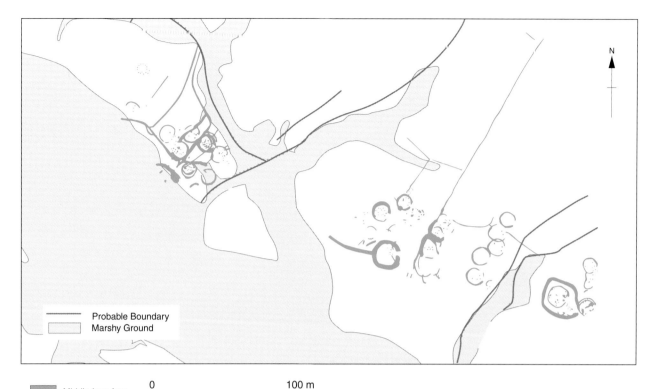

Probable Boundary
Marshy Ground

Middle Iron Age

0   100 m

Fig. 3.20   Middle Iron Age fields at (above) *Warren's Field, Claydon Pike;* (left) *Mount Farm, Berinsfield*

The sequence of development suggests that large hedges or banks adjacent to ditches influenced the way in which the pattern of enclosures evolved, including, for example, whether a ditch was simply recut or a new one was dug on the other side of a hedge. This seems to have depended on which enclosure was being maintained or redefined, and suggests piecemeal development with different parts of the complex being enhanced, modified or completely replaced in turn over a long period. This pattern of gradual evolution and adaptation spanned a period of perhaps 500 years from the middle Iron Age through to the later Roman period.

At Latton Lands ditches containing middle Iron Age pottery appear to define a group of coaxial fields respecting a middle Iron Age boundary ditch that followed a pre-existing land division marked by a linear early to middle Iron Age settlement. A broadly similar kind of development may be evident at Little Wittenham, where geophysical survey has revealed an extensive area of settlement and enclosures below the hillfort at Castle Hill. This includes a middle Iron Age curving ditch running for *c* 900 m from near the hillfort to the lower slopes of the adjacent Round Hill. Ditches at approximate right-angles are visible on either side of the ditch, forming sub-rectangular enclosures, and lines of pits were dug either to demarcate further boundaries or alongside boundaries marked only by fences or hedges that do not show on the geophysical survey. The detailed sequence of development is not clear, including how the ditch and enclosures relate to the extensive settlement in the area, though some of the

Allen 2004/5; Williams 1951; Hamlin 1963) there are traces of fence lines extending at right-angles to the essentially linear settlements into areas of arable which may represent field boundaries.

There is more evidence for middle Iron Age field systems than early Iron Age ones, and the evidence again tends to be piecemeal, perhaps in part due to the focus of excavations on settlements. As with the earlier Iron Age, most of the known examples of ditched fields and paddocks are not associated with those settlements on the higher gravel terraces regarded as prime arable producers.

At Mount Farm Dorchester a series of paddocks and fields and a trackway developed from middle Iron Age pens and a penannular gully (Fig. 3.20).

Fig. 3.21   *Middle Iron Age fields at Port Meadow, Oxford*

Bronze Age ring ditches
Iron Age settlements and paddocks
Gravel pits / allotments

0   500 m

enclosures contain penannular enclosure ditches characteristic of roundhouses.

Examples of paddocks and fields associated with small middle Iron Age settlements on lower-lying land have been investigated on or immediately adjacent to the Thames floodplain in the Lechlade area at Claydon Pike (Fig. 3.20), Thornhill Farm and Cleveland Farm, and extensive examples are well-preserved in ancient floodplain pastureland at Port Meadow, Oxford (Fig. 3.21; Lambrick and McDonald 1985). Such systems were not confined to floodplain sites. At Appleford (Hinchliffe and Thomas 1980) paddocks associated with middle Iron Age settlement were found during limited excavation of a complex that was probably more extensive.

Fig. 3.22   *Development of late Iron Age and early Roman fields at Mount Farm, Cippenham and Hengrove*

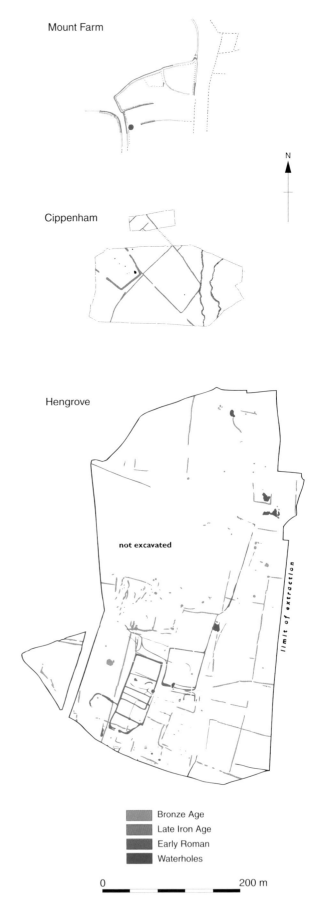

Mount Farm

Cippenham

Hengrove

not excavated

limit of extraction

Bronze Age
Late Iron Age
Early Roman
Waterholes

0   200 m

A similar pattern may be evident at Filkins, north-east of Lechlade, where parts of a possible middle to late Iron Age field system containing small enclosures were sampled in two pipeline excavations (Coleman and Hancock 2004). Other examples may be evident in more fragmentary form elsewhere, such as at Hatford (Bourne *et al.* 2000).

All of these sites produced evidence for subsequent development in the late Iron Age and Roman period, but at different levels of intensity (Fig. 3.22). Claydon Pike and Appleford became major estate centres (Booth *et al.* 2007), while the Thornhill Farm complex continued to develop alongside Claydon Pike, probably becoming part of the major estate until it was superseded in later Roman reorganisation. Several other sites, including Mount Farm, Latton Lands, Cleveland Farm, Port Meadow and Filkins, also continued to develop as minor late Iron Age and Roman complexes.

In the Middle Thames Valley there is generally less evidence of middle Iron Age field systems being established. At Eton Rowing Course, Dorney a long boundary ditch was cut diagonally across the larger of two middle Bronze Age field systems, avoiding two pairs of small enclosures that it contained. The middle Iron Age ditch had a smaller ditch alongside, which diverged from the main boundary and skirted one of the northern pair of Bronze Age enclosures, running alongside the long-since silted up Bronze Age ditch on two sides of the enclosure, suggesting the boundaries were still defined by hedges. A small middle Iron Age ditch that ran at right-angles to this boundary had a four-poster beside it, perhaps on the periphery of an area of domestic occupation, though the known middle Iron Age settlement was focused upon the adjacent gravel island 1.5 km away.

At Thorpe Lea Nurseries there is some evidence that the Bronze Age field system was either replaced or modified in the Iron Age with the addition of a long sweeping ditch, part of which had a parallel ditch forming a short trackway. It is difficult to discern fields as such, but despite the difference of alignment it is possible that parts of the pre-existing Bronze Age boundaries still survived as hedges. This may be borne out by the presence of other short lengths of gully that reflect the Bronze Age alignment but contained Iron Age and Roman pottery.

Late Iron Age

The late Iron Age is in many ways characterised up and down the Thames Valley by a proliferation of trackways, enclosure systems and fields close to and extending out from settlements that became the basis for more extensive Roman field systems. Almost all sites with evidence of late Iron Age occupation have at least some evidence of such fields and paddocks. There is no single pattern of development obvious, nor any particularly characteristic layout.

At some sites late Iron Age or Roman fields respected much earlier coaxial layouts with little sign of change during the Iron Age, including the middle Bronze Age fields at Appleford Sidings (Booth and Simmonds forthcoming), Hengrove (Hayman forthcoming d) and Lake End Road West (Allen *et al.* forthcoming c). In other cases such as Green Park there appears to have been little connection between Bronze Age field systems and middle to late Iron Age or Roman successors, or, as at Thorpe Lea Nurseries, it was at most only partial. At Aldermaston Wharf three parallel ditches appear to represent a possible co-axial field system of later Iron Age origin (Cowell *et al.* 1977-8, 3-7).

Some late Iron Age fields and paddocks, especially those originating from pre-existing middle Iron Age settlements or enclosure groups, or settlements of that type, display irregular, apparently organic layouts which later (often well into the Roman period) became more regular. This is apparent at Totterdown Lane, Horcott (Pine and Preston 2004), Thornhill Farm (Jennings *et al.* 2004 31-40, fig. 3.5) and Mount Farm (Lambrick forthcoming). At Wood Lane, Cippenham near Slough (Ford *et al.* 2003, 49-50, fig. 3.9) and Field Farm Bicester (Cromarty *et al.* 1999, 159-6 and figs 4, 5, 6) quite regular fields and paddocks were added to probable settlement enclosures. A similar sequence may also apply to Ireland's Land close to the Watkins Farm site, though the evidence of domestic settlement there was sparse (Norton 2006).

Other late Iron Age enclosures developed on land adjacent to existing settlements. These may either display broadly rather similar layouts, as at Claydon Pike (Miles *et al.* 2007) or represent new developments. At the Stanton Harcourt complex of settlements a recurrent pattern of establishing

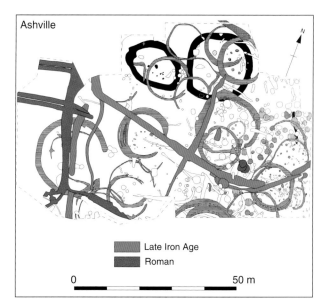

Fig.3.23 Late Iron Age and early Roman fields at Ashville

Stanton Harcourt

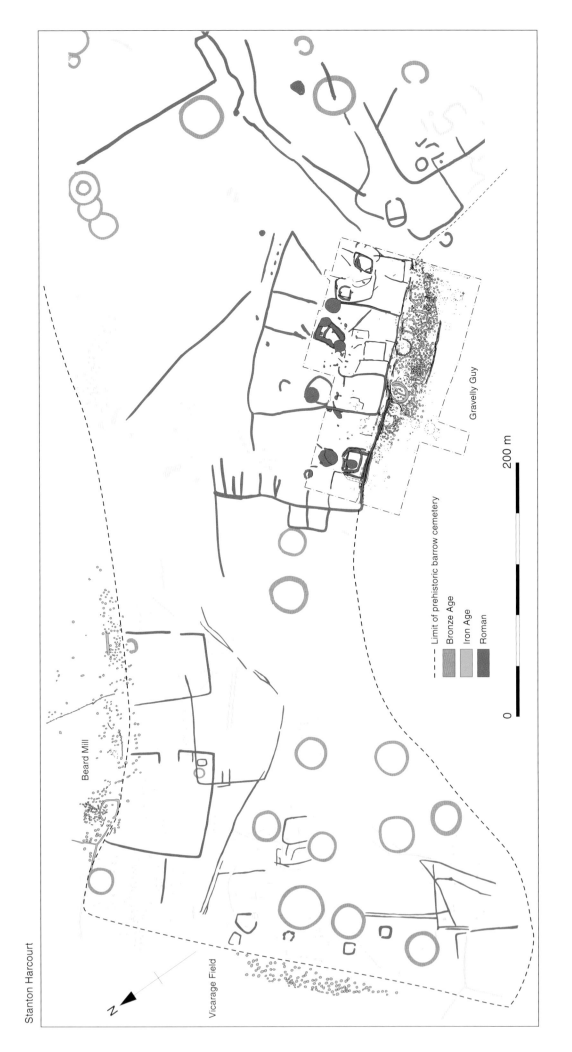

Vicarage Field

Beard Mill

Gravelly Guy

- - - Limit of prehistoric barrow cemetery
Bronze Age
Iron Age
Roman

0   200 m

Fig. 3.24   Late Iron Age and early Roman fields at Stanton Harcourt

rectilinear networks of fields and paddocks was associated with a shift in settlement across a landuse boundary. This has been investigated in detail at Gravelly Guy (Lambrick and Allen 2004) but is also evident at Beard Mill and Vicarage Pit (Case 1982, 115-6, fig. 59), and at Linch Hill (Bradford 1942a, 202). It is rare that such fields were laid out directly cutting across pre-existing settlements, as at Ashville (Fig. 3.23), and it is not clear in this case whether the settlement had already been abandoned, had shifted or was actively displaced (Parrington 1978, 36-9; Muir and Roberts 1999, 65).

Overall the redefinition or new establishment of ditched field and enclosure systems became very common in the late Iron Age and early Roman period, and often survived until at least the second century AD, when some were radically re-ordered or replaced with larger more extensive fields and tracks (Lambrick 1992 b, 101; Booth *et al.* 2007). The changes display considerable variation in character and sequences of development. Some were very piecemeal, others suggest coherently planned new arrangements or alterations, often in a varied and subtle mixture. If we look for explanations for this diversity of development in the late Iron Age it is reasonable to suggest that much of it would have resulted from local differences in how land was managed and organised. In some cases there would have been slow, piecemeal adaptation of existing arrangements, in others there would have been less constraint on new developments and rearrangement. For example, where middle to late Iron Age settlement became concentrated in part of the Perry Oaks/T5 complex, a subtle shift in landscape alignment took place, with the gradual loss of some Bronze Age boundaries and enclosures to new enclosure layouts, followed by early Roman fields reflecting parts of the new alignment. In another part of the complex Bronze Age boundaries were still reflected in medieval and later fields. The Stanton Harcourt complex suggests a relatively coherent communal adoption of new settlement and enclosure layouts in which there was very little alteration in the way people lived, how they gained their livelihoods or how they organised their land and resources (Fig. 3.24).

Chapter 4 – Settlements and settlement patterns

INTRODUCTION

Almost all late prehistoric settlements in the Thames Valley are represented by a standard repertoire of sub-soil features – postholes, pits, waterholes, gullies, ditches and a few less common deposits – which contain the debris of domestic living, farming and exchange. But while the basic building blocks of evidence that most commonly survive may be limited and fairly universal in their occurrence, they come in a variety of forms and combine in different ways to present a highly diverse range of forms of settlement. These vary considerably in location, size, layout and intensity, and also in the length, permanence and primary purposes of occupation. Floors, hearths, structural timbers, track surfaces, midden deposits, buried soils and other undisturbed surfaces rarely survive – at least on drier, heavily cultivated gravel terraces – but they can provide additional insights, especially where coupled with good preservation of biological remains.

This account of the character of late prehistoric settlements in the Thames Valley seeks to explore two very broad themes: the emergence of sedentary farming settlements, and the social and economic basis of 'open' and 'enclosed' settlements. Broader aspects of the development and interaction of settlements at a wider community level are discussed in Chapters 9 and 10.

It is difficult to decide how best to present the evidence. Here it is dealt with in terms of different forms of settlement while also taking account of chronological and geographical differences. This is not entirely satisfactory, both because morphological categorisation of sites is fraught with problems and because the form of settlements changed though time. The distinction between 'enclosed' and 'open' settlements and different morphological variations within these categories is not always clear and raises serious questions about whether such categorisations have any real validity. But equally, detailed investigations show that there is significant and in some cases recurrent variation in settlement morphology, and that much of this correlates with chronological, environmental or topographical considerations. Differences in settlement morphology still seems the best starting point to describe the variability of late prehistoric settlement, and we will return to broader themes of how and why settlements change in character in relation to other broader social, economic and political factors in Chapter 10.

In reviewing the character of later prehistoric settlements in the Thames Valley we cannot avoid the need to assemble and present archaeological evidence in the broad chronological pigeonholes of 'periods' and 'phases' that are commonly portrayed on plans. But in doing so it is important to recognise that these crude chronological distinctions provide only a broad framework within which more subtle evolution and development of settlement character took place. We also need to think about how settlements adapted and changed from other perspectives. How were they influenced by pre-existing conditions? How long might particular features like buildings or pits have lasted or been used and reused? Do broader spatial patterns and sequences help indicate social organisation and development of domestic activity?

Bearing in mind these provisos, the following sections start by considering possible evidence for the survival of seasonal mobile living presumed to have dominated earlier periods, moving on to look at a variety of dispersed open settlements and at domestic activity within later Bronze Age field systems. This is followed by a consideration of a range of farms and farmsteads, hamlets and villages characterised by unenclosed pit clusters, pens and paddocks and other enclosure complexes, ending with an examination of more fully enclosed settlements. Examination of settlement activity associated with defended sites and special midden deposits is left to Chapter 9, where they are considered alongside the wider communal roles of such sites. In Chapter 10 we return to look at the dynamics of settlement patterns from broader socio-economic perspectives in the context of all the other themes covered.

SEASONAL MOBILE LIVING

A key starting point of this discussion is the well-established, or at least not seriously challenged, view that the inhabitants of the Thames Valley did not generally live in permanent year round farming settlements before the middle Bronze Age (Hey *et al.* forthcoming c). Of key interest for the period is therefore how permanent farming settlements did emerge. Approaching this issue from the usual standpoint of seeing how far back one can project a scenario of permanently settled farms is liable to impose on the data a different interpretation from one that takes the more logical, but more difficult approach of trying to discover why, when, where and how a largely mobile pattern of farming and domestic life declined relative to the emergence of more permanent intensive forms of landuse and settlement.

A non-sedentary, possibly seasonally ordered mobile lifestyle is widely considered to have been the norm in the earlier prehistory of southern Britain, and domestic sites are usually typified by a few pits containing discarded material that often seems decidedly 'odd'. This is generally interpreted as carefully structured deposition, lending symbolic meaning to the discarded remains of day-to-day life, perhaps reflecting arrivals and departures or other events at recurrently visited places, rather than mere rubbish disposal. Although the view that such scattered remains reflect a non-sedentary way of life could be viewed more as 'received wisdom' than directly proven, there is a substantial difference from the abundance of structural, artefact and biological evidence of domestic occupation and farming that characterises fully-fledged late prehistoric permanent farms.

However, there is no reason to suppose, as often seems to be assumed, that these earlier patterns of impermanent non-intensive domestic occupation just ceased abruptly. It is more reasonable to expect a varied pattern in the survival of mobile seasonal farming and domestic activity. In the absence of overarching social or economic imperatives to change, it is reasonable to expect that up and down the Thames Valley a transition to more permanent farming settlements took place at different times and on different trajectories of change, depending on local as well as regional circumstances. Even when permanent year-round settlement was becoming common, this does not preclude survival of a complementary element of seasonal mobile activity, as envisaged by Barrett (1994, 136-46) and Brück (2000, 281-5). It is worth investigating whether there are small clusters of middle to late Bronze Age or Iron Age domestic material too small to be classified as 'settlements' but similar in character to ephemeral evidence of earlier prehistoric domestic activity that might indicate a continuance of mobile, mainly pastoral styles of living. This has not been considered exhaustively, but there is some evidence that this was the case.

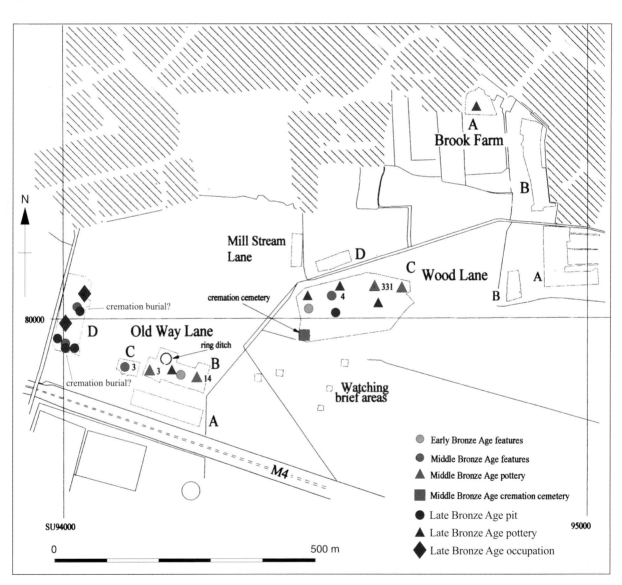

Fig. 4.1   Scattered Bronze Age domestic activity at Cippenham, Slough

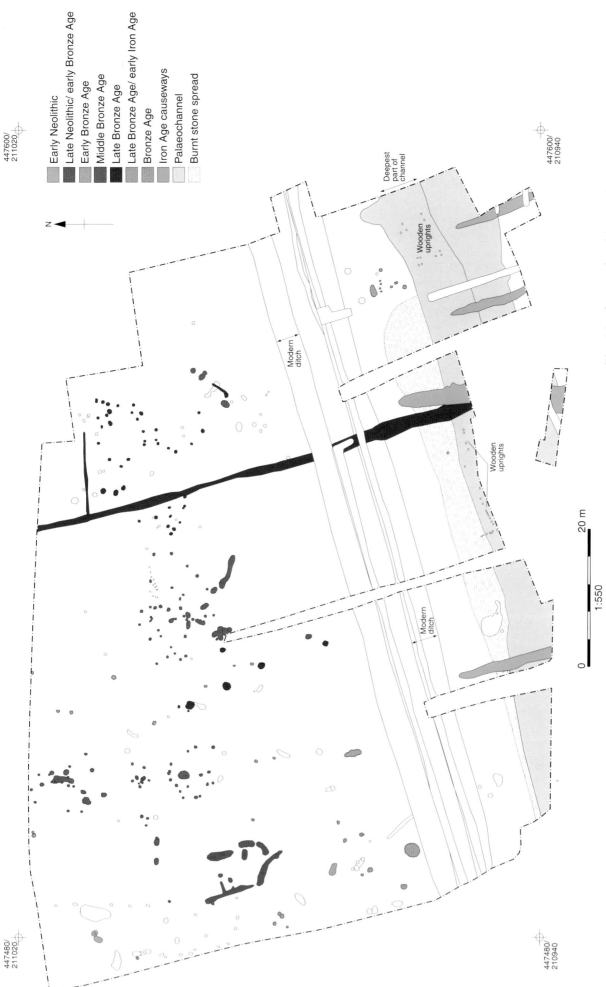

Early Neolithic
Late Neolithic/ early Bronze Age
Early Bronze Age
Middle Bronze Age
Late Bronze Age
Late Bronze Age/ early Iron Age
Bronze Age
Iron Age causeways
Palaeochannel
Burnt stone spread

N

447600/
211020

447480/
211020

447600/
210940

447480/
210940

Modern
ditch

Modern
ditch

Wooden
uprights

Wooden
uprights

Deepest
part of
channel

0   20 m

1:550

Fig. 4.2   Scattered prehistoric domestic activity at Yarnton

At Cippenham, Slough a number of small pits containing significant amounts of pottery, others with burnt stone, and a general scatter of pottery in later features provide evidence of middle Bronze Age occupation activity close to a ring ditch (Fig. 4.1). A cluster of late Bronze Age cremation burials and associated deposits is almost equally ephemeral (Ford *et al*. 2003, 155-9). A thin, widely dispersed scatter of middle to late Bronze Age pottery was found in later ditches. An equally sparse scatter of material characterises the late Bronze Age occupation at Hurst Park, East Molesey (Andrews 1996). At Blackbird Leys, Oxford one of a group of four small pits contained middle Bronze Age pottery, a decorated cylindrical loomweight and burnt stone (Booth and Edgeley-Long 2003). This was cut by another pit with burnt and worked flint and later Bronze Age pottery and further sherds of late Bronze Age pottery were redeposited in early to middle Iron Age ditches. The middle Bronze Age pit produced a significant amount of mainly oak charcoal and charred cereal grains were recovered from other Bronze Age pits. On the floodplain at Yarnton and Cassington sparse scatters of middle to late Bronze Age occupation material were present across large areas, in a few cases corresponding to a similar level of Neolithic and early Bronze Age activity (Fig. 4.2).

There are many other instances of sparse traces of late Bronze Age and Iron Age occupation activity, but being considered 'less important' than stereotypical late prehistoric permanent farming settlements, it is often assumed (and difficult to disprove) that such traces were peripheral to more intensive domestic activity 'nearby'. The possibility that mobile seasonal lifestyles may have remained part of the life of many communities alongside more permanent settlement has received little attention. As we shall see, a good case can be made for the existence of an ordered form of transhumant lifestyle in the middle Iron Age, possibly related to attempts to maximise economic production, but this raises a further question of whether some degree of transhumance and mobility had always been an element of later prehistoric settlement patterns and landuse.

DISPERSED OPEN SETTLEMENTS OF THE LATER BRONZE AGE AND EARLY IRON AGE

The distinction between such ephemeral traces of occupation and what one might call dispersed open settlements is one of degree. In some places on the Yarnton floodplain slightly more intensive domestic activity seems to have emerged almost imperceptibly from the middle Bronze Age onwards, represented by a few post built roundhouses, pits, waterholes and burnt mound material. A similar low level of activity continued in various parts of the floodplain into the late Bronze Age, but there were also areas of more concentrated domestic activity represented by small clusters and pairs of round, oval or D-shaped build-ings, fences, small pits, waterholes, and areas of activity next to a palaeochannel that generated burnt stones. Over much of the floodplain such traces of late Bronze Age domestic activity were still at a very dispersed, irregular and ephemeral level before the pattern of settlement changed in character and shifted topographical location onto the edge of the dry gravel terrace to the north. Here a much more focussed pattern of intensive occupation developed in a relatively restricted area in the early and middle Iron Age (see below). However, the middle to late Bronze Age settlement at Yarnton/Cassington seems also to have developed westward into a more ordered late Bronze Age settlement at Cassington West (see below). The sequence of development is relatively well dated by scientific means, though detailed chronological resolution is problematic, and dating of the Cassington West settlement is still awaited (Hey *et al*. forthcoming b).

The most extensive dispersed settlement of this kind so far excavated in the Thames Valley is at Shorncote/Cotswold Community, where excavations in advance of gravel extraction over the last 10 years have exposed features across an area of 40 ha, without yet fully defining the limits of occupation (Hearne and Heaton 1994; Hearne and Adam 1999; Barclay and Glass 1995; OA 2004). The density of features was generally low and only one type of structure was identified, and although there were apparently no clearly defined limits of occupation, some later boundaries seem to coincide with the limits of later Bronze Age and early Iron Age occupation evidence (Fig. 4.3). As at Cippenham and Yarnton, pits, funerary deposits and small-scale hengiform and other monuments indicate sporadic earlier prehistoric occupation, though there was no definite evidence of early Bronze Age domestic activity. The origins of the settlement were represented by a few isolated clusters of middle Bronze Age features, typically a waterhole, two to four possible roundhouses, pits and fences and an L-shaped ditch.

The evidence of late Bronze Age and early Iron Age settlement is more extensive, with numerous post built roundhouses, a similar number of four-posters and several waterholes and pits. However, the paucity of finds and infrequency of stratigraphic relationships made it very difficult to assign many features to particular periods within a broad middle Bronze Age to early/middle Iron Age time frame, and although there is certainly some clustering of features overall patterns in the distribution of structures and other features is difficult to discern. The character of the area seems to have altered little over as much as a millennium. Remains of waterlogged material from waterholes indicates pasture with secondary scrub and woodland in the Bronze Age with an increase of open pastureland over time.

Hearne and Adam (1999, 69-72) raised the possibility that occupation was not permanent, but based on mobile pastoralism. At any one time the level of occupation may have been slight. Overall, about 70

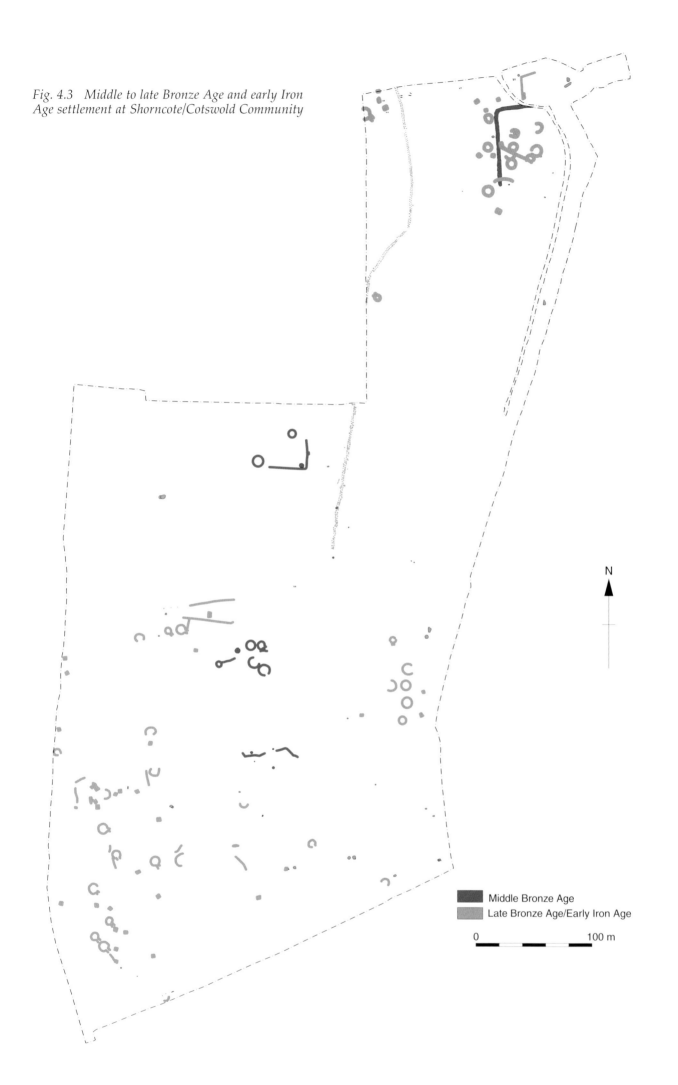

Fig. 4.3   Middle to late Bronze Age and early Iron Age settlement at Shorncote/Cotswold Community

N

Middle Bronze Age
Late Bronze Age/Early Iron Age

0   100 m

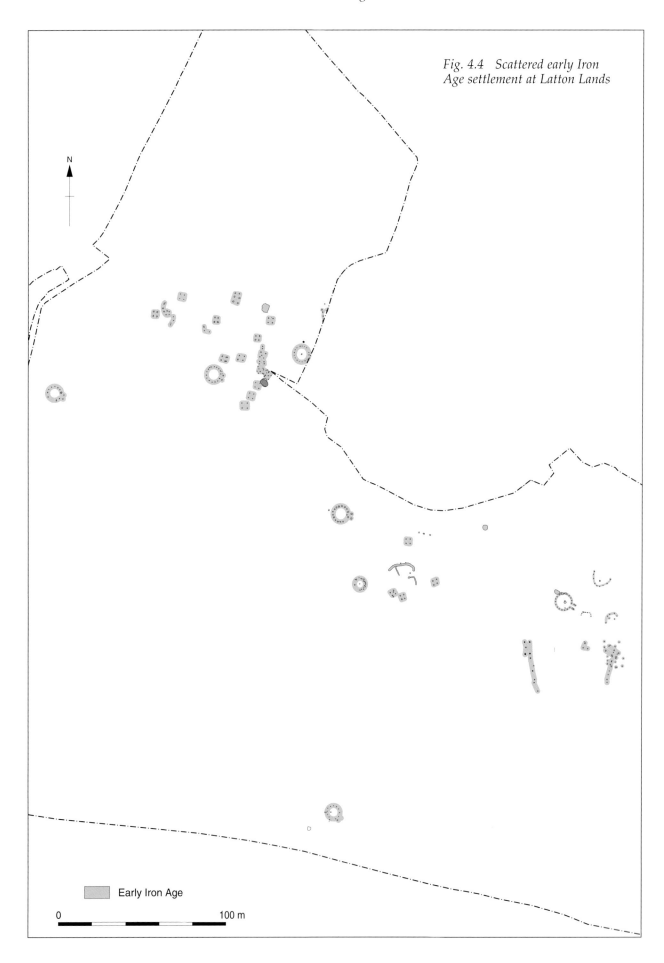

Fig. 4.4   Scattered early Iron Age settlement at Latton Lands

Early Iron Age

0   100 m

roundhouses, 75 four-post structures and 45 deep pits or waterholes were identified. Over a period of 750 to 1000 years only two or three houses may have been in use at any given time, even if each lasted a generation (Brück 1999). It is thus possible that the Shorncote/Cotswold Community area was a large, loose focus of seasonal occupation by a small number of families for the best part of a millennium before settlement and landuse intensified in the middle to late Iron Age and Roman period.

In the middle Iron Age the character of occupation changed, concentrating at two smaller areas on the edge of the drier ground. One was represented by a roundhouse and a few enclosure or paddock boundaries (Brossler *et al.* 2002) covering an area *c* 100 m by 40 m, the other by a fenced enclosure *c* 110 m by 95 m which endured as the main focus of

occupation with a complex sequence of intercutting enclosures into the Roman period, when a larger ditched field system was established for the first time (OA 2004).

Other sites in the higher reaches of the Upper Thames gravels display a similar pattern of scattered occupation extending into the early Iron Age. At Latton Lands three small groups of post-built roundhouses associated with four posters and at least two isolated roundhouses were spread over *c* 14 ha (Fig. 4.4; Powell *et al.* forthcoming). At Horcott Pit a group of four early Iron Age roundhouses with a few small pits was associated with a palisaded stock enclosure (Fig. 4.5; Lamdin-Whymark *et al.* forthcoming). Both sites subsequently evolved into tightly defined middle Iron Age settlements (see below).

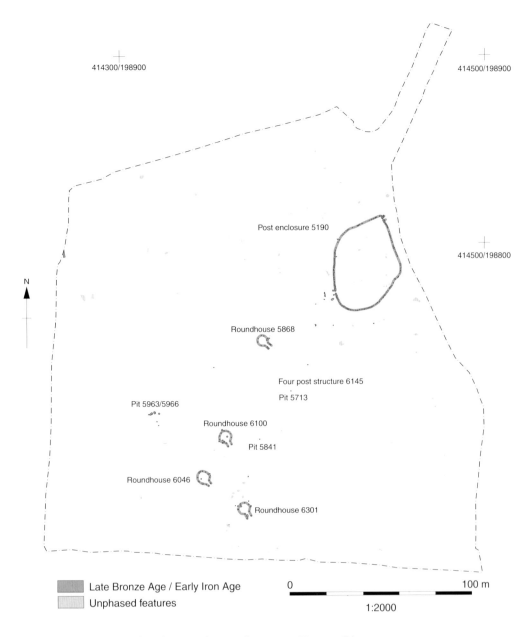

Fig. 4.5 *Late Bronze Age and early Iron Age settlement at Horcott Pit*

Other smaller late Bronze Age sites in the Upper Thames resemble in character the extensively investigated sites at Yarnton/Cassington and Shorncote/Cotswold Community. At St Helen's Avenue, Benson an amorphous scatter of pits, a possible quarry hollow and a number of postholes included a four-poster and three possible oval or D-shaped post rings and an arc of postholes (Pine and Ford 2003, 135). A significant concentration of early Neolithic activity was found on this site, and it is a measure of the ephemeral nature of the later Bronze Age settlement that there was significantly more Neolithic than later prehistoric pottery.

At Pingewood in the Middle Thames Valley part of a dispersed middle to late Bronze Age settlement was investigated in the 1980s (Johnson 1985, 19-23, figs 3, 5 and 6). Twenty pits and several post-built fences and structures, including two of semi-circular form, two possible roundhouses and a rectangular structure lay within an area *c* 50 m by 40 m. Two possible 'phases' of development were identified, despite a paucity of stratigraphic relationships.

Nearby at Knights Farm another area of highly dispersed settlement of similar date covering 2.2 ha was examined (Bradley *et al.* 1980). Features included 46 pits and 30 scoops, most unexcavated, but eight contained dense burnt material, and two pits with *in situ* burning were interpreted as possible 'ovens'. Burnt remains from a double pit were radiocarbon dated to 2141 to 1882 cal BC. Others produced dates of 1781 to 1257 cal BC. A large pond and various waterholes produced four radiocarbon dates ranging from 1499-1044 cal BC to 827-477 cal BC. Structures included four-posters and a fence line. A possible building may be represented by a group of nine small pits and postholes,

one within a ring gully 12 m in diameter dated to 1300 to 799 cal BC. No entrance was identified and little pottery was recovered. A small ring gully 3 m in diameter produced only fire-cracked flint and a cremation burial associated with coarseware pot lay 2 m away. Four other cremation burials were spread over an area *c* 150 m across, and other features contained small fragments of cremated bone. Like Yarnton, the broad spread of radiocarbon dates and the pottery preclude construction of a detailed sequence of development. However, both suggest a long period of recurrent low key domestic activity lasting several centuries from the middle Bronze Age to the earliest Iron Age, perhaps representing activity of a single peripatetic family group over several generations. As at Shorncote/Cotswold Community and the scattered floodplain occupation at Yarnton, carbonised cereal remains were uncommon, though a reasonable quantity of pottery was recovered.

At Furze Platt a similar scatter of pits, postholes, possible wells and burnt hearth type features covered an area about 150 m long and 40 m wide (Lobb 1979-80, 14-5, fig. 2). There was some clustering of features – most of the 25 pits and hollows lay within an area about 50 m by 40 m, and two posthole arcs suggested structures occurring close together.

In a few similar cases sparse occupation evidence in open areas adjacent to fields has been recorded, as at Hurst Park (Fig. 4.6; Andrews 1996, 64-9, 101-2, figs 35 36 and 57) and possibly Field Farm, Burghfield (Butterworth and Lobb 1992, 70). Along the Maidenhead to Windsor Flood Channel a middle Bronze Age roundhouse with a few associated features was found at Marsh Lane East, Lake End Road West and at Lot's Hole, but with only few

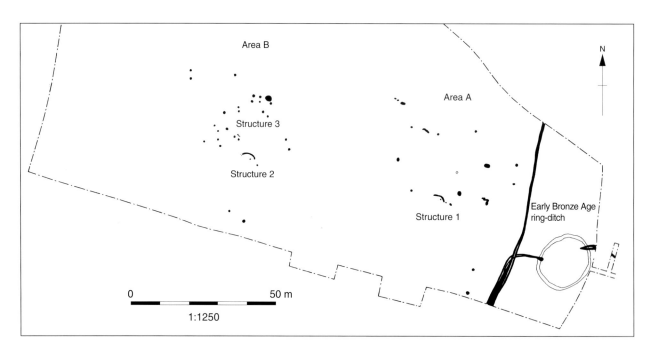

Fig. 4.6   Dispersed middle to late Bronze Age settlement at Hurst Park

Fig. 4.7   Reconstruction of an open Bronze Age settlement

concentrations of artefactual debris (Allen *et al.* forthcoming b). The limited adjacent area exposed makes it difficult to put such remains into context, and hints of field systems and relatively rich artefact and crop processing debris deposits at Lot's Hole suggest more intensive activity nearby. In these cases a deliberate division between open occupation areas and enclosed fields could be proposed, but in most cases the extent of excavation was insufficient to clearly demonstrate such an arrangement.

ORDERED OPEN SETTLEMENTS OF THE LATE BRONZE AGE (Fig. 4.7)

A few late Bronze Age open settlements display a more ordered and focussed layout than these dispersed occupation sites. At Aldermaston Wharf (Bradley *et al.* 1980) a settlement covering an area of at least 1350 m^2 included two post-built roundhouses, one of apparently high status, the other subsidiary. Forty-nine shallow pits formed four possible clusters associated with the structures and a pond and fence were also recorded. Finds included crucibles, mould fragments and fired clay pit liners. It seems plausible that metal working and possibly potting took place on the edge of site, and the pond acted as a communal shared water supply. Although not as clear, comparisons were made with the character of Deverel-Rimbury settlements in Wessex and Sussex which often have a major dwelling house plus one or more subsidiary huts and storage buildings (though not as clear as Black Patch in Sussex where Drewett envisaged a farm for an extended family with paired male and female huts correlating with complementary artefacts (Drewett 1980). Relatively abundant charred cereal remains were taken to indicate access to good agricultural land.

The settlement at Aldermaston produced radiocarbon dates of 1883-1207, 1386-1125 and 1014-839 cal BC, probably indicating a lengthy period of occupation, though the excavators felt that the pottery and stratigraphic evidence suggested otherwise. It is one of very few late prehistoric settlements in the Thames Valley where the density of pottery in deposits was calculated, suggesting that pit goups fell within three broad categories: 1:1,000-2,500 cc; 1:2,500-5,000 cc; 1:5,000-10,000 cc. This approach is probably not a very accurate method for analysing activity patterns but it could prove profitable if such calculations were to be carried out routinely as a means of providing a rough indication of the intensity and longevity of occupation. In comparing Aldermaston with Knights Farm, Bradley used other data to highlight the differences between the settlements. Although occupation at Knights Farm spanned a much longer period than that at Aldermaston Wharf, the density of features was only 1 per 88 m^2 compared with 1 per 12 m^2 at Aldermaston, and the evidence of associated flint scatters suggested that the extent of the Knights Farm occupation might be 75 times that of Aldermaston. Whereas the Knights Farm settlement exhibited some signs of shifting occupation, Aldermaston seemed a more permanent and ordered place. Aldermaston produced significant quantities of charred cereals in contrast to a complete absence at Knights Farm and the ratio of quern fragments to pottery was four times higher at Aldermaston.

In the Upper Thames Valley at Cassington West an area of more concentrated late Bronze Age activity has recently been exposed west of the scattered traces of middle to late Bronze Age domestic occupation on the floodplain at Yarnton (Fig. 4.8). Detailed analysis and dating is not yet complete but assessment indicates that there was almost no evidence of middle Bronze Age occupation compared with the other Yarnton sites, though there were a few early Bronze Age pits. The settlement contained a range of roundhouses, D-shaped structures, rectangular structures, four-posters, fencelines, waterholes, isolated and grouped pits, gullies, boundary ditches and middens. Although resembling such features elsewhere on the flood-plain at Yarnton, the layout here indicates a more concentrated and ordered settlement. Twelve possible roundhouses were identified, in some cases built at the same or overlapping locations. Three structures in the south-western corner of the site built in almost exactly the same location are partic-ularly noteworthy. Two overlapping structures and two directly adjacent structures were also identi-fied. Otherwise, most structures were 20 m to 25 m apart. Three D-shaped structures were examined, and a large rectangular structure, defined by long nearly parallel rows of posts stood near the centre of the site close to a curved enclosure ditch. There were sixteen four-post structures in three groups, the largest in the south-western corner of the site, the others near the centre and to the north of the settlement. Two rectangular structures defined by parallel rows of posts were constructed within the same area as the south-west group of four-posters.

Pottery of broadly late Bronze Age date was associated with almost all these structures, and unusually, seven of the roundhouses, two of the D-shaped structures, the large rectangular structure and the two smaller ones appear to have been associated with deposits of cremated human remains. With one possible exception, this did not apply to the four-posters.

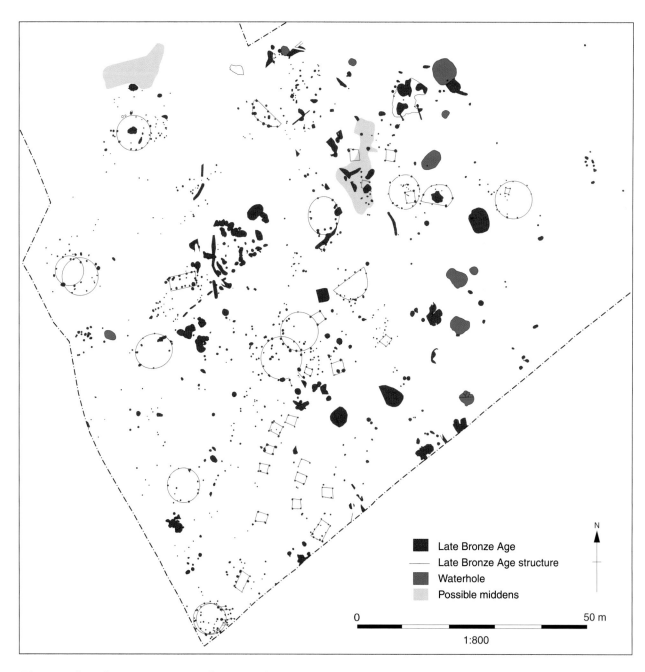

Fig. 4.8   Open late Bronze Age settlement at Cassington West

A total of 118 shallow pits were scattered across the site, some in clusters. Most of the pits would have been of insufficient depth for grain storage (see Chapter 7) and most produced few finds, but some pits near the middle of the site, just to the north of the long fence, contained substantial assemblages of pottery, animal bone and stone. Several further cremation deposits were found in waterholes and in small pits or postholes unassociated with structures. Nine waterholes up to 2 m deep were excavated, some with stepped or sloped sides, and with occasional dumps of material such as burnt stone. 'Decommissioning' deposits included waterlogged wooden artefacts, pottery and animal bone.

The north-western edge of the settlement was marked by a set of intercut ditches and the eastern side by a line of nine waterholes. Large quantities of finds from these features and from truncated midden deposits that overlay the northern edge of the settlement and the boundary ditches suggest that the edge of the settlement became a focus for deposition. The pattern defined by the distribution of features such as waterholes, rectangular structures, four-posters, fences, ditches, midden deposits and some pits, compared with the more dispersed distribution of roundhouses, cremation deposits and the remaining pits is striking. The overlapping roundhouses and intercutting pits indicate that the settlement developed over some time, and while the pottery is predominantly plain ware of the type normally dated to the beginning of the late Bronze Age, the presence of some decorated sherds suggests continuation into the later part of this period. However, while it is possible to define short, local sequences, and to observe relationships between some groups of features, it was not possible to determine a clear sequence of development or the size of the settlement at any given point.

Over 25 years ago Richard Bradley's comparison of Aldermaston and Knight's Farm highlighted both the potential and the difficulties in distinguishing long-lived but ephemeral occupation from intensive organised settlement. Unfortunately few comparable data have been published since. This makes further comparison difficult, especially in terms of quantities of finds per volume of soil relative to longevity of occupation. The Yarnton/Cassington complex provides an opportunity for similar analysis and the issue is also relevant to some middle Iron Age settlements.

SETTLEMENTS WITHIN MIDDLE TO LATE BRONZE AGE FIELD SYSTEMS

So far we have looked at settlement areas with no particular evidence of an enclosed landscape, but it is evident that at some sites occupation developed within, was part of, or was integrated into larger field systems. The level of occupation material is often sparse, reflected in small groups of pits, waterholes, concentrations of finds and

occasional evidence for houses sited within small paddocks or corners of fields. Some pits contain dumps of burnt stone and, less often, pottery and other domestic debris. These concentrations of material are notable within an otherwise sparse distribution during this period but become much more the norm in most Iron Age settlements. As with the dispersed open settlements, there are examples of intensive organised settlements as well as scattered areas of occupation.

Few examples of this type of settlement are known in the Upper Thames Valley. The clearest example is Eight Acre Field, Radley (Mudd 1995) where the gullies of a roundhouse lay within a triangular area defined by gullies, ditches and fences, with a waterhole nearby. Although contemporaneity of these features was not proven, the layout indicates that the house and the waterhole respected the field boundaries. Small areas of fields at Wallingford Road, Didcot produced more limited evidence of domestic occupation (Ruben and Ford 1992). At Appleford Sidings the settlement location is also unclear, though a number of waterholes and boundary ditches produced domestic debris. The Northfield Farm and Dorchester sites have not been sufficiently defined or investigated to identify associated occupation material. At Mount Farm middle Bronze Age pottery and animal bone was concentrated in and around the ring ditch respected by the field corner, but does not necessarily represent domestic rather than funerary activity (Lambrick forthcoming).

There is a great deal more evidence for the nature of domestic occupation within field systems in the Middle Thames Valley. The extensive excavations at Perry Oaks/T5 revealed several concentrations of domestic occupation within the middle Bronze Age coaxial field system. These are generally sparse concentrations of pottery and other artefacts in the tops of enclosure ditches and within waterholes, lacking obvious clusters of pits, hollows or structural features, though truncation may account for the absence of shallower features in many areas. In one of the better preserved parts of the site an area *c* 30 m by 22 m was enclosed by a sinuous ditch with a possible entrance between its terminal and a field boundary ditch. Two, presumably successive, post ring type roundhouses, a waterhole or well with the remains of a revetment lining, and a pit lay within the enclosure. Although six other possible settlement foci, represented by concentrations of domestic activity, were identified in the Perry Oaks area they were not particularly well defined (Framework Archaeology 2006, 113-32). Further examples have emerged from continuing fieldwork at T5 where a number of other characteristics of settlement areas were recognised, including the modification of major boundaries and the subdivision of fields. Waterholes were generally located a short distance from the main focus of occupation.

Some of the Perry Oaks/T5 occupation foci did not develop further during the later Bronze Age and may have been abandoned, while others, notably in the area of Settlement 5, became more distinct with greater concentrations of domestic debris in particular locations and fewer general scatters. It was suggested that some of this material might represent a scattered midden deposit (Framework Archaeology 2006, 133). No specific focus of early Iron Age occupation was recognised but the limited amount of early Iron Age material suggested that activity continued in an area that later evolved into a nucleated open settlement in the middle to late Iron Age (see below). This settlement was relatively intensive and began to redefine the broad orientation of the landscape which was by then open grassland (Framework Archaeology 2006, 190, 194, 200).

At Hengrove Farm within another middle Bronze Age coaxial field system, a group of postholes marked the position of a roundhouse of Bronze Age origin (Hayman forthcoming d). Pits and waterholes of prehistoric origin found close to the roundhouse may have been broadly contemporary with the field system. A substantial concentration of middle Bronze Age occupation evidence was found in one area, and elsewhere there were other small clusters of pits, some waterholes, including some with complex inter-cutting pits with concentrations of pottery and other debris in the subsidence hollows, which suggest separate small clusters of occupation activity elsewhere within the fields.

At Thorpe Lea Nurseries similar indications of middle Bronze Age settlement foci were indicated by concentrations of occupation material in the main spinal land division ditch of what may have been a coaxial field system. Few other boundary ditches were identified and no clear evidence of associated structures, possibly due to truncation. Compared with contemporary sites, the absence of waterholes is noteworthy. During the early to middle Iron Age, two more intensive areas of occupation were established at the site (Hayman forthcoming a).

At Home Farm, Laleham there was a significant concentration of domestic debris, including a large number of perforated slabs from a large rectilinear enclosure or L-shaped ditch. Nearby lay a substantial post built roundhouse with associated domestic debris. Dumps of domestic debris were present in some waterholes, but it was in general sparse within the field ditches and gullies (Hayman 1991b; forthcoming c).

At Painesfield Allotments, Chertsey an area *c* 45 m x 30 m revealed a small middle Bronze Age site with numerous features including pits, ditches and a waterhole, but with no evidence for structures. Despite the small size of the site, an unusually large number of artefacts were recovered, including a complete bucket urn with a cordon of finger impressed decoration and a hearth containing carbonised seeds and grain.

On the Maidenhead-Windsor Flood Channel a concentration of middle Bronze Age artefacts was found in a ditch terminal at Marsh Lane West,

possibly indicating a domestic focus in the vicinity, although the deposit, interpreted as a middening dump, may have been a structured special deposit.

At the Eton Rowing Course concentrations of both artefacts and ecofacts were found in both of the primary small enclosures of the west field system on Site F, and the presence of a waterhole in each, plus the deposition of a saddle quern in the terminal of one of the ditches, suggests that these were domestic foci. The increase in domestic debris may, however, have been due largely to the presence of the waterholes, which served as receptacles for special deposits. Concentrations of domestic finds and pits were also found in two other areas within the wider field system, and the general impression is of widespread and small-scale domestic activity rather than intensive permanent settlement. It is interesting to note that similar quantities of artefacts were recovered from waterholes and pits in the largely unenclosed neighbouring gravel terrace island (Allen *et al.* forthcoming b).

At Weir Bank Stud Farm, Bray, a middle Bronze Age roundhouse, a possible four-post structure and concentrations of domestic material were found in ditches that formed part of a regular, possibly coaxial, field system (Fig. 4.9; Barnes and Cleal 1995). The quantity of finds was considerably greater than the material recovered from Bronze Age domestic settlements at the Eton Rowing Course immediately across the river. The detailed sequence is not clear, but some of the ditches containing middle Bronze Age material cut earlier features with traces of domestic activity. It is possible that the field system had developed piecemeal, but the typical lack of stratigraphic relationships meant that it was not possible to establish precisely how the fields were laid out or how they related to the domestic activity. A possible late Bronze Age sherd from the roundhouse suggested that it was relatively late in the sequence. At the time the report was written very few other areas of middle Bronze Age domestic activity had been investigated and reported in the Thames Valley and comparing the results with well documented middle Bronze Age enclosed farming settlements in Wessex, Cleal highlighted the ephemeral nature of localised foci of domestic activity here, especially given the probability that it may have developed over a few centuries.

At Green Park and Moores Farm a number of middle to late Bronze Age field systems on different orientations have been investigated, with similarly ephemeral traces of middle Bronze Age occupation activity, much of it evident from accumulations of domestic debris in backfilled waterholes and ditches. Although numerous later Bronze Age houses and pits were recorded at Green Park, they were rare in the middle Bronze Age. Middle Bronze Age pottery was associated with one or more of the structures at Reading Business Park Area 5, although the excavators considered the houses to be later (Moore and Jennings 1992, 25). Apart from these sites, no structural evidence for middle Bronze Age dwellings has been found within the Green Park landscape, but the occurrence of middle Bronze Age pottery in boundary ditches, pits and waterholes (as well as occasional burials) provides evidence for occupation in and around the fields.

During the late Bronze Age at Green Park a substantial late Bronze Age settlement was established adjacent to a palaeochannel across or within part a middle Bronze Age field system, with another cluster of roundhouses *c* 400 m further east (Fig. 4.10; Moore and Jennings 1992; Brossler *et al.* 2004).

Fig. 4.9 Occupation areas associated with a Bronze Age field system at Weir Bank Stud Farm, Bray

Late Bronze Age pottery associated with the settlement was recovered only from the uppermost fills of the field ditches, and in places roundhouses assumed to belong to the later settlement postdated boundary ditches. On this basis the excavators concluded that the settlement superseded the field system, though it is interesting that the distribution of settlement features clearly reflected the preexisting field layout, implying the continued existence in several places of some form of above ground boundary – most likely hedges – and probably continued use of fields elsewhere.

This settlement contrasts with the much more dispersed nature of most middle to late Bronze Age settlements associated with field systems noted above. There were at least two main foci of settlement. One was established within the old field enclosures and consisted of two areas, one represented by at least 12 houses (some of them overlapping) straddling a former boundary, the other a more dispersed scatter of four-posters, waterholes, pits, postholes and hollows, and a large burnt mound deposit adjacent to the palaeochannel. On the other side of a former – possibly extant –

Fig. 4.10   Late Bronze Age settlement and middle Bronze Age field system at Green Park, Reading

boundary adjacent to this settlement was a separate cluster of at least four similar houses, several four-posters and other post-built structures, waterholes, pits and hollows, including a row of flax retting pits (Fig. 4.10).

The second main area of settlement lay to the east, on the other side of the palaeochannel, where there was a dense cluster of about 20 houses with intercutting features indicating successive rebuilds. There were a number of four-posters, fence lines and other structures but far fewer pits. This settlement apparently lay beyond the limits of the first middle Bronze Age field system, but possibly within or adjacent to another field system on a different alignment with a pond nearby (Moore and Jennings 1992, 29). Further possible clusters of settlement activity in the vicinity were not clearly defined.

At Church Lammas, Staines a middle Bronze Age rectangular enclosure 40 m long by 25 m wide with two entrance gaps was probably part of a rectilinear field system. Off-centre within the enclosure was an enclosed space *c* 8 m square defined by a flat bottomed gully surrounding a deep pit. Although a fair amount of middle Bronze Age domestic debris was found, the excavators considered this to be a ceremonial site (see Chapter 9)

LONG-LIVED OPEN SETTLEMENTS WITH PIT CLUSTERS

Middle Thames

A number of the ordered and intensively occupied late Bronze Age settlements in the Thames Valley exhibit relatively dense clusters of pits, as at Aldermaston, Reading Business Park/Green Park and Cassington West (see above). At Taplow a pipeline investigation close to the late Bronze Age hilltop enclosure and Iron Age fort at Taplow Court revealed about 100 pits and numerous scattered postholes of late Bronze Age to early Iron Age date within a 17 m wide swathe over a distance of *c* 150 m (Collard 2004). Such a large group of pits has not previously been noted in this part of the Middle Thames Valley. At the southern end of the site a ditch about 5 m wide apparently bounded the pit cluster, while a different sequence of pits and small ditches at the north end may have marked the other side of the settlement, leaving it unclear whether the site was enclosed as provisionally suggested (Collard 2004).

At the long-lived early to middle Iron Age settlement at Brooklands sewage works (Hanworth and Tomalin 1977) a group of 82 largely non-intercutting pits were located, but it was not clear that these represented the limit of activity. Other settlement features include numerous postholes, various gullies and at least one penannular house gully. The most notable feature of the settlement was significant evidence of iron smelting, an exceptional feature for the Thames Valley generally (see Chapter 6). On the adjacent racetrack site a large circular enclosure containing a roughly concentric inner penannular enclosure of unusually large diameter, probably a house site, was investigated. There were also pits, paddocks or fields, but less evidence of early Iron Age occupation than at the sewage works site, perhaps indicating a growth and shift in settlement focus (Hayman 1991c).

Upper Thames

In the Upper Thames Valley long-lived Iron Age settlements characterised by dense clusters of pits, small ditched enclosures and post-built structures are a distinctive feature of the higher gravel terraces and the sands and limestones of the Corallian Ridge (Fig. 4.11). Most examples of such settlements originated in the early Iron Age or the late Bronze Age to early Iron Age transition and lasted well into the middle Iron Age, often with late Iron Age successor settlements.

Stone's pioneering work in the 1880s at Standlake was the first to explore such a site (Stone 1856-9). His excavation examined only one of a number of such settlements at Standlake surrounding an earlier prehistoric barrow cemetery. At Stanton Harcourt settlements at Beard Mill, Vicarage Field, the Aerodrome site and Linch Hill have been examined surrounding the Devil's Quoits barrow complex.

At Gravelly Guy over 800 pits were investigated, the earliest containing All Cannings Cross style early Iron Age pottery and with a radiocarbon date of 780-400 cal BC (Lambrick and Allen 2004, 103-59 and 282). One of the most impressive aspects of this early to late Iron Age settlement is its cumulative density of features and their strict confinement within a sharply demarcated linear settlement zone. Another important feature is the existence of a number of subdivisions within the settlement that suggest it comprised six to eight family households. There was a fairly even spread of houses, two main complexes of successive interlocking enclosures (comparable to some of the pen and paddock type settlements referred to below) opening out onto adjacent pasture, and a dense spread of pits on the side of the settlement closest to the arable fields (Fig. 4.11).

Other pit cluster sites have been investigated at Hanborough (Case *et al*. 1964/5 42-50, figs 2, 17, 18) and Cassington (Case 1982b). Yarnton (Hey *et al*. forthcoming a) is of particular interest for the evidence it provides of such a settlement in relation to earlier dispersed occupation on lower lying ground. At Abingdon an extensive settlement with a dense pit cluster was excavated at Ashville/Wyndyke Furlong (Parrington 1978; Halpin 1983; Muir and Roberts 1999). Similar characteristics may

Fig. 4.11 (overleaf) Pit cluster settlements

PIT CLUSTER SETTLEMENTS

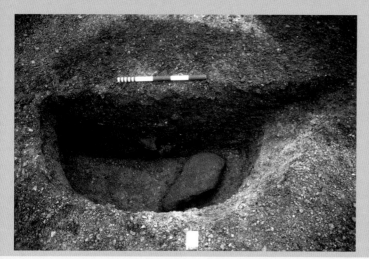

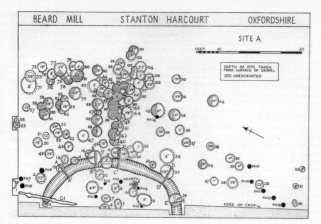

BEARD MILL   STANTON HARCOURT   OXFORDSHIRE

SITE A

Arable

Pasture

Long-lived Iron Age settlements characterised by dense clusters of pits are a distinctive feature of the higher gravel terraces and the Corallian ridge of the Upper Thames Valley. The pits were probably used for grain storage, and it is possible that this area, with its many pit cluster settlements, was the 'bread basket' of the Thames Valley in the second half of the first millennium BC. Such settlements display a particular emphasis on the physical organisation of arable and pasture land.

The pit cluster settlements of Beard Mill, Vicarage Field, Gravelly Guy, the Aerodrome site and Linch Hill at Stanton Harcourt formed a community surrounding the former early prehistoric barrow cemetery. Over 800 pits were excavated at Gravelly Guy, the earliest radiocarbon dated to 780-400 cal BC. The interpretation of the production dynamics of the Gravelly Guy settlement indicates that it could have produced a surplus of both animal and arable produce, even in bad years. Collectively the number of pits at the Stanton Harcourt group of sites may have been similar to or even exceeded that of a densely occupied hillfort such as Danebury.

Left page:
Clockwise from top left
* *Two intercutting pits at Gravelly Guy with a saddle quern on the base of the earlier one*
* *Intercutting pits at Gravelly Guy*
* *General view of Gravelly Guy showing dense layout along a boundary between arable and pasture land*
* *Beard Mill pit cluster excavated in 1944*
Right Page
* *Top Plan of Gravelly Guy showing interpretation of internal subdivisions*
* *Centre Dense cluster of pits and postholes at Gravelly Guy during excavation*
* *Below Map of the Stanton Harcourt Iron Age settlements surrounding the former barrow cemetery*

PIT CLUSTER SETTLEMENTS

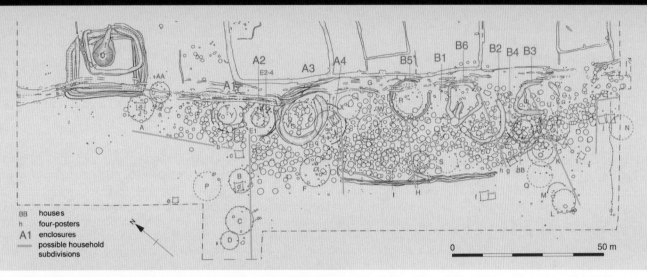

BB houses
h four-posters
A1 enclosures
—— possible household subdivisions

0   50 m

Environmental evidence indicates that pit cluster settlements engaged in mixed farming. Particular types and sizes of charred cereal and weed assemblages have been recovered from those pit cluster sites examined in detail. It is difficult to tell from the plant remains however whether these were 'producer sites' or 'consumer sites'. Pit cluster settlements were probably small communities of several households rather than the much larger populations envisaged for the large settlements inside so-called 'developed' Wessex hillforts.

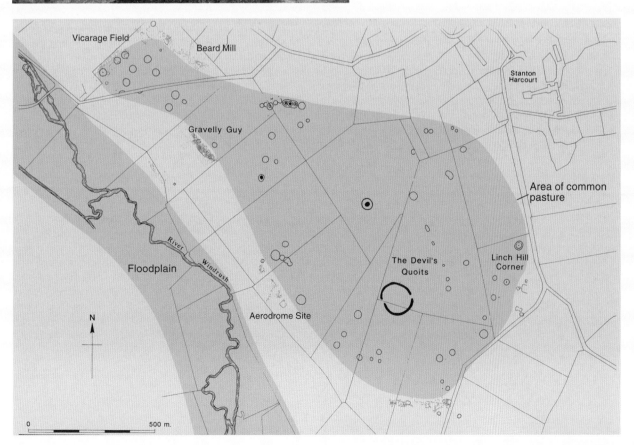

Vicarage Field
Beard Mill
Stanton Harcourt
Gravelly Guy
Area of common pasture
River Windrush
Floodplain
The Devil's Quoits
Linch Hill Corner
Aerodrome Site
N
0   500 m.

be evident from the dense presence of pits, gullies and other features at other large long-lived but less fully investigated settlements with early Iron Age origins at Abingdon, such as Spring Road and the Vineyard (Allen and Kamash 2008; Allen 1991; 1993; 1994 and Allen pers. comm.). Further west, on the Corallian Ridge, comparably long-lived open settlements with dense scatters of pits are known at Coxwell Road Faringdon (Weaver and Ford 2005; Cook *et al.* 2004), probably Frilford (Bradford and Goodchild 1939; Harding 1987; Lock *et al.* 2001) and perhaps at Hatford where extensive piecemeal discoveries have been made over several decades (Bourn 2000).

In the Dorchester area an extensive long-lived settlement, parts of which appear to be characterised by dense pits, was defined by geophysical survey and small-scale excavation outside the late Bronze Age and Iron Age hilltop enclosure and fort on Castle Hill, Little Wittenham, (Allen and Lamdin-Whymark 2005; Allen *et al.* forthcoming b).

Not all long-lived Iron Age open settlements on the higher gravel terraces were characterised by especially dense clusters of pits like those at Gravelly Guy. At Mount Farm an early to middle Bronze Age barrow and later waterhole and burning pit were ploughed prior to the establishment of two areas of early to middle Iron Age settlement represented by small clusters of pits (totalling *c* 50-60) and a few penannular gullies. These were extended and elaborated into a field system and trackway that continued to develop through the Roman period (see Chapter 3).

One particular feature of open settlements with dense clusters of pits on the higher terraces and Corallian Ridge is that they lasted throughout the Iron Age. No examples have yet been found that were first established later than the early Iron Age and none was abandoned during the Iron Age, although there may have been shifts or adjustments in location. For example, there was a distinct shift in the focus of settlement at Yarnton from the mainly early Iron Age activity at Cresswell Field to the mainly middle to late Iron Age activity at the main Yarnton site (Hey *et al.* forthcoming a). At Coxwell Road, Faringdon there was little evidence of middle Iron Age activity in the southern half of the site, but more in the northern area, strongly suggesting that settlement activity shifted (Weaver *et al.* 2004; Cook *et al.* 2004).

Pit cluster settlements were clearly engaged in mixed farming, and where examined in detail, as at Ashville, Gravelly Guy and Yarnton (and on a smaller scale Coxwell Road) charred cereal and weed remains are common and broadly similar in character. However they are variable in abundance, and it is now questionable whether charred plant remains can be used to differentiate reliably between 'producer' and 'consumer' sites (see Chapter 7). Settlements of this kind appear to represent small communities of one or two to several households rather than the much larger populations envisaged

for comparably dense but much larger pit cluster settlements inside Wessex hillforts such as Danebury (Cunliffe and Poole 1991 a and b). Collectively, however, the scale of the Stanton Harcourt community represented by half a dozen such settlements may have been similar to the scale of a densely occupied hillfort. But it is noticeable that some forts in the wider Thames Valley have settlements with more or less dense clusters of pits nearby *outside* the defended area, as at Cherbury, Salmonsbury, Madmarston, Castle Hill and Taplow (Hingley and Miles 1984; Miles and Lewis 1985; Nichols 2006; Allen 2000, 7, fig. 1.5; Allen *et al.* forthcoming a and b; Collard 2004). At least at Castle Hill, it appears that the late Bronze Age hilltop enclosure and Iron Age hillfort lacked intensive occupation remains of this sort themselves. Indeed, it is increasingly clear from several forts that have been subject to geophysical survey and sample excavation that most lack dense concentrations of pits (see Chapter 9).

Although small clusters and scatters of storage and other pits are a common feature of many Iron Age settlements, the distinctively dense linear pit cluster settlements of the Upper Thames Valley seem to be a particular phenomenon of the Iron Age settlement pattern. Settlements of this type may reflect a particular emphasis on the physical organisation of arable and pastureland, and the longevity of stable settlements. The rarity (so far) of major pit cluster sites upstream of Lechlade or downstream of Dorchester, including the whole of the middle Thames except for the sites near Taplow and the Brooklands complex, suggests that such settlements may have been a particular feature of a core area of the Upper Thames and the Corallian Ridge. The interpretation of the production dynamics of the Gravelly Guy settlement suggested that it would have easily been capable of producing a surplus of both animal and arable produce, even in bad years (Lambrick and Allen 2004, 484-8). Although not fully proven experimentally, the use of pits for grain storage on the gravels is widely assumed (see Chapter 7) and if the association with arable production as well animal husbandry is correct, it is tempting to see this core area with pit cluster settlements as the 'bread basket' of the Thames Valley in the second half of the first millennium BC.

Although this idea is attractive, it would be premature to conclude that less intensively explored parts of the wider Thames basin were not also important for cereal production. Apart from Madmarston hillfort, some enclosed settlements of the Cotswolds had quite dense, if not particularly extensive concentrations of pits just outside them, as at Guiting Power (Saville 1979) and probably Rollright (Lambrick 1988). In general, however, few extensive open settlements are known on the Cotswolds and dense scatters of pits have so far proved rare whether or not settlements were originally enclosed (Moore 2006 53; Lang pers. comm.). The extensive stripping of sites along the transect across the Cotswolds provided by the A419/A417 road scheme revealed a number of Iron Age settlements that lacked significant clusters of pits (Mudd *et al.* 1999, 35-97).

In many respects even less is known of pit cluster settlements on the chalk geology of the Thames Valley. Similarly dense clusters of pits do not particularly seem to characterise the interiors of hillforts or other enclosed sites, or at least not at the level of density of Gravelly Guy or Wessex hillforts such as Danebury, but at Castle Hill there is good evidence from extensive geophysics and sample excavations that the extramural settlement included dense concentrations of pits. There are further hints that significant clusters of pits may have characterised other, mainly middle Iron Age open settlements revealed in pipeline excavations on the chalk either side of the Thames at Halfpenny Lane, Moulsford (Ford 1990, 27-30) and Woodcote Road South Stoke (Timby *et al.* 2005, 210-27). Again the emphasis of the mixed farming economy of such sites is not entirely clear, but both sites had possible storage pits as well as smaller ones, and produced fairly abundant charred cereal remains.

So although dense pit cluster settlements are very distinctive, and seem to suggest particular aspects of settlement and land use organisation of a core part of the Upper Thames Valley, they can also be viewed as only an extreme form of the very common occurrence of pit clusters within Iron Age settlements, which were often engaged in mixed farming. If Iron Age pit cluster settlements on the higher gravel terraces, Corallian Ridge and limestone of the Upper Thames Valley were part of a regional 'bread basket,' it was certainly not to the exclusion of arable production elsewhere in the Thames basin, and perhaps was only one of many areas where cereal growing was important on well-drained fertile soils. The picture for the Middle Thames Valley is still unclear. Brooklands and the Taplow pipeline site suggest that the 'missing' early to middle Iron Age pit cluster settlements of this kind may reflect issues of discovery rather than a genuine absence.

IRON AGE HOUSE, PEN AND PADDOCK SETTLEMENTS

On the lower lying terraces and floodplain of the Thames open settlements and small farmsteads consisting typically of one or more groups of houses with associated (often interlinked) enclosed pens, paddocks and work areas are most readily recognisable from small penannular, polygonal, rectilinear and irregular enclosures demarcated by shallow ditches and gullies. Such farmsteads are usually characteristic of middle Iron Age settlement but it seems reasonable to consider that without these distinctive ditch arrangements such settlements are comparable with densely occupied late Bronze Age to early Iron Age settlements like Cassington West. In a growing number of cases relatively dense groups of enclosures succeeded more scattered settlements, whether in open areas as at Latton Lands and Shorncote/Cotswold Community in the Upper Thames, or within later Bronze Age field systems as at Perry Oaks/T5, Hengrove or Ashford Prison in the Middle Thames (see above).

In some cases such complexes of small gullies and ditches demarcating house sites, pens and work areas are part of a network of other irregular enclosures, ditched 'paddocks' and larger ditched enclosures. Many middle Iron Age houses were surrounded by penannular gullies that caught and drained away water running off the roof. They are such a common feature of house sites that they are widely considered to mark the location of buildings even where no direct structural evidence is present. The domestic attribution may, however, only be fully justifiable where there are clear concentrations of occupation debris in the terminals of the gullies either side of the entrance or other features nearby (eg Allen *et al.* 1984, fig. 6.3; Lambrick and Allen 2004, 129).

Gullies seem also to have demarcated pens and other small enclosures, perhaps work or storage areas. In a few cases these features originated as palisade fences (eg Lambrick and Robinson 1979), but generally they provided localised drainage. The topsoils of Thames gravel terraces are silty and even clayey on lower ground where they have not had sand and gravel mixed into them by ploughing or other disturbance, so drainage of surface water may have been an issue in relatively heavily used areas where the topsoil was compacted. It is noticeable that in many cases such features only just penetrate gravel, as though they were dug just deep enough to allow free drainage.

Although such gullies and ditches are particularly characteristic of middle and later Iron Age settlements, this may be misleading in terms of the origins of this kind of settlement that they represent. A number of examples of middle to late Bronze Age small circular or penannular ditched pens or enclosures are known as at Shorncote/Cotswold Community (Hearne and Heaton 1994, 32, fig. 4; Hearne and Adam 1999, 45-6, 50-1, 71, figs 10, 12), Eight Acre Field (Mudd 1995, 23-5 fig. 4) and much more fragmentarily, Hurst Park, East Molesey (Andrews, 1996, 64-6, fig. 36). It is also wrong to suppose that settlements of this kind did not exist just because their houses, animal pens and work areas were not surrounded by ditches and gullies. Such groups of enclosures occur within open settlements with extensive pit clusters. At Gravelly Guy, Yarnton, Ashville, and Mount Farm it has been noted that groups of middle Iron Age penannular gullies occupied areas already respected by earlier Iron Age pits, implying that there were already pens or small enclosures demarcated by hurdles or other barriers that left no subsoil traces. A few other cases of compact late Bronze Age and early Iron Age settlements of houses and other post-built structures and fences may similarly be the forerunners of a common form of middle Iron Age settlement.

Fig. 4.12 Middle Iron Age settlement along a boundary at Latton Lands

At Latton Lands three scattered groups of post built roundhouses and fenced pens and enclosures dated to the early Iron Age (Fig. 4.12 and see above Fig. 4.4) were succeeded by penannular gullies demarcating houses and pens. These probably continued to serve the same functions and occupied a more tightly constrained linear area along a boundary that was later demarcated by a long sinuous gated ditch with enclosures attached to its eastern side (Powell *et al.* forthcoming).

At Shorncote/Cotswold Community two or three clusters of middle Iron Age occupation, not necessarily contemporary, were spaced roughly 300 m apart along a terrace edge boundary that may have originated in the middle or late Bronze Age (see Chapter 3). One occupation site was a roughly square enclosure about 50 m across marked by a small gully with a penannular house gully outside and a few other gullies and pits (Powell *et al.* forthcoming); to the north there was a middle Iron Age house gully with posts of a V-shaped structure reminiscent of Yarnton and other workshops (see Chapter 6). Fragmentary remains of a series of irregular fields or paddocks were evident from recut ditches and odd lengths of fence, possibly representing a main north-south boundary with a series of irregular paddocks to its east, possibly representing three stages of development. It is suggested that land use was mainly pastoral (Brossler *et al.* 2002).

At Slade Farm, Bicester a series of individual penannular and other small enclosures were likewise laid out along a boundary marked by a long sinuous ditch with possible openings. Occupation debris suggests domestic use as well as livestock herding, and a fairly typical range of charred cereal remains was found. Land to the east may have been low-lying grassland subject to flooding from the river Ray, while landuse of somewhat drier ground to the west may have included cereal production.

At Farmoor a similar group of small enclosures and a waterhole were found along the edge of the first gravel terrace, the site of a sparse scatter of early Iron Age pits. These are rather different from the string of three small farmstead units on the floodplain (see below).

In other cases such settlements were established in previously unoccupied areas. This is especially noticeable on the floodplain of the Thames. A series of such settlements first established in the middle Iron Age have been investigated on parts of the Upper Thames floodplain and edge of first terrace at Cleveland Farm (Coe *et al.* 1981 43-6, fig. 3), Claydon Pike (Miles *et al.* 2007), Cassington (Hey *et al.* forthcoming b), Foxley Farm, Finmere (Hancocks 2003), Port Meadow (Atkinson 1942; Lambrick and McDonald 1985; Lambrick and Robinson 1988), Whitehouse Road (Mudd 1993), and Thrupp (Everett and Eeles 1995). In less clear cut topographical locations similar sites include a row of three clusters of penannular and segmental enclosures at Totterdown Lane, Horcott, two dated broadly to the

middle Iron Age and the third to the late Iron Age (Pine and Preston 2004). Further examples have been recorded at Hatford (Bourn 2000; Booth and Simmonds 2004) and perhaps Filkins (Coleman and Hancock 2004; Oxford Archaeological Unit 1993).

The basic components of such clusters were typically a house and between one and four attached pens and enclosures (or a larger surrounding enclosure), and sometimes separate penannular gullies and other facilities such as four-post structures. In some cases such settlements incorporated larger enclosures or paddocks, with associated houses and other structures, as at Cleveland Farm and Shorncote/Cotswold Community, and extensive linked networks of fields or paddocks defined by small ditches as at

Claydon Pike

Port Meadow

Fig. 4.13 Middle Iron Age house, pen and paddock settlements in the Upper Thames Valley at (above) *Claydon Pike and* (below) *Port Meadow*

Cleveland Farm, Claydon Pike and probably Port Meadow (Fig. 4.13). Orderly clusters of houses and pens are particularly evident at Claydon Pike, Foxley Farm and Port Meadow, suggesting very small social units of perhaps one or two family groups in each. Typically, such enclosures lay adjacent to each other, but did not overlap or face one another. Entrance gaps are generally east or south-east, but often with a few facing other directions (north and south at Port Meadow, south-west and north-east at Foxley Farm across the line of the boundary). Some of the enclosures at Totterdown Lane had asymmetrical double entrances like a number at Gravelly Guy thought to be associated with animal management (see Chapter 7).

The layout of the Claydon Pike and Port Meadow settlements was clearly linked to local topography, with the living areas of houses and pens occupying drier gravel 'islands' not normally subject to flooding. They were integrated with networks of curvilinear, straight and irregular ditches, often extending into lower-lying areas to define larger paddocks and fields. At Cleveland Farm one of the settlement enclosures was bounded on one side by a ditch over 160 m long which matched another long curving ditch to form a large funnel-shaped area suitable for gathering and herding animals. Finds indicate a fairly standard but seldom abundant range of pottery and other objects. Environmental evidence from Port Meadow suggests that these terrace edge and floodplain settlements were small pastoral farmsteads.

It is worth noting that in several cases these enclosures formed linear rows of three or four such clusters along low-lying terrace edges adjacent to the floodplain or on islands within it adjacent to palaeochannels – *c* 300 m apart at Shorncote/Cotswold Community, 50-150 m apart at Slade Farm, 50-260 m apart at Thrupp, with broadly similar groupings 300-500 m apart at Port Meadow and closer spaced clusters 20-100 m apart at Claydon Pike. It is not clear whether these represent separate family groups making up a larger community or successive changes in location. At Claydon Pike it seems that the relatively closely spaced settlement clusters on the dry gravel 'islands' were occupied successively, each following a period of modification to the settlement layout. The stratigraphic sequence of structures within the occupation areas on Islands 1 and 2 are especially complex, each with up to four or five phases of replacement. The evidence suggests occupation of only two or three houses at any one point over a period of perhaps 300 years and the pottery indicates a possible chronological shift between the islands. It was concluded that Claydon Pike was 'probably occupied year round by small family groups who over several generations shifted location' (Miles

et al. 2007, 59-61, 365-367). The evidence from Totterdown Lane suggests some sequence, but this was not so apparent at Slade Farm.

In the lower part of the Middle Thames Valley there are a number of relatively compact middle to late Iron Age settlements marked by penannular enclosures which in some cases emerged in areas of Bronze Age coaxial field systems. At earlier stages these seem to have been characterised by dispersed occupation activity, though in some cases an early Iron Age element is not apparent. They were typically succeeded by late Iron Age and Roman settlement and farming enclosures and field ditches.

At Perry Oaks/T5 evidence of occupation, probably beginning in the early Iron Age, extends over an area *c* 130 m by 185 m, later characterised by a cluster of penannular and other small enclosures (Fig. 4.14). Some of these formed linear groups on a different alignment to that of the pre-existing rectilinear Bronze Age field system, though the primary elements of the settlement may have been established within the remnants of the field system, with waterholes respecting the old boundaries. The new alignment of the middle Iron Age settlement endured into the Late Iron Age and Roman period when parts of the settlement were enclosed, cutting across the old Bronze Age field boundaries, with other enclosures and eventually a 'ladder' type field system added at later stages, broadly respecting the new alignment established by the unenclosed groups of houses and pens. The detailed sequence here is not yet fully understood, but it appears that the houses were not all built and occupied at once. This new settlement clearly superseded previous arrangements with the larger ditched enclosures, and a number of penannular gullies and other ditches and gullies assigned to this period intersect the Bronze Age ditched boundaries, suggesting that by this time the earlier layout had largely become defunct.

At Caesar's Camp, Heathrow, a complex of middle Iron Age penannular gullies and enclosures were located adjacent to the well known shrine site set within a banked rectangular enclosure (Grimes and Close-Brooks 1993, fig. 5). The area also produced evidence of late Bronze Age occupation. The ploughed out earthworks corresponded to the extent of some of the penannular enclosures, suggesting that the settlement was originally unenclosed. The relationship of the farmstead to the 'temple' or shrine, including whether some elements survived when the enclosure was constructed, remains uncertain.

At Hengrove Farm 17 complete and partial ring gullies, various ditches, pits, and postholes and a large waterhole occupied an area *c* 200 m long by 30 m wide, in places intersecting the ditched boundaries of the pre-existing middle Bronze Age coaxial

Fig. 4.14 (opposite) Middle Iron Age open settlement at Perry Oaks/T5 Heathrow (note the large enclosure which became a feature within the more extensive open settlement)

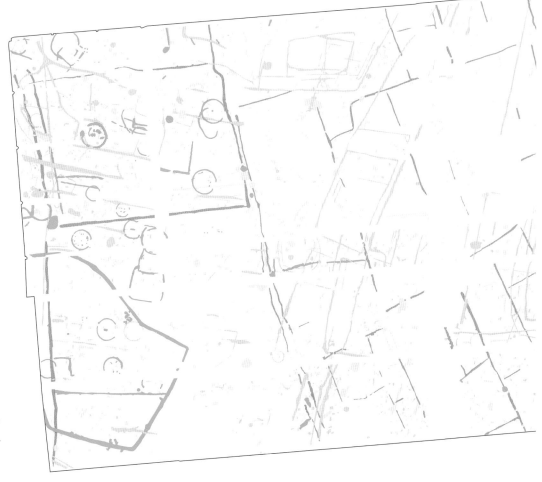

N

0   100m

Bronze Age trackways and ditches

Middle Iron Age features

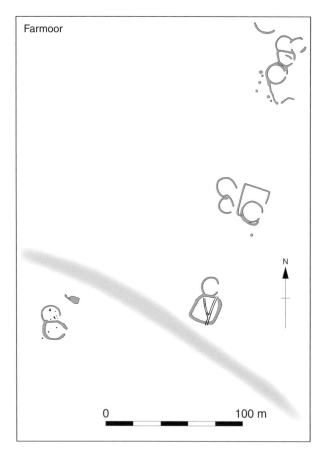

Farmoor

0   100 m

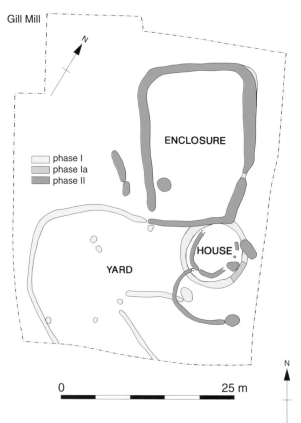

Gill Mill

N

ENCLOSURE

phase I
phase Ia
phase II

HOUSE

YARD

N

0   25 m

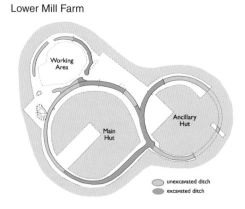

Lower Mill Farm

Working
Area

Main
Hut

Ancillary
Hut

unexcavated ditch
excavated ditch

*Fig. 4.15   Low-lying middle Iron Age single
family seasonal and temporary farmsteads*

field system (Hayman forthcoming d). Some of the ring gullies appear to mark the position of round-houses, but other smaller ones probably enclosed other types of structure (in one case a four-poster). The ring gullies were not enclosed by the ditches and appear to have belonged to an open settlement area. The finds from this period consisted mostly of late Iron Age pottery and animal bones, although some contexts may have been earlier. Occupation appears to have continued into the Roman period with no break, and a subsequent complex of late Iron Age and Roman settlement and agricultural ditched enclosures emerged from the middle Iron Age settlement on an alignment reflecting the Bronze Age coaxial layout.

Nearby at Ashford Prison a cluster of penannular enclosures with small pit groups and four-post structures was sited on a slightly raised area between the River Ash and a palaeochannel. The penannular gullies surrounded and apparently respected an earlier prehistoric ring ditch, which may have been still visible as an earthwork. There is less evidence at Ashford than at Perry Oaks/T5 of continuous development from the earlier Iron Age into a later Iron Age and Roman settlement and fields appear to have been focussed mainly in the Hengrove area.

Thorpe Lea Nurseries is another example of a mainly middle to late Iron Age settlement succeeding traces of domestic activity associated with a middle Bronze Age field system, with only limited evidence of early Iron Age activity (Hayman 1998; forthcoming a). This site, however, lacked the distinctive penannular house sites and animal pens. There were two main areas of middle Iron Age occupation and a third separate cluster of dispersed features, all characterised by small pits, postholes, four-posters, irregular gullies and two waterholes, all producing very few finds. They were established or later enclosed within part of a re-organised pattern of fields or large paddocks. Only the western area of the settlement was occupied for any length of time, surviving in use through the late Iron Age and much of the Roman period. Like several of the other middle Iron Age settlements that evolved within the relict Bronze Age field systems of the west London and Surrey gravels, the Thorpe Lea Nurseries site produced no carbonised crop remains or querns prior to the late Iron Age/Roman transition and no other evidence for cultivation. The most distinctive aspect of the occupation is its association with iron-working, including smelting (see Chapter 6), and relatively large quantities of spinning and weaving equipment (5 spindle whorls and 156 loomweight fragments).

Compared with the Upper Thames Valley, the west London and Surrey settlements of this type seem to have incorporated more penannular gullies, with little or no sign of associated networks of paddocks and even less evidence of crop processing There are also similarities such as the orderly rows of penannular gullies, and the possible survival of

above ground hedged boundaries surviving from the Bronze Age could mean that they were more similar to sites with paddocks and fields like Claydon Pike or Port Meadow than is at first apparent.

Most house pen and paddock settlements had complex histories of subsequent development, either on the same site, as at Cotswold Community and Park Farm, or more commonly shifting to an adjacent, sometimes drier location, as at Claydon Pike. Likewise, most seem to have been mainly pastoral farmsteads of varying sizes, though some of those on the drier terraces may have been more involved in mixed farming. The existence of similar groups of enclosures within major pit cluster settlements, such as those at Yarnton or at Gravelly Guy where they faced onto large open grazing areas, reinforces their association with pastoral aspects of farming settlements.

In some cases, even smaller settlements seem to have existed as isolated single family units with no large-scale ditched paddocks and fields, and no indication that they were part of a longer history of development (Fig. 4.15). At Farmoor a row of three such units, possibly not contemporary, was established on the Thames floodplain, not apparently on higher gravel islands (Lambrick and Robinson 1979). One was located on the low-lying edge of a palaeochannel and had a raised gravel path crossing it. The layout of these small farmsteads was much like others of their kind but what sets the Farmoor examples apart is the biological evidence. This demonstrates that they were set in open wet pastureland and, based on the lack of perennial weed species, that they were occupied for no more than a few seasons. Furthermore, aquatic snail species found in the surrounding gullies show that they were subject to flooding at the time they were occupied. They appear to represent short-lived specialist summer grazing camps. No other comparable sites have been confirmed but other examples may include Gill Mill, on the floodplain of the Windrush (Lambrick 1992) and Lower Mill Farm, Stanwell on or close to the floodplain of the Colne (Hayman 1991a).

LATE IRON AGE ENCLOSURE CLUSTERS

House, pen and paddock settlements established in the later Iron Age, including Langford Down (Williams 1944/4), are also quite variable in form. Some developed into complex networks of irregular and rectilinear pens and enclosures. At Thornhill Farm (Jennings *et al.* 2004) elaborate networks of irregular enclosures were continuously redefined and recut well into the Roman period (Fig. 4.16), whereas at Totterdown Lane, Horcott an increasingly well ordered pattern of regular rectilinear enclosures associated with a trackway emerged from the middle to late Iron Age clusters of houses and small pens or paddocks (Fig. 4.17; Pine and Preston 2004).

Key
■ Definite features
▨ Possible features
➳ Cropmarks
▨ Palaeochannels

0   200 m

Fig. 4.16   Later Iron Age pen and paddock settlement at Thornhill Farm

At Old Shifford Farm, Standlake (Hey 1995) a small farm evolved from a small D-shaped enclosure with an attached annexe to the north and a small ring gully and second enclosure to the south. Subsequently there was a long sequence of addition, subdivision, redefinition and amalgamation through the late Iron Age and Roman periods, creating a larger complex of enclosed spaces, probably linked to a wider system of paddocks and fields. Concentrations of finds clearly suggest that some of the small enclosures were foci of domestic occupation. Not far away at Smiths Field, Hardwick a similar pattern of intercutting and shifting smaller and larger enclosures of late Iron Age and Roman date has been observed and sampled (Allen 1981; 2000).

Nearby in the lower Windrush Valley west and south of Stanton Harcourt, there was a distinct shift of settlement into open pastureland from early to middle Iron Age locations around the periphery of the earlier prehistoric ceremonial and funerary complex. This has been most thoroughly explored at Gravelly Guy where small (in some cases heavily recut) enclosures were established within or

adjacent to regular networks of paddocks (Lambrick and Allen 2004, 161-79, figs 4.1, 4.2). A similar pattern also seems evident at Vicarage Pit and Beard Mill (Case *et al.* 1982, 113-6, fig. 59) and Linch Hill (Grimes 1960, fig. 57; Harding 1972, Pl 35).

A particular characteristic of some of these late Iron Age sites in the Upper Thames Valley is the extraordinarily dense redigging of enclosure ditches, notably at Thornhill Farm (Jennings *et al.* 2004, 30-58, figs 3.9, 3.11, 3.17, 3.19), Shorncote/ Cotswold Community (OA 2004) and Claydon Pike (Miles *et al.* 2007, 69-77, fig. 4.3). The recutting seems to have taken place over relatively short periods, apparently redefining the enclosed areas every two or three years. A similarly obsessive recutting of overlapping enclosures can be seen in the late Iron Age and early Roman period at Yarnton (Hey *et al.* forthcoming), while at Gravelly Guy (Lambrick and Allen 2004, 204-12) comparable sequences of intensive recutting are evident in three discrete enclosure groups set within wider networks of small paddocks. It appears that these heavily reworked and redefined enclosures are characteristic of

Fig. 4.17 (opposite)   Later Iron Age pen and paddock settlements

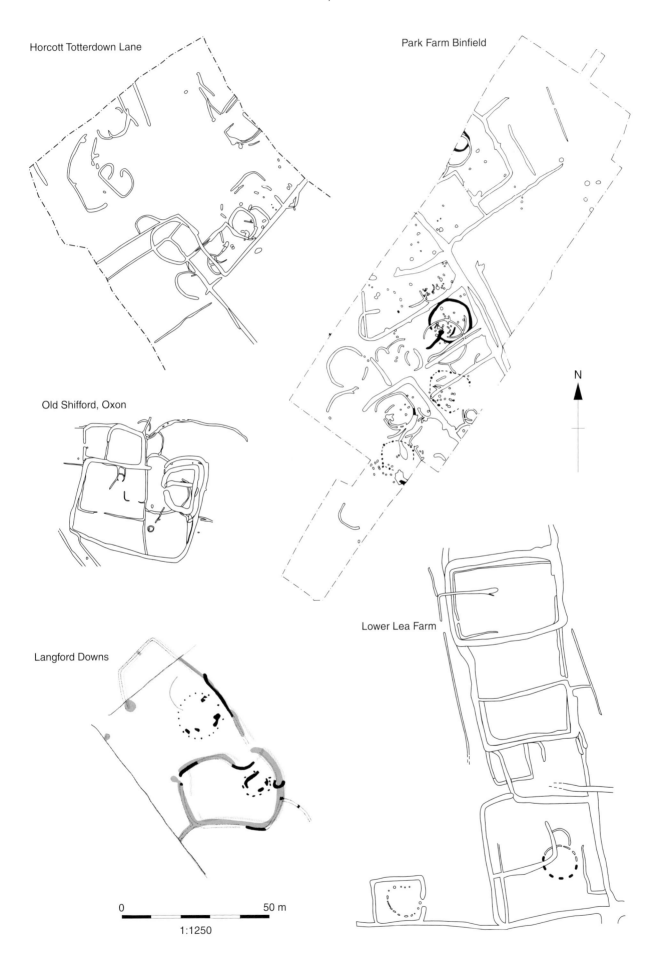

Horcott Totterdown Lane

Park Farm Binfield

Old Shifford, Oxon

Lower Lea Farm

Langford Downs

0   50 m

1:1250

N

predominantly pastoral settlements or, in the case of Yarnton and Gravelly Guy, perhaps the pastoral elements of mixed farming settlements. The extent to which these recut enclosures were foci of domestic activity seems variable. Some produced copious amounts of domestic debris, but many produced very little, suggesting that they were primarily stock enclosures. At Thornhill Farm there were a few possible domestic structures, though in general the level of domestic debris was very low. Some enclosures may have been used for smithing or other agriculturally related crafts, as seems to have been the case at Gravelly Guy and some enclosures at Thornhill (Lambrick and Allen 2004, 344, fig. 8.3; Jennings *et al.* 2006, 150).

In the Middle Thames Valley there is less evidence of late Iron Age enclosure clusters of this sort, but a comparable development of orderly rectilinear and sub-rectangular enclosures emerging from pre-existing small house, pen and paddock settlements has been recorded at Park Farm, Binfield on the clay east of Reading (Roberts 1995). The small enclosure cluster sites that grew up in the remnants of later Bronze Age field systems on the west London and Surrey gravels at Perry Oaks/T5, Hengrove and Ashford Prison continued to develop into the later Iron Age and seem to have been transformed through successive redefinition of enclosed areas into rectilinear Roman field systems (Framework Archaeology 2007, 202-14, Hayman forthcoming d).

ENCLOSED FARMING SETTLEMENTS

A distinction has long been drawn between 'enclosed' settlements, with most settlement components located within a space enclosed by a ditch, and 'open' settlements, which may include small pens and other enclosures but are not surrounded by a ditch (eg Harding 1972, 11). In the last two or three decades a good deal has been made of the social and economic status and symbolism of settlement enclosures (Hingley 1984; Hill 1996). In Wessex, both middle to late Bronze Age and Iron Age enclosed farms were standard, indeed dominant components of late prehistoric settlement patterns (Cunliffe 1993, 132-45; 179-84). In the Thames Valley the pattern is different, with more emphasis on the variety of 'open' settlements that we have reviewed above. Few examples of later Bronze Age enclosed farms – as opposed to communal hilltop or riverside enclosures – are known, and relatively few, generally small, enclosed Iron Age settlements have been excavated.

In his analysis of the distribution of sites based on cropmark morphology, Hingley (1984, 77-80, fig. 5.4) drew a distinction in the Upper Thames Valley between dense open settlements on the river gravels, and a more sparse pattern of enclosed settlements on the Cotswolds. This still seems to be a genuine pattern, and indeed has been supported by recent cropmark discoveries on the Oxfordshire

Cotswolds and the Berkshire Downs (Featherstone and Bewley 2000; Winton 2004). Some of these sites are large and highly elaborate, enhancing considerably the variety illustrated by Hingley and Miles (1984, 57, fig. 4.3). However, some caution is needed in building too much on this broad pattern.

Enclosed settlements are more easily recognisable from cropmarks than open ones and the picture becomes even more complex when chronological factors revealed by detailed excavation are brought to bear. As the late Bronze Age and middle Iron Age open settlements overlain by a substantial enclosure containing the Iron Age shrine at Heathrow illustrate (Grimes and Close Brooks 1992), it cannot always be assumed that settlements originated at the same period as their enclosure. And as excavations along the A417/A419 road scheme and elsewhere have shown, it also cannot automatically be assumed that late prehistoric enclosures were always significant as settlements (Mudd *et al.* 1999, 35-98).

Middle to late Bronze Age

So far, the Thames Valley seems to lack any clear-cut examples of middle Bronze Age enclosed farmsteads of the kind relatively common in Wessex and Sussex (Cunliffe 1991). Other than the special cases of hilltop enclosures and island sites (see below), there is no proven evidence for middle or late Bronze Age farming settlements fully enclosed within a specially created ditch and bank, but there are some incompletely understood sites that might qualify as such.

At Home Farm, Laleham, the corner of a ditched enclosure containing relatively large quantities of later Bronze Age pottery was found in or adjacent to a possibly pre-existing coaxial field system (Hayman 2002, forthcoming c). Like the site at Weir Bank Stud Farm, Bray (Barnes and Cleal 1995), however, this may have been an L-shaped arrangement of ditches or part of a larger field system rather than a complete ditched enclosure. Although, as noted above (Chapter 3) L-shaped 'enclosures' may have been associated with small settlement foci, the uncertainties of sequence and layout and the relatively modest ditches suggest that these cannot be regarded as enclosed settlements in the conventional sense. At Petters Sports Field Egham (O'Connell 1986) the upper fills of a very substantial ditch contained a dense deposit of late Bronze Age pottery, together with an important hoard of bronzes, but its primary fills contained very little domestic debris, and the evidence of settlement (probably the source of the domestic debris in the upper levels) was immediately adjacent to the ditch on the side opposite where the bank is thought to have been positioned. It is thus not clear that the ditch ever enclosed a settlement. The Petters site is discussed further below in the context of hilltop enclosures, forts and other high status sites.

In the Upper Thames Valley an unusual middle Bronze Age settlement defined by a complex of enclosures was excavated in the mid 1970s at Corporation Farm south of Abingdon (Fig. 4.18; Barclay *et al.* 2003, 37-40 fig. 3.8). It originated as a single open-sided sub-rectangular ditched enclosure of *c* 36.6 m by 33.6 m defined by a V-shaped ditch, redug with a U-shaped profile of similar depth, to which three subsidiary enclosures were later added. The smallest of these enclosed a possible house and small pits. A number of posthole alignments may have been fence lines, some parallel with and extending the line of the enclosure ditches, possibly defining the inner edge of internal banks or hedges, others perhaps for management of animals. Little is known of the settlement's economy as it was recorded in rescue conditions and only a limited amount of material was recovered. A notable feature was a series of deliberate animal burials at ditch terminals and in two pits defining the entrance to the proposed house enclosure. An undated, possibly unassociated, double inhumation burial lay outside the settlement. Although there are arguably similarities with areas of domestic activity associated with some field systems of this period at sites like Weir Bank Stud Farm, no other sites of this period in the Thames Valley are closely comparable to Corporation Farm. In layout it resembles somewhat the house, pen and paddock settlements of the early to middle Iron Age

(see above), but these were mostly on a significantly smaller scale.

Scattered finds of late Bronze Age pottery at the Corporation Farm enclosures may indicate some degree of continuing later use, although there is no evidence of more intensive occupation. As yet, there are no other definite examples of domestic scale enclosed late Bronze Age settlements in the Upper Thames Valley, though there was at least some domestic occupation within larger defensive hilltop enclosures (see below).

Early Iron Age enclosed settlements

A number of early Iron Age enclosed settlements have been investigated in the Upper Thames Valley, though these too are very ill defined. The best known is Allen's Pit, north of Dorchester-on-Thames where an enclosure 60 m by 40 m was revealed by air photography in the 1930s and investigated during its destruction by gravel digging (Bradford 1942b). The substantial enclosure ditch produced an important assemblage of pottery but little is known of the interior. A possibly similar but undated enclosure is known from cropmarks at Overy, near Dorchester-on-Thames (Harding 1972, 15-6), and another suspected enclosure that produced early Iron Age pottery was found across the river at Wigbalds Farm, Long Wittenham. The dimensions of the ditch and its relationship to the enclosed early Iron Age occupation were not reported (Savory 1937; Harding 1972, 15-16). Nearby at Neptune Wood, Long Wittenham a square enclosure of 0.36 ha. with an internal round-house enclosure was recognised from aerial photographs. The ditch has recently been sampled, suggesting an early Iron Age date, but it was much less substantial than the Allen's Pit ditch (Allen *et al.* forthcoming b). The enclosed area is of average size for those in the Upper Thames Valley (Hingley and Miles 1984, fig. 4.3) and it is best regarded as a simple domestic farmstead. The same might apply to a cropmark site at Culham Heights overlooking Andersey Island, on the other side of the river from Abingdon, from which early Iron Age pottery has been noted during fieldwalking.

On a spur of Wytham Hill, overlooking the Thames Valley just west of Oxford a large early Iron Age feature with an adjacent area of hard packed subsoil, investigated by the Oxford University Archaeological Society, was thought to be a ditch terminal, possibly marking the entrance to an enclosed settlement (Mytum 1986). It contained abundant domestic debris and was located towards the northern edge of the main concentration of a scatter of early Iron Age pottery covering an area of *c* 1000 m^2. The full extent and form of the settlement is unclear, and the possibility that the 'ditch terminal' was actually a waterhole in an open settlement cannot be entirely ruled out.

This patchy evidence for early Iron Age enclosed settlements in the Upper Thames derives from old

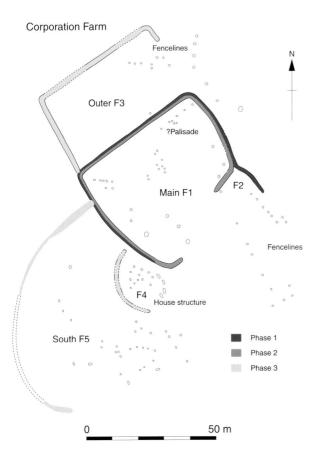

Fig. 4.18   Middle Bronze Age enclosed settlement at Corporation Farm, Abingdon

excavations and small sampling exercises, so the full character of these sites is uncertain, but some recent work has provided evidence for the character of early Iron Age enclosed settlements off the gravels.

On high ground west of Didcot an early Iron Age enclosed settlement with numerous grain storage pits, postholes and ditches has been identified (Smith 2006, 100), while on the chalk the small defensive enclosure at Alfred's Castle was excavated as a part of Oxford University's Ridgeway project (Gosden and Lock 1999; 2000; 2001). The enclosure had an impressive ditch and bank and has traditionally been regarded as a hillfort, but as Gosden and Lock point out, its location was more suited to a role as the centre of a large farming estate than a fort in the conventional sense, and the excavations have shown that its construction was unlike contemporary Iron Age hillforts. It also produced clear evidence of intensive early to middle Iron Age settlement, including large storage pits and rich assemblages of finds, which, unlike Wessex, can now be seen as uncharacteristic of hillforts in the Thames Valley (see below). But equally, its longevity, spanning both the early and middle Iron Age, sets it apart from other enclosed settlements in the Thames Valley which seem to be either early or middle to late Iron Age. Although its construction would have involved significant resources and labour, the scale of this was probably more comparable to Allen's Pit than larger hillforts. Nevertheless, the construction of such substantial enclosures may still have involved a significant degree of communal effort.

In the Middle Thames Valley a trapezoidal enclosed settlement, measuring 67 m east-west by at least 50 m north-south, was recently investigated at Hartshill Copse (Fig. 4.19; Collard *et al.* 2006, 367-422). It lay just north of an important late Bronze Age iron working site, though the detailed radio-carbon dating programme suggests that there was a break in occupation of the site, probably of a few centuries. The enclosure ditch was quite slight with at least two entrances, the narrower one coinciding with a much earlier cremation burial. The ditch, which was recut at least once, enclosed a moderate scatter of typical settlement features including four-posters, pits and a substantial roundhouse. The construction of this structure was radiocarbon dated to between 550 and 430 cal BC and its abandonment to between 390 and 320 cal BC, with other features dated to 760-380 cal BC, 410-210 cal BC and 400-200 cal BC. Some of these provided evidence of iron working, including smelting slag from a posthole dated to 550-360 cal BC.

Middle to late Iron Age enclosed settlements in the Upper Thames Valley

Apart from the unusual example of Alfred's Castle, the early Iron Age enclosed settlements do not appear to have continued in use into the middle Iron Age. Many probable later prehistoric enclo-

Fig. 4.19 Early Iron Age enclosed settlement at Hartshill Copse

sures known from cropmarks remain undated, but most of those sampled in the Thames Valley are of middle or later Iron Age origin. Many of these represented small farms that were either established anew or developed from previously unenclosed settlements of either early or middle Iron Age origin.

The most distinctive are so-called 'banjo' enclosures with entrances characterised by long trackways or funnel-shaped arrangements of ditches, once thought to be a form of middle to late Iron Age settlement almost exclusively confined to the Wessex chalk (Fig. 4.20). Over the last 20 years aerial photography has revealed a large number of previously unrecognised examples on the Cotswolds and the Berkshire Downs, exhibiting considerable variety of form (Featherstone and Bewley 2000; Winton 2004). A number are also known on the valley floor. Some sites display considerable elaboration and external features, suggesting more complex histories than apparent from aerial photographs alone. The increasing variety of form observed makes it difficult to define banjos as a truly distinctive type of enclosure. It is certainly reasonable to include other enclosures with elaborated entrances alongside them and even so detailed investigation (as at Watkins Farm) sometimes shows that the entrance features may not be original (Allen 1990).

None of the banjo enclosures on the Cotswolds or the Berkshire Downs has been thoroughly excavated, but one on the Corallian Ridge north of Swindon at Groundwell Farm and two broadly comparable enclosures with 'antennae' ditches on the gravels near Stanton Harcourt at Mingies Ditch and Watkins Farm have been examined in some detail and can be compared in character.

The early to middle Iron Age banjo enclosure at Groundwell Farm had two surrounding ditches and a south facing entranceway *c* 45 m long, from which the ditches splayed out, turning sharply east and west to form small paddocks either side (Gingell 1982). Excavation was confined to a wide strip across the middle of the enclosure and the more complex outer parts were defined only by geophysical survey, which suggests a complex sequence of development. A ditch crossed the southern entranceway, and indeed the geophysics did not suggest that the ditches flanking the entranceway were continuous. There was also evidence of a much narrower northern entrance with simple splayed antennae ditches, which gave access only through the outer ditch to the narrow space between the ditches, unless the inner ditch had been filled in. It was thus not entirely clear if the settlement had been enlarged (or reduced) during the life of the site, or was double ditched.

The more comprehensive excavations at Mingies Ditch revealed a double ditched enclosure laid out to incorporate a bow of the Mingies Ditch stream, presumably for watering livestock corralled in the outer enclosure. It was also clear that the inner ditch

had been infilled to provide a 'rear' entrance from this part of the enclosure. A sequence of paddocks had been added to the outside of the enclosure on the south side. The Watkins Farm enclosure had a single surrounding ditch.

The enclosure ditches at Groundwell Farm were not excavated, but at Mingies Ditch and Watkins Farm they were not of defensive proportions, being between 0.8 m and 1.2 m deep and around 2 m wide. The gravel upcast at Mingies Ditch survived, demonstrating that there had never been a substantial bank inside either ditch. At both sites waterlogged plant remains suggested that hedges were created as barriers by selective retention of scrub when clearing the site.

The inner enclosures at Groundwell Farm and Mingies Ditch were only 0.2 ha and 0.25 ha respectively, but the much larger outer enclosure at Mingies Ditch and the Watkins Farm enclosure were *c* 0.5 ha. It was thought that at Mingies Ditch animals were corralled in the outer enclosure whereas at Watkins Farm they would have been inside, with the central house having a correspondingly larger surrounding ditch to keep them out. It seems reasonable to suppose that the arrangement at Groundwell Farm would have been more like Mingies Ditch, with animals kept either in the outer enclosure or attached paddocks or both.

At Mingies Ditch the Iron Age ground surface and overlying occupation deposits survived, as did structural detail, while Watkins Farm was only partly preserved by a medieval headland and had been modified in the early Roman period. No such deposits survived at Groundwell Farm. All three sites had evidence of up to five houses, but at Groundwell Farm only one could have been in use at one time. This is likely to have been the case at both the other sites, suggesting that they were all farmsteads occupied by a single, possibly extended, family. Although varying in layout, each of the enclosures shows considerable internal organisation and both Watkins Farm and Mingies Ditch had a ditched trackway leading to the centre of the site, with a central house enclosure at a gate leading to separate houses, storage structures and a central open area. Externally, these sites had antennae ditches or tracks leading to small enclosures or fields, but not the classic 'banjo' necked external entrance ways leading through subsidiary paddocks, such as that at Groundwell Farm, which also had antennae ditches at the northern entrance. Unexcavated sites in the vicinity of Stanton Harcourt, including Black Ditch, had more conspicuous entranceways reminiscent of 'true' banjo enclosures.

Groundwell Farm lies on the top of the Corallian Ridge close to two springs, but Mingies Ditch and Watkins Farm are low lying, with waterlogged environmental evidence indicating that both were probably enclosed by substantial hedges and set in predominantly grazed grassland, possibly rather more scrubby at Mingies Ditch than Watkins Farm.

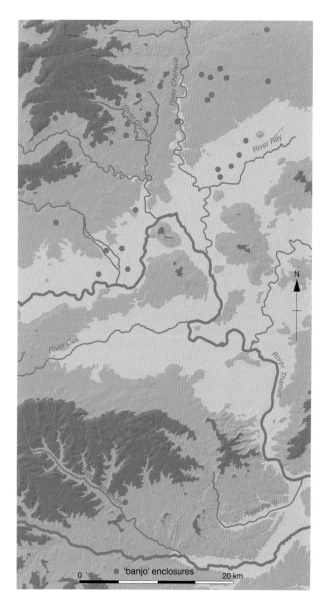

Fig. 4.20   Middle Iron Age banjo and similar enclosures in the Upper Thames Valley

Groundwell Farm

'banjo' enclosures

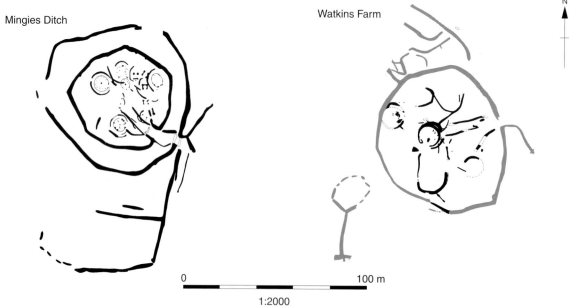

Mingies Ditch

Watkins Farm

0   100 m

1:2000

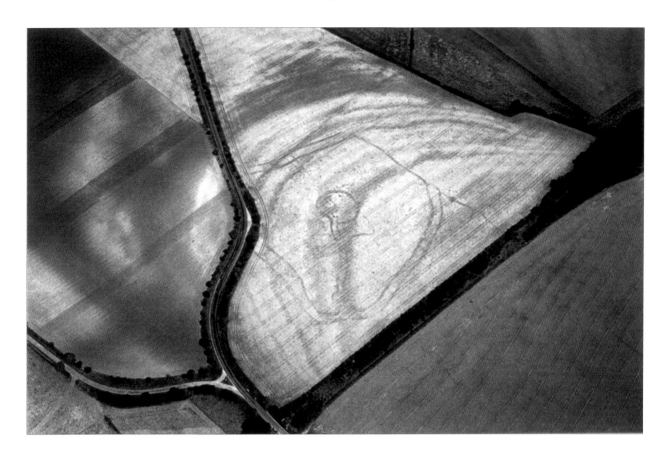

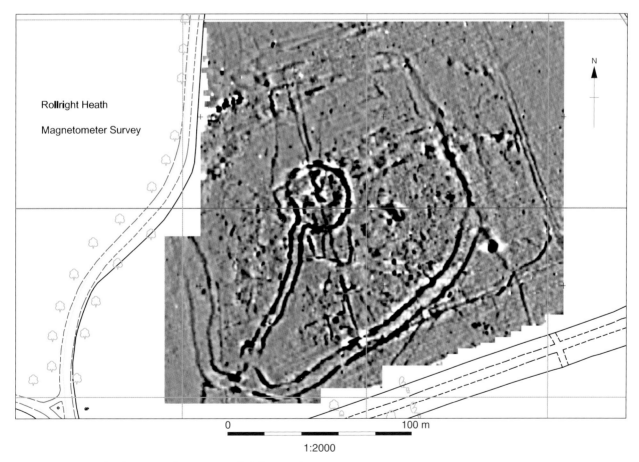

Rollright Heath

Magnetometer Survey

N

0   100 m

1:2000

Fig. 4.21   Complex banjo enclosure at Rollright Heath

This contrasts markedly with the arable and mixed farming environment on the higher gravel terrace nearby.

Mingies Ditch and Watkins Farm are part of a group of five enclosed settlements, at least two of which were banjo enclosures, on the first gravel terrace and floodplain in the lower Windrush Valley. As a group they are of particular interest for their spatial, economic and social relationships in the context of the very different ring of long-lived pit cluster sites surrounding an earlier prehistoric ceremonial and funerary complex on the higher, second gravel terrace at Stanton Harcourt (see above and discussion Chapter 10).

At Groundwell West, close to the Groundwell Farm enclosure, an unenclosed early to middle Iron Age settlement, probably including at least two houses, was superseded by a middle Iron Age enclosure with a funnel entrance and a single roundhouse, which was in turn replaced by a D-shaped enclosure in the later Iron Age (Walker *et al.* 2001). There were rows of pits along the inside of the earlier enclosure ditch but in the later enclosure pits were positioned outside it. This sequence of unenclosed to enclosed reflects an apparently widespread move to enclosures in the later Iron Age at a number of sites in the region (see Chapter 7).

On the north-eastern outskirts of Oxford, on the Corallian hills at Barton, a substantial ditch with an entrance gateway may represent an enclosed settlement of middle Iron Age origin with evidence of occupation into the early Roman period (Moore 2005). The ditch would have been over 2 m deep prior to truncation of the site and the entrance was marked by large gate-postholes. Some distance from the gate, on the same side as the postholes, was a group of pits. In the light of entrances through middle Iron Age boundary complexes at Slade Farm, Bicester and Latton Lands, where a quite elaborate gateway structure was found (Ellis *et al.* 2000; Powell *et al.* forthcoming), it is possible that the Barton site was no more than an area of occupation next to an entrance through a linear boundary, but the probable size of the Barton ditch makes it more likely that it was an enclosed settlement.

This illustrates a more general difficulty, especially with pipeline excavations, of characterising settlements associated with substantial ditches where the full layout of the ditches is not revealed by excavation and has not been clarified by air photography or geophysics as was done at Groundwell Farm. Other examples include middle Iron Age settlements near Radley (Cotswold Archaeology 2004); on the Chalgrove to Ilsley pipeline near Berwick Salome (Wilson and Cater 2005); at the Rutherford Appleton Laboratory, Chilton (Moore 2004), and a potential late Iron Age one on the Cleeve to Didcot pipeline at Moulsford (Ford 1990, 27-30).

A number of the much commoner late prehistoric enclosures on the Cotswolds have been investigated, but this has largely been restricted to relatively small simple enclosures and most of the excavations were small-scale, providing only an incomplete picture. In several cases, however, excavation was usefully combined with geophysics, greatly enhancing what is discernible from cropmarks.

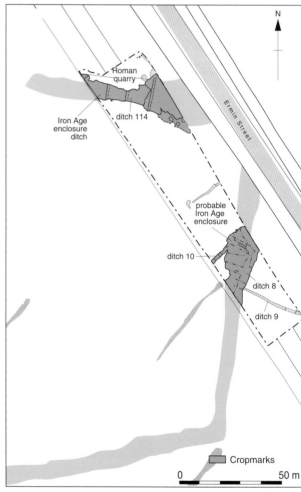

Fig. 4.22 Iron Age enclosures in the Upper Thames Valley: (above) *Preston;* (below) *Duntisbourne*

124

A number of middle and late Iron Age enclosures were found along the new A419/A417, notably a hexagonal site at Preston radiocarbon dated to the 4th to 3rd centuries cal BC (Mudd *et al.* 1999, 42-55). The enclosure had a central (unexcavated) circular ditched feature and apparently sparse internal occupation in the 25% of the site exposed (Fig. 4.22). Its role is rather enigmatic. Other subrectangular enclosed settlements on the Cotswolds, such as those at Guiting Power and Rollright had quite extensive areas of external pits (Saville 1979; Lambrick 1988), but in other cases there were few substantial pits and finds were generally sparse (Marshall 1990; 1991; 1995; Cook and Hayden 2000). Some of these middle to late Iron Age subrectangular enclosures appear to have been characterised by single large pits sited in one corner of the enclosure, referred to by Marshall as 'silos' and thought to represent a main store for seed grain. Some enclosures also appear to have had sudivisions or other arrangements of organising space, as at the Bowsings, where Marshall (2001) noted a possible trackway or other internal subdivision separating the northern and southern parts of the enclosure, with pits and domestic activity concentrated in the northern half. Environmental sampling has generally been limited or unrewarding, providing little detailed indication of the economic background of these settlements, which in itself may indicate something about the intensity of occupation. Where evidence is available it mostly suggests very typical mixed farming (eg Lambrick 1988).

The morphology of these enclosures is variable and there may be some chronological and other trends, such as the apparently late date of a group of trapezoidal enclosures in the northern Cotswolds noted by Marshall. There also seem to be distinct patterns in the relationship between different forms of enclosed settlement with soil type and topography (Featherstone and Bewley, 2000; Moore 2006; Lang pers. comm.). This may also be the case on the Berkshire Downs (Winton 2004), but so far insufficient excavation has been carried out to establish how this might relate to differences in social relationships or economic activity.

Overall, although there is a growing body of evidence relating to later prehistoric enclosures on the Cotswolds, the scale of most investigations has been limited, with a consequent lack of clarity about the organisation of domestic and other activities within or outside the enclosures. This and the relative dearth of finds and environmental data makes it difficult to define wider social and economic trends, patterns and relationships. An interesting, but largely unexplained phenomenon is the apparent clustering of banjo enclosures in the eastern Cotswolds, also noticeable on a smaller scale for the area of the Berkshire Downs south of Segsbury and a yet smaller group of banjos and related types of enclosure around Stanton Harcourt. As noted in relation to Rollright (Lambrick 1988) and subsequently (Moore 2006; Lang pers. comm.),

the more data recovered, the more the complexities of chronology and socio-economic activity increase, challenging the basis on which neat models can be constructed from the two dimensional evidence of cropmark analysis.

There are several cases where pre-existing early or middle Iron Age open settlements continued more or less unchanged well into the later Iron Age, but at others larger enclosed elements were added, replacing or enclosing existing elements, or were established on adjacent land. The chronology of these changes varies within the middle to late Iron Age, or even into the early Roman period, and it is difficult to date them (especially pre- or post-Roman conquest). The mundane character of most of the pottery and the dearth of closely datable artefacts makes the task no easier. A general characteristic of these enclosures is their relatively small size, seldom more than 30 m across, which, coupled with the relative poverty of domestic material, suggests that they were simple family farms – and not all need have been occupied.

At Latton Lands the linear boundary settlement (see above) continued in use, though the focus shifted to a particular area where a gateway interrupted the boundary. Immediately adjacent to the gate a ring gully marked a probable new house site within a pre-existing enclosure complex, and two enclosures were remodelled on the south side, one associated with a remarkable series of ritual burials (see Chapter 8).

At Cotswold Community a small rectangular enclosure defined by a narrow gully containing only slight traces of middle Iron Age occupation was redefined as the focus of more intense occupation as a small farm in the late Iron Age. This was modified with multiple recutting of ditches and was again substantially remodelled at least twice in the Roman period, eventually ending up with masonry footed buildings, a corndrier and small cemetery.

Half a kilometre to the west of the middle to late Iron Age house pen and paddock settlement and Roman settlement and field system at Totterdown Lane, the scattered early Iron Age settlement and animal stockade was succeeded at Horcott by a long middle Iron Age boundary ditch with a rectangular enclosure at the end of it containing pits, four-posters and a possible roundhouse (Fig. 4.23; Lamdin-Whymark *et al.* 2007).

At Finmere, on the lowest slopes of the Cotswold dip slope north of Bicester, a middle Iron Age enclosure with a north-east facing entrance succeeded a linear house, pen and paddock type settlement (Fig. 4.23; Hancock *et al.* 2003). Full analysis and publication is awaited, but the interim results suggest several phases of development, and it appears the enclosure may have included a roundhouse, a four-poster and a few pits.

At Bicester Fields Farm a square ditched enclosure of *c* 0.15 ha shared its alignment with a group of rectilinear fields or paddocks defined by narrow gullies to its west, which it may have respected (Fig.

4.23; Cromarty *et al.* 1999). No internal features were definitely attributable to the initial middle to late Iron Age phase of the enclosure, though it is possible that a recut roundhouse gully could have been an original feature. The south-west side of the original enclosure was later recut and extended north-westwards to enlarge the enclosed area to approximately 0.2 ha, and on the south-west side a trapezoidal annexe of *c* 0.13 ha was added. The enlarged enclosure contained two further phases of the roundhouse gully cutting the phase 1 enclosure ditch. There was no obvious entrance for any stage of the enclosure, though various dumps of limestone in the ditches may represent infilling to create causeways. A cattle burial radiocarbon dated to 334-326 cal BC or 200 cal BC to 60 cal AD was found at the centre of the annexe, and a human burial was found 30 m south of the original enclosure in a circular pit with a small assemblage of mid-late Iron Age pottery. The corner of another enclosure lay to the north and an irregular, recut ditch roughly parallel to the western side of the annex and cutting the earlier rectilinear gullies could define the eastern side of another enclosure. It is more likely, however, to belong to a realigned system of fields and paddocks.

The Bicester site in some respects resembles the late Iron Age enclosed settlement at Barton Court

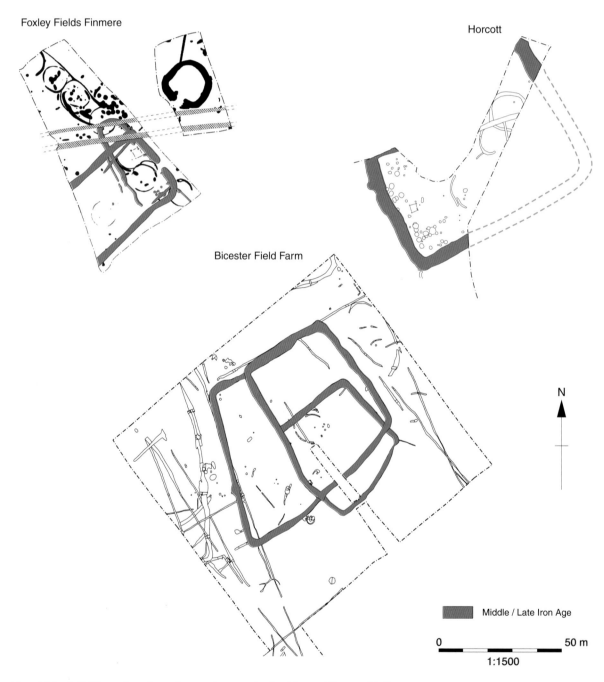

Fig. 4.23 *Middle to late Iron Age enclosures in the Upper Thames Valley*

Farm, Abingdon where a large ditch with no obvious entrance gap defined a square enclosure of *c* 0.35 ha,. This was subdivided to create a smaller sub-rectangular area of about 0.1 ha in one corner. A circular post built structure with an inhumation burial of uncertain date stood in the corner of the inner enclosure, close to the middle of the large enclosure. In the opposite corner there was part of what may have been a penannular ditch for a house and two pits which contained evidence of burning. Within the larger enclosure lay a rectangular ditched area 20 m by 14 m, with a west-facing entrance. An undated cremation burial was placed just inside it and a linear cluster of 14 pits outside. The pits were probably seed grain stores, and it was calculated that the contents of one large one would have accommodated the produce of 7.5-10 ha or more.

These examples of later Iron Age enclosed settlement seem to have been single farms, some reflecting a increased concentration of activity in a particular area succeeding dispersed clusters of middle Iron Age occupation. In other cases, like Barton Court Farm, they seem to represent new foundations, although their precursors may lie in unexplored areas away from the excavated site.

In some cases, as the hints of other enclosures at Bicester might suggest, relatively substantial enclosures may have developed as elements of larger complexes of domestic occupation and fields, making clear distinctions between 'enclosed' and 'unenclosed' settlements of dubious value. For example, at Stanton Harcourt between Linch Hill and the middle Iron Age enclosure at Watkins Farm, a small middle to late Iron Age open settlement at Ireland's Land was succeeded by or incorporated into a redefined rectilinear enclosure in the corner of what developed as a late Iron Age or early Roman field system. However, the extreme dearth of occupation debris may indicate that this was not a settlement, but rather an enclosure for managing animals (Norton 2006).

Middle to late Iron Age enclosed settlements in the Middle Thames Valley

On the gravels of the Middle Thames Valley relatively few Iron Age enclosures are known. Three small settlement enclosures less than 3 km apart have been investigated in recent years in the Slough and Eton area, one at the Eton Rowing Course and two at Cippenham, Slough. Another single enclosure was identified on the edge of the floodplain at Thames Valley Park, Reading (Allen *et al.* 2000; Ford *et al.* 2003; Barnes *et al.* 1997). All were single ditched enclosures, and all were damaged by ploughing. None contained waterlogged environmental remains, but the high water table probably prevented pit storage on all of these sites. There is some consistency in the size of these enclosures, ranging from 0.25 to 0.5 ha, and their ditches were of similar dimensions, about 1.0 to 1.5 m deep, clearly not intended primarily for defence.

The square 0.5 ha enclosure at the Eton Rowing Course occupied the edge of a dry gravel island with alluvium to the west and to the north, where there was extant river channel nearby (Fig. 4.24). The entrance was in the northern part of the east side, opening out onto dry ground. There was no gateway structure but a probable house was represented by a length of gully and an arc of shallow pits, some containing large pieces of middle Iron Age pottery. There was a six-post structure on the south side of the interior and a four-post structure on the opposite side, apparently deliberately sited on a former barrow next to the river channel. The enclosure ditch was almost completely redug in the 1st century AD, leaving little material associated with the original Iron Age occupation.

The trapezoidal enclosure at Wood Lane Cippenham occupied *c* 3.5 ha defined by a ditch with opposing 11-12 m wide entrances. No features were exposed in the interior but placed deposits recovered from the ditch included middle Iron Age pots in fresh condition and numerous bones, including some articulated cattle bones and part of an ox skull. The enclosure was recut late in the Iron Age, and the northern entrance narrowed to 2 m, while the southern entrance remained unchanged. Rectilinear paddocks were added in the late Iron Age or early Roman period. The Thames Valley Park enclosure was subrectangular and also covered 0.25 ha, again with no internal features and only a scatter of small pits nearby (Fig. 4.25).

On the south side of the Kennet Valley at Riseley a low-lying middle Iron Age curvilinear enclosure – possibly not domestic in character but connected with pottery production and iron working – was replaced by a late Iron Age, probably domestic, rectilinear enclosure about 300 m away on slightly higher ground. This area was associated with iron working, indicated by smelting and smithing slags, a hearth bottom and pieces of bog ore. The enclo-

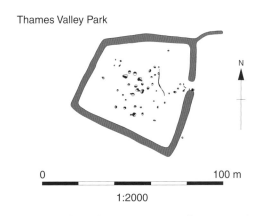

Thames Valley Park

0   100 m

1:2000

Fig. 4.25   Middle to late Iron Age settlement in the Middle Thames Valley at Thames Valley Park, Reading

Fig. 4.24 (overleaf)   Bronze Age and Middle Iron Age enclosed settlement at Eton Rowing Course

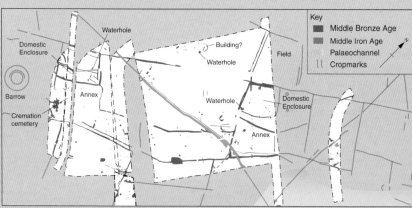

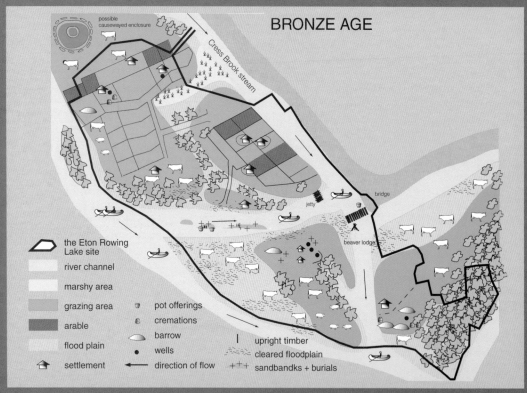

BRONZE AGE

Key
- Middle Bronze Age
- Middle Iron Age
- Palaeochannel
- Cropmarks

Waterhole
Building?
Waterhole
Field
Domestic Enclosure
Domestic Enclosure
Barrow
Annex
Waterhole
Annex
Cremation cemetery

possible causewayed enclosure
Cress Brook stream
jetty
bridge
beaver lodge

the Eton Rowing Lake site
river channel
marshy area
grazing area
arable
flood plain
settlement

pot offerings
cremations
barrow
wells
upright timber
cleared floodplain
sandbandks + burials
direction of flow

Left page

Clockwise from top left
* *Bronze Age waterhole*
* *Phase plan of excavated Bronze Age and Iron Age features*
* *The Bronze Age settlement*

Right page

Clockwise from top left
Middle Iron Age pottery from Eton
Cropmarks showing the Iron Age settlement enclosure occupying a corner of a dry gravel terrace next to a former river channel
Iron Age potin coins (105-0 BC)
Four post structure in the middle of a Bronze Age barrow
Plan of the Iron Age enclosure and contemporary features

At Eton Rowing Course in the Middle Thames Valley two areas of middle Bronze Age enclosures and fields were identified from cropmarks and the larger area was subject to substantial excavation between 1994 and 1997. The enclosures and fields together covered about 40 ha and were part of a varied and extensive exploitation of this landscape. Waterholes, pits and animal burials lay within a largely unenclosed grazing tract on one side of the former Thames channel, with flint-knapping scatters and burnt areas indicating temporary encampments on the floodplain.

The baseline boundary from which the Bronze Age field system was laid out was a straight ditch traced for 600 m running north-east across a peninsula of gravel from the River Thames to the Cress Brook, formerly a major channel of the river. The symmetrical mirror-image layout of two pairs of enclosures and associated fields is unusual. There was also some evidence of late Bronze Age occupation and, although the fields seem to have been 'abandoned' in the early Iron Age, the hedges surrounding them may have been maintained, allowing continued use of some fields while the focus of domestic activity and the management of water supplies changed, leaving little archaeological trace within that area.

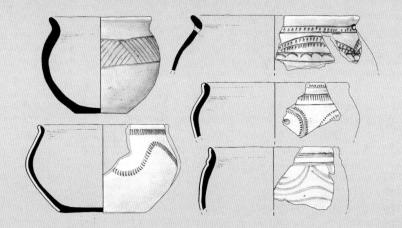

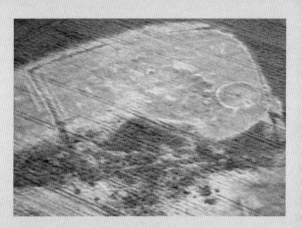

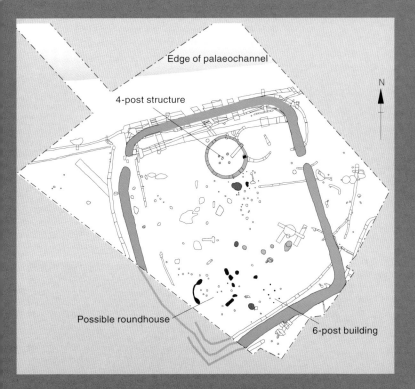

Edge of palaeochannel

4-post structure

N

Possible roundhouse

6-post building

A middle Iron Age boundary ditch respected a pre-existing middle Bronze Age field system, skirting one of a northern pair of Bronze Age enclosures. A smaller middle Iron Age ditch which ran north at right angles to this boundary had a four-post structure beside it, perhaps part of an unexcavated area of domestic occupation. The main middle Iron Age settlement on the site was focused upon the adjacent gravel island nearly 1.5 km away.

The middle Iron Age gravel island settlement lay within a 0.5 ha square enclosure occupying the edge of a dry gravel island close to an extant river channel. An east-facing entrance opened out onto dry ground. A possible roundhouse in the south-west corner of the enclosure was marked by a gully and an arc of shallow pits which contained middle Iron Age pottery. A six-post structure lay to the east of the house and a four-post structure on the opposite side of the enclosure was sited on a former barrow next to the river channel. The enclosure ditch was almost completely redug in the 1st century AD.

sure ditch was recut several times within a short period in the first half of the first century AD. Pottery imitating imported wares and the locally distinctive 'Silchester ware' suggests the influence of Silchester 9 km away, but there were no imports (Lobb and Morris 1991-3).

South-east of Silchester, on the western border of Surrey in the Blackwater Valley, investigation along a road scheme near Runfold revealed four substantial settlement enclosures dated by the pottery to the middle to late Iron Age (4th-2nd centuries BC). These include a substantial middle to late Iron Age enclosed settlement at Tongham Nurseries immediately adjacent to the river Blackwater, which appears to have formed its western boundary. The northern end of the enclosure was not exposed but a fairly modest ditch defined its southern and eastern sides, enclosing an area about 60 m wide and at least 80 m long. An 'inner' enclosure defined by a more substantial ditch was added to its eastern side away from the river. The outer enclosure contained seven houses represented by wall slots and penannular gullies ranged along the bank of the river, together with a number of four-posters. A waterhole at the end of the enclosure adjacent to the river contained a log ladder. The 'inner' enclosure contained two substantial roundhouses, which may reflect a social distinction between the occupants of the outer and inner enclosures.

At Perry Oaks/T5 a moderately substantial irregular ditched enclosure about 100 m across covering 0.95 ha with an entrance to the east was added to the early to middle Iron Age open settlement in the remains of the Bronze Age field system. It was defined by a ditch *c* 2.5 m wide and 1 m deep, with a smaller ditch across its southern side creating a subdivision of 0.23 ha. Of four penannular house gullies within the enclosed area, it is not very clear

how many were contemporary, but one which produced the latest pottery occupied a position so close to the enclosure ditch that it would have cut any internal bank, suggesting that it may have post-dated the enclosure. The extent of the excavations at Perry Oaks/T5 demonstrate that this enclosure is only the best defined of several irregular enclosed paddocks that succeeded the open middle Iron Age settlement of smaller pens and paddocks. As such it again blurs any clear distinction between 'enclosed' and 'unenclosed' settlement.

A similar sequence is apparent at Thorpe Lea Nurseries where two early to middle Iron Age settlements were characterised by scatters of pits, postholes and gullies. One of the settlement clusters was enclosed by an irregular group of ditches pre-dating a more definite late Iron Age or early Roman enclosure, together with a trackway and other boundaries which superseded it whilst partly retaining an earlier Bronze Age field system. The Roman layout developed from the western Iron Age settlement area and involved further ditch rearrangements. At other sites, such as Fairylands, Laleham there is evidence of middle to late Iron Age and later settlement with ditches, but the excavated area was too limited to determine the precise form of the settlement.

DISCUSSION

It is increasingly clear that the general distinction between 'open' and 'enclosed' forms of settlement and typological distinctions of enclosure shapes encompass such a degree of variation that the distinction is as likely to frustrate as to aid analysis. Within the range of bounded space in and around settlements noted above we can see significant variety in whether or not houses were

Fig. 4.26   Enclosed or unenclosed? This artist's impression of a house within its own enclosure depicts part of the middle Iron Age open settlement at Claydon Pike (see Figure 3.20, bottom right of plan)

enclosed and within what size of area; whether pits and four-posters were inside or outside (or both); whether animals are likely to have been corralled within such enclosures or outside them in separate areas; whether water supply was inside or outside; and whether they were related to other surrounding areas of sub-divided or enclosed land (Fig. 4.26).

Where ditched boundaries and other settlement divisions were located suggests that space was segregated in diverse ways between living areas, storage of agricultural produce, management of animals, access to water and disposal of waste – and this seems to apply to both 'enclosed' and 'unenclosed' settlements. Instead of pre-judging how settlements should be categorised on simple morphological grounds it thus seems more profitable (though beyond the scope of this review) to look at which elements of settlements were enclosed or separated by boundaries, what form such boundaries took and how impressive they might have been. While the labour of creating a substantial ditched boundary may be some measure of its social significance, the social strength of bounded spaces need not have been expressed only by ditches.

Whether settlements were enclosed or not was probably less socially significant than whether they represented single or multiple households. Likewise, the longevity of a settlement and its rootedness in land rights and traditions may have been as or more important than Hingley's (1984) social modes of production in determining how space needed to be defined and managed. Additional to these issues are a range of other practical as well as symbolic factors that would have determined the form of settlements.

Although social status may have been important, it is seldom overtly evident from the morphology of ordinary farming settlements alone. There can be quite marked differences in material culture between otherwise similar settlements, like the strikingly different quality of the pottery at Mingies Ditch and Watkins Farm. In Chapter 9 we will come back to the issue of status, settlement and community in the context of major midden sites and fortified enclosures, but it is worth noting here that their role as settlements seems to be one of their least distinctive characteristics, and this is best seen within the context of their other communal roles. In the meantime we will turn to look at the details of day-to-day life.

Chapter 5 – Hearth and home: buildings and domestic culture

In this chapter we look first at the evidence for the buildings in which people lived and worked, how they were used and how they reflect abstract aspects of domestic life. We then consider the evidence of family and personal life – health, food preparation, cooking and eating, personal appearance, dress and ornaments and recreation.

HOUSE ARCHITECTURE AND USAGE

Common to all parts of Britain in late prehistory, the vast majority of structures recognised as houses in the Thames Valley were more or less circular, though an increasing number of alternative structural forms are being identified (Fig 5.1). Roundhouses were built of timber, straw, daub and turf, even on the Cotswolds where limestone for dry stone walling was used for other structures but seldom for houses. A range of different types of roundhouse have been distinguished in terms of layout and construction, size, presence or absence of porches, internal facilities, orientation and other observable design elements. Some of this apparent variation results from survival of evidence and confidence of interpretation rather than necessarily reflecting the original intentions of the builders.

During the past 20 years there has been much debate about how the design and use of houses reflected not only practical considerations of daily living, but also how these may have been structured within a range of cosmological and social concepts. These ideas have usefully moved interpretation forwards from the largely functional and environmental factors recognised in the 1980s (eg Allen *et al.* 1984), but to some extent, have also left them behind. In emphasising cosmological interpretations to the virtual exclusion of practical and environmental considerations, debate in the 1990s has effectively replaced one limited set of interpretative constructs with another, both failing to recognise that how people live in their houses has always been a mixture of practical needs, social norms, personal relationships and cosmological outlook. The extent to which these are an overt or almost subliminal part of daily life can vary and change through time, and one-dimensional static models are seldom helpful, often relying too much on selective evidence. Recently this has been discussed by Rachel Pope (2007) in a critique of the theoretical and evidential limits of cosmological models as an adequate basis for the interpretation of the design and use of domestic space.

Methods of Construction

From what is known of available technology, the basic construction methods available to build houses remained much the same throughout later prehistory, but there were changes in their usage.

Post-rings

From the middle to late Bronze Age to the late Iron Age the use of rings of posts as the main structural framework was the norm. The size and layout of buildings varied considerably but the basic structural principles were simple enough, reliant on a continuous ring-beam of solid timber or of woven rods to prevent the main structural supports from splaying outwards. Stability against sideways twisting movement was reinforced by the solid wall to which the outer ends of the rafters were anchored.

Within these basic principles considerable variation in the form and size of buildings could be achieved, a clue to their form being the position of the door. Often represented by a pairing of large postholes on the easterly to southerly side of a post-ring, doorways were set either within the ring of posts or as an additional pair of posts set outside the main ring, indicating a 'porch' or 'vestibule' (see below).

Buildings constructed with close-set posts, stake rings and wall trenches

Some large diameter early and middle Iron Age roundhouses were built of close-set posts or planks or posts set in continuous wall trenches. These include an impressive early Iron Age circular building constructed with a double ring of close-set posts at Dunston Park and two substantial middle Iron Age buildings with wall slots at Groundwell Farm (Fitzpatrick *et al.* 1995, 72-4, figs 35, 36; Gingell 1982). To these might be added the middle Iron Age 'stake' ring structure at Frilford, where a 9.6 m diameter ring of small postholes with a wide post-built entrance was found beneath the Romano-Celtic temple. Harding (1987, 5-9, fig 3) concluded that the diameter was too large to have supported a roof on the basis that Reynolds (not referenced) had found experimentally that stake rings of more than 7.5 m could not support the roof structure. At Mingies Ditch, however, there is good evidence that Reynolds' comments might only apply to the particular combinations of stake sizes and roofing materials used in his experiments, and would not

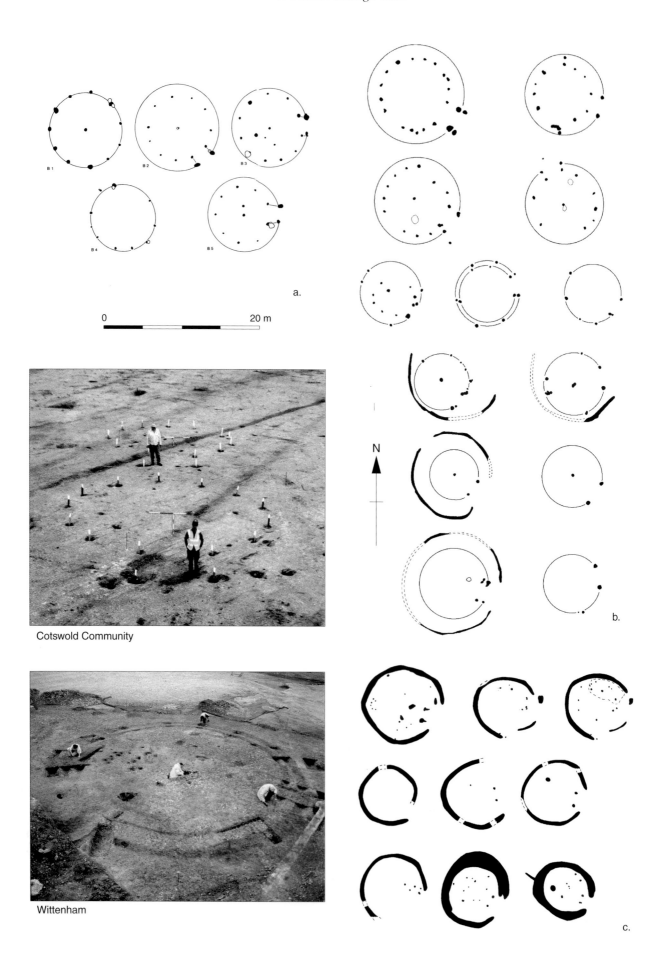

a.

0   20 m

Cotswold Community

N

Wittenham

b.

c.

apply if the 'stakes' were actually small posts, as Harding's account of the Frilford structure suggests.

By the middle Iron Age, and possibly before, it was realised that structurally sound buildings could be built with lighter materials requiring fewer posts than the standard post-ring structures. Posts were still needed for the door, but walls could be made from a closely spaced ring of stakes woven with horizontal rods and stiffened with daub without relying on a full ring of posts to provide the principal load-bearing support. Posts were often still used at points within the wall circuit, but they seem to have been used more selectively, perhaps placed at particular points where additional load-bearing was needed or for other, non-structural reasons.

This type of construction was recognised at Mingies Ditch (Allen and Robinson 1993, 54-9 Building 5) where an 8.4 m diameter building, including hearth and other typical characteristics of an Iron Age roundhouse, was excavated (Fig. 5.2). This type of construction is also suggested for a number of roundhouses where 'ring-grooves' consisting of narrow, often shallow, steep sided slots marking the wall line of the building are thought to have contained close-set vertical planking or poles. Some may actually be closely spaced stakeholes that have coalesced into a narrow gully through post depositional erosion (cf Lambrick and Robinson 1979, 12, fig. 4; Allen and Robinson 1993, 54-9, fig. 26). The outer wall of Structure 15 at Claydon Pike (Miles *et al.* 2007, 63) may reflect this type of construction, as might the narrow curving slots inside roundhouse gullies in Trench 19, Hill Farm, Little Wittenham (Allen *et al.* forthcoming b) and Park Farm Binfield (Roberts 1995, 100 and fig. 50), both tentatively dated to the middle to late Iron Age. At Ashford Prison, Surrey several middle to late Iron Age penannular gullies suggesting the positions of roundhouses had curved secondary gullies inside them, which may similarly indicate the positions of the walls. There are other good middle to late Iron Age examples at Tongham Nurseries and at Perry Oaks/T5 (Framework Archaeology 2006, 176-91).

Walling materials: wattle-and-daub, turf and other mass walling

It is generally assumed that wattle and daub was the standard material used to form the walls of Iron Age houses, though it is extremely rare to find any direct evidence, either *in situ* or as panels that might have come from a building. Unfired daub would generally have disintegrated once left exposed to the elements. On the other hand, partly fired fragments of daub with impressions of woven 'sails' and 'wattles' are quite common on Iron Age

settlements. Some may have come from burnt buildings but other sources are also possible, including clay ovens (eg Lambrick and Allen 2004/5, 386). Analysis of 'slag' at Segsbury and elsewhere has led Salter to suggest that some material recorded as 'slag' may in fact be daub accidentally heated to the point of semi-vitrification (Lock and Gosden 2005, 123).

As an alternative to post- or stake-ring houses with wattle and daub infill, some houses had walls substantially built of turves or other earth-based mass walling, such as cob or witchet. Mass walling was probably used in conjunction with a basic framework of posts or stakes, and indeed could account for somewhat irregular arrangements of posts which, apart from the door posts, were largely incidental to the structural integrity of the building. Because mass walling on level ground need not disturb even the topsoil, let alone the subsoil, it is rare to find direct evidence of it in the Thames Valley.

The existence of Iron Age houses with mass walling was initially inferred from evidence of turf stripping in the one of the floodplain settlements at Farmoor (Lambrick and Robinson 1979, 25-7), though very difficult salvage conditions prevented adequate investigation of actual house sites. Good evidence of mass walling was recovered at Mingies Ditch, where there had been just sufficient alluviation to ensure preservation of floor levels (Fig. 5.2). The floors, in addition to irregular rings of posts, indicated the position of wall lines. The walls were poorly preserved, and if made from turf would in any case be difficult to distinguish from the natural soil, but it was noted that spreads of clay loam and gravel overlying several of the house sites could have been the remains of disintegrated turf or cob walls (Allen *et al.* 1984, 94). On other sites remains of walling may be represented as soil spreads or daub in hollows and surrounding gullies.

Floors and external surfaces

Evidence from a small number of sites with surviving roundhouse floors indicates that they were often simply trodden earth mixed with occupation debris. There is clear evidence from Mingies Ditch, however, of gravel being used as a base for floors, perhaps to fill hollows and provide a porous surface (Allen and Robinson 1993, 43-49, figs 19-23 and pl. 13 and 14). At Farmoor there was evidence that a layer of cobbles had been removed from the interior of a house sited on the low-lying floodplain in Enclosure III. Here there was also *in situ* evidence that the original ground surface had been stripped from the house enclosure, as well as for raised gravel walkways leading to it. These features suggest an attempt to minimise problems of trampled mud creating an impervious floor that

Fig. 5.1 (opposite)   Houses in the Thames Valley: outline plans: a) late Bronze Age, Reading Business Park; b) early to middle Iron Age, Gravelly Guy; c) middle Iron Age, Claydon Pike

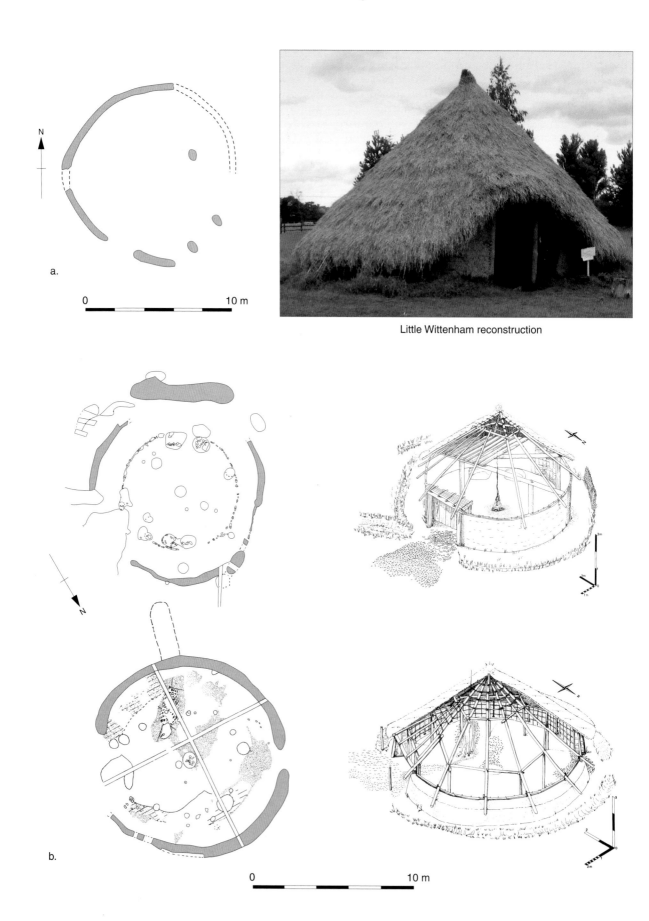

Little Wittenham reconstruction

Fig. 5.2   Middle Iron Age stake-wall, ring-groove and mass wall roundhouses a) Claydon Pike; b) Mingies Ditch

136

would not drain after seasonal floods (Lambrick and Robinson 1979, 25, figs 14 and 15). There is also evidence from other low-lying sites, such as Claydon Pike and Port Meadow, of the incorporation into floors of burnt and unburnt limestone, possibly deliberately spread as cobbled surfaces (Miles *et al.* 2007, 64; Anon 1946-7, 163). The entrance of a probable house at Milton Common had a compacted cobbled entrance between the terminals of the enclosing gully (Rowley 1973, 31 and fig. 3).

At Castle Hill, Little Wittenham the corner of a packed chalk floor bounded by postholes, interpreted as a rectangular building (Rhodes 1948), has been recently re-examined. The chalk and pebble surface was as Rhodes described it, stratified within an early Iron Age midden deposit, but no further trace of posts or other wall supports was found to confirm the existence of a building, and it is suspected that it represents a platform built within the midden rather than a domestic building (Allen *et al.* forthcoming b). Other sites with evidence of cobbled surfaces, though not clearly within a building, have been recorded at Hatford and at Abingdon Vineyard (Bourn 2000; Allen pers. comm.).

Less common is evidence that hard paved floors were sometimes created by the simple expedient of removing soil to expose a level surface of natural bedrock – of gravel, sand or limestone. This includes examples of 'hearths' represented only by areas of burnt subsoil within buildings and a few instances of apparently compacted subsoil or patches of cobbling as at Langford Down (Williams 1947).

Roofing materials

There is no direct evidence for any of a wide variety of materials appropriate for roofing, but the most likely materials would be coppice grown poles for rafters, bound together by successive horizontal rings made from thin poles, rods, withies or bound ropes of bramble, clematis or other materials, and straw, reeds, rushes, brushwood or other plant material (less likely turf) for a waterproof covering. Straw roofing seems most probable where it was available since the naturally tall growing varieties of cereals in cultivation in later prehistory are good for thatching, and there is recurrent evidence that cereals were cut low on the straw (Moffet 2004, 445; see below Chapter 7). It has been suggested that heavy weights were used to anchor roofing materials rather than, or additional to, the common interpretation of clay weights as warp-weighted loomweights. This might be the case, but these objects have not been found particularly concentrated in or regularly distributed round the ditches and gullies surrounding houses as might be expected, and in general the distribution of loomweights (allowing for broken ones being reused as pot-boilers) is more consistent with their traditional interpretation reflecting domestic crafts, or as 'oven bricks' (see below).

Changes in construction methods

The construction techniques for late prehistoric buildings changed over time. During the middle to late Bronze Age and early Iron Age there seems to have been a strong preference for forms largely reliant on earth-fast posts. In the middle to late Iron Age, preferences shifted to construction techniques for which such posts were less critical to the structure, except at doorways. This was apparently not the result of any particular technological innovation as all the basic building materials and construction techniques had been used for a long time. In many cases only partial rings of posts survive for middle to late Bronze Age and early Iron Age sites (eg Moore and Jennings 1992, 14-27; Hey *et al.* forthcoming) and, although by the middle Iron Age a shift away from post-ring structures is clear, at sites like Gravelly Guy (Fig. 5.3) and Yarnton, where early and middle Iron Age houses were identified, and Mingies Ditch, where the evidence was especially well preserved, there is considerable variation in apparently broadly contemporary houses. The plans and construction details indicate no clear division between buildings reliant on earth-fast post-rings and those that were not. Details of such variation are observable in the five well-preserved houses at Mingies Ditch, where it is also instructive to consider what evidence would survive if the site had been truncated.

In essence, it is clear that earth-fast posts, which on truncated sites may be the only surviving evidence of roundhouses, were only ever one component of any building structure. The observed variability suggests that there may never have been a distinct template for either post-ring or non post-ring 'types' of construction. Where not attributable to later truncation, the presence or absence of postholes is more likely to reflect choices about whether posts were desired or could be dispensed with as part of an integrated structural concept. While it might be the case that it was only gradually realised that the traditional ring of earth-fast posts was not structurally indispensable, it is as or more likely that the changes in construction methods were a matter of stylistic taste, fashion or individual preference.

Design, size, layout and facilities of roundhouses

Doorways, porches and vestibules

In considering the design and use of late prehistoric buildings, it is appropriate to start with the entrances, not just because they were the natural way in, but also because archaeological recognition of this element is crucial to the identification and interpretation of such buildings and their practical and social role. The outward and inner appearance of the main entrances to houses is very commonly a means of expressing something of the occupants' outlook on the world and their place in society.

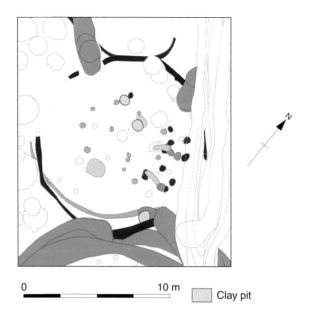

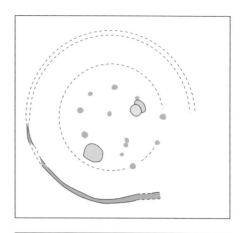

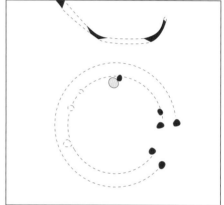

0   10 m   ▨ Clay pit

Fig. 5.3   Sequence of House E at Gravelly Guy: the initial post-ring construction was succeeded by three rebuilds with fewer posts

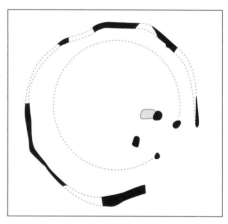

Most recognisable late prehistoric roundhouses had doorways marked by pairs of often larger than average postholes, sometimes slightly wider- or narrower-spaced than others in a post-ring, often recut, and typically (but certainly not always) oriented so that the doorway would face in a broadly easterly to southerly direction. Whether associated with obvious rings of postholes or less direct evidence of superstructure, such posthole pairs are often the most consistent and distinctive evidence of a roundhouse site. From the middle Iron Age onwards, when deeply set earth-fast posts ceased to be such a common feature of house construction, an appropriately spaced and oriented pair of postholes, together with a range of other features – typically a concentric drainage gully – are often virtually the only surviving evidence of a house.

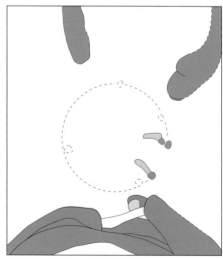

The spacing of door posts, typically falling within a range of 1.4 m to 2.8 m apart (Moore and Jennings 1992, 19, 35; Brossler *et al.* 2004, 20; Lambrick and Allen 2004, 132-3) is distinctly wider than typical modern front doors, or indeed the doorways of most ordinary Roman and medieval buildings. It is usually assumed that doorways were low, and it is worth noting that there may have been some advantage in their width to let more early morning light into the building (see below). Various characteristics of the doorway postholes suggest that entrances to houses were emphasised to a greater extent than a purely functional arrangement would require. They were not only often significantly larger (which may have been structurally necessary to hold a wide door) but were also often doubled, and such doubling cannot always be dismissed as replacement of original door posts.

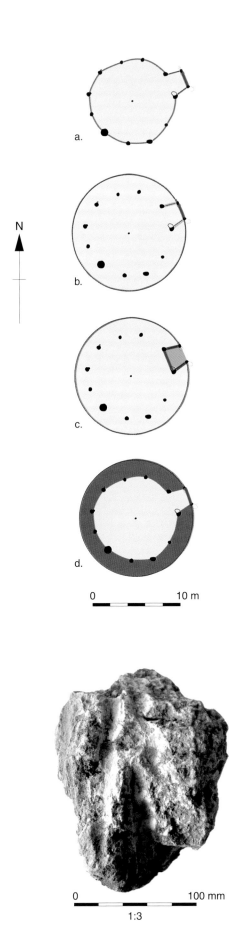

a.

b.

c.

d.

0   10 m

0   100 mm

1:3

There is also evidence from the middle Bronze Age onwards that the entrances of some round-house were characterised by external 'porches' or internal 'vestibules.' It is not always obvious whether such structures were internal or external as plough-truncated sites often lack direct evidence for the position or size of external walls. There would have been substantial variation between turf or other mass constructed walls and wattle and daub walls. On this basis post-rings with apparent 'porch' structures protruding from them can be interpreted in different ways, the post-ring either representing the wall of the building with a protruding porch, or an internal structure leaving an aisle (or possibly space for a thick mass wall) but no external porch. Interpretations tend to be subjective but other evidence, such as the depth of the 'porch' structure or the position of surrounding drainage gullies, can be useful (Fig. 5.4).

Despite these difficulties there is evidence that some large roundhouses did have external porches, other doorway structures or inner vestibules (Fig. 5.5). Circular buildings at Home Farm Laleham (late Bronze Age); Dunston Park (earliest Iron Age); Crickley Hill (early Iron Age); Gravelly Guy Building C (early Iron Age); City Farm Hanborough (early Iron Age); Groundwell Farm (middle Iron Age) and Frilford (middle Iron Age) exemplify this type of structure, all with large (typically 8.5-10 m) diameter post-rings, close-set posts or wall slots (Hayman forthcoming; Fitzpatrick 73-4 figs 35, 36; Dixon 1973,56-9; Lambrick and Allen 2004 135, figs 1.23, 3.12; Harding 1972 pl 26; Gingell 1982; Harding 1987, 5-8 fig. 3).

The layout of house entrances – double door posts, inner vestibules and porches – are sometimes, but not always, neatly rectangular. The series of late Bronze Age houses at Reading Business Park/Green Park had variable entrances, some with narrow doorways under 1.5 m wide, others marked by small posts and porches or vestibules, sometimes positioned slightly askew to the inner post-ring (Fig. 5.1). Entrances were either parallel sided or tapered outwards. The middle to late Bronze Age house at Weir Bank Stud Farm, Bray also had an entrance structure that tapered outwards. By contrast, early and middle Iron Age houses seldom had doorways less than 2 m wide, or outer door posts smaller than inner posts. Iron Age doorways and entrance porches or vestibules were usually parallel sided or splayed outwards, and generally not skewed.

Although this possible chronological change in the layout of entrances does not apply to all later

Fig. 5.4 Alternative interpretations of Building 86 at Reading Business Park a) single cell dwelling with outer porch; b) aisled interior inner vestibule; c) aisled interior external porch or entrance way; d) single cell dwelling with thick turf wall and covered entrance way. Photograph: Wall daub showing wattle impressions, Castle Hill, Little Wittenham

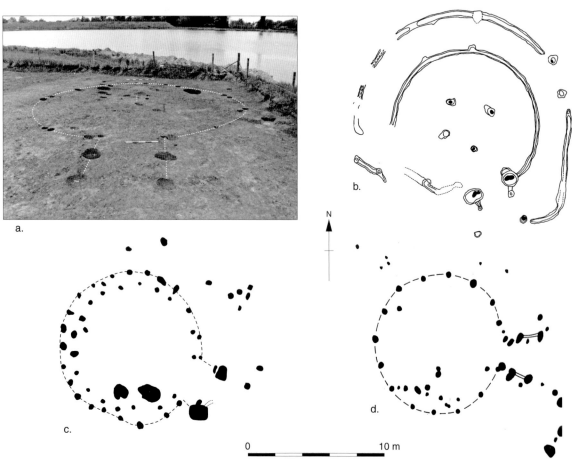

prehistoric houses, it may nevertheless indicate a subtle but important change in social interaction. The middle to late Bronze Age houses with distinctly narrow, skewed and/or outwardly tapering entrances would have had doorways restrictive from the outside but opening up inside, perhaps acting as an indication of the privacy of interior space as compared with the exterior world. The more consistently wide doorways and common outward splay and larger posts forming the entrances of Iron Age houses might have had structural benefits, but they may also have conveyed status or social display, with the splay suggesting a gathering of attention inwards from the outer world, while also tending to provide light to a more private interior. Whether such emphases would have seemed welcoming or forbidding might have depended on the relative status of inhabitant and visitor.

The entrances to houses also varied in appearance depending on the size and number of postholes. Differences in the size, shape and height of posts could have conveyed different impressions of the role and status of the house and its inhabitants within the wider community. Some large houses had especially large post pits at their entrances and it is conceivable that these outermost posts were free standing. More generally, door posts could have been carved or painted or may have projected above the roof line. Entrances might also have been emphasised by decorated gables or lintels. Although evidence of the actual appearance of doorway structures does not survive the evidence that they were emphasised suggests that they could have been used to reflect important social distinctions within communities.

Subsidiary entrances

Evidence from a number of sites indicates that some houses had back or side doors as well as the more conspicuous 'front' entrances. Most examples are indicated by the layout of surrounding gullies or wall trenches, and occasionally additional door post structures, and most are middle Iron Age. A possible middle Bronze Age example at Eight Acre Field, Radley is worth noting but is not altogether convincing (Mudd 1995, 23-5 fig. 4). House 3 at Mingies Ditch had an area of trodden gravel floor that spread through an apparent gap in the mass wall of the house opposite a gap in the surrounding gully. At Claydon Pike House 17a appears to have a second doorway to the rear, aligned on a gap in the surrounding drainage gully (Miles *et al.* 2007, 61-4). At Gravelly Guy, a penannular gully enclosing a probable house (enclosure A1, house Y) had a gap opposing the main entrance, and another (enclosure A2, house E) had a clear pathway respected by

other features leading to the rear side of a penannular enclosure containing a house (Lambrick and Allen 2004, 131-44).

The stake-walled structure at Frilford (which may not have been a domestic house even if it is accepted as a building) appears to have had an especially wide (2 m) porched entrance with gaps in the close-set ring of small posts on one if not both sides, as if leaving two narrow entrances similar to the large early Iron Age house at Pimperne, Dorset (Harding *et al.* 1993). At Groundwell Farm, Building 2 was a complex structure with an inner and outer wall slot, the inner one with a clear single doorway marked by substantial posts, but the outer circuit, conceivably unroofed, with one entrance corresponding with the inner one but another to one side (Gingell 1982). In the Middle Thames Valley there is less direct structural evidence of subsidiary doorways, but they have been inferred for a number of buildings, including Penannular Gully 3 at Perry Oaks/T5 (Framework Archaeology 2006, 186-7).

Evidence for subsidiary doorways often relies on exceptional preservation as at Mingies Ditch, ill-defined posthole arrangements as at Claydon Pike, or tenuous evidence from the position of other features as at Gravelly Guy (Fig. 5.1). The existence of subsidiary doorways is, therefore, often difficult to substantiate and they may have been much commoner than the recorded examples suggest. One advantage of a back door would be, as it is today, the convenience of allowing movement between the building and separate activity areas. At Gravelly Guy these may have been activities related to arable farming or animal husbandry. Subsidiary entrances would also have provided additional daylight (see below), but in terms of being weatherproof, there may have been disadvantages. The provision of a second access point and separate source of daylight on the opposite side of the building would also have made a substantial difference to the natural dynamics of movement through and within the house and the use of internal space that has seldom been considered in the socio-cosmological models recently devised for organisation of space within roundhouses.

Interior layout and space

Whether or not they also had outer aisles, most late prehistoric roundhouses had core open circular spaces that were quite spacious, with diameters of about 7.5 m to 8.5 m, giving floor areas of 44 m^2 to 58 m^2. Some were as small as 5 m – 6 m, with floor areas down to about 20 m^2. Others were substantially larger, with inner diameters of 9 m or 10 m (occasionally larger) increasing the range of inner floor areas in some cases to over 80 m^2. As we have seen, these include a number of large houses with

Fig. 5.5 (opposite)   Large roundhouses with porches: (top) *reconstruction; a) Home Farm, Laleham; b) Groundwell Farm; c) Dunston Park; d) Cassington*

clear outer porches, but several others had less elaborate entrances, including two or three simple, unaisled and apparently unporched roundhouses probably dating to the middle Iron Age at Gravelly Guy (Lambrick and Allen 2004 138-9, table 3.11 and fig. 3.14, buildings F, K and T).

Orientation, order and use: symbolic and practical

General orientation

Although there are exceptions, the vast majority of main doorways of houses in the Thames Valley were oriented between north-east and south, especially broadly easterly, in common with late prehistoric houses throughout Britain (Oswald 1997). A number of explanations for the very strong eastward orientation of late prehistoric round-houses have been proposed. One prevalent in the 1970s was that this orientation ensures that build-ings had their doors facing the least windy quarter, and hence least draughts and driving rain. This correlates well with modern weather patterns for the region (Guilbert 1975; Lambrick 1978). However, Oswald (1997, 89-90) raised a number of objections, including the lack of ethnographic paral-lels for the orientation of houses linked to environ-mental conditions, and this included the notion that house orientation was related to making the most of the morning light (Hingley and Miles 1984). Oswald's view reflected a recognition that a complex range of cosmological, social and spiritual concepts and practice are likely to have been impor-tant influences in determining the social norms for domestic architecture. These ideas suggest that late prehistoric houses were constructed to face the east for symbolic and spiritual reasons, making the connection between sunrise, awakening and life and reflecting broader integration between the ordering of architectural space with reference to symbolism of the human body and the cosmos, including the agricultural cycle (Parker-Pearson and Richards 1994 47-54; Parker-Pearson 1996; Oswald 1997).

Brück (1999) has been sceptical of relatively static cosmological models, emphasising the need to recognise that the way a house is used can change over its 'lifecycle' with the changing personal and social circumstances of its inhabitants, and she raised the possibility that houses might have been coterminous with the lives of their inhabitants. More recently Pope (2007) has been even more trenchant in her criticism of the theoretical, method-ological and evidential basis on which the cosmo-logical models have been developed as being too simplistic in ignoring the role that environmental and topographical factors might have played. She noted that Oswald had found almost no preference for eastward-facing houses in Wales, and from her own work on houses in northern Britain, suggests that preferred orientations between east and south-

east would have achieved an optimum balance between shelter from prevailing weather and morning light that may even have varied with latitude (Pope 2007 211-4).

Other variations in orientation have also been noted. Brück (1999, 155-6) found that most middle Bronze Age house doors were oriented south-east (58%) or south (20%) and noted a divergence in late Bronze Age and Iron Age houses which tend to have a more easterly orientation. Oswald (1997, 93) noted that a divergence of orientation between two broadly easterly ranges is a feature of Iron Age circular buildings at both national and regional level, clustering in the ranges 90-100° (ESE) and 125-150° (SE). It was suggested that this clustering of orientation might reflect house construction at particular times of year – broadly the equinoxes or midwinter.

However, at some sites a similar clustering of orientations is evident but at different points of the compass. For example, at Gravelly Guy a similar clustering was noted, but within the ranges 65°-81° (ENE – 10 examples) and 100°-140° (ESE to SE – 15 examples). This might suggest, using Oswald's rationale, that construction or usage took place at other times of year – high summer and winter either side of the equinoxes. It is perhaps more likely that other site factors were important in modifying the basic easterly orientation. The settlement at Gravelly Guy respected a major landuse division on a broadly NW-SE alignment which meant that clustering of orientations was broadly on the line of the settlement as a whole or roughly at right-angles to it. The settlement at Green Park, Reading devel-oped within a pre-existing field system laid out roughly NNE-SSW and WNW-ESE and the orienta-tion of houses there clustered SE with some ESE (Moore and Jennings 1992, 14-25; Brossler *et al.* 2004, 19-29). However, at the neighbouring Site 5 Reading Business Park, with no such constraint, orientations were more variable (Moore and Jennings 1992, 35-9). At Mingies Ditch, Allen and Robinson (1993) concluded that the principal factor determining house orientation was that they broadly faced the south-east entrance of the enclosure.

North- and west-facing buildings

Westerly or northerly facing roundhouses are generally unusual (Fig. 5.6). The exceptionally large building immediately inside the main hillfort entrance at Crickley Hill is perhaps most noteworthy and is thought to have had a communal function. The other Crickley roundhouses faced SE or SSE (Dixon 1976). At Gravelly Guy Building G is very unusual in facing only just west of north (Fig. 5.6; Lambrick and Allen 2004, 131-6). At Claydon Pike a middle Iron Age penannular house gully with an internal wall-groove building (Structure 15) faced north-west (Miles *et al.* 2007, 63-4), while a similar building at Park Farm, Binfield faced south-west, as did other subsequent late Iron Age and early Roman houses (Roberts 1995, 100-3, figs 50, 51). At the ironworking site at Brooklands a west-facing penannular gully contained a post-ring thought to represent a house (Hanworth and Tomalin 1977, 12, fig. 8).

A number of west-facing middle to late Iron Age penannular gullies may or may not have enclosed buildings. At Caesar's Camp, Heathrow a west-facing penannular gully may have reflected its position, set into the inner side of the eastern bank of the enclosure (Grimes and Close Brooks 1993, 324-5 fig. 5). Nearby at Perry Oaks/T5 a single substantial westerly-facing penannular gully was found amongst a group of predominantly east or south-east oriented ones (Framework Archaeology 2006, 184-6, fig. 4.10). At Mount Farm a repeatedly recut west-facing penannular gully containing concentrations of pottery and slag had a scatter of postholes within it, though no definite building (Lambrick 1979; forthcoming).

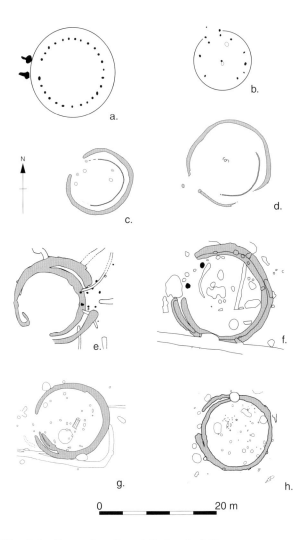

N

0   20 m

Fig. 5.6   Examples of west-facing buildings:
a) Crickley Hill; b) Gravelly Guy; c) Claydon Pike;
d) Park Farm, Binfield, and penannular gullies:
e) Watkins Farm; f) Perry Oaks; g) Mount Farm;
h) Segsbury

At Segsbury a circular ditch that may have started as a penannular gully facing east (the plans show a possible residual terminal on the east side) was recut with the opening to the west. On the grounds of a surrounding scatter of human remains and ethnographic parallels the excavators inferred that this structure was associated with death, though the gully did not produce human remains and the contexts which did either belonged to an earlier phase or were undated (Lock *et al.* 2006, 59-67, figs 3.1a, pl 3.6). Such an association does not seem to be apparent from other west-facing structures in the region and the gully did contain significant quantities of daub and slag, possibly indicative of the rebuilding of a workshop or other structure, which is better paralleled at other sites in the region (see Chapter 8).

Some house enclosures in the Upper Thames Valley show complex sequences of recutting which cut across earlier entrances or shifted their location, suggesting changes in the orientation of previous structures. This seems evident in at least one, possibly four or more cases of mainly east-facing enclosures at Ashville and Wyndyke Furlong (Parrington 1978 11-9, figs 3, 12; Muir and Roberts 1999, 16-22, figs 2.13, 2.14). At Watkins Farm the central house gully originally had a south-west entrance, later modified to face east (Allen 1990, 12-4). At least two of the penannular gullies thought to indicate roundhouse sites at Little Wittenham had west-facing entrances replaced by continuous gullies (Allen *et al.* forthcoming a). At Yarnton a south-facing penannular enclosure had been similarly recut (Hey *et al.* forthcoming a, Enclosure 390). This may indicate a change of use or of attitude to these structures.

The ordering of internal space

Internal post positions, partitions and other internal structures

As Reynolds (1979; 1995, 194) observed and demonstrated experimentally there is no need for a central post to support the roof of even very large circular buildings. Nevertheless, many late prehistoric roundhouses from the later Bronze Age through to the middle Iron Age did have centrally placed postholes (8 out of 20 at Reading Business Park; 1 out of 5 at Green Park; 4 out of 12 at Yarnton; 15 out of 30 at Gravelly Guy; 2 out of 5 at Mingies Ditch), though on some sites they seem to be absent (Gingell 1982; Miles *et al.* 2007, fig. 3.11). At Salmonsbury a cluster of three postholes was found at the centre of one of the houses, and two, which Dunning (1976, 82) took to be roof supports, in another.

However, it is unlikely that central posts were intended to support the roofs of these houses. Any post reaching the apex of a roundhouse would need to be twice or even three times as long as a wall post, with a commensurate increase in base diameter. But unlike doorway postholes, which

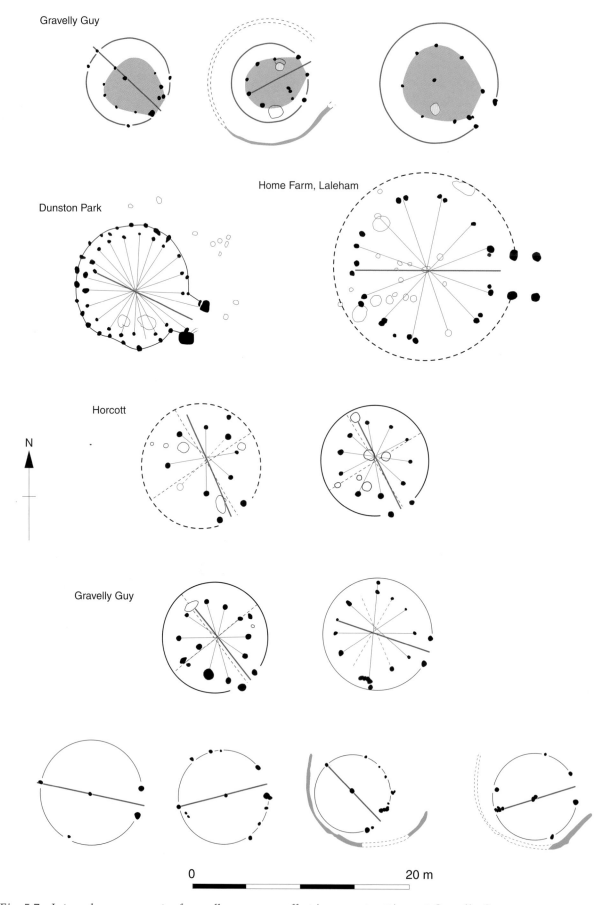

*Fig. 5.7 Internal arrangements of roundhouse space: offset inner post settings at Gravelly Guy;
axial and diametrically placed posts at Dunston Park; Home Farm, Laleham; Horcott Pit; Gravelly Guy*

often seem to have taken larger posts, whether for structural strength or display, central postholes are rarely especially large. It is more likely that they existed to support partitions dividing the interior of the house (eg with radially placed hurdles) and/or floors to create loft spaces.

At Mingies Ditch a central post in Building 5 was removed to make way for a hearth, and two other posts were placed diametrically either side of it. Together with other modifications these may have been intended to support a potentially smoky storage space over the rear half of the house. Other evidence for partitions or upper floors might be indicated by the positions of extra postholes that could represent strengthening or repairs at particular points of load-bearing, including the extra laterally positioned posts in buildings at Gravelly Guy (Building L) and Horcott (Roundhouses 6100 and 6046). Other scatters of postholes within buildings may also have supported internal partitions (Miles *et al*..2007, 63-4; Harding 1987, 5-9; Allen and Kamash 2008). In Scotland stone brochs are the ruins of multi-floored prehistoric buildings that in some cases still stand to above first floor level, and Pope (2007 220-1) has stressed the range of full attics, half lofts and large shelves that could have been constructed for storage or other purposes in the roofs of timber-framed roundhouses.

Some structures interpreted as roundhouses had what look like four-posters placed centrally within them, as at Reading Business Park Building 9, Rams Hill Building C, Cotswold Community Structure 2430, Groundwell Farm Building 2 (Moore and Jennings 1992, 22, fig. 15; Bradley and Ellison 1975, 55, fig. 2.23; Gingell 1982). These could be supports for internal superstructure, but as with central supports, there is no indication that these were especially tall posts. Given that there are many other cases of four-posters and roundhouses overlapping in non-concentric positions, it is possible that they were not part of the same structure. There are also instances of four-posters sited centrally within small penannular gullies, as at Castle Hill, Ashville Ditch 346, Perry Oaks Penannular Gully 9 (Allen *et al.* forthcoming a; Parrington 1978, 11, fig. 10; Framework Archaeology 2006, 180-2, fig. 4.8). One possibility is that these are all cases of conventional four-post structures that were deliberately enclosed, either being built within small fenced enclosures marked by gullies, or, to achieve the same effect, in the shell of ruinous houses.

Central and peripheral space

In roundhouses with inner post-rings and outer aisles there is much variation in the ratio between the inner and outer spaces as defined by circles drawn through the post-ring and doorposts. At Gravelly Guy for example, of the nine buildings of this type recognised, there were three with the inner core much smaller than the outer ring (26 m^2/53 m^2, 33 m^2/62 m^2 and 13 m^2/30 m^2), two where they were about equal, and two examples with the inner core significantly larger than the outer ring (66 m^2/55 m^2, 61 m^2/34 m^2, 50 m^2/35 m^2). It is usually assumed that the relatively poorly lit outer 'aisles' in such buildings were used for storage, sleeping and other purposes involving little coming and going or requiring little light. Hingley (1990b) has suggested a distinction between central 'public' – ie shared – space and peripheral 'private' space. Such differences in the sizes and relative ratios of available space indicate, as others have observed (Pope 2007, 217-9), that the internal architecture of aisled post-ring houses was not dictated purely by structural considerations of distributing the weight of the roof, but also may indicate, as Pope has also found, that applying a single interpretation to how 'peripheral' space was used is inappropriate.

At Gravelly Guy two, or possibly three, buildings had apparently oval or pear-shaped inner post-rings set closer to the door, as though to ensure that the inner core area was as close to the entrance – the main source of light – as possible. In the case of building A2 this appeared to be a modification of a more conventional concentric early Iron Age aisled roundhouse; building E1 was subsequently rebuilt three times in the middle Iron Age. These plan forms seem unusual, but a similar building, House 2, at Mingies Ditch reinforces the impression that this modified layout may have been part of the transition away from standard concentric post-built houses to more varied types in the middle Iron Age.

Although a few post-built 'aisled' roundhouses are known from middle Iron Age settlements, in general there seems to have been a shift towards buildings with the whole interior left unencumbered by structural posts. In a sense this was not new, because such buildings had always existed, so it may simply have been that formal aisled plans ceased to be favoured. This is unlikely to reflect improvements in construction methods, and it is more likely that changes in living styles made formal division of interior spaces inconveniently inflexible or inappropriate, even if practical usage still differentiated central and peripheral space.

Internal orientation and symmetry

We have seen that the entrances to houses may have had a symbolic as well as a functional role, as do our own front doors, and it is also reasonable to suppose that posts also had multiple functions within buildings. At a number of sites (eg Moore and Jenings 1992, 19; Lambrick and Allen 2004, 131-2) it has been noted that late prehistoric post-ring buildings often have a post set in the post-ring or the wall line on an axis that passes through the doorway. There is no particular structural requirement for such posts and, although some may be fortuitous, it is noticeable that in some cases where few posts survive on the wall line, one on this axis is often one of them. At Gravelly Guy axial posts were noted in six or eight of the 30-odd early and middle Iron Age houses (Lambrick and Allen 2004

131-44). The large early Iron Age concentric post-ring house at Dunston Park had an extra post placed inside the wall line in this position (Fig. 5.7). Fitzpatrick suggested that this could represent the position of a visible feature emphasising a symmetrical division of the house down the middle, with either side devoted to different activities or associations (Fitzpatrick *et al.* 1995, 87, fig. 35; 1994, fig. 20.4). If, as seems likely, axial posts did have a symbolic role, they may have been decorated, carved or highlighted to be more visible from the entrance than other posts. It is worth noting, however, that they occur both in houses with central posts and without them, so visibility from the doorway may not have been a prime consideration. One possibility is that such axial posts marked the most private place in the house, a kind of inner sanctum, that could fit with several cosmological models of arrangement of space (Parker Pearson 1996; 1999, 47-51, fig. 7).

Axial symmetry is also expressed in houses with posts placed in diametrically opposite pairs (Musson, 1970; Guilbert 1982; Brück 1999, 155). Again, this was not structurally necessary, but may indicate a method of laying out the ground plan that reflects a concept of symmetry and ordering of life that is not geometrically concentric but more segmental. In 'circular' buildings this kind of pairing can result in the structural centre of the building where 'diameters' cross, not actually being at the centre of a best-fit circle round the ring of posts. Indeed, this kind of diametrical pairing can be applied to non-circular plans. Several of the houses at Gravelly Guy exhibited this characteristic, including the large porched building C and building L, which both had axial posts. It may also apply to the large buildings at Home Farm, Laleham (Fig. 5.7) and Dunston Park with axial posts, and to City Farm, Hanborough and Crickley Hill without. Among four such buildings at Horcott, two had small pits in the position of axial posts (Fig. 5.7).

Such symbolism, or hints of structured behaviour in the use of domestic space, discernible in the structural design of buildings, may reflect the kind of social ordering of space that ethnographic parallels suggest. In these different areas are assigned to different groups within the family and visitors, and wider cosmological concepts underlie what is regarded as the appropriate organising of space (Parker Pearson and Richards 1994; Parker Pearson 1996; Oswald 1997; Hingley 1990b). The general principle that different degrees of privacy and social interaction take place in different parts of domestic accommodation is a more or less universal trait of human society. But the details differ considerably both between societies and at different levels of society and families, depending on factors such as social status and family size, composition and age profile. A further factor in the physical expression in domestic architecture of abstract social relationships is the scope offered by the size of the accommodation concerned. The relationship between social, symbolic and spiritual norms and practical issues of daily living related to natural lighting, heat and access arrangements are complex, each factor both influencing and being shaped by the others in ways that cannot readily be disentangled. While we might expect some of these norms to be reflected in physical remains of daily living such as the distribution of pits and finds within and around houses, we should not necessarily expect patterns to be consistent. In addition to the complex relationships between patterns of behaviour and the social norms that shaped them, the archaeological evidence reflects a wide range of depositional and post-depositional factors.

Light sources

Oswald (1997, 92) was perhaps too dismissive of Hingley and Miles' (1984) suggestion that light might have been an important factor in determining doorway orientation, misleadingly stating that 'direct sunlight would hardly ever have entered those buildings with east facing doorways during winter months', though his own research indicated a preponderance of orientations over a wide spread between east and south-east. While his remark that the sun does not always shine is more pertinent, the strength of daylight from the southern sky is still determined by the position of the sun except on the most overcast days.

The combined need for light and shelter, the superiority of daylight over any artificial light and the need for better light for some activities than others would have been key practical considerations, inextricably bound up with access and heating, in determining how space within a prehistoric roundhouse was used. These practicalities would have influenced when and exactly where daily indoor activities took place as well as being interwoven with cosmological associations of dawn, awakening, new activity and life.

In the absence of direct evidence for purpose made oil lamps, dishes or other holders in which tallow wicks might have burned, it is assumed that the hearth would have been the main source of artificial light, and this unsteady, not very bright light would not have been very effective for domestic tasks needing good illumination. Both from ethnographic and structural considerations there is a well-established assumption that late prehistoric roundhouses in Britain did not have windows. However, this is unproven and it is possible to envisage windows equipped with shutters or even translucent skins, or some kind of opening in the roof allowing light in (Jarett and Wrathmell 1981, fig. 36) as reconstructed at Castell Henlys, though there are also some good practical reasons not to let smoke out (Reynolds 1995). However, even allowing for these caveats, it is probably reasonable to suppose that the best natural light would have come through the door.

The general effectiveness of a doorway as a light source would have depended on its orientation relative to the changing position of the rising or setting sun, which would have had a significant seasonal effect on which parts of a house were best lit. This would have further been affected by the size and proportions of the entrance, width being important to catch low winter sunlight (Fig. 5.8).

The issue of light may have been relevant in the design of porches or vestibules. Any such structure with solid walls or screens at each side would have reduced the time during which the sun could shine directly into the interior of a house, significantly restricting the amount of light entering the building. This would be avoided if these structures had open sides, and if they incorporated open-ended gables they could have enhanced the light available from the entrance, allowing some light in even if the door was closed (Bersu 1940).

Although direct stratigraphic and structural evidence is usually lacking in the Thames Valley, it is generally assumed that the relatively dark 'aisle' space and walls away from doorways would have been used mainly for storage and sleeping. The

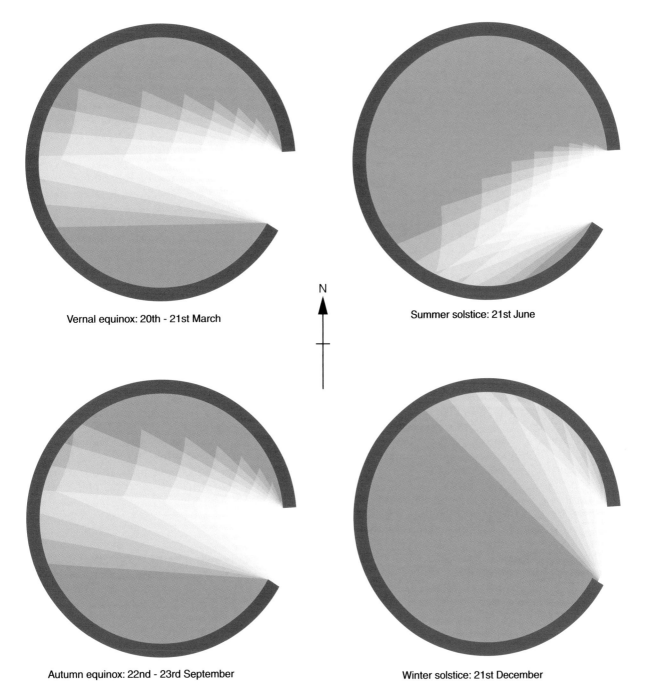

Vernal equinox: 20th - 21st March

Summer solstice: 21st June

N

Autumn equinox: 22nd - 23rd September

Winter solstice: 21st December

Fig. 5.8   Computer generated diagram of the parts of a roundhouse interior directly lit by sunlight shining through the door at different times of the year. The assumed height of the doorway is 1.8 m-2.0 m

central space around a hearth and inside the doorway is the area most likely to be used for general family and social activity and the craft activities needing good light would be carried out in the interior immediately inside the doorway and in the doorway itself. However, this would not always mean the same thing in every house. Apart from the uncertainty about windows and openings at the apex of the roof, a more pertinent point is that some buildings had secondary doorways with other orientations than the general easterly norm. Moreover, since these secondary doorways tend to be recognised as much or more from spatial relationships than from conspicuous doorposts, it is possible that subsidiary doorways were much more common than has been recognised. This too would have had practical implications for the internal organisation of space, radically altering the assumed dynamics of access and egress.

Hearths, clay pits and other pits

The position of hearths is rarely established because, along with floor surfaces, they are often truncated by later disturbance, generally ploughing. At Mingies Ditch, five houses had surviving internal surfaces and three had hearths constructed of gravel and/or blocks of conglomerate, two placed centrally and one off-centre to the left of the doorway looking inwards. A fourth had a charcoal filled hollow, possibly a hearth, on the main axis of the house offset towards the door. At Claydon Pike remains of three hearths or fire pits and a possible oven base were found just inside the doorway of a house surrounded by a penannular gully within an outer enclosure (Miles *et al.* 2007, 40-2, fig. 3.6 pls 3.3, 3.4).

In the Upper Thames Valley small, shallow circular or rectangular pits packed with raw clay and burnt limestone are associated with several houses, as noted at Claydon Pike and Gravelly Guy (Miles *et al.* 2007, 63-4; Lambrick and Allen 2004, 142-4). These are variously placed, often middle or rear left (Claydon Pike buildings 1, 2, 6, 7, 9, 10, 11, 17; Gravelly Guy E2) but sometimes front left (Claydon Pike 2, 13, 14; Gravelly Guy E1, E3, T) or front right (Gravelly Guy A1/A2, G), and in one or two cases central (Claydon Pike 20, Gravelly Guy G). These positions generally accord with siting within or on the edge of the varying seasonal lighting of roundhouses.

The clay and limestone in these pits usually represents their general fill rather than a lining. It has been suggested that this material may have come from clay-lined pits that functioned as tanks for heating water with hot stones, or that the clay had been stored to make loomweights and other ceramic objects, then discarded with the burnt stone intended to consolidate the floor surface. At Mingies Ditch, a small pit in House 2 contained fired, partly fired and unfired loomweights (Allen and Robinson 1993, 43 and Pl. 12).

The available evidence suggests that other small pits were placed in almost any part of a house, though often close to walls, as with one containing a cache of querns in Building 5 at Mingies Ditch (Allen and Robinson 1993, 54-9).

Finds distributions and depositional circumstances

For most sites in the Upper Thames Valley artefacts from postholes and small pits associated with houses are too sparse for concentrations to be evident. So far as they are discernible, as at Horcott for example, a variable pattern between houses is suggested (Lamdin-Whymark *et al.* forthcoming).

In the Middle Thames Valley a similarly varied picture emerges. At Home Farm, Laleham a range of domestic refuse was found in small pits and postholes associated with the east-facing late Bronze Age porched roundhouse (Hayman forthcoming c). Assuming the 'porch' was indeed the entrance, rather than a four-poster beside a post-ring house, it appears that most pottery and other domestic debris, including querns, perforated clay slabs, spindle whorls and a bronze object, were concentrated at the back of the house, with two small pits within the 'aisle' and a larger elongated pit outside just to the right of the entrance.

At the late Bronze Age ironworking site at Hartshill Copse there were clear differences in the quantities of pottery and relative distributions of bowls and jars between contemporary structures and also a distinction between a concentration of secondarily fired pottery towards the rear of one house and pottery of a different character closer to its entrance (Collard *et al.* 2006, 374-80).

At Dunston Park an unusually large amount of pottery and burnt stone was found in the postholes of the porch and the southern side of the large ESE-facing early Iron Age house and also in two small internal pits on that side. Decorated pottery seemed particularly concentrated in the well-lit area of the porch. This was taken to suggest that much daily living activity took place in the right hand side of the house looking out, the line of axis marked by an extra axial post at the rear of the building (Fitzpatrick *et al.* 1995, 85-9, fig. 40; Fitzpatrick 1997).

Votive Deposits

The unusually rich quantities of artefacts from the houses at Dunston Park, Home Farm, Laleham and Hartshill Copse were associated with both pits and postholes and did not obviously include deliberately buried deposits. But in a few cases pits lying within or close to houses produce more unusual collections of finds. For example, at Reading Business Park a pit probably associated with one of a number of late Bronze Age buildings contained five smashed pots (Moore and Jennings 1992, 28). At Horcott Pit four early Iron Age post-built roundhouses had small pits, one with a substantial deposit of crushed pottery and a spindle whorl, and another, slightly larger pit with a complete angular jar and four spindle whorls. At Gravelly Guy loomweights and circular clay slabs were found in a pit possibly associated with an early Iron Age house (Lambrick and Allen 2004, 143, and plate 3.2, Pit 503).

Special deposits were occasionally placed either side of roundhouse entrances, as with a horse skull and jaw in the terminals of a pennanular house gully at Farmoor (Lambrick and Robinson 1979, 23, fig. 13). Some late Bronze Age and, more rarely, early Iron Age roundhouses appear to have associated cremation burials (see Chapter 8). The Tower Hill bronze hoard was placed or hidden at the entrance of a roundhouse (Miles *et al.* 2003, 145-7, fig. 8.5). At Latton Lands (Powell *et al.* forthcoming) three or four post-built circular structures had young animals (three calves and a foal) buried close by, one of these clearly placed on the axis of the house either just inside or just outside the wall. These burials might have been foundation deposits. At Mingies Ditch a pair of saddle querns and their rubbers deposited in a pit in Building 5 were interpreted as a possible buried cache of valuables, indicating that abandonment of the site was not intended to be permanent (Allen and Robinson 1993, 54, 89). They might, alternatively, have been a votive deposit.

The social context of deposits such as these is seldom clear, and may have ranged from the practical need to hide valued objects to tokens of good fortune (like nailing a horseshoe to a barn door) or serious spiritual offerings. One issue they raise is whether in some cases they reflect particular superstitions connected with making or leaving a home. It is suspected, for example, that some of the heavily burnt houses and distributions of broken pots at sites like Dunston Park and Hartshill Copse might represent explicit decommissioning of houses rather than accidental destruction.

Overview

Throughout the later prehistory of the Thames Valley, as elsewhere in Britain, houses were usually deliberately oriented towards the east, probably for a number of reasons, including social, cultural and spiritual beliefs or traditions interwoven with a range of practical considerations such as shelter and light. The rising sun may have represented life and awakening but it is also reasonable to suppose more pragmatically that the early morning may have been a good time to carry out indoor activities, especially in winter . This may have been as much a part of the socially acceptable norms of daily living as more abstract cosmological concepts. Other practical considerations would have played a part in how houses were ordered to reflect socially accepted family and community life. Some houses had subsidiary entrances facing in other directions that would have altered the dynamics of how space

was used. Similarly, it would be unwise to suppose that the few northerly or westerly facing buildings were always intended to symbolise death, or were only meant to have been used in the evening. All these considerations seem likely to have been tempered by practicalities of site layout, especially where orientations were already established in the settlement layout, or where other requirements of access needed to be taken into account. Thus while the easterly orientation of houses seems likely to have reflected some deep-seated social and cosmological norms, and there were aspects of symmetry and demarcation of space that suggest social ordering of space, there was plenty of scope within that for varied individual practice and adaptation to the practical constraints of settlement layout and needs of physical access.

The variability in the distributions of small pits and objects in relation to the layout of houses in the Thames Valley accords with Brück's (1999, 155-8) observations for a larger cross section of middle Bronze Age houses in southern England. The patterns are more complicated than the symbolic bilateral division of space related to light/dark right/left proposed for Dunston Park might suggest. Exceptional collections of querns, spindle whorls or other objects such as those at Horcott, Laleham or Mingies Ditch may not reflect where they were used. The distribution of finds must reflect several different circumstances of deposition, including the direct discard of objects close to where they were used; the storage of objects not in use; deliberate deposition of symbolic offerings; the results of accidental (or possibly deliberate) destruction by fire or other means; or symbolic abandonment or closure deposits. The seasonal variation in the lighting of buildings adds further complexity.

To look at how houses were used purely in terms of either utilitarian, symbolic or social models is too simplistic. All three are likely to have played a role in influencing human behaviour and none need have been an overriding factor in the division of space and distribution of artefacts associated with houses. Indeed, these different influences are likely to have varied in importance from one household to another. As Brück (1999) noted, changes over the lifetime of houses through construction, use, reuse and abandonment or closure, together with the changing social circumstances, status or age of their inhabitants introduce further reasons to treat over-simplistic models with caution.

EXTERNAL LIVING

Although access and light, together with social and spiritual traditions, seem likely to have had an important influence on the use of houses and the distribution of the activities that took place within them, it is likely that much daily living would have taken place outside, leaving interior living spaces relatively clean.

Most ordinary small pits associated with buildings produce little of note. At Reading Business Park Site 3100 the pits located within buildings were notably devoid of occupation material apart from one with a large sherd of decorated pottery (Moore and Jennings 1992, 42). At Weir Bank Stud the eastern half of a post-built middle Bronze Age roundhouse with a south-east facing porch overlapped an area of truncated ground surface outside the house. A small hearth was set within the left hand side of the house about 2 m from the doorway, but finds from the interior were sparse compared with the concentration of worked and burnt flint and pottery found outside to the north of the porch (Barnes and Cleal 1995, 11-12 fig. 10, pl 3). At Mingies Ditch where very extensive remains of the Iron Age ground surface survived, there was a noticeable concentration of external occupation debris and some hearths in the centre of the site, while the floor layers and other deposits within houses were relatively clean, with debris typically thrown out into surrounding gullies (Allen and Robinson 1993, 90-1). This is a recurrent, though seldom plotted, pattern (Allen *et al.* 1984, 91, fig. 6.3). While it is not entirely clear how much external occupation debris was due to clearing rubbish out of houses rather than external living, the presence of external hearths is a clear indication that much domestic life took place out of doors.

Clustering and Pairing

It is difficult to tell whether particular buildings were contemporary and even more difficult to demonstrate that they complemented each other in function. Ethnographic parallels suggest that there might have been distinct houses for men and women, that an extended family might have occupied a small cluster of houses, and that houses may have been complemented by workshops or store houses. However, despite the investigation of well over 100 houses in the Thames Valley, there are few examples for which such arrangements can clearly be discerned.

One of the most convincing examples of paired buildings is the recently excavated pair of late Bronze Age house/workshops associated with very early ironworking at Hartshill Copse, where distinctions in the distribution of pottery and metalworking debris clearly differentiate between different living and working activities (Fig. 5.9; Collard *et al.* 2006, 400-05). Moore and Jennings (1992, 38) suggested that three, or possibly five pairings are identifiable in the cluster of late Bronze Age buildings at Reading Business Park Site 3100, though this was less evident in the subsequent excavation in the adjacent area (Brossler *et al.* 2004, 122). The sequence of circular buildings on 'Island 3' in Warrens Field at Claydon Pike suggested that they may have been used in groups of two or three, and similar arrangements seem to have occurred as the settlement shifted to

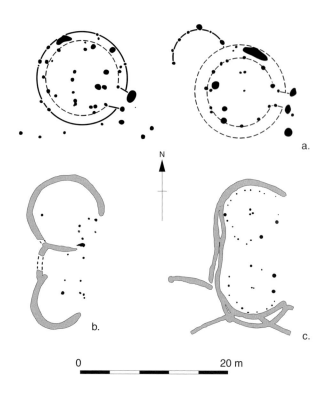

Fig. 5.9   Pairings of roundhouses: a) Hartshill Copse; b) Claydon Pike; c) Salmonsbury

other patches of dry ground (Fig. 5.9; Miles *et al.* 2007, 59-61, fig. 3.10).

In a few cases buildings clearly faced each other, and on the whole their fairly uniform size, distribution of domestic rubbish, clay-lined pits and hearths suggest that most were domestic, though some may have been small workshops or pens. In the Middle Thames Valley at Ashford Prison, Surrey a group of nine middle to late Iron Age penannular gullies containing much domestic debris similarly suggest that houses were sited to respect each other, although taking account also of nine four-posters, it is unlikely that all were contemporary. Lower Mill Farm may also suggest a pairing of houses (Hayman 1991a). In the Upper Thames Valley at Salmonsbury two post-built houses were enclosed by a single ditch forming a kind of double penannular gully (Fig. 5.9; Dunning 1976). Artefacts showed these buildings to be middle to late Iron Age, one with possible hearths to one side. At Yarnton a similar double enclosure was identified, but without convincing traces of buildings or significant amounts of domestic debris (Hey *et al.* forthcoming a).

Ancillary buildings and annexes

At Hartshill Copse one of the houses seems to have been residential but with an elongated pit and a semi-circular annexe associated with blacksmithing. The other roundhouse produced less evidence of residential use and was associated with bloom-smithing (Collard *et al.* 2006). This level of evidence for craft activity, in this case based on the incidence of different kinds of hammerscale, and the contrasts in the quantity and types of pottery associated with structures is unusual. A similar arrangement of a post-built roundhouse with adjacent semicircular arc of postholes was recorded at Gravelly Guy, but with no clear evidence of ironworking or other craft activity (Lambrick and Allen 2004, 144, fig. 1.22).

Other examples of paired buildings generally show less clear evidence of specialised usage. At Ashville a middle Iron Age penannular gully which probably enclosed a roundhouse had an annexe enclosing a succession of circular and rectangular structures, but again there was no clear evidence of craft activities. At Farmoor an irregular penannular gully with significant domestic debris also had an annexe enclosing a semi-circular building (Parrington 1978, 11-5 fig. 12; Lambrick and Robinson 1979, 9-13 fig. 4).

Other Buildings

Rectangular Buildings

Although small 4- or 6-post square and rectangular structures, generally interpreted as storage facilities, are common (see Chapter 7), convincing rectangular buildings have been rare. Recently a growing number of convincing examples have been investigated, most of which are late Bronze Age or early Iron Age (Fig. 5.10). While several of these rectangular structures appear to be simple animal pens or workshops, some are associated with deposits or sites that suggest less utilitarian functions.

At Church Lammas, Staines a small rectangular slot was interpreted as a sill beam trench of a small structure surrounding a large pit, probably of middle Bronze Age origin and possibly a shrine (Hayman 1991; forthcoming b; see Chapter 9). At Runnymede a structure constructed of widely spaced postholes within the late Bronze Age midden deposits appears to have been deliberately decommissioned (Fig. 5.10; Needham and Sørensen 1988, 113-26). It is also worth noting two other rectilinear settings of postholes within the early to middle Iron Age midden deposits at Woodeaton (Harding 1987, fig. 10) and Castle Hill (Allen *et al.* forthcoming b), the latter associated with a chalk floor.

At Perry Oaks/T5 a rectangular 6-post structure measuring 3 m by 2.5 m abutted a field boundary within a general area of domestic occupation. At the middle to late Bronze Age settlement at Pingewood a small, irregular setting of posts was identified as a possible building (Johnston and Bowden 1985), while at Hartshill Copse a rectangular structure of irregularly set posts thought to be a stock pen was identified. This produced late Bronze Age plain-ware pottery and was located close to a 10th century ironworking workshop and house on a site with possible ceremonial connotations (Fig. 5.10; Collard *et al.* 2006, 377, fig. 5). Recent work at Cassington

West has identified a distinctive rectangular structure within the late Bronze Age settlement (Fig. 5.10), together with two smaller structures resembling elongated four-posters, all associated with cremated human bone. Nearby at Yarnton, a roughly rectangular setting of 16 irregularly spaced postholes was interpreted as a rectangular building, of possible early Iron Age date. Some of the postholes contained burnt stone and a pit and two postholes contained fragments of human bone. One of these postholes belonged to the rectangular structure and produced cremated animal bone and a burnt fragment of a human femur.

At Crickley Hill a series of rectilinear settings of regularly spaced posts flanking the entrance road of the early hillfort were interpreted as possible long rectangular buildings (Dixon 1976). Some of them had central hearths, providing good evidence, along with the increasing number of newly discovered late prehistoric rectangular buildings, to counter suggestions that these structures were rows of four-posters.

Rectangular structures are less common on early to middle Iron Age settlements, though at Eton Rowing Course a 6 m long sub-rectangular six-post structure was identified within the middle to late Iron Age enclosed settlement (Allen *et al.* forthcoming b). On a pipeline route on the gravels north of Radley, Oxfordshire a 4.5 m long rectangular building consisted on one long side of seven close-set posts, with three and four posts along the short sides, but only one small post on the other long side, suggesting it was an open-sided building, such as a workshop (Cotswold Archaeology 2004). Another rectilinear setting suggesting an open-sided workshop was found on the metalworking site at Brooklands (Hanworth and Tomalin 1977, 17, fig.10).

Late Iron Age structural remains are generally sparse, but there is some evidence for rectangular buildings of sill beam construction, especially at Silchester, where several such structures fronted onto the first streets of the late Iron Age town (Fulford and Timby 2000). At Bierton, near Aylesbury, a possible rectangular structure defined by wall trenches was described by the excavator (Allen, 1986) and another possible 5 m by 9.5 m rectangular post-built structure is visible on the published plan (S Kidd pers. comm.). The best known of all later prehistoric rectangular buildings in the Thames Valley is the concentric setting of beam slots and close set posts at Caesar's Camp Heathrow, interpreted as a celtic shrine (Grimes and Close-Brooks 1993; see Chapter 9).

The interpretation of most rectangular structures poses numerous problems. Finds are generally sparse, making domestic use at best doubtful without much other indication of their use. Associations with a hillfort, possible shrines or ceremonial sites, midden deposits and deposits of human bone suggest that at least some of these structures were religious or ceremonial, some may have been domestic and others are more likely to have been workshops or animal pens.

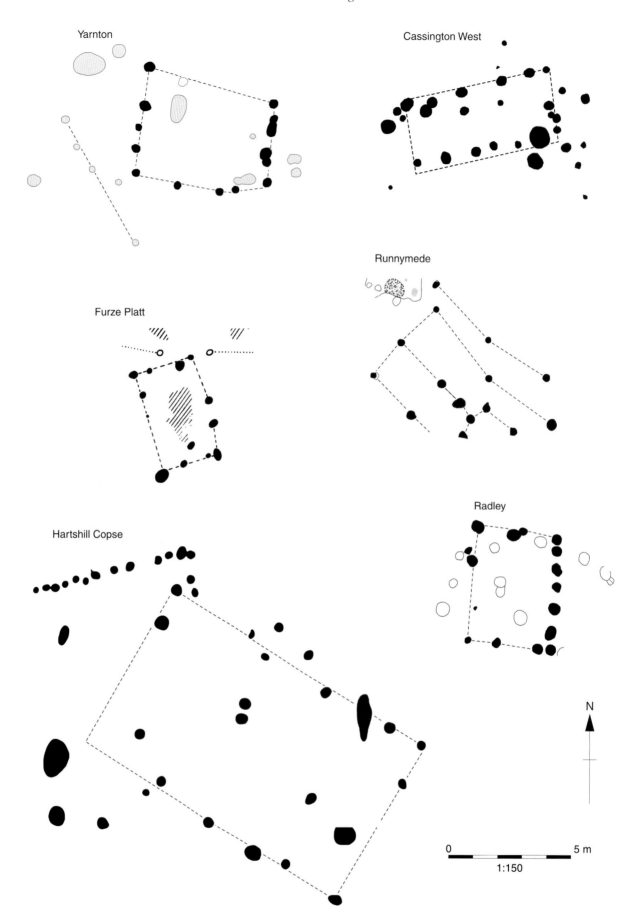

Fig. 5.10   Possible late prehistoric rectangular buildings in the Thames Valley

Workshops and other non-domestic buildings

Most domestic, farming and manufacturing crafts could have been carried out either in domestic houses or in the open air with little in the way of specialised structures or facilities, and many need not have left obvious archaeological traces. For the want of evidence to the contrary, most circular buildings are regarded as houses which were also used for domestic crafts like sewing and weaving. But it is also widely recognised that some circular buildings, especially where they are grouped, could have been ancillary structures used as specialist workshops or for storage. While it is common to find objects that reflect various crafts in and around late prehistoric buildings, it is normally very difficult to prove that the buildings were specifically built for, or limited to ancillary uses.

D-shaped, oval or boat-shaped structures

Structure A at Rams Hill was a sub-rectangular or horseshoe setting of eight posts 6.1 m across, open to the north-east (Fig. 5.11; Bradley and Ellison 1975, 52-4 fig. 2.21). It had no obvious doorposts and two of the postholes were cut by postholes associated with the timber framed rampart, suggesting that it predated the enclosure or was associated with its earliest phase around the end of the 12th century BC.

About half a dozen possible semicircular or D-shaped settings, most likely to be late Bronze Age and early Iron Age, but with possible middle Bronze Age and middle Iron Age examples, have

tentatively been identified at Shorncote (Hearne and Heaton 1994; Hearne and Adam 1999), and further possible examples have been found at Latton Lands (Powell *et al.* forthcoming).

At Yarnton several distinctly D-shaped post settings, most dating from the middle/late Bronze Age to the early Iron Age, were identified, several associated with pits containing charcoal and burnt stone (Fig. 5.11). These range from near oval rings to distinct semicircles, indicating the difficulties of formal classification or interpretation of these structures. There is no particular reason why some of them might not have been domestic houses. Amongst the five early Iron Age D-shaped examples, four were positioned close together, possibly built as pairs.

Another example might be discerned in posthole cluster D below the South Oxfordshire Grims Ditch at Mongewell (Cromarty *et al.* 2006, 166-7, fig. 5.5).

An early Iron Age semicircular or D-shaped setting of posts at Beard Mill, Stanton Harcourt was interpreted as a workshop in the early 1950s (Williams 1951) but was reinterpreted 20 years later as a series of drying racks represented by paired postholes (Harding 1972, 37-9 fig. 7; cf Reynolds 1995, 205). Subsequent observations of less complex semicircular posthole clusters suggest that the original interpretation might be justified, though it may also be noted that the idea of 'drying racks' has gone out of fashion, very seldom even being discussed as a possibility in modern reports.

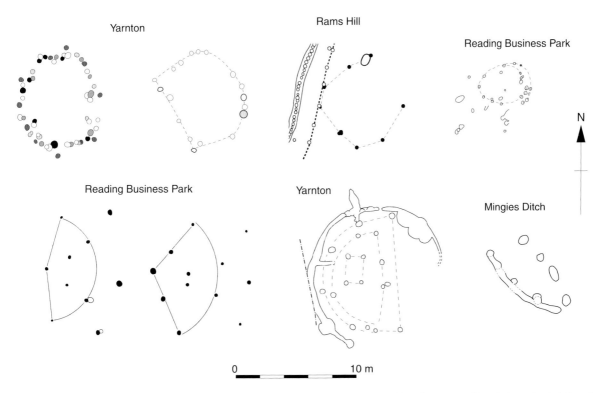

Fig. 5.11   D-shaped semicircular, segmental and boat-shaped structures in the Thames Valley. (Note the left hand plan for Yarnton is a composite of several different structures to show their similarity of size and form.)

Segmental and semicircular structures

Segmental structures (arcs of postholes with the other 'sides' formed by symmetrical radial settings) have been advanced for the late Bronze Age at Reading Business Park (Moore and Jennings 1992, 38, figs 24, 25), and there are possible early and middle Iron Age examples at Yarnton and Shorncote (Hey *et al.* forthcoming a; Brossler *et al.* 1992, 46). A middle Iron Age penannular enclosure ditch at Yarnton surrounded two concentric semicircular settings of posts with their flat sides to the east, one within the other (Fig. 5.11). A concentration of slag was noted in the general area (Hey *et al.* forthcoming a). At Farmoor a distinct middle Iron Age semi-circular building was enclosed by a small penannular gully, originating as a palisade fence, abutting an area that became a larger horseshoe-shaped enclosure or pen (Fig. 5.12). The semicircular structure measured 8.0 m by 4.3 m with the flat side to the west, away from the entrance to the surrounding enclosure. There was no particular concentration of craft related finds from the structure, although several loomweight fragments were found in an adjacent ditch (Lambrick and Robinson 1979, 12, fig. 4, Pl II and IV; finds, 57). A similar middle Iron Age semicircular gully may have originated as a palisade fence at Thrupp (Everett and Eeles, 1999, 125, fig. 9). A middle Iron Age gully at Shorncote enclosed a curious V-shaped post-built structure comparable to 'workshop' structures at Yarnton and elsewhere (Brossler *et al.* 2002, 46). At Gravelly Guy (structure R) and Mount Farm middle Iron Age penannular gullies with possible semicircular or segmental settings of posts were exposed, but neither was as convincing as the Farmoor and Yarnton examples.

Oval and boat-shaped structures

Oval rings of postholes can indicate the existence of non-circular houses or of circular structures with oval or pear-shaped inner post-rings. But there are also a number of more extreme oval and boat-shaped structures which appear inappropriate as houses but are sufficiently well-defined and spatially discrete to be free-standing structures, although not necessarily roofed. These include building 3110 at Reading Business Park, probably dating to the late Bronze Age along with the rest of the settlement (Fig. 5.11; Moore and Jennings 1992, p 38 fig. 22). Another late Bronze Age cluster of postholes was found beneath the South Oxfordshire Grims Ditch at Mongewell (Cromarty *et al.* 2006, 163, fig. 5.5), and a middle Iron Age boat-shaped structure was investigated at Mingies Ditch (Fig. 5.11; Allen and Robinson 1993, 63-5, fig. 31).

Other structures

On the basis of Gerhard Bersu's ethnographic observations applied to British Iron Age archaeology it was common until the 1980s to interpret pairs of postholes as settings for free-standing racks used for drying fodder or other materials (Harding 1972, 37-8) and this was tested experimentally by Reynolds at the Butser Iron Age Farm experimental project (Reynolds 1995, 205; 1987 figs 27, 39). It is not very clear why this interpretation has largely disappeared from the literature in recent years, but it is probably due to the plethora of candidates for such structures on many extensively dug sites, and the impossibility of proving their existence and function.

Another type of structure that figures commonly amongst possible facilities for craft or agriculturally

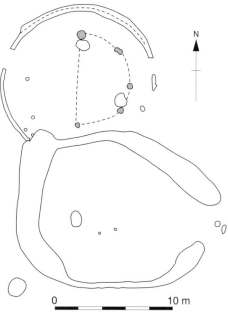

Fig. 5.12   Semi-circular structure at Farmoor

related activities is the 'windbreak.' In many cases this is an interpretation of arcs or groups of post- or stakeholds that are not entirely convincing as semi-circular and other workshop buildings. Again these are difficult to prove either way.

The role of non-circular buildings and other structures

Late prehistoric non-circular structures are generally difficult to interpret. Just as some 'round-houses' may have been workshops or other ancillary buildings, as at Hartshill Copse, some non-circular structures could have been houses. As we have seen, rectangular structures tend to have associations with sites that are in some sense 'special' or with human remains, but at least some make more sense as workshops or houses. D-shaped structures are in some ways the best candidates as houses, but other roles as workshops, storehouses and open stock pens are possible. An increasing number of convincing semi-circular structures seem to make most sense as workshops, but the lack of exceptional associations with craft-related objects makes this difficult to substantiate. The identification of structures that were specifically used as workshops or other craft-related facilities is thus problematical, but we should almost certainly envisage a mix of domestic and craft-related uses, some buildings more or less specialised than others.

DIET, FOOD PREPARATION AND DRINKING

What people ate

The late prehistoric diet was probably rather dull by modern standards. Throughout the period people ate food that was almost entirely the produce of farming rather than from hunting and gathering, which had been more important in the Neolithic and earlier Bronze Age. Much of what we know of this change comes from the waste products of food preparation and consumption, and to a limited extent residues from cooking, so the evidence of what people ate is in many respects the starting point from which wider conclusions about the development of farming can be inferred, as well as telling us something of daily life.

The consumption of hunted game became rare in later prehistory. Where significant groups of wild animal bones do occur it usually seems to be in the context of special symbolic deposits, for example the late Bronze Age or early Iron Age deer bones at Westcroft Road, Carshalton (Procter 2002) or the deer skeleton "complete and articulated but for its hind quarters" beneath a collapsed revetment wall at Blewburton (Collins 1952/3).

Stray deer bones occur quite commonly on later prehistoric settlements but usually only in low and generally declining numbers, from typically 2-5% in the later Bronze Age to 0-1% in the middle Iron Age

and hardly any in the late Iron Age (Fig. 7.3). The 17.5% of later Bronze Age deer bones at Anslows Cottages (admittedly of only a low total) and even the 5% for the middle Iron Age at Latton Lands are exceptional (Butterworth and Lobb 1992; Powell *et al.* forthcoming).

There is little evidence of hunting in terms of archery or other hunting equipment. Flint arrow-heads do not appear to have been produced from the middle Bronze Age onwards, and they are notably absent from funerary deposits. At Hatford a carefully worked perforated bone object decorated with a carved lattice pattern was reported as an 'archer's wristguard' (Bourn 2000, 45, fig. 23 no 3), but it was broken and may be a decorative 'plaque' or other object. Spears are much more common, especially as river finds and in late Bronze Age metalwork hoards, but in the absence of more bones of game animals, they appear not to have been used much for hunting compared with their role as personal weaponry and status symbols. Clay sling shots are quite common, though far from numerous finds on later Bronze Age and Iron Age settlements, but while these might have been used for hunting, their use as weapons is well-attested, as reflected in their much more frequent occurrence on hillforts (see Chapter 9).

The extent to which fishing was practised as a regular source of food is uncertain. Fish bones do not survive as well as animal bones and sample sizes are often too small to recover them, or suitable small mesh sieving has not been carried out (Wilson 1993, 172). Nevertheless their absence from deposits at sites such as Runnymede and Whitecross Farm, where these problems are less of an issue, suggests that like wild mammals, fish were not an important practical source of food. Nevertheless there are some finds of fish bones from Iron Age sites. Pike bones were found in the 'well' at Watkins Farm and pike was found at Castle Hill, Little Wittenham, along with a few eel bones, in early and middle Iron Age pits, though these occurrences might reflect symbolic behaviour rather than an element of the normal diet. Dobney and Ervynck (2007) have recently reviewed the incidence of fish bones on 117 Iron Age sites in England and found they occurred on only 2% of sites in the Midlands and none in the north, whereas they occur on 6-8% of Roman settlements. They concluded that while survival and recovery issues were a factor, 'Iron Age interest in freshwater fish was extremely low', and that 'this has little to do with the vagaries of preservation and/or sampling and recovery.' They go on to observe ethnographic evidence of taboos against the consumption of fish.

Wild plant foods were no doubt collected but do not seem to have contributed significantly to the diet. Hazelnuts occur in only small numbers amongst charred plant remains, as do the edible tubers of the grass *Arrhenatherum elatium*, though the latter, a frequent component of Bronze Age cremation burials, may have been accidentally incorporated in grass tinder. Compared with water-logged plant remains from waterholes and wells in later periods, there is no evidence that fruit was cultivated and the use of wild resources to vary the diet seems to have been negligible. Indeed it is to be wondered how a sufficient intake of vitamin C was obtained from such a diet. Perhaps the raw leaves of wild plants, such as *Rumex acetosa* (sorrel), *Chenopodium album* (fat hen) and *Stellaria media* (chickweed), were eaten. Seeds of elder, sloe, crab apple and blackberry regularly occur in water-logged samples but there is little evidence for the consumption of wild fruit, although at Mingies Ditch, numerous blackberry seeds (*Rubus fruticosus* agg.) were found in a possible cesspit (Allen and Robinson 1993, 117). The leaves of a variety of wild plants, such as sorrel (*Rumex acetosa*), fat hen (*Chenopodium album*) and chickweed (*Stellaria media*) could have been eaten. At Farmoor edible plants of damp ground included watercress (*Nasturtium offic-inale*), and mint (*Mentha* sp.) though there was no evidence that they were eaten (Lambrick and Robinson 1979, 115).

Meat derived from a wide range of body parts of domestic animals would have provided a good variety of beef, mutton and pork, with some goat and horse, and this was occasionally supplemented by deer and probably dog. Chickens were a late Iron Age introduction and their bones are very rare on pre-Roman sites in the region, from which it may be assumed that eggs were not a significant part of the diet, though wild birds' eggs may have been eaten. Dairy products of milk and presumably butter and cheese were derived from cattle, sheep and probably goats. The occasional occurrence of pottery, usually relatively fineware jars or bowls with perforations may indicate they were used for the preparation of curds (Lambrick 1984, 169; forth-coming).

The main crop staples were cereals consisting very largely of emmer and spelt wheat and six-row hulled barley, of which emmer became unimportant after the late Bronze Age. Rye may have been consumed in small quantities and less certainly oats. A charred piece of spelt bread, with glume fragments in it, was found at Ashville (Jones 1978, 98). Iron Age bread was unleavened and comprised rough-ground grain with some chaff remaining, and cereals were probably consumed as much or more in porridges, stews and perhaps dumplings.

Field (or Celtic) beans and peas were eaten as pulses, though it is uncertain to what extent, since they do not tend to be preserved in any great quantity by accidental charring or waterlogging and it is not clear how far they were grown as crops. Similarly infrequent in the record but possibly significant, are opium poppy and perhaps brassicas that may have been grown for oils.

In general terms all food was home-grown or at least locally sourced throughout the period, but by the late Iron Age there is evidence from a few sites that wine, olive oil and other preserved foods were being imported from the continent in amphorae and possibly other imported pottery containers. This applies especially to high status late settlements like Salmonsbury, Bagendon, The Ditches, Abingdon, Calleva and Verlamion. At Calleva there is other evidence of an unusually Romanised diet, including oysters which are otherwise unknown from inland Iron Age sites, and the consumption of fowl and proportions of pork and beef to other meats suggest habits quite different from the diet of local farming communities (Fulford 1992, 23-38).

Processing of farm products

The production of food from farming and storage is mainly discussed in full in Chapter 7. Here we are concerned with how the products of animal and crop husbandry were converted to food ready to be cooked.

Slaughter and butchery

The large bone assemblages at Runnymede revealed recurrent axial splitting of vertebrae, suggesting that carcasses were typically divided into two halves. However, at Whitecross Farm this seems to have been less common and there was evidence of carcasses being divided into lengths across the backbone, though this might indicate further subdivision into smaller, pot-sized pieces. Evidence of skinning, removal of brains and tongues suggests careful division of carcasses to maximise both meat and other products (Done 1991, 340; Serjeantson, 1996; Powell and Clarke in Barclay *et al.* 2006, 109-10).

An interesting point to emerge from the Runnymede bone assemblage was that horses were butchered and prepared for human consumption (Done 1991). This is common amongst Iron Age assemblages, and at Gravelly Guy the variety of skeletal elements of horse with marks of butchery was even higher than for pig, suggesting that horse was routinely eaten. Butchery marks are less common on dogs, but there are sufficient examples to suggest that they too occasionally contributed to the diet.

The examination of cut marks on bones at Ashville showed that Iron Age butchery involved the removal of limbs and disarticulation of joints (Fig. 5.13). There was evidence that cheek and tongue meats were cut out of cattle skulls, while chopping or sawing of horn cores suggests recovery of horn for use as a secondary product. At Mount Farm interesting early to middle Iron Age and Roman evidence of butchery was found amongst articulated limb bones and segments of backbone, mainly of cattle, some horse, and a sheep (Fig. 5.13). Carcasses were often dismembered into large portions. Commonly, the limbs were detached from the ribcage and pelvis and sometimes the hind limb was disjointed further between the femur and the tibia. Since the bones were articulated, the cut

Fig. 5.13   Food preparation: Evidence of butchery methods from cuts on cattle bones from Ashville and cattle with butchered limbs in a pit at Mount Farm

marks around the carpal and hock joints cannot indicate further disjointing but confirm hints from the bones at Ashville that such marks resulted from the removal of skin as far as these joints. Cut marks on other bones show skinning as far as the hooves of cattle. The remaining cut marks and absence of charring on the upper limb bones suggest that meat was removed before cooking and deposition of the bones. This seems to have been common practice with cattle, whereas the less frequent butchery marks of sheep and pig bones may indicate more of the meat was cooked on the bone.

A study of Iron Age butchery at Mingies Ditch suggested that carcasses were cut up on the ground (Wilson 1993, 124-30). Larger animals, such as cattle, seem to have been dismembered on the periphery of the settlement whereas smaller animals, such as lambs, were cut up in the vicinity of the houses and hearths, where there were also concentrations of burnt bone debris and boneworking offcuts. A similar study was carried out at the late Iron Age enclosed settlement at Fields Farm, Bicester (Charles in Cromarty *et al.* 1999, 219-20). This site lacked the *in situ* hearths and occupation soils found at Mingies Ditch and the distribution study covered a wider area, but nonetheless there was a similar change in the species representation more than about 20 m away from the presumed round-house close to the centre of the site. Gnawed bones increased to a peak *c* 50-60 m away, perhaps reflecting the activity of domestic dogs taking bones to an area where they would not be disturbed. The

proportion of burnt bones peaked 80-90 m away, suggesting clearance and dumping of refuse, perhaps also reflected in the relative scarcity of bone debris close to the centre.

For the most part butchery techniques remained unchanged throughout the later prehistory of the Upper Thames Valley and into the early Roman period on ordinary farms, but at the early Roman military garrison at Alchester the butchery techniques used to dismember and divide up the sheep were not in the British Iron Age tradition. Instead of careful cuts made with a fine sharp blade, the butchery was characterised by haphazard cut marks made with a heavy tool.

Briquetage fragments from several sites showed that salt was imported to the Upper Thames region from Droitwich and elsewhere, but it is unlikely that salt was available on a large enough scale for the preservation of meat in this way to have been other than an occasional delicacy. Smoking or drying, which leave no directly discernible evidence, were perhaps more common means of processing meat for long term storage.

Processing of cereals

After preliminary threshing and winnowing in the harvest fields grain was stored on the ear either in pits or granaries within settlements (see Chapter 7). Further parching, pounding and sieving of the grain was then needed to release the grain from its husks and remove the chaff. From the middle Bronze Age onwards it is clear that these final stages of crop processing occurred within settlement areas when grain was taken from storage, and this is when accidental charring of both grain and chaff is most likely to have occurred. Grain which had been stored in pits would certainly have needed to be dried before it could be dehusked, and it is likely that the grain stored above ground was also parched to make the glumes brittle.

The equipment needed for crop processing was simple. No special kilns or ovens were needed for drying grain, and although the density and distribution of carbonised cereal remains is variable within and between settlements, this does not seem to differ from other concentrations of general domestic rubbish. This suggests that much grain processing was carried out by individual households rather than communally. Various activities required to prepare grain for grinding into flour can be inferred from the character of charred plant remains, but detailed interpretation is often hampered where material from several different activities has become mixed. Other unrelated plant remains were often accidentally incorporated into fires along with cereal processing waste and charred crop remains are also likely to have been redeposited through movement of soil in the digging and backfilling of pits, ditches and postholes. The evidence of crop processing practices that can be gleaned from charred plant remains is therefore only what can be glimpsed through the 'noise' created by other mechanisms determining the composition of charred plant samples.

Cereal processing remains are seldom abundant on middle to late Bronze Age sites, but at Bradford's Brook glumes of emmer and emmer or spelt dominated the waterlogged and charred cereal remains (Robinson 2006b). The charred remains from Taplow and Runnymede Bridge provided evidence for de-husking and final cleaning of emmer and spelt wheat. The high concentration of charred plant remains from Whitecross Farm suggested that crop processing was an important activity. Grain, cereal chaff and weed seeds were well-represented, suggesting de-husking and final cleaning of emmer and spelt wheat and six-row barley. Similar activity was probably occurring on other late Bronze Age settlements, including Eight Acre Field, Radley, although the concentration of crop processing remains from a waterhole dated to 1020-800 BC was lower (Robinson 1995 b).

Charred waste from cereal de-husking and final cleaning of the grain is more commonly found on some early Iron Age settlements such as at Ashville, Gravelly Guy and Yarnton (Jones in Parrington 1978; Moffett 2004; Pelling and Stevens in Hey *et al.* forthcoming a). In the case of grain stored in pits, once the pit had been opened it would have been necessary to process all the grain promptly before it germinated or rotted.

The results of the analysis of charred plant remains from the early Iron Age and Roman settle-ments settlements at Dorney contrasted markedly. The Iron Age settlements were certainly using six-row hulled barley and spelt wheat, but processing seems on a very small scale whereas processing of cereals was a major activity within the Roman settlement, which produced rich deposits of grain, cereal sprouts, chaff and weed seeds. Grains of six-row hulled barley were parched and de-husked both prior to milling and as part of the malting process for beer making. There is no evidence for the use of sprouted grain to brew beer until the Roman period.

Grinding of flour

Once cleaned and dried, grain would have been kept ready to use whole, or to be ground by hand into flour using quernstones. This was mainly done with saddle querns and loaf-shaped rubbers. Although very simple in design, saddle querns were carefully shaped to ensure stability on the ground and a smooth rubbing surface (Fig. 5.14). There are few examples in the region of rotary querns from middle to late Iron Age contexts,. They include two Upper Old Red Sandstone fragments (upper and lower stones) at Claydon Pike (Fig. 5.14; Miles *et al.* 2007, 52-3) and 15 fragments of Lodsworth upper and lower stones from a pit at Castle Hill, Little Wittenham dated to 200 cal BC to 1 cal AD (Roe in Allen *et al.* forthcoming b). Pieces of rotary Lodsworth quern have also been found in association with middle Iron Age pottery at Abingdon Vineyard (Roe pers. comm.).

Rotary querns, especially heavy 'beehive' forms, have advantages in their mechanical efficiency in that grain is gradually fed onto the grinding surfaces and a steady pressure assisted by the weight of the upper stone can be exerted. The sources of stone used for rotary querns, extending into the Roman period, differed from those for saddle querns. However, it is not clear whether this was a technical issue related to the suitability of different rocks for the more sophisticated rotary querns, and the availability of suitable tools to make them or socio-economic issues connected to status and exchange networks (see Chapter 6). It appears that the technical advantages of rotary over saddle querns for grain processing had rather little influence on their adoption in the later Iron Age, in the face of possible constraints on the new technology being taken up.

Tom Moore (2006, 119) has suggested that the apparent absence of saddle querns from Bagendon suggests that by the 1st century AD rotary querns were dominant, but high status sites may not be representative. Although unusually there were middle Iron Age rotary querns at Claydon Pike, there were no late Iron Age or early Roman ones and definite rotary quern fragments are generally seldom found at ordinary farming settlements of this period in the Upper Thames. None were found in late Iron Age and early Roman contexts at

Fig. 5.14   Food preparation: a) rotary quern from Claydon Pike; b) saddle quern and rubber from Gravelly Guy

a.

b.

0   250 mm

1:5

Thornhill Farm, Old Shifford, Gravelly Guy, Watkins Farm, Yarnton, Bicester Fields, Barton Court, Ashville and Mount Farm, though in several cases no querns of any kind were attributable to this period. Rotary querns are also rare at Middle Thames sites of this period.

Drink

Virtually nothing is known of the range of liquids drunk or their preparation. Apart from the obvious cases of water and milk, a multiplicity of infusions and brews could have been produced from natural and cultivated plants. Charred and waterlogged fruit stones are rarely present on sites, but they could reflect either eating the fruits or the waste resulting from drink preparation, or both. Although cereal-based beers and ales may have been made during late prehistory, there is no firm evidence of pre-Roman malting. The brewing of mead might be one explanation for the beeswax residues detected in pots from Yarnton (see below), but this is merely speculative.

Cooking

Burnt stones and cooking places

Food can readily be roasted, baked, boiled or steamed when placed with very hot stones in a pit, tank, large pot or other container. Since the heating is achieved indirectly there may be little evidence for the use of small pits in this way, except that boiling requires a waterproof lining. The use of hot stones placed along with food in pits or in tanks of water or as 'pot-boilers' is a well-documented and flexible method of cooking, and can encompass a wide variety of cooking modes, including boiling, stewing and simmering (O'Kelly 1954). This is complicated by the fact that hot stones are also thought to have been used to heat water on a larger scale for other purposes (see below). However, on most sites burnt stone is a characteristic component of deposits and hearths associated with houses and other areas of domestic occupation, suggesting it was commonly used for cooking in individual houses. Abundant deposits of burnt stone mixed with pottery, bones, charcoal from fires and other domestic debris are often found in ditches close to house doorways or as dumps in pits, hollows or other midden deposits. Sometimes burnt stones mixed with other domestic debris were used to make cobbled surfaces, as at Mingies Ditch (Allen and Robinson 1993, 91).

The ubiquity of this material has long been noted and the dense concentrations of burnt stone in the fills of some pits and waterholes from the middle Bronze Age onwards have often attracted comment. These stones seldom derive from the gravel deposits underlying sites, but were brought some distance, far outweighing in quantity and weight the stones imported as querns and rubbers, indicating how vital an element of ordinary life this was. Fragments of old querns, loomweights and other stone or ceramic objects were also recycled as 'pot-boilers' and burnt stones were often reused until they disintegrated.

Cooking pits and hearths

Pits with signs of *in situ* burning and/or very dense burnt debris in their fills are fairly common, and may have been used for cooking. A specific form of fired or semi-fired clay with no sign of wattles and smooth on only one side has been noted on late Bronze Age sites in the Middle Thames such as Aldermaston Wharf and Reading Business Park/Green Park, and in Surrey at Weston Wood Albury (Bradley *et al.* 1980, 244-5; Moore and Jennings 1992, 89; Brossler *et al.* 2004, 94; Russell, 1989). Such fragments are generally flat or slightly concave and it has been suggested that this material comes from pits that had clay linings fired *in situ* which may have acted as the base of ovens set in shallow pits or scoops. Another possibility for pieces that have flat or slightly concave surfaces is that they are smooth clay hearths (Brossler *et al.* 2004, 94). This type of fired clay has not specifically been noted for late prehistoric sites in the Upper Thames Valley but, like the under-reporting of burnt stone, this may be more a matter of recognition and reporting than real absence.

The notion of 'hearth and home' makes us think of hearths as an essential part of a house. In the very few cases where floor layers survive, as at Mingies Ditch, this usually seems to be the case. However, evidence from Mingies Ditch and other sites also indicates that hearths, at least in the sense of a particular place of domestic fires, were also an outdoor feature (Fig. 5.15). Some hearths were deliberately constructed of packed gravel or stone slabs, some were in small pits, others were formed from a densely packed layer of burnt limestone or flint and some survive only as areas of *in situ* burning surrounded by domestic debris (Allen and Robinson 1993, 37; Miles *et al.* 2007, 42). At Mingies Ditch as many outdoor hearths were found as indoor, though none of the outdoor ones were as carefully constructed as the indoor ones. Together with the evidence of burnt stones this indicates that outdoor living and cooking were features of late prehistoric life, and perhaps more common than is reflected in the modern-day phenomenon of permanent barbecue stands.

Cooking Vessels

Observation of sooting deposits on pottery (Lambrick 1984; forthcoming) suggests that pots were often placed directly on or immediately above the flames and also sometimes hung above them. Varying the height of cooking pots relative to the fire would been a standard way of controlling the level of heat. Although more elaborate equipment for cooking over hearths, such as cauldrons, chains, firedogs and spits are known in British late prehistory, the only evidence from the Thames Valley is a few finds of cauldrons, mostly scraps. The notion that certain large round-bodied T-rimmed pots

found at Mount Farm and elsewhere might be pottery cauldrons (Bradford 1942, 12; Harding 1972, 75-8) has probably been refuted by the discovery of a similar vessel with a flat base at Appleford (Hinchliffe and Thomas 1980, 24), though some distinction is to be drawn between true T-shaped rims and merely thickened ones like the Appleford vessel, which had a longer currency into the middle Iron Age. Recently part of a very large coarse ware pottery vessel of non-local form was found in the ditch of the late Bronze Age enclosure at Castle Hill (Allen *et al.* forthcoming b). Metal cauldrons and buckets were objects of high prestige in later prehistory, and may have been used both for cooking and serving feasts or special meals (see below).

As the postulated pottery cauldrons indicate, the form of vessels is not always a reliable indication of function. Use of pottery vessels for cooking, however, can be examined by observing the presence of sooting and macroscopic burnt cooking residues, limescale and leaching on their surfaces, and, more recently, by analysing sherds for biochemical traces of the food itself (Fig. 5.15). Lambrick (1984) showed how useful information about cooking practices can be gleaned from analysis of macroscopic use wear residues, leaching and abrasion of pottery. This was based on an analysis of the early to middle Iron Age pottery at Mount Farm, where 6% of the sherds exhibited such residues. The level of occurrence of such residues has also been noted elsewhere, 4.5% for middle to late Bronze Age pottery at Green Park (Morris 2004) and 5.3% for Yarnton (Booth in Hey *et al.* forthcoming a). In most cases, however, the rate of occurrence is seldom reported, so it is not clear that the relative 'lack of visible use wear evidence' at Green Park is as noteworthy as Morris suggests. It may be that cooking vessels were generally kept reasonably clean, but it is also noticeable that, where forms can be determined, the proportion of sherds exhibiting residues can be very high for some vessel types.

The analysis of residues and wear on early to middle Iron Age pottery from Mount Farm suggested a number of broad patterns (Lambrick 1984; forthcoming). A wide range of vessel sizes was used in cooking, including some small ones with capacities of 0.6 litres or less. There is no positive evidence from limescaling or thick carbonised residues for cooking pots over 2.2 litres in capacity, suggesting that in general cooking and eating was carried out at a small family scale. Pots for cooking relatively solid food such as thick soups and stews tended to be used low on an open fire and were almost exclusively unburnished and often coarsewares. These coarse vessels used for cooking had both limescale and carbonised residues, sometimes

Fig. 5.15 (opposite)   Cooking pits, hearths and equipment used in cooking: a) Distribution of hearths at Mingies Ditch; b) late Bronze Age perforated slab fragment from Home Farm, Laleham; c) fired clay slabs from Gravelly Guy; d) and e) cooking residues on Iron Age pottery from Mount Farm (position of residues shown on profile) and f) Castle Hill, Little Wittenham

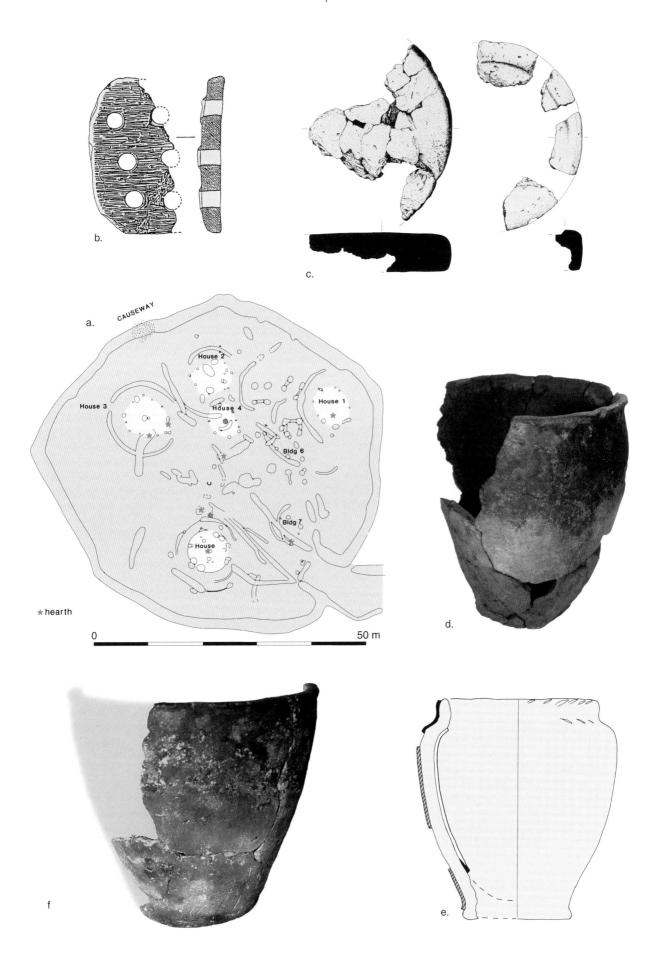

b.

c.

a.

CAUSEWAY

House 2

House 3

House 4

House 1

Bldg 6

Bldg 7

House

★ hearth

0   50 m

d.

f

e.

both occurring on an individual vessel, showing some diversity in function. However, a notably high proportion of vessels associated with heating water were burnished fineware bowls, sometimes decorated, so although there was no simple distinction between fine 'table ware' and coarse 'kitchen ware', the 'kitchen' use of fineware was significantly restricted. Three sherds from smallish bowls had limescaling extending through holes in the pots and extending across the base, a phenomenon also noted on a sherd from Castle Hill (Edwards in Allen *et al.* forthcoming a). These could reflect either a double cooker arrangement (fitting in with the occurrence of limescale on the rim of some larger pots) or more likely might be the result of straining curds in cheese making. Occasional differential leaching of the inside of pots with calcareous temper might indicate boiling of relatively acidic fruit or vegetables, but could result from physical wear and tear from cycles of soaking in hot liquid and drying and mechanical abrasion from stirring contents during cooking or serving.

At Claydon Pike (Jones 2007, 48-9) between a third and half of middle Iron Age pots and jars with shaped necks, internally bevelled rims and barrel-shaped or globular profiles had external sooting and/or internal burnt residues, indicating consistent use in cooking or heating, but only 10-20% of bowls had cooking residues. Some vessels, such as expanded rim forms, were seldom used for cooking. Of 38 vessel bases recovered there were no deposits of external soot, consistent with the evidence from Mount Farm that vessels were usually placed low in the fire or on the hearth during cooking. As at Mount Farm, internal abrasion and leaching was noted on some vessels. A wide range of vessel sizes were used for cooking at Claydon Pike, mostly small to medium pots and jars of 100-200 mm diameter (*c* 0.5 to 6 litres capacity), but seldom larger vessels within the same groups, though sooting was noted on two very large vessels of 360 mm and 380 mm diameter (up to 30 litres capacity). Such large vessels suggest the preparation and consumption of food on a communal scale, but like Mount Farm, this was very rare and in general the conclusion is that people prepared and consumed food in relatively small family groups.

At Gravelly Guy and Yarnton (Lambrick and Allen 2004, 278; Hey *et al.* forthcoming a) less correlation was found between fine- or coarse-wares and types of cooking residue, but unlike Mount Farm, the distinction of 'wares' was based more on fabrics, not finish. This may indicate that if a distinction between 'fineware' and 'coarseware' vessels is to be drawn, it should be on the basis of finish, and perhaps form, not fabric. At Yarnton similar observations about forms were noted, with carbonised residues commonest on simple barrel-shaped jars, less commonly shouldered, angular or globular forms, but this was not related to vessel size.

In other cases in the Upper Thames Valley, including several with large assemblages, use wear evidence has been noted but with no quantification or detailed analysis. This applies also to Middle Thames Valley sites where large assemblages of middle and late Bronze Age pottery have been recovered, in some cases with sequences stretching into the Iron Age. Although the conclusions of the Mount Farm study have been partly confirmed by the evidence from Claydon Pike, most subsequent investigations have not been sufficiently specific to confirm or refute these observations, even where the assemblages were sufficiently large with copious discussion of pottery forms and fabrics. For example, it has been suggested that the cordons on Deverel-Rimbury bucket urns would have facilitated hanging above a fire, but this has not been tested by examining patterns of sooting and residues.

The examination of bio-chemical traces of food preparation and consumption absorbed as lipids into pottery fabrics is a relatively new technique that has not been extensively applied to later prehistoric material in Britain. The largest such study carried out to date has been for Yarnton, where 28 of 49 samples submitted produced some residues (Copley in Hey *et al.* forthcoming a). Nearly all the residues recovered were degraded animal fats, but it was possible to show that five of the sherds came from pots that had been used for food containing ruminant adipose fats (eg beef or mutton stews), a further three from vessels which also contained porcine adipose fats (pork or ham as well as beef and mutton) and that 11 sherds came from pots that contained dairy products. A further two sherds produced evidence of beeswax, possibly remnants of food containing honey. None produced leaf wax compounds derived from vegetables. No particular correlation with vessel form or finish was noted, though one of the beeswax samples came from an All Cannings Cross type decorated vessel. In general this evidence seems to confirm multipurpose use of vessels, as indicated in less detail by the macroscopic residues. What these results do not convey is the extent to which residues may have accumulated through cooking or serving food.

Ovens, griddles and other cooking equipment

While hearths and pots provide evidence for boiling, braising and roasting, ovens suggest that food was also baked. No *in situ* oven bases have

Fig. 5.16 (opposite)   Fine ware decorated pottery and wooden bowls: a) early Iron Age All Cannings Cross style bowl from Yarnton; b) middle Iron Age swagged bowl from Abingdon; c) early Iron Age decorated lid from Castle Hill; d) early Iron Age haematite-coated bowl from Castle Hill; e) middle Bronze Age wooden bowl from Perry Oaks/T5; f) middle Bronze Age bowl from Latton Lands; g) late Bronze Age ladle from Green Park, Reading

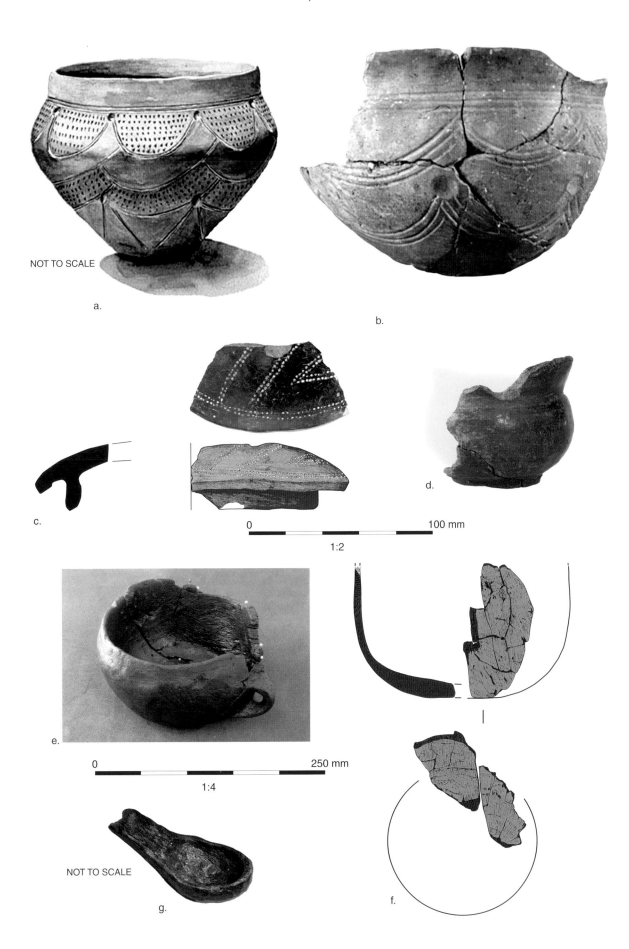

NOT TO SCALE

a.

b.

c.

d.

0   100 mm

1:2

e.

0   250 mm

1:4

NOT TO SCALE

g.

f.

been found in the region, but several sites have produced fragments of daub-like material with concave surfaces that could have come from ovens built of fired clay. An unusual object that may provide evidence of baking was a small (*c* 20 mm³) piece of charred material found at Ashville which had chaff on its surface, tentatively identified as bread (Jones 1978, 98).

Perforated square or rectangular fired clay slabs are a specific type of late Bronze Age artefact often assumed to be associated with cooking, partly by analogy with ovens with perforated clay components from continental Europe, though it is not clear how they were used (Fig. 5.15). They are usually rectangular or square, about 10 mm thick and perforated with *c* 6-10 mm diameter holes before firing. They are sometimes interpreted as 'cooking stands.' Complete examples are rare but fragments are commonly found in small numbers with domestic refuse on settlement sites in eastern England and in the Middle Thames Valley as far upstream as west of Reading. They have not so far been found in the Upper Thames area.

Thick circular fired clay slabs found on later prehistoric sites may also have been associated with cooking. At Gravelly Guy 13 or so slabs up to 440 mm in diameter and 68 mm thick were found, all but one in two early Iron Age pits associated with a post-built roundhouse (Lambrick and Allen 2004, 339-40; 384-6, fig. 8.13, 118, Pl. 3.2; 249). These differ in size and character from the fired clay discs or pot lids of Roman date (Lambrick and Robinson 1979, 53-4; Hey 1995, 136-8; Bradley *et al.* 2005, 168-9). One slab had what appeared to be a 'lip', perhaps a thumb-hold and another had a flange round the outer edge of one side. They may be griddle plates which were heated in a fire and then removed for slow-cooking dough, batter or pancake mixtures, hence the low flanges. Another possibility is that they were oven furniture. They are not common artefacts, but late Iron Age or early Roman examples were found at Mount Farm (Lambrick forthcoming). A range of ceramic discs and plates, some with perforations resembling examples from Wessex, were found at Castle Hill (Allen *et al.* forthcoming a).

Fired clay objects of various types cannot conclusively be associated with cooking, and other possible explanations, such as cheese-making or multiple functions, have been noted. None has been subjected to detailed scientific analysis, either for food or other residues, and they are too rare for patterns of contextual associations, even as rubbish, to be explored much further.

Serving, eating and feasting

Throughout the period a distinction can be made between fineware and coarseware pottery that may broadly reflect the use of vessels primarily for preparing or serving food. However, the range of forms used for serving food remained limited for most of the period, consisting mainly of bowls, pots and jars. It was only at the end of the Iron Age under the influence of a Romanised Europe that a wider range of serving dishes, beakers and flagons began to appear. Nevertheless, throughout the period there are well-finished, sometimes carefully decorated medium and small jars and bowls clearly designed for presentation of food, even if not on a daily basis (Fig. 5.16).

The existence of non-ceramic serving or dual purpose cooking and serving vessels is evident from a few fragments of bronze cauldrons, buckets and wooden vessels. In recent years with a proliferation of waterhole excavations, especially of middle to late Bronze Age date, a number of wooden bowls and other vessels have been found. These include a wooden bowl or ladle at Runnymede (Needham 1991, 141, fig. 63 Pl.54), four wooden vessels at Perry Oaks/T5 (Barrett *et al.* 2001; Framework Archaeology 2006 and forthcoming), an unfinished maple bowl from Wey Manor Farm (Hayman 1999, forthcoming e), a wooden bowl, a spoon or ladle and part of another vessel at Green Park (Taylor in Webley *et al.* forthcoming), a shallow bowl from Yarnton (Taylor in Hey *et al.* forthcoming a) and a fragmentary bowl from Latton Lands (Stansbie and Laws 2004,). Most of them are simple semi-spherical or slightly ovoid with no footring. A bowl from Perry Oaks/T5 is more elaborate than the others in having a lug handle and a stitched repair, but none of the examples so far discovered is decorated. Although rare survivals as archaeological finds, these objects may have been common items of eating and drinking.

Feasting and other special meals are generally assumed to have been an important aspect of late prehistoric society, though direct evidence is relatively scarce (Fig. 5.17). On a number of sites concentrations of animal bones have been interpreted as remains of feasting events (Fig. 5.18), sometimes in a funerary or religious context. For example, at Mount Farm a scatter of butchered cattle bones were found in a ring ditch associated with middle Bronze Age cremation and inhumation burials (Lambrick forthcoming). At Castle Hill, Little Wittenham a large assemblage of animal bone and pottery was recovered from a single early Iron Age pit (Allen *et al.* forthcoming a). The 621 identifiable bones included a disproportionate number of lambs and piglets, possibly representing the slaughter of numerous young animals at one time for a feast. Butchered cattle, deer and horse bones were also present, together with the articulated skeleton of a raven and an unidentified fish bone. The pit also contained 11.5 kg of pottery, representing a significant number of vessels, dominated by large T-rimmed cooking pots, formerly called 'cauldrons',

Fig. 5.17 (opposite) Feasting vessels and debris: (left) *a) the Weybridge cordoned bucket; b) the Battersea cauldron; c) the Brentford tankard;* (right) *late Bronze Age/early Iron Age 'feasting set' from a waterhole at Perry Oaks/T5*

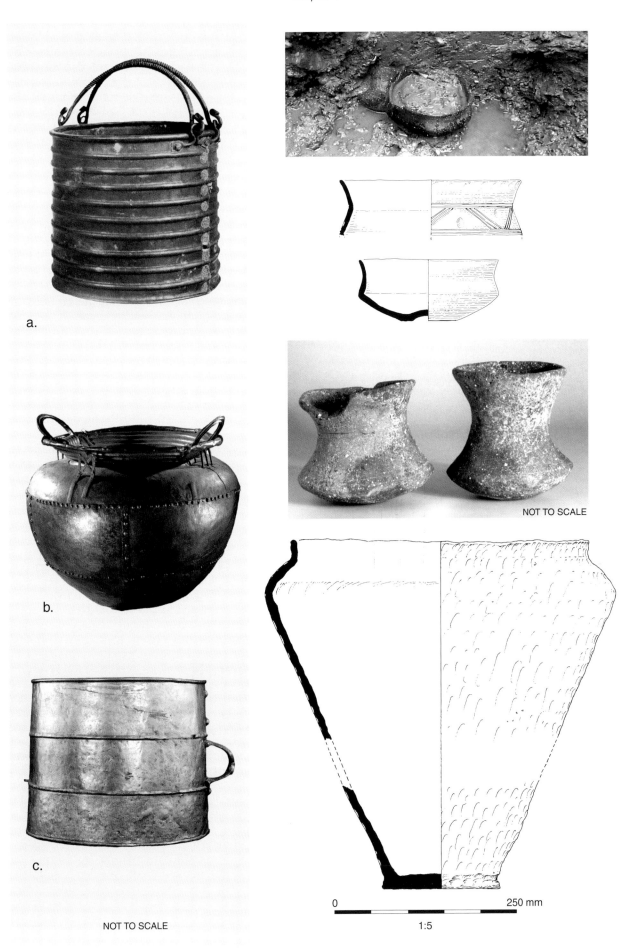

a.

b.

c.

NOT TO SCALE

NOT TO SCALE

0 250 mm

1:5

165

and small red-finished round-bodied bowls or cups. This distinctive assemblage suggests communal eating and drinking. A pottery lid of possible continental origin was also recovered from this clearly significant deposition context. In the hillfort at Aylesbury a bizarre deposit of human remains and bones of numerous lambs and kids suggests a combination of ritual sacrifice and feasting (Farley 1986a, b). Wilson (1992; 1996) has suggested that feasting could account for the relatively frequent occurrence of exceptionally dense animal bones and articulated carcasses.

Metal vessels and elaborate wooden ones, along with highly finished pottery may have been reserved for feasting. The earliest examples of cauldrons are late Bronze Age or earliest Iron Age and various types evolved through the Iron Age and into the Roman period. The very fine early Iron Age bronze bucket from Weybridge near Brooklands is a rare import from the Alpine region of Italy, thought to belong to a wine mixing set (Fig. 5.17; Smith 1908). Relatively few examples of late prehistoric high status metal vessels are known from the Thames Valley, and excavated examples are usually fragmentary. Some, like a substantial fragment from Shepperton Ranges, are from riverine contexts but are more commonly elements of hoards of scrap metalwork (Needham 1990, 63-7). Very few fragments of metal cauldrons or buckets have been found on settlement sites in the Thames Valley, but one such example is a fragment of a repaired 1st century BC Stanton 1 type cauldron

from a pit at Gravelly Guy (Lambrick and Allen 2004, 340, 362, fig. 8.5 no.4).

Higher status wooden vessels are also rare, due partly to adverse conditions for preservation on dry sites. The most impressive example from the Thames Valley is a late Iron Age three litre oak-staved tankard bound in beaten bronze sheeting with a separately cast decorative handle from a river hoard at Brentford (Fig. 5.17; Corcoran 1952). Both the tankard and doubtless its contents would have been highly valued, probably reserved for ceremonial feasting.

Apart from pottery and other vessels, few known implements can unambiguously be associated with eating or serving food and drink. The unusual find of a wooden ladle at Green Park is one of the clearest. Carved from a single piece of wood, it has an oval bowl with a short handle set at a shallow angle. Much commoner, but more ambiguous as serving or eating implements, are a variety of bone tools, notably scoops and 'knives', made more or less throughout later prehistory.

Metal knives are much less common and are equally ambiguous as eating implements. Indeed it may be misleading to suppose they were restricted to particular uses. For example, in the late Bronze Age small cutting implements usually described as 'razors' and/or 'knives' are mostly recovered from settlement sites with other imported and relatively high status finds, such as Runnymede and Whitecross Farm. Such objects are generally referred to as 'razors' (some tanged, others not) because of their delicate, sometimes elaborate form that seems unsuited to use as common domestic implements, and their association with continental – but not British – male graves (see below). However, they may have been used as knives, perhaps for only special purposes.

Larger socketed knives are known from later Bronze Age contexts, usually hoards or riverine deposits. At Whitecross Farm several socketed knives were possibly from a scattered hoard deposited or eroded into the river (Cromarty *et al.* 2006, 48, 55-7, fig. 53 no. 6). One is also known from occupation deposits of the similar site at Runnymede, where an unfinished antler object thought to be a knife handle was also found (Needham 1991; Needham and Spence 1996, 190 no. B22). Most Iron Age knives are tanged, made of iron, and assumed to have been for general use, though some of the smaller curved cutting implements may have been predominantly for domestic rather than agricultural use (Harding 172, Pl 76, D, E; Lambrick and Allen 363-5, fig. 8.7, no 510). A small, straight, short-bladed example from a pit at Hill Farm, Little Wittenham might have been specifically for food preparation or eating, but is unusual in that it is double-edged (Scott in Allen *et al.* forthcoming a). Handles for knives are known from several sites, including Standlake, where a curved knife or cutting hook was found complete with its handle. Another possibly unfinished handle compa-

Fig. 5.18   Pit containing animal bone fragments, Gravelly Guy

rable with others probably intended for knives was found at Yarnton (Harding 1972, 172, Pl 76 C, D; Hey *et al.* forthcoming a). A bronze knife handle shaped as a bull or ox head was one of a group of grave goods at Birdlip (Green 1949).

HEALTH AND SICKNESS

Limited information can be gleaned about health and disease from archaeological evidence. A certain amount can be assumed about quality of diet from remains of what people ate, and hence some idea of health, but while this gives us some idea of potential nutrition, it provides little indication of the actual availability or abundance of food and whether there were significant risks of food shortages. We also have only the faintest indications of what herbs and other remedies were available as basic medicines. The bulk of the evidence we have about people's health, or more particularly disease, in later prehistory comes from the people themselves, whose skeletal elements are well-preserved where soils are calcareous or neutral, especially in the Upper Thames region. However, it is important to be aware of biases both in the incidence of burials, which is affected by varying soil conditions along the Thames Valley, and who was buried where. We will see that this is unlikely to be fully representative of the general population.

Food supply and nutrition

In very general terms it seems that the region was easily capable of providing sufficient food for people. It is also clear that the range of subsistence food consisted of a variety of cereals, pulses, meat and dairy products which, as long as they were properly stored, would have been healthy and nutritious. The region is a lowland valley with generally fertile soils, less vulnerable to climatic and other factors that are likely to have affected the viability of more marginal upland areas of Britain. There is no *prima facie* reason to believe that there were famines or food shortages during this period, though outbreaks of plant or animal disease and human illness or conflict, not obvious in the available evidence, could have caused problems. Most settlements were probably at least self sufficient and/or capable of producing a tradable surplus in either animals or cereal produce. The Gravelly Guy calculations suggested that settlements of that kind would have been capable of generating a sufficient surplus to weather the odd crop failure or relatively poor harvest, though this may have depended on the size of reserve retained for such contingencies after trading the bulk of any surplus (Lambrick and Allen 2004, 484-8). If some communities or family groups led a transhumant pastoralist existence for much of the time, it remains likely that they would have been capable of growing or obtaining sufficient cereals to supplement food from animal produce while also generating the wherewithal for exchange.

The inevitable outbreaks of infection, poor harvests and other setbacks would not automatically have precluded the enjoyment of a broadly healthy life style, at least as far as diet was concerned. However, it is a common characteristic of many societies that producing sufficient animals and crops not only to feed your family but also generate a surplus is not an automatic guarantee that communities are well-fed. There are innumerable social and economic reasons for inequalities that may result in poor nutrition. In recent years careful examination of teeth of late prehistoric people in the Thames Valley has revealed the common incidence of hypoplasia, fine cracks in tooth enamel, associated with poor nutrition and mainly evident in youths and young adults. However, as it has been recorded only in recent analyses it is only just becoming apparent how common it may have been and, as discussed below, the sample may be biased in terms of the status of people whose remains are found.

Stature is another broad indicator of general health and nutrition, but not very reliable given small and potentially biased samples. Taking 24 relatively complete adult skeletons, mostly women, from later Bronze Age to late Iron Age pits and graves in the Thames Valley and 17 in the middle Iron Age cemetery at Yarnton, stature averaged 1.65 m (pits) to 1.68 m (cemetery) for men, and 1.53 m (pits) to 1.58 m (cemetery) for women. This compares with site assemblages from northern and southern England with averages ranging from 1.65 m to 1.71 m for men and 1.56 m to 1.62 m for women (figures quoted by Hey *et al.* forthcoming a) and national averages calculated by Roberts and Cox (2003, 396) of 1.68 m for men and 1.62 m for women. This compares with national averages of 1.65 m and 1.57 m in the Neolithic (1.69 m and 1.60 m for a sample of eight Thames Valley burials), and 1.72 m and 1.61 m in the Bronze Age (1.75 m and 1.63 m for a sample of 14 Thames Valley burials). The national figures for the Roman period are 1.69 m and 1.59 m, and for the early medieval period, 1.72 m and 1.61 m. Local populations in the Thames Valley fall within a centimetre or two either side of these figures (Booth *et al.* 2007, 162-3, 174).

The extent to which such variations are genuine, based as they are on a small and disparate late prehistoric sample, is debatable, but worth noting if only to raise questions. The figures for the Thames Valley initially suggest a late prehistoric break in a gradual increase in stature, with a decline after an increase from the earlier Neolithic to the Bronze Age, and then another increase through the Roman and Saxon periods, consistent with national trends. This might superficially be taken to indicate that the late prehistoric transition to more permanent settled farming was initially not especially conducive to improved general health. But there were also changes in burial practice that might have produced a bias in the comparison of the earlier prehistoric and later prehistoric samples relative to socio-economic advantage and disadvantage (see below). It is also worth noting that there was not more difference between the Yarnton cemetery and some Roman ones.

Another broad indicator of health is longevity, although there are the usual *caveats* of relatively limited numbers of late prehistoric burials and the biases that arise from excarnation and the possibly unrepresentative social status of those buried in pits and graves (see Chapter 8). So far as the available skeletal remains can shed any light on this, it appears that about a quarter of people who survived their first year did not reach their twenties; a further quarter were probably dead before they were thirty and only a few lived much into or beyond their forties.

Despite a reasonable diet, the absence of sophisticated medicines would have meant that childhood and adult diseases and complications arising from accidents or infections would have been common causes of early death. The issue of neonatal death is difficult to assess. In general terms the relative frequency of neonatal infant remains, including one double burial of a woman and neonate (Birbeck 2001, 231, 271) and another of a woman and foetus (Allen *et al.* 2000, 83, Pl 6), suggests that childbirth was often traumatic and infant mortality would have been common. This may, however, be distorted by social attitudes if very small infants (eg in the first year of life) were not regarded as fully-fledged members of society, as discussed in Chapter 8. Although neonatal human remains are common on Iron Age settlements, the pattern is highly variable; even those sites with the highest occurrence are unlikely to reflect the true incidence of infant mortality. For example, the exceptionally numerous deposits of 43 infant burials and stray bones at Gravelly Guy represent only about one case per 100 years per family, if the interpretation that the settlement represented about six households over 700 years is correct (Lambrick and Allen 2004, 223-36, tables 6.2, 6.3). While infant burials may reflect some natural instances of perinatal death, there were more complex social factors that determined whether or not the remains were disposed of within settlements, and infanticide cannot be ruled out.

Indications of chronic disease suggest that many people, especially from their 30s onwards had bad teeth, suffered back and joint problems and a variety of other painful and crippling ailments. Some, like spinal and joint disease, are not much more curable now than they were then, except that we probably have much better pain relief. Although the sugarless diet of prehistoric people was in some ways less likely to cause caries or other dental disease than is the case today, natural sugars and honey (for which the honey bee at Mingies Ditch provides indirect evidence) would have triggered tooth decay and there was less effective prevention or cure than today. Caries is present in some younger people of the later prehistoric period, but

most tooth losses and abscesses are evident in those of twenty-five and more. Most of these older people must have suffered severe toothache. In general it appears that the incidence of tooth problems in the small sample collated for the Thames Valley is worse than the national picture (Roberts and Cox 2003, 89-104) but both sets of figures are affected by the nature of the samples – the national picture dominated by Yorkshire barrows and other cemeteries; the much smaller Thames Valley sample being mainly settlement burials, though the Yarnton cemetery is not very different in several respects.

Although pain relief might have been crude, a wide range of remedies and potions could have been made from natural plants, fungi and animal parts, and it is likely that the worst pain was relieved with mind-altering drugs. Their existence is almost impossible to prove but plant remains provide a degree of evidence. These include opium poppy, which is sufficiently common in later Bronze Age deposits to suggest that it was probably deliberately grown, although it is not clear to what extent this would have been for medicinal rather than culinary purposes (see Chapter 7). A wide range of native plants commonly found in waterlogged deposits could have been used for a variety of treatments including antiseptic, diuretic, antibiotic, laxative, digestive, analgesic, anti-rheumatic, sedative and general tonic effects (www.herbal-medicines.org/explorer_index.html). However, while biological evidence indicates the availability of many species of herb and plant sources as potentially useful natural remedies, it is not possible to demonstrate their actual use from existing evidence. It is possible that residues identified from lipids or waterlogged deposits might in future shed more light on this.

While it is very difficult to demonstrate the use of drugs and potions, there is clearer evidence that at least basic medicine was practised. Dental treatments were probably very limited, but examples of healed tooth losses, probably from extraction before death are moderately common. Broken bones do not seem to have been especially common, and while some were clearly not properly set, there are examples of healed fractures of long bones that are sufficiently clean and straight to suggest crude setting (eg Allen *et al.* 2000, 93, Pls 14 and 15).

An interesting example of a late prehistoric medical procedure is the practice of trepanning – removal of a disc of bone from the skull of a living patient. In the samples examined by Roberts and Cox (2003) they found five or six cases each for the Neolithic, Bronze Age and Iron Age. The reasons for carrying out this procedure probably include both medical and magico-ritual purposes (Piggott 1940). Possibilities range from relief of pressure on the brain causing severe headaches or convulsive fits, to brain infections (probably the cause of death of a child at Bourton-on-the-Water) and epilepsy or mental ailments, perhaps including conditions that caused irrational behaviour. Assuming that little was understood about brain function, the most likely practical reason for trepanning would have been to relieve obvious and severe pain, but it is possible that broader cultural and spiritual attitudes to the human head were also involved, and in some cases trepanning was carried out after death (Piggott 1940). Unhealed trepanning holes like one at Hunsbury, Northamptonshire could also be cases where the operation failed or caused death.

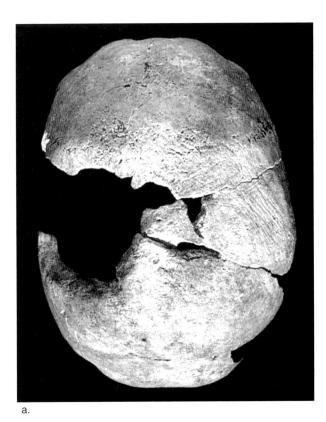

a.

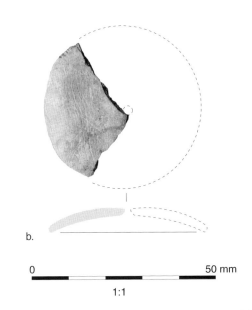

b.

0 ———————— 50 mm

1:1

Fig. 5.19 a) Trepanned male skull from Watchfield; b) perforated human skull pendant from Green Park, Reading

The massive healed trepanning hole in a male skull from Watchfield (McKinley 2001, 272, fig. 16) is testimony to the fact that these crude operations, presumably done with no anaesthetic or at best only natural sedatives or mind-altering drugs, did sometimes work (Fig. 5.19). The Watchfield skull represents one of the largest trepans known from Britain. The discs of human skull from trepanning operations or post-mortem mutilations are occasionally found and were sometimes turned into pendants, like late Bronze Age and early Iron Age examples from Green Park (Fig. 5.19) and Gravelly Guy (Brossler *et al.* 99, fig. 4.23; Lambrick and Allen 2004, 386, fig. 387). It is conceivable that these were worn by their owners as talismans of good fortune after successful operations. Some operations were probably not successful: additional, unhealed scraping of the Watchfield man's trepanned skull around the time of death may indicate that a second operation to treat a recurrence of the problem or some other condition was not successful, though it might alternatively suggest a post-mortem investigation of a remarkable survival.

Although there is thus some evidence of medical treatment, including basic dentistry and surgery, it is not possible to establish with certainty the attitudes to the chronically sick and disabled in late prehistoric communities. There is wider evidence that celtic societies respected women and cared for the sick and the elderly, but as we shall see in Chapter 8 that does not mean that they were always well cared for.

DRESS, ORNAMENT AND PERSONAL APPEARANCE

For some periods the objects found with burials are highly informative about modes of dress, but this is not the case for later prehistory. Most people were excarnated or cremated or their remains were scattered, so relatively few burials are found (see below, Chapter 8). Even amongst the not insignificant number of inhumation burials that have been recorded, grave goods are very rare before the late Iron Age and not very informative about dress. A spindle whorl, toggles and pendants at Gravelly Guy, a pot at Gallows Leaze, a bone ring at Abingdon, and a bracelet associated with a burial at Cassington are about the limit of the evidence. Some late Iron Age burials, however, were exceptionally richly furnished, especially in the heartlands of the Catuvellaunii on the dip slope of the Chilterns north of London, though most of these are cremation burials that offer no clear evidence of how personal ornaments were worn. The exceptionally richly furnished burial discovered in 1879 at Birdlip on the edge of the Cotswolds was one of three, or possibly four, associated inhumation burials, but no detailed record was made of the finds distributions within the main grave. Such burials are therefore generally uninformative about how personal ornaments were worn or their gender associations, but they do provide useful evidence of associations between objects from which possible gender attributions can be guessed, albeit at some risk of making stereotypical assumptions that are not demonstrable. They also provide additional evidence of the range of objects regarded as important to the deceased, although again much caution is needed in distinguishing the personal, communal and spiritual connotations involved.

Dress

What we know of dress comes from the evidence of the materials used and crafts involved in making clothes and, for personal ornaments, from objects that were lost. Although some items were probably made of animal skins or pelts, most clothes would have been made from woven, and possibly knitted, wool. There is also good evidence for the growing of flax, particularly in the late Bronze Age, suggesting that linen may also have been important. The greater use of woven or knitted fabrics is generally thought to be evident from the common appearance of spindle whorls and weaving equipment and from the increasing proportions of sheep in animal herds, suggesting that wool was an increasingly important by-product. Leather would have been used for belts and thongs and natural fibres are likely to have been used to make the cords that may be inferred from the existence of toggles and pendants (see below). Seeds and other plant remains, including weld, recovered from waterlogged deposits could have been used in dyeing (Campbell 1992, 34-40). There is no evidence from the region to indicate what footwear may have been worn. Likewise, there is very little direct evidence for the shape or form of clothing – certainly nothing to add to other, more informative sources (eg Lloyd-Morgan 1995, 98-102). Some evidence of dress comes from personal ornaments associated with the fastening of clothes.

Dress pins and brooches

In the middle to late Bronze Age and early Iron Age large decorative pins were probably used as a means of fastening loose garments, though they have also been interpreted as large hair pins. In the late Bronze Age these pins displayed a wide range of forms. Nail headed pins were recovered at Woodeaton, Eynsham, Whitecross Farm and Marsh Lane West (Northover forthcoming). Others with sun disc and other decorative heads, including imports from the continent such as a wart headed pin from Lower Saxony at Runnymede (Needham and Spence 1996, 188, M26) or a Picardy pin from Siddington, Gloucestershire (Enright 1999), suggest that they would have been seen as valuable, even exotic objects of some status.

In the early Iron Age swan-neck and ring-headed pins with a distinctive kink at the neck, which would have helped secure the fastening, are characteristic forms made both in bronze and iron. Swan-necked pins, as exemplified by three from Woodeaton (Harding 1972, 90, 170, pl 73; 1987, 39) and a recent find from Castle Hill (Allen *et al.* forthcoming a), are considered a particular regional speciality of south-west England, in which the Thames Valley is on the periphery. An unusually large number of early Iron Age ring-headed pins are known from the Woodeaton midden deposit. Several of these have bent shafts, though it is not clear if this was connected with their practical use in fastening clothes, dress or hair, or with votive associations. Some ring-headed pins had relatively elaborate heads, such as an example from Syon Reach, but most are plain, and iron pins, such as a recent find from Warborough/Berwick Salome (Major 2005, Appendix H), would probably have been more functional than ornamental.

From the end of the early Iron Age onwards fibula style brooches, offering more secure fastening, became fashionable. These display a fairly distinctive evolution of styles that reflect continental forms, best known from the major deposits of objects in peat deposits at La Tène on the shores of Lake Neuchâtel in Switzerland. From the middle Iron Age onwards, penannular brooch forms became fashionable. Both iron and bronze were used to make pins and brooches in the Iron Age and they vary quite significantly in the quality of finish and degree of decoration, the Woodeaton midden providing a notable range of examples (Harding 1972, 94, 170-1 pl 74; 1987, 39).

At Gravelly Guy the body of a 10 or 11 year old child with a fragmentary Nauheim derivative iron brooch and the pin of another brooch in front of his/her face was found in a small grave amongst the ditches of a late Iron Age or early Roman enclosure complex (Lambrick and Allen 2004, 233-6, 249, 394, figs 6.3 and 8.18). This is unusual in providing *in situ* burial evidence of the use of such brooches, but their fragmentary condition and the rarity of such associations makes interpretation difficult. They might indicate the use of two brooches fastening a garment at the shoulder or high under the chin, but they could alternatively represent the fastening of a bag or shroud in which the body was buried.

Toggles and strap unions

Objects associated with cords, thongs and straps that may have accompanied clothing include two small decorated bone toggles found with a burial at Gravelly Guy, two others from the same site, one with a transverse hole, and a similar one from Yarnton decorated with a flower motif (Lambrick and Allen 2004, 389, fig 8.14; Hey *et al.* forthcoming a). Larger toggle-like objects are also known, but less obviously accompanying personal dress. An unusual late Bronze Age ornament is a so-called bugle fitting found in the Petters hoard (Needham

1990, 61 fig. 14). Other examples in different variations are one from the river at Sion Reach (Wheeler 1929, 11-13, pl II fig. 1) and a two-piece example from the Berkshire Downs at Waylands Smithy (Whittle 1991, 87-8, fig. 12), for which patterns of wear suggest use as a strap union. Although very different in detailed shape and style, two decorated middle Iron Age antler objects from Mount Farm and Rollright of comparable form were independently identified as possible strap unions (Lambrick 1988, 96-7, fig. 65, no 1). The precise way in which these objects functioned is not clear, but apparently they allowed one strap to cross over another strap or a cord to hold each in position while held tight and also allowing easy adjustment if loosened. The size of these decorative objects suggests they were most likely to have been for personal use rather than harness.

Personal appearance and toiletries

Items such as late Bronze Age 'razors', tweezers and late Iron Age mirrors demonstrate concern with personal appearance in addition to the impression created by clothes, ornaments and personal tools and other equipment (Fig. 5.20). Personal and social status was expressed through all these means. The relative rarity of what might be termed 'toiletry' items and their more common occurrence on high status sites suggests that an overtly particular concern with personal appearance was in itself a mark of high status.

A number of well-preserved 'bog bodies' in Britain and Europe suggest that some attention was paid to how people wore and cut their hair and manicured their nails (Glob 1969; Stead *et al.* 1986; Parker Pearson 1999). Both men and women seem to have worn their hair long, and it is possible to imagine the use of the long pins, rings and possibly 'strap unions' mentioned above to hold hair in position. There are few depictions of people from the region but two probably late Iron Age heads, one of bronze from Welwyn, the other of sculpted chalk from Chelsea, show men with large trimmed moustaches in the manner typical of other Celtic depictions of warriors (Lloyd Morgan 1995, 95-8).

The objects most suitable for cutting hair are small knife-like implements, commonly referred to as 'razors', which are known in a variety of both single and double-bladed forms from the late Bronze Age onwards. Exactly how they might have been used as knives for cutting hair or razors for shaving is uncertain, including whether they were used on a regular basis, retained for special occasions, or even only for the preparation of dead bodies before burial. Razors are not very common. They are sometimes found in hoards, some are known from the river and a few from late Iron Age burials. Only a few have been found on Thames Valley settlements, most from relatively high status sites including Rams Hill (Bradley and Ellison 1975, 89, fig. 3.1), and they were probably not items of everyday use. Late Bronze Age razors of continental styles have been found at Runnymede (Needham 1987) and another rare continental type of semi-discoidal razor-knife was found at the late Bronze Age eyot site at Whitecross Farm (Cromarty *et al.* 2006, 49-51 and fig. 3.1). A typical double-sided example is known from the late Bronze Age or early Iron Age settlement within the defensive enclosure at Ivinghoe Beacon (Cotton and Frere 1968, 204 fig. 10, no.1), and a very small example of an early Iron Age single-bladed Hallstatt type was found in a middle Iron Age pit at Slade Farm, Bicester (Ellis *et al.* 2000, 249-50 and 264, fig. 21 no. 1). The Runnymede and Whitecross Farm, and possibly Ivnghoe examples are from midden and occupation deposits on sites where other metalwork was found. They might have belonged to collections of metal intended for exchange, hoarding or recycling. The Slade Farm razor was worn, broken and scratched but its occurrence in a later pit that may have been at a focal point in the site layout suggests that it was likely to be a curated heirloom. Other examples come from the river at Syon Reach and Brentford, where there may have been another important riverside occupation or midden site (Piggott 1946, 121-41). A common feature of such razors is that they usually have one or more suspension holes and are often decorated, suggesting that they were worn as shiny pendants, perhaps symbolically reinforcing the importance of the personal appearance of the wearer.

Early and middle Iron Age razors are not particularly common but they are again evident in the late Iron Age, perhaps because inhumation and cremation burials were accompanied by grave goods during that period. Complete razors are rare, but a fine razor handle was found at Silchester and another possible example or handle is amongst the grave goods from a late Iron Age burial at Birdlip (Green 1949), in both cases 'mirror' burials presumably of women.

Occasional finds of tweezers, assumed to be for plucking hair, also suggest attention to personal appearance throughout later prehistory. A few examples are known from Runnymede (Needham and Spence 1996, 187 no. M24) and four were found in close proximity along with a large pin within the early Iron Age midden deposit at Woodeaton (Harding 1987, 43, fig. 12). One, possibly two, late Bronze Age or early Iron Age examples in bronze were found at Ivinghoe (Cotton and Frere 1968, 208-9, fig. 11, nos. 16 and 19) and others at Brentford (Old England) and from the river nearby in Syon Reach (Piggott 1946). A pair of iron tweezers was found in an early or middle Iron Age pit at Slade Farm, Bicester (Ellis *et al.* 2000, 250, fig. 21). Bronze tweezers were amongst the toiletry items, jewellery and other personal grave goods in the late Iron Age burial at Birdlip (Green 1949), and they sometimes occur as grave goods in other late Iron Age burials, cemeteries and settlements (Hill 1997).

Evidence from bog bodies (eg Stead *et al.* 1986) suggests that some people had surprisingly well

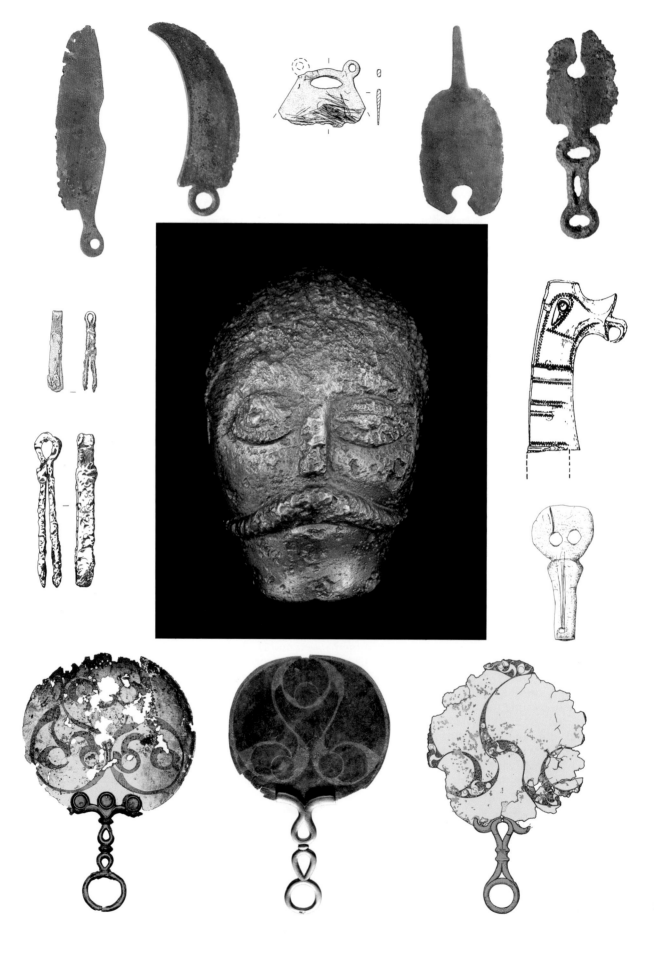

manicured hands. Two of the late Bronze Age or early Iron Age swan-necked bronze pins from Woodeaton have small flattened forked ends that could have acted as nail cleaners (Harding 1972 Pl 73 A and B). Remarkably, a 1-2 mm human nail paring found in a late Iron Age well at Silchester showed that it had been cut using a sharp knife working from two directions. The edge of the paring also showed that this was not the first time it had been cut (Firth in Fulford 2000, 505). Body painting and tattooing are attested for the late prehistoric period (Carr 1995) but there is no direct evidence from the Thames Valley.

By the late Iron Age high status interest in personal appearance is evident from late La Tène III mirrors exhibiting considerable artistry in the curvilinear design engraved on their backs. Most examples are from burials which often contain other toiletry items and jewellery. The example from Birdlip, high on the Cotswolds at the edge of the Thames catchment, was found along with a bead necklace, tweezers, and other grave goods associated with the inhumation of a woman in a stone-lined cist. Others are associated with cremation burials, as at Dorton, north of Thame, Latchmere Green near Calleva and Aston near Welwyn (Farley 1983; Fulford and Creighton 1998; Rook *et al.* 1982). These were clearly high status objects and there is little evidence for smaller, less showy examples, though it was suggested that a late Iron Age antler handle at Ashville might be from a mirror (Parrington 1978, 81 fig. 60 no. 33).

Jewellery and other personal ornaments
(Figs 5.21, 5.22)

Before the late Iron Age, when some high status burials were accompanied by jewellery, most late prehistoric personal ornaments found in the Thames Valley are from settlement sites, hoards or the river. Even in the rare instances where there are associations with burials there is little direct evidence of how jewellery and personal ornaments were worn, in what combinations or whether such objects were worn by men or women or both. There is equally little to indicate whether children wore such ornaments, though there are a few exceptionally small versions that would suggest this. Most evidence thus comes from the objects themselves. Common to jewellery the world over, most personal ornaments were made from colourful, shiny materials that in most cases were not commonplace.

Although not common, 'ornament' hoards of jewellery and sometimes other personal or household objects are well-attested for the middle to late

Bronze Age. Few have been subject to excavation and the reasons for their deposition are seldom clear, though many must represent unrecovered valuables hidden for safe-keeping. This is likely for the middle Bronze Age hoard of two twisted gold arm or neck ornaments and three plain penannular gold bracelets discovered during a metal detecting rally at Crow Down on the Lambourne Downs (Fig. 5.21; Varndell *et al.* 2007). Jewellery and other personal ornaments also occur in mixed hoards associated with the activities of metalworkers, representing collections of newly made objects, items of exchange, or broken objects for recycling. For example the Tower Hill hoard, consisting mainly of newly made and unfinished axes, also contained several personal objects, including bracelets and rings (Miles *et al.* 2003, 215-20).

Hair ornaments and earrings

A range of objects could have been worn in the hair. Large decorative pins of the middle to late Bronze Age and early Iron Age which come in a variety of forms are usually seen as dress pins, but it is also possible that they were hairpins. Similarly, a range of rings and other hollow objects could have been used in the hair.

Two elegant tear-drop gold earrings with embossed decoration of middle Bronze Age date from the Thames are amongst the most attractive examples of late prehistoric jewellery from the region. Other small rings that may have been used as earrings, or perhaps nose-rings, include a small bent decorated penannular ring found in the Tower Hill hoard of late Bronze Age metalwork (Miles *et al.* 2003, 215 fig. 11.14, no. 26) and a horseshoe-shaped jet penannular ring from a middle Iron Age context at Yarnton (Hey *et al.* forthcoming a). The absence of any means of securing such rings other than pressure suggests that they would have been used on special occasions as they would easily have been lost. There is no clear evidence of more elaborate forms of earrings or objects that might have been used to pierce ears or other parts of the body.

Neck rings and torcs

Large neck torcs were amongst the most prestigious of personal ornaments in later prehistory but are seldom recovered from excavation. A particularly fine middle Bronze Age gold torc ploughed up in a field near Moulsford in 1960 (Wymer 1961) was probably from a disturbed hoard. It is made of four square-sectioned twisted gold bars held together in two places by twisted gold wires and bent into a hoop with gold caps covering the terminals, decorated with finely engraved alternating bands of cross-hatched rectangles and triangles. A recent find

Fig. 5.20 (opposite) Personal appearance: (centre) *rare depiction of a late prehistoric person from Welwyn;* (clockwise from top left) *razors and razor handles from Runnymede, Slade Farm and Silchester; possible mirror handle from Ashville; mirrors from Latchmere Green, Hants., Aston, Herts. and Dorton, Bucks.; tweezers from Slade Farm and Runnymede*

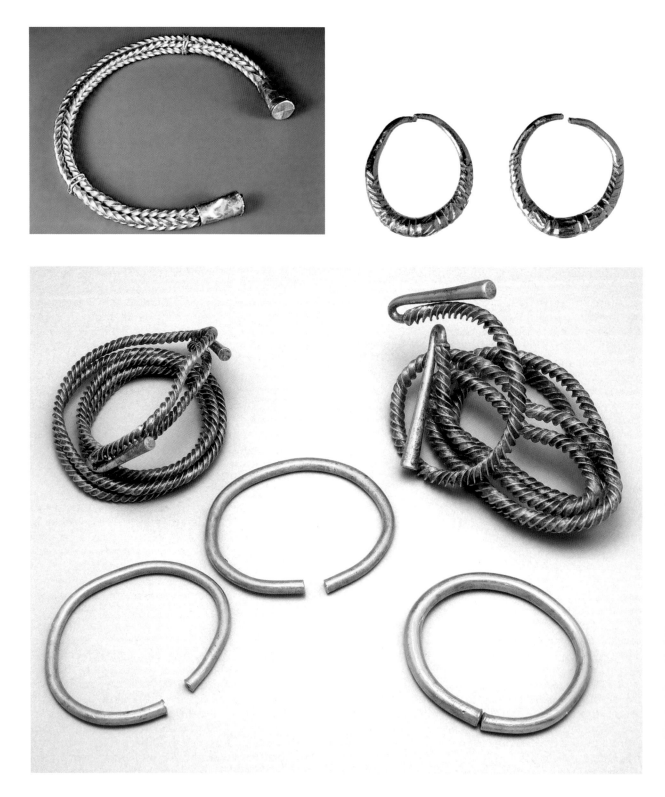

Fig. 5.21   Late prehistoric gold jewellery from the Thames Valley: (above) Moulsford torc; (centre) middle Bronze Age earrings from the Thames; (below) the Crow Down hoard

of a similar torc in the vicinity may be from the same hoard. Two twisted gold torcs (or possibly armlets) dating to the later middle Bronze Age (*c* 1300-1100 BC) were recently found along with three plain gold penannular bracelets in the Crow Down hoard on the Berkshire Downs (Fig. 5.21). A few later Bronze Age and Iron Age torcs have come from the river in London, including at Hammersmith and the Walbrook (Wait 1985, 313, 314; Read 1909). A torc was reportedly found somewhere near the high status burials at Birdlip (Green 1949).

The size and, in many cases considerable value of torcs coupled with their prominent placing round the neck suggests that they were particularly powerful symbols of the personal and social status of the wearer. Occasionally such symbolism may have been used to convey a negative rather than a positive message. Outside the Thames Valley at Brackmills near Northampton a trussed and bound woman with a lead torc around her neck was buried face down in a pit (Selkirk 1998). In this case the torc was made of a heavy base metal and may have been symbolic of the need to quell a restless spirit, or as a sacrificial symbol reflected in the nooses round the necks of Danish bog bodies (Glob 1969).

Beads, necklaces, amulets and charms

Beads from necklaces, amulets and other personal ornaments worn round the neck are more commonly found in excavations though still quite rarely, perhaps because they are easily missed in gravel soils. The relatively few examples from settlement sites tend to be of somewhat exotic materials. Amber beads come from a middle Bronze Age context at Appleford (Booth and Simmonds forthcoming) and possibly Perry Oaks/T5 (Framework Archaeology 2006, 116) and from late Bronze Age contexts at Runnymede (Needham and Spence 1996, 188), Carshalton (Needham 1987) and Cassington (Hey *et al.* forthcoming a). Glass beads are recorded from late Bronze Age Runnymede and Whitecross Farm (Henderson 1989; Cromarty *et al.* 2006, 57-8), and from middle Iron Age Mingies Ditch (Allen and Robinson 1993, 79). A small unfinished bronze ring with casting webs still present amongst the Tower Hill hoard could have been intended as a bead (Miles *et al.* 2003, 217, 11.14 no. 78). At Ashville a bronze bead with continental parallels and a stone one of uncertain source were found together in an Iron Age pit. It was suggested that this unusual juxtaposition might indicate that they were from a charm or amulet (Parrington 1978, 81 and fig. 59, nos. 19 and 20). The extent to which natural bead-like stones and fossils were kept and used as beads or amulets is difficult to ascertain but a hollow flint pebble found in the late Iron Age cremation burial at Watlington (Harding 1972, 170 Pl 72 B) suggests that this source of beads may often go unrecognised. Occasionally clay beads (eg Runnymede – Needham and Spence 1996, 184) are also found, but these are even less common than those made of more exotic materials.

The most impressive example of a late prehistoric necklace from the Thames basin is the richly furnished grave of a high ranking person, usually assumed to be a woman, at Birdlip on the edge of the Cotswolds (Green 1949; Gloucetser City council u.d). The remains of an impressive complete or near complete necklace of twenty beads consists of seventeen large amber ones, two of shale, and one of the mineral pyrophillite, of which there are deposits in Scotland, although the closest match is with Chinese specimens. These materials might have been regarded as embodying 'magical' properties – amber for static electricity, shale and pyrophillite for stone that burns. Beads are also recorded from other late Iron Age burials, such as the Welwyn burial which contained one amber and two glass beads (Stead 1967).

Pendants

Bone, antler and teeth do not seem to have been used much to make beads but there are examples of pierced dogs' tooth pendants from Gravelly Guy and Bourton-on-the-Water Primary School, which seem to have been solitary items rather than belonging to a necklace (Lambrick and Allen 2004, 386 fig. 8.14, no. 630; Cool 2006, 42, Pl. 3). Although they are often interpreted as pendants they might alternatively be beads or toggles, but it is worth noting that both were found in association with human remains (a disarticulated neonate burial and a femur fragment respectively). The perforated human trepanning discs from Gravelly Guy and Green Park, are other examples of bone pendants that may have been thought to bring good fortune to the wearer.

As noted above, most 'razors' have suspension loops, suggesting that they too were worn as pendants. Other possible metal pendants include large decorated rings such as two from the Tower Hill hoard (Miles *et al.* 2003, 215-7, fig. 11.14). One is like a bracelet but with a hole assumed to be for suspension. Another more elaborate ring with an added suspension loop had a continuous groove round each ring face with eight slots cut through it joining up the slots. Comparisons are made with other rings with rectangular slots (but no grooves or suspension loop) interpreted as strap distributors, but this one seems different and the report does not offer a specific explanation. One possibility, especially as other items in the hoard are freshly made and unfinished, might be that this ring was another unfinished pendant of a more elaborate form, awaiting the addition of metal, enamel, clay, or organic inlay to fill the two grooves, and joined through the slots to make a bicolour ring when seen from either side.

A number of other late Bronze Age pendants are riverine finds, including one from Syon Reach. Although such items could have been worn by people it is possible that they were decorative harness fittings. Bronze pendants seem less common in the Iron Age but a possible example in

the form of a miniature axe was found at Bourton-on-the-Water Primary School in a pit with the disarticulated remains of a new- or still-born baby in a cist and fragments of at least two adults (Cool 2006, 39, 41, Pl 1).

Bracelets, armlets and anklets

Bracelets, and to a lesser extent armlets, and other rings are probably the commonest form of personal adornment found on later prehistoric settlements and in middle to late Bronze Age hoards. Some gold examples are known, but most late prehistoric bracelets are made either of bronze or, especially from the middle to later Iron Age, Kimmeridge shale, more rarely jet. They come in a wide variety of forms and were decorated to different degrees.

Gold bracelets are rare finds but three plain gold penannular examples were part of the Crow Down hoard dated to *c* 1300-1100 BC. Bronze examples are much more common in hoards of various types, though the great variety of sizes and forms make it difficult to determine whether they were worn on the wrist, arm, leg or ankle or as pendants. It is also possible that some rings were not personal ornaments at all, but were harness fittings or cauldron ring handles, though the latter are often distinctively square-sectioned. The Petters hoard included part of a hollow-section bracelet (Needham 1990, 62, fig. 14, no. 30). Eight rings or parts of rings in the Tower Hill hoard, some decorated, may have been bracelets and another larger plain ring might have been an armlet (Miles *et al.* 2003, 215-20, figs 11.14, 11.15). River finds, especially from London, include a wide variety of middle Bronze Age to Iron Age bracelets and armlets of both complete and penannular rings, mainly bronze, though a few in gold, some decorated, others plain. Bronze bracelets are less common on settlement sites, but a Ewart Park type bracelet was found in an occupation deposit, possibly a house site, within the hillfort at Taplow (Allen and Lamdin-Whymark 2000, 23) and examples are known from Runnymede (Needham 1987).

Shale bracelets or the material for them are likely to come from Kimmeridge in Dorset, where exploitation of the resource was intermittent in the Bronze Age and became extensive in the Iron Age (Lawson 1976, 242). A middle Bronze Age example was found at Petters Sports Field, Egham (Johnson 1975), and another, either middle or late Bronze Age, was found at Green Park (Webley *et al.* forthcoming). At 92 mm diameter the latter was quite large (perhaps an armlet), resembling a late Bronze

Age example from Runnymede Bridge (Longley 1980, 31). Four fragments were found in Harding's relatively small-scale excavations at Woodeaton, two of late Bronze Age or early Iron Age date and one from the upper early to middle Iron Age deposit (Harding 1987 43, fig. 12, nos. 19, 20, 21, 10).

Shale bracelets or armlets are more common on Iron Age settlements, especially from the middle Iron Age, in keeping with the growth of the industry at Kimmeridge, but this could also be a function of the much greater volume of soil excavated on many of these sites. Nine unfinished examples of varying sizes have been found at Bourton on the Water (Cool 2006, 39-40) and another at Latton Lands (Powell *et al.* forthcoming). Most shale bracelets are found as finished articles. Four examples were found at Gravelly Guy (Lambrick and Allen 2004, 368, fig, 8.8, nos. 42, 439, 582, 734) and two at Yarnton (Hey *et al.* forthcoming a), in each case from both early and middle Iron Age contexts. Single examples are known from Preston enclosure near Cirencester (Mudd *et al.* 1999, vol ii, 413, fig. 7.40, no. 675), Ashville, Abingdon (Parrington 1978, 81 fig. 59, no. 21) and Whitchurch (Wood 1954, fig. 4). Jet, usually from North Yorkshire near Whitby, is less common, but a small fragment of a ring or bracelet suspected of being jet came from a middle Iron Age context at Mount Farm (Lambrick forthcoming). Few shale bracelets have been found on Iron Age sites in the Middle Thames Valley but one is known from Brooklands (Hanworth and Tomalin 1977, 45, fig. 27, no. 11).

Although it is generally assumed that most of these objects are made of shale (or jet) this is not easily demonstrated without geological analysis, and it has also been suggested that coal measures such as those in the Forest of Dean were an alternative source of shiny black stone objects (Allason-Jones and Jones 1994, 265-72; Cool 2006, 39).

Rings

Finger and/or toe rings are quite common, especially in the spiral wire form which was generally prevalent from the late Bronze Age onwards. The most usual Iron Age examples were made from tightly twisted wire that was then coiled into a hollow spiral (eg Lambrick and Robinson 1979, 55 fig. 29, no. 1). A plain, highly polished bone finger ring, 16 mm internal diameter with a circular cross section, made from a large mammal long bone, was found by the head of the middle Iron Age burial of a four-five year old child at Spring Road, Abingdon (Allen and Kamash 2008).

Fig. 5.22 (opposite)   Late prehistoric and early Roman personal jewellery and fastenings: (clockwise from bottom left) *phalera from Syon Reach; Hallstatt brooch from Tetsworth, Oxon.; pendant ring from Tower Hill; Bronze Age pins from Syon Reach and Whitecross Farm; swan's neck pin from Wittenhams; ring-headed pins from Gravelly Guy, Syon Reach, Frilford, and Ilsley (Oxon) and Hammersmith; glass beads from Richmond, Brentford and Birdlip; amber, shale and pyrophillite bead necklace from Birdlip; bronze brooches from Hammersmith, Heathrow and Cotswold Community; bone toggle from Wittenhams; spiral finger rings from Perry Oaks and Cotswold Community*

Other personal ornaments

A number of other objects may have served a broadly similar ornamental function. These include small bronze chains, such as one from a middle Iron Age context at Farmoor (Lambrick and Robinson 1979, 55 fig. 29, no. 2) and a number of 'plaques' – small, usually polished and sometimes decorated rectangular pieces of bone or antler. They resemble squared-off pieces from the mid-sections of weaving combs or 'rib knives' and might have been made from broken or worn out implements of those types if not carved anew. Most seem to lack any perforation; some such as an example from Mount Farm were apparently made of deliberately charred bone or antler and polished to produce a shiny black finish. An 'archers wristguard' – a polished bone plaque decorated with a carved lattice and with a perforation through one end – might be a plaque or pendant of this kind (Bourn 2000, 45, fig. 23, no 3).

The similarity of these 'plaques' to weaving combs emphasises a point discussed below, that certain craft tools, especially spindle whorls and 'weaving' combs, and fineware pottery share qualities of finish and decoration which many personal ornaments exhibit, thus blurring any hard-and-fast distinction between personal ornaments and craft implements or household equipment. It is perhaps less surprising that metal tools, particularly weapons, which can be assumed to have been of high intrinsic value and social status, also often have finish and decoration that must have been intended to enhance them as symbols of wealth, power or personal status.

Issues of artistic expression and design in personal objects and ornaments and their relation-ship to craft objects and other aspects of prehistoric life are discussed further at the end of Chapter 6.

RECREATION, GAMES AND TOYS

The remains of structures and objects clearly associated with sporting and recreational activities, games or toys are common in some societies, but not, it seems, in later prehistoric Britain. That is not to say that people did not have recreational pursuits or that children did not play games and have toys, but it appears that such interests were not so strong or of a type that required provision of special places, structures or objects to pursue them.

It is possible that very small loomweights (Lambrick and Allen 2004, 377, 380, 384, fig. 8.12, no. 222) and some tiny pots were children's playthings, but they are very uncommon. Objects such as the bone or antler 'plaques' described above might have been used as counters. But overall the absence of obvious recreational objects and structures suggests that leisure activities were pursued using facilities and objects that served in everyday life. Leisure activities may not have been seen as a distinctively identifiable aspect of social life, or did not involve overt expression in the possession of special objects or the construction of special facilities. When gaming pieces (and even a possible games board) do appear, as for example, in a late Iron Age grave at Welwyn (Stead 1967), it is clear that these were high prestige items, perhaps more symbolic of the leisured existence of an aristocrat than of the ordinary farming communities who owed them allegiance.

Chapter 6 – Making a living: production and exchange

Work areas and structures

Burnt mounds and associated features

Large deposits of burnt stone are known by the generic term 'burnt mounds,' although these deposits vary significantly in character. Although normally used to refer to heaps or thick layers of burnt stone resting on the ground surface, similar deposits occur in hollows, as deliberate infill of the upper layers of waterholes and as pit fills, often close to natural or artificial water sources. In Ireland and elsewhere such mounds of burnt stone are associated with structures such as water tanks, workshops or shelters.

There has been much debate and experimentation seeking to determine what activities generated such large quantities of burnt stone. Three broad categories of use, as cooking places (O'Kelly, 1954; Hedges 1975), as baths or saunas (Barfield and Hodder 1987) and areas for washing fleeces, fulling and dyeing (Jeffrey 1991; Denvir u.d.) are both plausible and supported by successful experiment. In addition, other uses such as funerary pyres or burial places have also been suggested (Harding 2000; Roberts 1998).

In the Middle Thames Valley at Eden Walk in the middle of Kingston-upon-Thames a large dump of burnt flint associated with Deverel-Rimbury pottery rested on a dump of brushwood within a palaeochannel, but investigations were not sufficiently extensive to define its wider context (Searjeantson *et al*. 1991-2). At Reading Business Park/Green Park an extensive burnt mound deposit 85 m long, 25 m wide and 0.2 m thick, consisting of *c* 70% burnt flint and accompanied by late Bronze Age domestic debris, occupied the bank of a former stream channel (Fig. 6.1; Brossler *et al*. 2004, 39, 128-9, figs 3.7, 3.22, Pl. 3.9). Given the presence nearby of flax-retting pits and remnants of fired clay pit linings made of a pottery-like fabric (Moore and Jennings 1992, 89), it is possible that the mound was the by-product of heating water, perhaps associated with the manufacture of linen or woollen cloth or with cooking or other activities (Brossler *et al*. 2004 128-9). At Anslows Cottages, 1.5 km to the north, the end of a small burnt mound lay adjacent to a small river channel just beyond the end of a ditch and post alignment that followed the river bank, close to a small platform or jetty dated to 840 to 510 cal BC (Butterfield and Lobb 1992, 90, figs 28, 29). The relationship between the mound, riverside boundary and timber platform in the slow-flowing water was not chronologically or spatially clear, though the boundary could have

demarcated a section of river bank round the platform, with the burnt mound debris just down stream. Both were superseded by another late Bronze Age or early Iron Age ditch along the river-bank. The site is notable for the relative lack of domestic debris and unusually high proportion of deer bones, and the general environment was grassland and marsh with patches of alder carr. In this case a function associated with cooking or intensive domestic crafts seemed unlikely (Butterfield and Lobb 1992, 165-6).

In the Upper Thames Valley at Yarnton spreads, hollows, pits and other features packed with burnt stone and charcoal dating to the middle and late Bronze Age and earlier lay close to palaeochannels and waterholes some distance from the main foci of domestic activity (Hey *et al*. forthcoming b). Like Anslows Cottages, the level of domestic activity was fairly slight. Waterlogged stems and seeds of flax were recovered and some features might have been retting pits, but there were no features or remnants of pit linings like those at Reading Business Park/Green Park. At Cassington West, a kilometre or so to the west, midden-like deposits with abundant burnt stones were found along a boundary of the late Bronze Age settlement.

At a number of other sites, pits or hollows filled with burnt stone are sited adjacent to waterholes. At Mount Farm a shallow oval pit containing a mass of burnt fractured quartzite pebbles and charcoal and sherds of middle Bronze Age globular urn lay immediately next to a ramped waterhole, both dug into the hollow left by a ring ditch (Lambrick 1979; forthcoming). At Perry Oaks/T5 a number of features containing deposits of burnt stone were also found close to middle to late Bronze Age water-holes. One of these is referred to as a 'burnt mound complex' although no actual mound survived (Framework Archaeology 2006, 145-7, 150-1, fig. 3.35). Many of the waterholes at Shorncote/ Cotswold Community and Reading Business Park/Green Park also contained large quantities of burnt stone.

The debate about the origins and functions of burnt mounds and similar deposits originated as an attempt to reach agreement about classification as archaeological monuments, but this is now seen as a restrictive approach. They may have served various or multiple functions. Whether they had a communal role as suggested by Ray (1990) is open to speculation, but they should not be seen in isolation. It is generally agreed that burnt mounds reflect activities involving indirect application of heat through water

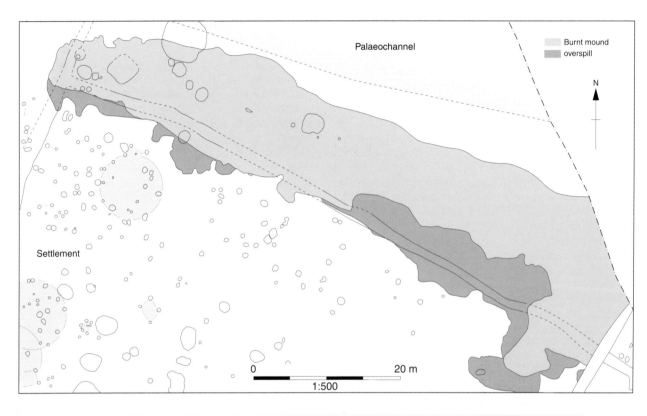

Fig. 6.1 Craftworking or processing features: burnt mound deposits at Green Park, Reading

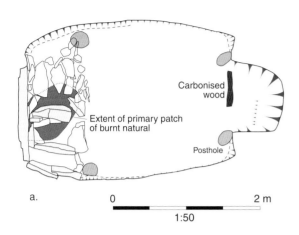

Carbonised wood

Extent of primary patch of burnt natural

Posthole

a.

0   2 m

1:50

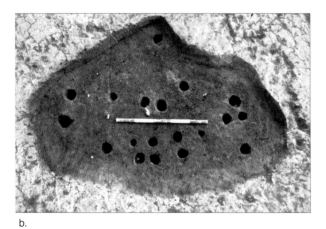

b.

Fig. 6.2 Unexplained early Iron Age craftworking features: a) sunken-floored structure with stone lined hearth at Ewe Farm; b) pit with stakeholes and burning at Moores Farm

or air in confined spaces, sometimes on a relatively large scale and/or in locations, often waterside, where recurrent practice led to a substantial build-up of burnt stones used for transmission of heat. As we have seen in relation to cooking, this type of heating also took place routinely on a smaller scale at settlements, whether or not in the vicinity of burnt mound deposits. Burnt mounds may thus reflect a scale and location of activities requiring hot water, not separate activities unconnected with the dumps of burnt stone that occur in pits, waterholes and other depressions within settlements or in the fields. This raises the question of why these smaller deposits of burnt stone continued to be generated throughout the Iron Age, whereas large-scale burnt mound deposits are especially a middle to late Bronze Age phenomenon. It may be that the activities with which they were associated came to be organised in different ways, perhaps on a different social or physical scale.

Pits and hollows associated with burning

Pits with clear signs of burning but no obvious metalworking or crop-processing debris were common features at late Bronze Age sites, including Aldermaston, Knights Farm and Pingewood and fragments of possible fired pottery pit linings were found at Aldermaston and Reading Business Park (Bradley *et al.* 1980; Johnstone and Bowden 1985; Moore and Jennings 1992, 89). Heavily burnt pits have also been exposed on Iron Age sites, some associated with carbonised grain or high temperature craftwork (Lambrick and Allen 2004, 112). The direct association of such features with craft or working areas is rare but not unknown (see below). A number of unusual pits, gullies and trenches have also produced exceptionally dense concentrations of burnt stone not obviously connected with domestic activity.

At Moores Farm two shallow pits lying 4 m apart had clusters of 13 and 22 stakeholes driven into their bases through layers of primary fill, which contained pottery and amorphous fired clay, with further pottery, hearth lining and fired clay in their upper fills (Fig. 6.2). Surprisingly, given the unusual character of these features but close similarity and juxtaposition, one contained middle Bronze Age pottery whereas the other produced early Iron Age sherds. Whether they were of different dates or whether the pottery was redeposited is uncertain, and their original form and purpose is unclear. At Wickhams Field, Reading an early Iron Age rectangular pit with a collapsed clay lining contained a deposit of dense burnt stone and black silt (Crockett 1996 118-9, fig. 68, Pl. 17). The vertical sides of the fill suggest that the lining originally continued upwards, perhaps as timbers. It is possible that it was a tank for heating water. Ironworking slag was found in nearby features not directly associated with the pit. At the middle Iron Age enclosure at Risely an unusual triangular arrangement of three gullies leading to a deeper, broader central hollow contained a high concentration of burnt flint, charcoal and pottery, including a sherd with burnt clay adhering to it (Lobb and Morris 1991-3, 51-3). Another mass of burnt clay suggested a possible clay-capping superstructure. Charcoal from the primary deposit was dated to 405 to 171 cal BC. Ironsmithing residues but almost no crop remains were found in other features on the site. The triangular gully arrangement might have been associated with some aspect of pottery manufacture, such as artificial drying of pots, but there were no wasters or other remains to attest to firings. At Cleveland Farm a number of so-called 'exclamation mark' features, 4-5 m long gullies with a separate pit at one end, contained dense concentrations of burnt stone, but with no other evidence of their function (Coe *et al.* 1991).

Sunken-floored industrial building

An early Iron Age sunken-floored subrectangular building 3 m long and 2 m wide was recently discovered at Ewe Farm, Newington (Fig. 6.2; Paul Booth and Tim Allen pers. comm.). The floor was about 0.3 m deep with a ramp leading in from a door at one end. At the opposite end were three heavily burnt cells constructed of Corallian limestone slabs. These extended beyond the area defined by postholes at the sides and the entrance, which presumably supported a roof. The floor beneath the cells and the slabs defining the side of the feature behind them were also heavily burnt, suggesting that they were a modification of an originally single hearth. The base of the whole structure was covered with a layer of charcoal, and the interior, except for the cells, was filled with burnt clay and charcoal-rich soil. There was no sign of slag, charred grain or burnt stones other than in the structure itself. Apart from the ramped entrance, the sides of the sunken-floored area were vertical with no sign of weathering. A dark band along the vertical edges of the feature and small areas of charred timber in one or two places suggest that the sides were plank-lined. Lumps of well-fired clay were concentrated along the edges of the interior, suggesting that a clay superstructure had collapsed in. A significant quantity of late Bronze Age pottery, including large sherds from at least a dozen vessels, was found within and immediately outside the cells.

The building lay on the edge of a low hill with a capping of drift deposits similar to Clay-with-Flints, and extensive deposits of clay surrounded the site. There were also ponds nearby. This unusual building was clearly used for a purpose involving relatively careful control of heat. The absence of burnt stones and tank structures suggests that it was not concerned with heating water, although the form of the building would otherwise not be out of place as part of a burnt mound complex (Hedges 1975). There was no metalworking debris, or signs of particularly high-temperature heating and no

charred crop remains. Although it could have been used as a pottery kiln there are no obvious wasters amongst the recovered pottery. There were no objects to suggest a religious function and, pending further analysis, this unique structure is interpreted as a craft or industrial building, either a series of ovens or kiln.

Work areas, compounds and 'windbreaks'

The layouts of many settlements include areas defined by gullies, arcs of postholes, circular enclosures, subcircular, rectangular or irregular areas defined by gullies. These may have served a variety of functions, as animal pens, storage areas or work areas for a variety of crafts. In some cases remains of this sort are associated with clusters of pits and other features. Possible craft-related use of such clusters of features is usually very ill defined. Similarly, the numerous examples of annexes attached to penannular house enclosures seldom produce clear evidence of function.

Specialised use of areas within settlements has been identified, however, and this tends to be related to activities involving heat and fire. At Hurst Park, East Molesey two concentrations of postholes, gullies and pits, between 55 m and 70 m across and 40 m apart, produced very different collections of artefacts. The larger area contained much pottery, together with quern fragments and perforated clay tablets, the smaller area almost no pottery but significant quantities of burnt stone, a polishing stone and a couple of clay tablet fragments. These were interpreted as 'baking' and 'boiling' areas respectively but, depending on the interpretation of the clay tablets and burnt stone, other food- or craft-related activities can be postulated (Andrews 1996, 64-9, 101-2, figs 35, 36, 57). Another example of distinctive work areas represented by concentrations of features and areas of burning was identified at the ironworking site at Brooklands and the late Bronze Age ironworking site at Hartshill Copse, where different types of debris distributed around two roundhouses indicated different usage (Hanworth and Tomalin 1977 9-22, fig. 8; Collard *et al.* 2006; see below).

Less specific evidence of craft-related working areas is discernible in some relatively fully excavated settlements. This suggests that some activities were more specifically focussed in some areas than others. At Whitecross Farm an examination of finds distributions, including flints displaying different types of use-wear, demonstrated that implements used for boring were concentrated in one area and implements associated with scraping, cutting or whittling had a more general distribution (Cromarty *et al.* 2006 38, 63-7, fig. 2.10g). At Gravelly Guy slag associated with ironworking was concentrated in particular areas, whereas objects associated with textile working were spread across the site (Fig. 6.3; Lambrick and Allen 2004 336-9, figs 8.1, 8.2, 8.3).

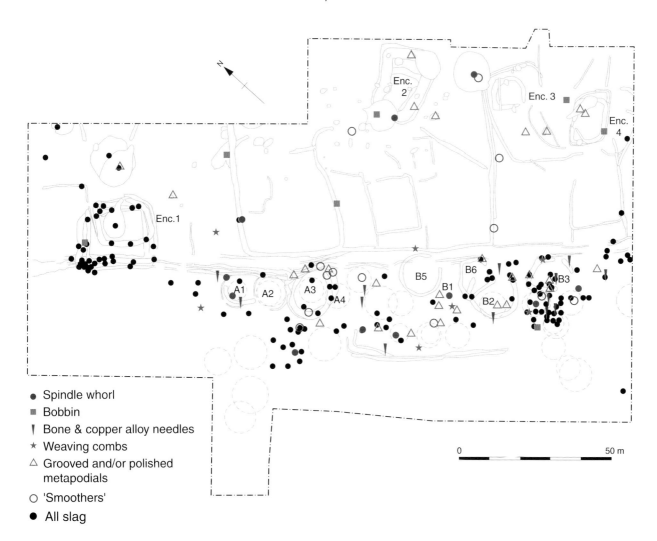

Spindle whorl
Bobbin
Bone & copper alloy needles
Weaving combs
Grooved and/or polished metapodials
'Smoothers'
All slag

Fig. 6.3   Distribution of craft and industrial activities at Gravelly Guy

Domestic and communal crafts: evidence of tools, products and waste materials

Most of the tools and household equipment were produced by domestic or communal crafts, but some may have been made by itinerant craftsmen or acquired through exchange. Artefacts and other evidence from later prehistoric sites in the Thames Valley illustrate not only a wide range of crafts that supported daily life but also something of the complex pattern of domestic, communal, specialist and foreign production that merges with local and regional patterns of exchange. With the exception of the manufacture of flint tools, which became a dying art after the widespread supply and adoption of metal implements, a number of crafts became more sophisticated during the later prehistoric period, albeit not consistently.

Flint-knapping

Manufacture of flint blades, scrapers, arrowheads and points reached its apogee in the late Neolithic and early Bronze Age, and by 1500 BC was in decline as metal tools became more common. The

characteristics of flint-knapping in the metal age were summarised by Ford *et al.* (1984) using material from the Thames Valley, the Wessex Chalk and elsewhere. There is some difficulty in interpreting late prehistoric flintwork because of the almost ubiquitous occurrence of redeposited earlier prehistoric material. Even so, a broad trend towards more opportunistic exploitation of flint with less careful control of knapping and form is clear, reinforced by the appearance of one or two new but very crude forms. Several later Bronze Age assemblages show how the retouched flints are dominated by scrapers, flakes, points, denticulates and notched pieces.

The late Bronze Age material from Whitecross Farm is especially significant as it was from relatively well sealed contexts, providing a well-preserved assemblage almost entirely uncontaminated by earlier material (Fig. 6.4). Rather than adopting a purely typological approach, it was possible to characterise the selection mechanisms for flint pieces and modification for different uses through a study of use wear, reduction strategies and refitting (Brown and Bradley 2006). This meant

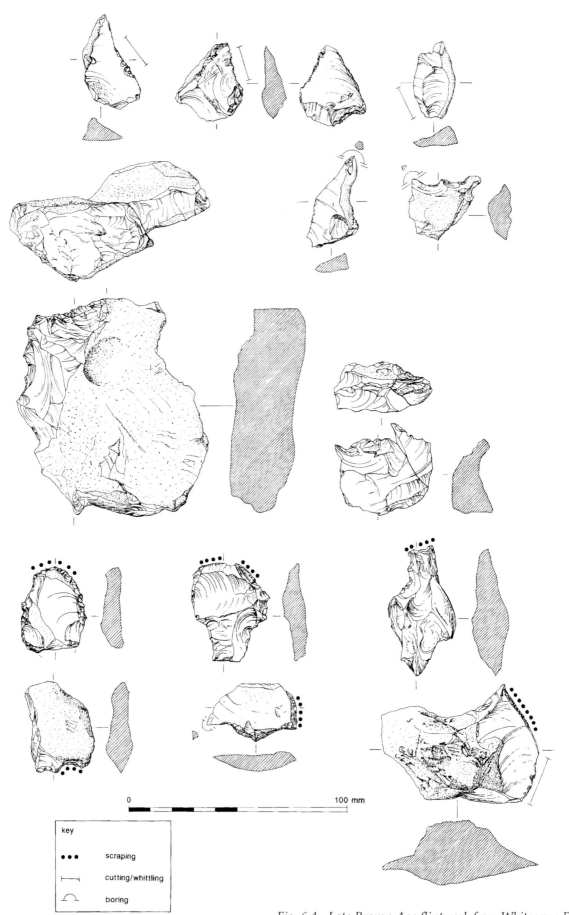

key

●●● scraping

├──┤ cutting/whittling

⌒ boring

Fig. 6.4 Late Bronze Age flintwork from Whitecross Farm

0   100 mm

the flintwork was characterised on its own merits rather than reflecting abstract preconceptions linked to degeneration of knapping competence from earlier periods. Of a total of 410 unburnt and potentially usable flakes, only 19 flints were retouched and 59 had evidence of use-wear visible under low magnification. All retouched pieces had been used on at least one edge but so had many other flints with unretouched edges. It appears that short lengths of useable edge were usually adequate, the mode of use depending on what the edge angle most suited.

Flint pebbles or cobbles, commonly fist sized, which can be found in the Thames gravels in parts of the catchment draining the chalk and on surrounding hills, were the main sources. The approach to converting this material to pieces with useable edges seems to have been based on fairly crude bashing rather than careful maintenance of a core with prepared striking platforms. The effect of such bashing was to weaken the structure of the cobbles so that they fractured, often with sharp changes of angle. 'Cores' and debitage therefore tended to be irregular. Trimming flakes were outnumbered by preparation flakes, indicating that cores were not exhaustively reduced and that fresh platforms were created rather than existing platforms maintained by further trimming and rejuvenation. On average each core recovered had yielded only about seven flakes of all types. Experimental flaking of similar raw material to reproduce similar waste suggested that useable flakes were made in four basic ways – directly off a cobble; using a natural break or old platform for new removals in different directions; splitting the pebble to create platforms for use in multiple directions (probably the most common method); and using pieces removed from the core to obtain further flakes (Brown and Bradley 2006, 62-3).

Denticulates are the most distinctively innovative late prehistoric flint implements. They have coarse-toothed edges, often formed by just two or three 'teeth' separated by concavities that were produced by single, relatively large retouch removals. The intention may have been to create either the points or the concavities, but it is also possible that some denticulates were an accidental effect of trying to use a flake as a core or anvil for *écaille* flaking. Many of the Whitecross Farm pieces had a denticulated edge, but low-power microscopic examination of use-wear patterns identified only six cases where either the 'teeth' or concavities had been used. Of the other used pieces at Whitecross Farm, scraping edges were frequently unretouched, but two scrapers with retouch had been resharpened, one of which may have broken during this process or subsequently during use.

The lack of control over the final form of later prehistoric retouched pieces (which makes their categorisation difficult) and the *ad hoc* usage of retouch to create short sections of useable edge, contrasts markedly with the use of retouch during the Neolithic and earlier Bronze Age. In their review of later prehistoric flintworking, Ford *et al.* (1984) showed that the range of classifiable retouched forms declined through the Bronze Age but the unclassifiable 'deliberately modified pieces' rose as a proportion of total assemblages.

However, on the Yarnton floodplain 55% of worked flint of all periods showed some evidence of use and only 10% of pieces used for boring or piercing had also been retouched (Hey *et al.* forthcoming). It thus seems likely that the changes that took place in later prehistory were less to do with the introduction of *ad hoc* and opportunistic utilisation of flints (which had probably always happened) than a decline in careful reduction of nodules and shaping of implements. This is evident in the raw materials and methods used to create useable pieces of flint. Both the character of the waste and its much lower general rate of utilisation can be seen as a more profligate use of the raw material, generating more unused shattered waste, less use of potentially usable pieces, and less core preparation and retouch to maximise use of the raw material and prolong the life of implements.

The lack of care in shaping tools, despite broadly similar proportions of use for boring, cutting, scraping or whittling suggests that flint tools were still useful in much the same ways as before, but that after the introduction of metal it was no longer socially necessary to demonstrate adeptness in making, possessing and using them. Nor was it now economically, or perhaps socially, relevant to make the most of the raw materials. There is no reason to suppose that late Bronze Age flint points and cutting, whittling or scraping implements were any less effective than earlier prehistoric ones, so the decline in manufacturing care may have been more a matter of changes in personal value attached to them as mundane but desirable objects than any major technological difference in their effectiveness (Brown 1991). As a craft, skills in flint-knapping may have largely ceased to have much social cachet.

A major obstacle to the examination of when and how lithic technology declined may be the reluctance of excavators to collect struck flint and stone from late prehistoric sites with the same care as from earlier periods (Brown and Bradley 2006, 66-7). This can be particularly true of sites on flint bearing gravels where crudely bashed material may not always be easily distinguished from naturally broken pieces.

Whether flint-knapping continued into the Iron Age after *c* 750 BC remains a matter of debate, though Young and Humphrey (1999) have proposed a strong case for it on some sites as late as the middle Iron Age in eastern England. Although no one suggests that flints were the principal or even a common form of tool after this period it can be difficult to demonstrate whether or not flint-knapping debris and implements found in Iron Age contexts were entirely redeposited from earlier activity. At Gravelly Guy the character of 1357 flints recovered from Iron Age and Roman contexts, leaving aside chips recovered by sieving, is similar to those recovered from excavated Neolithic and early Bronze Age contexts (Lambrick and Allen 2004 93, table 2.11). Moreover, this similarity includes relatively formless categories such as 'shattered pieces' and 'miscellaneous retouched pieces' that might be expected to be more common if later Bronze Age styles of flint-knapping continued into the Iron Age. But some Iron Age sites have produced little or no evidence of other earlier prehistoric activity, and the character of the flintwork recovered is more in keeping with later Bronze Age than earlier prehistoric styles of flint-knapping. This was the case at Segsbury, where there was no evidence of Neolithic or Bronze Age activity, suggesting that the 60 flints recovered could represent low level flint-knapping activity continuing into the early Iron Age (Humphrey 2005).

Poor recovery of crudely worked flints is cited as a contributory reason for the relative lack of late prehistoric flintwork, but on the limestone gravels of the Upper Thames this is less likely to be a problem. Some Iron Age sites which lack evidence of earlier activity also lack any contemporary significant flint assemblages. For example, only three flints were found at Watkins Farm (Allen 1990, 55); about three from Claydon Pike (Miles *et al.* 2007), 17 from Farmoor, all of which could be Neolithic or Bronze Age (Lambrick and Robinson 1979, 61), 24 from Thornhill of Mesolithic to Bronze Age type (Jennings *et al.* 2004, 89) and 58 from Mingies Ditch, of which the majority were clearly Mesolithic, Neolithic and in one case Upper Palaeolithic, leaving a small handful that might be Iron Age (Allen and Robinson 1993, 16-19). Therefore, even if some level of flint use did continue into the early Iron Age or later on non-flint geologies, it is likely to have been limited, *ad hoc* and adventitious and would not have contributed significantly to craft activities.

Carpentry, wood- and wicker-working

Woodworking tools

A variety of stone tools, especially axes, served woodworking functions in the Neolithic and earlier Bronze Age but the considerable increase in the availability of metal from the middle Bronze Age onwards allowed basic carpentry and woodworking equipment to become more sophisticated and effective (Figs 6.5 & 6.6). Several types, like some later Bronze Age socketed chisels or the Iron Age adze-hammer from Yarnton (Hey *et al.* forthcoming a) reached a basic form that has remained largely unchanged to this day. The developing designs of axes and other tools display

adaptations that may have signified status but also demonstrate awareness of the possibilities for improving mechanical effectiveness.

There are no extant examples from the region of wooden wedges and mallets that would have been key tools in converting larger round timbers into planks, rails, beams and other baulks of wood, but there is good evidence of axes and billhooks designed for felling and trimming timbers. By the later Bronze Age the basic repertoire of woodworking tools consisted mainly of axes (also usable as adzes) and chisels, supplemented by knives. Together these would have provided the basic means of shaping timber and cutting joints and holes. From the late Bronze Age onwards lathes were used in conjunction with chisels to make small bowls and drills and saws become more evident in the Iron Age. Finishing timbers would probably initially have been achieved with flint scrapers and later knives. Sharp grit and sand or grinding stones could have been used to achieve a smooth finish on bowls and other fine objects, but surfaces of recovered timbers are usually too decayed to preserve the fine detail of finishes.

Choice of woods and conversion of timber

The increasing catalogue of recovered worked timber and the range of trimmings, offcuts, structural timbers, tools and wooden objects that they represent demonstrate a clear appreciation of the properties of various species to suit different purposes. Oak was routinely, but not exclusively, selected for structural timbers, hazel and some other species were managed to produce straight rods, ash was often used for handles and a variety of fine grained woods such as alder and maple were used for bowls. Maisie Taylor has noted (pers. comm.) that virtually all structural oak piles, beams and planks so far found in the Thames Valley must have been coppice- or pollard-grown to achieve suitably long straight timbers for jointed frame construction. These qualities must have been discovered through experience during the early stages of woodworking development. It was certainly nothing new by later prehistory, and the same basic appreciation has lasted ever since. The use of broad planks from old trees is much less apparent, with the notable exception of the Bronze Age plank-lined well at Cassington (see Fig. 7.15).

Structural carpentry and hurdles

No superstructures (as opposed to the vertical piles) of bridges, jetties or other structures are known to survive *in situ*, nor have any carefully constructed timber trackways or causeways been found across former marshes, such as those known from the

Fig.6.5 (opposite) Woodwork: (above) log ladder from Perry Oaks/T5; (centre) charred structural timbers and coppice rods in the river channel at Whitecross Farm; (below) hurdling panels at Eton Rowing Course

a.

b.

1985 Trial trench

N

0   2 m

○ Wooden piles

▨ Pot

⌁ Antler

◆ Flint

○ Charcoal spread

☐ *Quercus* sp; oak

☐ *Corylus* sp; hazel

■ *Prunus* sp; blackthorn, wild cherry

☐ *Pomoideae* sp; hawthorn, apple,
   whitebeam, mountain ash

☐ *Alnus* sp; alder

■ *Fraxinus* sp; ash

☐ Unidentified

c.

a.

b.

c.

d.

e.

f.

g.

h.

i.

Lower Thames Valley, Somerset, the Fens, and other wetlands. Nevertheless, there is growing evidence from the Thames Valley for the techniques used in structural carpentry, both for *in situ* structures in rivers and waterholes, mainly piles for bridges and jetties and timber well linings, and discarded or reused remains of structures. Dry sites are generally less informative, although some indication of shapes of timbers and general structural use of timber is evident from voids and post-pipes, and occasionally charred timbers survive within the earthworks of timber-framed ramparts.

For the most part, piles for riverine structures were substantial oak posts sharpened to a point using axes, then driven into the riverbed. A massive straightened-off piece of tree trunk with somewhat battered ends found in one of the channels at Eton is thought to be part of a pile driver (Fig. 6.18). Tool signatures reveal a typical range of standard axe forms. Piles were usually selected from straight-grown young oaks, used in the round but stripped of bark. Sometimes split timbers were used, as for example for a well lining at Shorncote dating to 1110-1100 or 1077-811 cal BC (see Fig. 7.15; Brossler *et al*. 2002, 44-5, fig. 8), where both radially and tangentially split logs survived. On dry sites postholes seldom retain discernible shapes of post pipes, and voids of rotted posts are even less common, but it is clear that split timbers were used for the timber ring at Gravelly Guy (Lambrick and Allen 61-3 fig. 2.13) and in the timber-framed ramparts of Segsbury (Lock *et al*. 2005, 102).

Handling large timbers would have been an important task during the middle Bronze Age. At Eton Rowing Course large cigar-shaped uprights up to 0.5 m in diameter had holes axed in opposite sides like the central tree at Holme (Taylor in Allen *et al*. forthcoming b). Such holes may have been used to help drag large timbers into position but may also have been used to anchor ropes around the timbers so that they could be drilled into the ground by rotating the uprights. The lower end of the largest recovered timber at Eton was worn almost flat, probably by rotation within the coarse flint gravel used to help drive it into the ground. With the piles in position the lugs could have been used as tying points for other purposes during construction and use of the structure.

Such timbers do not generally survive above permanent water level, and since most superstructures were designed to stand above water, the means by which timbers were attached to the tops of piles is seldom clear. At Whitecross Farm a jetty or bridge extended out from a former eyot in the river into an adjacent silted river channel (see Fig. 7.18). The top of one of the piles had a V-shaped notch in its tapered top, as though acting as a tenon for a plank with a mortise hole which could have been fitted over it and held in position by driving a wedge into the notch to tighten the joint (Taylor *et al*. 2006). At the Eton Rowing Course, two types of plank and mortise hole joints were recorded, one represented by pieces of roundwood trimmed flat on one side and halved in thickness at the ends, probably to form lengthways ties between upright piles. The other was represented by squared planks with smaller mortise holes that may have formed the lateral crosspieces tying the rows of piles together.

Occasionally, as at Mingies Ditch, the bases of posts survive, but otherwise woodwork from houses or other structures is rare and it is hardly surprising that no timbers survive still jointed together. This does not mean that evidence is entirely lacking, as shown by the unusual discovery of what may be the remains of a burnt down structure found dumped in the late Bronze Age river channel at Whitecross Farm (Cromarty *et al*. 2006 26-30, figs 2.7-2.9). This suggests that a variety of round, half-split, squared oak timbers and planks were used as the main structural elements, with straight hazel coppice rods to provide the basis of lighter infill elements.

Examples of *in situ* hurdles or other structures made of uprights and woven wattles from the Thames Valley survive. This technique was used to make fences, revetment steps in waterholes, and a track- or pathway, and it was probably a standard element in the construction of roundhouses and other buildings. A broad distinction can be made between the weaving of long, straight coppiced stems between earthfast posts or stakes to create fixed fences and walls, and portable panels of hurdling made of thinner 'sails' and wattles, which would have been woven for use either in conjunction with fence posts as gates and temporary fencing, or just tied together to provide flexible means of controlling animals in temporary enclosures and compounds. Both types have been found at the Eton Rowing Course (Fig. 6.18 & 6.19; Allen *et al*. forthcoming b)

Scabbards, handles, hafts and sticks

Wooden hafts of weapons and implements have been found in waterlogged conditions, occasionally still *in situ* in the socket of the object or bound in sheathing. A number of later prehistoric swords and chapes have remains of wooden scabbards bound in bronze, and there are a few more complete scabbards. The handle of the Chertsey shield was made of wood sheathed in bronze (Stead 1987).

Fig. 6.6 (opposite) Woodworking tools and woodwork: a) and b) wooden axe hafts from Bronze Age waterholes at Perry Oaks/T5; c) hafted socketed late Bronze Age axe from Shepperton; d) reconstruction of a Bronze Age gouge; e) Bronze Age chisel from Oxfordshire; f) Middle Bronze Age palstave from Richmond; g) Bronze Age flanged axe from Syon Reach; h) Late Bronze Age/early Iron Age socketed axe from Syon Reach; i) The Yarnton wooden trough

Socketed spears and implements rarely contain remains of their shafts but they would have been made from straight grown coppice poles. A long smooth, straight oak pole found in a waterhole at Vicarage Road, Sunbury might have been a staff or shaft for an implement (Hayman forthcoming e). In waterholes at Perry Oaks/T5 two oak hafts for socketed axes or adzes were found, one of them associated with a Neolithic axe head within a votive deposit (Fig. 6.6; Framework Archaeology 137-42, figs 3.29 and 3.31). A fine example of a socketed axe with its original haft was found in the river channel at Shepperton Ranges (Fig. 6.6; Poulton forthcoming a). A late Bronze Age wooden ard share and a late Iron Age scythe blade or sickle with the end of its wooden handle attached found in a river channel at the Eton Rowing Course are examples of the use of wood in agricultural equipment (see Fig. 8.3).

Log ladders

Finds of larger domestic and agricultural wooden equipment are rare except for log ladders, which survive relatively frequently in waterlogged wells (Figs 6.5 & 7.15). These simple objects were formed by cutting deep asymmetrical notches in the side of a substantial log, commonly alder. Seven examples have been found in waterholes at Perry Oaks/T5 (eg Framework Archaeology 135, fig. 3.30), and others at Yarnton, Cassington and Eight Acre Field, Radley (Hey *et al.* forthcoming; Mudd 1995). One of the upright piles at the Eton Rowing Course was also a log ladder. It is unclear whether this was a reused piece or was intended as a structural part of the bridge itself.

Turning, carving and coopering

Although late prehistoric turning, presumably on a pole lathe, is well attested from shale objects found in the region, there is limited evidence of lathe-turned wooden objects. Carved wooden objects other than vessels are rare and a doughnut-shaped wooden disc of uncertain purpose, *c* 120 mm in diameter with a central perforation, is an unusual exception (Taylor 2004b, 101-3, fig. 4.24).

The range of wooden vessels and ladles found in waterholes in recent years (see above) illustrate a variety of manufacturing techniques. Close-grained woods such as alder were selected for this purpose, and Taylor (2004c) suggests that the lack of similarity with contemporary pottery forms might indicate that the character and grain of the wood was as influential as other considerations in determining the shape of wooden bowls. The ladle from Reading Business Park/Green Park was carved from a piece of wood with a naturally bulbous shape, possibly the join between a side branch and the trunk of a small tree (see Fig. 5.16; Taylor forthcoming). A wooden bowl from the waterhole at Wey Manor Farm (Hayman forthcoming f) was apparently unfinished. This might

be coincidental, but it suggests that more readily worked green wood was used and the roughout was soaked in water prior to finishing it to prevent the wood drying out and cracking, but was then lost or not recovered.

Taylor's (forthcoming) catalogue of wooden bowls found at Reading Business Park/Green Park includes a turned example and a carved one. The latter was fragmentary, but was apparently oval with straight sides and a rebated rim, perhaps a lid seating. This type is unparalleled amongst middle to late Bronze Age wooden vessels. It was almost certainly of two piece construction originally, although single piece vessels do occur in the Bronze Age (Taylor 2001, fig. 7.66). A third vessel from the site was too fragmentary to type, but seems to have been a sewn or two part vessel.

Evidence for sewn birch bark vessels is known from the Neolithic onwards, such as the three birch bark buckets from Horton (Ford *et al.* 2003, 52-62). Techniques of constructing wooden vessels from multiple pieces of wood are evident from the base of a sewn or two piece vessel from a middle Bronze Age waterhole at Reading Business Park/Green Park (see above), a bucket base found in a late Bronze Age waterhole at Vicarage Road, Sunbury and remains of a bucket from Cassington (Hayman forthcoming e; Hayden pers. comm.). These illustrate the well-documented existence of constructed vessels from the middle Bronze Age onwards. Well-preserved stave built buckets, tubs and other vessels remain exceptional. The bronze sheathed stave built late Iron Age ceremonial gallon tankard with a decorative cast bronze handle dredged from the river at Brentford is especially fine, but not necessarily made in Britain. The Brentford tankard shows that some such vessels had metal fittings, offering the possibility of recovery of similar pieces from non-waterlogged contexts. This is still rare, however, and the suggestion that two curved iron binding strips riveted together found at Gravelly Guy belonged to a small bucket is only a possibility (Lambrick and Allen 2004, 363, fig. 8.7, 378). The rim and handle of a bucket from Cassington, and a handle from Groundwell Farm are more convincing examples (Harding 1972, 172, Pl 76; Gingell 1981, 64, fig. 18 no. 8).

Other containers are represented by semicircular-profiled rim binding strips (Lambrick and Allen 2004/5, 361-3; figs 8.5, 8.7). A group of 12 rim binding strips were found in a posthole at Hill Farm, Little Wittenham (Scott in Allen *et al.* forthcoming a). It is possible that such bindings come from leather containers, or from lids, perhaps for baskets, as suggested for a D-shaped frame of strips associated with decorative studs, ringlets and eyelet fastening holes from one of the Arras culture graves in Yorkshire (Stead 1991, 56-7).

Basketry would have been a practical and common means of making containers during later prehistory in the Thames Valley, but such finds are rare in waterlogged deposits. There are no definite examples of objects such as fish traps, domestic or agricultural containers, though fragments of such material were recovered from a waterhole at Perry Oaks/T5, which, along with a few other sites, also produced examples of withy ties.

Conclusion

Although the evidence is slim, woodworking techniques such as coopering, fine carving, turning and basket making as well carpentry are clearly represented for the later prehistoric Thames Valley. The variety of surviving examples of the craft illustrates a high level of sophistication. The careful selection of form, growth habit and species evident in utilised wood and timber shows both that woodland management was geared to growing raw materials that were fit for purpose and that the natural properties of wood were well understood and fully exploited. Most basic woodworking techniques of converting and shaping timber for different purposes with axes and adzes were already well established by the middle Bronze Age, but the development of new tools (eg socketed chisels from the middle Bronze Age and simple lathes from the late Bronze Age and iron saws and drills in the Iron Age) represent improvements that established methods of woodworking still familiar today as non-mechanised techniques.

Textiles and cordage

Finds of textiles and cordage are rare in the Thames Valley but small traces are occasionally preserved in the corrosion products of metal objects. Evidence for the spinning of plant and animal fibres into thread for weaving or knitting into cloth is not common before the middle Bronze Age. Compared with using animal skins and furs, the manufacture of fabrics is labour intensive, but equipment for spinning, sewing and perhaps weaving is very well represented by finds on settlements in the Thames Valley from the middle Bronze Age onwards. The basic range of objects – stone, pottery and bone spindle whorls, bone and bronze needles, fired clay and stone 'loomweights,' and a variety of bone 'bobbins,' 'combs' and 'weft beaters' – remained standard throughout later prehistory (Fig. 6.7) Variations in detailed form over time are useful chronological indicators. For example, there was a change in the form of ceramic and stone 'loomweights' from cylindrical in the middle Bronze Age, and pyramidal in the late Bronze Age to triangular from the early Iron Age into the early Roman period.

A serious problem arises in relation to the functional interpretation of many of these objects. There is not much difficulty with spindle whorls and needles, nor with bobbins formed of animal bones with a simple transverse hole. However, as discussed below, almost every other type of artefact proposed as evidence of textile production is ambiguous.

Sources of fibre

Both plant and animal fibres were used to make cloth in later prehistory. Hurcombe (2000) has reviewed the use of plant materials for crafts in Neolithic Britain and these are likely to have continued in use throughout later prehistory. Numerous wild plant species can be used to create fibre, including nettle, lime bast, clematis and other climbers. Apart from sheep wool, hair from goats, horses and other animals may have been minor sources for textile production.

Over the last 15 years a number of middle to late Bronze Age sites in the Thames Valley have provided evidence of flax growing (see Chapter 7), although not as yet of processing flax fibres. It is striking that while there is growing evidence of flax growing in the middle to late Bronze Age in the Thames Valley, there is none yet for the Iron Age. It is unlikely that this is a reflection of the large number of later Bronze Age waterlogged waterhole deposits compared with Iron Age ones, as numerous other waterlogged deposits associated with middle Iron Age settlements have been investigated, and there is evidence of flax growing again in the Roman period. The apparent demise of flax growing in the Iron Age roughly corresponds to a significant increase in the numbers of sheep reared during the early to middle Iron Age. This declined in the late Iron Age and Roman period, when flax growing is again evident. The trend is, therefore, probably linked to wider changes in landuse and land control and the production of secondary products in the Iron Age (see Chapter 7).

Late prehistoric sheep are generally believed to have resembled Soay and other breeds that naturally moult their fleece in the summer, so that wool could be plucked and collected without the need for shearing, for which there is no evidence of specialised implements. Once gathered, the wool would need to be cleaned and untangled by carding or combing. It has been suggested that so-called 'weaving' combs were used for this purpose (Cunliffe and Poole 1991b, 357), but presumably other means were also available and must have been used in the later Bronze Age before such combs were developed.

Spinning

Spinning woollen or other fibres into yarn was accomplished with simple spindles equipped with a weight to act as a flywheel, giving momentum to the spinning stick. Spindle whorls are found on most later prehistoric settlements and are quite commonly found in association with houses. At a late Bronze Age or earliest Iron Age settlement at Horcott a small pit within a possible roundhouse or workshop produced four spindle whorls buried with a complete pot. Another spindle whorl was

Fig.6.7 (overleaf) Textiles and cordage

TEXTILES AND CORDAGE

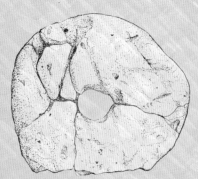

Late Bronze Age cylindrical spindle whorl from Yarnton

Ceramic spindle whorl from Castle Hill

Spinning, weaving and sewing equipment are well-represented on settlement sites in the Thames Valley from the middle Bronze Age onwards, although evidence of actual textiles is rare. The standard equipment throughout prehistory included stone, ceramic and bone spindle whorls, bronze and bone needles, clay and stone loomweights and a variety of bone combs, bobbins and weft beaters. The typological development of these objects is a useful chronological indicator. Loomweights, for example, evolved from a cylindrical shape in the middle Bronze Age to pyramidal in the late Bronze Age to triangular in the Iron Age.

Wool and hair from sheep, goats and horses along with fibres of nettle, lime bast, clematis and other climbing plants were used to make textiles. Cordage and rope could have been made from honeysuckle, bryony, wild clematis and hemp. There is evidence for flax growing (though not for processing) during the Bronze Age in the Thames Valley but none for the Iron Age, perhaps reflecting an increase in wool production during that period. A range of natural mineral pigments and plant dyes were used to colour fabrics. At Lower Bolney a pit tentatively dated to 380-100 cal BC (Campbell 1992, 34-40) produced a broken spindle whorl and specimens of dyers rocket (*Reseda luteola*).

TEXTILES AND CORDAGE

Polished and worn sheep metapodials from Eton Rowing Course and Gravelly Guy

Vertical warp-weighted looms were used for weaving yarn into broad cloth and a variety of tablet-weaving techniques were used for narrow cloth. The main evidence for warp-weighted looms comes from the numerous loomweights recovered from a variety of features on domestic sites. Bone implements were used as pin-beaters to ensure a tight weave. Late Bronze Age polished blade-like implements made from longitudinally split animal bones were found at Runnymede and Bray (Needham and Spence 1996, 189; Morris 1995, 34) and 'weaving combs' and grooved and polished sheep metapodials are present on many Iron Age sites. Highly polished surfaces and other wear marks on such implements may indicate multi-functional uses in textiles, cordage and leather working, and perhaps other crafts.

Textile making objects were clearly highly valued personal belongings. A shale spindle whorl was found at the hip of a woman buried in a middle Iron Age grave at Gravelly Guy (Lambrick and Allen 2004, 23) and decorated chalk examples from the site were imports or gifts. Prolific and well-executed decoration on some weaving combs also indicates they had more than mere utilitarian status

Left page:
Reconstruction of tablet weaving; Antler combs from (left) Yarnton and (right) Agar's Plough, Maidenhead; Bone needle from Castle Hill

Right page:
Chalk loomweight from Castle Hill; reconstruction of a warp weighted loom with pyramidal loomweights

found with a broken pot crammed into a small hole inside a another roundhouse (Lamdin-Whymark forthcoming). More generally spindle whorls are found amongst general domestic waste, and at Gravelly Guy no clear concentrations were noted (Lambrick and Allen 2004, 336-8, figs 8.1, 8.2).

Late prehistoric spindle whorls were made from a variety of materials, mainly fired clay, pottery, stone and antler or bone. An unusual lead spindle whorl from Thrupp near Abingdon resembles examples from Glastonbury (Everett and Eeles 1999, fig. 22 no. 1). They vary a great deal in quality. While many are plain and seem to have been merely functional, others may have been personal belongings of some value, as suggested by a shale example found at the hip of a 35-40 year old woman buried in a middle Iron Age pit grave at Gravelly Guy (Lambrick and Allen 2004, 232 Pl 6.4). Two examples, also from Gravelly Guy, were of chalk, one broken prior to completion, and both decorated with linear devices. The chalk would have been imported from some distance. Some pottery and bone examples are burnished and/or decorated (for pottery see Lambrick and Allen 377, fig. 8.11, no. 159; for bone see Muir and Roberts 1999, 48, fig. 3.7 no. 4), though most are crude, some made from bases of ceramic vessels (Lambrick and Allen 2004, 377, fig. 8.11, no. 516).

Dyeing

Dyeing may have been carried out both before and after thread was woven into cloth, depending on whether a coloured woven pattern was intended. Such patterns may have included the check depicted on some representations of late celtic dress. A wide range of natural soil-based mineral pigments and plant dyes would have been available. Four specimens of the yellow dye source weld or dyers rocket (*Reseda luteola*) and a broken chalk spindle whorl were found in a pit at Lower Bolney. It contained no datable material but was sealed beneath alluvium, and a nearby pit produced a radiocarbon date of 380-110 cal BC (Campbell 1992, 34-40). Many other wild plants that could have been used for dying include madder and dyer's woodruff for reds, dyer's greenweed for yellow and woad for blue.

Weaving

While the role of spindle whorls for spinning fibres is uncontroversial, the interpretation of most equipment attributed to weaving is in dispute. A variety of card-weaving techniques may have been used for narrow widths of cloth and this might explain the highly distinctive grooved and polished sheep metapodials (see below). For weaving yarn into broad widths of cloth, however, it is generally accepted that vertical warp-weighted looms were used, formed from a framework based on two side poles set in the ground or leant against a wall.

In the absence of direct remains of looms the main evidence for their existence relies on the standard interpretation of perforated cylindrical, pyramidal or triangular blocks of fired clay or stone as 'loomweights.' But this widely accepted interpretation of such objects has been questioned in some detail in a review of 'loomweights' at Danebury (Poole 1991 b, 380), where it was suggested that they might be reinterpreted as 'oven bricks'. In recent years this alternative interpretation has been proposed for sites in the Thames Valley, sometimes with as much assurance as the more generally accepted interpretation. The issue is difficult to resolve, not least because although broken triangular blocks are often found with burnt stones, it is likely that whatever their original function they would have been reused as pot boilers.

Associations of fired clay 'loomweights' with other cooking equipment, such as circular clay plates at Gravelly Guy (see above), is perhaps worth reviewing but unlikely to be conclusive. However, a wider review of such concentrated collections might be worthwhile. So far there has been no systematic study of wear patterns on the perforations in the Thames Valley, though this might anyway be inconclusive if rows of weights had been arranged on rods to spread the weight evenly, leaving little or no evidence of wear (Lisa Brown pers. comm.).

In the middle Bronze Age these weights or perforated blocks were often cylindrical, including several from Home Farm Laleham (Hayman forthcoming c). Late Bronze Age examples were typically tall pyramidal or occasionally cylindrical shapes (Longley 1980, 411). Iron Age forms were typically equilateral triangles with perforations through one, two or all three corners, but most recovered are fragmentary. Of the several hundred fired clay triangular blocks found at Gravelly Guy, only 21 were complete. It was tentatively suggested, given the small sample, that three size ranges were made: large – 1750-2000 g; medium – 1375-1500 g; and small – up to 300 g. This variation could represent loomweights of different sizes intended for larger or smaller lengths or widths of cloth, the heavier weights being used to hold more warp threads or to keep longer lengths of warp tight.

This issue is not easily resolved as it is extremely rare to find loomweights in groups. However, a cache of 16 from a middle Bronze Age pit at Imperial College Sports Field could represent a set of weights (Crockett 2001). At Gravelly Guy two early to middle Iron Age pits, one inside the other just outside a post-built roundhouse (Building A) produced concentrations of triangular blocks (Fig. 6.9). Pit 503 just inside the back wall of the building produced twelve, three complete, and Pit 326 contained six fragments. Their association with lumps of partly burnt conglomerate, burnt limestone and fragments of fired clay slabs in Pit 503 suggests the group might represent a cache of stone and fired clay objects awaiting recycling as pot boilers, while the comparable associations, plus a dog forelimb and a human trepanning disc, suggest a ritual deposit, but neither provides good evidence of the original use of the triangular blocks (Lambrick and Allen 2004, 118, pl 3.2; 377-8-, fig. 8.12 and 8.13; 253). More generally, 'loomweights' are found in pits and postholes in houses but seldom in deposits that indicate their function. For example, a pit with semifired triangular blocks in House 2 at Mingies Ditch (Allen and Robinson 1993, 43, fig. 18) and similar groups in pits at Gravelly Guy and Mount Farm demonstrate that they were made on site in a domestic context, but not what they were used for.

General distributions of 'loomweights' within settlements, including pastoralist settlements, provide limited additional insight. The 48 fragments at Park Farm, Binfield and a large number at Ashridge Wood nearby are exceptional given the limited extent of excavation, the limited life of the settlement in the later Iron Age and early Roman period and the small numbers of finds (Roberts 1995; Ford 1987). At the much longer-lived, intensively occupied and completely excavated settlement at Gravelly Guy 564 triangular blocks or fragments and one pyramidal one were found, representing a total weight of 49.27 kg, but their disparate distribution along with other textile associated objects suggests only common household usage.

A variety of bone and antler tools may have been equipment used in weaving or other cloth manufacture. Bobbins, which may also have served as shuttles, are fairly common finds. They were made from a variety of animal bones in a wide range of sizes, and only some of them might have been associated with clothmaking.

In the late Bronze Age thin, highly polished knife- or sword-like implements made from longitudinally split and pointed animal long bones, usually cattle as at Runnymede (Needham and Spence 1996, 189, B19-20), but also sheep as at Home Farm, Laleham (Hayman forthcoming c), may have been pin-beaters used to beat up the weft ensuring a tight weave on the loom. However, the evidence from Runnymede suggests alternative functions. Other examples have been found at Bray in Berkshire and other sites of middle Bronze Age date across the country (Morris 1995, 34). These implements do not seem to occur in quite this form on Iron Age sites, though bone 'knives' or 'gouges' made from tapered rather than split bones might have served a similar purpose. Alternatively, the same function may have been achieved with so-called weaving combs which would have allowed the weft to be beaten up at several points at once.

The function of 'weaving combs' is uncertain. Although Sellwood's (1984b, 375-8) study of use-wear provided some support for their interpretation as beaters-in, other uses, notably as hair combs or for working animal skins, have also been suggested. It is probably misleading to imagine that they had a single function and a multifunctional tool for

preparing skins, carding wool for spinning and beating up the weft in spinning is quite plausible (see below).

Another type of object possibly connected with weaving is the highly distinctive, but still largely unexplained, 'grooved and polished sheep metapodials' (Fig. 6.7 and see above). Their often highly polished surface, and characteristic pairs or sets of heavily worn grooves set on opposite faces of the bone, typically 50-60 mm apart, are of unknown origin. They may have been a form of lease rod, the grooves caused by the friction of the warp and the weft. Not all weaving need have been done on a large vertical warp-weighted loom. There is much ethnographical and historical evidence for a variety of ways of weaving strips of cloth without recourse to a framed loom, such as 'tablet' weaving, which might be a particular context for the use of metapodials.

Sewing and making clothes and other objects from fabrics

Production of clothes, bags and other objects from woollen and linen fabrics and animal skins is reflected in finds of antler, bone and bronze needles for sewing, and awls, points or punches. From the later Bronze Age onwards bronze and bone or antler needles are found in both single and double-ended forms, bone and antler examples being fully shaped from splinters made using the groove-and-splinter technique of bone working. Awls varied considerably in size and shape dependant on the bones from which they were made, with a variety of bronze, and later iron forms, including both tanged and untanged variants. Most needles and awls are quite worn but some are still very sharp. Some large settlement assemblages display a wide range of such implements (eg Needham and Spence 1996, 187-9; Lambrick and Allen 2004, 339, 361 365, 388 395, figs 8.5, 8.7, 8.14, 8.19).

Sewing together of strips or tubes of woven fabric is only one way of making garments from spun thread or wool. 'Nalebinding', a single needle precursor of knitting, is also known as knotless netting, looped needle netting, needle looped fabric and single-needle knitting, and may have been commonly practised. The technique is a simple means of producing woollen fabrics or coarse netted bags based on a darning technique using a needle and coarse yarn, passing the thread for each stitch through the loops of at least two previous stitches. It is attested from Neolithic times in the Mediterranean and north-west Europe, including fabrics from later prehistoric Danish bog bodies (Bender Jørgensen 1990; Hald 1980), but there is no direct evidence for this technique from the Thames Valley.

Although there is reason to assume routine use of thread, string, cords and rope, finds of cordage are rare in the Thames Valley and relatively few objects provide indirect evidence of its use. For example, it

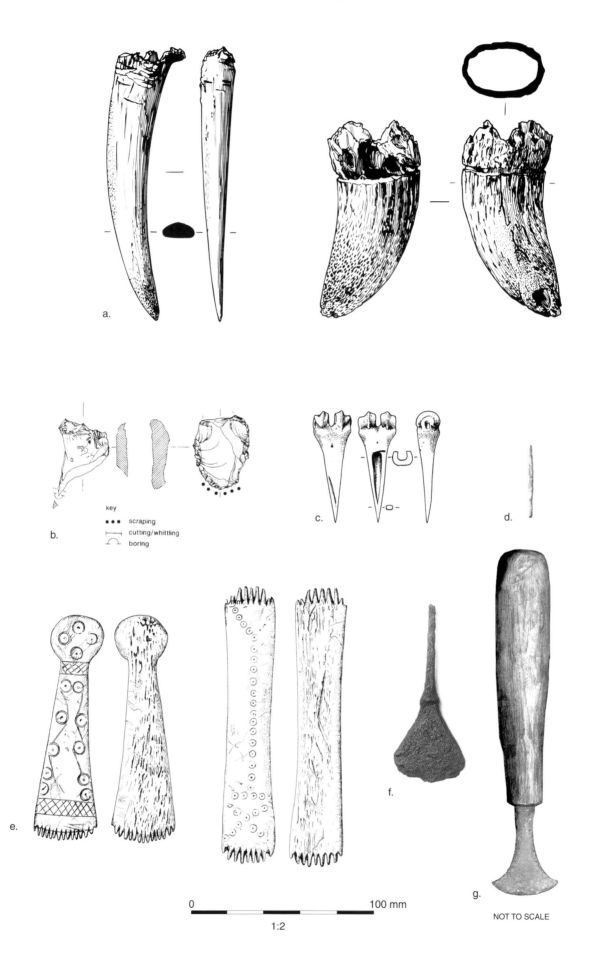

key
●●● scraping
├──┤ cutting/whittling
⌒ boring

a.

b.

c.

d.

e.

f.

g.

0   100 mm
1:2

NOT TO SCALE

largely ceased to be used as a means of making impressed decorative designs on pottery by the later prehistoric period. Cordage and rope may have been made from several plant fibres, including hop/hemp, wild clematis, bryony, honeysuckle and nettle. These plants are all recorded at various later prehistoric sites in the Thames Valley. Bark bast, especially from lime trees, is another possible source of material for rope. Other objects that may reflect the use of cordage include small toggles, beads and small bronze tubes that may have served as tag ends (eg Ashville, Parrington 1978, fig. 59 Nos. 17, 18). Bone bobbins for winding thread, string or cord are common and, amongst other things, could have been used for net making. Various bone points and spikes could have had uses that involved ropes and knots.

Bone and antler working, animal skins and leather

Bone, antler and horn

Bone and antler were essential raw materials for late prehistoric tools and ornaments, and are generally well preserved on the more calcareous soils of the Thames Valley (Fig. 6.8). Offcuts, unfinished objects and completed tools and ornaments provide a range of evidence for utilisation and working of bone.

Bones were selected for their practical qualities to suit different uses. Antler in particular has a high tensile strength and antler picks continued to be used as digging tools at least into the middle to late Bronze Age at Home Farm Laleham, and possibly Mount Farm (Hayman forthcoming c; Lambrick forthcoming). Although no antler picks were found at Rams Hill, toolmarks indicated that they had been used to lever out chalk blocks that were then shaped with metal axes or adzes, as was the ditch itself (Bradley and Ellison, 11, 90, fig. 3.2). This restricted use of antler for a specific task where tensile strength was needed makes sense when hafted axes and adzes would not have been as strong for exerting leverage. Antler was also the commonly preferred material for smaller items requiring tensile strength, such as handles, combs and some strap unions (see above).

Off-cuts suggest that shed antlers were collected as a raw material and, while most other bones were selected from the normal range of domestic animals reared for food and other purposes, pig bone was seldom used, probably because it is more porous and liable to split than that of other species (Seager Smith 2000, 222-40). Bird bones, probably mostly collected from dead birds found in the wild as domestic poultry was rare before the end of the Iron Age, were used to make fine needles and pins and were used, sometimes unmodified, for decorating pottery. Many other parts of animal carcasses would have been put to good use. Horncores with evidence of cutting round the base, such as one from Gravelly Guy (Fig. 6.8; Lambrick and Allen 2004 391 and fig. 8.14 no. 723), suggest that horn as well as antler was valued, perhaps both as material for handles and drinking vessels.

Where large bones required splitting or shortening to create basic roughouts a number of techniques were used. These included the 'groove and splinter' techniques practised since the Mesolithic using flint tools (in later prehistory probably metal ones) to create controlled lines of weakness along which bones splintered into long thin strips, rods and points. Although stone and flint knives, drills, choppers and fine saws were used for boneworking in the Neolithic and earlier Bronze Age, and use-wear suggests that some flint tools were still used on hard materials such as bone and antler in the later Bronze Age (Fig. 6.8; Brown and Bradley 2006 60-1), the development of metal versions of such tools in later prehistory would have greatly facilitated boneworking. Fine knife cuts, drilled holes, chopped ends, and sawn fragments commonly provide evidence for the use of a range of metal tools in converting bone and antler into objects.

For most purposes it was necessary to carve, shape, drill, and sometimes smooth and polish initial roughouts to create finished articles. For some items such as needles, the bone from which they were made has been so worked down that the species of animal is no longer identifiable. However, in many cases only the 'business' ends of bone tools were worked so it is possible to observe that certain bones were preferred for particular types of implement. More rarely bones needed no modification at all for their purpose. The grooved and polished sheep metapodials demonstrate preference for a single unmodified skeletal element of a particular species for a particular (unidentified) function. In many cases the polish that accumulated on bone and antler tools resulted purely from their use, but there are objects with deliberately smoothed and polished, glossy surfaces (Fig. 6.7).

A few objects, particularly personal items like toggles and strap junctions and so-called bone or antler 'plaques', were polished and decorated using a wide range of decorative devices, sometimes achieved with very fine knife cuts. More rarely, antler (less frequently bone) was deliberately charred black and then polished and/or decorated to create a high glossy black finish, perhaps intended to resemble shale. Generally, however,

Fig. 6.8 (opposite) Worked bone, bone-working and leather- and skin-working: a) horncores from Gravelly Guy; b) flint scrapers and piercer from Whitecross Farm; c) bone awls from Runnymede; d) bronze awl from Whitecross Farm; e) Iron Age antler combs from Yarnton; f) tanged, semi-discoidal knife from Whitecross farm; g) reconstruction of an Iron Age chisel

bones were not large and dense enough to allow direct imitation of shale bracelets, spindle whorls and other items. For the most part utilitarian tools – awls, gouges, knives, spatulas, bobbins, needles, grooved metapodials – were seldom decorated, but the antler combs are an exception. The vast majority were at least shaped and polished all over and were commonly elaborately decorated. Whether the hypothesised functions are valid, the quality of finish suggests a stronger personal association for these objects than other tools.

Animal skins and other soft tissue

Given the greatly increasing occurrence of spindle whorls and weaving equipment in the later prehistoric period, woven fabrics apparently became more common, or the equipment for making them more efficiently was developed at this time. The established tradition of craftsmanship in the preparation of furs, hide and leather probably used for clothing and a wide variety of belts, containers and other uses probably endured. It is also likely that animal sinew, gut, leather strips and horsehair were used for thongs and cords. Evidence for these is largely absent apart from butchery techniques that hint that these elements were deliberately removed. It may also be assumed that the carcasses of animals were processed to make grease, tallow, oils, and perhaps glue and other useful by-products that rarely survive.

Evidence of the preparation of animal skins and leather comes from knife marks on animal bones that indicate the careful and systematic removal of hides (Wilson 1992), and from tools that would have been useful in their preparation. In the middle to late Bronze Age crude flint scrapers are thought from use-wear evidence to have been used on soft materials including animal skins (Brown and Bradley 2006, 60-1). Other available tools include late Bronze Age tanged knives with broad chisel-like blades, commonly believed to be leather-working tools.

The highly distinctive and often decorative antler combs common on early to late Iron Age settlement sites may also have been used in processing animal skins, though interpretations of these combs vary (Hodder and Hedges 1977). The teasing out of fleeces or tamping down of wefts is supported to some degree by use-wear studies (Sellwood 1984b, 375-8) but another common suggestion is that they were used for scraping hides (Cunnington 1923, 94-5). Similar Inuit implements were used for preparing seal skins, as illustrated by examples in the Pitt-Rivers Museum, Oxford. Stubby bone awls such as the late Bronze Age examples at Runnymede, and bronze and iron tanged or plain awls are also common artefacts on settlement sites, and are likely to have been used for making holes in animal skins or leather. One interpretation of grooved and polished sheep metapodials is that they were thong stretchers.

Prehistoric leatherwork seldom survives, partly because tanning techniques were not well developed. Iron Age sword scabbards, such as that found at Shepperton, were clearly made of leather, in this case from a calf, with metal mountings (Poulton forthcoming b). A few scraps of leather were found in a waterhole at the late Bronze Age site at Watkins Farm (Allen 1990, 56) and in a middle Iron Age waterhole at Wyndyke Furlong (Muir and Roberts 1999, 49), but these were not recognisably crafted objects. Small toggles could have been used with laces to tie leather or cloth bags, but in general there are few fittings that would have been necessarily associated with leather bags, shoes or boots, so unambiguous evidence for them is lacking. However, a wide variety of fittings for leather belts are commonly found on settlements, in hoards and other contexts.

Pottery and other ceramics

Techniques used in potting

Little can be said of clay preparation methods, but in the Upper Thames the presence of freshwater snails in some alluvial fabrics, the natural occurrence of abundant fossil shell in some surface deposits of Kimmeridge Clay, of calcareous gravel in some river channel clays, and of abundant glauconitic sand in some Gault clays all point to the possibility that some clays were selected as naturally 'ready-tempered' (Lambrick forthcoming). However, various tempering materials such as sand and fossil shell were added to improve the firing properties of clay. It has been suggested that querns and other grinding stones were used to prepare flint or other inclusions for pottery production at Runnymede, in addition to their use in food preparation (Needham and Spence 1996, 162-4).

The clearest evidence of the addition of temper to potting clays at Runnymede and elsewhere is the common use of crushed calcined flint and quartzite, which was standard practice in the late Bronze Age in all parts of the Thames Valley. Indeed, this is more than a regional pattern as it applies equally to many other parts of England (Barrett 1980). It may merely reflect the considerable abundance of calcined flint and quartzite left from cooking and other activities involving heating water (see above) and its suitability as tempering material as compared with the less suitable reuse of burnt limestone at later periods.

The change in choice of materials used in pottery tempering from calcined flint or quartzite to other local materials may thus be linked to a technical or cultural change in the practice of heating stones. In the Upper Thames Valley this change was from a type of stone suitable to act as potting temper to one that was not, but even in areas where flint continued as the favoured material for heating stones there was a similar shift away from using it as temper. It appears that, compared with earlier and later periods, there was a cultural, not merely technical reason for this widespread use of calcined flint and quartz as the standard tempering agent in the later Bronze Age. This may reflect a cultural, symbolic or technological link between pots and the red-hot stones used for cooking, which ceased to be important from the early Iron Age onwards.

In the Upper Thames Valley quartzite pebbles are abundant in 'Northern Drift' deposits stretching in a linear band from the Cotswolds in the north-west through Stanton Harcourt and Yarnton to Culham, Dorchester and the Goring Gap. Within the more northerly part of this band above Abingdon, where flint is almost absent from the gravels, later Bronze Age pottery was typically tempered with calcined quartzite rather than flint, and burnt mound material is also predominantly quartzite before limestone became the standard source of heating stone from the early Iron Age onwards. Further upriver contemporary pottery in the Shorncote/ Cotswold Community and Latton area is usually shell-tempered (Hearne and Heaton 1994; Barclay and Glass 1995; Hearne and Adam 1999; Barclay 1999, 319; Timby 2004a).

Needham (Needham and Spence 1996, 162-4, pls 20-21) suggests that flint-tempered late Bronze Age pottery was made at Runnymede This is based on the presence of deposits reflecting stages in the crushing of calcined flint, which include clusters of complete nodules, smashed pieces and thoroughly crushed material, together with stone hammers or pestles used for crushing, grinding stones (probably also used as querns), lenses of raw clay, burnishing implements and possible firing locations (Fig. 6.9). A spalled pot was also recovered from the site. Each of these elements can be interpreted in other ways, but their concurrence lends some weight to the interpretation.

Almost throughout the later prehistoric period until the last decades before the Roman conquest, pottery was made without the benefit of a wheel. A variety of techniques for forming pots is known, including slab-building, ring- and coil-building and simple 'thumb-pot' techniques. Slab-building is evident in a badly fired pot from Bampton and coil-building is often evident in the rounded bowls of the middle Iron Age, with horizontal coils clearly visible and tangible in the variable thickness of the pot wall. Sometimes the junctions of coils and slabs are visible in cross-section (eg Parrington 1978, fig. 33, no. 28) but generally details of pot formation are not observed or systematically recorded.

While most ordinary utilitarian pots and jars were undecorated and crudely finished, a high degree of care and skill is evident in the highly finished and decorated finewares. Glazing was not introduced until after the Roman conquest, but high polishes were achieved through burnishing. In the early Iron Age this was sometimes coupled with the application of an iron-rich slip of haematite or the burnishing of haematite rich clay to create a polished, deep red surface. This was especially favoured for pottery of the earliest Iron Age of the Wiltshire All Cannings Cross style, but was imitated locally within the Thames Valley. More commonly burnishing was applied to pots that were then fired to achieve an all-over reduced (black) or oxidised (brown, orange or reddish) finish enhanced by the silky sheen of a burnished finish. The detailed texture of the finish was sometimes enhanced by the direction of burnishing.

Decorative motifs were incised (especially in the later Bronze Age and early Iron Age) or tooled (especially middle Bronze Age and middle Iron Age) onto surfaces. Raised cordons, sometimes with finger impressions or slashes, are a feature of later Bronze Age and early Iron Age pottery. White inlaid decoration using the white apatite content of bone is a particular feature of some early Iron Age finewares characteristic of the Chinnor area of the Chilterns, found at sites on the Upper Thames gravels. Bone tools, including bird bones sawn off to make small impressed circles or used to create curiously shaped impressions from their natural joint ends, were used to create a considerable variety of impressed, incised or tooled motifs. Bone or metal knives were used for decorative slashing and scoring of the wet clay, and potters used their fingers to make rows of impressions round rims and shoulders. Larger dimples, piecrust cabling and other features were impressed or moulded onto pots.

Until the end of the Iron Age pottery was fired at low temperatures without the use of a kiln, and there are examples of severely overfired, distorted and vitrified pots. It seems clear from examples of spalled, cracked and distorted pots that the wedging of potting clay, preparation of tempering materials and/or drying and firing of pots was not always carried out with sufficient care. Although there is evidence for kilns in the immediate pre-conquest period at Yarnton, they were small and unsophisticated, perhaps only a limited improvement on bonfire and clamp methods of firing that had been the prehistoric norm. They did not attain the high temperatures or quality of firing achieved by specialist potters elsewhere (whose imported products occasionally appear on late pre-conquest sites) or in the much larger sophisticated later Oxfordshire Roman pottery industry. Nevertheless, there is evidence throughout later prehistory in the Thames Valley, as elsewhere, that despite the lack of kilns, a significant degree of control over firing conditions was achieved. This is especially clear from the choice of reducing or oxidising conditions in the manufacture of finewares.

The organisation of pottery production

While a good deal is known from the pots themselves about basic potting methods, direct evidence for the location of manufacturing sites and

Fig.6.9 (overleaf) Ceramic crafts

CERAMIC CRAFTS

Decorated pottery from Castle Hill, Little Wittenham

Until the end of the Iron Age most pottery found on Thames Valley sites seems to have originated within the Thames catchment area. It was handmade and fired at low temperatures in bonfires or 'clamp kilns'. Primitive kilns of the immediate pre-conquest period were identified at Yarnton and Hanborough. Unfired or partly fired ceramic loomweights from Mingies Ditch and Gravelly Guy suggest on-site manufacture and spalled, cracked and vitrified pottery wasters recovered from various sites are likely to have been produced nearby.

The range of ceramic artefacts from later prehistoric sites in the Thames Valley include loomweights, spindle whorls, crucibles, briquetage and, most commonly, pottery. Evidence for raw materials sources and manufacturing sites is slight. No specialist production centres have been identified, nor is it clear whether pottery was made by women or men, whether each household made its own pots or whether production was communal or the work of itinerant craftsmen.

Evidence for the preparation of pottery temper by grinding of calcined flint was found at Runnymede along with bone 'burnishers'. Pottery production was only one of many crafts that a late prehistoric agricultural community engaged in for its own use and for production of goods for exchange. However, whereas every family probably did its own spinning and weaving, made its own bone tools and undertook other crafts, it is unlikely that they made all of their own pottery.

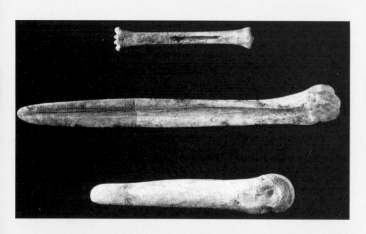

CERAMIC CRAFTS

Late Bronze Age vessel with impressed finger prints visible on rim

Although some potting clays were naturally tempered, sand, fossil shell and flint were often added to improve firing properties. Handmade pots were formed by slab, ring- and coil-building and simple 'thumb-pot' techniques. Burnishing produced a high polish and iron-rich slips created deep red surfaces. Raised cordons with finger impressions or slashes feature on later Bronze Age and early Iron Age pottery, and decoration inlaid with white apatite derived from bone was applied to early Iron Age finewares from the Chinnor area.

There would have been some level of exchange of pottery between the Upper and Middle Thames River Valleys in late prehistory. A Frilford-style swag-decorated globular bowl was found at Thames Valley Park, Reading, while geometric decorated sherds characteristic of Middle Thames types were found at Blewburton and Hill Farm, Little Wittenham. Malvernian pottery and Droitwich briquetage were transported from the West Midlands to Claydon Pike in the upper reaches of the Thames Valley in the middle Iron Age. The late Iron Age, particularly the first half the first century AD, was marked by a significant increase in the diversity of traded pottery, especially evident at major centres such as Silchester, but also in ordinary farming settlements.

Left page:
(centre) Unfired clay loomweights in a small pit at Gravelly Guy
(below left) Bone pottery burnishers from Runnymede;
(below right); Production of flint temper at Runnymede: calcined flints, quern and stone pounders
Right page
(top left) This late Bronze Age or early Iron Age jar from Bampton, Oxon, lost its base and was cracked and spalled in firing
(bottom left) Irregular firing: the unusual pattern of cracking suggests this irregularly fired middle Iron Age pot from Castle Hill was slab-built
(right) Late Iron Age/early Roman pottery kiln at Yarnton

the identity of the makers is extremely sparse for the period. There is some evidence that children helped add finger-impressed decoration, even if they were not more fully involved in potting. Otherwise we have no clear evidence whether women or men made pots, whether every household made its own pottery, or whether it was a communal effort or the work of itinerant craftsmen. The classic archaeological indicators of *in situ* pottery manufacture are kilns and wasters, but these are rare for the period.

The discovery of primitive kilns at a few late Iron Age sites in the Upper Thames Valley tells us something of the manner of pottery production before the emergence of specialist production on an industrial scale in the Roman period. All were found on settlement sites, not apparently 'specialist' pottery production facilities, but this is hardly surprising as, even at its height, the major Oxfordshire Roman pottery industry was embedded in the local agricultural economy. It is unlikely that late prehistoric pottery production was anything more than one of a number of crafts undertaken by an agricultural community for its own needs, or as a way for some individuals to produce goods for exchange.

Pottery 'wasters' are the unusable by-products of severe misfirings. Wasters of wheelthrown, kiln fired pots are often distinctive by their obvious distortion, cracking, and other physical flaws or from overfiring to the point of vitrification. This can also be discerned in handmade low-fired pots, but is a less typical kind of pot failure as some level of distortion is almost inevitable (eg Allen and Robinson 1993, 71 and fig. 34, no.14) and firing problems were as likely to be due to under- as to over-firing. Most failed pots would have disintegrated, reverting to their raw materials, perhaps to an archaeologically unrecognisable state. Where they failed less catastrophically and were usable it becomes a moot point whether they are really evidence of on-site manufacture. There are several cases of misfired late prehistoric pots from the region which suggest this, though it is very difficult to distinguish clearly between firing accidents and post-firing damage through overheating during use or from accidental fires.

A higher proportion of middle Bronze Age and earlier cremation urns, as opposed to domestic vessels, are cracked or distorted. This may reflect the deliberate, symbolic use of broken pots that have no useful 'life', and so in a sense are themselves 'dead', to contain the remains of dead people. Pots that went wrong in firing may have been retained for this purpose.

'Spalling', the flaking off of the surface of pots, can be the result of impurities in the clay, but most commonly is the result of poor drying of the clay. Moisture trapped in the fabric of the pot cannot escape and expands explosively as it turns to steam on firing. It can also occur as a result of thermal shock during use of pottery under conditions that puts it under abnormal stress. At Perry Oaks/T5

two waterholes contained substantial deposits of pottery with evidence of over- or misfiring which may have occurred in their manufacture (Framework Archaeology 2006). One of these assemblages (927 sherds; 9841 g) consisted of up to 13 fineware bowls and 7 medium sized coarseware jars, all of a single broad fabric type, many of which had been burnt or overfired to varying degrees. Some sherds exhibited a friable, powdery texture and were (re)fired to a pale grey colour, and others had blistered or spalled surfaces. The basal fill of another waterhole produced 117 sherds from six vessels, including a short-necked fineware jar, a biconical bowl, a shouldered bowl and an extremely large shouldered fineware bowl or jar. At least three of the vessels bore signs of over- or refiring, and two vessels had surface spalling.

Another example of a large spalled and cracked vessel is an almost complete late Bronze Age or early Iron Age shouldered jar from Bampton, Oxfordshire, which had vertical cracks (suggesting it was slab-built) and major spalling in several places, including the loss of most of its base (Mayes *et al.* 2000, 278-9, figs 9 and 10). At Castle Hill a large part of an unevenly fired, distorted pot had broken after firing with a vertical crack from top to bottom, around the base and diagonally around the pot, suggesting a complex sequence of slab-building.

At Gravelly Guy seven pits, variously of early and middle Iron Age date, contained sherds of spalled pottery (Lambrick and Allen 2004, 274-5 and fig. 292, no. 25). At least one was an almost complete vessel, almost certainly perfectly usable, as were the others before they were broken. Three of the pots were in a distinctive sandy ware. However, as this accounted for only 3% of the assemblage it seems unlikely that the pots were made on the site. The other four pots were in fabrics tempered with calcareous gravel, which was more obviously local, though again not conclusive evidence of manufacture on site (Lambrick and Allen 2004, 285-6, fig. 7.6, no 25). Several fire-damaged and broken pots were noted at Whitecross Farm, including a near complete jar with a drilled hole beside an old break, indicating a post-firing repair that eventually failed (Cromarty *et al.* 2006, 84, fig. 3.10, no. 1).

The difficulty of achieving controlled high temperatures to fully fire pottery means that until the late Iron Age most prehistoric pottery was fired without a kiln at relatively low temperatures, often only just above the point of ceramic change at around 500° C. Although the use of kilns was not a routine part of late prehistoric pottery manufacture, this does not mean that higher temperatures could not be achieved deliberately on a smaller scale, as it clearly was for metalworking, or that they did not occur accidentally whilst firing pottery or in other circumstances. Apart from crucibles, sherds of overfired pottery were found at Reading Business Park/Green Park (Brossler *et al.* 2004, 90) and Cookham (A Barclay pers. comm.), but these are not necessarily wasters. They were often overfired as broken sherds and, while this could happen during firing if the pot exploded, it is more likely that they were incorporated in accidental fires in buildings or ovens (Barclay 2002; Morris 1992).

Evidence of late prehistoric pottery manufacture is thus seldom clear-cut from wasters. Firing damage, cracking, spalling and distortion did not necessarily mean that 'failed' pots were regarded as useless or valueless, nor does it provide good evidence for manufacturing sites.

Other evidence for pottery manufacture within settlements is rare and often ambiguous. The possibility of preparation of tempering agents and bone burnishers at Runnymede has been cited above (Needham 1996) as evidence of *in situ* manufacturing. But even if this tentative interpretation is accepted, it does not tell us much about wider organisation. Within the broader scenario that Needham envisages for Runnymede – as a place of both long-term inhabitants and visitors who may have been temporary residents for reasons of social contact, exchange, or specialist craftsmanship – pottery manufacture could have been carried on by either residents or visitors. The same applies to virtually every other late prehistoric settlement in the Thames Valley.

Perhaps the most convincing evidence is the use of a pottery-like fabric for the lining of pits or oven bases at Aldermaston Wharf, Reading Business Park/Green Park, and possibly Albury (Moore and Jennings 1992, 89; Brossler *et al.* 2004, 69). Although no pots made in quite the same fabric were found, other, denser coarse fabrics used for large jars were similar and it is easy to imagine that only a modest adaptation of ingredients and methods would have been needed to make both materials. Furthermore, it seems highly unlikely that the raw materials for the pit linings would have been brought from elsewhere.

Apart from the late Bronze Age pit linings in the Kennet Valley, some of the clearest evidence of local manufacture of ceramic objects is the presence on a few sites of unfired or partly fired loomweights in small pits along with ordinary domestic debris, usually with other fully fired loomweights and sometimes other fired clay objects. One such deposit was found at Mingies Ditch (Allen and Robinson 1993, 43 and 78, Pl 12), and three at Gravelly Guy (Lambrick and Allen 2004, 118, 336), both in the lower Windrush Valley, and one at Mount Farm.

From various perspectives it thus seems plausible that there were specialist potters operating within some communities and others as seasonally or continuously active itinerant craftsmen. This is, however, difficult to prove without 'signature' pots. The closest we get to a possible 'school' of potting is the very distinctive style of decoration of early Iron Age pottery from Chinnor (Harding 1974, 162; Gibson 2002, 126). As yet no detailed analysis of fabrics and highly distinctive decorative styles has been carried out for late prehistoric pottery in the Thames Valley to

match that which defined Glastonbury ware and other pottery from geologically more distinctive parts of Britain. Superficially it appears that no such correlation between fabrics and decoration would be found in the equivalent middle to late Iron Age swag-decorated bowls of the 'Cassington/Frilford' tradition since a variety of fabrics characterise vessels within each of the two main sub-styles (Fig. 6.10; Lambrick 1984).

In general, the variation in pottery fabrics in all parts of the Thames Valley demonstrates the use of local clays and tempering in the manufacture of pottery throughout the period. Indeed, until the end of the 1st century BC there is only limited evidence of pottery that did not originate within the Thames catchment. Recurrent changes in fabric proportions on long-occupied sites that do not obviously reflect technological advances, together with changing fashions of form, finish and decoration, all seem to indicate regional or local preferences in the production of domestic pots that had little to do with technical production. Such common stylistic trends are thus not good indicators that all pots were made in specialist centres of production. This might be true of some, but in general they are more likely to be the result of imitation in response to commonly shared preferences, as seems evident from the wide range of fabrics used for some of the most distinctive regional styles of decoration.

So 'local' production of pottery does not automatically equate to purely domestic crafts, like spinning and weaving, but equally, there is an absence of sites or physical infrastructure (like kilns) providing clear evidence of specialist pottery production until the latter end of the period. Even then, with the advent of kilns, pottery production is likely to have been only a marginal activity of some farming communities. In a sense the question is not so much whether there were people who sometimes specialised in making pots, either within farming communities or as itinerant potters, as whether there were families and communities who did *not* make at least some of their own pots. It seems probable that whereas every family probably did do its own spinning and weaving, made its own bone tools and undertook some other crafts, they probably did not generally make all or possibly any of their own pottery, even if someone else in their community did so.

Morris (forthcoming) noted that post Deverel-Rimbury pottery assemblages from settlements in the Middle Thames display wide variation in vessel forms and decoration, which cannot be entirely explained by chronological factors. The pottery of each settlement appears to display a different character or specialisation, perhaps reinforcing evidence for local production, or reflecting different degrees and patterns of interaction with wider exchange networks. Runnymede Bridge has a high proportion of decorated wares and a much wider range of forms than most other sites. Caesar's Camp has a predominance of specific coarseware jar and

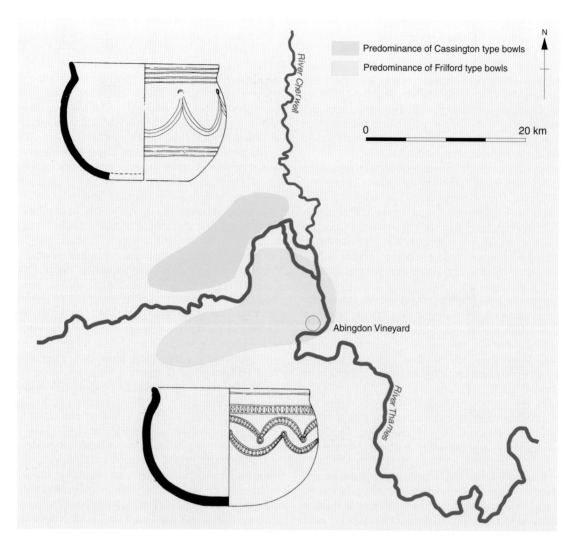

Fig. 6.10   Local distribution of pottery styles: Since this distinction between Cassington and Frilford swagged bowls was first published in 1984, new finds have tended to repeat the pattern but with some exceptions. Notably, the site of the oppidum at Abingdon Vineyard has produced almost equal numbers of the two styles

fineware bowl forms. St Mary's Hospital, Carshalton, produced a high number of handled jars (Adkins and Needham 1985), while a small assemblage from Coombe Warren, Kingston Hill comprised a range of notably small vessels (Field and Needham 1986). A similar observation has been made of the diverse early to middle Iron Age pottery assemblages from sites in the Stanton Harcourt area, where significant variations can only partly be accounted for by chronological differences (Lambrick and Allen 2004, 288-9). The relative diversity of fabrics, finishes and decoration of the pottery from Watkins Farm compared with the limited range at the otherwise similar settlement at Mingies Ditch is especially striking. While this may be due partly to chronological differences, both assemblages differ from the material at Gravelly Guy, which spans the chronological range. Such variations seem best explained by differences in how settlements were linked to wider exchange networks and, although this might be related to

'status' and issues of inter-dependence, this is a complex issue.

Morris's (1981) study of Iron Age ceramics in western England suggested that there may have been three levels of pottery production and exchange, with a few very distinctive wares widely traded on a regional and wider basis, a wider range of more locally traded pots and the bulk based on local production. No comparably systematic analysis of pottery styles and fabrics has been attempted in the Thames Valley and the sedimentary geology tends to be less distinctive, so only tentative observations can be made. Despite being broadly 'local,' the fabrics found on most late prehistoric sites in the Thames Valley demonstrate other trends in pottery manufacture and distribution that have a bearing on production sites and methods. The recovery of some distinctive localised fabrics at sites with raw materials that could not have been used to make those fabrics shows that locally made pottery was part of wider local exchange networks within the Thames Valley. A particularly good example of this is the distribution of pottery made from a fabric including glauconitic sand from the Upper Greensand. This mineral outcrops in a relatively narrow strip of land at the base of the chalk escarpment and in out-wash alluvial material along streams springing from its interface with the underlying Gault clay. Unsurprisingly, pottery made from fabrics containing glauconitic clay is common on sites within this zone, but it also occurs in smaller proportions outside it at, for example, Mount Farm Dorchester. It accounts for 6% of pottery from Gravelly Guy 17 km to the north and a single sherd was found as far north as Rollright, on the scarp of the Cotswolds about 50 km distant.

Stylistic pottery links are also discernible within Thames Valley assemblages. Haematite-coated pottery and jars and bowls decorated in the All Cannings Cross style characteristic of the late Bronze Age and earliest Iron Age seem likely to have come from north Wiltshire, though this has not yet been demonstrated through detailed fabric analysis. Similarly, early Iron Age pottery with the distinctive style of decoration from the Chinnor area has been found on the Thames gravels, though again without proof of its source. Exchange along the river valley between the Upper and Middle Thames seems evident from the presence of a Frilford style swag-decorated globular bowl at Thames Valley Park, Reading (Mepham in Barnes *et al.* 1997), and, in the reverse direction, pottery with geometric decoration characteristic of Middle Thames types was found at Blewburton and at Hill Farm, Little Wittenham (Allen *et al.* forthcoming).

More distant movement of pottery is evident from Malvernian pottery brought from the West Midlands along with Droitwich briquetage (see below) to sites in the upper reaches of the Thames Valley such as Claydon Pike (Miles *et al.* 2007, 13-27).

The late Iron Age, particularly the first half of the first century AD, was marked by a significant increase in the diversity of traded pottery. This is especially evident at major centres such as Silchester (Fulford 2000) but to some extent it also filtered down to ordinary farming settlements. There are a few finds of imported amphorae, especially of Dressel I type, that reflect overseas trade in wine and other commodities from the Mediterranean.

Stoneworking, quarrying and collection

Collection of stone would have been a continual occupation of late prehistioric communities in the Thames Valley. Stone would have been required as potboilers for heating and for a wide variety of other uses. Some sites have been excavated on a sufficient scale to calculate the total quantities involved. For example, the burnt mound at Reading Business Park/Green Park was *c* 85 m long, 25 m wide and up to 0.2 m thick, consisting of 70% burnt

flint in a black charcoal-rich soil matrix, representing over 100 m^3 of stone. Settlements where the burnt stone did not originate on site but had to be brought some distance are of particular interest in demonstrating the lengths to which people would go to collect this material. Burnt limestone is ubiquitous on Iron Age sites in the Stanton Harcourt area, around Cassington and Yarnton and at Lechlade, all 5-10 km from the nearest source, where outcrops of cornbrash mark the tail end of the dip slope of the Cotswolds. Elsewhere in the valley (and in the later Bronze Age for much of the Upper Thames) quartzite or flint were most commonly used for heating and were more readily available from the gravel terraces or other drift deposits.

Stone was also collected for other purposes, an impressive case being the limestone causeway at Yarnton (Fig. 6.18) and the cobblestone and limestone ones at Thrupp. The surfaces of the stones used in the Yarnton construction were worn and rounded even where not exposed to traffic, suggesting that they had been collected either from the surface of fields or from streambeds where the stone outcrops at least 4 km away. The total volume of stone was not calculated but must have been in the order of 13 m^3. Even with carts a significant effort would have been required to collect, load up and transport it to the site. The limestone at Thrupp is most likely to be Corallian stone from a similar distance.

In areas with horizontally laminar stones, especially oolitic limestone on the Cotswolds and Pusey flags on the Corallian Ridge in the Upper Thames Valley, drystone walling was practised, as it had been since the Neolithic. Substantial defences were built with drystone construction on the Cotswolds at hillforts like Crickley Hill (Dixon 1994) and Rainsborough (Avery *et al.* 1967). Elaborate entrances involving timber bridges and massive gates with sentry boxes and guardrooms were built into the core of the ramparts constructed of rubble faced with drystone walling. On the Corallian ridge a slightly different construction technique, with walling revetting a largely earthen bank, was used on a less impressive scale for the inner rampart of the low-lying fort at Cherbury, built on a tongue of Pusey flags surrounded by former marshland. Excavations by Bradford in 1939 exposed a 24 m length of drystone walling and indicated that it probably ran all the way round the inner rampart. In places up to 9-10 courses survived *in situ*, standing about 1.5 m high. Taking into account the fallen material, it would have stood to over 2 m (Bradford 1940, 17). A very clear straight joint and step in levels suggested that construction involved gang work.

It is well known that in the earlier Neolithic Pusey Flags were transported *c*15 km to Waylands Smithy on the edge of the chalk to create a Cotswold-style long barrow. It is interesting in this context that similar material, perhaps from further east along the Corallian Ridge around Marcham,

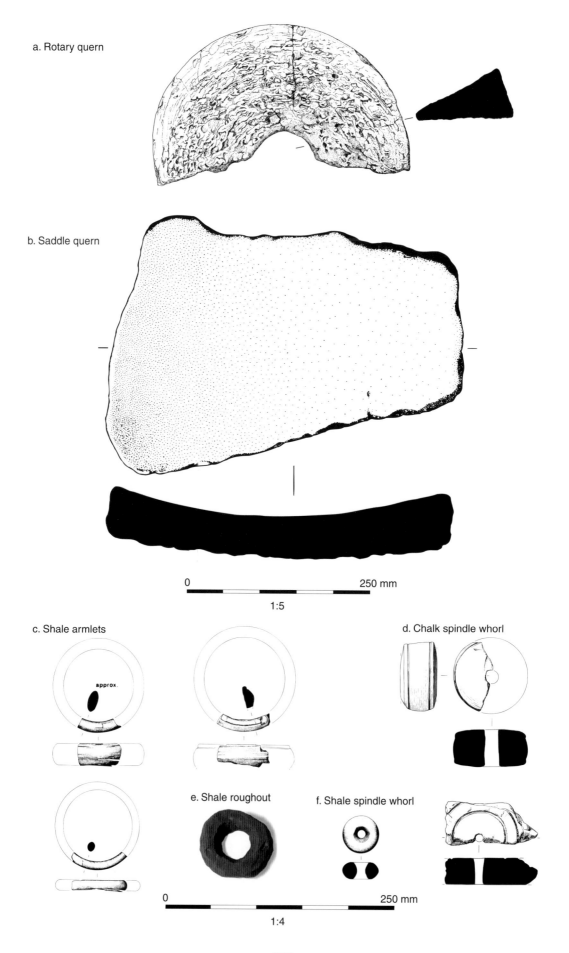

a. Rotary quern

b. Saddle quern

0 _____ 250 mm

1:5

c. Shale armlets

approx.

d. Chalk spindle whorl

e. Shale roughout

f. Shale spindle whorl

0 _____ 250 mm

1:4

was taken 15-20 km to make the drystone walls for the entrance passage of the hillfort at Blewburton Hill (Collins 1952-3, 38, Pls IIIa and IVa). Corallian beds are also likely to be the source of a few large slabs of limestone used in the late Bronze Age or early Iron Age kiln or oven structure at Ewe Farm between Brightwell Salome and Warborough, probably 10 km from the source.

Apart from hillforts, there is little evidence for stone walling, but large ditches dug into the Cotswold limestone for enclosures at Rollright (Lambrick 1988, 83) and examples excavated along the line of the A417/A419 (Mudd *et al.* 1999, Chapter 3) suggest that the extracted stone could have been used to make walls, which, with the rock-cut ditches, would have created formidable barriers. Stone was sometimes used for building houses in the Cotswolds (Moore 2006).

Querns

Stone was also collected and worked to make querns, whetstones and other stone tools such as hammerstones (Cromarty *et al.* 2006, 72, fig. 3.7, no. 5) and objects such as door and gate pivot stones. Some suitable rock types such as sarsen would have been collected as surface stone and others would have been taken from natural exposures (eg river gravels and streambeds). At least some material had to be quarried, though no definite late prehistoric quern quarries have been identified in the area. From Neolithic times onwards throughout later prehistory, saddle querns and rubbers were in use. They typically have one worked grinding surface. A suitably shaped stone would have been selected for shaping by pounding with other stones to obtain an even grinding surface. This would then have been rubbed smooth, initially by grinding grit rather than grain. In the majority of cases (eg 44 out of 56 pieces from Gravelly Guy) one or more of the other surfaces were also dressed, often including the base. Toolmarks and evidence of coarse flaking or pounding to shape the stones is sometimes visible, while the grinding surfaces were roughened by pecking. It is conceivable that the evidence of grinding of flint grits thought to be for pottery manufacture at Runnymede (Needham 1991, 137; Needham and Spence 1996, 162-4, pls 20-21), might also or alternatively reflect the process of preparing the surface of the quern before it was used for grain. Smaller rubber stones would have been selected and their shapes refined in similar ways. Thereafter, saddle querns and their rubbers would have been worn and shaped by use. In some cases stones were turned and fresh faces prepared for reuse.

Rotary querns, known from the middle Iron Age onwards but not common until later, involved significantly more shaping. It was necessary to create closely matching convex and concave grinding surfaces, to obtain at least a roughly circular form (sometimes quite finely shaped) and, more particularly, to create a central hole in the upper stone through which the grain was fed, along with a socket for a wooden handle to turn the stone. The basic shape would probably have been achieved by chipping with an iron pick and hammer and perhaps also by pounding and grinding as for saddle querns, and the holes are likely to have been formed by application of the same basic techniques, but focused specifically on one spot.

With very few exceptions the natural underlying geology of the floor of the Thames is gravel overlying clay, neither of which are good sources of quernstone, although cobbles of quartzitic sandstone from the Thames gravels were sometimes used as rubbers. In a few places suitable sandstones and gritstones outcrop close to the river, most notably where it cuts through the Corallian and Lower Greensand ridge south of Oxford in the vicinity of Sandford-on-Thames and Culham. Otherwise most grinding stones from sources within the Thames basin would have been Tertiary sandstones such as sarsen (either from the surface of the chalk or reworked into Plateau Drift deposits) and Upper and Lower Greensand. However, these were not the only sources exploited for grinding stones in later prehistory, and from at least the late Bronze Age onwards sandstones were also brought in from much further afield. They provide some of the best evidence of late prehistoric exchange networks, which is the subject of detailed research by Fiona Roe, to whom I am grateful for providing the basis of the following account.

The main sources of quernstones in the Upper Thames Valley throughout the prehistoric period were a specific well-cemented outcrop of Lower Greensand at Culham and Lower Calcareous Grit, a hard Jurassic sandstone probably obtained from several sources along the Corallian Ridge from Oxford west to Highworth, and east to Thame. Querns of Culham Greensand have been found as far south and east as Reading Business Park/Green Park (*c* 35 km) in the late Bronze Age, as far north as Steeple Aston (*c* 36 km) and as far west as Claydon Pike (*c* 43 km) in the middle Iron Age (Fig. 6.12). Roe has suggested (Brossler *et al.* 2004, 97-8) that the distribution might reflect riverine transport of these querns, while also noting that away from the river two have been recorded from hillforts, at Blewburton *c* 10 km south of Culham and at Segsbury Camp 23 km south west of Culham. Apart from Lower Calcareous Grit and Culham Greensand the other main natural source of material for querns in the Upper Thames basin, as well as further downstream, would have been sarsen. Although sarsen boulder fields like that near Ashdown House west of

Fig. 6.11 (opposite)   Later prehistoric stoneworking: examples of stone and shale artefacts from a) Yarnton , (b-d,f) Gravelly Guy and (e) Latton Lands

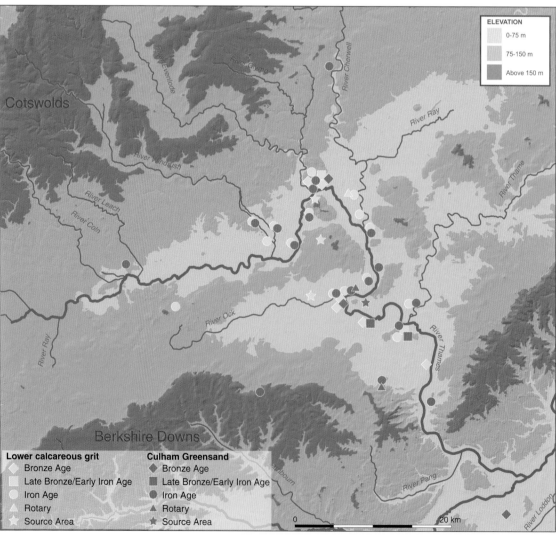

Uffington are now rare on the Berkshire Downs and in the Chilterns, they would have been much more common in the past. Sarsen boulders also occur in plateau drift deposits not far from the river. Sarsen querns have been found as far north of the chalk as Faringdon (11 km), Lechlade (Roughground Farm, *c* 18 km) and Yarnton (*c* 30 km).

While it is suspected that Lower Greensand querns from deposits like those at Culham were transported up and down the river by boat, and this may have had some influence in extending the range covered by this material, it was not the only factor that determined patterns of exchange. If convenient sources had lain close to the Thames where it cuts through the chalk escarpment at the Goring Gap it would have been another useful link to river transport, but sarsen was not recorded amongst the worked stone from later prehistoric sites at North

Stoke (Timby *et al.* 2005, 268-4), Moulsford (Ford 1990, 13) or Whitecross Farm, Wallingford (Cromarty *et al.* 2006, 71-2), where querns of other stone types have been found. Moreover there is no obvious broader pattern of sarsen querns to suggest that riverine distribution was important. Querns from further afield have been found at many late prehistoric sites in the Upper Thames Valley, including a number around Abingdon close to the source of the Culham greensand.

North of the Corallian Ridge May Hill sandstone was brought over 80 km from near Newent, west of the Severn as far as Stanton Harcourt, Yarnton and Bicester (Fig. 6.13). Along the ridge it has been recorded at Hatford and Abingdon, but has not been found south of the Ock. North of the Corallian ridge it may have travelled into the valley along the same trade routes as Droitwich briquetage and

Fig. 6.12 (opposite) (above) *Culham Greensand quern from Castle Hill, Little Wittenham;* (below) *distribution of querns from geological sources within the Upper Thames Valley. IPR/117-40C British Geological Survey. © NERC 2009. NEXTMap Britain Elevation Data from Intermap Technologies. All rights reserved*

Fig 6.13 Distribution of querns from sources outside the Upper Thames Valley. IPR/117-40C British Geological Survey. © NERC 2009. NEXTMap Britain Elevation Data from Intermap Technologies. All rights reserved

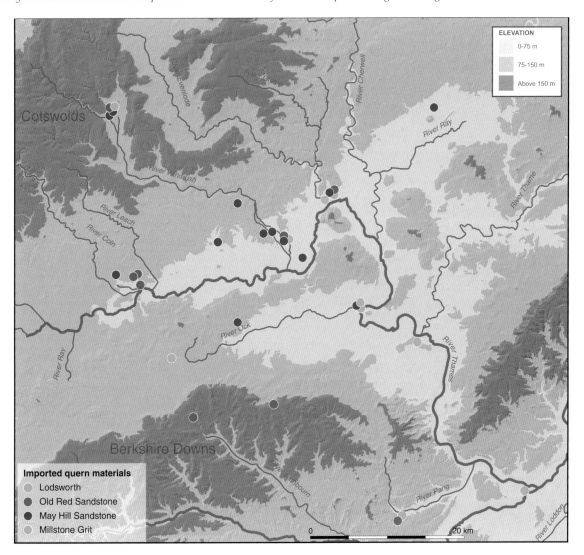

Malvernian pottery with which it shares a similar distribution, but the absence so far of Droitwich briquetage and Malvernian pottery south of the Thames, except at Uffington, suggests that the Hatford and Abingdon material came by a different, more southerly route. Old Red Sandstone, probably from the Forest of Dean about the same distance away, is much less common than May Hill sandstone in the early to middle Iron Age, with only three pieces found in middle Iron Age contexts at Gravelly Guy compared with 28 pieces of May Hill sandstone. But it has also been found in late Bronze Age contexts at Tower Hill (c 80 km), at Gassons Road Lechlade (King 1998, 278) and at Upper Bucklebury (c 120 km distant), with rotary querns in later contexts at Lechlade (Roughground Farm), Faringdon and Yarnton. In the middle Iron Age rotary querns from Lodsworth in West Sussex reached Castle Hill (c 94 km), Abingdon (c 104 km), and one fragment was found at Gravelly Guy, and others at Faringdon are about 120 km from the source (Lambrick and Allen 2004; Weaver et al 2004, 173; Cook et al 2004, 241-3).

From the north and east a quern made of Northamptonshire sandstone was found at Finmere, and in the later Iron Age granite from Mount Sorrel, Leicestershire (c 120 km) reached Bourton-on-the-Water and possibly also Bagendon (Fiona Roe, pers. comm.). Distinctive beehive querns of Millstone Grit from Derbyshire over 150 km away were found at the late Iron Age defensive enclosures at Salmonsbury, Abingdon Vineyard and probably also Cassington Big Ring (Fiona Roe pers. comm.).

The occurrence in the middle to late Iron Age of small numbers of rotary querns made of stone from distant sources, such as Lodsworth greensand, Old Red Sandstone and Millstone Grit, presage what by the Roman period was a radical change in the sources and exchange networks for querns. This seems to have been closely bound up with the transition from saddle to rotary querns, but the factors that influenced this change are not fully understood. There may have been technical issues concerning the grinding properties of the stones or their suitability or the availability of specialist skills for the more elaborate carving required to make them. But it is perhaps more likely that the whole question of quern exchange was bound up with economic and social value.

The sources of quernstones in the Middle Thames catchment also include sarsen from the chalk and Plateau Drift and a range of greensand and other sandstones. As with the Upper Thames Valley, local sources predominate, especially greensand and sarsen. For example, a variety of sources are represented amongst querns and other grinding stones brought to the late Bronze Age settlement at Runnymede, including sarsen, perhaps from the area around Chobham Common (10 km away), and two varieties of greensand, Bargate stone from around Godalming in Surrey (Fiona Roe pers.

comm.) and Lodsworth stone, both transported, in all likelihood, via the rivers Wey and Thames. Other stone types include a fossiliferous sandy limestone thought to be from south Oxfordshire (Fiona Roe pers. comm.) and a number of fine-grained stones of uncertain origin (Needham 1991 138; Needham and Spence 1996, 165-9**).**

In middle to late Bronze Age occupation areas at Home Farm Laleham ten quern fragments comprised seven of lower greensand, including both Bargate and Lodsworth stone (Fiona Roe pers. comm.), two other sandstones and one sarsen (Hayman in prep.). Greensand was also found at Hurst Park (Andrews 1996, 80).

At the middle Bronze Age site at Weirbank Stud Farm, Bray there was one coarse grained ferruginous sandstone rubber and a sarsen saddle quern (Barnes and Cleal 1995, 24-5). In the Burghfield area late Bronze Age querns at Reading Business Park/Green Park include sarsen, other tertiary sandstones and two pieces of Culham Greensand from 35 km upriver to the north (Moore and Jennings 1992, 94-5; Brossler et al 2004, 94-7). At Knights Farm a quern fragment in altered gabbro was found (Bradley *et al.* 1980, 245, 275) thought to be Squilver gabbro from the Shelve area of Shropshire (Fiona Roe pers. comm.). Further up the Kennet Valley sarsen was found at the early Iron Age settlement at Dunston Park (Fitzpatrick 1995, 77). The presence of Old Red Sandstone at the early ironworking site at Upper Bucklebury near Hartshill Copse is intriguing, given the possibility of the Forest of Dean as a source for both the quern and a connection with iron or ironworking skills.

Although somewhat different in chronological span and size of assemblages, the overall picture for the Middle Thames Valley is similar to the Upper Thames, with a predominance of querns coming from a variety of relatively local sources probably less than 15 km away but with a distinct element of more exotic sources represented.

It is clear throughout prehistory that people obtained quernstones from a much wider range of geologies than the closest convenient source, even when, as at Abingdon, these sources were extremely close. To some extent, at least with a range of different local sources, this might reflect the varied destinations of outgoing produce as well as incoming materials. The networks of contacts and exchange routes through which querns were obtained from much further away seem to involve more than just the practical procurement of crop processing equipment. That querns had a social and symbolic value is evident also from their occurrence in special deposits, such as the child burial at Carshalton (Adkins and Needham 1985, 17) and possible hoards. It seems likely that, along with smaller items of exotic stone, there was prestige in possession of querns from remote places, and the acquisition of salt and pottery through the same routes would have consolidated the kudos gained through such exchange.

Other stone tools and ornaments

Broadly similar, but more refined methods may have been used for shaping other hard stone tools (eg whetstones and smoothers), but softer rock could have been carved with metal or other tools. Where precise shaping was not required, as with whetstones, working would have been minimal because stones would have been selected as being roughly the right shape. However, other items such as spindlewhorls and personal ornaments needed more care. The most sophisticated stoneworking is evident in a variety of objects, bracelets, spindle whorls, rings etc, made of shale.

At Aldermaston Wharf there was a piece of worked igneous rock (Bradley *et al.* 1980, 245), which may have been part of a mould. Thin sectioning has shown that this rock was a syenite comparable with another worked piece of stone from Castle Hill, Little Wittenham (Allen *et al.* forthcoming b). Both of these pieces probably relate to a group of stone moulds for casting Stogursey axes (Needham 1981 and in prep.).

Objects were carved from shale throughout prehistory, but by the later Iron Age were also lathe-turned and polished, resulting in some extremely fine finished products. Although it is thought that the shale originated from the Kimmeridge area in Dorset over 150 km away, where the distinctive remains of a prehistoric industry include specialised flint tools for the working of shale (Calkin 1953; Lawson 1976; Woodward 1987; Cox and Woodward 1987), the identification of items as Kimmeridge shale rather than jet or other coal-measure rocks is a matter for scientific analysis (Allason-Jones and Jones 1994). In terms of distance, this may make a substantial difference. Whitby as a possible source of jet is over 350 km from the Thames Valley, Kimmeridge 175 km away, and the Forest of Dean, the nearest coal measures, about 80 km from some of the more easterly parts of the Upper Thames, though much the same distance as Kimmeridge from west London. Whatever the source, it is clear that black rock that takes a shiny polish was a valued material that was procured from some distance. However, it is not entirely clear in what form the shale was brought to the Thames Valley. In their finished form shale bracelets are relatively fragile and, while they may have been carefully packed for the long journey overland or by sea and river, it would have been less risky to import raw materials or roughouts to finish locally. At Bourton-on-the-Water 29 fragments of shale were recovered, the majority being roughouts ready to be turned into bracelets or other objects (Cool in Nichols 2006, 38-41; www.gloucestershire.gov.uk/index.cfm?articleid=5322). This suggests that the final shaping of pieces was done locally, perhaps by a middleman craftsman based at sites like Bourton-on-the-Water, where the number of shale objects is exceptional. The same may apply to other objects made of soft stone imported to the Thames Valley.

At Gravelly Guy a broken, partly roughed-out lump of chalk brought from *c* 20 km away was broken during carving into a spindlewhorl (Lambrick and Allen 2004, 368, fig. 8.9, no. 50), and there are many other cases of unfinished chalk spindle whorls on sites closer to the chalk.

Other 'exotic' materials would have been obtained from distant sources, including beads of amber, present in middle to late Bronze Age contexts at Runnymede, Carshalton and Appleford Sidings, middle to late Iron Age at Risely, and in the late Iron Age necklace at Birdlip which also contained beads of shale and pyrophilite, a rare rock possibly from Scotland or overseas. Glass beads would also have been acquired through gift or exchange. A late Bronze Age bead at Whitecross Farm was made of high magnesium glass, probably imported from the Mediterranean or the Near East, and six were found at Runnymede. (Cromarty *et al.* 2006, 57-8; Needham 1991). An Iron Age cobalt blue bead recovered at Mingies Ditch was possibly from Somerset (Allen and Robinson 1993, 79).

Salt

Although a few natural salt springs, such as Marcham, are known in the Thames Valley there is no evidence that they were significantly exploited as a source of salt at any time in later prehistory. Salt was a commodity generally traded in ceramic vessels of distinctive character. By the early Iron Age the use of salt becomes evident from the crude but distinctive fired clay 'briquetage' containers used to import it. This was well documented by Morris's analysis of Droitwich briquetage (Morris 1981). It has now been recorded on several sites north of the river in the Upper Thames Valley above Oxford, such as Claydon Pike and Thornhill Farm, penetrating as far as Stanton Harcourt and Yarnton, where its occurrence is noted in both early and middle Iron Age contexts. There is also good evidence, reinforced by recent finds, of an association between the distribution of Droitwich briquetage, Malvernian pottery (Morris 1981, 67-71) and possibly sandstone querns from May Hill, all sharing a west Midlands origin and probably indicating a form of piggy-back commerce sharing the means of transporting bulky materials.

The investigations at Bourton-on-the-Water produced one fragment of briquetage from Dorset (Morris in Nichols 2006), indicating that Droitwich was not the only supplier to the area on the north side of the Thames. Although it is a single find, it would not be surprising if, like the Droitwich material, it came with other goods, in this case the exceptionally large number of shale objects of probable Kimmeridge origin.

South of the river and downstream of Oxford finds of salt containers are generally much less common, though pieces of Hampshire briquetage have been found in late middle Iron Age deposits at the Abingdon Vineyard, Castle Hill (Allen *et al.* forthcoming a) and Segsbury (www.arch.ox.ac.uk/ _data/assets/pdf_file/1527/daubreport.pdf accessed 1/12/2006 4-5). These provide evidence of transport of salt from the south coast, complementing the better substantiated provision of salt from Droitwich on the other side of the river to the north. Although there is not such an obvious pattern of piggy-back trade as that associated with Droitwich salt, there is increasing evidence that the Abingdon area and Corallian ridge may also have been the approximate limit of the distribution of querns from Lodsworth, West Sussex before the Roman conquest, though there is one find from Gravelly Guy (Lambrick and Allen 2004, 357, 368-70).

Very few finds of briquetage have been reported in the Middle Thames Valley, but salt coming from the south coast over the Chalk and Weald, or up the Thames estuary from Essex and Kent coastal wetlands would not have had to travel further than that brought into the Upper Thames Valley from Droitwich or the south coast.

Metalworking and smithing

Metalworking evidence: raw materials, equipment, products and waste

The range of evidence for later prehistoric metalworking in the Thames Valley reflects all stages of production and recycling: raw materials, normally scrap metal, very rarely lumps of iron ore, a few furnaces and hearths used for various stages of metalworking and various types of equipment including crucibles and moulds. Waste products in the form of various kinds of slag and furnace linings and of hammerscale from smithing activity are the commonest evidence for metalworking. Other

waste products such as casting droplets and flashings are occasionally associated with bronzeworking debris along with scrap metal, mould fragments and crucibles (Cromarty *et al.* 2006; Needham 1990). The raw materials and manufacturing methods used in making objects are also well documented from metallurgical analysis of the chemical and physical composition and visible form of finished products (Northover 1995). Finds of metal or other tools such as tongs used in metalworking are rare, and are largely limited to the Iron Age. A possible semi-circular sectioned file, a punch and a curious curved tool, possibly some sort of graver, were found in association with bronzeworking debris in the early Iron Age midden at Woodeaton (Harding 1987 33, 43, fig. 12). Quern-like stones may have been used as anvils and stones may also have been used as hammers, though there is no clear evidence of microscopic traces of metal embedded in late prehistoric hammerstones. By the Iron Age axe- and adze-hammers illustrate the availability of metal hammers. There is much technical literature about metalwork typologies and manufacturing, which includes evidence from the Thames Valley, but the remainder of this overview will focus on evidence for the relationship between metalworking and late prehistoric social and economic life in the Thames Valley.

Bronzeworking

Later Bronze Age bronzeworking

The middle, and more particularly late Bronze Age saw a substantial expansion in the range, quantity and size of bronze artefacts made, reflecting major technical advances in metallurgy and casting and

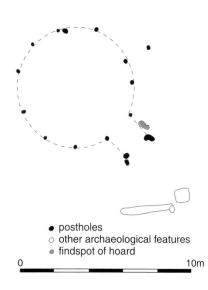

- ● postholes
- ○ other archaeological features
- ● findspot of hoard

0   10m

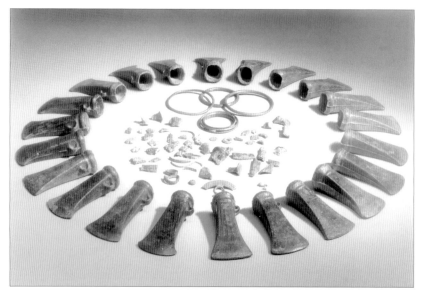

Fig. 6.14   Late Bronze Age metalwork hoards and their context: the Tower Hill hoard

Fig. 6.15 (opposite)   Late Bronze Age metalwork hoards and their context: the Petters Sports Field hoard

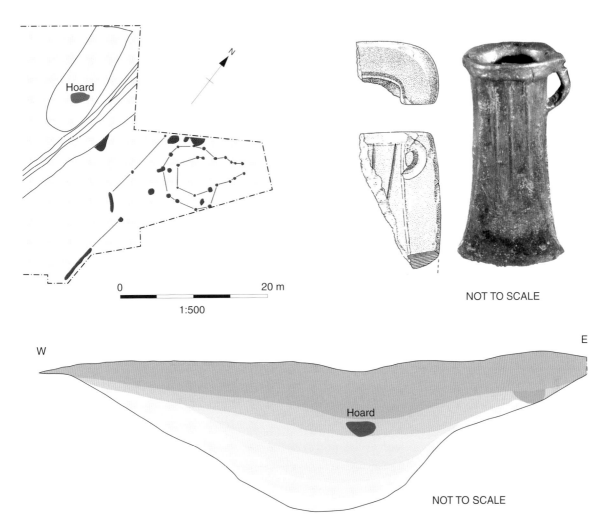

0   20 m

1:500

NOT TO SCALE

W

E

Hoard

NOT TO SCALE

forging techniques, as well as important social and economic trends in how metalwork was valued, traded and used in both practical and symbolic ways. Many bronze objects recovered in the Thames Valley were made outside the region, including a significant proportion from overseas sources (Northover 1995).

As noted above, various aspects of metal-working, such as the raw materials, casting and forging techniques and the high levels of skill involved comes from the metallurgy and detailed morphology. The bronze objects themselves also shed useful light on economic issues based on the movement of raw materials and finished products (Northover 1995). But the principal evidence for the organisation and location of bronzeworking as a craft within the region comes mainly from bronze founders' hoards and occasional finds of metal-working equipment or waste, especially slag, crucibles and casting moulds, less commonly other casting debris, such as flashings and metal droplets.

The hoards at Petters Sports Field, Egham and at Tower Hill on the Berkshire Downs are particularly notable in the Thames Valley in having been investigated *in situ* (Figs 6.14 & 6.15). This makes them all the more valuable in shedding light on metal-working practices. The Petters hoard consisted largely of broken objects with some evidence of metalworking, and can be classed as a 'founder's' hoard in traditional terms. The Tower Hill hoard recently excavated on the Berkshire Downs (Coombs *et al.* 2003, 203-21) was dominated by finished and part-finished axes, along with some scrap and metalworking debris. This was not a simple 'axe hoard' or a simple 'founder's' hoard. Characterised by significant numbers of unfinished, pristine or unsharpened items, it might once have been seen as a 'merchant's' hoard.

These types of classification can obscure as much as they enlighten. If such hoards were deposited by itinerant specialist craftsmen, the distinction between a 'founder' and a 'merchant' may be no more than an issue of when the material was buried in relation to the manufacturing cycle. Crudely speaking, a 'founder's' hoard might reflect burial at the time of arrival at a new working locality and a 'merchant's' hoard might reflect departure from a locality, and either might reflect transit between working places. Although classifications of hoards may be useful shorthand indicators of the broad character of hoards, their composition is seldom exclusively of one type or another. Needham (1990) and Bradley (1990) have argued the need to avoid simplistic approaches to a highly complex subject. It cannot be assumed that all hoards were buried with the intention of recovering them rather than being votive offerings, nor can we automatically assume that all bronzeworking was carried out by itinerant smiths (eg Harding 2000, 236-7). Investigating the archaeological context of hoards is thus an important, but all too rare step towards better understanding.

The Petters hoard was placed in the hollow of a largely infilled ditch terminal and then covered over while the Tower Hill hoard appears to have been buried in a shallow hollow in the doorway of a house. Both locations are often associated with other 'special' deposits and could be votive, but other votive deposits in such positions are seldom composed of conventionally valuable material. Neither hoard was properly buried but both were placed in locations that would have been easy to relocate within a few months or years. On balance the excavators and specialists consider it most likely that these hoards were concealed rather than votive.

Both hoards suggest *in situ* bronzeworking, and with other, non-hoard evidence they provide some insight into where bronzefounding and smithing took place. As noted above, the large ditch at Petters, together with other evidence of finds, the density of occupation and its proximity to Runnymede Bridge suggests that it was not just an ordinary farming settlement. In terms of other high status sites, further evidence of earlier on-site bronzecasting comes from moulds and casting debris at Runnymede itself (Needham 1991). A miscellaneous collection of bronzes from the river and nearby settlement at Whitecross Farm, Wallingford apparently represents middle Bronze Age river deposits mixed with a scattered hoard and objects associated with domestic activity and midden deposits. The presence of an unusual solidified bronze droplet is direct evidence that bronze was being melted there, although there were no fragments of moulds to attest to casting (Northover in Cromarty *et al.* 2006, 55-7). Metalworking was also carried on at the hilltop enclosure at Rams Hill and Carshalton (Bradley and Ellison 1975; Proctor 2002, 68).

Bronze casting and smithing were certainly not confined to high status sites. The Tower Hill hoard comes from what appears to be an ordinary late Bronze Age farming settlement with sparse features and no particular density or richness of other finds. Fragments of moulds and or crucibles have also been found at a number of farming settlements on the Thames gravels, notably at Aldermaston (Bradley *et al.* 1980, fig. 20) and Green Park (Brossler *et al.* forthcoming) in the Middle Thames Valley, and at Shorncote/Cotswold Community (Powell *et al.* forthcoming), Roughground Farm (Allen *et al.* 1993, 34) and Cassington (Hey *et al.* forthcoming b) in the Upper Thames Valley.

It is often assumed, because of the specialist skills involved, that such metalworking was done by itinerant bronze founders. This is difficult to prove, but possible evidence for the existence of such craftsmen is a mould fragment for a Stogursey type axe, characterised by three ribs, a simple moulded top and side loop high on the axe, amongst the debris from Petters Sports Field. Axes of this type are found thinly scattered across southern England and more densely in south Wales, but stone moulds are mainly from the West Country rather than locations where most of the axes have been found.

214

The Petters mould (Fig. 6.15), of non-local stone is thus thought to have been brought by a smith from the south-west (Needham 1990) as is also suggested by the syenite mould fragments from Aldermaston and Castle Hill.

However, while this evidence seems to point to the existence of itinerant craftsmen, it does not mean that they were not also farmers who settled in one place for much of the year. In questioning the assumptions behind the notion of smiths as peripatetic specialists, Harding (2000, 236-7) noted the lack of good ethnographic parallels for this. He raised the possibility that hoards might actually be the property of the community, not the itinerant craftsman, and the association of the Petters and Tower Hill hoards with settlements is consistent with this idea. However, if smiths were part time farmers with permanent workshops, the small quantity of metalworking debris, even allowing for one-off deposited hoards, and lack of evidence for permanent metalworking areas, suggests that their permanent bases have not yet been identified amongst the farming settlements investigated in the region.

The existence of small quantities of metal-working debris on a wide range of sites and the occasional need to conceal collections of scrap still seems to fit best with a fairly straightforward scenario of late Bronze Age metalworking carried on by itinerant specialists who spent some of their time farming and perhaps building up stocks of new objects to be exchanged for scrap or other goods. Within such a scenario it is also possible to envisage some communities having their own metalsmiths, or accumulating scrap for recycling into new objects by a visiting craftsman.

Needham (1990) suggested that the date and content of scrap hoards raise further problems of interpretation. Firstly, while in general late Bronze Age hoards are much commoner than middle Bronze Age ones, scrap hoards are exclusively late Bronze Age, and the vast majority come from the so-called Ewart Park stylistic group, long recognised as belonging to the period of transition to the Iron Age, now dated to 1020 to 800 cal BC (Needham *et al.* 1997, 55-107). There has been some discussion as to why earlier hoards of scrap are not commoner, and whether this might relate to the introduction of ironworking technologies.

Iron Age bronzeworking

Although so-called founders' hoards are very much a feature of the late Bronze Age, the manufacture and use of bronze ornaments, and less often tools and other objects, continued through the Iron Age. The metallurgy and patterns of waste material from Iron Age bronze smithing have been analysed more systematically in the last 20 years than previously, and a clearer picture has emerged of the nature of Iron Age bronzeworking (Northover 1984; 1995).

Like the late Bronze Age midden sites at Runnymede and Whitecross Farm, there is evidence of bronzeworking from the Iron Age midden at Woodeaton, the lower layer of which may have had late Bronze Age origins but continued into the early Iron Age, overlain by middle Iron Age deposits, including a number of postholes and pits and a layer of cobbling. A small pit cut through the cobbling and covered with a stone slab contained bronzeworking slag, a fragment of crucible and a piece of a stone mould. It is thought that this might represent a metalworking area, also reflected in three iron implements (Harding 1987). There is also plentiful evidence of *in situ* bronzecasting in the early to middle Iron Age from ordinary farming settlements on the Thames gravels such as Gravelly Guy (Lambrick and Allen 2004), Yarnton (Hey *et al.* forthcoming), Mingies Ditch (Allen and Robinson 1993, 77, fig. 36) and possibly Roughground Farm (Allen *et al.* 1993, 44-5). Gravelly Guy is unusual for the number of crucibles, mould fragments and quantities of slag that were found, but it is not clear how exceptional this is given the unusual complete-ness of excavation (Fig. 6.16).

The lost wax method of casting bronze objects was an Iron Age development which Northover (1984) noted as rare prior to the late Iron Age, but is evident from the chape of the Minster Ditch scabbard (Harding 1972), indirectly supported by the discovery of a honeybee from Mingies Ditch, which provided confirmation of the availability of beeswax in the middle Iron Age (Allen and Robinson 1993, 117).

Ironworking

The geology of the Thames catchment contains many iron-bearing formations, including the Lias and other Jurassic beds, Upper and Lower Greensand, Tertiary sands and iron concreted gravels. However, very few deposits seem to have been of high enough grade quality for iron smelting, especially given the difficulty of reaching the high temperatures that allow impurities to be removed from lower grade ores. Salter and Ehrenreich (1984, 146-9) noted that for every kilogram of finished iron produced, approximately 20 kg of iron ore, 90 kg of wood fuel and 40 kg of clay would be needed. They identified four stages of iron production – ore roasting, smelting, bloom smithing and black-smithing – of which evidence for roasting and smelting is rare in the Thames Valley and smithing evidence is quite common.

The introduction of iron

Based largely on finds from settlements, not hoards, Turnbull (1984) suggested that the transition from mainly bronze to mainly iron tools and weapons took place over a period from the 9th to 7th centuries BC, after which iron was manufactured and used at a fairly constant level across Britain where ore was relatively close at hand. In the Thames Valley, where good iron ore deposits are relatively scarce, few sites have produced evidence

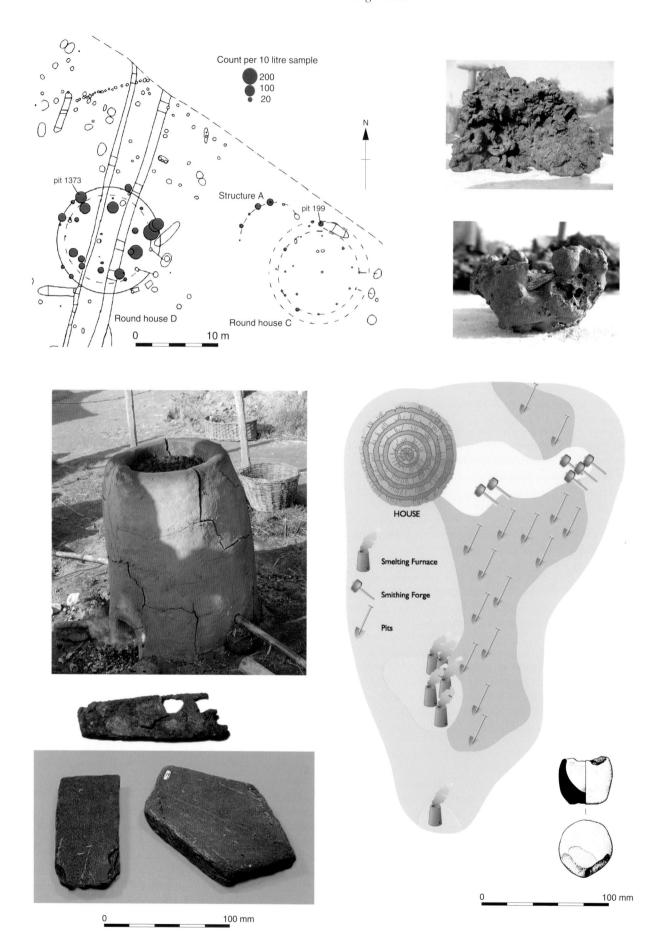

of ironworking as early as this. Recently, however, excavations at Hartshill Copse, on the north side of the Kennet Valley at Upper Bucklebury, funded by the Aggregates Levy Sustainability Fund, revealed hammerscale and other remains of ironworking dating as early as the 10th century BC (Fig. 6.16), with radiocarbon dating for the two houses associated with ironworking suggesting (68% confidence) that Round-house C was in use from 1030–940 to 970–880 cal BC, and Round-house D from 1060–940 to 960–840 cal BC (Collard *et al.* 2006, 382-4).

This is the oldest known ironworking site in Britain and provides valuable new insights into the development of prehistoric metalworking. Most of the evidence for ironworking at Hartshill Copse came from the area of two post-built roundhouses (Round-houses C and D), each with a porch to the south-east, and one with a semicircular post-built structure (structure A) on the opposite side (Fig. 6.16). Elongated pits were also closely associated with the two roundhouses. The settlement produced several hundred sherds of late Bronze Age plainware pottery and other domestic debris, including charred cereals, but notably few crop-processing residues.

Soil samples taken from the remains of the structures produced thousands of tiny hammerscale fragments. Although this was only equivalent to about a tenth of a smelt, the fragments displayed a clear spatial distribution that makes it unlikely they were intrusive. Particularly high concentrations were recovered from the postholes of Round-house D, the semicircular annexe (A) attached to Round-house C, and from both the elongated pits, but very little came from the postholes of Round-house C itself. The proportions of flake to spheroidal hammerscale recovered suggest that different processes were carried out in the different structures, with spherodial hammerscale mainly associated with bloom smithing coming from Round-house D, and flake hammerscale resulting from blacksmithing associated with Structure A, adjacent to Round-house C. Varying concentrations of pottery (559 sherds mainly from jars associated with Round-house C, compared with only 34 mainly from bowl sherds associated with Round-house D) seem to confirm differential use of the buildings. This provisionally supported an interpretation of a residential use for Round-house C with ancillary workshops for different purposes in buildings A and D. These distributions are of interest not only in providing an insight into the early origins for ironworking, but also because they provide an unusually clear indication of the role of different buildings as houses and workshops.

It is not known what, if any, artefacts, as opposed to iron blooms and billets, were being made at Hartshill Copse, but in revealing something of the character of an exceptionally early example of ironworking, the site also provides evidence against which much later evidence can be compared. For example, the apparent absence of evidence of ore roasting or primary smelting of ore, and evidence for both the later stages of smithing (converting the initial bloom into useable metal and the blacksmithing of metal into products) is also typical of settlements throughout the Iron Age. The Hartshill Copse evidence is exceptionally early, but it is worth noting that one of the very few other examples of relatively early ironworking is the evidence of smithing slags from an early Iron Age pit as early as the 7th century not far from Hartshill Copse at Coopers Farm, Dunston Park (Fitzpatrick 1995).

There was little evidence for rebuilding at Hartshill Copse, which together with the tightly clustered radiocarbon dates suggests that the settlement was short-lived. The broader social context of the ironworking at Hartshill Copse is less clear, but it appears that it could have been part of a ceremonial complex. There were earlier barrows in the vicinity and an acute intersection of two palisade fences on which the ironworking roundhouses were aligned is most unusual for the region (Collard *et al*. 2006, 405, fig. 18, Pl 1). These are taken as indications of the high prestige that might have been attached to such an innovative technology. The excavators also note that much of the pottery found in Round-house C had been burnt and then redeposited in the postholes after the removal of the posts, perhaps suggesting symbolic 'killing' of the site, though other more prosaic explanations are possible.

The evidence of very early ironworking at Hartshill Copse confirms suspicions of a long period of overlap, of perhaps 200-300 years, in the shift from predominantly bronze to predominantly iron metalworking technologies. The early stages of this change, such as at Hartshill Copse, coincide with a period of metalworking associated with the currency of the 'Carp's Tongue' style of bronze sword, when many hoards of scrap bronze were deposited in southern England. This widespread hoarding has been seen by some as a possible reflection of the increasing use of iron (Needham 1990), even though evidence of ironworking such as that at Hartshill Copse and actual iron objects are both extremely rare. It was a period of considerable innovation in bronze working in northern Europe, prompted by developments further south and east in central Europe, the earliest iron tools being

Fig. 6.16 (opposite)   Late Bronze Age and Iron Age metalworking in the Thames Valley (top left) *plan of late Bronze Age ironworking workshops and distribution of hammerscale at Hartshill Copse;* (top right) *slag;* (centre left) *reconstruction of an iron smelting furnace;* (centre right) *interpretative plan of early to middle Iron Age iron smelting site at Brooklands, Surrey;* (below left) *Iron Age currency bar and whetstones from Gravelly Guy;* (below right) *crucible from Gravelly Guy*

punches and gravers that may have been used for decorating the surface of bronze objects. Iron-working clearly grew out of bronze smithing needs and technologies, but it seems to have been some time before it was sufficiently well developed to produce large tools and weapons comparable to their bronze equivalents, such as appeared in the so-called 'Halstatt' period in the 8th to 7th centuries BC. The earliest directly dated iron object in Britain is an iron socketed axe from dredgings beside the River Thames at Buscot Lock, Oxfordshire (Barclay *et al.* 1995), of which the remains of the ash haft have been radiocarbon dated to 790-410 cal BC (Needham *et al.* 1997, 99).

The close connections in the exchange of metal and metalworking technology with northern France and the Low Countries meant that despite being an area with little high quality iron ore, the Thames Valley was nevertheless at the forefront of the adoption of ironworking technology, and the Hartshill Copse site is notable for the evidence of both smelting and smithing. As the excavators argue, it is probably no coincidence that its position on the upper slopes of the Kennet Valley not far from a notable concentration of late Bronze Age settlements suggests that it was part of a flourishing agricultural economy.

Iron Age ironworking

Apart from the exceptional evidence from Hartshill Copse, there is no other evidence for the roasting and smelting stages of iron manufacture in the Thames Valley before the middle Iron Age, and it is very rare even then. When Salter and Ehrenreich examined the evidence for Iron Age iron smelting and smithing in the Thames Valley over 20 years ago, they showed that while evidence for smithing was quite common, the only sites revealing smelting activity were at Brooklands near Weybridge in the middle Iron Age and Berkhamstead in Hertfordshire and Bagendon in Gloucestershire in the late Iron Age (Salter and Ehrenreich 1984, 149 and fig. 10.3 – note reversal of symbols for smelting and smithing sites in key). The many excavations that have taken place since then have strongly reinforced this general picture. Only two additional roasting/smelting sites have been found in the Thames Valley, one being the middle to late Iron Age settlement at Thorpe Lea Nurseries (Hayman 1998; forthcoming a), the other the late Iron Age enclosure at Risely (Lobb and Morris 1991-3). But evidence of smithing activity has been found at almost every extensively examined settlement (and many that have only been sampled). Smithing for processing blooms, and even more commonly the making and repairing of tools and other objects, thus seems to have been a routine craft of most farming settlements. Exceptions, like the middle Iron Age site at Perry Oaks/T5, where not only slag but also querns and other artefacts were notable by their absence, raise issues about what sort of settlement they were (Framework Archaeology 2006, 170-201).

Primary iron smelting usually but not always appears to have been done close to the source of the ore (Salter and Ehrenreich 1984, 146-7). This was the case at Brooklands (Fig. 6.16), the most extensively investigated smelting site in the Thames Valley, where a range of iron smelting and working facilities were investigated in two main concentrations (Hanworth and Tomalin 1977, 15-22). In the western area used for smelting the iron there were five small furnaces, three of which lay within a trapezoidal-shaped area or workshop defined by six postholes. One of the other two (which were only 0.5 m apart) was central to a short curving gully and there were spreads of unfired clay lumps and reddened clay nearby. Various patches of stones, a few lumps of slag, areas of charcoal, reddened or stained sand and a number of pits were investigated. The best preserved of the furnaces had a bowl-shaped base acting as the hearth with the natural sand beneath it scorched bright red and remains of fired clay super-structure. The walls of the furnace had been strengthened with broken potsherds burnt to a friable pumice. Although an arc of stained sand leading away from it was thought possibly to have been the result of tapping molten slag, this was not otherwise in evidence, and several finds of slag cakes or 'furnace bottoms' – the iron 'bloom' that was allowed to cool, coalescing on the furnace base – suggest that the remains reflect use of a non-slag tapping type of bowl furnace, also known in eastern Europe and at Kestor in Devon (Fox 1954, 21).

In the other ironworking area there was a circular hearth 1 m across surrounded by a semi-circle of stones, a heap of mixed slag and stones, and a patch of bright red burnt clay, with another patch of burnt clay, possibly remains of superstructure, overlying another area of stones and slag nearby. This part of the site did not have obvious furnaces and appears to have been used for forging the initial iron blooms into solid metal by repeated heating and hammering to remove slag impurities, consistent with the smithing slags found in this area. Lumps of fired clay with wattle impressions, likely to have been fragments of furnace superstructures, were found in the fills of 18 pits and 9 other features, one with over 15 kg of such material. Other traces of burning, charcoal, burnt stone and reddened soil were also probably connected with the ironworking activity, but overall there was surprisingly little slag.

The excavators concluded, and subsequent authors like Salter and Ehrenreich have empha-sised, that the scale of ironsmelting and forging at Brooklands was very modest (Hanworth and Tomalin 1977, 22). Assuming the reuse of the furnaces four or five times for smelting 5-10 kg of metal from each smelt, the excavators suggested production of perhaps around 200 kg or more, allowing for some features not found within the areas excavated. Although not large, this would be enough for a fair number of weapons, tools or small objects. But Salter and Ehrenreich (1984, 150-1) pointed out that over 12 times the amount of slag actually found would be expected to be derived from this scale of production. The total amount of fired clay recovered would also hardly account for more than a single firing. It thus seems likely that unless it was only the periphery of a much larger area, the Brooklands site was never a major production centre, though there was equally limited evidence of agricultural activity. Fieldwork in 1990-91 on a nearby site to the south-east within the Brooklands racetrack produced further evidence of broadly contemporary mid to late Iron Age settlement, including carbonised grain indicating arable farming, but no further indication of ironworking.

At Thorpe Lea Nurseries, evidence of smelting rather than smithing came from finds of especially dense, iron-rich slag from a number of Iron Age and Roman contexts, the majority classified as dense slag or furnace bottoms. This included distinctive material with charcoal inclusions and wood impressions that indicate use of a type of pit furnace known in Norway in the Iron Age, but not previously recognised in Britain, in which the slag was allowed to flow down through the base of the furnace into a pit packed with chopped wood. Most of the iron smelting debris at Thorpe Lea was found in and around groups of postholes in the eastern area of Iron Age settlement, but the full extent, focus and duration of ironworking in the Iron Age (and Roman period) was unclear. Two pieces of smithing hearth indicated some smithing activity as well as the smelting, but were not closely dated and need not be prehistoric. The total quantity of slag (only 27.6 kg) does not suggest a long-term or large-scale operation, but it is possible that the focus of ironworking lay beyond the excavated area. No definite furnaces or other *in situ* evidence of ironworking was found, and the limited amount of relevant debris occurred in small quantities widely distributed amongst Iron Age and Roman deposits, and may have been redeposited.

Possible fragments of incompletely smelted ore resemble furnace linings and/or slag, but the chemical compositions of neither these nor the other slags or furnace bottom material indicate an ore source, though high levels of phosphorous are considered consistent with bog ore. Although it is not clear what or where the source of the ore was, it seems that, unlike Brooklands, ore would have had to be brought from some distance to be smelted at Thorpe Lea Nurseries. This can be compared with Risely, where smelting and smithing slags, a hearth bottom and pieces of bog ore were found (Lobb and Morris 1991-3), while at Bagendon significant amounts of slag were associated with haematite ore imported from the Bristol area or the Forest of Dean (Clifford 1961).

While there may have been many smelting sites in the Thames Valley, others probably await discovery. However, very few ordinary farming settlements were involved with the initial conversion of ore to iron, and it is possible that the raw materials for making iron tools and other artefacts were brought in from other regions as blooms of semi-processed iron, or as iron ingots in the form of currency bars (see below). But while evidence for smelting is rare in the Thames Valley, most farming sites, including small pastoralist settlements like Farmoor or Mingies Ditch, produced some evidence of on-site smithing activity. This takes the form of various types and densities of slag, and sometimes crucibles, hearth bases and, when adequately sought, hammerscale. Such remains indicate a variety of iron forging and blacksmithing tasks to make, mend or refashion tools and other objects, or to melt down billets of iron or recycle scrap iron into new billets from which fresh objects could be made. Fragments of 'currency bars' and 'hooked billets', thought to be the remains of iron bars ready for forging into new tools, are occasionally found on farming settlements, as at Gravelly Guy (Lambrick and Allen 2004, 365, fig. 8.7, nos. 267, 277). But neither these nor other iron objects that could have been used for recycling into new tools are particularly common on most late prehistoric sites, and it is generally assumed that irreparable and worn out ironwork was saved and recycled into new objects.

The uneven distribution of smithing debris within multiple household sites like Gravelly Guy (Fig. 6.3) or Yarnton (Lambrick and Allen 2004, fig. 8.3; Hey *et al.* forthcoming) suggests that was not a craft common to the repertoire of every household. Indeed the necessary skills would make that unlikely, especially for the activities involving melting down scrap or smithing fresh billets of iron. On the other hand, the relative ubiquity of smithing debris could indicate that in some settlements there were individuals who had at least picked up basic smithing skills for day-to-day purposes. It may be, as envisaged for the late Bronze Age, that itinerant smiths did much of the primary melting and shaping of iron into new objects and basic blacksmithing and running repairs were done by local craftsmen. With respect to more elaborate and larger objects, especially swords, scabbards and large tools, a high degree of craftsmanship was required, unlikely to have been locally accessible.

Hybrid high temperature craftsmanship

Although ironworking involves different processes and skills from bronzeworking, and glass and enamel working is different again, it is clear that from the middle Iron Age onwards the techniques of producing hybrid artefacts of iron, bronze and/or enamel were being mastered in the quest to create objects of especially high prestige value compared with simple bronze or iron counterparts. Such objects included scabbard chapes and horse bits made from a forged or cast iron core with a highly finished, sometimes decorated, cast bronze inlay, and a range of horse gear, mirror handles, brooches and other objects made of cast and sometimes engraved bronze with coloured enamel inlay. It is not entirely clear how or where such craftsmen operated, but it is possible that high levels of skill in more than one of these high temperature crafts were mastered by some individual master craftsmen, or perhaps by pairs or small groups of specialists working together as workshops producing high prestige items. Many of these hybrid objects were also the vehicles for the execution of some of the best celtic art and design, and it is clear that the combination of very high technical skill, combined with striking colour combinations and sophisticated artistic decoration would have given such objects a value that clearly expressed the high status of their owners. Such status may have been accorded no less to the master craftsmen who made them. The technical skills involved in creating such beautiful objects out of fire might well have seemed magical – the 'mystery' of great craftsmanship that seems to transcend any ordinary mortal accomplishment.

Metal and metalwork exchange

Compared with other commodities, exchange networks for metalwork were especially complex because, in addition to trading of raw materials and finished objects, metal can be melted down and made into new artefacts. This results in multiple ways in which materials and objects reflect complex histories of exchange. For example, the metallurgy of the Petters Sports Field founder's hoard shows local smiths recycling stocks of scrap metal that had north French origins, but impurities suggest that the metal had been progressively altered in recycling by addition of other metal types from another source area (Needham 1990). This hoard also suggests the work of a craftsman familiar with the traditions of the bronze founding industry in Wessex, bringing in scrapped pieces of Stogursey socketed axes, alongside the products of local smiths (Needham 1981, 52; Needham 1990). A fragment of Cornish syenite from an early Iron Age deposit at Castle Hill, Little Wittenham resembles late Bronze Age fragments from moulds at Aldermaston and Runnymede (Allen *et al.* forthcoming).

In commenting on patterns of metalwork exchange in later Bronze Age Surrey, Needham (1998) noted the presence of continental razors, pins, bracelet and ring attachments at Runnymede, a European socketed axe from Kensington, an Irish axe in the Beddlestead hoard, an Aunernier sword fragment at Wickham Park and a Moringen type sword from the river at Chertsey. Links eastwards from the Upper Thames Valley down river are suggested by Bronze Age metalwork of continental origin found in the river (eg around Wallingford, Dorchester and Little Wittenham) and also further west, a 'Picardy' type pin from Siddington, Gloucestershire (Enright 1999).

Compared with bronze and its component metals, iron is intrinsically difficult to source by scientific means and so the origins of the metal used in objects are less clearly understood. However, the evidence of how limited smelting activity was compared with smithing indicates that the raw materials for metalworking and/or finished products must have been circulated through exchange networks after the initial smelting of ore at places like Brooklands. It is likely that once the main impurities had been removed, more or less usable iron was circulated in a variety of forms for further refinement and smithing more locally. Amongst the most distinctive manifestations of this is the occurrence of currency bars, iron billets and scrap objects which with little more refinement could be forged into new implements. A number of currency bars have been recovered from the Thames and others have been found in hoards, sometimes with other objects. These include the currency bars and other objects found in a small cache at the rear of the defences of the hillfort at Madmarston Camp (Fowler 1960, 41-3 and fig. 18), another hoard at the valley fort of Salmonsbury (Dunning 1931, 489-91) and a recently discovered small hoard possibly associated with a boundary close to a small open farming settlement at Totterdown Lane, Horcott (Pine and Preston 2006). Such hoards may have been valuable collections of ingots and scrap iron hidden for security equivalent to bronze founders' hoards. Hingley (2006), however, has highlighted the spatial distribution of later prehistoric and Roman ironwork hoards and special deposits, suggesting that the close correlation of currency bars and boundary contexts indicates something more than just the hoarding of valuable raw materials, although burying valuables near a recognisable feature is a way of helping to ensure safe recovery. As with bronze hoards, a range of motivations for hoarding iron may have applied in different circumstances, but the deposition of currency bars in the river certainly suggests that they were sometimes deposited as votive offerings and as Hingley notes, many other single iron objects occur in what may be classed as 'special deposits' (see below Chapter 8).

With far fewer hoards of metalwork in the Iron Age, there is much less evidence for the circulation of scrap metal than in the late Bronze Age. This may have more to do with the particular socio-economic reasons for the prevalence of bronze hoarding at the beginning of the first millennium BC rather than that iron was not circulated in the form of scrap along with fully processed ingots. Indeed, even if hoards of currency bars and scrap were often deposited as votive offerings as Hingley (2006) suggests, the existence of such collections may still reflect how fully processed iron was traded as a valued raw material, most of which would never have entered the ground but was used to make new implements.

It is not within the scope of this study to review in detail the complexities of later prehistoric metal circulation, especially as it has been the subject of specialist studies (eg Rohl and Needham 1998). The circulation of raw materials for metalworking (including scrap) and of metal ornaments, tools and weapons was clearly of considerable practical importance in procuring tools and other useful objects. On the continent there is good evidence that bronze sickles were used as standard units of metal (Sommerfeld 1994). The circulation of metal, however, was also intimately bound up with the expression of status, wealth and prestige. Particularly in the later Bronze Age, the value placed on metalwork is thought to have been a key part of social, political and economic intercourse (Burgess 1980; Needham 1990; 2007; Thomas 1999). This significance was increased by the variety of roles that the possession and use of metal objects and materials could play in symbolic, personal and communal interaction and religious activity through various forms of votive offering or symbolic sacrifice, as well as representing a potent component of a culture that was much concerned with the display and use of arms. The proliferation of metalwork, both in terms of the diversity of ornaments, weapons and tools and its sheer quantity in the later Bronze Age has led a number of authors to suggest that, although the growth of agricultural production was important, it was the acquisition, possession and exchange of metalwork that was the driving force of a prestige goods economy, a pattern that eventually collapsed with the advent of iron and further changes in the social and economic development of farming (Needham 2007).

Coinage

Although the deposition of metalwork in the river continued in the Iron Age there is little other indication apart from the enigmatic role of so-called currency bars (Hingley 1997) of high prestige items of exchange until the late Iron Age when coins appeared. The role of late Iron Age coinage has been much debated (eg Fitzpatrick 1992; Haselgrove 1996; Creighton 2000) and, as with the circulation of late Bronze Age metalwork, the chronological and typological patterns are complex. Even when found in hoards, the context of use, loss or deliberate deposition are very seldom resolved by excavation. There is little evidence that coinage functioned effectively as a general currency of exchange and trade in the Iron Age, and it is noticeable that most Iron Age coins found on settlement excavations, even where there are late Iron Age phases, come from Roman rather than Iron Age contexts, as at Barton Court and Gravelly Guy (Miles 1984, 8; Lambrick and Allen 2004, 391). It is possible that Iron Age coins remained (or became) acceptable currency in the early Roman period.

The earliest coins to reach south-east England in the latter part of the 2nd century to the mid 1st century BC were Gallo-Belgic imports, while the first indigenous coins may have appeared just before Caesar's British campaigns in the middle of the 1st century BC (Fitzpatrick 1992, 12-5). Various functions for these coins have been proposed. They may have been part of a wide pattern of cross-channel economic social or political contact, served as payment for mercenary services or for straight-forward money exchange in the course of trade.

It is increasingly considered (eg Creighton 2000) that late Iron Age coins served as a means of displaying a combination of political and social status and wealth, whatever their actual role in exchange. By the 1st century AD coins were becoming the vehicle not just for the expression of tribal and ultimately dynastic authority reflecting a new politics of individual leadership and kingship, but as an overt symbol of tribal identity and allegiance that we will explore in Chapter 9.

Artistic design and fashion

It would be a mistake to leave this discussion of later prehistoric crafts and production without giving some consideration to the importance of crafts and construction as vehicle for artistic expression and style. Artistic and decorative expression is a powerful vehicle for communicating personal and communal identity, status and taste, as well as representing a means of expressing spiritual or aesthetic values that may be a source of inner well-being or pleasure. Changing fashions in decorative style often transcend the more immediate consideration of function, technology, locality or materials that dictate how objects, structures or places are designed. Within social groups it is often the case that basic features of design are so widespread and familiar that they may not consciously be recognised as a purely stylistic expression, especially where such basic styles remain unchanged over large areas and many generations. In these circumstances they become not an outward and deliberate expression of identity and status, but an unconscious sense of shared cultural roots.

Any discussion of art and fashion in later prehistory is inevitably limited by what survives, mainly personal ornaments, objects of everyday living, tools, weapons and to a limited extent structures. We certainly cannot assume that these are fully representative of how people expressed themselves artistically. Albeit limited and biased, the evidence nevertheless provides an insight into aspects of artistic and aesthetic expression that reflect changing fashions in style and design. To some extent we can also glimpse how some of the characteristics of artistic expression reflect complex symbolism or meaning.

Design on the small scale – the application of decorative techniques to objects

Although we have a wide range of decorative objects, many forms of decoration do not survive. Painted posts or walls and personal painting or tattooing may have been equally important media for artistic expression. Although we have virtually no evidence for how decorative arts were created in organic media such as dyes and paint, or applied to objects made of organic materials such as woollen or linen fabrics, leather or basketry, it is clear that techniques and materials were available to create a wide range of decorative schemes. These include techniques directly used in the basic manufacture of objects, such as patterns woven into fabric or basketry or applied as a special way of finishing them, such as cutting and punching leather, dyeing and painting. However, the mere existence of techniques of creating or applying decorative schemes on organic objects or structures does not necessarily mean that they were commonly applied. It is obvious that people apply artistic decoration for reasons other than the mere technical ability to do so.

The rapidly growing collection of wooden artefacts and worked timber recovered from water-logged waterholes and river channel deposits in the Thames Valley in recent years means that there now exists a large sample of wooden artefacts, but we still lack evidence of decorative carving. This is not particularly surprising as the vast majority of wood recovered to date represents offcuts of round wood and below-ground structural timbers, stakes and wickerwork, mostly well linings. Aboveground structural timbers, such as the burnt structure dumped in the river at Whitecross Farm (Cromarty *et al*. 2006) or the collapsed aboveground wooden elements of the causeway at Yarnton, are rare survivals and extremely fragmentary. Likewise, virtually no aboveground timbers have been recov-ered from Runnymede or Eton. Even in wetlands such as the East Anglian Fens, Somerset Levels or Irish bogs, smaller carved sculptures and decorated wooden objects are rare, so it is unsurprising that none have yet been found in the Thames Valley. Likewise, the small number of carved wooden bowls known from the region do not include decorated examples. It is possible that wooden vessels were common artefacts, and it is worth bearing in mind that only a small proportion of pottery (often less than 1-5%) is adorned with impressed, incised or tooled decoration equivalent to what might be expected on wooden bowls, so the absence of decorated late prehistoric wooden objects amongst the very few recovered to date is again not surprising.

Excavations in the Thames Valley in recent years have not, on the whole, added much to what is known of the styles of later Bronze Age and Iron Age metalwork, though exceptional hoards such as Petters Sports Ground and Tower Hill and a steady accumulation of individual objects from excava-tions (especially larger and/or more productive ones like Runnymede, Whitecross Farm, Gravelly Guy or Yarnton) have provided useful material to take such studies forward. There has also been important new research on existing material, such as the detailed chronology of late Bronze Age metal-work styles (Needham *et al*. 1995).

A much larger corpus of new material has been accumulated for more mundane objects, especially pottery, bone and antler, though there has not been any serious effort to update or revise early attempts at synthesising decorative pottery styles at a regional (Ellison 1980; Cunliffe 1991), sub-regional (Lambrick 1984) or chronological (Barrett 1980) level, nor to update analysis of decorative schemes on other objects such as combs (Hodder and Hedges 1977). Such a synthesis is beyond the scope of this book but a number of general observations can be made about the extent to which new evidence has reinforced or altered traditional views.

Style and fashion

As a highly plastic medium for craftsmanship and a common, durable, but easily broken finished product, pottery is an ideal vehicle for tracing changes in cultural fashions at the level of daily life. Although Cunliffe's (1991), and to some extent Ellison's (1980) regional style zones for Iron Age and middle Bronze Age pottery respectively have been the main basis for analysing stylistic fashions, it is probably more realistic, as Lambrick (1984 170-3) suggested, to think about this more in terms of a range of cultural and economic influences operating at different local, sub-regional, regional or larger scales.

The basic shapes of middle Bronze Age bucket urns and baggy globular bowls, of late Bronze Age to early Iron Age angular jars and bowls, of middle Iron Age saucepan pots, barrel jars and globular bowls and of late Iron Age necked jars and butt beakers reflect very broad changes in cultural fashion and taste that transcend regional and sub-regional variations. Similarly, tastes in decorative motifs, such as late Bronze Age and earlier Iron Age finger impressions and incised angular ornamenta-tion, or middle to late Iron Age curvilinear designs, have a very wide currency. The extent to which these patterns also reflect broader cultural styles in western Europe, such as the well-known La Tène cultural style, and what that means in terms of cultural fashion, economic or social contact or movement of peoples has long been a matter of debate. What does seem clear is that these matters were more issues of very broad cultural fashion and taste than technical, utilitarian or perhaps even symbolic considerations.

Beneath these very broad trends in cultural fashion are highly complex variations. The idea that these reflect 'regional' style zones of the kind long championed by Cunliffe is now well entrenched in the literature, if only because no systematic attempt has been made to provide an alternative broad-brush interpretation despite misgivings (eg Collis 1977). But numerous sub-regional and local variants may nevertheless be discerned, which are far from homogeneous and seem to reflect a more complex mixture of style, production and exchange (Lambrick 1984, 170-3). For example the sub-regional difference in Cassington as opposed to Frilford type swags in the Upper Thames Valley observed by Lambrick (1984, 170) has to some extent been confirmed by recent finds, but has also been modified with the occurrence of each style within the zones dominated by the other. The extent to which such differences might reflect personal, communal or tribal identity with an area is thus more complicated than might first appear, but one where detailed re-examination of the fabrics of such pots using a rigorous standard methodology might prove fruitful.

The artistic content of design

British celtic art includes a significant number of carved stone and, less commonly wooden, human figures, though the vast majority of these are late Iron Age and Romano-British (Green 1995). They mainly depict or celebrate deities or mythical beings, though the appearance of heads on a few late Iron Age coins imitating Greek originals seems to have adopted the political and economic symbolism of connecting a personality with power. The depiction of animals, especially in cast bronze, is less restricted both in terms of period and special context, but nevertheless, they are largely confined to high prestige objects and very seldom occur on settlement sites. It may be that humans, animals, and plants contributed more to the content of art in other media than those that survive archaeologically, but the overall impression has been that the vast majority of later prehistoric art and design was abstract. However, Fitzpatrick (2007) has recently suggested that this may partly be due to the traditions of art history in which formative studies were conducted and has drawn attention to the depiction of highly stylised pairs of mythical beasts on weaponry from the Thames and elsewhere, including the Chertsey shield, two shield bosses from Wandsworth and a scabbard from Hammersmith. He suggests that such fantastical beasts and birds may have symbolised a relationship between warrior elites, death and the spirit world, perhaps to convey prowess in warfare as the warrior grasped the weapon.

The most impressive artistic style observable on late prehistoric artefacts for the Thames Valley, as more widely in Britain, is the well known celtic scroll motif which appears in endless variety on high status metal objects, mostly from the river and burials, including sword and dagger scabbards, shields, a chariot wheel boss, horse bridles and mirrors (Fig. 6.17; Fig. 8.2). This reflects La Tène influence from the continent and appears in the Thames Valley from about the 3rd century BC onwards. The Standlake sword scabbard is one of the earliest examples. It is not possible to point to anything like such a strong, distinctive style of artistic impression before then, even in high prestige metalwork. This is not to say there were not stylistic trends in the design of late Bronze Age and Iron Age metalwork, only that they do not display such a distinctive style of exuberant artistic decoration.

To what extent multi-regional fashions in design and specific decorative motifs and design styles symbolically reflected other social or spiritual considerations is debatable. Some distinctive early Iron Age pottery from the Chinnor area might include motifs representing the rising or setting sun. Middle Iron Age bowls in the Frilford and Cassington style have swags that could represent hanging ropes, and a sherd from Gravelly Guy had a rim that seemed to represent a twisted rope. None of these can be substantiated and most decorative schemes appear to be straightforward geometrical or abstract ornamentation, despite the suspicion that complex symbolism might be involved (MacDonald 2007). In relation to how art and ornamentation was reflected in the lives of most people it is arguable that too rigid a distinction tends to be made between art – often restricted to ornamented high status metal and stone objects specifically in the 'celtic' style – and design in a more general sense. For example, an intriguing but unexplored issue is whether differences in angular and curvilinear ornamentation, present both in the early Iron Age when pottery styles were dominated by angular forms and in the middle to late Iron Age when rounded and globular forms predominated, have any wider symbolic significance, or are merely a natural realisation that the style of decoration should echo the form of the object.

Surface finishes

A common feature of many classes of late prehistoric artefact in different materials is the effort made to achieve a smooth, often shiny finish. This applies to objects made of stone, especially shale and amber, antler, bone, pottery, glass beads, and bronze. It may also apply to other materials like iron, where corrosion products often obscure the original finish, and probably wood, where polished surfaces do not survive, but some bowls have clearly been finished to a smooth enough surface for tool marks made in shaping the object to be almost invisible. The proportion of objects given a high finish differs according to the properties of the material from which they were made and their function, but also other factors. The proportion of burnished finishes in pottery, for example, varies considerably with vessel form and fabric, but also between sites (Lambrick 1984 170; Allen 1990, 37-8; Wilson 1993, 72).

Taking quality of finish as a general attribute, the items most commonly finished to a high lustre were, as might be expected, personal and family ornaments and prestige objects. These include fineware pottery bowls (Fig. 5.16), shale bracelets and spindlewhorls, pins and brooches, bone and antler toggles and pendants (Fig. 5.22), weaponry and probably some tools like bronze axes. There is nothing odd about this: such an association can be traced throughout prehistory and history. In contemporary society it is more evident than ever in personal jewellery, furniture, cutlery, personal tools and utilitarian status objects such as cars. What is perhaps worth noting is that in later prehistory, as in the Roman, medieval and later periods, the range of materials and objects to which such finishes could be applied increased significantly. A great expansion of metal production replaced what could be achieved on stone axes, and techniques for achieving a high lustre of pottery improved. Within later prehistory the basic techniques for achieving particular effects seem to have developed, particularly in metalworking. However, as we have already seen, they also seem to have been subject to the vagaries of fashion, along with changes in the basic shapes of objects and decorative motifs, that had no particular connection with the function or fitness for purpose of the objects concerned.

Colour

The drab appearance of most worn, abraded, corroded, and patinated surfaces of surviving metal and ceramic objects, and the missing organic dyes and paints that would have decorated buildings, structures, clothes and other objects leaves us with a misleading impression of the role of colour in later prehistoric art and design. Except by extrapolating the possible colours that could be achieved from dyes derived from plants of which seeds or other parts survive, we are largely reliant on imagining the original appearance of materials that are resistant to decay, where we can see how colours were selected through choice of raw materials or created in manufacture.

Apart from the use of organic materials for dyeing textiles and selection of woods of different colours, the crafts and activities that would have achieved decorative colouring effects as by-products of manufacture involved relatively high temperature firing, especially of ceramics and metalwork. Bone and antler was also deliberately charred to create black polished surfaces for toggles, 'plaques,' and possibly combs (Lambrick forthcoming). Glass beads demonstrate how firing technology was used to achieve decorative colour effects, both in the late Bronze Age and Iron Age (Fig. 5.22).

Throughout later prehistory, as in both earlier and later times, pottery was fired to achieve particular colour effects, particularly exploiting the properties of iron-rich clays to fire red, orange, brown or yellow in an oxidising atmosphere and to fire black or grey in reducing (anoxic) atmospheres. There is clear evidence, both from the consistent final finish of some pots and from layers or zones of different colours beneath the surface, that the firing atmosphere was deliberately controlled to achieve such effects. These techniques had been known since the Neolithic and earlier Bronze Age, but were enhanced in the late Bronze Age and later by the use of iron-rich coatings and fully reducing atmospheres to create distinctively red or black pots. For the most showy pots, such as burnished bowls, the finished product was often deliberately fired black, red, orange or brown. In the earlier Iron Age some fineware bowls in the Upper Thames Valley were coated with an especially iron-rich 'haematite' slip which was dried, burnished and fired to create a rich red glossy surface (Fig. 6.9).

Another interesting colour effect of early Iron Age pottery is the application of crushed bone, pure white clay or chalk as an inlay of incised decoration, dramatically highlighting the white design against a glossy black or red surface. This was a distinctive trait of the style of pottery from the southern Chilterns around Chinnor. This sophisticated application of colour by use of special slips and inlays does not seem to have survived into the middle Iron Age, but striking colour effects achieved through simple manipulation of firing conditions are nevertheless apparent in middle to late Iron Age globular bowls. In the late Iron Age higher firing temperatures, use of slips and other techniques, some applied to pots imported to the region, represent another stage in the technological exploitation of pottery to achieve desirable colouring effects.

In metalworking too a range of techniques was exploited to achieve colour effects. At the most basic level, there can be little doubt that the original off-gold raw metal colour of bronze was attractive, especially when polished. This could have been maintained by waxing or greasing the surface and perhaps occasional abrasion and repolishing to prevent tarnishing. It is equally likely that the various turquoise blue, green and brown effects of bronze patination may have been considered aesthetically desirable throughout prehistory. Similar considerations may have been applied to iron, but prevention of rusting is more difficult and, at least to the modern eye, leaves a much less aesthetically pleasing surface than bronze patination.

By the middle to late Iron Age both bronze and ironworking had become sufficiently sophisticated for designs of objects to incorporate colour through the juxtaposition of different materials – iron and bronze, iron or bronze and enamels, and metal with wood or leather. A variety of scabbards, tankards and bridle bits from the Thames Valley display such juxtaposition of materials. Fitzpatrick (2007, 344-5) has drawn attention to the use of colour in Iron Age weaponry and grave goods, suggesting an association of red with death and blue with life and possibly females. Such symbolism could have been more complex, both in relation to the range of colours that were available and the range of objects through which colour was clearly carefully controlled and exploited. It is clear that materials of particular colours were selected to make objects, as for example spindlewhorls made of white chalk or black shale, pots fired to shiny black or cherry red finishes, bones and antler tools polished to a fine creamy yellow or deliberately charred and polished black and beads of golden amber or bronze, or blue, purple, green or yellow glass.

On a much larger scale, the natural raw materials of packed white chalk set against a green grass background of the Uffington White Horse display the use of colour in design at a landscape scale (Miles *et al.* 2003). While this particular figure is undoubtedly artistic in concept, the choice of such colour schemes of contrasting natural bedrock against natural vegetation may have been a very deliberate aspect of the architecture of hillforts, not just on the chalk but also on other geologies (see below). The texture and colour of drystone walls used in forts, including the Corallian limestone imported to Blewburton (see below) can also be seen as an architectural design feature that went well beyond the purely pragmatic needs of construction.

The application of decoration to ordinary objects

In common with personal items at all periods the world over, objects such as brooches, bracelets, rings, pins, toggles, strap unions and rarer, more obviously showy items such as torcs demonstrate a range of decorative finishes and occasional applied, incised or moulded designs (see Chapter 5). There is nothing unusual in this, but an interesting issue is why some tools and other functional objects were decorated while others were not. This may relate to their role in personal, family or community life, and perhaps the 'character' imparted to such objects. For example, as we saw in Chapter 5, spindle whorls were made of many different materials (pottery, shale, chalk, and other stone) and were often highly finished and decorated, whereas many other mundane objects like bobbins were used with little or no modification. Both were items used for making textiles that would have been in constant use within the household, but spindle whorls may have been personalised prized possessions.

Most bone implements, awls, gouges, polished metapodials and the like were not decorated, nor shaped beyond what was required to function. Their high polish derives from use, not deliberate decoration. But within this broad class antler and bone combs were often deliberately polished and decorated, usually with abstract curvilinear or angular freeform designs, circlets or other motifs. They stand out amongst antler and bone tools in the full shaping and decoration of the whole object, not just carved or adapted to the minimum extent required to make an effective tool. Whether these combs were used for weaving, for preparing skins and pelts, or even as personal hair combs, their exceptional decoration places them on a par with spindle whorls as highly personal objects of dress and ornament.

The decoration of spindle whorls and combs might indicate that making spun and woven textiles and preparing animal skins for clothing was as personal as wearing them. Even more intriguingly, a number of combs clearly seem to display a phallic form, suggesting that these objects were amongst the most personal of all domestic equipment, adding further complexity to understanding their role and the gender of their users. Anthropological evidence suggests that either men or women (or both) took part in the time-consuming domestic crafts involved in making personal garments. The sexual overtones suggest a particularly strong personal association that could have been symbolic of the partnership of men and women in making the clothes they wore, a craft that would probably have filled part of most days in every household.

Art and design in later prehistoric society

Art and design in later prehistory is thus a complex and intriguing, but ultimately puzzling topic. Some aspects – broad changes of fashion, the desire for shiny objects to make statements about personal and family status or wealth and the different levels at which stylistic fashions and local distinctiveness seem to have worked – are typical of most societies. Other, more specific features, such as the lack of representation of people or creatures on many classes of artefact, or the mysteries of sexual or other symbolism on items of everyday personal equipment, remain poorly understood (Fig. 6.17).

A rich vein of inquiry into issues of individual, communal, spiritual and cultural identity awaits exploration through the evidence of art and design in the later prehistory of the Thames Valley that is only hinted at here. If art and design were considered from a broader perspective than the specific intricacies of 'celtic art' to synthesise the material now available and explore in depth the function and use of some classes of object, a better understanding of the role of art and design in late prehistoric society might emerge. Although the apparent abstractness and obscurity of symbolism in most later prehistoric art and decorative design in the region poses challenges of interpretation, there are other aspects of design in a broader sense that might also be explored.

Transport and communications

Means of transport

Boats

Unlike other rivers no definite prehistoric boats are known from the Thames. At Brentford G F Lawrence recorded the discovery of three undated dugout canoes lying side by side on the Thames foreshore in an area that has been particularly prolific for finds of late prehistoric metalwork (Lawrence 1930). Two of the boats were excavated

Fig. 6.17 (overleaf)   Art and design in the late prehistoric Thames Valley

ART AND DESIGN

Prehistoric crafts and production served as vehicles for artistic expression and style. They communicated concepts of personal and community identity, status and taste and expressed spiritual and aesthetic values. Decorative style often transcended the prosaic considerations of function, technology, locality and materials that dictated how objects, structures or places were designed. Within social groups it is likely that the basic features of design were not only an outward and deliberate expression of identity and status, but also an unconscious sense of shared cultural roots.

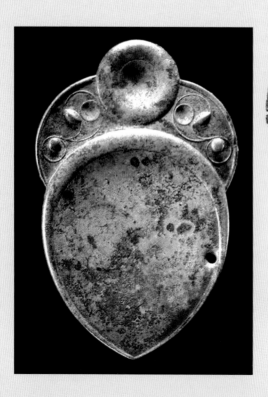

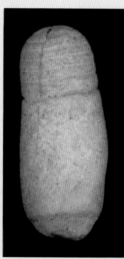

Late Iron Are ritual bronze spoon from the Thames at London (British Museum)

Iron Age spearhead from the Thames (British Museum)

Two views of a late Bronze Age or early Iron Age phallic object from Taplow pipeline site

The discussion of art and fashion in later prehistory is essentially limited to what survives - personal ornaments, tools, weapons and carved stone - but other elements, such as painted organic objects and structures, tattooed skin and textiles may have been equally important media for expression. The apparent abstract quality and obscurity of symbolism in much late prehistoric art and decorative design in the Thames Valley region poses a constant challenge of interpretation. For example, why does pottery lack figurative decoration although it occurs on metal and stone objects?

ART AND DESIGN

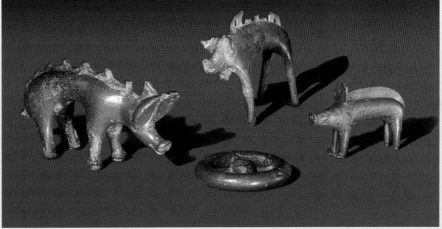

Chariot hub from Brentford (Museum of London)

Late Iron Age glass counters from Welwyn (British Museum)

Bronze boar figures from the Hounslow hoard (British Museum)

Aesica brooch recovered by metal detecting at Cerney Wick, Glos.

1st CAD cruciform harness mount, South Cerney (Corinium Museum

Decorated bone comb from Agars Plough, Maidenhead

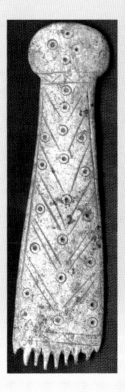

Recent excavations in the Thames Valley have not enhanced to a significant degree what is known of later Bronze Age and Iron Age metalwork, although the Petters Sports Ground and Tower Hill hoards, along with individual objects from Runneymede, Yarnton, Gravelly Guy and Whitecross Farm, have provided useful comparanda. A much larger corpus of new material has been accumulated for commoner objects, especially pottery, bone and antler, but only limited revision and updating of decorative style sequences at a regional or chronological level has been attempted to date.

by the Port of London Authority, but fell to pieces during extraction so that virtually nothing is known of them. There are also references to log boats in the Lea Valley (www.english-heritage. org.uk/server/show/ConWebDoc.5400) though the only one dated there proved to be Saxon. Nineteenth century discoveries of log boats at Marlow and Woodburn were thought by Clinch (1905) to be Bronze Age, but are not confirmed. These tantalising references to undated log boats and the finds from other river valleys merely highlight the potential for such discoveries, and the absence of prehistoric boats from the Thames so far is no indication that they were not important. As relatively small features deeply buried in river sediments, any sort of boat is inherently difficult to detect through survey. They are almost bound to be discovered accidentally during cleaning out drainage channels or extensive excavation of areas of floodplain for gravel extraction, as in the case of two late prehistoric log boats found recently at Shardlow quarry in Derbyshire.

Despite the absence of direct evidence, river transport was no doubt important in the Thames Valley during the later prehistoric period. Several heavy and bulky commodities exchanged up and down the valley in prehistory would have been well suited to river transport, including querns and salt. More speculatively, we can imagine grain being moved by river. Metalwork and other objects from overseas, and likewise the important export of later Bronze Age metalwork from Britain to Europe must have been by water. The Thames-Rhine route is seen by McGrail (1995) as one of three main cross-channel routes likely to have been in use from the 2nd millennium BC onwards, with additional routes developing in the first millennium.

Pedestrian transport

By far the commonest means of overland transport and, perhaps for a few centuries at the beginning of the later prehistoric period the only means was pedestrian. However, it is an aspect of daily life in later prehistory for which we have almost no evidence at all. An exception to this dearth of information is the existence within the palaeochannels at Yarnton and one of the small farmsteads or shielings at Farmoor of raised gravel paths so narrow and smoothly compacted that they could only have been used by people on foot (see below). Perhaps comparable, but less compelling, are the narrow double ditched tracks that look like footpaths rather than droveways within some Bronze Age field systems, but as we have seen (Chapter 3), these can also be interpreted as double ditched hedge banks.

Animal transport and wheeled vehicles

Items of harness indicate better control of animals for transport than can be achieved with a rope tied around their necks. Antler cheek pieces, known from the middle Bronze Age into the Iron Age, are the most distinctive elements of early harness.

Several late Bronze Age examples were found at Runnymede (Needham 1991) and an early Iron Age one is recorded at Yarnton (Hey *et al.* forthcoming). Other strap fittings with less explicit functions might also be harness parts or decoration, including late Bronze Age bronze 'bugle fittings', of which there are examples from Petters Sports Field and Waylands Smithy. Two middle Iron Age antler objects from Mount Farm and Rollright are also possible strap joiners (Lambrick 1988).

Oxen, with their qualities of strength and endurance but not speed, were probably used for heavy traction of ploughs, carts and sleds and as pack animals. By contrast, the stamina, physiology, manoeuvrability and speed of horses suit them to riding and other forms of transport, such as chariots, requiring speed more than strength. It is usually assumed that harness elements such as cheek pieces and bits would have been used for controlling horses rather than steering oxen, which are more likely to have been controlled by a combination of leading and prodding, tapping and beating with a stick.

Bones of horses are rarely found before the middle Bronze Age and it is likely that they were introduced to Britain and became highly valued principally for riding and later for wheeled transport, already well-established in continental Europe. A major technical improvement in the middle to late Iron Age was the introduction of the horse bit, essentially the same design utilised until the modern era. These are found as various one-two- and three-link types. Large rings replaced the earlier straight form of cheek-piece and they were forged so that they could swivel in the holes formed at the ends of the bit itself, which might be a single bar, or made from two or three linked pieces held in the horse's mouth. This gave the rider considerably greater control over the horse, and hence significant advantages for speed and manoeuvrability.

Several horse bits have been found in the region, including two corroded single-link iron ones with fragmentary traces of bronze binding in an Iron Age pit at Wytham (Harding 1972, 172, Pl. 76). A broken outer segment of a three-link iron bit originally cast in bronze was found in a middle Iron Age pit at Cassington (Harding in Case 1964, 86, fig. 88). A much finer pair of three-link bits made of decorated cast bronze with an iron core, probably of late Iron Age date, was found in a hoard of metalwork at Hagbourne Hill on the Berkshire Downs in 1803 (Harding 1972, 172, Pl. 77). Other very fine examples of three-link bits include river finds from Old Windsor and Strand-on-the-Green, Kew.

The Hagbourne hoard is problematic as it, or other deposits now combined with the group, also contained later Bronze Age metalwork and late Iron Age or early Roman coins (Harding 1972, 91). The collection also contained three terret rings of similar manufacture to the horse bits which are probably from the same hoard, dating to the late Iron Age (after 100 BC). The occurrence of a *pair* of horse bits, especially if associated with the terret rings, implies their use with a horse drawn vehicle. Given the quality of the objects, the vehicle is more likely to have been a relatively high status form of transport such as a chariot rather than an ordinary cart. The pairing of the bits from Wytham may also imply an association with wheeled transport. Although as found they were much less impressive than the Hagbourne pair, the traces of bronze binding suggest that they were originally as impressive in appearance, even if less well made. Although neither of these enigmatic, poorly recorded finds is likely to be from a chariot burial such as those of the so-called Arras culture burials of East Yorkshire (Stead 1991), the design of the three-link bits seems to be derived from the Arras area in northern France, although these examples may be much later.

A number of other terret rings are known from the region, including one resembling the Hagbourne rings found on the Thames foreshore at Isleworth in 1975 (Cotton 1978). These objects often came in sets of five mounted on a yoke for a pair of ponies, the central largest one probably used to attach it to the central draw-pole, the others to guide the reins (Stead 1991, 47-52, fig. 42). Most terrets are found as casual losses and one is a metal-detected find from Steventon, Oxfordshire (Fig. 6.18). Like bits, they were both functional and showy – a characteristic of harness and other fittings of wheeled transport down the ages. Strap unions were also used in harness. Decorative figure-of-eight examples from the Yorkshire cart burials have been found in positions corresponding to the ends of the yoke, suggesting that they were for tightening the girth that held the yoke to the backs of the ponies or bullocks (Stead 1991, 49). There are few other finds that belonged to carts or chariots, but these include the occasional linch pin, including a simple iron example recovered from an Iron Age pit at Gravelly Guy, likely to be from a small cart (Lambrick and Allen 2004, 365 and fig. 8.7, no. 278). At the other end of the decorative spectrum is the highly ornate cast bronze finial or 'chariot-horn cap' recovered from the river at Brentford. Indirect evidence of carts also comes from the wheel ruts set about 1.5 m apart in the entrance roadway at Cherbury (Bradford 1940, 17-18), and possibly in the limestone causeway at Yarnton (Fig. 6.18; Hey *et al.* forthcoming a).

These sparse finds are sufficient to indicate the use of wheeled transport and the range of sites from which the evidence comes does not suggest it was a particularly exclusive form of travel. At the same time, the care and attention paid to the manufacture and decoration of some horse gear and chariot parts indicates that wheeled transport certainly could be used as an overt display of wealth, prestige or social status.

Structures associated with river and floodplain communication

In general little remains of the physical infrastructure of late prehistoric communications but the special conditions provided by old river channels and the alluvial covering of the floodplain mean both that particular structures were needed and have been preserved in ways that do not apply to dry ground locations.

Revetments, waterfront structures and jetties

Remains of revetted river banks and jetties that would have facilitated the loading and unloading of boats provide some evidence of the infrastructure of prehistoric river transport. Given the very shallow draft of log boats, they would have been like a modern punt in facilitating access along quite small channels. We should not assume that river transport was restricted either to large river channels or used only for transhipment of goods. Some structures in or beside river channels are more likely to have been connected with nearby land-based activities rather than river traffic, and it is seldom easy to establish how 'waterfront' revetments, 'platforms', 'jetties', 'bridges' and other structures were actually used or how they were associated with votive deposition in the river. It is likely that most were used for a variety of purposes, which may or may not have included landing stages.

Some riverside structures may have been minor reinforcements of riverbanks. At Anslows Cottages near Burghfield a 7th or 8th century BC rectilinear timber structure consisting of 10 or 11 stakes in two rows oriented along the side of a small river channel could represent a small landing stage. There was a broad hollow, possibly a trackway, leading towards the channel and a small burnt mound deposit was cut by several irregular, interrupted ditches running parallel to the channel. The latest of these contained abraded late Bronze Age pottery. An alignment of 31 irregularly spaced postholes formed a fence or revetment along the south bank of the channel, cutting across the line of the holloway.

Other revetment structures consisting of closely spaced rows of posts have been found at the late Bronze Age high status riverside settlement sites at Whitecross Farm and Runnymede. At Runnymede a water edge palisade type structure and an inner row of more widely spaced posts may have formed part of an elaborate superstructure for which various reconstructions have been proposed, including a tall palisaded enclosure. Only a short length of the Whitecross Farm revetment was exposed and there was no clear indication that it was more than a simple revetment. It was located at a point where a jetty or bridge extended into the river and so might have been designed only to reinforce that particular part of the river bank, but it could equally have been used as a landing stage.

Fig. 6.18 (overleaf)   River Crossings and Transport

RIVER CROSSINGS AND TRANSPORT

The Thames and its tributaries provided a key means of transport in the late prehistoric period and heavy commodities like querns and salt would probably have been transported by river. No boats definitely of this date have been found, but possible jetties and waterfronts that could have been used for mooring have been investigated at Runnymede, Whitecross Farm and Eton Rowing Course.

Bridges, fords and causeways facilitated communication across the Thames floodplain. At Eton Rowing Course a series of six later Bronze Age and Iron Age timber bridges crossed a channel of the Thames. They were constructed of oak roundwood uprights and mortised planks were used in at least one phase. A hurdle trackway anchored between upright piles may have served as a pedestrian ford during the Iron Age.

Left page:
Eton Rowing Course:
(top left) Possible pile driver; (bottom left) Iron Age hurdle;
(upper and lower right) excavating timber bridges
Right page:
(above) Excavating the Iron Age stone causeway at Yarnton;
(centre) the stone causeway, Yarnton,
(below left) bone cheek pieces from Yarnton;
Iron terret ring from Steventon;
Iron Age bridle bit from Hagbourne Hill

RIVER CROSSINGS AND TRANSPORT

Most journeys were made by foot in the prehistoric period. Some narrow double-ditched tracks within Bronze Age field systems may have been footpaths rather than droveways. Before the onset of the late Iron Age-Roman alluviation, palaeochannels took the overspill when water levels were high and 'islands' of well-drained land formed causeways crossing low-lying areas. These are a notable feature of middle Iron Age sites on the Upper Thames floodplain. At Yarnton there was a major stone causeway with many ritualistic deposits, and both there and at Farmoor there were narrow compacted gravel causeways that formed well-used footpaths crossing seasonal channels.

Oxen were used for heavy traction of ploughs, carts and sleds and horses were used for riding and, later in prehistory, for wheeled transport. Manoeuvrability and control of horses was achieved by use of harnesses. Bone and antler cheek pieces, distinctive elements of late Bronze Age harness gear, were found at Yarnton, and middle Iron Age antler objects from Mount Farm and Rollright are possible strap joiners. A major technical improvement in the middle-late Iron Age was the horse bit. Large metal rings were forged so that they could swivel in holes at the ends of the bit, allowing for greater control. Cart or chariot fittings are rare in the Thames Valley but indirect evidence for carts comes from wheel ruts in the entrance roadway at Cherbury (Bradford 1940, 17-18) and the limestone causeway at Yarnton.

There was no evidence to determine whether the revetment and jetty/bridge structures were contemporary. The layout of the timber piles interpreted as a jetty or bridge allows for two successive structures, one based on a layout of pairs of posts placed along the structure at intervals that roughly equal its width, the other formed by narrow rectangular groups of four uprights spaced at intervals slightly longer than the width of the structure. It was not clear whether they formed short jetties protruding at right angles to the river or continuous bridges across the channel. An alternative interpretation, that all the piles belonged to one structure – a jetty or bridge with short narrow landing stages set at right angles to it like a modern marina – seems less likely. One pile had a notch cut in the top and a slight taper suggested that the superstructure was positioned at that level. This would have been only a few centimetres above the contemporary normal river level, in which case the structure is more likely to have been a jetty or landing stage, easily accessed from a log boat, than a bridge. At the Eton Rowing Course hurdles were used to make a fence stretching for more than 50 m alongside the river and for lesser jetties and other structures in mid-channel.

Bridges, fords and causeways

It would have been necessary during late prehistory to communicate across and within the extensive floodplain of the Thames and its tributaries. Before the Thames was dredged for navigation in the 19th century it would have been much more easily fordable than it is now, as is attested by the many 'ford' place names of early medieval riverside settlements. These sometimes record the character of the ford (eg 'shingly' in Shillingford) or seasonal availability at low water (eg Summerford) or the suitability for heavy traffic (eg for ox-carts at Oxford). But this does not preclude the likelihood that there were bridges, causeways and raised walkways to permit both localised movement and wider communication.

At the Eton Rowing Course there was a series of at least six late prehistoric timber bridges (Fig. 6.19 and see Chapter 8). The earliest was a middle Bronze Age bridge represented by two parallel rows of oak uprights crossing a channel of the Thames. The rows of posts were set opposite each other in pairs. Another five possible bridges, all constructed of oak roundwood uprights and dating to the early or middle Iron Age were found, together with

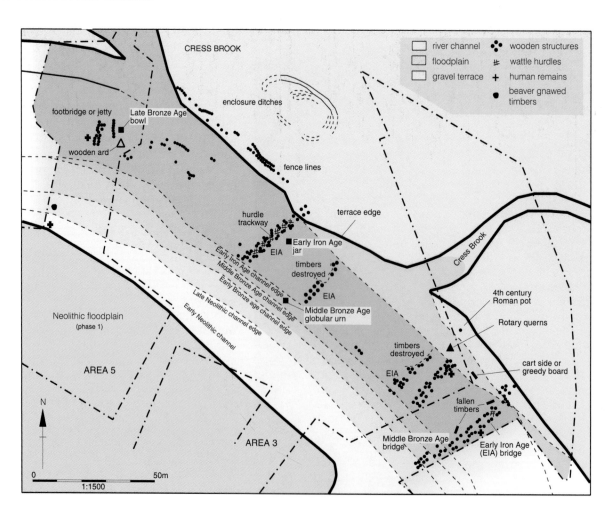

Fig. 6.19   Late Bronze Age and Iron Age timber bridges at Eton Rowing Course

mortised planks that probably belonged to the superstructure of one or other of these bridges. The design of the supports of the various bridges included regularly spaced single rows of uprights and paired groups.

Floodplain causeways, trackways and paths

At the Eton Rowing Course an Iron Age hurdle trackway was found lying on river silts, anchored between the upright piles of an earlier bridge. The trackway was supported on long horizontal timbers and consisted of pairs of hurdles laid side by side between each pair of bridge uprights, overlapping in the middle. At the south end of the structure the individual hurdles were replaced by longer lengths of wattle fencing. The hurdles showed little sign of wear, and it seems that quantities of small twigs and brushwood found on top had been laid as a surface, but not anchored into the structure.

A notable feature of some Iron Age sites on the Upper Thames floodplain is the creation of raised paths and causeways to cross low-lying areas and to prevent the ground becoming boggy along well-used routes. Prior to the onset of alluviation in the later Iron Age and Roman period palaeochannels would have taken natural overspill when water levels were high. In between such channels there were slightly higher 'islands' of drier, better-drained land. The topography and hydrology of the floodplain would thus have been different from the present day, offering more diverse resources, but also difficulties in traversing it. The need to negotiate palaeochannels that had not yet been infilled with alluvium would have become more difficult as the general water table of the valley floor rose during the Iron Age, especially at times of high water (Chapter 3). As a result, there was an increasing need to construct fords, causeways and raised pathways, to allow access locally or to get from one side of the valley to the other. Although it is reasonable to see such features as a practical response to changing environmental conditions, it is also important to recognise that some were elaborate constructions, three built of stone imported from some distance, and at least one associated with votive deposits. They may have been intended to afford some type of 'special' access across wet areas.

At Thrupp, east of Abingdon salvage work by the local archaeological society has exposed two middle Iron Age stone and gravel causeways. One, at least 12 m long, ran north-south across a palaeochannel (Ainslie 1999, 30, fig. 4). Wooden stakes driven into channel silts were covered with horizontally laid sticks, with pieces of limestone providing a base about 4 m wide on which a 2 m wide strip of gravel was laid down the middle. At the edge of the channel the stakes and sticks were not needed and the limestone was laid directly onto exposed natural gravel and the causeway forked, a branch diverging to the south. A large posthole in the centre of the main track at the point of divergence may represent a marker post to indicate the position of the

causeway when it was covered at times of high water. Middle Iron Age pottery, including a globular bowl sherd, and much animal bone was recovered from associated deposits. Fragments of human skull found on the quarry spoil heap may have been from the site.

The second causeway was a curving stone built roadway at least 30 m long, 3-5 m wide and 0.20 m-0.25 m thick (Ainslie 2002). It was founded on 0.3 m of alluvial clay sealing natural gravel. The causeway was constructed of large pieces of limestone at the base with limestone and burnt limestone cobbles above and a patchy surfacing of gravel. It was overlain by 1.3 m of peat and alluvium. Fragments of triangular loomweight, pottery sherds including middle Iron Age globular bowl, and smithing slag were found amongst the cobbles. The bone assemblage included a few human fragments. The character of the finds suggests that part of the material used to build the causeway was ordinary domestic debris derived from a nearby settlement like the one previously investigated nearby on the edge of the floodplain (Everett and Eeles 1999). However this would not account for the large quantities of stone required to build the main structure, which must have been brought from some distance. The purpose of the causeway is not very clear. It may have been designed to provide access to the edge of open water, but this would not account for its curved course, turning almost through a right angle. Traces of a timber causeway probably associated with earlier finds were also found at Thrupp (Ainslie 2002, 38).

At Yarnton a particularly diverse range of causeways and trackway structures was found in the intensive exploration of the floodplain and the numerous palaeochannels crossing it (Hey *et al.* forthcoming a). The most impressive was a large middle to late Iron Age limestone and gravel causeway crossing a palaeochannel between two gravel islands and sealed beneath Roman and later alluvium (Fig. 6.18). As the stone would have had to be brought at least 4 km from the nearest source of lower cornbrash, construction of the causeway would have been a major undertaking. It developed in several stages, possibly from an initial wooden trackway, and finds of small late Bronze Age metal objects nearby suggest that it had been a habitual crossing point long before the causeway was built. Evidence of trampling beneath the base of the earliest deposits associated with the causeway might confirm this, although it may have been connected with construction work. Two parallel wooden structures were either contemporary with or pre- or post-dated the stone causeway.

The original wooden elements of the causeway consisted of an irregularly spaced 11.8 m row of vertical roundwood uprights of mixed species only 38-55 mm in diameter, and an irregular 1.5 m by 0.7 m patch of small diameter roundwood, possibly the remnants of an earlier brushwood trackway. However, a date of 400-340 or more likely 330-230 cal BC for this material is close to the date of 380-210 cal BC obtained for the construction of the limestone causeway. The two may have been elements of the same construction process. The stone surface was spread across the palaeochannel over a length of 32.5 m, 3.7 to 5.0 m wide and 0.1 to 0.2 m thick. It was made of rounded flat brashy limestone pieces with occasional quartzite pebbles, laid in up to three broadly horizontal beds.

Numerous animal bones, of which 402 were identified to species, were embedded within and below the causeway along its entire length. These seem to have been a deliberate element of the make up of the structure. Most were cattle, a smaller element horse, and deer bones were present in larger proportions than is normal in Iron Age assemblages. The most remarkable feature of these bones was that there was a significant bias towards the right sides of the animals.

The stone was laid around a series of *in situ* timber uprights, spaced at intervals forming a double row 2.3 m apart down the middle of the causeway. Some of the limestone covered the backfill of the postholes, suggesting that they were an original part of the structure, although it is possible that some of the stones been displaced by wear. Radiocarbon dating gave results for the posts that were statistically indistinguishable from other dates for the construction of the causeway. The posts clearly demarcated a carriageway where the limestone surface of the causeway was worn and disturbed through use, with hints of wheel ruts midway along it over the deepest part of the channel. The outer margins of the causeway were relatively unworn. Towards the northern end of the deepest part of the crossing about 11 narrow timbers roughly 1.5 to 2 m long were embedded in the surface across the middle of the causeway. They might have been remains of a vertical structure or, more likely, reinforcement of the surface to reduce rutting. There were numerous additional horizontal timbers and pieces of twine, originally thought to belong to handrails, though they might be pieces of the uprights that had broken off. Whether or not the uprights held horizontal rails, they presumably would have acted as guide markers for the crossing when the water was high and would have helped ensure the edges of the causeway were not damaged by traffic.

At a later stage, perhaps in response to wear, changes in the type of traffic using the causeway and rising water levels, a narrower raised gravel walkway was laid on the worn surface of the limestone. It was up to 0.14 m thick and probably deposited as a series of resurfacings. The narrowness and smooth compacted surface of the gravel indicate that it was intended for and restricted to human pedestrian use. Dating is not clear but it is likely to have been a middle to late Iron Age modification.

This narrower gravel causeway was one of several found crossing a number of palaeochannels at Yarnton, all of which were narrow paths with

smooth compact surfaces constructed of sand and gravel obtained from channel silts. In another part of the Yarnton floodplain a series of possible brushwood tracks or walkways were partially preserved. These included collapsed late Bronze Age or early Iron Age wattle work, followed by a period of ponding and silting before a large quantity of roundwood was dumped later in the early Iron Age date. This was succeeded by another structure consisting of two parallel rows of five uprights that may have held some sort of brushwood track or boardwalk in place. Elsewhere on the floodplain two very large and two smaller posts found in an evaluation trench on the northern edge of a palaeochannel, together with a small concentration of roundwood debris, might have been the end of a jetty or another trackway across the channel.

At Farmoor a narrow, raised gravel pathway similar to those at Yarnton was designed to provide access to the lowest lying of the three floodplain farmsteads there (Lambrick and Robinson 1979, 25, figs 3, 14, 15). Prior to the discoveries at Yarnton this was the only such pathway known on the Thames floodplain, and by the time the site was identified in salvage conditions little survived and only a small area was investigated. The path branched out in the area of the farmstead and crossed the infilled ditch of a paddock attached to the house. Another path was confined within the paddock. It is not known where the other end of the path led, but it seemed to lead to a deeper part of the damp hollow left by an infilled palaeochannel, probably to gain the higher ground of the adjacent gravel terrace, where a possible section of it was observed in about the right position 40 m to the south on the other side of the palaeochannel. Like the Yarnton examples, the path was narrow (1.5 m wide) but had accumulated to 0.3 m thick through successive resurfacing. Its level and hard-packed smooth surface suggested regular use and careful maintenance.

The enclosed floodplain settlement at Mingies Ditch had a metalled track approaching the site and turning at right-angles through its entrance into the centre of the site (Allen and Robinson 1993, 28-31, 65-6). Just inside the inner enclosure was a short branch leading to the doorway of what may have been the latest house. The metalling consisted of a thin layer of gravel upcast from adjacent ditches, which were modifications of the original antennae ditch entrance to the enclosure. At the entrance to the outer and inner enclosure the roadway was cut through by blocking ditches probably associated with the abandonment of the site. No evidence of wheel ruts was observed, and the track was only about 3 m wide, so it may have been intended for mainly pedestrian use.

Another metalled entrance road was excavated at the valley fort at Cherbury. Here, a series of 3 m trenches was opened in 1939 to locate and characterise the roadway approaching the eastern entrance of the fort between the ends of the surrounding ditches (Bradford 1940). A roadway with metalling of compacted small stones was compressed by wheel ruts suggesting a 'wheel gauge of 5 ft or a bit less.' The metalling yielded a 'fair amount' of middle Iron Age pottery. At least one remetalled surface, a response to a build up of thick mud, had Roman pottery embedded in its surface.

Further downstream in the Middle Thames Valley there is less evidence for causeways and more for timber structures, such as those described above. Although there may be topographical or other reasons for this, it currently seems most likely to have arisen fortuitously due to circumstances of discovery.

Overland routeways

In terms of paths, tracks and roads crossing drier ground, there is little direct evidence of the physical character of overland transport routes other than localised tracks associated with enclosed field systems. For the most part these provide little idea of how such local routes fitted into use of the broader landscape, other than giving access to fields.

Apart from the river, the flat, well-drained and long-occupied gravel terraces, largely cleared of thick woodland, would have played a vital role in communications along the valley. These terraces had inhibited drainage in the valley floor back from the river, hence several 'marsh' and 'moor' names for these areas, such as Crowmarsh, Cowley Marsh, Moreton and the Moor Ditch in the Upper Thames Valley. Furthermore, the lower reaches of almost all the tributary valleys just above their confluence with the Thames had been notably narrowed by the deposition of the level, well-drained gravels either side, thereby minimising natural barriers to overland communication routes along the main gravel terraces.

However, there is some evidence that by the middle Bronze Age such access was already constrained. At Perry Oaks/T5 the extensive coaxial field system appears to have developed from a series of four or more broadly parallel narrow trackways or paths crossing a large expanse of gravel terrace roughly parallel to the floodplain of the river Colne to the west, and at right-angles to the River Thames to the south (Fig. 3.6; Framework Archaeology 2007, 105-12). These routes would have facilitated access between the river and higher ground through areas where access may have been restricted by closely controlled grazing rights. Within the area investigated at Perry Oaks/T5 there was no indication of comparable east-west tracks designed to traverse the valley across these areas, suggesting that by the middle Bronze Age large field systems may have consolidated pre-existing restrictions on general 'through traffic' across important grazing lands, making it necessary to skirt round them.

In this context, the large east-west boundary ditch found at Stanwell to the south of Perry Oaks/T5 might indicate demarcation of an area where such restrictions did not apply, though this area too was later absorbed into the field systems (O'Connell 1990). Although the details are far from clear, it is reasonable to postulate that intensification of landuse, tight control and ultimately enclosure of land would have restricted the natural freedom of movement that the Thames gravel terraces would in principle allow. By the Roman period, networks of roads crossing the gravel terraces between areas of fields or open ground become very evident, such as that at Long Wittenham (Baker 2002, 9-13). The origins of such roads can often be traced back into the Iron Age, as at Mount Farm (Lambrick forthcoming).

Looking beyond the gravel terraces and valley floor the range of objects imported to the region shows that communication with other areas, both locally within the wider Thames basin and beyond its natural borders, took place. Such communication was probably a routine part of the lives of those who lived in the valley: nowhere are the edges of the Thames sub-catchments more than one or two days walk from the river.

Topographically, the main 'natural' communication routes off the gravels were along the watersheds between river catchments. The major sub-catchments of the Thames basin are bounded by the ridgeline scarps of the Chalk, Corallian and Oolitic Limestone hills, each with river valleys or dry valleys extending down their dip slopes, creating minor ridges and watersheds that link the main valley floor with the surrounding hills. The Ridgeway along the chalk scarp of the Marlborough and Berkshire Downs and the Chilterns, the Icknield Way along the Upper Greensand bench at the foot of the Downs and Chilterns and the so-called Jurassic Way along the scarp of the Cotswolds, are traditionally recognised as ancient routeways. A Corallian ridgeway would be another plausible routeway.

GIS techniques could provide an ideal starting point to examine the distribution of later prehistoric settlements, communal gathering points, such as fortified enclosures, and sources of bulky raw materials like querns and briquetage in relation to the natural topography and traditional and documented ancient routeways. Although no attempt has yet been made to analyse this issue taking account of all these factors, a limited exercise examining the route of the modern Ridgeway in relation to a theoretical 'least cost' surface route and the location of hillforts on the Berkshire Downs has produced interesting results (Miles *et al.* 2003, 131-3, fig. 7.7). This showed that the hillforts of Liddington Castle, Hardwell Camp, Uffington Castle and Rams Hill are all located on or, in the case of Uffington, close to the 'least cost' surface route, whereas the modern course of the Ridgeway, at least in places, differs markedly from this line. At Uffington the 'least cost' route passes north of the hillfort, whereas the present day route of the Ridgeway south of the hillfort is intersected by a boundary ditch, probably of later prehistoric origin (Miles *et al.* 2003). Elsewhere along the Ridgeway numerous other ditches cross it, many still visible as lines of deep rutting where agricultural traffic and off-road vehicles have sunk into their soft fill in wet weather. At the Avebury end of the Ridgeway a whole Roman field system intersects it, casting doubt on its ancient origin. However, this does not necessarily detract from its existence as an ancient routeway of a less formal nature.

While the natural ridges of the Thames basin might have provided long distance south-west to north-east routes, minor ridges, dry valleys and tributary valleys may have provided routes at right-angles to the main grain of the land. It would be erroneous, however, to assume that these 'natural' topographic routes were always preferable. As a general rule, pedestrian and animal transport routes usually take a steep direct route in preference to a longer diversion with gentler gradients, and it is likely that many communication routes were established before the introduction of wheeled transport. It is also highly characteristic of later settlement patterns, especially along the scarps of the Chalk in Oxfordshire, Buckinghamshire, Berkshire and Surrey, that Saxon and medieval estates, as reflected in parish boundaries, straddled these areas to provide a diversity of resources. Many historically ancient routes, far from running with the natural grain of the land, crossed it at right-angles to provide access to resources, and it would not be surprising if some of these routes proved to be prehistoric in origin.

Case (1964/5; 1982) argued for a possible north-south route for prehistoric communications across the Upper Thames Valley. Recently Edward Bull (1993) drew attention to a 'bi-axial' pattern of existing roads and trackways across the Chilterns and north Buckinghamshire, which he suggests pre-dated the Roman road network and might be prehistoric in origin, akin to co-axial field systems recognised in Essex and elsewhere (Rodwell 1978; Fleming 1987; Williamson, 1987; 1998). The discovery at Site B on the Aston Clinton bypass of a trackway of Iron Age origin running along a historic parish boundary perpendicular to the Chilterns on the same alignment as this system, provides supporting evidence for Bull's hypothesis (Masefield *et al.* 2003).

Chapter 7 – Living off the land: farming, water, storage and waste

So far we have examined the natural environment, the physical infrastructure of land division and fields, different forms and patterns of settlement and how people lived their daily lives and made and traded goods. This chapter explores the day-to-day relationship between people and the land from which they obtained their means of subsistence and agricultural produce for exchange, and to which they consigned their waste. This was not just a functional cycle of rural living, but one in which spiritual values played an important part. People relied heavily on the land, arguably an increasingly contested resource, to make their living. There are good reasons why earth and water, domestic animals and crops, their safe keeping and all that could be made from them may have been seen both as the physical source and a spiritual repository of people's fortunes. It was a matter not only of what could be taken from the ground but also what should be put back. As we shall see in Chapter 8, that could involve complex traditions and rituals that we do not yet fully understand.

LATE PREHISTORIC FARMING IN THE THAMES VALLEY

Little is known about the organisation of Bronze Age agriculture in the Middle and Upper Thames Valley before 1500 BC. As noted in Chapter 3, there is little evidence for ditched field boundaries in this period and soils sealed beneath Bronze Age monuments do not show signs of cultivation, but other archaeologically less visible forms of land division may have existed. Although pollen evidence suggests that cultivation was occurring, as exemplified by deposits at Daisy Banks in the vicinity of Barrow Hills, Radley in the Upper Thames Valley (Parker 1999), this is patchy and most assemblages of charred crop remains and animal bones are too small to provide a detailed picture of crop and animal husbandry.

But as we shall see in this chapter, the evidence is much more plentiful, though by no means uniformly so, from the later Bronze Age onwards.

Tools for farming and subsistence

General Farm Implements

Many later prehistoric tools seem to have had multiple applications not specifically related to farm work (Fig. 7.1). Implements like axes, awls, saws, punches, bobbins and knives used for woodworking and other crafts (Chapter 6), together with containers such as buckets, barrels and baskets, would have had more general applications around the farm. Similarly, many ordinary items related to harness and carts were probably used on and around farms as well as for wider communication (Chapter 6). Other metal fittings, bone objects, etc may have had uses round the farm that are not clear to us, and there must have been wooden implements that have not survived.

Cutting Hooks

Of the implements that might be considered primarily of farm use, the most distinctive is a range of sickle- and hook-shaped cutting implements (Fig. 7.2). Amongst these are middle to late Bronze Age socketed 'sickles' with short cutting blades set at right-angles to the handle, a basic form of which there are also early Iron Age examples made of iron. Such sickles are quite common components of later Bronze Age scrap hoards, including Petters (Needham 1990), and some relatively high status settlements such as Whitecross Farm have also produced examples (Cromarty et al. 52-4, fig. 3.2, nos. 2 and 3), one of which is of the regionally distinctive 'Thames' series (Fox 1939). A number have been recovered from the river, further suggesting that they probably had a more than purely utilitarian role, perhaps as potential votive tools connected with harvest, or some non-agricultural uses. On the Continent bronze sickles were used as standard units of metal (Sommerfeld 1994).

So-called 'reaping hooks' are moderately common finds on ordinary Iron Age farming settlements, though there is a wide range of curved iron blades within which these fall. Most have sockets for wooden handles (Jennings et al. 2004, 82, fig. 4.7, no. 79; Hey et al. forthcoming b), but some, such as a sickle from Ashville, had tangs onto which wooden handles would have been driven, accompanied by iron collars to prevent the wood splitting (Parrington 1978, 78, fig. 58 5; cf. Lambrick and Allen 2004, 394, fig. 8.19, no. 119 for a collar). Less robust examples had riveted tangs for antler or bone handles. These sometimes survive, occasionally as complete implements (Harding 1972, 172, Pl 76 C, D and E; Parrington 1978, 78, fig. 58, 7; Fowler 1960, 43 fig. 18, no. 6; Lambrick and Allen 2004 363-4, fig. 8.7, no. 510). The extent to which these curved cutting implements were used for reaping or as heavy duty billhooks or lighter knives depends on their size and shape. Small sharply curved hooks with riveted tangs were clearly not designed for a chopping action, but could have been used as reaping hooks for cutting handfuls of cereal heads just below the ear. This and perhaps other uses (eg trimming hedges) may also apply to longer sickle-like examples that are too big to be handy as knives. Smaller, straighter examples may have been curved knives used for a variety of purposes. The larger hooks might have been used for reaping, but could also, or alternatively, have been used as billhooks for hedging, coppicing, making hurdles, collecting firewood and cutting branches to provide leaf fodder.

The doubling up of implements to serve more than one function is even more evident in shaft-hole adzes and axes on which the back of the socket doubled as a flat hammer head (Hey *et al.* forthcoming a; Fowler 1960, 42-3 fig. 18, no. 5). These might have been particularly useful for fencing and splitting timbers with wedges as well as shaping them.

Ploughs

Apart from spades and hoes, for which there is little physical evidence, the main prehistoric cultivation implement was the ard or simple scratch plough. These implements worked on the principle of dragging a single wooden share, sometimes tipped with metal or stone, through the ground at a shallow angle, thereby lifting the soil and breaking it up. This principle could be applied in two ways, either using a manually pushed 'breast plough' or an animal-drawn 'ard'. It is possible that very worn old axe- and spearheads doubled as tips for digging sticks or simple breast ploughs: axes were certainly used for digging (see below).

Ards had the great advantage of making use of animal traction – almost certainly pairs of oxen – to provide considerably more power. There are various forms of ard, all based on the principle of a substantial naturally bent draw beam through which the ard 'stilt' and head and a handle would be fitted through a mortise at the rear end, and an attachment for a yoke through another hole at the front end. Reynolds (1987, 28-9) defines three basic kinds for different stages of cultivation. The 'sod-buster' or 'rip' ard with the share set at a relatively steep angle to the draw beam would have been used for breaking up old grassland for the first time. The 'bow' ard with a shallower angled share would have been the main regular cultivation implement for use in previously cultivated soil. The third type of ard envisaged by Reynolds (but without direct archaeological evidence) is a furrow ard made from a simple forked branch used to make a seed drill and facilitate between-row hoeing with consequential benefits in terms of crop establishment, weed suppression and crop yield.

No ard frames have been found in the Thames valley but there are a few later prehistoric ard shares. An almost complete late Bronze Age or early Iron Age wooden ard share, radiocarbon dated to 940-760 cal BC (or 11% chance to 690-550 cal BC) was recovered from a river channel at Eton (Fig. 7.11

TOOL MARKS

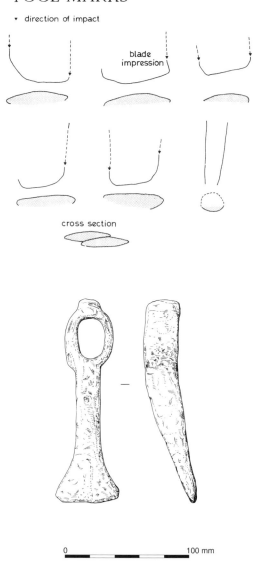

Fig. 7.1 Tools for land management and construction: (above) late Bronze Age socketed axes from Tower Hill; (centre) *toolmarks on chalk blocks from Rams Hill;* (below) *iron adze head from Yarnton*

238

& Fig. 8.3). This may be the oldest such ard share so far dated in Britain, though stone tips and ardmarks are known from earlier contexts. The triangular-shaped head of the ard was still intact, and largely unworn, though the stilt was broken. This would have made it unusable but it is not clear if this represented an accident during an early stage of use or a deliberate 'killing' of the implement prior to votive offering, like other objects deposited in the river (Allen *et al.* 2000, 94).

A short iron ard tip (an iron sleeve covering the wooden ard tip to prevent rapid wear) was recently found in the secondary fill of an early/middle Iron Age ditch during excavations of an extensive settlement found on a pipeline near Berwick Salome (Wilson and Cater 2005). Although short ard tips were considered to be relatively early by Rees (1979, 51) there are examples as late as the 1st century AD, as at Gorhambury in Hertfordshire (Neal *et al.* 1990,

142). The complete, apparently still usable, condition of this example and its location in a ditch terminal suggest that it was a deliberate deposit rather than a discarded piece of worn out farm equipment, which one might expect to have been recycled.

Another complete ploughshare was found in a posthole of the penannular ditched 'shrine' at Frilford (Fig. 7.11; Bradford and Goodchild 1939, 13, Pl. V, c). Harding (1987, 10-16) doubts whether this site really was a shrine as originally supposed and widely accepted, including in his earlier writings (Harding 1972, 61-4), but as discussed in Chapter 9, this dismissal of the original interpretation may be too emphatic. Frilford is certainly of interest as another possible example of a votive deposit of a ploughshare, emphasising that even if such deposits are not common, cultivation equipment would have been believed to have more than a merely functional value.

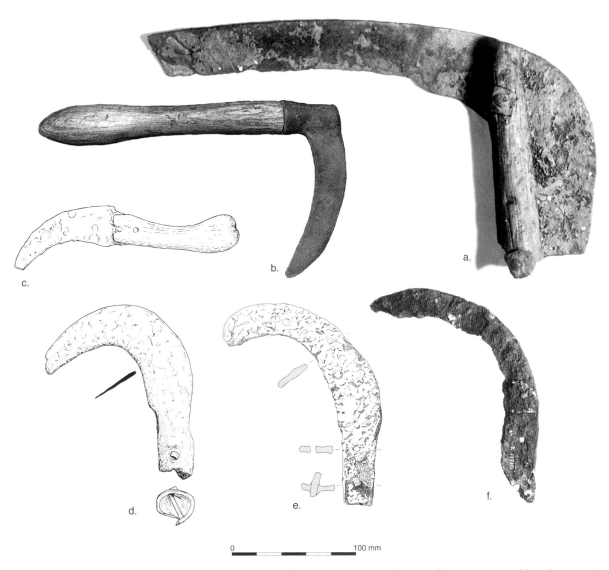

Fig. 7.2   Agricultural tools: a) Late Iron Age scythe from Eton Rowing Course; b) reconstructed late Bronze Age sickle; c) knife with bone handle from Standlake; d) - f) socketed and tanged cutting hooks from (left) *Yarnton,* (middle) *Slade Farm and* (right) *Kingston*

A short ard tip comparable to those at Berwick Salome and Frilford was found in the lower fill of a well at Thames Valley Park together with a number of oak timbers to which it was 'possibly attached.' The excavators did not suggest that the timbers were an ard frame, but their character and the precise relationship to the iron tip is not described. The date of the ard tip is also uncertain: fragments of handmade Iron Age or Saxon pottery were found in the fill of the well but with no other finds, and the wood was not radiocarbon dated. The excavators' tentative conclusion was that the ard tip might be earlier than the early Roman date suspected for the feature. As we have seen in relation to objects deposited in wells and waterholes, this may be another votive deposit, of a late date. It is also worth noting that the wooden ard share from Ashville, Abingdon had been stuck upright in the bottom of a Roman well (Parrington 1978, 83).

Digging Equipment

Considering the increasing scale of excavation of pits, ditches and fortifications during the later prehistoric period there is relatively little evidence of the tools used for digging. It is likely that some tools commonly found but not necessarily regarded as digging tools had more uses than we would normally recognise today. For example, especially worn or blunted 'axes' and 'adzes' may have doubled as what archaeologists would now call 'handpicks' 'backhoes' or 'mattocks', complementing and eventually replacing antler picks of earlier prehistory; some 'ferrules' and worn out spearheads could have been used as the points of digging sticks. Marks of antler picks were found in primary silts of the ditch of the middle to late Bronze Age enclosure at Rams Hill and tool impressions found on lumps of chalk and the sides of the ditch indicate the use of some sort of digging stick and of bronze axes, presumably hafted as adzes (Fig. 7.1; Bradley and Ellison 1975, 11, 90, fig. 3.20). An Iron Age iron adze deposited in a ritual burial context in the hillfort ditch at Blewburton may or may not have been a digging implement (Collins 1952-3, 50 fig. 17, no 1).

Cattle scapulae could be used as 'hand shovels,' but the small beasts characteristic of later prehistoric times would have provided less satisfactory material for this purpose than the larger beasts of earlier prehistory. If wooden spades or shovels existed there is no evidence of their having been shod with metal blades, equivalent to the ard tips noted above. Soil may still have been raked back into baskets rather than picked up with shovels.

Traction

The evidence for harness and other equipment associated with traction has been dealt with in Chapter 6 in relation to communications (Fig. 6.18), but this was obviously an important part of farming life, vital for ploughing areas of any size, and probably for dragging timber from woods and transporting heating stones, querns and any other heavy commodity. Cattle would have been bred to ensure a reliable provision of oxen for traction as well as for meat, milk and secondary products, and cattle leg bones which show pathological conditions that are typical of stress from use in traction are common on Iron Age settlements (Wilson 1978, 118-9).

Hunting and gathering

As noted in Chapter 5, bones of wild vertebrates that could have been hunted for food remained an unimportant and diminishing part of the later prehistoric diet. They nevertheless indicate that some hunting did take place in the Thames Valley in late prehistory

It seems likely that many wild plants were gathered and eaten to supplement and flavour the staples of cultivated crops, but this was largely incidental to the main means of generating food and secondary products through crop husbandry and the raising and management of domestic animals for meat, dairy and traction.

Animal husbandry

Representation of species

Middle Bronze Age

The main domestic animals in the middle Bronze Age, as earlier, in the Upper Thames Valley were cattle, sheep and pig. Dogs were also present at most settlements. Horse bones that have been found on a few sites are among the earliest records of horse for the region. Unfortunately few assemblages of sufficient size have been found to allow detailed analysis of management strategies. One of the largest groups is from Latton Lands (Hamilton in Stansbie and Laws 2004, 128-33) where the assemblage, mostly derived from waterholes, pits and an L-shaped ditch complex, was dominated by cattle bones.

Cattle tend to dominate bone assemblages of this period (Tinsley and Grigson 1981, 210-49), and though comparative sites in the Thames Valley are rare, this is also true of the small assemblage from Mount Farm, most of which came from the upper fill of a ring ditch. Cattle also dominated the middle Bronze Age animal assemblage from Corporation Farm, Abingdon (Shand *et al.* in Barclay *et al.* 2003, 39), although no detailed breakdown of species was given, nor any details of five complete cattle and sheep skeletons. It was observed that this material was strongly influenced by special deposits with abnormally high proportions of skull and jaw bones which might bias the picture, but unfortunately no analysis of age data based on tooth-wear was carried out. It was nevertheless noted that, where identifiable, most of the cattle and half the sheep were females, perhaps indicating an emphasis on dairying and other secondary products. Most of the other 'later Bronze Age' assemblages shown in Figure 7.3 are from late Bronze Age or a mixture of middle to late Bronze Age contexts.

A similar poverty of good animal bone assemblages of this period applies to the Middle Thames Valley despite several large-scale investigations. This is partly because bone preservation is often poor in less calcareous soils except in some waterlogged deposits. For example, at Weir Bank Stud Farm, Bray (Barnes and Cleal 1995) only 115 fragments were identifiable, of which cattle comprised 57%, sheep 37% and pig 6%. It was not possible to establish kill-off patterns. Cattle predominated amongst the even smaller number of animal bones from the extensive investigations at Perry Oaks/T5, but sheep and pig were also present (Knight 2006). Again there is insufficient information on the kill-off patterns of the domestic animals to establish herd structures and management systems. The availability of plentiful pasture there means it is likely that many animals were kept for their secondary products of milk and wool.

Late Bronze Age

The same range of domestic animals – cattle, sheep, pigs, horses and dogs – were kept in the late Bronze Age. It was possible to confirm the presence of goat as well as sheep at Whitecross Farm (Powell and Clarke 2996, 106) and at Runnymede Bridge (Done 1991, 334).

So far the only published late Bronze Age site in the Upper Thames Valley for which the bone assemblage was large enough for detailed analysis is Whitecross Farm, Wallingford (Powell and Clark 2006). It was atypical in that it was a high-status midden site on an island in the River Thames. Sheep bones (39% of the total identifiable fragments, 47% by minimum number of individuals) outnumbered cattle (21% fragments, 13% MNI). However, the proportion of pig bones (33% fragments, 27% MNI) was exceptionally high compared with many other late Bronze Age settlements in southern England, probably because meat formed a larger part of the diet of the occupants of the site than was usual amongst the general populace. This may reflect the special status of the site, and there was also a relatively high proportion of deer bones (6% fragments, 7% MNI). Although both pigs and deer may reflect exploitation of woodland resources, it has been suggested that plants of river margins, such as the rhizomes of waterlilies during times of low water, could have made an important contribution to the diet of pigs (Powell and Clark 2006).

The age profile of pigs and sheep from Whitecross Farm showed that both were being raised for meat production, with a high proportion of animals slaughtered at less than two years old. While such a kill-off pattern is typical for pigs, which yield no secondary products, the lack of many older sheep suggests that wool or milk

production did not play an important part in the economy of the site. In contrast, a greater proportion of older animals was represented among the cattle bones, which would be consistent with the use of some animals for traction or milk. Interestingly, some of these characteristics (a high proportion of pigs and sheep exploited for meat) are also apparent in the high status riverside midden side at Runnymede (see below), but are not evident from the species composition or limited ageing data in the small assemblages of bone from the defensive enclosures at Rams Hill and Castle Hill, Little Wittenham, or the late Bronze Age to early Iron Age midden at Castle Hill (Bradley and Ellison 1975, 118-22; Allen *et al.* forthcoming a).

Bone preservation is poor on most Middle Thames sites but large assemblages were found at Runnymede Bridge (Done 1991). Bones of sheep (41% of fragments) and pig (30%) were the most abundant, with cattle third (28%) which like Whitecross Farm, probably reflects a meat-rich diet on a high status site, coupled to some extent with the particular characteristics of their role as middens. As at Whitecross Farm, both the pigs and sheep tended to be slaughtered at the optimum age for meat production. Cattle bones were slightly less abundant than sheep. Horse was present and the incisors of one animal showed a wear pattern which suggested that it had repeatedly gnawed a solid fixed object, as often occurs with an animal tethered to a post or kept in a stable. Other possible evidence for the housing of domestic animals, or at least their confinement, was that the horns had been removed from three cattle skulls. Red deer were present but at a lower level than at Whitecross Farm and seem to have comprised only a very small part of the diet.

Taken together, a moderately large group of assemblages has been reported at the Reading Business Park/Green Park settlements (Levitan 1992; Wilson 2004), but it was not possible to obtain sufficient age-at-death data to establish the kill-off patterns for the various species. However, the sheep were mature animals, indicating animals kept for secondary products. There were no certain examples of goat present.

The proportions of the various large and medium-sized mammal species from Reading Business Park/Green Park and other late Bronze Age settlements in the Middle Thames Valley display significant variation in the relative dominance of cattle or sheep and other animals. Even the immediately adjacent sites of Reading Business Park/Green Park display some of this variability. In general cattle predominate, but this may in part be a reflection of the poor preservation of bones on some sites, although the proximity of water would have facilitated the raising of cattle.

The predominance of sheep and a relatively high proportion of horse is unusual at Home Farm Laleham. The low proportion of pig and deer suggests that woodland exploitation was unimportant. By contrast, the very small assemblage from

Anslows Cottages with 13% pig and 18% deer fragments is exceptional, but perhaps not fully representative.

Early Iron Age

There was no change in the species of domestic animals kept during the early Iron Age for which cattle, sheep, goat, pig, horse and dog are all represented. Once again proportions of the main species are very variable, but the range of variation shifted significantly. There was less emphasis on cattle (maximum 90% to minimum 20% of fragments in later Bronze Age assemblages compared with 50% to 15% in early Iron Age ones) and more on sheep (maximum 56% to minimum 5% of fragments in later Bronze Age assemblages compared with 78% to 30% in early Iron Age ones). The range of proportions of pig remained much the same (with an interestingly high proportion from the Castle Hill fort not much less than Whitecross Farm), but those of horse increased (maximum 4% to minimum 0% of fragments in later Bronze Age assemblages compared with 20% to 0% in early Iron Age ones). Most early Iron Age sites have less than 7% horse, but there are unusually high proportions of 20% at Latton Lands and 12% at Gallows Leaze on the Chalgrove-Ilsey pipeline (Powell *et al.* forthcoming; Wilson and Carter 2005).

The much larger assemblages available for study (three early Iron Age sites with over 1000 fragments, a further four with over 500 and two over 200; compared with two later Bronze Age ones with over 500 and a further two of 200 or more) provide greater scope for understanding the pastoral management strategies of the period (see below).

Middle Iron Age

The main domestic animals found on middle Iron Age sites in the Upper Thames Valley were still cattle, sheep, pig and horse (Fig. 7.3). Goats are also recorded and dog is also usually present, but domestic fowl bones from Gravelly Guy, Stanton Harcourt were regarded as intrusive (Mulville and Levitan 2004, 474).

Once again proportions of the main species are very variable, but the range of variation shifted less significantly. The proportions of cattle and sheep bones on any one site were seldom equal, but the range of variation became much smaller with slightly more cattle (maximum 50% to minimum 15% of fragments in early Iron Age assemblages compared with 61% to 16% in middle Iron Age ones) and fewer sheep (maximum 78% to minimum 30% in early Iron Age assemblages compared with 65% to 18% of fragments in middle Iron Age ones). The range of proportions of pig remained much the same, with again one site, the banjo enclosure at Groundwell Farm, having an exceptionally high proportion. More striking is the greater emphasis on horse rearing, all assemblages having some horse, accounting for 20-21% of fragments in three assemblages ranging down to a minimum of 2-3%. Apart from Woodcote Road on the edge of the chalk and Slade Farm on the edge of the limestone, the other seven sites with more than 10% of horse bones are all situated on low gravel terraces or the floodplain. Only two sites investigated within this topographical zone, Claydon Pike and Thrupp, did not have over 10% horse bones. From butchery marks, it is clear that horses were eaten, but very few young horse bones are found, suggesting that they were bred for use or exchange as riding and traction animals, and perhaps for the prestige of ownership, not primarily for meat. Where young horses are present, as at Gravelly Guy, it is suspected that settlements may have been engaged in horse breeding, and there seem to be a number of sites in the lower Windrush Valley where this was the case (Wilson 1993; Mulville and Levitan 2004, 477-8).

Although goat can only be differentiated from sheep on a few skeletal elements, on the sites where the ovicaprid remains have been studied in detail

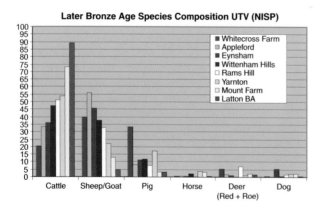

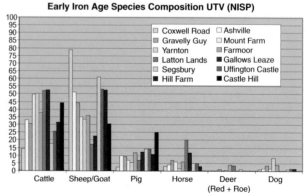

Fig . 7.3 (above and opposite)   Proportions of domestic and wild animal bones from late prehistoric settlements in the Upper Thames Valley by period. Percentages are based on the number of identifiable species present. The sites are grouped topographically: pink to red limestone slopes; strong yellow Corallian ridge; pale yellow to ginger high gravels; green to pale blue low gravels and floodplain; dark blue and purple chalk

Middle Iron Age Species Composition UTV (NISP)

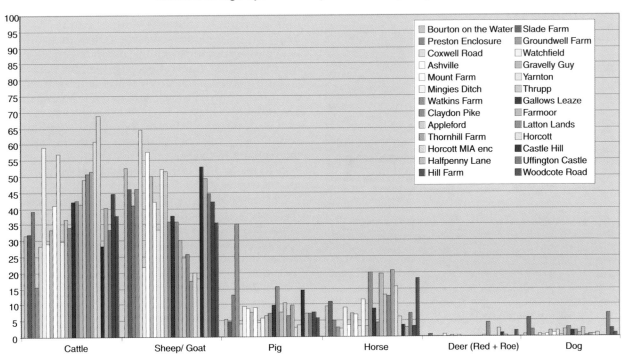

Late Iron Age & Early Roman Species Composition UTV (NISP)

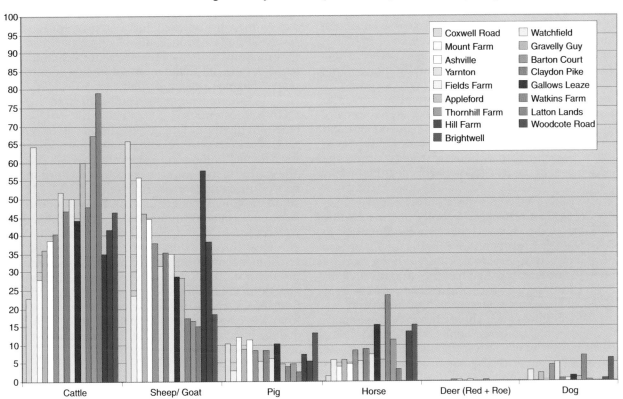

Middle Iron Age Age Species Composition MTV (NISP)

Fig. 7.4 Proportions of domestic and wild animal bones from middle Iron Age settlements in the Middle Thames Valley. Percentages are based on the number of identifiable species present

(eg Mingies Ditch, Wilson 1993, 238), goats were greatly outnumbered by sheep. At Gravelly Guy the ratio of goat to sheep in early Iron Age deposits was 1:13 but 1:57 from middle Iron Age ones (Mulville and Levitan, 2004). Goats are particularly effective at browsing on developing thorn scrub and eating the regrowth of cut scrub, but they are not as productive as sheep on pasture. A declining proportion of goats in relation to sheep between the early and middle Iron Age may thus indicate pasture being brought into better management.

There is again a dearth of reasonable sized animal bone assemblages from the Middle Thames Valley, due in part to poor preservation. There are few assemblages of any size, virtually none large enough for detailed analysis beyond species representation, and that may be distorted by preservation factors (Knight 2006, 1). Such material as there is, for example from Perry Oaks, Cippenham and Fairylands Laleham displays a rather similar variation in species proportions to middle Iron Age settlements in the Upper Thames Valley (Fig. 7.4).

Late Iron Age and Early Roman

All domestic animal species noted for the middle Iron Age in the Upper Thames Valley continued to be kept during this period. Domestic fowl may also have been introduced as evidenced by several bones from late Iron Age contexts at Barton Court Farm (Bramwell, Cowles and Wilson 1986). Caesar noted that in Britain, domestic fowl were kept for pleasure but not eaten. Three cat bones were identified from late Iron Age contexts at Barton Court Farm but at least one was thought more likely to have been from *Felis sylvestris* (wild cat) rather than the domestic cat *F. domesticus* (Wilson 1986).

Proportions of cattle and sheep varied within much the same ranges as in the middle Iron Age, but cattle more consistently outnumbered sheep at sites

on the lower gravel terraces and floodplain. Unlike previous periods, no late Iron Age site has yet been found with an exceptional proportion of pigs. It is also notable that fewer of the low lying sites have high proportions of horse, Watkins Farm with 23% being an exception, increasing rather than diminishing the proportion of horse bones compared with the middle Iron Age period. The Watkins Farm site is also notable for the survival and refurbishment of the middle Iron Age enclosure in the Roman period. The other two sites with over 10 % horse had middle Iron Age phases in which they were significantly commoner. This may indicate that the special interest in horse raising that characterises low-lying sites in the middle Iron Age was on the wane except for a few sites where it survived.

The animal bones from the military phase at Alchester included remains of the principal domestic species: cattle, sheep, horse, pig and dog (Grant 2000, 63). There was a relatively high proportion of horse bones, consistent with the assumption that the garrison at Alchester included cavalry (Sauer 2000). It is likely that the horses were brought from the continent because of the time it takes to train a horse for military use. In contrast, the small size of the sheep suggested that they had been obtained locally.

Patterns of late prehistoric animal husbandry and breeding

Evidence of how animals were bred and strategies for their management for meat and secondary products relies on significantly larger site assemblages than are needed for a basic indication of species representation. This means in effect that the vast majority of data available are for the Iron Age, largely restricted to the more calcareous soils of the Upper Thames Valley.

Animal morphology

Due to a dearth of large bone samples little can be said of middle Bronze Age animal morphology in the Thames Valley, and seldom across all species. The Latton Lands cattle were a small shorthorned type with average withers height of 1.10-1.15 m, similar to Iron Age animals. However, an unusually large cattle bone from a middle to late Bronze Age waterhole at Mount Farm seems more like an aurochs, though this could not be confirmed (Wilson in Lambrick forthcoming). Measurements for the various domestic animals at Runnymede and Whitecross Farm are generally typical of later Bronze Age material, which does not differ much from the Iron Age. At Whitecross Farm, however, one pig bone was significantly larger than the norm, suggesting the presence of wild boar (Powell and Clark 2006, 109).

A thorough study of the morphology of these animals was made for the Iron Age on the bones from the settlement on the second gravel terrace at Ashville, Abingdon (Wilson 1978). The cattle, all horned, were small beasts compared to modern breeds, with shoulder heights averaging 1.08 m. The sheep, all small-bodied, long-legged and horned, resembled the Soay breed, with withers height up to 0.64 m. The pigs were small animals of wild boar appearance but had a third molar shape confirming a domestic variety. The horses seem to have been pony-sized animals standing 1.20-1.43 m (10.5-12.5 hands) high at the shoulder. Most of the dogs were 0.48-0.53 m high at the shoulder. Subsequent studies have generally confirmed these observations and in some cases refined the picture. For example, the much larger samples of bones from Gravelly Guy and Yarnton (Mulville and Levitan 2004; Hey *et al.* forthcoming a) suggest cattle and sheep of similar size with no obvious change through the middle to late Iron Age and into the early Roman period. Eighteen dog burials at Gravelly Guy fell within a slightly wider range of 0.43-0.55 m. Horses at Gravelly Guy and Yarnton were of similar size, but the larger number of measurable bones at Gravelly Guy indicates that the horses there tended to be slightly smaller (1.18-1.37 m) than at Ashville or Yarnton. There is also a slight indication, based on small samples for the early and late Iron Age, that their stature may have increased slightly over time (from 1.24 m to 1.29 m).

The morphology of domestic animals remained much the same until the end of the prehistoric period. Although there was a tendency for Roman domestic animals to be somewhat larger than their Iron Age counterparts, this trend did not necessarily begin until after AD100 (Wilson 1986).

Kill-off patterns

Because of the limited number of large site assemblages, evidence for the sex and age of slaughter of later Bronze Age domestic animals is limited. Where identifiable, most of the middle Bronze Age cattle bones at Latton were cows but there was some suggestion that some male cattle were killed young for meat with cows kept until older for breeding and secondary products (Hamilton in Stansbie and Laws 2004). The two late Bronze Age midden sites at Whitecross Farm and Runnymede present similar patterns of species and kill-off to each other, but these are highly exceptional assemblages with complicated underlying patterns of animal exploitation which are likely to have differed from ordinary farming settlements. Particularly noticeable are the high proportions of pigs and the early kill-off patterns for both pigs and sheep, suggesting a strong emphasis on exploitation for meat (Powell and Clark 2006, 110).

Much fuller patterns are available from several Iron Age sites (Fig. 7.5). The kill-off pattern for sheep at Ashville, on the second gravel terrace at Abingdon, based on a study of tooth eruption and tooth-wear patterns in mandibles, showed that around 60% of animals were overwintered once and 30% overwintered at least twice (Wilson 1978). Assuming lambing to have been in March, the first

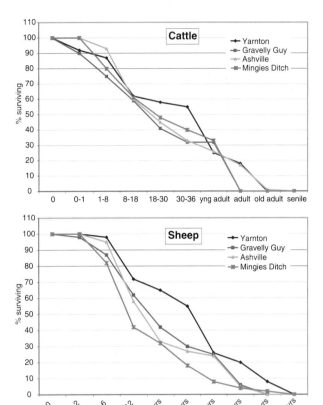

Fig. 7.5 Kill-off patterns for cattle and sheep at four Iron Age sites in the Upper Thames Valley

peak of mortality was around October of the first year and the second around October of the second year. A study showed a general immaturity of male pelvises, suggesting rams tended to be killed early. There was also evidence that some of the males could have been castrated (wethers). After the fusion of the acetabulum at 6-10 months the proportions of the pelvises indicated an Iron Age flock cohort of about 75% ewes and 25% rams and wethers. Such a kill-off pattern suggests that the production of wool and possibly milk were important in addition to meat.

Bulls, castrates and cows were identified among the cattle from Ashville. Most males were killed for

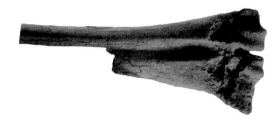

Fig. 7.6 Cattle metatarsal (probably castrate) with side growth resulting from prolonged stress on back legs due to traction, Ashville

meat or castrated at an early age. The remaining animals were kept for milk, breeding or traction and died at over 4-5 years. The pathology of foot bones suggested the use of some animals for traction (Fig. 7.6). For example, a metatarsal from a probable castrate showed a marked lateral extension of bone deposition on the distal articulation surface (Wilson 1978, 118). This probably resulted from prolonged stress on the back legs as occurs when an animal is used for draught purposes.

Pigs were the only domestic animal kept solely for the products of death – meat and perhaps leather and bristles. Most pigs were slaughtered before reaching full maturity, as might be expected with animals kept for meat.

The horses ranged from 2.5 to 12-18 years old. Although some horse bones showed signs of butchery, the raising of horses is not an efficient means of meat production and they were presumably used for riding or traction. Goat was present at Ashville and it is possible that they were grazed amongst other domestic animals to reduce the regeneration of thorn scrub. Dogs could have been used for protection and management of stock and possibly for sport, though if used for hunting, their prey does not seem to have contributed significantly to the diet.

The kill-off pattern of domestic animals suggests that flocks and herds retained their importance for secondary products. This became more pronounced in the early Roman period when there was an increase in the average age at death of most species. Epiphyseal fusion and tooth-wear data for sheep from the early Roman phase at Barton Court Farm were appropriate for a flock kept for wool production, although young sheep may have been killed and eaten away from the site (Wilson 1986).

Work on other sites in the Upper Thames Valley has revealed broadly similar patterns of animal husbandry, but with some variation in emphasis. For example, Gravelly Guy shows a much more even kill-off rate for both cattle and sheep. At Mingies Ditch fewer cattle were killed as very young animals but fewer survived to adulthood, while sheep, and more particularly pigs, were killed off earlier. The sheep at the similar site at Watkins Farm had a similarly strong peak of first year mortality, but then another at 3-4 years. At Yarnton cattle were killed off in much the same pattern as Ashville, but more sheep survived until their third year.

The large assemblages at Gravelly Guy and Yarnton have enabled the examination of trends through time on single sites. At Gravelly Guy cattle tended to be killed off later in the middle Iron Age and late Iron Age to early Roman period than in the early Iron Age. Sheep had a more marked peak in culling at six months to two years with another peak around 4-6 years, and this more obvious culling pattern intensified in the late Iron Age and early Roman period with peaks of culling at 6

months to 1 year and 2-3 years. Pigs were slaughtered at a distinctly younger age in the middle Iron Age than before. At Yarnton more cattle, more sheep and more pigs were slaughtered at a younger age in the middle Iron Age than before, but for cattle and sheep, though not pigs, this trend reversed in the late Iron Age and early Roman period.

All these trends suggest adjustments in animal husbandry practices to optimise the balance between production of meat and secondary products. The variations between sites and through time suggest that within a broadly similar overall pattern of husbandry detailed management of livestock was tailored to particular environmental conditions or economic or social requirements. The evidence of more systematic culling in the middle Iron Age, and to some extent, a clearer distinction between meat production and secondary products may indicate a more systematic approach to managing animals that reflects broader changes in social and economic structures and in how land was managed and farmed for subsistence or surplus.

Living herds

The number of bones of species such as those quoted above are useful to indicate broad trends, but it is difficult to determine the precise ratio between different domestic animals on a settlement because not all the animals kept on a site enter the archaeological record. Furthermore, there are usually biases in patterns of deposition, scavenging, disturbance and recovery that introduce a range of distortions. To some extent this is overcome by using measures such as the minimum number of individuals from which fragments are derived, but this too introduces other biases, as do measures based on bone weight.

It is even harder to determine live herd ratios between domestic species because as we have seen, different species were allowed to live to different ages. At Mingies Ditch, for example, horses were nearly four times as long-lived, on average, as sheep. This ratio must be taken into account to arrive at an idea of the living herd. While on average sheep were more numerous than horses in the live herd structure, a single horse would be equivalent to three or four generations of sheep. A ratio of 'beast years' represented by the bones of the main domestic animals at Mingies Ditch was obtained by multiplying the fragment totals of each species by the average age at death of the species (Allen and Robinson 1993, 143-4), giving an indicative live herd/flock structure of 10 cattle: 12 sheep/goat: 1 pig: 10 horses.

If such results are to be related to the area grazed by different species, it must be noted that cattle and horses have a food requirement at least four times greater per individual than sheep. Such considerations also apply to meat yield. Thus, at Mingies Ditch, although sheep bones outnumbered cattle bones, a greater area was probably grazed by cattle than by sheep and cattle would have contributed more meat to the diet than sheep. Even though horse bones are significantly less numerous than either cattle or sheep, making allowance for the extra longevity means that between a third and half of the available grazing for settlements like Mingies Ditch supported horses that were eventually eaten for food. This figure may have been much higher where horses were bred for external exchange, as is suspected for this and other sites in the Lower Windrush Valley. In terms of pasturage, therefore, the increase in horse bones in the middle Iron Age may have been more significant than the bare figures suggest.

Another approach to considering herd structure was explored at Gravelly Guy. Here it was possible to consider this within the context of a fully excavated mixed farming settlement where the extent of available land for arable and pastoral use could be estimated from the layout of the site in relation to contemporary neighbours, and the scale of crop growing and animal raising could be related to the estimated number of households in the settlement. While many assumptions underlay the model, it was suggested that the settlement might have had about 50 head of cattle 65 sheep, 15 pigs and 11 horses (Lambrick and Allen 2004, 484-8). In this case no allowance was made for 'beast years' but this may be less significant here. As noted above, the difference in kill-off patterns for sheep and cattle was less marked than for Mingies Ditch, with more cattle killed earlier and more sheep and pigs surviving longer (Mulville and Levitan 2004, 475-8, fig. 11.7). However, the proportion of horses in particular may be underestimated. Unlike some sites, including nearby Watkins Farm, whole or partial burials of horses were not included in the general species count (Mulville and Levitan 2004, 467, 477-8) and while young horses were present in the ordinary bone debris, adult horse bones were almost exclusively from 'special deposits', suggesting that they are not representative. Situated half way between the lower-lying enclosed settlements of Mingies Ditch and Watkins Farm, Gravelly Guy can perhaps be seen as one of a group of lower Windrush Valley sites engaged in horse breeding, and it seems likely that most adult horses in the living herd would have been bred for exchange, thereby not registering in the archaeological record.

In one sense this extra emphasis on horse rearing might be seen as having exacerbated pressure on the availability of grazing land, but equally, and perhaps more convincingly, it could indicate that the farming economy had shifted from simple subsistence to providing more produce for exchange. At Gravelly Guy the modelling of land use relative to the size and structure of the settlement suggested that it should have been easily capable of producing a surplus, probably with room to spare for more horses (Lambrick and Allen 2004, 484-8).

Animal husbandry in the Upper Thames Valley from a wider perspective

Hambleton (1999) carried out a review of Iron Age animal bone data on regional basis, including a sample of Upper Thames Valley sites consisting of Ashville, Farmoor, Mingies Ditch, Watkins Farm, Barton Court, Claydon Pike and The Ditches. Since then a large number of other assemblages have been analysed and reported and Dr Hambleton has recently undertaken a new review of data across southern England covering the same period as this book, which may elaborate on her principal conclusions and go further than the review presented here. Her original observations about Iron Age animal husbandry in the Upper Thames Valley as compared with Wessex (Hambleton 1999, 88-9) may be summarised as follows:

- There is no evidence of increased numbers of sheep during the Iron Age such as occurs in Wessex, but, except for The Ditches outlier, the two regions otherwise display broadly similar species proportions and mortality patterns

- Culling age of cattle varies within the region, with intense culls at different stages but all are prime meat bearing ages. There are some differences in sheep mortality in the 2-6 month range; and there is low variability in pig culling, all aimed at meat production.

- Evidence of the role of sheep is similar to Wessex – well suited to better drained land (gravels/chalk); perhaps integrated with arable (stubble grazing and manuring), with more sheep through time in Wessex possibly associated with increased arable. Split mortality at stage C yearlings indicates some were kept to maturity for secondary products, others more often killed off for meat. In Wessex similarities to the Bronze Age pattern may indicate survival of a pattern established earlier.

- The higher proportion of cattle and differences in their management from Wessex sites may mean that cattle were more important in the Upper Thames Valley than in Wessex, despite the role of sheep being much the same.

- Different mortality rates for cattle between Wessex and Upper Thames Valley suggest that in the Thames Valley cattle were mainly raised for meat with a small number kept to old age for milk, traction and manure. This strategy could be achieved by maintaining reasonably large herds to sustain high levels of sub-adult mortality and still retain viable herd structure, in keeping with high proportions of cattle. In Wessex lower proportions of cattle and older mortality show that higher proportions of older animals were needed to maintain the reproductive potential of small herds.

- The similar strategy for sheep and pigs, but raising of more cattle for meat, may reflect a pattern of husbandry more suited to the river valley (more water but also danger of liver fluke disease on the valley floor) than upland chalk.

- It was not possible to demonstrate from the bones Lambrick's (1992) suggestion of an intensification of pastoral farming during the Iron Age in the Upper Thames region, but in general data was insufficient to prove intra-regional variations.

Hambleton's conclusion was that the different strategy for cattle husbandry argues against Cunliffe's (1991) view that Wessex and the Upper Thames Valley had essentially the same pattern of pastoral farming. The evidence reviewed above may reinforce this conclusion, but a more considered opinion must await Dr Hambleton's updated analysis of late prehistoric animal husbandry in southern England.

The physical management of herds

Many enclosures and pen-like features display little evidence of domestic activity. One of their principal roles may have been to corral, subdivide and manage herds and individual animals for a variety of purposes, ranging from protection of animal wealth to specific roles in animal husbandry. Yates (1997; 1999) has suggested that some riverside enclosures known from cropmarks might be middle to late Bronze Age community stockyards on the model proposed by Pryor (1996), but none of these has been investigated properly and the only two where salvage observation took place (Bishop's Court, Dorchester and Field Farm, Burghfield) no evidence was found to support this. The idea of such stockyards is not unreasonable, but depends on specific models of social organisation and herd management in the Fens that do not necessarily transpose to other areas and are not easy to prove archaeologically. At Perry Oaks/T5 some areas might have acted as communal or farm stockyards rather than ordinary fields, but the idea is not generally favoured (Framework Archaeology 2006, 152-4). Although subsequent work for the Terminal 5 development has defined a central D-shaped enclosure which in layout is of a different character to other parts of the field system, there were no obvious facilities for herding large numbers of animals into it or out of it (rather than round it), and although there were numerous wells and water-holes within it these could have been more to do with settlement than the watering of large herds.

The idea of large enclosed sites acting as communal refuges or gathering places for animals has also been put forward for the Iron Age, both in the context of fortified and smaller enclosed sites. Most fortified sites in the Thames Valley region have not produced evidence of the large scale grain storage or intensive domestic occupation that

characterises 'developed' hillforts in Wessex (Cunliffe and Poole 1991a, b). Nonetheless, they could have been connected with communal protection of animals, which would have been important both in terms of family wealth and exchange patterns, while also being significant for social, cultural and religious reasons, as suggested for Segsbury (Lock *et al.* 2005). At the level of individual farms, there are several instances of enclosures that have little or no domestic occupation that may have acted as stock enclosures, such as some along the A419/A417 road scheme (Mudd *et al.* 1999).

More unusual is an oval palisaded enclosure, possibly of early Iron Age date, that may have been connected with animal rearing at Horcott Pit (Fig. 7.7; Lamdin-Whymark *et al.* forthcoming). It had two narrow opposing entrances marked by large double posts like a house porch. The palisade contained virtually no evidence of internal domestic activity and was undated but for predating an early to middle Iron Age ditch and a few postholes containing possibly late Bronze Age/early Iron Age pottery. A small group of early Iron Age round-houses was found nearby. It might have been a corral but if so, its entrances were hardly wide enough for a small cow or horse to be led through, and lacking any hint of funnel structure, they would have been unsuitable for herding beasts unless moveable hurdles were used. If it was used in animal rearing, a connection with training horses or draught oxen is perhaps plausible.

A good example of specific provision for corralling animals is the outer enclosure at Mingies Ditch where there was direct evidence of animal trampling within the enclosed space surrounding the inner domestic living area, and provision had been made to allow animals direct access to a local stream for water (Fig. 7.8; Allen and Robinson 1993, 35-6, figs 8-10, Pl. 11).

As we have seen in discussing the form of Iron Age fields, some layouts suggest specific provision for the management and movement of animals, including trackways and funnelled entrances. In a few cases this includes gaps in boundaries associated with gateways and pens, as in later Bronze Age field systems at Perry Oaks/T5 (Fig. 7.8; Framework Archaeology 2006, 153 fig. 3.39) and middle Iron Age land divisions at Latton Lands (Fig. 7.8; Powell *et al.* forthcoming) and Bicester Slade Farm (Ellis *et al.* 2000, 262).

At Yarnton fences were used to divide a water-filled palaeochannel, possibly to control access to water by animals grazing different land parcels either side of the boundaries in a manner still common in shallow streams and lake margins.

Pens and structures within Iron Age settlements provide other hints of animal management. Asymmetrical entrances of different widths may have facilitated dividing and managing of groups of animals or separating individual beasts. Small enclosures with asymmetrical entrances were a characteristic form of middle Iron Age enclosure at

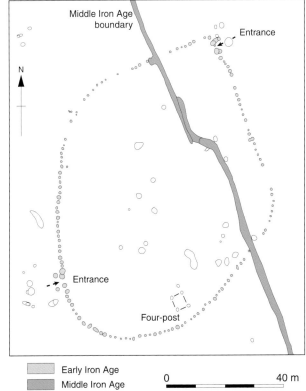

Middle Iron Age boundary

Entrance

N

Entrance

Four-post

Early Iron Age
Middle Iron Age

0   40 m

Fig. 7.7   Facilities for the management of animals: palisaded corral at Horcott Pit

Various post built buildings or structures might also have been used for housing or managing animals, such as some rectangular structures (see Chapter 5) or the enigmatic elongated building 6 at Mingies Ditch (Allen and Robinson 1993, 63-5). In general, however, there is no indication that animals were kept indoors in significant numbers.

Crops and their cultivation

Cereals

The cereal record for the Bronze Age prior to 1500 BC is very sparse. Results from large-scale flotation for charred plant remains at Yarnton in the Upper Thames Valley and Dorney in the Middle Thames Valley confirm the use of emmer wheat (*Triticum dicoccum*), free-threshing bread or rivet-type wheat (*Triticum* sp.) and hulled barley (*Hordeum* sp.), and in the case of Yarnton six-row hulled barley (*H. vulgare*), during the Neolithic (Robinson 2000c, 88). All these crops probably continued in use during the early Bronze Age. Barley and free-threshing wheat was identified from Bronze Age ring ditches at Ashville, Abingdon (Jones 1978), whereas a few indeterminate grains were the only cereal remains from early Bronze Age cremations at Barrow Hills, Radley (Moffett 1999). Other crops recorded from elsewhere in southern England during the early Bronze Age and likely to have been present in the region include naked barley (*Hordeum* sp.) and flax (*Linum usitatissimum*). However, it must be stressed that, even in comparison to the Neolithic, evidence for Bronze Age crops in the region prior to 1500 BC is very limited. With the exception of cremation deposits, the concentration of charred plant remains is usually so low that it is questionable whether they were

Gravelly Guy (Fig. 7.9; Lambrick and Allen 2004, 119-31), while at Mount Farm the spacing of gaps between a series of gully terminals suggests that they were laid out to accommodate different dispositions of standard sized hurdles for sorting animals in different ways using variable widths of opening (Lambrick forthcoming). It may be possible to discern comparable arrangements of asymmetrical entrances in other sites known from excavation or cropmarks (eg Lambrick and Robinson 1979, 23-4; Ellis *et al.* 2000, 262; Pine and Preston 2004; Framework Archaeology 2006 186-7, fig. 4.11).

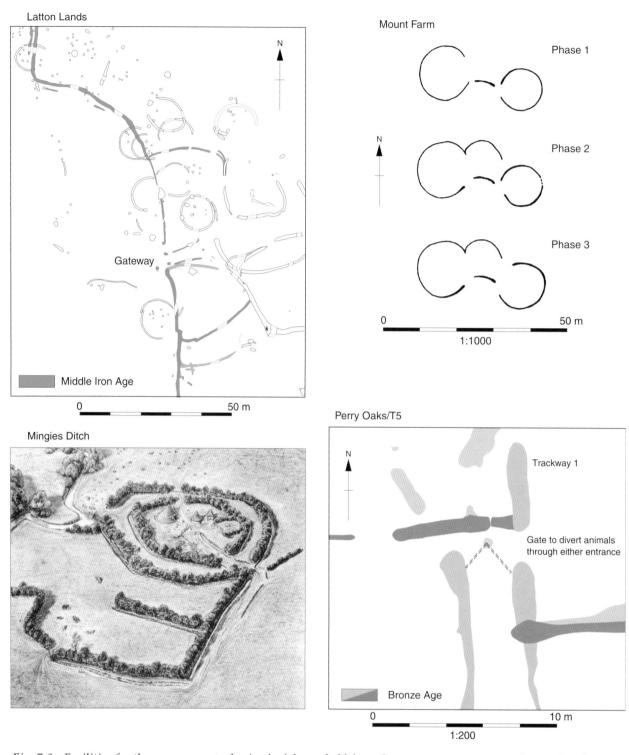

Fig. 7.8 Facilities for the management of animals: (above left) *boundary gateway structure at Latton Lands;* (below left) *enclosures and gateways at Mingies Ditch;* (above right) *drafting pens at Mount Farm;* (below right) *drafting gate arrangement at Perry Oaks/T5*

contemporaneous with the deposits or simply intrusive background presence from later activity.

Middle Bronze Age

Evidence becomes more plentiful in this period with more deposits in which crop remains are trapped, including ditches, pits, postholes and waterholes, but in most cases concentrations of remains are still extremely low.

In the Upper Thames Valley a waterhole at Eight Acre Field, Radley dated to 1680-1420 cal BC contained waterlogged glumes of emmer wheat (*Triticum dicoccum*). Both charred and waterlogged glumes of emmer along with a charred hulled grain

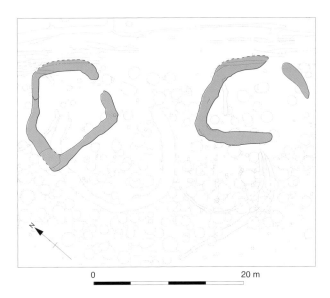

0   20 m

Fig. 7.9   Facilities for the management of animals: asymmetrical enclosures at Gravelly Guy

of *Hordeum* sp. (barley) were also found in a water-hole at Bradford's Brook with radiocarbon dates of 1740-1410 and 1440-1120 cal BC (Robinson 1995; Robinson 2006b).

Spelt wheat (*Triticum spelta*) makes its first appearance in the Upper Thames Valley during the middle Bronze Age. A carbonised grain of spelt from a well at Yarnton was dated to 1740-1410 cal BC (Robinson, unpublished) and a charred spelt glume came from a ceremonial ditch complex on the same site with a date range of 1630-1320 to 1420-1210 cal BC. Spelt wheat has recently been identified from a second middle Bronze Age site in the Upper Thames Valley, Appleford Sidings, where it was associated with emmer, six-row hulled barley and flax (Robinson, unpublished).

Similar evidence is emerging for the agricultural economy of the Middle Thames Valley. Charred plant remains were recovered from a middle Bronze Age settlement on the floodplain gravel at Weir Bank Stud Farm, Bray (Clapham 1995), many of the samples from postholes of a roundhouse associated with a field system. The main cereal crops identified were emmer, spelt wheat and hulled barley along with a few grains of *Secale cereale* (rye). While it is possible that the rye was growing as a weed at Weir Bank Stud Farm, this very early record demonstrates its presence in the region during the middle Bronze Age. Waterlogged spikelets of emmer and spelt wheat were present in waterholes set amidst small rectangular fields dated to around 1325 cal BC at Perry Oaks/T5 (Carruthers in Framework Archaeology 2006). Spelt wheat has also been recovered from the middle Bronze Age enclosures at Dorney.

Late Bronze Age

All the cereal crops recorded for the middle Bronze Age, six-row hulled barley and emmer with some

spelt wheat, remained in cultivation, again in the Middle Thames Valley including rye (*Secale cereale*), which has been identified from midden deposits in a palaeochannel of the Thames at Runnymede, dated to around 900 cal BC. It was found in sufficient quantity to suggest it was a crop in its own right, though not as abundant as the other cereals (Greig 1991).

The ratios of the numbers of charred grains of different cereals do not give a direct indication of the area under cultivation for the respective crops, but results from sites such as Whitecross Farm (Robinson 2006a, 118) suggest that both hulled wheat (emmer and spelt) and six-row hulled barley were the major crops. This seems consistently the case at other sites in the Upper Thames Valley, though some like Yarnton and Shorncote produced only very low levels of charred crop remains.

In the Middle Thames Valley only small quantities of charred cereal remains were found on two 11th-9th century BC settlements at Prospect Park on the floodplain of the Colne and at Hurst Park, East Molesey (Hinton in Andrews and Crockett 1996, 143-7, 95-9). Hulled six-row barley and hulled wheat, probably both emmer and spelt, were the main crops. A bread type wheat at Prospect Park may be intrusive from Saxon activity on the site. Cereal grains at Hurst Park were outnumbered by hazelnut shell fragments. Much larger quantities of charred cereal remains came from a 10th century BC roundhouse on the gravel terrace at Taplow (Robinson, unpublished). Wheat predominated with both emmer and spelt well represented.

The Lower Kennet Valley near its confluence with the Thames seems to have been a centre of agricultural activity. The late Bronze Age settlement on the First Terrace of the Kennet investigated at Reading Business Park/Green Park (Moore and Jennings 1992; Brossler *et al.* 2004) related to and partly extended over a ditched field system. Carbonised remains were dominated by cereals with six-row hulled barley, emmer and spelt. Aldermaston Wharf, Berkshire also produced a large amount of emmer and six-row hulled barley (Robinson 1992, 54).

In general, emmer and spelt wheat remains tend to occur together in late Bronze Age samples and no large pure assemblages of either type have been found. It is possible that they were being grown together as a mixed crop or 'maslin', not in the sense of one in which pure components were mixed prior to planting, but rather one in which the product of the mixed harvest was re-sown.

Early Iron Age

In the Upper Thames Valley charred crop remains generally occur more commonly and sometimes in greater abundance in the early Iron Age than was the case in the later Bronze Age, but this is not universally the case. There was apparently some variability in the degree of involvement of settlements with arable production and crop processing.

By the early Iron Age the main cereal crops had been reduced to spelt wheat (*Triticum spelta*) and six-row hulled barley (hulled *Hordeum vulgare*). Emmer wheat (*Triticum dicoccum*) had declined in importance to such an extent that, although present, it was probably not a crop in its own right. If maslins were typical of the later Bronze Age, emmer may have declined as a component of mixed crops either by deliberate choice or more likely as a result of other changes in husbandry, possibly related to increased autumn sowing (see below).

In rare cases almost pure prime grain was charred after it had been fully prepared for use, possibly because it had been burnt as a result of spoilage due to poor storage (eg infected by fungus) or as a result of domestic accidents. At Gravelly Guy over 18,000 charred grains of pure hulled barley were found, possibly the result of an accident in the parching needed to remove the 'hull' for consumption (Moffat 2004, 438). The fact that this assemblage was pure barley rather than a mixture of barley and wheat suggests the growing of monocrops rather than maslins. This could imply increased specialisation, higher yields and various advantages in cultivation and harvesting, but also more risk of serious crop failure.

In the Middle Thames Valley emmer, spelt, rye and six-row hulled barley were present in small quantities in late Bronze Age to early Iron Age samples from Thorpe Lea Nurseries, Egham (Robinson, unpublished). A single barley rachis and some unidentified cereal grain came from a settlement of the 7th century BC at Dunston Park, Thatcham in the Kennet Valley (Clapham in Barnes *et al.* 1995, 84-5). However, large quantities of charred spelt glumes along with a few possible emmer glumes, grain, including six-row hulled barley, and wheat were found in early Iron Age features at Wickhhams Field, near Reading (Scaife 1996).

Middle Iron Age

The arable economy in both the Upper and Middle Thames Valley continued to be based on the cultivation of spelt wheat and six-row hulled barley, although the evidence from the Upper Thames is again most abundant. Traces of emmer wheat (*Triticum dicoccum*) continue to be found in middle Iron Age assemblages of charred cereal remains but they only occur as a very small proportion in assemblages dominated by spelt wheat, so it is possible that emmer was merely a contaminant in the spelt crop. Bread-type wheat (*Triticum aestivum* – the name *T. aestivocompactum* was formerly used by archaeobotanists) may also have been present but some grains attributed to bread wheat were short grains of spelt, while the tough rachis segments identified as bread wheat could have been basal segments of spelt. It is also possible that there were occasional mutations of spelt giving rise to plants with free-threshing ears. A few rachis nodes of rye (*Secale cereale*)

were found at Mingies Ditch (Jones 1993). Oats (*Avena* sp.) is also commonly present in low numbers, but there is no evidence that it was cultivated as a crop rather than a wild species (either *Avena fatua* or *A. sterilis* spp. *ludoviciana*) growing as a weed.

A morphological study of rachis segments of Iron Age barley at Ashville, Abingdon found them to have been very variable (Jones 1978), showing that the plants grown ranged from very dense-eared to lax-eared. The genetic variability in the barley suggested by the morphology implies that there was also variability between the individual plants in the conditions required for their optimal growth and their range of environmental tolerances. Thus the barley could cope with a range of soil and weather conditions with at least some plants giving a good yield. This is in contrast to modern cereal crops bred for genetic uniformity to achieve maximum yield under known conditions created by the farmer.

The Iron Age agricultural economy of Britain showed strong regional variations in cereal crops (eg van der Veen 1992). Spelt wheat and six-row hulled barley predominated throughout most of southern England and the Midlands (Fig 7.10). In the extreme south-west wheat was less important and in East Surrey and Kent emmer wheat had remained a major crop since the Bronze Age, grown alongside spelt and barley. There is also variation in the concentrations of cereal remains found on settlement sites. More cereals occur on Upper Thames Valley sites, excluding the floodplain, than on sites in the Middle Thames Valley but not as much as on settlements on the Hampshire Chalk. In contrast, although cereals were used in the Bedfordshire Ouse Valley, concentrations are very low and occur in company with wild food plant remains, producing assemblages that resemble Neolithic charred assemblages from the Thames Valley (Robinson, unpublished).

Fig. 7.10   Middle Iron Age crops from Mingies Ditch: (left) *carbonised grains and rachis of six-row hulled barley (*Hordeum vulgare*) and* (right) *grains and glumes of spelt wheat (*Triticum spelta*)*

Late Iron Age

All the main cereal crops that were farmed in the middle Iron Age continued to be exploited in the late Iron Age, principally spelt wheat and six-row hulled barley. Free-threshing bread-type wheat is occasionally present in very small quantities, but on most sites it need have been no more than a minor weed of other cereal crops. Better evidence that bread-type wheat (*Triticum aestivum*) was a minor crop comes from Barton Court Farm where both grain (named as *T. aestivocompactum*) and chaff were identified (Jones 1986). Jones placed a much greater emphasis on the importance of the cultivation of bread wheat in the late Iron Age and into the Roman period, suggesting it could have been linked to increased manuring. However, his evidence was largely based on evidence from Bierton in Buckinghamshire where there was also a significant Saxon settlement, raising the possibility of intrusive material (bread wheat was the main wheat of the Saxon period). Recent work in the Upper Thames Valley has not substantiated any significant cultivation of bread wheat at this period. Grains and chaff of emmer wheat (*Triticum dicoccum*) occur more frequently in late Iron Age and early Roman deposits than middle Iron Age charred assemblages. It is possible that it was once again being grown as a crop in its own right, but as it has only been found as a small component of mixed assemblages, it need have been no more than a volunteer in spelt crops. Oats (*Avena* sp.) is somewhat more likely to have been a crop during the late Iron Age than in the middle Iron Age but most early Roman examples are likely to have been wild oats.

Other Crops

Middle to Late Bronze Age

A feature of the middle to late Bronze Age is the emergence of flax (*Linum usitatissimum*) as a crop. A large quantity of flax seeds were found in postholes around the entrance of a roundhouse at Weir Bank Stud Farm in the Middle Thames Valley (Clapham in Barnes and Cleal 1995, 35-7). Whereas the charred cereal remains, which included much chaff, probably derived from crop processing, the flax seeds were probably accidentally carbonised as the result of a fire that burnt down the house. Charred fragments of hazelnut shells were abundant at the site, showing that wild food plants were still being exploited. Middle Bronze Age flax pollen was identified at Green Park (Scaife in Brossler *et al.* 2004). A waterhole at Dorney dated to 1410-1120 cal BC produced remains of opium poppy (*Papaver somniferum*), which may have been grown as a crop for seeds or oil, if not as a drug.

In the Upper Thames Valley a single seed of flax was present in a waterhole at Eight Acre Field, Radley, dated to 1680-1420 cal BC and a seed was also found in a waterhole at Appleford (Robinson in Booth *et al.* forthcoming). Waterlogged flax seeds radiocarbon dated to 1370-790 cal BC were found in the bottom of a pit at Yarnton on the Thames floodplain. Waterlogged seeds of opium poppy were quite well represented in a waterhole at Bradford's Brook, radiocarbon dated to 1740-1410 and 1440-1120 cal BC.

Late Bronze Age

At Reading Business Park, where significant quantities of waterlogged flax capsules and some seeds were found in a row of pits, it is likely that flax was a major crop in addition to cereals (Campbell in Moore and Jennings 1992). There is a strong contrast between the carbonised and waterlogged crop remains from this site. While cereals dominated the charred plant assemblages, flax remains were abundant in some waterlogged deposits but there were few waterlogged cereal remains. Flax was probably being threshed at Reading Business Park, the bundles of dry flax plants beaten or combed (rippled), to remove and break up the seed capsules, releasing the edible oily seeds. Some of the pits and waterholes that produced flax debris may have been used for retting (soaking bundles of flax stems to free the fibres) for the production of linen (Moore and Jennings 1992), but no stems or fibres were found to confirm this.

Seeds of *Papaver somniferum* (opium poppy) have been noted in other Bronze Age contexts including the Wilsford Shaft (Robinson 1989, 83), but they were sufficiently abundant (203 seeds) in one sample from Whitecross Farm, Wallingford to suggest that it was being cultivated for its oily seeds (Robinson 2006a, 139).

There is also evidence from the late Bronze Age onwards of field or Celtic bean (*Vicia faba*) cultivation, with a single charred seed from Reading Business Park (Campbell 1992, 106). Seeds of brassicas (wild turnip, mustard etc.) occasionally occur in later Bronze Age samples but not sufficiently abundantly to suggest that they were deliberately grown.

Early Iron Age

While there have been many finds of flax from late Bronze Age contexts in both regions, it seems to disappear from the archaeological record with the start of the Iron Age. Although this could in part be a result of fewer early Iron Age waterlogged deposits being discovered on settlements, it may also be a genuine shift in preferences related to sources of oil and fibre.

The trend coincides with a change of emphasis in animal husbandry from cattle to sheep accompanied by greater interest in secondary products, which would have included wool (see above). Flax may well have been grown for its fibres as well as its oil-rich seeds, and if so there are several good reasons why wool might have taken over as the principal if not exclusive source of textile fibres, while animal fats and lanolin may also have been a more convenient source of oils. Flax is not just a crop that needs cultivation, sowing, tending, weeding and harvesting, but also relatively fertile soils (which may have meant manuring) and involves a particularly obnoxious retting process to extract the fibres before they can be cleaned and prepared for spinning. Wool by contrast naturally grows yearly on animals that are also much valued for dairy products while they are alive, and for meat and many other useful by-products from the carcass when they are dead.

Middle Iron Age

Despite large samples of carbonised seeds and many more waterlogged deposits having been analysed than for the early Iron Age, there is still only slight evidence for non-cereal crops in the middle Iron Age. Flax has not yet been found in the many middle Iron Age waterlogged deposits investigated, and although seeds of opium poppy (*Papaver somniferum*) have been found in very small quantities on several sites, it may only have been growing as a weed.

Pulses present a problem of interpretation. These crops tend to be under-represented in the charred record because fire need not be part of their processing prior to cooking and their seeds are not readily preserved by waterlogging. A single seed of field or celtic bean (*Vicia faba* v. *minor*) was present in a middle Iron Age deposit at Gravelly Guy, but it was not recorded at Yarnton or Ashville. A seed of vetch or pea was recovered at Coxwell Road Faringdon (Pelling in Cook *et al.* 2004, 268). As with the few later Bronze Age and early Iron Age finds, it is possible that both peas and beans were minor crops in the region during the Iron Age and into the Roman period.

Late Iron Age and early Roman

Flax continued to be absent from late Iron Age and early Roman sites in the region until after AD100. Peas and beans may well have been grown in the region during the late Iron Age and early Roman period, but their occurrence is again very low; for example a single carbonised seed of field or celtic bean was identified from the settlement at Yarnton in the Upper Thames Valley while three carbonised examples of *Pisum sativum* (pea) were identified from the early Roman settlement at Dorney in the Middle Thames Valley.

The Roman invasion of AD 43 had an immediate impact in terms of exotic food plants introduced with the Roman army. Waterlogged remains from the early sediments of the ditches of an auxiliary fortress annexe at Alchester were given a dendrochronological date of October AD 44 to March AD 45 for the felling of the timber used for its gateposts (Sauer 2001). A fragment of a seed of coriander (*Coriandrum sativum*) was found in a

deposit containing many fragments of cereal bran and a fragment of a seed of corn cockle (*Agrostemma githago*) (Robinson 2000b). Such material is characteristic of human sewage. Sediment trapped between the sieve and spout of a bronze wine strainer found in a waterlogged ditch contained 24 seeds of celery (*Apium graveolens*). Small quantities of charred cereal remains, including glumes of spelt wheat, were found in the annexe ditches, while a charred grain of common millet (*Panicum miliaceum*) came from the early silting of the outer ditch.

Coriander is a Mediterranean herb valued in the classical world for the flavour it imparts to cooked dishes. Celery is a plant of brackish marshes which has a wide distribution in Europe, including a few coastal marshes in Britain. Its seeds too were valued in classical cookery and it is unsurprising that food flavourings were imported by the army. However, celery seeds were also used to sweeten wine which had deteriorated, a likely reason for their presence in the wine strainer. Spelt wheat could have been obtained locally. Millet never seems to have been a crop in Iron Age or Roman Britain but it was grown in Northern Gaul. The occurrence of the millet and the grain weevil *Sitophilus granarius* suggests that grain was imported to Alchester from the continent, an insurance that a failure to obtain sufficient grain from the Britons did not jeopardise the invasion.

What is striking, although not surprising, about Alchester is the clear differences that did come with the Roman army, in some respects paralleled with the deliberate Roman acculturation at Silchester, and how strongly this contrasts with the continuance otherwise of Iron Age practices.

Cultivation and Harvesting

Direct evidence of cultivation in terms of digging or plough marks or even the equipment used for it is very sparse, but some indication of the soil conditions in which crops were grown, such as changes in fertility and drainage conditions, can be deduced from weed seeds associated with crop remains and occasionally from buried soils.

Much cultivation, especially in the middle to late Bronze Age, is believed to have been carried out on a horticultural scale with a variety of hand tools – picks, mattock/adzes, hoes, digging sticks, possibly breast ploughs and spades – many of these the same tools as those used for digging pits and ditches. It is perhaps less surprising, given subsequent cultivation and other landuse, that undisturbed soil horizons providing evidence of late prehistoric cultivation seldom survive in the Thames Valley. While some cultivated soils are sealed beneath later earthwork monuments, few reveal direct evidence of cultivation methods.

Fig. 7.11 (opposite) (above) *Artist's impression of prehistoric ard cultivation in the Middle Thames Valley;* (below left) *late Bronze Age wooden ard share from Eton Rowing Course;* (below right) *middle to late Iron Age iron ard share from Frilford*

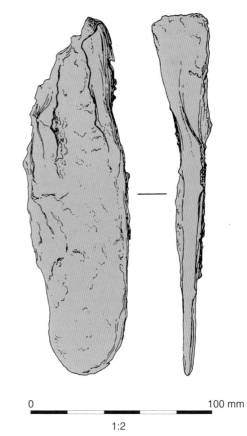

0   100 mm

1:2

It is argued above that initially crops were probably still being grown on a small horticultural scale in many parts of the Thames Valley, perhaps even when extensive fields were laid out for managing pasture. Such plots would have been small and perhaps cultivated with hand tools, but as yet there is no direct evidence of toolmarks below a contemporary cultivation soil. By the time cereal production was beginning to expand to field-scale cultivation, methods of hand cultivation would have been inadequate. As we have seen, this expansion probably happened at different times in different parts of the Thames Valley, but large-scale cereal cultivation had certainly become well established in some areas by the early Iron Age, and probably the late Bronze Age in some places. The main tool used to plough whole fields would have been the ard, sometimes equipped with an iron shoe to protect the point from rapid wear. Peter Reynolds (1981) has argued that in most cases parallel or crosscutting ardmarks found beneath ploughsoils result from initial sod-busting rather than regular cultivation, which would generally be confined to the already disturbed soil

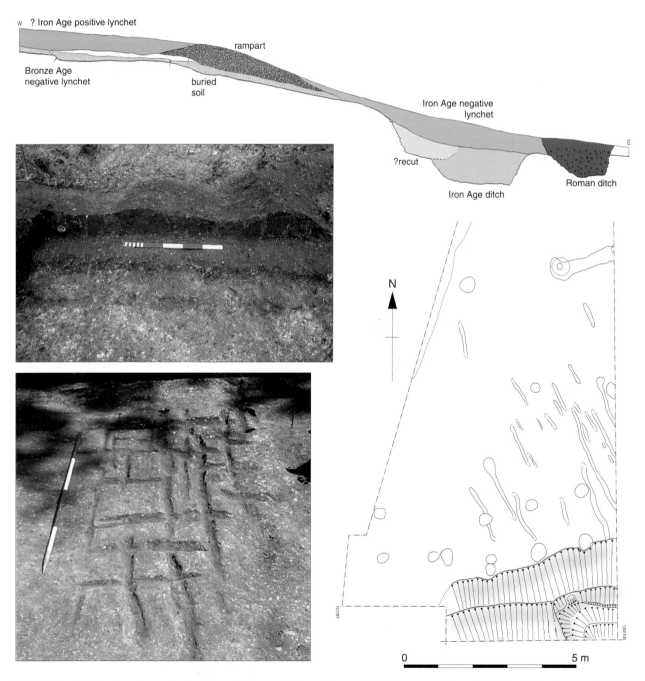

Fig. 7.12 *Cultivation traces in the Upper Thames Valley:* (above) *Section across Rams Hill lynchets;* (centre left); *cord rig below Grims Ditch;* (below left) *ardmarks in the tail of Grims Ditch;* (right) *ardmarks at Segsbury*

horizon and would be obliterated by repeated cultivation.

A group of irregularly spaced parallel ardmarks found beneath the terminal of the rampart at Segsbury Camp on the Berkshire Downs interpreted as the result of initial ground-breaking may have been associated with site clearance for the fort rather than pre-existing fields (Fig. 7.12; Gosden and Lock 1998, 60, fig. 13). Although there was evidence of plough lynchets sealed beneath the Iron Age rampart at Rams Hill these were not associated with ardmarks (Fig. 7.12; Bradley and Ellison 1975). Possible ardmarks have been noted at Alfred's Castle but were not sufficiently coherent or datable to be interpreted (Gosden and Lock 2001, 83).

An unusual example of ardmarks surviving on a largely plough truncated site on the Thames gravels was found at Mount Farm. Here, the shallow earthworks left by an early to middle Bronze Age ring ditch and middle to late Bronze Age waterhole were ploughed in the early Iron Age, filling the hollows that had hitherto been naturally silting up. Parallel ardmarks were also found below an Iron Age ploughsoil on the eroded inner lip of the ring ditch (Lambrick 1978; forthcoming).

The most impressive sequence of ploughsoils and ardmarks in the Thames Valley was found beneath the bank of the South Oxfordshire Grims Ditch on the eastern bank of the river at Mongewell (Cromarty *et al.* 2006, 162-72). At the base of the sequence was a small patch of cross-ploughed ardmarks regularly spaced and oriented at right angles to each other. The date of this episode is uncertain (and could be earlier prehistoric) but the overlying ploughsoil was cut by a series of postholes of three possible structures reflecting probable late Bronze Age domestic activity. The soil was disturbed by later tree-throw holes. These need not all be contemporary and one was cut by one of the postholes, suggesting partial reversion to tree cover prior to the settlement.

At a later stage the area reverted to cultivation before the South Oxfordshire Grims Ditch was constructed in the late Iron Age (Fig. 7.12). This took the form of 'cord-rig' cultivation consisting of narrow parallel ridges and furrows about 1 m apart, traces of which were found over a distance of over 40 m beneath the bank of the Grims Ditch.

Cord-rig is a well recognised feature of northern England and Scotland (Topping 1989) but has only rarely been found in southern Britain (Entwistle *et al.* 1994; Russell 1989). There is some debate as to whether such ridges were created by ploughing (which would be possible with a winged ard) or spade dug. The extent and other characteristics of the northern examples of cord-rig led Topping to conclude that they were probably created by ploughing connected with increased cereal production in a wetter climate. This need not apply at Mongewell, but it is clear that this was an area of cultivation at least 50 m across and possibly very much larger.

At about the same level as the cord-rig, and cutting the same soil horizon were further patches of crosscutting ardmarks. The stratigraphy is difficult to interpret and it appears that these may have been made both at the time and after construction of the bank of Grims Ditch as some of the ardmarks contained chalky material not derived from the underlying soils.

This succession of cultivation episodes interstratified with domestic occupation and other activities reflects several episodes of cultivation spread over several hundred years. It is not possible to tell how long each episode lasted, or to what extent they obliterated intervening episodes of cultivation, but they illustrate the use of different methods of cultivation, possibly related to growing different crops.

Archaeobotanical Evidence of Cultivation Practices

The weed seeds identified amongst charred crop processing remains give an indication of the ecological conditions of arable fields on the gravel terraces. A pioneering study by Jones (1978) of the charred plant remains from Ashville Trading Estate, Abingdon demonstrated how a mature arable weed flora grew amongst the Iron Age cereal crops in the fields of the Iron Age settlement. They included species such as chickweed (*Stellaria media* gp.), orache (*Atriplex* sp.), vetches and tares (*Vicia* or *Lathyrus* sp.), black bindweed (*Fallopia convolvulus*), dock (*Rumex* sp.) and corn gromwell (*Lithospermum arvense*). The occurrence of small quantities of seeds of grassland plants such as red clover (*Trifolium pratense*) could have been due to ploughing grassland for arable, episodes of fallow in which grassland plants became established or because scratch plough cultivation with an ard would have been less effective in destroying perennial weeds than mould board ploughing was in later times.

Some of the samples contained seeds of spike rush (*Eleocharis palustris* or *uniglumis*) and other marsh plants, suggesting that the cultivated area at Ashville extended beyond the edge of the terrace, perhaps onto the clay slope where there could have been wet areas resulting from a spring line. Spike rush is no longer considered an arable weed (indeed its presence amongst a crop would now be very unusual) but it regularly occurs in charred seed assemblages, suggesting suitable conditions for this plant in or on the edge of cultivated fields. Other weed species are indicative of light, well-drained soils, as might be expected on the higher gravel terraces, limestone and sands of the Thames Valley. There was also an element of the late prehistoric flora of charred seeds characteristic of light acidic soils, including sheep's sorrel (*Rumex acetosella* agg.), but which also occurs on the circumneutral soils of the gravel terrace.

A key result of Jones' work at Ashville was the detection of changes in the proportion of some key weed species during the Iron Age which he interpreted as indicative of changes in methods of arable husbandry and/or areas and soils under cultivation.

Recent work by Stevens (2003) has re-examined several of the issues and others have also commented on trends.

Campbell and Hamilton (2000) have argued that autumn sowing would have been the norm in prehistoric times and that spring sowing is a late Iron Age development. However, the evidence from the Thames Valley is mixed. There are a number of indications from weed seeds associated with charred plant remains or arable crops that both autumn and spring sowing was practised to varying extents.

Middle Bronze Age assemblages of charred weed seeds from crop processing are small but they include goosegrass or cleavers (*Galium aparine*) which tends to germinate in autumn and winter but not after the preparation of spring seed beds. This species remains a consistent, though generally not very common, component of arable weed assemblages throughout the Iron Age into the Roman period, making it likely that at least some crops were autumn-sown. Trends are difficult to determine – for example at Ashville and to a lesser extent Mount Farm and perhaps Coxwell Road goosegrass tended to occur less frequently with time, but at Gravelly Guy it became more common, especially in late Iron Age and Roman samples. Stevens suggests that autumn or spring sowing may be reflected in how seasonal fluctuations in soil nitrogen related to the abundance of these species of Chenopodiceae that require relatively high levels of soil nitrogen and Leguminosae that do not (Stevens in Hey *et al.* forthcoming), but the relative abundance of Chenopodiceae and Leguminosae is usually considered to be connected to longer term changes in soil fertility.

The transition from both emmer and spelt as important wheat crops in the late Bronze Age to spelt as the only major wheat in the early Iron Age is striking, and may relate to an increase in autumn sowing. Archaeologists formerly believed that emmer was a spring sown crop of light soils whereas spelt was an autumn sown crop of heavier soils. This was based on the work of Percival (1921) on localities in Europe and Anatolia where these wheats remained in use together with associated cultivation traditions. Subsequent cultivation experiments, including those of Mark Robinson, have shown that in Britain both wheats can be grown successfully from either autumn or spring sowings and that emmer can tolerate wet heavy soils. There is thus no intrinsic limitation in the viability of emmer as a crop to explain the switch to spelt. While deliberate choice is still a possible explanation, it is unclear why spelt would have been preferred over emmer. Both are hulled with similar de-husking requirements (their grains are tightly held in spikelets which need to be parched and pounded before they are released). Both provide straw suitable for thatching. However, if emmer and spelt were grown together and regarded as a single crop, another possible explanation is that changing practices of cultivation could have indirectly caused spelt to displace emmer. In cultivation experiments Robinson planted two plots with seed mixtures starting with equal mixtures of emmer and spelt. One plot was sown in autumn, the other the following spring. Each plot was then re-sown with grain in the species ratio that had been harvested from that plot and at the same time of year as previously planted. After five years, spelt wheat had almost entirely displaced emmer on the autumn sown plot and emmer had almost entirely displaced spelt on the spring-sown plot. This suggests that the decline of emmer at the end of the Bronze Age was the result of competition because more mixed wheat crops were being autumn sown.

This is not to say that some spelt wheat was not spring sown in the Iron Age, and there would have been advantages in maintaining some spring sowing. Despite the slightly higher yields of autumn sown cereals, sowing a significant part of the crop in the spring would have had the advantage of spreading risk and extending the harvest period because spring sown crops ripen a little later. The burden of cultivation would have been spread, and it would also have provided stubble grazing in the autumn and over the winter when floodplain pasture was wet. There would have been a greater opportunity to graze animals on land which was not going to be planted until spring, though this would not enhance its fertility unless the animals were grazed elsewhere by day and then driven to the fields to drop dung at night, as in the case of sheep-folding.

Changes in soil fertility may be reflected in the changing proportions of certain arable weeds. Leguminous species such as vetches and tares fix atmospheric nitrogen through a bacterial association in nodes on their roots and can therefore tolerate nitrogen poor soils, whereas some Chenopodiceae prefer nitrogen rich soils. At Ashville there was a steep rise in the presence of leguminous weeds from the early Iron Age through to the Roman period suggesting declining soil nitrogen levels (Jones 1978, 109), and Jones' analysis at Mount Farm shows that a similar increase in these weeds was matched by a decrease in the occurrence of Chenopodiceae (Lambrick forthcoming). At Gravelly Guy the proportion of leguminous weeds remained fairly static during the early to middle Iron Age before seeing a substantial rise in the late Iron Age and early Roman periods (Moffett 2004, 445). At Yarnton there was only a slight rise in leguminous weeds for the early to middle Iron Age and the Chenopodiceae also increased (Pelling and Stevens in Hey *et al.* forthcoming).

The ability to utilise atmospheric nitrogen gives legumes a selective advantage where soil nitrogen is low (Warrington 1924). On this basis the rise in leguminous weeds can be explained in terms of progressively diminishing soil nitrogen, until the process was reversed in the later Roman period. But as a general trend, Lambrick (1992) noted that the marked increase in leguminous weeds in the late Iron Age and early Roman period does not reflect the evidence of early Roman manuring, which ought to have slowed down or checked loss of fertility, and at Yarnton the model has also been questioned. Stevens (2003; Hey *et al.* forthcoming) observes that nitrogen is only one aspect of soil nutrient status. While legumes are good at competing on nitrogen-poor soils, they do not necessarily flourish on soils with generally low nutrient levels. He also cites evidence that nitrogen levels in soil do not change in an ever-diminishing manner but tend quickly to reach a natural base level. They moreover vary seasonally, being higher in the spring. The nitrogen-loving Chenopodiceae readily germinate in the spring, and Stevens therefore suggests that the changes in leguminous weeds and Chenopodiceae could reflect changes in spring or autumn sowing of crops.

The evidence for direct management of soil fertility is inconclusive. While Lambrick (1992) noted an apparent discrepancy between the supposed decline in late Iron Age and early Roman soil fertility and evidence of manuring from late Iron Age or early Roman pottery scatters, it is uncertain earlier on how far fields were manured with midden material from settlements because handmade prehistoric pottery does not survive well. Iron Age artefact scatters detected by field-walking at Yarnton, however, were likely to have been from manuring, suggesting that the practice was relatively widespread.

At Ashville it was noted that the rush *Elocharis palustris* substantially declined between the middle and late Iron Age and that a number of other damp ground taxa (*Carex* sp., *Mentha* sp. and *Montia fontana* Subsp. *chrondrosperma*) disappeared completely. A similar trend was noted at Mount Farm where, like Barton Court Farm and Abingdon Vineyard, damp ground species reappeared in the Roman period (Stevens 1996). At the Ashville site the changes in the occurrence of damp ground weeds were explained in terms of changing landscape organisation whereby arable fields and areas of unfavourably damp ground were somehow distanced from one another. In a more general consideration of crop production in the British Iron Age Jones (1981) suggested that this might have been connected with improvements in field drainage in the late Iron Age which kept pace with continuing arable expansion on more water reten-tive soils until at least the 3rd century AD, after which damp ground species occur in carbonised cereal assemblages. Subsequent work suggests a more variable picture. Evidence of Roman expan-sion of arable onto the floodplain in the form of ardmarks and/or ploughsoils containing pottery indicative of manuring has been found at Drayton and Yarnton (Lambrick 1992; Barclay *et al.* 2003; Hey *et al.* forthcoming), and at Yarnton this is accompa-nied by an increase in damp ground species. But at Gravelly Guy there was no evidence of changes in species indicative of damp ground. This is consis-tent with the evidence that early Iron Age organisa-tion of arable and pastureland around Stanton Harcourt remained unaltered until the 2nd century AD (Lambrick and Allen 2004).

Although there are finds of 'reaping hooks' or sickles which are likely to have been the main harvesting implements, more specific evidence comes from charred plant remains, in particular the seeds of arable weeds likely to have been incorpo-rated accidentally with the gathered crop or with straw. The latter could have been used for thatching and domestic objects such as mats and containers, but also animal bedding and, in the case of barley straw and associated weeds, fodder.

Charred plant assemblages typically do not include debris from the initial stage of threshing and winnowing which therefore seem mostly likely to have been carried out in the fields. Stevens (1996), however, highlights differences in proportions of larger and smaller weed seeds that suggest differ-ences in how grain was stored prior to de-husking. At sites like Yarnton some grain may have been stored above ground only partially threshed or even as sheaves rather than ears or spikelets. At Yarnton the common presence in most samples of clover (*Trifolium* sp) and the grass *Poa annua*, which grow to only 0.2-0.3 m high, was also taken to indicate harvesting low on the stalk. Stevens (1996) has suggested that the ubiquity of these species in carbonised plant assemblages may indicate that this was a common Iron Age practice in the region. At Gravelly Guy charred seeds of other low growing weeds like chickweed (*Stellaria media*), parsley piert (*Aphanes arvensis*), ivy-leaved speedwell (*Veronica hederafolia*), field madder (*Sherardia arvensis*) and cornsalad (*Valerianella dentata*) indicate that straw was cut low to the ground (Moffett in Lambrick and Allen 2004, 445). Although some samples appear to correspond closely to 'fine sievings' from the later stages of crop processing, others are more mixed and may have resulted from the incorporation of various sorts of waste into fires used for parching grain prior to dehusking, or from some batches of grain being stored more fully cleaned than others. Another possibility, raised by Reynolds (1995, 185) is that straw was harvested separately.

The evidence of change in the arable weed flora of the Upper Thames Valley and the ecological and taphonomic interpretation of changes in farming practice and settlement activity have become more complex as further sites have been investigated. Several lines of evidence that once seemed clear-cut are now less apparent and the picture is more complicated as it is realised that the varied environ-mental circumstances and access to land of each settlement may have influenced how and where crops were grown, and how far changes in soil conditions were precipitated or countered by local farming practice. However, it still seems valid to interpret some cereals as being autumn sown and at least some areas on the Upper Thames terraces appear to have experienced declining soil fertility during the Iron Age.

Woodland management and products

The main evidence for the exploitation of woody plants in the Bronze Age prior to 1500 BC comes from human cremation burials. Woodland species such as oak (*Quercus* sp.) and hazel (*Corylus avellana*) and species of thorn scrub were used as fuel. A high degree of selection was apparently exercised in the choice of wood for cremation (Thompson 1999). From the middle Bronze Age onwards the character of timbers that survive in river channels and waterholes provides clear evidence of careful management and possibly enclosure of woodland to produce the materials needed for construction, which may have much earlier origins. Charcoal from settlements indicates the resources being exploited for fuel, and there is also evidence for the exploitation of other heathland and woodland resources.

Structural timbers and other wood

At the Eton Rowing Course a series of timber bridges and other structures ranging in date from the middle Bronze Age to middle Iron Age was exposed, all built of oak uprights from straight-grown, probably coppiced, trees. None of the 150 plus straight oak uprights had more than 35-40 rings, so none could be dated by dendrochronology. The largest were four middle Bronze Age timbers *c* 0.5 m in diameter, the rest (mostly Iron Age) were generally 0.15-0.32 m in diameter. This pattern is repeated at Runnymede (Needham 1991, 83-105) and Whitecross Farm (Cromarty *et al.* 2006), and similar sized timber can also be inferred from the size of many postholes and post pipes at settlements and defensive sites. Massive timbers seem mostly to have been reserved for major structures like hillfort gateways.

There is plentiful waterlogged evidence from the Eton Rowing Course and elsewhere that hazel and other coppiced rods were used in hurdles, and larger oak timbers were used to make structures (Fig. 7.13). At the late Bronze Age site at Whitecross Farm the remains of a burnt structure were found in the shallow margin of the river channel next to the island. The structural timbers were all of oak, and almost all the straight-grown rods were coppiced hazel. This typical optimum use of the growth habits and strengths of these tree species had been practised since the Neolithic (Talyor *et al.* 2006). Remains of *in situ* Iron Age structural timbers are rare but include an oak doorpost from an Iron Age house at Mingies Ditch (Allen and Robinson 1993).

The occurrence of well grown straight coppice rods indicates careful management of woodland, probably including protection of young shoots from deer (Fig. 7.13). This does not necessarily imply enclosure of woodland in the style of medieval woodland management but there may have been a similar level of care taken to produce products

Fig. 7.13 Modern coppice woodland (left) *and ancient coppiced poles and rods in a hurdle from Eton Rowing Course* (right)

necessary for making everything from major structures to tools, household objects and ornaments. Whitecross Farm produced some evidence for woodland management: oak piles of the waterfront structure had grown rapidly under well-illuminated conditions, suggesting regeneration in woodland, which had been felled. There were detailed morphological characteristics of typical coppiced poles, such as a piece of oak with three stems and a long hazel rod with a curve at the base, both characteristic of rods cut from a coppice stool (Talyor *et al*. 2006).

The scale of woodland management, at least in local terms, would have been significant. Experimental reconstruction led Reynolds (1995, 200-1) to conclude that allowing for posts, poles and wattles, the products of about 12 coppiced trees would be needed to build a four-poster, 100 for a modest roundhouse and perhaps 200 for a large double post ring building. While many such structures would have lasted for years with only occasional repairs, fencing could have presented an even greater demand for woodland products, being much more susceptible to rotting, animal damage and periodic reorganisation. Reynolds suggested that this might have required the supply of coppice products from a few hundred trees for an ordinary farming settlement, though presumably this would depend on the extent to which stock-proof hedges were used rather than fences. Additionally there would have been a constant demand for firewood. Apart from managing trees to grow in forms to provide timber, poles, wattles and withies, it is also likely that natural bends and branches were selected to make objects such as ard stilts, where maximum practical strength would be ensured by the natural pattern of the grain. Young stems of hedgerow or woodland trees and bushes may have been deliberately bent to grow into desired shapes to achieve the same effect.

Reynolds observed that a hectare of coppice woodland can typically produce 12,000 wattles, but also that a single coppice stool might produce only three to seven good timbers, and these would have to grow for 30 or 40 years to achieve an appropriate size for structural use. Furthermore, only a proportion of trees in natural woodland would be oak, the species most favoured for use in buildings. It is likely that some sort of rotation or selective management was applied, so that in any one year a hectare might only produce between 30 and 100 decent timbers.

Allowing for all the needs for timber, wattling, fencing materials, equipment and firewood, even the smallest settlements would probably have needed access to a few hectares of woodland. However, supplies of straight-grown timber of a different order of magnitude would have been needed for large communal structures like the palisades and ramparts of timber built or timber laced fortifications and ones built on a corduroy of timbers such as at Burroway and Taplow. Charles Griffith calculated that the number of timbers required for the initial palisade and timber framed rampart phases of construction at Rams Hill (Bradley and Elison 1975, 225-8) would have been 2200 and 1020 posts respectively, not allowing for cross-members, though these could have been taken from the upper ends of the same coppice stems. The larger figure might have needed in the order of 350 to 700 trees. As it is unlikely that a hectare or more of woodland would have been clear-felled, planted or kept in strict rotation to create a stand of uniform 30 or 40 year old single species coppice, it would have been necessary to scour several hectares of managed woodland to provide sufficient trees to build Rams Hill.

Early Iron Age forts with timber frame and dump rampart construction tended to have less closely spaced timbers but more elaborate framing and much longer circuits than a simple palisade. Uffington had two rows of posts, the outer one spaced at *c* 1 m intervals, the inner one alternating small and larger posts at about 0.5 m intervals. Allowing for cross members, it was reckoned that the timber required was equivalent to a tree for every metre of the 700 m circuit (Miles *et al*. 2003, 96-8). The amount of timber required to build the rampart at Segsbury has not been calculated, but the structure seems to have been broadly similar to Uffington and with over double the length of circuit (1.5 km) may have had to be supplied from as many as 1,500 trees. If the timber corduroy beneath the probable timber framed rampart at Burroway was complete over the 600 m circuit, over 1800 timbers might have been needed just for the corduroy, and about 1200 trees needed altogether. Forts such as these would probably have required tens of hectares each of intensively managed woodland to supply the timber required for their construction.

To put this into perspective, however, even the most timber greedy construction projects could have been supplied by areas of woodland that in modern terms are large, but nonetheless smaller than some large ancient woods such as those at Appleton, Wytham, Bagley, Culham, Goring or Henley that overlook the Thames today.

In terms of labour, Griffiths calculated that the main timber rampart at Rams Hill would have involved 3604 man hours for the timber cutting and hauling alone, and the Uffington, Segsbury and Burroway figures are likely to have been correspondingly greater. Doubtless many people were deployed to undertake these tasks, but even for the more mundane daily and seasonal living of later prehistoric farmers, the gathering of fire wood, timber and other woodland produce, and grazing of pigs would have occupied a significant part of the working year, especially in the winter.

Evidence of the wood used to make hafts for tools and weapons and other objects is noted in Chapter 6, reinforcing the evidence for good working knowledge of the properties of wood from different species of trees for particular purposes.

Fuel and other uses of plants

In the middle to late Bronze Age woodland and scrub provided wood for fuel, with charcoal showing that in both the Upper and Middle Thames the main species collected were hawthorn, apple etc. (Pomoideae), sloe etc. (*Prunus* sp.), hazel (*Corylus avellana*) and oak (*Quercus* sp.). Charcoal from Iron Age sites in the region commonly includes the same range of species, sometimes with more oak (*Quercus* sp.), rather smaller quantities of hazel (*Corylus avellana*) and a range of other species. This suggests that both scrub or hedgerow and woodland were being exploited. For example, in the early Iron Age at Gravelly Guy Rowena Gale (2004) found that oak (*Quercus*) and plum or more likely sloe (*Prunus* sp.) predominated, with some hawthorn etc (Pomoideae indet.) and hazel, alder and willow. The oak probably derived from a woodland source but the high proportion of sloe could have resulted from scrub clearance as areas of rough grazing were being brought into more intensive agriculture. In the middle Iron Age at Gravelly Guy there was much less *Prunus* and more hazel and alder, with maple and ash also present, perhaps suggesting more reliance on woodland, riverside resources and mature hedgerows and less on scrub.

At Perry Oaks/T5 Challinor (2006) found that there was a significant change in the wood species exploited for fuel, with the use of oak in particular increasing from about 50% of fragments in the Bronze Age to 70% by the Iron Age, while field maple increased from 1% to 6% and pine appeared at 2%, again perhaps suggesting more reliance on woodland (and perhaps off-cuts from structural timber work) and less on scrub.

Charcoal from late Iron Age and early Roman sites suggest that both scrub or hedgerow and woodland were still exploited for fuel, with hawthorn, apple etc (Pomoideae), sloe etc (*Prunus* sp.), oak (*Quercus* sp.) and hazel (*Corylus avellana*) all commonly present. At both Gravelly Guy and Perry Oaks/T5 there was a trend towards fewer species and even more dominance of oak and other timber trees (accounting for 88% of the Roman charcoal at Perry Oaks).

There is evidence from both the Middle and Upper Thames Valley that heathland or acidic woodland resources were also exploited to provide bracken and other materials from at least the late Bronze Age onwards. The midden deposit in the palaeochannel at Runnymede contained much waterlogged bracken (*Pteridium aquilinum*) and bog moss (*Sphagnum* sp.) (Robinson 1991, 325). Almost half the waterlogged samples from the waterfront site at Whitecross Farm contained frond fragments of bracken (Robinson 2006a, 140), and most middle Iron Age settlements on the floodplain of the Upper Thames Valley such as Farmoor (Lambrick and Robinson 1979) preserve bracken fronds. Bracken was still imported to settlements in the late Iron Age, although perhaps on a smaller scale than in the

middle Iron Age. It is a plant of light acidic soils and would not have colonised the circumneutral soils of the Thames floodplain. The nearest likely sources, in most cases, were acidic sands on hillsides a few kilometres away. Bracken has a reputation for reducing attacks by biting insects and it is likely that it was brought in as bedding for humans or litter for animals. It might have been collected with other materials or at the same time as nearby woodland was being used for pannage.

Overview of the development of late prehistoric farming in the Thames Valley

The overall basis of the late prehistoric economy in the Thames Valley as elsewhere in southern Britain was mixed farming. This is very evident not only from animal bones and structural evidence but also from the basic management requirements of arable production which were heavily reliant on animals, not least as a key source of traction (Reynolds 1995). However, within this very broad basis there was significant variation in the balance between pastoralism and mixed farming, both chronologically and geographically. Low intensity residentially mobile pastoralism seems to be the basis from which later prehistoric sedentary mixed farms developed, and pastoralism seems to have remained a key general factor in how agricultural systems developed, alongside the growth of arable farming.

The period from the middle Bronze Age until the end of the Iron Age saw a transition on the Thames gravels from a landscape of perhaps lightly grazed rough pasture with some thorn scrub to a fully organised agricultural landscape. Prior to 1500 BC the area under cultivation was very small indeed, probably much less than 1% of the total area of gravel terrace and floodplain. By the end of the Iron Age perhaps as much as 20% – 30% of the gravel terraces were under cultivation in the Upper Thames Valley and that figure would have been even higher if much of the floodplain had not been experiencing seasonal inundation by this date. In the Middle Thames Valley the area under cultivation was almost certainly less, partly because soils on the gravel terraces were more vulnerable to acidification and nutrient depletion, but also due to wider socio-economic factors that will be examined in Chapter 10.

In the middle Bronze Age, the first signs of significant measures to increase agricultural production through physical division and enclosure of land are reflected in the creation of small, probably hedged, fields which were perhaps being farmed almost at an individual household level, but probably not on a permanently settled basis (see Chapters 3 and 4). These fields were used both for the cultivation of crops and the raising of domestic animals and the area beyond them was also used as rough grazing. By the beginning of the late Bronze Age some settlements were becoming more sedentary and more land may have been brought under careful management, although there was no shortage of rough pasture between settlements.

The late Bronze Age was perhaps the period of greatest agricultural productivity in the Middle Thames Valley. This was perhaps in part because the control of the bronze trade up the Thames enhanced the prosperity of the Middle Thames region, enabling a more rapid population growth (see Chapter 10). But the soils of the Middle Thames terraces were not as resilient to agricultural exploitation as the soils on the Upper Thames gravels, and they suffered deterioration at much the same time as other social and economic changes were to alter the region's economic and political influence.

Although the later Bronze Age is clearly the period when settled farming communities with extensive fields began to emerge in the Thames Valley, there were some places, sometimes adjacent to more fully farmed areas, where settlements and land management remained ephemeral, in many respects resembling their earlier prehistoric predecessors. This is especially true of the higher reaches of the Upper Thames Valley, but is also apparent for parts of the Middle Thames that were not characterised by extensive field systems.

From the early Iron Age onwards agricultural expansion associated with more permanently settled farms accelerated in the Upper Thames Valley and much of the remaining rough grazing between settlements was probably taken into controlled management before the end of the early Iron Age. As the population rose so there was an increasing emphasis on the use of domestic animals for secondary products before they were butchered for meat. It is likely that grazing land on the clay hinterland of the gravel terraces began to play an important part in the agricultural system but there was still much pasture on the gravels. While in the middle to late Bronze Age networks of small ditched fields represented the main areas of fully managed agricultural production, they became less relevant for larger scale (perhaps more communally based) management of land, and the small paddocks and enclosures that were created around some middle Iron Age settlements were perhaps used to keep domestic animals or to grow non-cereal crops. The main areas of cultivation and pasture on the gravel terraces were probably large blocks of land divided by unditched boundaries, fences, hedges and natural boundaries such as streams.

The attempted expansion of cultivation onto the floodplain of the Upper Thames Valley in the late Iron Age and the early Roman period, despite rising flood levels which made the floodplain unsuitable for arable, shows continued pressure to increase the area under cultivation. This was met in the Roman period by a reduction in grassland on the gravel terraces and probably increased cultivation of other geologies.

In the Middle Thames Valley the pattern of agricultural development in the Iron Age is very different on the gravels. There is little evidence of the emergence of permanently settled farms there before the middle Iron Age, and the small quantities of carbonised cereal remains indicate little significant growth in arable production. Stagnation, if not decline, may have been the norm, with the region ceasing to be economically important.

The trajectories of change in the development of farming between the two main sections of the Thames Valley were very different, with the Upper Thames taking over from the Middle Thames as the main area of development at around the end of the Bronze Age. But within this broad trend, there were many sub-regional variations in the character and pace of change, so that many key recurrent features of the development can be seen to have taken place at different times in different parts of the valley over periods of several centuries. The idea that there was a sudden middle Bronze Age 'agricultural revolution', as Yates (2001) claims, seems to be an exaggerated view of what was probably a much more complicated and diverse pattern of change.

We will return to some of the general factors that may have shaped this diversity of change in Chapter 10, but here it is worth having a closer look at some of the wider interpretative issues that this overview has touched upon.

Issues concerning the emergence of settled farming communities

Subsistence and surplus; intensification and specialisation?

The period from the middle Bronze Age to the late Iron Age is widely recognised as one in which there were major changes in agricultural production and the socio-economic systems that supported it. This is often referred to in terms of 'intensification,' in some instances leading to 'over-exploitation,' and reference is also often made to 'specialisation'.

Brück (2000, 276-80) has suggested that regarding the appearance of fields in the middle Bronze Age as evidence of 'intensification' is misleading, relying too much on unsubstantiated assumptions that imply more intensive cultivation regimes, and misinterpretation of evidence of colluviation as reflecting erosion due to over-exploitation. She pointed out that the appearance of fields does not imply intensification in the sense of increased productivity per person: 'social units may simply have produced the same amount from a smaller area of land', or, put another way, a growing population may have produced more from the same amount of land. She also suggests that it is anachronistic to see agricultural development in terms of economic maximisation and over-exploitation driven by primarily economic motives.

In relation to 'specialisation' there has been much debate about Jones' (1985) concept of differences between settlements as predominantly 'producers' or 'consumers' of arable produce (see below).

Hambleton (1999) has suggested that it is difficult to find any animal bone evidence to support seasonal patterns and 'specialisation' in pastoral farming.

It would certainly be inappropriate to think of 'intensification' and 'specialisation' in the modern sense of different elements of an economic system focusing on particular skills, technologies or management systems as deliberate strategies to maximise the productivity of every aspect of the work that people contribute to the output of the whole. A more realistic way to consider the development of farming in later prehistory is to see it as an essentially social issue, based primarily on subsistence living but adapting to demographic, cultural, economic or political pressures to increase production. Increased production would have been required to support the general subsistence needs of the population if it was growing, and surpluses would have been necessary to provide emergency stores in case of bad harvests, disease or low reproduction of animals. In addition, many authors have seen the apparent 'intensification' of farming (in this sense of increased production) as having been required to underpin higher level economic and political activity. This could have included the need to provide resources for major communal construction works, to supply commodities to underpin exchange systems supporting the widely recognised prestige goods economy of the late Bronze Age and perhaps later to provide other kinds of political tribute or economic levy, which by the end of the Iron Age might have resembled a form of taxation.

The issue of 'intensification' thus principally concerns the ways in which land was managed and organised and how social, economic and political relationships developed to meet increased levels of production required for subsistence and social obligations. If this involved ways of managing animals and crops that also increased productivity, it would have been a beneficial side effect, not a goal in itself.

Pastoralism, animals and topography

Lambrick (1992) and Pryor (1996) drew attention to the fact that in the past far too little attention was paid to the importance of the pastoral element of later prehistoric farming systems. This is now less of a problem and, for example, it has become widely recognised that field systems could have been established in the context of primarily pastoral farming systems (Fig. 7.14). We have seen above the extent to which animal husbandry underpinned farming patterns in all parts of the Thames Valley. Nevertheless, there is still much to be learnt about how animal husbandry was practised and how it related to the natural resources of the valley.

In general terms sheep were often especially prevalent on the chalk, sands, limestone and drier gravel terraces, while cattle and horses were more prevalent on lower, damper ground, in keeping with the natural suitability of species for varying topographical zones of the valley. However, a rapid collation of more results for this study than were available to Grant (1984) or Hambleton (1999) shows that, although the very broad trend in species preferences may be valid, there is considerable variation in the proportions of domestic animals at

Fig. 7.14   Pastoral landuse in the later Iron Age

settlements within these geological zones (Fig. 7.3).

Unusually high cattle to sheep ratios on the second terrace site at Yarnton, on the Corallian Ridge at Watchfield and, to a lesser extent, the chalk at Woodcote Road and Hill Farm can be compared with unusually low cattle to sheep ratios for lower-lying sites at Mingies Ditch. The seemingly anomalous 'results' may be explained to some extent if horses are taken into account with cattle and pigs with sheep, but there remains substantial variation in species proportions even so. The high proportion of sheep at the floodplain settlement at Mingies Ditch may reflect issues of special preservation, and this could have affected other sites, but seems unlikely to account for the full range of variability.

The most likely explanation is that the character of the bone assemblages reflects the character of the predominant grazing available, not the specific topographical location of the settlement. Thus the low proportion of sheep at the second terrace site at Yarnton suggests that the extensive floodplain immediately adjacent would have provided most of its grazing land, whereas the higher proportion of sheep at Gravelly Guy, also on the second terrace, is consistent with the premise that the former early prehistoric ceremonial complex was the principal grazing area for the surrounding settlements. Likewise, it may be that the sheep-dominated assemblage from Coxwell Road reflects extensive grazing on the well-drained main ridge of the Corallian sand, whereas nearby Watchfield on the edge of the sandy dipslope may have been exploiting adjacent clays, with its extensive paddocks and fields designed primarily for cattle herding.

Pastoral 'specialisation' and cereal 'producers' and 'consumers'

Although mixed farming is clearly the general basis of late prehistoric agriculture, there is a fundamental issue of how far communities were engaged in arable agriculture. On some sites, carbonised crop processing remains are absent or sparse despite thorough sampling. This applies to several middle to late Bronze Age settlements, but is rarer amongst Iron Age ones, at least in the Upper Thames Valley. The relative dearth of such remains on some sites compared with others suggests that not all were equally involved in arable production, but this must be seen in the context of other lines of evidence. For example, amongst 500 samples at Perry Oaks/T5 none of the later prehistoric ones contained sufficient charred cereal and weed seeds to warrant individual analysis and reporting (Challinor 2006), but there was nevertheless pollen evidence, at a relatively high level in a few cases, to indicate the presence of cereals within the predominantly grassland environment.

Because so much effort is expended on interpreting charred plant assemblages where they are large enough to support comparative analysis, little attention has been paid to the reasons why some settlements produce little or no charred crop processing debris despite thorough sampling. It is also worth noting that in some cases samples of charred plant remains from late prehistoric sites seem to share some characteristics of earlier prehistoric ones (presence of low levels of grain and some hazelnut shells but little chaff or weed seeds) that might reflect the survival of a different type of agricultural regime than the typical later Iron Age farm.

In relation to early and middle Iron Age settlements Jones' (1985) model of distinguishing between 'producer' and 'consumer' sites on the basis of differences in composition of their carbonised plant remains has again been debated. Both the methodological basis and socio-economic assumptions behind this influential idea have been repeatedly challenged (Van der Veen 1987; 1999; Smith 2001; Stevens 2003). In the most recent critique Van der Veen and Jones (2007) have also suggested that other explanations of differences between archaeobotancial carbonised plant assemblages in the Upper Thames Valley, such as those proposed by Campbell (2000) and Stevens (2003), are also flawed. The problems arise from the difficulty of interpreting assemblages of plant remains that are the product of highly complex multi-stage, potentially multi-source and varied depositional and post-depositional formation processes.

What is clear is that in the Upper Thames Valley other biological and topographical evidence strongly suggests that long-lived Iron Age settlements with many storage pits on the higher terraces, such as Ashville and Gravelly Guy, had a major involvement in cereal production. Lower lying middle Iron Age settlements produce greater evidence for pastoralism, although they may also have been self-sufficient in grain. Confirmation of at least some level of agricultural interdependence between settlements is seen in the occurrence of settlements on the floodplain such as Port Meadow, Mingies Ditch and Farmoor, which not only have other biological evidence to suggest they mainly engaged in pastoralism but were also situated in localities ill-suited to cultivation. Indeed, the settlement enclosures at Farmoor experienced seasonal inundation and, while Mingies Ditch did not experience flooding contemporaneous with occupation, the preserved Iron Age palaeosol showed no evidence of cultivation. However, the charred plant remains from Mingies Ditch showed that spelt wheat was certainly being dehusked on the site, implying that grain was brought to the site in spikelet form.

This still leaves at issue whether more consideration should be given to the nature of settlements that produce extremely sparse charred crop remains, especially where these are similar in character to earlier prehistoric ones.

WATER SUPPLY, STORAGE AND WASTE

Water sources

Water is obviously essential to sustaining the life of people and their animals, and can also be important in hygiene, social interaction, ritual practices and a variety of crafts (Fig. 7.15). Not surprisingly there is plentiful, though far from complete evidence of how a range of means of access to water were developed and used in later prehistory. These can be reviewed within some broad categories, distinguishing first between natural and artificial water sources and then the means of exploiting, developing, accessing and using each of these broad categories.

Use of natural water bodies

Natural springs, streams, rivers and lakes would have been important sources of water for both domestic consumption and animals and, to a considerable degree, such use would leave no archaeologically recognisable trace. The importance of such water bodies is reflected in the frequent deposition of objects in them, such as an Iron Age sword from a spring at Little Wittenham and the extensive deposits of objects in river channels. Unusually, there is specific evidence of the use of a natural water supply for watering animals at Mingies Ditch, where the layout of the enclosed middle Iron Age floodplain settlement was specifically designed to provide access to a channel of the river Windrush for watering animals corralled within the outer enclosure of the settlement. As noted above, a series of fences and other structures within a palaeochannel at Yarnton may have been designed to manage access of animals to water.

Structural timbers at several sites indicate the existence of revetments, jetties and bridges that could have served as platforms giving access to water for a range of purposes. Other general evidence for wooden buckets and large pottery containers (together with the likelihood of leather water skins) indicates the potential for collecting water from nearby springs, streams and rivers. It is worth noting complete or near complete pots recovered from channel deposits at Whitecross Farm and Eton, even though these might be symbolic deposits rather products of accidental breakage or loss when drawing water.

At Yarnton and Green Park, Reading extensive burnt mound deposits provide evidence of activities involving the heating of water carried out adjacent to natural palaeochannels that provided a convenient source of water, at least seasonally, even if the channels were not still flowing. Deeper parts of former palaeochannels are likely topographical locations of natural lakes and ponds. Sequences of deposits at Yarnton and the complex sequence of channel and alluvial development at Runnymede illustrate the variation over time of hydrological regimes of such places, between active flowing channels, pools, ponds and seasonal drying out. It is not entirely clear how far the exploitation of such water bodies varied with their hydrological status or with more general patterns of settlement farming and ritualistic behaviour.

Natural springs may have been another significant natural source of water in prehistoric times, but few areas around springs have been archaeologically investigated. Topographically the Thames gravels are not obviously characterised by strong spring lines. Most of the gravel terraces were laid down over impermeable clays and, where they are sealed from contact with the gravels underlying the river, water seepage and small springs often occur around their edges, reflecting perched water tables. These are seldom sufficient to start permanent streams and may not have been very important. Springs emerging from other geological formations may have been more significant. At Little Wittenham an Iron Age sword was recovered during the creation of a pond near a spring at the base of the chalk outliers on which the major late Bronze Age enclosure, Iron Age fort and extramural settlements at Castle Hill were located, with the Dyke Hills oppidum just across the river.

Creation and use of artificial water sources – collection of rainwater and dew

Artificial sources of water were developed extensively in later prehistory, both in terms of *in situ* use and collection and transport in containers. These can broadly be divided between the collection of rainwater (or dew) and the creation of artificial access to groundwater by means of wells, waterholes and ponds. As the collection of rainwater can leave no archaeological trace, there is less direct evidence for this than for constructed access to groundwater.

Rainwater and dew must have been significant and practical sources of water. Potential evidence of rainwater collection takes the form of ditches and gullies surrounding houses and enclosures, particularly in the middle Iron Age. A number of such gullies at Farmoor had deepenings or sumps that may have been designed both to facilitate drainage and for temporary collection of water (Lambrick and Robinson 1979) and relatively deep sumps were noted at Cleveland Farm Ashton Keynes (Coe *et al.* 1991, 45). Evidence for drainage sumps acting as underground storage cisterns is less obvious, but a possible example was recorded at Gravelly Guy, where a roundhouse gully ended in a large clay lined pit (Lambrick and Allen 2004, 109-10). Whether such a pit would have been effective for storing water is unproven.

However, such arrangements are not common, and there may have been other ways of collecting rainwater from house roofs that are not visible in the archaeological record. The existence of rainwater collection devices such as stretched leather hides held on posts with a hole to channel water into a container beneath, can only be speculated and there has been little consideration of water collection by promoting formation of dew.

Creation and use of artificial water sources – waterholes, wells and ponds

The development of artificial access to groundwater is well documented archaeologically, and is a particular feature of middle to late Bronze Age settlements and field systems. Although there are some earlier Bronze Age examples, as at Yarnton, the majority of all prehistoric waterholes investigated in the Thames Valley are middle to late Bronze Age, with far fewer Iron Age examples.

The common term 'waterhole' has come to embrace a wide range of large holes in the ground designed to provide access to groundwater and has even been applied to some large pits where there is little or no evidence that they held water. Three kinds of waterhole that may have worked in different ways can be distinguished. Those that might be termed *wells* were compact in plan with more or less vertical shafts, with or without linings, intended to have water drawn from them in buckets, skins or other vessels, or were accessed by use of log ladders. Examples of such wells have been investigated at Perry Oaks/T5 (Framework Archaeology 2006, 140), Yarnton (Hey *et al.* forthcoming b), Eight Acre Field (Mudd 1995) and elsewhere. *Ramped wells* were pear-shaped (or teardrop- or tadpole-shaped) in plan, very steep sided, occasionally somewhat undercut, but with a shallower angled access ramp and sometimes a revetment step or other structure to allow people (and more doubtfully animals) direct access to the water. *Ponds* can be seen as large, sometimes sprawling in plan, often with at least some shallow-angled sides but some still steep or even undercut, intended to allow direct access to water by animals as well as people, often exhibiting extensive digging out, recutting and modification.

While these distinctions are probably genuine, the morphology of waterholes is not clear-cut. Many archaeological reports do not seek to make such distinctions, and in any case it is useful to retain 'waterhole' as a more generic term. At Perry Oaks/T5 all such features are termed 'waterholes' but a distinction is made between 'steep-sided' and 'ramped' examples. Not all 'waterholes' are investigated sufficiently to establish their precise physical characteristics; many are more amorphous than the definitions above suggest, commonly including a range of simple large round or oval pits with sloping sides and no particular distinguishing characteristics beyond size and evidence of water-logged fills.

Middle to late Bronze Age

A clear example of a teardrop shaped ramped well was recorded at Stanwell (O'Connell 1990). The ramp stopped a short distance above water level, ending in a small pegged wooden revetment board creating a step from which water would have been drawn. Another particularly large recut pond-like feature had been cleared out at the bottom and contained a possible log ladder. There were two more amorphous waterholes and a very large and heavily recut, though not waterlogged, hollow that may have been a quarry rather than a pond.

At Perry Oaks/T5 several waterholes were dug and used within the middle Bronze Age field system during the period 1700–1150 BC (Fig. 7.15). Some lay in the middle of fields but most in positions that clearly reflected the layout of the boundaries. In some cases they apparently cut ditches, suggesting that they were dug after the fields were laid out, but a few were cut by field ditches. There was no particular chronological distinction in the occurrence of the 'steep-sided' and 'ramped' waterholes, but several had been recut, sometimes more than once, as distinctive vertical-sided shafts. A number of the ramped waterholes had a step revetment arrangement similar to that at Stanwell, including one constructed of timber and wattle dated to 1500 to 1100 cal BC (Framework Archaeology 2006, 145-6, fig. 3.4, Pl 3.5). Wicker or wooden revetments were preserved in several of the steep sided waterholes. These would have stabilised the sides of the shafts and acted as filters to maintain a clear pool of water at the base.

There are some instances of multiple phases of recutting and reuse and areas of intercutting waterholes. Some such sequences continued into the Iron Age. In one case a new sump had been scoured out of the base of a large vertical-sided waterhole, leaving an access platform. It was later abandoned and allowed to silt up after a Neolithic stone axe, a wooden axe haft, a wooden 'beater' and a broken log ladder dating to 1502-1116 cal BC had been deposited. In another case, an axe haft and 'beater' were deposited in a waterhole that had been allowed to fill completely before a revetted shaft was sunk though it. Between 1150 and 750 BC many waterholes were recut and reinstated and new ones excavated, exhibiting a more even distribution across the landscape in the later period. In one case a steep-sided waterhole was excavated through a ditch that formed part of one of the spinal boundaries or 'trackways', possibly indicating either the abandonment of this 'trackway' as a route or that it was in fact a double ditched boundary.

An *in situ* post in a waterhole at Vicarage Road, Sunbury might have been part of a lining or platform (Hayman forthcoming e) and one of two waterholes or wells excavated at the site produced

Fig. 7.15 (overleaf) Late prehistoric waterholes, wells and ponds

WATERHOLES, WELLS AND PONDS

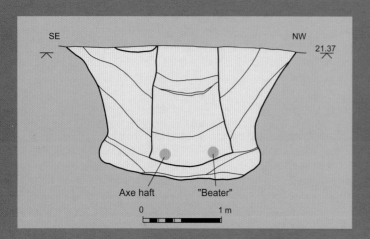

SE   NW

21.37

Axe haft   "Beater"

0   1 m

Features that provided artificial access to groundwater are highly visible in the archaeological record of the Thames Valley. They are particularly characteristic of middle and late Bronze Age field systems in the region but Iron Age examples have also been identified, sometimes in association with earlier field systems.

The term 'waterhole' embraces a wide range of large holes dug to obtain water, but at least three distinct types can be distinguished. Wells are generally compact in plan with more or less vertical shafts, with or without linings, from which water was drawn in buckets, pots or skins. Some were accessed by log ladders, such as those found at Perry Oaks / T5 and Yarnton. Ramped wells are pear-shaped in plan, steep-sided with a shallower angled ramp or revetment step designed to allow access for people or animals (or both). Animals were also watered at ponds, generally irregular sprawling features with both shallow and steep or undercut sides.

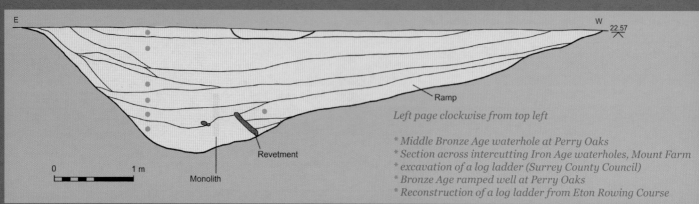

E   W

22.57

Ramp

Revetment

Monolith

0   1 m

Left page clockwise from top left

* *Middle Bronze Age waterhole at Perry Oaks*
* *Section across intercutting Iron Age waterholes, Mount Farm*
* *excavation of a log ladder (Surrey County Council)*
* *Bronze Age ramped well at Perry Oaks*
* *Reconstruction of a log ladder from Eton Rowing Course*

WATERHOLES, WELLS AND PONDS

Yarnton has provided the best dated sequence of waterhole features in the Upper Thames Valley. An early Bronze Age waterhole dug into the base of a dried up palaeochannel contained a log ladder and wooden bowl, both alder, dated to 1660-1520 cal BC and 1640-1450 cal BC. Another waterhole, dug on the bank of the channel nearby after the palaeochannel became seasonally active, was dated to the 15th century cal BC from charred residue on a potsherd. Elsewhere on the bank of a palaeochannel a square-sided pit was filled with burnt stone and charcoal, and spreads of burnt stone were found next to another waterhole that had been recut four times. In addition to their practical uses, waterholes were important symbolically as a source of life and perhaps a connection to the underworld, and often attracted a variety of votive deposits.

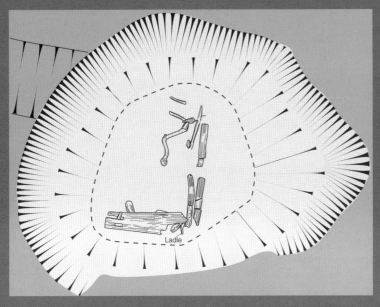

In the Middle Thames Valley at Perry Oaks / T5 waterholes dug along boundaries of the field systems were dated to between 1700-1150 BC. There was no obvious chronological distinction between 'steep-sided' and 'ramped' waterholes, but a number had been recut with distinctive vertical-sided shafts. Wicker or wooden revetments designed to filter the water survived in some of the steep-sided waterholes.

Right page clockwise from top left

* *wattle lining from a later Bronze Age waterhole at Perry Oaks*
* *Late Bronze Age or early Iron Age timber-lined well, Shorncote*
* *Plank-lined well at Yarnton/Cassington*
* *Late Bronze Age waterhole with ladle, Green Park, Reading*

the base of a wooden bucket made of willow or poplar wood along with a long thin pole.

Numerous waterholes have been found amongst Bronze Age field systems at Hengrove, Home Farm Laleham and Imperial Sports Ground (Hayman 2002b; forthcoming b and c; Crockett 2001). At the Eton Rowing Course there were two middle Bronze Age wells, one with wooden planks forming a revetment around three sides of the base, the other with an upright post and another timber at the base. The much-decayed remains of another one plank deep lining survived at the base of a late Bronze Age well.

'Ponds' were investigated at Aldermaston Wharf and Knights Farm, though only the Knights Farm pond was an obvious large open water source rather than an ordinary waterhole (Bradley *et al.* 1980). At Reading Business Park/Green Park there were several rather amorphous broad waterholes. A timber structure at the base of a waterhole dug through unstable gravel subsoil at Green Park was probably a plank built revetment retained by driven stakes. Disarticulated timber debris in two other waterholes may have derived from similar constructions.

At Appleford Sidings in the Upper Thames Valley 17 waterholes were associated with a middle Bronze Age field system (Booth *et al.* forthcoming). They were circular or occasionally oval in plan, ranging from 2.0 m to 6.75 m across and up to 1.9 m deep with steeply sloping sides. The smaller examples had concave bases and the wider ones steep sides and generally flat bases. Two examples of intercutting waterhole complexes were identified.

At Mount Farm Dorchester a large ramped well dated to 1310-980 cal BC was cut though a ring ditch utilising the hollow of the silted ditch as the starting point for the ramped access. Timbers near the base were not definitely worked nor obviously an *in situ* revetment step. At Eight Acre Field, Radley the earlier of two waterholes investigated was dated to 1680-1420 cal BC. It was an elongated, possibly ramped pit located in a gap in a field boundary adjacent to a possible house site. The later one, dated to 1020-800 cal BC, was a steep-sided well sited at the other side of the boundary not blocking the gap. There was a log ladder at the base and a possibly votive dump of early Iron Age pottery and animal bones in the upper fill (Mudd 1995, 25-30, figs 3b and 5).

The Yarnton excavations provided the most thoroughly dated sequence of waterhole features in the Upper Thames Valley. An early Bronze Age waterhole dug into the base of a dried up palaeochannel included a log ladder and a wooden bowl, both alder, radiocarbon dated to 1660 to 1520 cal BC and 1640 to 1450 cal BC. Another waterhole was dug nearby on the bank of the channel, probably after the earlier waterhole had filled. Charred residue on pottery produced a date in the 15th century cal BC, by which time the palaeochannel may have become at least seasonally

active. Elsewhere on the bank of a palaeochannel spreads of burnt stone and a square sided pit filled with burnt stone and charcoal were found next to another waterhole that had been recut on four occasions. Four radiocarbon dates indicated that the second and third recuts and infilling occurred over less than 100 years during the 15th century cal BC. A date in the 13th or 14th century cal BC was obtained for the pit with burnt stone, which may have been contemporary with the infilling of the fourth recut. Nearby at Yarnton a well lining was constructed of massive timber planks forming a 2 m long box (Fig. 7.15; Hey forthcoming b).

At Watkins Farm a ramped well contained remains of a plank and, most unusually, a whole human skeleton lay near one side of the base. Layers of burnt limestone may have been used to consolidate the base of the well. At the time of publication the early radiocarbon date of 1490-1130 cal BC was considered anomalous on the basis of what was then known of the hydrological history of the Upper Thames (Allen 1990, 10) but is now regarded as consistent with the picture that has emerged from Yarnton (Tim Allen, Mark Robinson pers. comm.).

At Shorncote/Cotswold Community several large pits more than 2 m deep were interpreted as waterholes or wells, though not necessarily permanently retaining water (Hearne and Heaton 1994; Hearne and Adam 1999; Brossler *et al.* 2002). Four had 'sumps' in the bottom which may have served to deepen them if they had dried up or were created by the scraping action of buckets when water levels were low. A cluster of postholes around the top of one pit (Hearne and Heaton 1994) suggested the presence of a timber wellhead structure for drawing of water with a bucket. Most of the compact, steep-sided pits that penetrate the water table and can be regarded as wells have not produced *in situ* evidence of linings, but a number certainly were lined and others have produced collapsed timbers possibly representing linings. Another part of the Shorncote complex exposed a steep sided well lined with a ring of vertical split timber revetments driven into the base (Fig. 7.15; Brossler *et al.* 2002, 44-5).

Iron Age

Compared with the middle to late Bronze Age very few Iron Age waterholes, wells and ponds have been found anywhere in the Thames Valley, but they seem to be most common where associated with pre-existing field systems, apparently continuing previous practice. This is an important feature of the Perry Oaks/T5 field system where it is mainly the waterholes and wells that can be shown to be early or middle Iron Age, often clearly respecting the layout of the fields. This suggests the continued use of the field system into the Iron Age, although the ditches had ceased to be maintained by that stage. In one case a carinated bowl and two drinking vessels were placed on the base of a vertical well shaft that had been cut through the backfill of a ramped waterhole. Other waterholes were commonly located close to the boundaries or corners of extant Bronze Age fields. Water for the middle Iron Age settlement was provided by several waterholes, including two located on the eastern edge of the settlement and two within it. These were substantial features, open for considerable periods of time, one probably used into the late Iron Age. Some waterholes out in the fields, including one containing significant proportions of slag, were apparently associated with craft activities.

At Watkins Farm, Northmoor a deep vertical sided pit that penetrated the water table lay just outside the original south-west entrance of the central roundhouse, possibly outside a rear entrance when the house was re-oriented to face north-east, and adjacent to an enclosed area to the south. The well contained a wooden plank radiocarbon dated to 390-30 cal BC and the remains of a pike (Allen 1990 14, fig. 3).

At Farmoor a probable waterhole lay immediately adjacent to a small domestic structure and workshop on the edge of the gravel terrace overlooking the floodplain (Lambrick and Robinson 1979).

A series of middle and late Iron Age and Roman waterholes or ponds were exposed at Mount Farm towards the edge of an isolated patch of higher gravel terrace, exploiting the perched water table. These very large features were only trenched and so their full morphology and sequence are unclear, but they provide good examples of artificial ponds that seem to have been extensively disturbed, recut and remodelled to maintain a water supply. No waterlogged samples were recovered from the Iron Age contexts, but the level of dung beetles in the Roman deposits was extremely low, suggesting that they were not used by animals.

Considering the extent of excavation in the Upper Thames Valley the absence of more waterholes and wells clearly attributable to the Iron Age is noteworthy. While this might partly be attributable to differences in their character and location in comparison with later Bronze Age ones, this is unlikely to account adequately for their absence. It is more likely that changes in social and economic circumstances meant the provision of an artificial water supply in this form became less important. It is noticeable in this context that a wide variety of ramped waterholes, lined and unlined wells and ponds became common again in the mid to later Roman period.

Storage of produce

Four posters and similar structures

So-called four-post structures, usually square and sometimes rectangular settings of postholes, are characteristic features of late prehistoric settlements (Fig. 7.16). Where they can be assigned to a period within later prehistory, the majority of four-posters

in the Thames Valley are late Bronze Age or early Iron Age, but there is an interesting group of low-lying middle Iron Age sites where they have also been recorded. Most are simple square settings of four posts usually set 1.2 m – 2.5 m apart, but other common layouts include a variety of six- and eight-posters, four-posters with apparent extensions of a different size and examples placed side by side. Frequent rebuilding or replacment of individual posts is evident from recutting of postholes.

Based largely on grain-rich farming settlements in Wessex, ethnographic parallels noted by Bersu (1940) and an interpretative approach to late prehistoric farming dominated by an emphasis on arable (eg Fowler 1983), the 'default' interpretation of four-posters has been that they were granaries. They would have kept consumption grain in safe, dry, accessible conditions out of reach of mice and other predators, whereas seed grain was kept moist underground. A standard four-poster could be calculated to hold between one and six tonnes of grain, easily enough to supply a small to large extended family for a year (Gregg 1988).

In reviewing the then available evidence, Gent (1983) found that grain storage is amongst the most plausible explanations for these structures, but the assumed association with grain was far from clear and difficult to prove. He noted that where such structures appear to have burnt down, there was no very obvious association with remains of stored grain, though there was an example of an association with beans. However, Gill Cambell (pers. comm.) notes that since Gent's analysis good charred plant assemblages have been recovered from four-posters at three sites, Stanwick (Northamptonshire), St Osyth (Essex) and Sutton Common (Yorkshire), which confirm that some were used as granaries, both for storing grain and possibly fodder. Some of the recent discoveries had clearly burnt down when full of grain. However, ethnographic parallels suggest a variety of uses such as fodder ricks (Bersu 1940) and other, non-storage functions have also been mooted, including platforms for exposing the dead (Carr and Knüsel 1997) or sleeping or cooking huts or saunas, but again no clear association with human remains, environmental evidence objects or burnt mounds supports these ideas.

There are no cases in the Thames Valley of four-posters clearly associated with grain or other stored produce, or with evidence to suggest other specific functions, but superficially there is a case for assuming that they were mostly connected with pastoral farming. They occur very commonly on highly dispersed and densely occupied late Bronze Age and early Iron Age settlements in the Upper and Middle Thames Valley, thought to have had predominantly pastoral economies (see Chapters 4 and 7), and they are also a feature of low-lying middle Iron Age, predominantly grazing settlements at Claydon Pike, Mingies Ditch and Port Meadow.

Needless to say, a general association with settlements mainly engaged in animal husbandry does not mean they were not grain stores. It would still have been necessary to store grain for consumption even if settlements were not producing much themselves, and yields of experimentally grown prehistoric cereals indicate that the harvest from a single hectare would probably be enough to fill a small four-poster, enough to keep a family supplied for perhaps a year. Grain storage is thus still plausible, but if this was the predominant use of four-posters, we might expect it to be reflected in their location within a settlement (eg near houses or in areas given over to storage), but the evidence for this is ambiguous.

In and around late Bronze Age settlements of both highly dispersed and more nucleated form, four-posters seem to have been as widely scattered as houses and waterholes, but seldom with a very close association in their distribution, though there is some pattern in relative degrees of clustering. Thus at Shorncote, houses, waterholes and four posters are all widely scattered with little obvious clustering (Fig. 4.3). At Cassington West (Fig. 4.8) there were orderly rows of rectangular structures but no direct association with houses (Hey and Hayden forthcoming). In the middle Thames Valley at Green Park some four-posters seem to have been closely associated with a concentration of roundhouses, but others were clustered further away in work and storage areas (Brossler *et al.* 2004). Amongst the dispersed traces of domestic activity within the field systems on the Surrey and west London gravels four-posters and similar structures have so far proved rare, and again with ambiguous associations with domestic occupation.

In a few cases four-posters appear to be associated with major field systems or other land divisions, as at Roughground Farm and Eton (Allen *et al.* 1993, 36, fig. 26, Pl. 28; 89; Allen pers. comm.). At Horcott Pit undated, and hence not necessarily associated, four-posters lay within and outside the early Iron Age palisaded stockade (Lamdin-Whymark *et al.* 2007).

Gravelly Guy is one of the few major Iron Age pit scatter sites with a significant number of four-posters in the Upper Thames Valley (Lambrick and Allen 2004, 144-6). Among the 19 four-posters identified a row of three respected the same alignment as three early Iron Age roundhouses sited alongside an access path between the settlement and fields. However, one of the four-posters impinged on one of the houses and none was demonstrably contemporary with the houses. In other respects the four-posters at Gravelly Guy were more scattered and were exceptional as the only structures *not* confined within the otherwise constrained limits of the settlement, occurring in both the arable and pastoral areas either side of it. At Yarnton four of the seven four-posters identified may have succeeded houses (Hey *et al.* forthcoming a). At Ashville/Wyndyke Furlong only one, contained within a small penannular

gully, was recognised though others might be disguised within dense clusters of postholes (Parrington 1978; Muir and Roberts 15-23). At Coxwell Road Faringdon five four-posters were exposed (with a possible sixth missing one post), again representing a mixture of some close to structures within the settlement and others more isolated beyond the main cluster of features. At Mount Farm no four-posters were identified amongst a moderately dense scatter of postholes in areas where there were few other features (Lambrick forthcoming).

It is probably wrong to assume that all four-posters and similar structures had the same function, but in so far as anything might be gleaned from the evidence above they seem as likely to have been stores for fodder as for consumption grain, and there is no apparent correlation with disarticulated human bone, waterholes or burnt mounds to support the idea that they were excarnation platforms, sauna huts and the like.

Most four-posters and similar structures found in the Upper Thames Valley have fairly modest sized post holes (usually less than 0.4 m across), and of those that have produced dating evidence most are late Bronze Age or early Iron Age, though there are a few middle Iron Age and later examples. This is largely the case in the Middle Thames Valley, though middle to late Iron Age examples have been found at Eton Rowing Lake, Ashford Prison and Perry Oaks/T5.

'Mega-posters'

There is a class of particularly strongly built four-posters and similar structures, here termed 'mega-posters', generally associated with middle Iron Age enclosures and/or low-lying pastoral settlements in the Upper Thames Valley. They are represented by large post pits, typically 1 m across with post pipes upwards of 0.35 m, in some cases linked by gullies, which may have held bracing timbers.

A 'mega-poster' found at Horcott Pit with post pipes of *c* 0.4 m diameter lay just inside the south-west corner of the rectangular early to middle Iron Age enclosure (Lamdin-Wymark *et al.* 2007). At Mingies Ditch four or possibly five 'mega-posters' were grouped within the domestic inner enclosure in an area possibly set aside for storage and general work, each apparently associated with one of the succession of five houses (Fig. 7.16). Two had single linking gullies, two had parallel ones and the fifth had three such gullies. Where post pipes were discernible they too were about 0.4 m across. One of two structures identified at Claydon Pike resembled the Mingies Ditch examples, with parallel linking gullies, the other a more conventional layout but with particularly large postholes (Miles *et al.* 2007). An unexcavated example at Port Meadow has postholes large enough to show up on air photographs (Lambrick and McDonald 1985; Lambrick and Robinson 1988). At Groundwell Farm a similar distinction was apparent between

Fig. 7.16   Four post structures: (above left) as excavated at Gravelly Guy; (above right) interpretative reconstruction as structures for storage or excarnation platforms; (below left) 'mega-posters' at Mingies Ditch; (below right) a variety of four post structures at Hill Farm, Little Wittenham

Gravelly Guy

Mingies Ditch

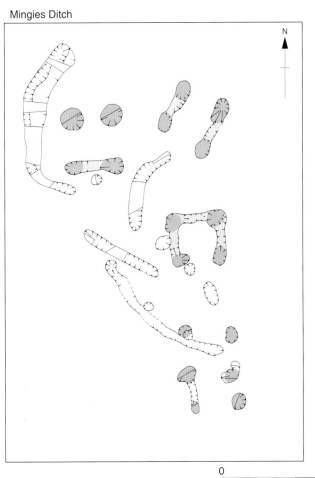

Hill Farm

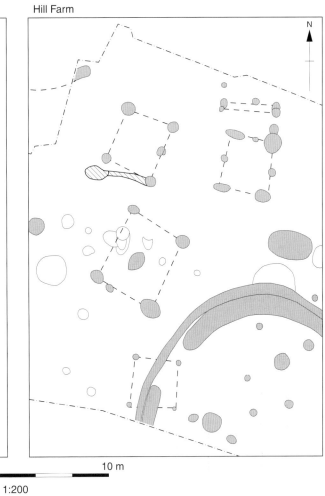

0   10 m

1:200

conventional four-posters and a number with much larger linked postholes similar to those at Mingies Ditch. In addition, there were a number of similar parallel slots with post positions that formed rectangular groups. Several four-posters with especially large postholes have also been found at Hill Farm, Little Wittenham (Fig. 7.16). Although most of these 'mega-posters' are in the Upper Thames Valley, there are some examples of four-posters with unusually large postholes at Ashford Prison in the Middle Thames Valley (Carew *et al.* 2006).

These particularly robust structures appear to have been built to take considerable weight. Storage of grain and other bulky and heavy materials are clear possibilities, but other non-storage functions should be considered. They may have served as tall watch towers to guard against cattle rustlers or functioned as sturdy structures to restrain individual animals for a variety of treatments connected with animal husbandry.

Other possible storage structures

Above-ground storage facilities not interpretable as houses or workshops may also have existed, but are seldom recognised. On the Windrush floodplain at Mingies Ditch a structure with a possible D-shaped plan was exposed (Allen and Robinson 1983, 63-5, fig. 31). While this group of postholes could be merely overlapping arcs of two circular buildings or successive screening structures, this site was sufficiently well preserved to make the former unlikely, while the latter can be dismissed on the basis of the substantial size of the postholes. The stratigraphy did not provide evidence of how this structure was used, and there were no obvious craft related objects, which led the excavators to suggest that this was more likely to be a storage building than a workshop.

Conclusion

Considering the combined evidence, the traditional explanation of four-posters as granaries for storing grain or pulse crops for consumption is plausible, but not conclusive. Where they occur on late Bronze Age and Iron Age pastoral settlements they are present in appropriate numbers relative to round-houses to make sense in terms of feeding the inhabitants. On some sites they share with houses a broadly similar pattern of clustering and distribution within settlements, but in others the spatial patterning is complementary and in some cases they occur beyond the boundaries of settlements. Overall these patterns would make as much sense if four-posters were structures for storing fodder or other material connected with pastoral farming. Apart from the unusually sturdy 'mega-posters', they are mostly late Bronze Age and Iron Age in date and seem to be most common on sites that were not heavily engaged in the production or processing of grain. Nonetheless it is most likely that four-posters served a variety of functions.

Storage pits

From an archaeological perspective it is easier to find evidence for storing materials underground than above ground. In most cases this is no more than the hole in which the stored commodity was buried, which was later emptied, perhaps reused, and finally deliberately filled in, or more rarely just abandoned. Commodities that were never recovered sometimes survive if they consisted of materials resistant to decay. Advantages of underground storage include its effectiveness as a method of keeping stored material in good condition, avoiding taking up valued space above ground, and provision of a hiding place for valued goods that might be stolen, either in mundane or exceptional circumstances of crisis.

The essence of underground storage that distinguishes it from votive offering is the intent to recover the material, but this is not always easy to infer from the evidence left in the ground. Holes in the ground also have many valuable uses other than storage, especially for getting rid of unwanted waste of various kinds. It is obvious that most late prehistoric pits did normally end up being filled with soil relatively rich in domestic debris – categorisation of fills suggests that very few were just left open (eg Lambrick and Allen 2004, 114-5 fig. 3.4, no. 815). A more problematic issue is the extent to which pits were dug as latrines or other waste disposal facilities without having first been used for underground storage.

Use of pits for grain storage

Since Gerhard Bersu's (1940) seminal report on his excavations at Little Woodbury was published, the ethnographic evidence for underground storage of grain has been a well-established explanation of large late prehistoric pits – so much so that pits have become more or less synonymous with the idea of underground storage in late prehistory in a way that does not apply to other periods. The basic principle of storing grain underground is that it is especially applicable to seed grain, because in permeable bedrock and with an impermeable seal over the top, the temperature, moisture and atmospheric conditions that develop (including initial sprouting of grain to generate carbon dioxide levels that prevent further germination) are ideal for keeping the grain alive but ungerminated, and free from predatory rodents and insects (Reynolds 1974). This is ideal for seed grain and emergency reserves, which are best kept in large quantities and only opened to be used all at once. It is less satisfactory for consumption grain, for which above-ground granaries, coupled with jars and other containers, are more practicable to provide small amounts on a regular basis.

Compared with four-posters, the evidence of storage of grain in pits is more robust. Bersu's observations were based on good ethnographic evidence and since then both the science and practical effectiveness of such storage has been demonstrated in some detail by the experiments of Peter Reynolds on the Hampshire chalk at Butser (Reynolds 1979). It is very unusual to find storage pits with their contents charred *in situ* but one such example was investigated on the Hampshire Chalk at the hillfort of Danebury (Jones 1984). This showed that both spelt wheat and six-row barley were stored in the hulled state, the spelt as spikelets and the barley as ears. Although it has not been demonstrated scientifically, it seems likely that such storage would also work on the gravel, sand and limestone geologies of the Thames Valley. At first sight this appears to be borne out by the proliferation of pits on some settlements but detailed interpretation of pit storage is complicated by a number of factors.

The key issue is that while storage of seed grain in pits clearly works, not all pits are likely to have been used for this purpose, not least because many were probably too small for the correct balance of moisture, temperature and atmospheric conditions to develop. This is a particular issue for interpreting the possible use of pit storage in the Thames Valley. It has long been recognised (eg Case *et al.* 1964/5) that the maximum size (volume and depth) of late

prehistoric pits on the Thames gravels tends to be significantly smaller than the classic grain storage pits found on chalkland sites such as Little Woodbury or Danebury, and they are also much less undercut. Both of these factors can usually be attributed to the characteristics of gravel as a less stable medium for digging deep pits than chalk. However, the physical limits of effective grain storage in pits dug in gravel sand or limestone have never been established. Although Reynolds (pers. comm.) thought that storage pits had to be at least a metre deep and/or a cubic metre in capacity to be effective, it has not been demonstrated either from the science of underground storage or by practical experiment that smaller pits would not work. Moreover, while some storage pits dug into the chalk, as at Alfred's Castle, are much larger than those on the Thames terraces, and probably could not be replicated in gravel, many late prehistoric pits dug into limestone and chalk in the Thames basin are no bigger than those dug into gravel or sand.

Depth to width ratios differ quite markedly from site to site. Unlike many classic grain storage pits on the Hampshire chalk, average diameter almost

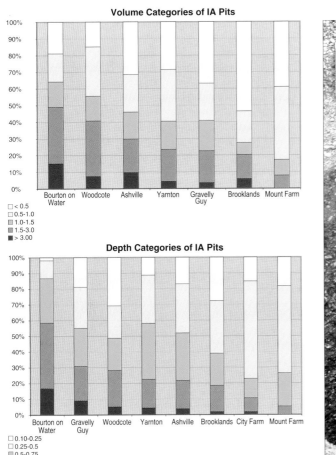

Fig. 7.17 Pit storage in the Thames Valley: (left) *proportion of differently sized pits at eight Iron Age settlements;* (right) *an undercut storage pit at Gravelly Guy*

always exceeds depth, even on several chalkland sites in the Thames Valley, and in most cases average diameter to depth ratios range from 1.8:1 to 3:1. These 'as found' dimensions do not allow for topsoil, erosion and other truncation, and all sites display considerable variation. As measured from the subsoil surface, pit depths in the Thames Valley seldom exceed 1.6 m (Fig. 7.17). Overall, between 60% and 90% of pits are usually less than 0.75 m deep, and between 10% and 30% are less than 0.25 m deep. Volumes are also variable. The proportion of pits with a volume more than 1 m³ was 65% at Bourton-on-the-Water, 55% at Woodcote Road, 45% at Ashville, 40% at Gravelly Guy and Yarnton, but only 26% at Brooklands and 18% at Mount Farm.

A review of the detailed distribution of depths and volumes for several sites reveals a recurrent pattern of a small number of exceptionally large pits that vary in size, and a much more numerous group of medium to small ones that exhibit a more even spectrum of sizes. Sites like Gravelly Guy with the largest samples suggest there are no sharp breaks in size range.

Pit shapes are also considered important in relation to grain storage, those with vertical and more particularly undercut sides being most effective (Reynolds 1979, 74). At Gravelly Guy undercut pits were the deepest, averaging 0.87 m deep with average volumes of 1.62 m³, and accounted for a quarter of both early and middle Iron Age pits (Fig. 7.17). Cylindrical pits were shallower at 0.62 m and smaller at 0.93 m³, accounting for another 40% of pits. The occurrence and depth of pits with undercut sides at a similar level at Coxwell Road (20%; 0.81 m) were much less frequent in the more fully excavated and mostly earlier part of the site to the south (8%). Undercut pits were also rare at Yarnton (7% for the Cresswell Field area; 2% for the rest of the Yarnton settlement). Taken together undercut and vertical sided pits account for between 30% and 60% of all pits, averaging about 0.8 m and 0.6 m deep respectively.

Most pits were unlined, but some had clay linings. It is also rare to find direct evidence of crops that have been stored in them in the form of charred remains resulting from burning the outer 'crust' of stored seed grain (cf Reynolds 1979).

Overall, there is no indication that pits fall into distinct size categories or signs of use that might clearly distinguish storage pits from others. If the maximum size of pit that could be dug in gravel sand or limestone had limited the amount of grain that could be stored in each batch, we might expect a much clearer clustering of large pits around the maximum practicable size that could be dug on that geology. This is not the case, so maximum physical constraints do not seem to be the limiting factor. Similarly, if grain storage was only effective in pits above a certain size and the amount required for storage was seldom much above this minimum (assuming large pits were not needed for other purposes) we might expect a clear basal threshold for larger sized pits, in effect splitting the overall range of pit sizes into two populations of 'grain storage pits' and 'other pits'. Again, this does not seem to be the case. Although most settlements had a small number of exceptionally large pits, these are highly variable in size, so it is unlikely that they reflect routine year-on-year seed grain requirements. Indeed, we cannot be sure that such very large (often very broad rather than particularly deep) pits were for grain storage at all, but if they were they might be explained in terms of special circumstances such as bumper harvests or some other reason for doubling up storage, or the need to store a particularly large surplus for exchange.

Taking all these factors into consideration, it is difficult to say how far pits were used for storage of seed grain in the Thames Valley, but in the absence of experimental data it seems premature to suggest, as Chris Stevens (2003) has, that grain storage in pits would not have worked on the Thames gravels. It seems more reasonable to assume that grain storage in pits was routinely practised in the region. Although the minimum practical size of pits used for grain storage may be unclear, larger pits with vertical or undercut sides are likely to have been suitable. Given that there are a few very substantial pits in gravel, the size of most is likely to have been determined by the quantities of grain needing to be stored, not the physical constraints of the bedrock. But equally, it is very unlikely that all pits (especially the smallest ones) were used for grain storage, even if some were used for storing other commodities. However, there is no obvious particular minimum depth or volume that stands out statistically in the dimensions recorded.

Without clear experimental evidence little more can be said about the practicalities of underground grain storage on different geologies in the Thames Valley. No doubt well designed experiments like those of Reynolds would help to resolve much uncertainty. Clarifying basic technical issues about the suitability of pits of different sizes and in different geologies for storing seed grain would provide a good basis for considering the socio-economic issues of storage of seed grain in the agricultural cycle and the subsistence and surplus capacity of settlements.

This complex issue involves some unknown factors, but has been tentatively explored at Gravelly Guy. Here the potential storage capacity of a long-lived, fully excavated Iron Age settlement was examined in the context of a reasonable basis for assessing household and population levels and the area of arable land available relative to neighbouring settlements (Lambrick and Allen 2004). On the basis of the projected area of arable plus the inferred structure of the settlement and its needs for nutrition and surplus, it was calculated that, if pits were used as stores for seed grain, only one or two medium to large pits would be needed annually. In the early Iron Age, with 92 pits over 1 m³, this might have meant reusing pits for 4 or 5 years, but for the middle to late Iron Age there were almost twice as many pits over 1 m³, suggesting either that they were not reused as often, or that more capacity was being provided for storing surpluses. On the basis of possible nutritional requirements in relation to arable area and likely crop yield it was concluded that a significant surplus could have been generated most years (Lambrick and Allen 2004, 484-8).

However, there would have been little point in storing seed grain if it were to be sown only a few weeks after harvest, and Fenton (1983) viewed such pits as long term storage of surplus rather than seed corn stores. In this case the pits at settlements like Gravelly Guy could have played a different role, with significantly more in use (or reuse) at any one time, especially if each household stored its own share of surplus.

At other sites the evidence for expansion or contraction of storage capacity is less clear and is intrinsically difficult to demonstrate due to lack of clarity about the key parameters to be taken into account. For example, there are the questions of how storage capacity of a settlement is measured (average size and number of pits, number above a certain size or total capacity, reuse) as well as issues of whether sampling strategies fully reflect shifts in occupation, and whether the area of arable available to a settlement can be estimated. So far as it is possible to discern such trends, at Ashville many fewer pits were definitely datable to the middle Iron Age, there were proportionally fewer large ones and maximum depths and volumes were smaller; Mount Farm shows a similar pattern though with a much smaller sample. At Yarnton fewer pits were datable to the middle Iron Age, though this may be due to survival levels and sampling in areas with more middle Iron Age occupation. Otherwise the average depths and volumes of pits decreased somewhat in the middle Iron Age, with slightly fewer undercut, but the maximum depths and volumes became slightly larger.

It has been demonstrated experimentally that reuse of pits is feasible for several years (Reynolds 1995). Cunliffe and Poole (1991) suggest that the storage pits at Danebury were only used once; others (eg Weaver *et al.* 2005) argue that it would be a waste of effort not to reuse pits. On the chalk, the condition of the pit walls can indicate how freshly cut they were but this is not possible on sand and gravels. However, at Gravelly Guy it was observed that pits with rounded bottoms were typically 0.1-0.2 m deeper than their flat bottomed counterparts of the same basic shape, which is consistent with a similar initial depth before repeatedly cleaning. Two thirds of pits with undercut profiles, those most likely to have been used for grain storage, had rounded bases, compared with less than half of cylindrical pits (Lambrick and Allen 2004, 112-3, Table 3.5). Furthermore, calculations of storage capacity in relation to the socio-economic dynamics of the settlement suggested the need for some reuse (Lambrick and Allen 2004).

Although a range of small pits are found on most settlements, the large deep pits that are best candidates for surplus or seed grain silos mostly occur on higher gravel terraces and other well-drained soils above the water table. On the first gravel terrace of the Upper Thames Valley pits tend to be shallow and on the floodplain they hardly exist. Below ground storage may have been difficult here because of the high water table, though it may be that storage of seed grain was not important given the mainly pastoral economic basis of settlements in lower lying areas. An unusual example of a deep pit occurring on the first terrace recorded at Appleford (F105; Hinchcliffe and Thomas 1980) was late Bronze Age and may predate an Iron Age rise in the water table (Robinson and Lambrick 1984).

Similar considerations apply on the gravels further downstream, but this is much less clear cut because large storage pits, and pits in general, are a less conspicuous feature of most settlements in the Middle Thames Valley and Surrey. Most pits there are either small or exceptionally large and broad like waterholes, rather than clusters with many deep cylindrical and undercut pits. Considering also the relative paucity (and in some cases virtual absence) of charred grain or crop-processing debris it is debatable to what extent Iron Age communities in the Middle Thames were much engaged in production and storage of surplus grain.

While there is some doubt about the efficacy of underground storage of seed grain in relatively small pits on gravel, sand and limestone soils, as compared with the chalk, there are variations in the occurrence of larger pits suitable for storage, which are not easily explained except in terms of varying economic needs for grain storage. The topographical constraint of a high water table as well as economic considerations would have influenced pit forms on the first terrace and floodplain, but their use on the higher gravel terraces would not have been subject to such constraints and thus may more genuinely reflect the economic basis of settlements.

Use of pits for storage of other commodities, objects and hoards

The use of pits as underground storage features for commodities other than grain is plausible, but in the absence of more experimental data, is difficult to demonstrate. Nevertheless short term underground storage could have been appropriate for meat and other products needing to be kept cool, damp and protected from vermin, especially if they were also prepared for preservation against organic decay through salting, smoking or other treatments. Some deposits of articulated meat bearing animal joints might reflect such storage rather than being 'special' votive deposits.

Fenton (1983) suggests the use of shallow pits to store hay or fodder rather than grain. At Farmoor and Thrupp, the early pits on the first terrace were shallow and on the floodplain there and at Mingies Ditch, Watkins Farm and Claydon Pike the only pits were very small shallow ones (Lambrick and Robinson 1979; Everett and Eeles 1999); Allen and Robinson 1993; Allen 1990a; Miles and Palmer 2007).

Some small pits were probably used for storing clay or burying waste; others seem to have finally been used for placing special deposits or hiding objects such as quern stones (Allen and Robinson 1993, 54, fig. 37), spindlewhorls (Lamdin-Whymark forthcoming), loomweights and other fired clay objects (Crockett 2001; Lambrick and Allen 2004, 118, Pl 3.2) and scrap metalwork (Miles *et al.* 2003 144-5, Pl 8.2). These tend variously to be regarded as 'hoards' or 'votive' or 'special' deposits. This is perhaps most obvious in the case of metalwork hoards.

Since Sir John Evans' work on Bronze Age metalwork in the 19th century there have been attempts to understand 'hoards' in terms of what their content says about the circumstance of burial, and in particular the role and motives of the person who buried clearly valuable objects. It was assumed that there was always an unfulfilled intention to recover such hoards, and they tended to be classified according to the roles and motivations of imagined owners, some being the notional property of 'merchants' or 'founders,' others being caches of valuable tools (often axes) or 'ornaments' (Needham 1990; Bradley 1990).

Exceptional groups of objects buried in pits are difficult to interpret. We do not know the possible symbolic significance of different commodities in later prehistory, their relative economic value, or the dangers of theft. While there are certainly objects that offer no explanation other than their being votive deposits buried in the ground, it is not always easy to distinguish these from objects meant to be recovered. Metalwork hoards and evidence of underground grain or meat storage may share several common objectives: to preserve valued commodities or raw materials and objects; to hide them from possible theft; and to allow later recovery when required. This may have applied equally to other things put in the ground for safe keeping, from meat to querns to almost anything else of value not needed for immediate use – including the collection of stones, broken loomweights and fired clay slabs that might have been kept as a source of pot boilers in a house at Gravelly Guy (Lambrick and Allen 2004, 143, and Plate 3.2).

Rather than seeing 'hoarding' as invariably reflecting 'special' behaviour, it might be more appropriate to see it as a standard means of safeguarding valuable commodities that was extended to encompass some categories of material for special reasons. These might have been technical (eg underground storage of seed grain is very effective), but could also be tempered by other considerations. For example, was this also a good way of hiding produce from those to whom tribute might be owed? They might also reflect a period of temporary abandonment. This was suggested for the cache of querns at Mingies Ditch, which is seen as possibly contemporary with the blocking of the entrances to the site (Allen and Robinson, 1993 89), and might obviously apply to hoards of jewellery such as the Crow Down hoard or valuable metalwork such as the Tower Hill collection, which might reflect a danger of theft, mugging or raiding.

In a sense therefore, we might see routine underground 'storage' in terms of safe-keeping in suitable conditions as part of a continuum, with underground 'hoarding' of valuables in more special circumstances. Both are different from 'special' or 'votive' deposits, which may also have involved objects of value but are more likely to have been overtly symbolic in the manner of burial not with the intent to recover the material. For example, the querns at Mingies Ditch could have been a special votive deposit marking the formal closure or departure from the house where they were found. It is obviously difficult to infer motivation and valued objects might still have been buried for later recovery in places like boundaries and entrances (Hingley 2006) which might have been symbolic while also providing ease of relocation. Before we explore this in more detail in Chapter 8, it is important to try to understand waste disposal as another related aspect of material buried in the ground, for which it is just as difficult to distinguish the ordinary from the 'special'.

Waste, rubbish disposal and recycling

General patterns

Three broad but complex factors contribute to the patterns of deposition and distribution of discarded artefacts and other material. These patterns reflect a mixture of deliberate and unconscious human behaviour and extraneous factors. 'Structured deposition' is not the same as 'special deposits', which denote conscious behaviour with spiritual or symbolic connotations. Disentangling the two, however, is not simple.

Firstly, there is an issue as to what constitutes 'rubbish' or 'waste': in reality there is no black and white distinction between what is actively useful and what is utterly discarded as 'waste' or 'rubbish'. As Stuart Needham has discussed in relation to how the midden at Runnymede accumulated (Needham and Spence, 1996), we know from our own behaviour that things actually go through several stages of ceasing to be useful, being put aside for potential use, abandoned and finally disposed of (Fig. 7.18). They may also be reused, recycled or altered for other purposes at any point. During this process of use turning to disuse or reuse, objects may shift location. In modern domestic terms this equates to whether we put things on a shelf, in a cupboard, the loft, a garden shed, the compost heap, a bonfire or in the dustbin.

Secondly, although patterns of rubbish location can often spatially reflect where particular activities took place and/or where waste was discarded, such patterns may also reflect the accumulation for discard of waste from different activities and at different stages in the waste cycle. So spatial patterns are actually the product of highly complex factors that may have disguised, or at least diluted, original patterns of behaviour.

Thirdly, even when 'finally' disposed of, rubbish is not static. Waste left exposed may be reworked by a variety of processes, including human recycling and scavenging animals, and buried rubbish is often subject to physical redepositon by people digging pits and ditches or moving fertile, rubbish-rich soil, and to disturbance by people, foraging pigs or burrowing animals. As a result, different sources of waste, locations of disposal and periods of use and discard may become mixed.

Interpretations about rubbish generating activities that we might wish to derive from disposal patterns are thus inevitably fraught with hazards. But as Lambrick (1984, 162-77) noted, the trend of most of these factors is to homogenise and disguise patterns, so that any which do emerge may still be informative, even if their interpretation is not straightforward.

Late prehistoric settlements in the Thames Valley have been used on several occasions to explore the general issue of how patterns of waste disposal shed light on society and social behaviour factors such as those outlined above may bias the picture when only certain parts of settlements are investigated (Bradley *et al*. 1980; Lambrick 1984; Allen and Robinson 1993, 123-30; Needham and Spence 1996, 242-8, fig. 19). To a large extent, these considerations apply to any archaeological material, but it is worth examining some key types of deposit that reflect deliberate and unconscious patterns of late prehistoric waste disposal and recycling in the Thames Valley.

Middens

A number of sites in the Thames Valley are characterised by superficial artefact-rich deposits, most notably Runnymede, Whitecross Farm and Castle Hill, to which we should almost certainly add Woodeaton (Fig. 7.18; Harding 1987). As applied to Runnymede (and thence to some other broadly similar sites, but not necessarily these) Needham and Spence (1996, 248) have defined 'middens' as specialist sites that were not just areas of 'undirected refuse aggregation' that resulted in large, refuse-rich deposits, but were 'a set of deposits with a particular structure and certain kinds of spatial and temporal interrelationships'. More specifically, they observed that while refuse accumulation seems to have been generally endemic, midden sites like Runnymede retained accumulations on a much grander scale than is likely to have derived merely from a resident community. Middens in this sense are not just 'rubbish heaps' but places to which more material

was brought than was taken away and where much was reworked, reflecting a much higher level of communal interaction and status than applies to ordinary farming settlements (see Chapter 9).

Runnymede in particular is comparable with a few other exceptional sites like Chisenbury and Potterne that seem to have been special places where unusually rich and complex deposits accumulated. Restricting the term 'midden' to such exceptional places, as Needham has proposed, is not uncontentious. In ordinary parlance 'midden' means any surface dung- or rubbish-heap to which material is periodically added. Indeed, it is sometimes used archaeologically in this sense to refer to any rubbish-rich soil such as that which accumulated in hollows left by gradually settling fills of deep waterholes (eg Hearne *et al*. 1999). Another problem is that there are distinctions of richness and scale that may be obvious at the extremes at sites like Runnymede, Potterne or Chisenbury, but which are much more difficult to discern at lesser scales.

The Whitecross Farm, Castle Hill and Woodeaton sites have not been investigated and quantified in as much detail as Runnymede or Potterne, and it is not entirely clear how comparable these deposits are in terms of their relative volume, richness and longevity. It does seem clear, however, that all these deposits contrast with the thin, relatively artefact poor occupation deposits that have been found *in situ* at a small number of low-lying sites like Mingies Ditch (and perhaps Farmoor and Burroway), but possibly not so different from some hillfort interiors, such as Ivinghoe Beacon (Cotton and Frere 1968, 187-260).

Needham and Spence (1996, 248) acknowledge that it is not very clear how middens differed in kind from truncated occupation sites. At one such site, Gravelly Guy, the pits alone accounted for 790 m^3 of finds-rich soil, which if spread over the c 3,400 m^2 surface of the site from which it derived, would have been 0.23 m thick. Allowing for the fills of some substantial ditches and the disturbed plough-soil machined off the site, the quantity of occupation-rich soil originally created at Gravelly Guy could easily have been equivalent to a total thickness of 0.5 or 0.6 m had much of it not ended up in pits and ditches. The accumulation of dumps of 'midden'-like deposits in the tops of middle to late Bronze Age waterholes is also well recognised and deserves more investigation.

It may thus be too simplistic to assume that all sites with unusually thick occupation deposits fit within a single class of specialist 'middens', or that plough-truncated sites do not reflect similar activities of generating and reprocessing waste. Almost any settlement would have been involved in the accumulation and recycling of more or less high value waste on some scale. While it is clear that

Fig. 7.18 (overleaf) Midden sites

MIDDEN SITES

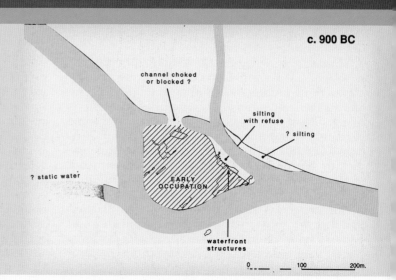

c. 900 BC

channel choked
or blocked ?

silting
with refuse

? silting

? static water

EARLY
OCCUPATION

waterfront
structures

0 ─ ─ ─ 100 ─ ─ ─ 200m.

Middens are generally defined as any surface rubbish or dung heap to which material is periodically added and reworked, which can include rubbish rich soils accumulating as the upper fills of waterholes. They are a phenomenon of the late Bronze Age and early Iron Age. Thames Valley midden sites have been identified at Runnymede, Whitecross Farm, Castle Hill and possibly Woodeaton.

On some sites these deposits reflect a higher level of communal interaction and status than would be normal on ordinary farming settlements. They represent special places where unusually rich and complex deposits accumulated, including a wide variety of artefacts and a larger proportion of high status items than most contemporary settlements. The deposition of materials was not haphazard discard of ordinary refuse, but possibly derived from high status communities and gatherings of people from further afield bringing items of particular value. Chalk platforms and other structural evidence within middens suggest that they were more than rubbish heaps. Riverside midden sites like Runnymede, Whitecross Farm and possibly Bray may even have been trading entrepôts.

Left page
Top left: Excavations in progress at Runnymede
Top right: Plan of the island midden site at Runnymede
Below left: Waste disposal and recycling at Runnymede
Below right: Distribution of types of wear on worked flint at Whitecross Farm showing variation of activity in different parts of the site
Right page
Top left: Excavation of midden deposits at Castle Hill
Top right: Trench across the island midden site at Whitecross Farm showing buried palaeochannel with contemporary timbers
Below: Artist's impression of the Whitecross Farm midden site

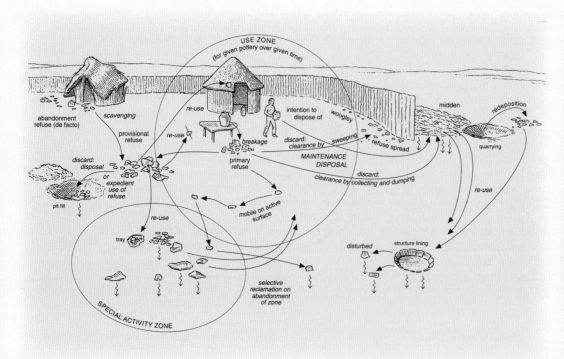

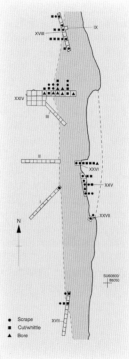

MIDDEN SITES

Not all sites with unusually thick occupation deposits were specialist midden sites. Most settlements would have accumulated and recycled waste on some scale. While it is clear that sites like Runnymede did so on an exceptional scale, there are no sharp dividing lines. At Gravelly Guy, for example, the finds rich soil that ended up in subsoil pits and ditches would have been equivalent to a deposit 0.4- 0.6 m thick if spread over the surface of the site.

Runnymede and Whitecross Farm occupied low-lying 'islands' in the river, while Castle Hill, Little Wittenham and Woodeaton were on higher ground. At Runnymede the late Bronze Age midden was the largest in the Thames Valley, covering an area of about 1.5 ha, from 0.2 m to at least 0.45 m thick (Needham 1991, 66-8, figs 20-25; Needham and Spence 1996, 41-6, figs 5-7; Needham 2000,232-4figs 11.9-11.10). The midden was at least partly enclosed by timber palisades or waterfront structures and surrounding rectangular posthole structures. The vast amount of refuse at Runnymede represents activities, notably food consumption, pottery breakage and craft production in the context of large gatherings of the resident community, visitors (perhaps vassals or subjects) expert craftsmen and traders.

some like Runnymede did this on a grand scale that sets them apart from ordinary settlements, there are no sharp dividing lines. The scale of deposits, the quality, density and character of finds, evidence of specific reprocessing activities and time scale of accumulation are all critical factors for characterising midden activities.

Ditches, pits, disused waterholes and latrines

Once ditches, storage pits and waterholes ceased to be used for their original purpose they were normally filled in with soil that contained, or had added to it, varying amounts of occupation debris and sometimes other deliberate deposits. Partially infilled ditches were often used as convenient places to dump rubbish, as reflected in the dense occupation debris in top of the large ditch at Petters Sports Field and concentrations of rubbish in ditch terminals close to house entrances. Pits were also used to dispose of domestic rubbish, and given that not all pits seem well suited for storage, it is possible that many were dug as repositories for waste and rubbish. Although this is difficult to demonstrate, some contain distinct layers of artefacts, bones and burnt stone, others sometimes have evidence of burnt soil and charcoal or dumps of burnt stone that could be the result of clearing out accumulated debris. Various attempts have been made to classify the fills of pits in ways that reflect the extent to which they silted up naturally, were filled in with clean subsoil, with well mixed soils containing general occupation debris, or heterogeneous deposits that reflect more specific dumping of debris. This generally indicates that pits were hardly ever left open to silt up naturally and very seldom filled in with freshly dug material (eg from a new pit), but were very commonly backfilled with mixed occupation soils. Pits with heterogeneous fills may reflect a more drawn out process of backfilling with material from a variety of sources. At Gravelly Guy the proportion of pits with heterogeneous fills declined with time (from 70% in the early Iron Age to 57% in the middle Iron Age) suggesting increased mixing of soils with time, also reflected in redeposited pottery.

Waterholes in particular are large features that tend to display distinct stages of backfilling, with some layers especially rich in occupation debris, particularly the hollow left by initial fills sinking as the soils compact beneath. Although in some cases such variation may have had strong symbolic connotations, in others it seems likely to be no more than the use of convenient hollows for dumping loads of soil containing pottery, burnt stone and bones that accumulated in and around houses. Similar fills can be seen in ditches used in the same way (see below).

The possible use of pits as latrines is an aspect of waste disposal that has received much less attention but the issue was examined on a number of sites in the Thames Valley in the 1970s and 1980s. At Brooklands Tomalin examined the character of pits and pit fills in the context of his observation of latrine pits in Africa (Hanworth and Tomalin 1977). At Mount Farm it was noticed that the natural gravel forming the base of pits was in some cases concreted, possibly as a result of their use as latrines, though analysis of this by Peter Fisher was inconclusive (Lambrick forthcoming). At Mingies Ditch it was suggested that a waterlogged pit containing an unusually high concentration of blackberry seeds, but not other scrub species that were present in the enclosure ditch, might have contained cess (Allen and Robinson 1993, 117). Perhaps the clearest evidence is from Rollright, where small semi-digested bones and mineralised remains characteristic of medieval and later cess pits were found, and it was noted that similar material occurred at Gravelly Guy, though this was not confirmed (Lambrick 1988). It is not entirely clear what these remains are, but they may be calcium phosphate castes of vesicles within faecal material.

Where residues from samples are examined a wider range of mineralised material is found. Mineralised material is increasingly identified in pit fills from the early to Middle Iron Age, but this type of material has not been found in late Iron Age features, suggesting a change in waste disposal (Campbell 2000). These remains are distinctive, survive reasonably well on sites with calcareous soils and are recoverable by sieving, but reports seldom indicate whether sample residues were examined for such remains, so their apparent rarity may partly be because evidence is not routinely being sought, despite its relevance to whether or not pits were dug or reused as latrines.

This important issue adds another dimension to the rationale behind pit digging and filling. If the layering observed by Tomalin is an indicator, then a high proportion of pits might have been used as latrines even if this was not their original function. Perhaps the most significant point about this proposed use of pits is that there are implications for how other pit deposits are interpreted. As indicated below, there is no hard-and-fast distinction between 'ordinary' rubbish disposal and so-called 'special' deposits; how they are interpreted relies partly on how the context of the place of deposition may have been seen. A 'special' deposit placed in a pit used as a latrine could have very different connotations from the same kind of deposit placed in a disused grain storage pit.

Chapter 8 – Attitudes to life and death

The sacred and profane were deeply intertwined throughout prehistory, but this relationship seems to have become especially evident in a great variety of 'special' deposits in late prehistoric domestic contexts that cannot adequately be explained in terms of ordinary rubbish disposal. This widely recognised characteristic of later prehistoric Britain is as evident in the Thames Valley as elsewhere, but it is often difficult to interpret what social, religious or spiritual beliefs, superstitions or traditional customs and ritualistic behaviour were reflected in the remains that ended up in the ground – especially since the context of deposition is seldom clear.

Another strong characteristic of life in later prehistory is that fewer monuments were overtly designed for ceremonial and funerary activity than in previous eras, though a variety of natural features, especially rivers, but also hills, woods and other natural or topographical features remained or became more important for a wide range of ritual activities.

In this chapter we examine a wide range of such evidence, including the expression of abstract aspects of social interactions and relationship with the world and wider cosmos. We start with some of the more mundane aspects of material culture and move towards the obviously sacred and aesthetic in terms of religion, human death and burial, and what this indicates about social status.

'Special deposits' and hoards

'Special deposits' in settlements

So-called 'special deposits' in settlements cover a wide range of material remains that appear to reflect something more than 'ordinary' rubbish disposal. As Lambrick and Allen (2004, 489) noted, the definition of what is regarded as 'special' is bound up with recognition and recording in the field. A degree of pragmatism is inevitably involved, reflected in the need to adopt methods of recording deposits that seem 'unusual'. The selection of material for burial in pits as 'special deposits' is known from the Neolithic and earlier Bronze Age and, if anything, the range of special deposits seems to have increased in later prehistory, reflecting a general increase of deposition of domestic and other debris in subsoil features and middens.

In the broadest sense 'special' deposits can include a wide variety of human burials, 'stray' human bones, burials of whole animals, articulated animal limbs, skulls and other bones, pottery, other objects and probably organic material that has not survived. In many cases a mixture of such materials, together with other characteristics such as concentrations of burnt stone may be present (Fig. 8.1).

The great variety of such deposits and complexity of the possible background beliefs and depositional processes that determined their character makes interpretation difficult. A wide range of types of deposit have been classed as 'special'. At Gravelly Guy about eighteen categories of human, animal and artefactual deposit were distinguished as being out of the ordinary and potentially ritualistic, and these are only part of the full range of such deposits that are known from the Thames Valley.

Various approaches have been adopted towards the recognition and classification of 'special' deposits, and a number of frameworks for interpretation of such deposits have been explored. In general these distinguish between undifferentiated deposits where no particular patterns are discerned; 'structured deposition' reflecting general patterns of behaviour and spatial differentiation that may be influenced by social and spiritual beliefs or traditions; and 'special deposits' which more specifically reflect non-pragmatic or ritualistic motivations.

A number of means of examining this in more detail have been attempted. At Segsbury, sherd size was taken as a key indicator of special status of deposits, although other studies (Bradley *et al.* 1980; Lambrick 1984; Needham and Sørensen 1988; Lambrick and Allen 2004 488-91) suggest that, given the range of materials and complexity of taphonomic processes involved, there is no need to expect a correlation between sherd size and ritualistic behaviour. Hill (1995, 125) argued most surviving archaeological material derives from deliberate, often ritualistic behaviour, but did not seek to make further distinctions in how deposits derive their characteristics. The taphonomic complexity of deposition has been studied in some detail at Runnymede, suggesting that it is often difficult to distinguish ritualistic behaviour (Needham and Spence 1996, 242-8).

Lambrick and Allen (2004, 489-90) saw the 'special deposits' at Gravelly Guy as the product of two factors – the behaviour that generated the material and the taphonomic processes involved in its deposition. The six behavioural factors ranged from direct veneration, through discarded waste or by-products of ritual activity, to incidental unrelated domestic rubbish. The depositional factors ranged

Fig. 8.1 (overleaf) 'Special deposits'

SPECIAL DEPOSITS

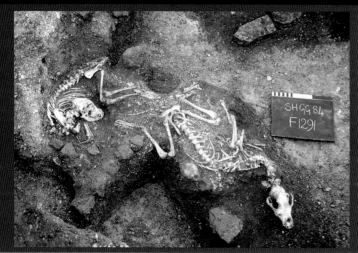

The social sphere

Life

Death

Utilisation (routine)
and Commissioning
(explicit)

Decommissioning

Disuse

Use/disuse

Use

Waterhole

Top left to right:
* *Double dog burial at Gravelly Guy*
* *Horse foreleg in a pit, Gravelly Guy*
* *Partially fired and over-fired
  loomweights, Yarnton*
* *Human skull fragment on the base of a
  pit, Castle Hill*

Left page:
* *(centre) Theoretical symbolism of
  deposits in a waterhole at Green Park,
  Reading*
* *(below right) Quern, pot and skull
  fragment: 'special deposits' at Castle
  Hill*
* *(below left) Reconstruction of pit finds
  from Horcott*

Right page:
* *Horse skulls in a ditch terminal,
  Gravelly Guy*
* *Bone and pottery deposits in middle
  Bronze Age pits and ditch junctions
  and terminals at Corporation Farm,
  Abingdon*

Special deposits involve a wide range of materials and reflect activities distinct from ordinary disposal. The selection of material for burial in pits, ditches, middens and other features is known from the Neolithic period onwards but an intensification in this particular type of activity and an increase in the range of materials is apparent in later prehistory. The definition of what is 'special' is highly dependent on recognition and recording in the field.

SPECIAL DEPOSITS

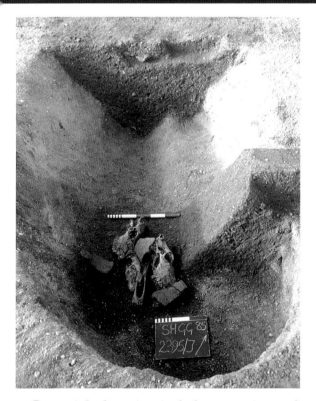

At Gravelly Guy 18 categories of human, animal and artefact deposits in pits and ditches were identified as extraordinary or possibly ritualistic. These were interpreted as the products of two factors - the behaviour that generated the material and the taphonomic processes involved in its deposition (Lambrick and Allen 2004; 489-90). Similar deposits were recorded at Castle Hill, Little Wittenham and occur at least in low numbers on most Iron Age settlements.

Placement of artefacts as 'closing deposits' within waterholes, pits and postholes was common practice in later prehistory and is highly visible in the archaeological record. Selective deposition of material in boundary features is also a recognised feature of prehistoric sites, as exemplified by artefacts placed in Bronze Age ditch junctions and terminals at Corporation Farm (Barclay *et al.* 2003, 31-40)

Special deposits include a variety of human and animal burials, selected limbs or skulls, pottery, metalwork, querns, burnt stone and probably a wide range of organic materials that have not survived. The variety of deposits and the complexity of the underlying behaviour and belief systems makes interpretation difficult. Various approaches have been adopted towards recognition, classification and interpretation of such deposits. These generally distinguish between undifferentiated deposits with no obvious pattern, 'structured deposition', which reflects general patterns of behaviour or spatial differentiation influenced by social and spiritual beliefs and traditions, and 'special deposits', which more specifically reflect non-pragmatic or ritual motivation.

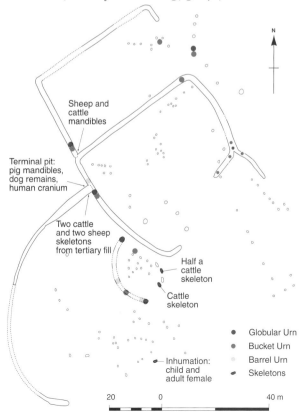

Sheep and cattle mandibles

Terminal pit: pig mandibles, dog remains, human cranium

Two cattle and two sheep skeletons from tertiary fill

Half a cattle skeleton

Cattle skeleton

- Globular Urn
- Bucket Urn
- Barrel Urn
- Skeletons

Inhumation: child and adult female

20   0   40 m

from deliberate placing of carefully selected items at one extreme to accidental redeposition at the other. It was found that different types of deposit could be interpreted in very different ways. It may also be the case that the symbolic significance of the object is grounded in the very fact that it has a role to play in everyday life (Hill 1995; Fitzpatrick 1997). Thus in one context an object may have no special status while in another it may be regarded in a different light, resulting in a quite different treatment.

Even though it is difficult to interpret the practices and ideas that lay behind particular deposits, they collectively appear to provide evidence of a wide range of superstitions, taboos, spiritual beliefs and votive activity. They say something about the status of people, animals and objects, and their relationships to each other beyond their routine roles. This may relate to a range of cosmological or religious ideas linking the natural and agricultural cycle with everyday living and the ordinary vicissitudes of personal and family life to more abstract beliefs and customs (Fitzpatrick 1997). While this provides much scope for theorising and speculation, it may be over-ambitious to expect to determine the meaning of such deposits with any precision.

The contents of most such deposits are various combinations of domestic objects and animals in varying states of completeness, but some special deposits have a distinctive element reflecting the natural world. For example, at Westcroft Road Carshalton (Proctor 2002) the top fill of a pit or shaft over 2.14 m deep contained an unusual group of finds, apparently consisting of raw materials such as flint nodules, 'raw potting clay', antlers, other selected material such as a horse skull and two red deer skulls but no post-cranial bones, and general domestic debris including worn broken querns – some conjoining between features – fragmented burnt sheep bone, pottery, perforated slabs, a fragment of briquetage, a broken piece of a bronze axe and worked flints.

Location

A further factor explored by Hill and others, commonly noted in excavation reports, is the location of special deposits. This has been subject to extensive scrutiny, including the position of deposits within pit and ditch fills as well as their broader spatial location in relation to houses, enclosures, boundaries, entrances and so on.

Many deposits do not obviously reflect specific associations with precise locations. For example, the position of deposits within pits and the stage of digging or infilling them is highly variable, reinforcing the impression that the beliefs and superstitions reflected were very much part of everyday life, although there may have been nuances of meaning that we cannot recognise. A specific issue in this respect is the need to understand what the context of deposition was and what it may have meant. The occurrence of such deposits in pits is commonly associated with the assumption that they were used as storage pits and the deposits were intended as propitiation to ensure fertility and good harvests, or offering thanks for successful storage. While this might make sense for deposits placed in empty pits which had gone out of use, it is more questionable when they were placed within the fill. Whatever their original use, if the infilling of pits was connected with their use as latrines or rubbish disposal, these provide an entirely different social context for interpretation of the deposits. This might reflect either a deliberate symbolic connection with waste and discard or a more incidental relationship. If the ritualistic act was not particularly concerned with how the remains were disposed of, they could still be archaeologically distinctive.

In other cases, special deposits were clearly made in particular localities within and around settlements, including ditch terminals and junctions. In this respect there seems a clear indication of superstitions or spiritual beliefs associated with concepts of boundaries and entrances as spiritual as well as physical points of liminality between spaces that had different social and economic roles. These particularly include deposits of animal skulls and jaws and sometimes querns or pots at ditch terminals. Animals or domestic objects also sometimes occur in entrances to houses or enclosures. Such deposits can also include human remains (see below).

In the Thames Valley such ideas were clearly well-established by the middle Bronze Age, as exemplified by the remarkable range of animal deposits associated with the terminals and junctions of ditches at Corporation Farm (Barclay *et al.* 2003, 37-40). Some of the middle Bronze Age L-shaped enclosure ditches produced unusually large pieces of pottery and other objects.

Foundation deposits, decommissioning and closure

In addition to the notion of spatial liminality, special deposits are often made, even today, to mark important times of change – a kind of temporal liminality marking new beginnings, the foundation or completion of objectives and closure or decommissioning of a place or structure. The most impressive deposits of this kind come from defensive enclosures such as foundation animal burials in the entrance of Rams Hill, and macabre human burials in hillfort ditches at Aylesbury, the Big Ring, Cassington and Blewburton (see below). At Blewburton a remarkable group of burials lay beneath the collapsed remains of the final phase of the fort entrance passage. These consisted of the skulls of a horse and a cow in the centre of the street close to the gate structure, an articulated deer skeleton lacking its hind quarters under the fallen stones of the southern revetment wall of the entrance passage, two complete horse skeletons under the fallen northern revetment wall and parts of the skull and forearm of a small child in the centre of the street nearby (Harding 1976b).

At Hartshill Copse, the 10th century cal BC ironworking site was deliberately closed with the removal of structural posts from the roundhouses and, in House C, the deposition of a large amount of burnt pottery in the postholes (Collard *et al.* 2006). There was no scorching to suggest that the posts were burnt *in situ*, but they might have been used as a kind of pyre for the building on which specially selected pots were placed. The final act in the 'closure' may have been the deposition of a complete burnt vessel in an axial posthole directly opposite the entrance of the structure. Other possible examples of 'closing' acts on broadly contemporary sites have been noted by Brück (2001b, 151–2), and the practice may also be evident on some early Iron Age sites (Collard *et al.* 2006).

These types of deposits are also found in more ordinary circumstances. It has been suggested that a recurrent pattern of finds from different levels in the backfill of waterholes reflects changes in the types of deposit symbolically associated with their use, disuse and final closure. As we have seen in Chapter 5, a variety of deposits seem to be associated with the initial foundation and/or closure of houses, including cremation or other burials.

'Special Deposits' and social dynamics

It is very difficult in most cases to get a good grasp on how often in the lives of people such deposits were made. Hill (1995, 100-1) suggests that they were episodic, Wait (1985, 83) implies that they were routine and commonplace aspects of everyday life and Fitzpatrick (1997, 79, 83) suggests that such deposits were made every five to 10 years. Perhaps the best evidence for the Thames Valley comes from the complete excavation of the early to late Iron Age and early Roman settlement at Gravelly Guy. Here, about 135 'special deposits' of human and animal remains were identified, distributed (not very evenly) across the periods represented (Lambrick and Allen 2004, 490-1). It was estimated that this equated to one every six or seven years for the early Iron Age, one every four or five years for the middle Iron Age and one every seven or eight years for the late Iron and Roman period, the lower frequency of the last figure possibly reflecting the smaller scale excavation of the late Iron Age to early Roman occupation area. Given a proposed six to eight family households occupying the Iron Age settlement, it was reckoned that human and animal deposits occurred only about once or twice per generation in any nuclear family, even though they were probably more frequent for the whole community or wider family groups (Lambrick and Allen 2004, 490-1).

However, we should not necessarily assume that Gravelly Guy is typical. It is more difficult to estimate such rates for other partially excavated settlements with less intensive sampling, but allowing for differences in sampling strategy, such deposits do appear to have been less common at the long-lived sites at Ashville, Yarnton and Coxwell

Road. In terms of human remains they seem to have been more common at sites like Castle Hill and Bourton-on-the-Water. On some low-lying and pastoral sites special deposits are apparently also rare, though in the light of the relatively short life of some of these settlements this may not be significant.

Hoarding

Hoards of metalwork are a particular feature of the late Bronze Age and pose major challenges of interpretation, partly because few have been excavated *in situ* but also because they can reflect a great variety of different social and economic contexts, and reasons for deposition, especially whether they were votive deposits or buried with the intent to recover them. This has been discussed at some length by Needham (1990) in connection with the hoard found from a large ditch at Petter's Sports Field, Egham (O'Connor 1986). Needham suggested that hoards were broadly distinguishable on the basis of content, first between 'weapon hoards' and others, with 'scrapped weapon hoards' of mainly broken items distinguished from small 'personal arms hoards' and larger 'armoury hoards' of weapons with little damage. Amongst the non-weapon hoards he suggested three kinds exhibiting limited damage to the objects can be distinguished, predominantly 'axe hoards', or with a more mixed range of tools, 'tool kit' hoards, and other specialised hoards. Those in which damage is frequent are seen as 'scrap hoards', of which those with a component of metalworking debris or equipment can be termed 'founders' hoards'. This type of classification is perhaps more useful as a general description of the range of hoards than necessarily providing clear-cut explanations of the motivations and exact circumstances of hoard deposition.

Hoarding is generally seen as a 'special' activity, whether for votive purposes or concealment. As Needham (1990, 138) noted, while weapon hoards are often regarded as votive deposits this need not always have been the case, and conversely it does not mean that other categories were not votive. Any collections of metalwork, whether complete items or scrap, would have been extremely valuable, hence both appropriate as important votive offerings and worth concealing for later recovery if in danger of being stolen. This is discussed by Needham (2001) in relation to hoards whose contents could have been partly removed during the Bronze Age. Conversely there may be a danger that deliberately buried non-metallic objects are too readily seen as 'special deposits' rather than as hoards of valued items stored in small pits.

Hingley (2006) discusses these issues in relation to late prehistoric iron objects, arguing that few can be regarded as casual losses or rubbish, though he only considered individual objects recognised as 'special deposits'. He found a notable correlation of such deposits with ditches or boundaries, especially hoards of currency bars. In the Upper Thames

Valley these include the hoards of 12 currency bars from the back of the ramparts at Madmarston (Fowler 1960, 11, 13, 14) and Salmonsbury (Dunning 1976) and a corroded mass of *c* 10 bars at Totterdown Lane, Horcott close to a boundary outside a middle Iron Age enclosure (Pine and Preston 2004, 45, 69-70). To these might be added several currency bars from the river.

Another notable iron object in a boundary context is the adze hammer found beneath a horse and human burial in the hillfort ditch at Blewburton (Collins 1952-3, 50, fig. 17, no. 10) but another one, from a pit within the settlement at Yarnton (Hey *et al.* forthcoming a), does not seem to have the same connotations. Hingley found few instances of deposits of iron objects in Iron Age pits, wells and waterholes, and it is noticeable in the Thames Valley that, although Bronze Age and Iron Age metalwork is common in natural watery contexts (river channels and occasionally springs like that at Little Wittenham), few metal objects have been found in middle to late Bronze Age waterholes.

Hingley also noted an association of iron objects with shrines, including the ploughshare from Frilford (Bradford and Goodchild 1939, 13), but it is worth noting the varied contexts of the iron and wooden ploughshares found in the Thames Valley – waterhole at Thames Valley Park, a ditch at Berwick Salome and a river channel at Eton (see above Chapter 7). This raises the question of how far it is sensible to consider complex relationships between hoarding and votive deposits in terms of the parent material rather than the part they played in everyday life or special events.

Whereas small scraps of iron that could not easily be fashioned into other objects are common as casual losses and general living debris, most objects of any size (ie too valuable not to recycle) are found in some sort of hoard or votive deposit. For these larger objects the issue was not just that they were iron, and hence valuable, but also that they had other functions and values and so might be deposited in a wide variety of places. At Gravelly Guy the most complete large iron object was a spearhead from a child burial, but the next largest items – a scrap fragment of a currency bar and an almost complete knife blade – had no such association, though a smaller fragment of possible currency bar came from a pit with a dog burial (Lambrick and Allen 2004, 362-66; 249-57).

The river and other watery places as a focus for deposition

The River Thames is one of the most prolific sources of late prehistoric metalwork in North West Europe (Bradley 1998). Jill York (2002) examined the distribution and character of Bronze Age metalwork, three-quarters of which is weaponry, in some detail (Fig. 8.2). Compared with a relatively even distribution of early Bronze Age metalwork in the Middle Thames, she found substantial variation in later

Bronze Age deposition. In the 20 miles between Runnymede and Teddington this was almost twice as substantial as in an equivalent stretch of the river between Bisham and Windsor, which in turn was much more than in further 20 mile sections of the river upstream. In each case the increase was fundamentally middle Bronze Age in origin, sustained into the late Bronze Age (York 2002, fig. 3). York also found that the proportion of objects deliberately destroyed steadily increased from none in the early Bronze Age to 21% in the middle Bronze Age and 50% in the late Bronze Age. Most of the destroyed objects had been used.

The nature of the places where there are particular concentrations of weaponry and other metalwork is still not entirely clear. Some concentrations of later Bronze Age weaponry and other metalwork from the river are near major fortified enclosures or other high status sites, and this probably applies also to Iron Age metalwork. There is a concentration of finds from the Thames in the vicinity at Days Lock and from a spring at Little Wittenham, not far from the late Bronze Age enclosure and Iron Age hillfort at Castle Hill and the late Iron Age enclosure of Dyke Hills. Another concentration is known from Taplow, close to the similar sequence of late Bronze Age enclosure and Iron Age fort (Allen *et al.* forthcoming a and d). If the supposed Marshalls Hill enclosure is real, a similar picture may apply at Reading, as suggested by Bradley (1984, 122-2, fig. 5.4), and a similar case might be made for Iron Age objects in the river Wey below the St Georges Hill hillfort. Another instance might be Windsor, where a major concentration of river finds is close to the naturally defensive bluff on which the medieval castle may obscure a prehistoric fortified enclosure (see below, Chapter 9).

If late prehistoric riverside middens are also taken into account, a notable concentration of middle to late Bronze Age material is known from Wallingford in the vicinity of the Whitecross Farm site (Northover 2006, 56-7). Below Taplow there is another concentration at Bray close to another suspected high status site. Just downriver from Runnymede a concentration of Bronze Age metalwork is recorded in the 'Staines' reach and downstream from Teddington the major concentration of metalwork in the Brentford Syon Park reach of the river is close to what may be another high status, possibly multi-period site, though as yet there is only inconclusive evidence (Bell 1996). This leaves two further concentrations of metalwork at Kingston and Weybridge where there is insufficient evidence of a known high status terrestrial or island site, though they might be expected in these positions, like the other sites near the confluences of tributaries with the Thames or associated with river eyots.

Excavated examples of riverine deposits of metalwork are rare, but during gravel extraction at Shepperton Ranges a late Bronze Age hafted axe and an Iron Age sword and scabbard were recovered from a buried loop of the Thames close to the Wey confluence (Fig. 8.2). These were part of a long sequence of deposits in the channel, stretching from the Neolithic to the medieval (Poulton forthcoming b).

At Abbey Meads monitoring of dragline excavation of a palaeochannel produced a series of deliberately discarded objects including a Neolithic stone axe and a range of later prehistoric metalwork (Jones in prep.). These include a late Bronze Age sword of 10th century BC Wilburton type in good condition. The most important object from the quarry is the Chertsey Shield (Stead 1987). It was made entirely of bronze except for the wooden core of the handle, which provided a radiocarbon date of 750-190 cal BC (*c* 400-250 cal BC at one sigma level). Stead concluded that it had probably been made only for display or ritual purposes and in art historical terms was 'very probably La Tène 1' (Stead 1987, 22-3). It had almost certainly been in good condition and complete when it entered the river. Although it was slightly crumpled and had lost its handle when it was recovered, this was probably damage that resulted from its retrieval in a drag-line bucket. A late Iron Age or more likely early Roman coarse ware beaker of unusual form was also recovered from this area. A human skull and neck vertebrae were also found (see below).

The most thorough investigation of the issue of deposition in ancient river channels has been undertaken at the Eton Rowing Course (Allen *et al.* 2000; forthcoming b) where prehistoric waterlogged deposits were found either on sandbanks within the former Thames palaeochannel or in the main channel adjacent to timber structures interpreted as bridges across the channel (Fig. 8.3). This is the first time that a good picture of the long-lived range of funerary, farming and settlement uses of the adjacent land has been brought together with detailed investigation of old river channels. These revealed bridges, other timber structures and channel deposits that contained a range of human body parts and domestic and agricultural objects, though no major weaponry or other metal objects. There was a long tradition of deposition in the river at Dorney, with human bones (and possibly whole individuals), large parts of vessels and deliberately placed animal skulls and antlers being found at the channel edge from the Neolithic onwards.

There is some indication that the detailed nature of this behaviour at Eton changed in later prehistory, perhaps connected with the construction and use of a series of six timber bridges across the main palaeochannel (Fig. 6.19). The first bridge dates to the middle Bronze Age when much of a fineware globular urn was deposited in the river. In the later Bronze Age animal and human bones appear on the sandbank and in the main channel, and an ard share, much of a pot and a deposit of charred cereal grains were deposited on the channel edge. Human bones were also found, and especially notable are a series of late Bronze Age to early Iron Age longbones which show evidence of modification. Cuts on the bones imply deliberate defleshing and disarticulation, while gnawing by carnivores implies that bones were either excarnated or simply left in the open close to the river. Further bridges were constructed in the early Iron Age, and are accompanied by pots and timbers driven into the sandbank, while in the middle Iron Age whole bodies may have been put into the water next to the last bridge.

At Eden Walk in the middle of Kingston-upon-Thames a long sequence of palaeochannel deposits was investigated (Serjeantson *et al.* 1991-2). Some of the earlier levels were Neolithic and produced flints, the frontal bone of a human skull and human femurs. These deposits were overlain by a layer of brushwood which may have been a deliberate foundation for a large dump of burnt flint with Deverel-Rimbury pottery on or in the top, possibly a 'burnt mound' deposit, though conceivably some sort of deliberately constructed platform. Subsequent deposits indicate a change from clogged organic mud to a more sandy silt, suggesting a change to freer flowing conditions in the Iron Age but with no further deliberate deposits

At Brimpton, south of the River Kennet, a watching brief during gravel extraction in 1978-9 revealed a palaeochannel of the River Enborne which had been cut by later Bronze Age features (Lobb 1990, Site A). Conditions were not suitable for detailed investigation, but a side-looped socketed spearhead was recovered along with a significant quantity of late Bronze Age pottery and animal bone, a bronze-working crucible and a bun-shaped clay weight from layers deposited in the river channel which sealed these features. The lack of abrasion on the pottery and the good to moderate state of bone preservation suggests that this material had not been heavily reworked but was dumped in a relatively fresh condition, possibly from a nearby settlement that was not located. It was not suggested at the time that the deposition of this material might have had special connotations and it seems to have been different from the material at Eton, which appears to have entered the river as individual acts of deposition rather than general dumps of material.

This is comparable to the situation at Whitecross Farm where there was some debate about the nature of the metalwork finds relative to objects from the river. It is now clear that while some metal objects were deposited in the river, they are reasonably distinct from the material from the island midden which was partly a scattered hoard of scrap and partly objects associated with domestic occupation on the site. But there was also other evidence of

Fig. 8.2 (overleaf) Deposits from the River Thames and its tributaries

RIVER DEPOSITS

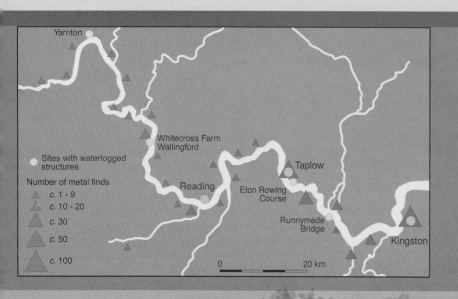

Sites with waterlogged structures

Number of metal finds

c. 1 - 9

c. 10 - 20

c. 30

c. 50

c. 100

Yarnton

Whitecross Farm
Wallingford

Reading

Taplow

Eton Rowing
Course

Runnymede
Bridge

Kingston

0   20 km

Deposits of late prehistoric metalwork, mainly weaponry, human body parts and other artefacts, have been recovered from the Thames and its tributaries. The overall distribution shows that much more metalwork was deposited in the Middle and Lower Thames than the Upper Thames, both in the late Bronze Age and the Iron Age.

A distribution of late Bronze Age riverine deposits (York 2002) suggests a correlation with fortified enclosures and other high status sites. River deposits have been found at Days Lock and at a spring at Little Wittenham close to the Bronze Age enclosure and Iron Age hillfort at Castle Hill and the late Iron Age enclosure at Dyke Hills. Other concentrations are known from Taplow, close to the late Bronze Age enclosure and Iron Age fort and from below Taplow at Bray.

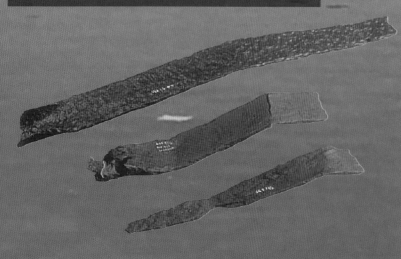

RIVER DEPOSITS

Clockwise from top left:

* Distribution of Thames River deposits (York 2002)
* Dredging the River Thames
* The Chertsey shield
* Iron Age shield from Abbey Mead, Chertsey
* Iron Age dagger from the Thames at Mortlake
* The Waterloo helmet
* Bronze Age sword from the Thames at Mortlake
* Iron Age sword with bronze scabbard mounts, Shepperton Ranges
* Deliberately damaged currency bars from the Thames at Reading

Such deposits are also associated with high status late Bronze Age island midden sites, for example a deposit from the 'Staines' reach down river from Runnymede and from Wallingford close to Whitecross Farm. Excavated examples of riverine deposits are rare but a late Bronze Age hafted axe and Iron Age sword and scabbard came from a loop of the Thames close to the Wey confluence at Shepperton Ranges (Poulton forthcoming b).

RIVER DEPOSITS
ETON ROWING COURSE

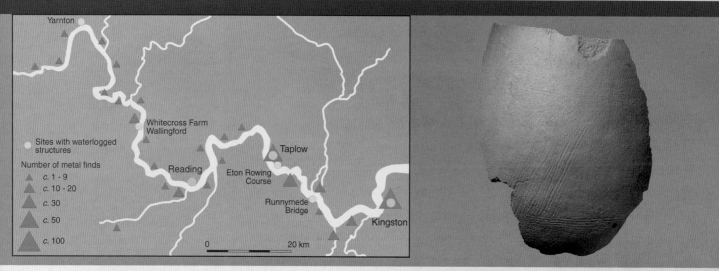

A thorough investigation of ancient river channel deposition was recently undertaken at Eton Rowing Course. Waterlogged deposits found on sandbanks within the former Thames palaeochannel and in the main channel provide a good picture of a long-lived range of funerary and settlement use of the adjacent land. The tradition of deposition in the river at Dorney began in the Neolithic period with the placing of human bones, pottery, animal skulls and antlers.

With the construction of a series of bridges across the palaeochannel from the middle Bronze Age onwards, these deposition rites evolved. Human body parts, domestic and agricultural objects (but no major weaponry or major metal objects) were associated with the bridges. A middle Bronze Age fineware urn was deposited during the life of the first bridge and in the late Bronze Age animal and human bones, an ard share, pottery and charred cereal grains were placed in the river

RIVER DEPOSITS
ETON ROWING COURSE

Clockwise from top left:

* Distribution of Thames River deposits (after York 2000)
* Bronze Age globular urn from the Eton Channel
* Eton Rowing Course site during excavation
* Human bone from the river channel: Neolithic skull and late prehistoric limb bones
* Late prehistoric limb bones with evidence of gnawing, cut marks and possible marrow extraction
* Late Iron Age scythe blade and late Bronze Age wooden ard share
* Amber bead
* In situ late Bronze Age pot placed on the edge of a sand bank

and on the channel edge. Late Bronze Age/early Iron Age human long bones from these deposits show cut marks consistent with defleshing and disarticulation, and gnawing marks attest to exposure on the riverbank. During the middle Iron Age the dead were placed in the water next to the final phase bridge.

deliberate deposition from an almost complete pot and possible demolished hearth dumped (or placed) in the channel immediately adjacent to the site (Cromarty *et al.* 2006, 45-6).

Bradley and Gordon (1988) showed that there is a strong correlation in the occurrence of human skulls with that of artefacts, usually weaponry, deposited in the Thames, and they suggested that the skulls probably span a similar date range to the artefacts. While some human bones have been found on riverside sites (such as a skull from Runnymede), it is thought that most were deliberately deposited in the river, not eroded from riverside sites or burials. The extent to which this was a novel practice is uncertain, but we will now turn to look in more detail at changing burial practices.

Burials in monuments and cemeteries

Middle to late Bronze Age

In very broad terms, one of the clearest features of later prehistory that distinguishes it from earlier periods is that communities gave up building large formal monuments for the dead. While this undoubtedly reflects a change in attitudes to treatment of the dead and may reflect much deeper-seated changes in social relationships, it is not something that happened suddenly. In the middle Bronze Age in particular, pre-existing burial monuments continued to be used, were respected and sometimes remodelled and used afresh; less commonly new earthwork barrows were built, albeit on a smaller scale than many of their Neolithic and early Bronze Age predecessors. The Thames Valley has a rich legacy of burial monuments in earlier prehistory (Hey *et al.* forthcoming c) and extensive excavations on the gravels and elsewhere have provided valuable insights into how funerary practices gradually moved away from formal burial in monuments to a wide range of other locations.

During the earlier Bronze Age, as compared with the Beaker period, formal burial practices had shifted from a normal rite of inhumation, almost always in crouched position, to cremation and only occasionally inhumation. Cremation deposits were quite varied, sometimes enclosed in pots, which might be upright, inverted or on their side and sometimes with other objects, including pottery, struck flints, burnt stone, bone or metal and more rarely items of 'exotic' materials like amber or jet. Some deposits represent a substantial proportion of the burnt bones of a single individual, others the mixed remains of more than one person. Often the cremated bone was only a token amount, which might be associated with urns or other objects. In many instances there are other cremation-like deposits that do not actually contain cremated bone although they are close to others that do. Essentially

these practices continued into the middle Bronze Age, and in addition inhumation burials became more common.

Although cremation burial began to decline in the late Bronze Age in favour of inhumation and probably excarnation, there is increasing evidence from the Thames Valley that cremation continued into the late Bronze Age and even the early Iron Age, though such remains are rare and seldom accompanied by grave goods. There is no clear evidence that this means of disposing of the dead continued in the middle Iron Age before it re-emerged in the late Iron Age when, once again, some burials were accompanied by grave goods.

In addition to these changes in *how* the dead were treated, there were complex patterns of *where* their remains were disposed of, which raise a wide range of issues concerning the nature of prevalent belief systems and social status.

Maintenance and reuse of pre-existing monuments

The visible, permanent commemoration of the dead through the building of substantial barrows as monuments for the burial of important members of society reached its apogee in the early Bronze Age. Such monuments were constructed in a wide range of forms and varied concentrations, from single isolated mounds to pairs, small scattered groups, and some major barrow cemeteries that developed over several hundred or even a few thousand years. Much older monuments, some dating to the early Neolithic, also survived as visible earthworks, either within the later barrow cemeteries that grew up around them or in more isolated locations. Whether through continued use or long tradition such monuments were still identified as burial places and for the most part continued to be respected in the middle to late Bronze Age. There are several cases where they continued to be used, or were re-used afresh for burials in the middle Bronze Age, sometimes re-defined, re-emphasised or remodelled in the process. This can be seen for a variety of types of earlier prehistoric monument, not just those particularly dating from the immediately preceding centuries.

Perhaps the clearest example of reuse of a Neolithic monument as a middle Bronze Age cemetery is at Shorncote/Cotswold Community, south Gloucestershire (Barclay and Glass 1995). Here a small, deep hengiform ring ditch with a narrow (0.2 m) gap in the northern ditch was recut on the inside forming a slightly broader, shallower ditch 0.8 m deep and over 2 m wide, leaving an interior diameter of 9 m and retaining the narrow northern gap (Fig. 8.4). A posthole set in the narrow causeway might belong to either phase. Inside the enclosure there were 16 small pits, a few with Deverel-Rimbury cremation burials, including a central pit containing one of the larger

Fig 8.3 (previous spread)   River deposits at Eton Rowing Course

burials (298 g) together with a bucket urn with horseshoe lugs. The main cluster of features lay south-west of a diametrical axis through the entrance and its posthole, the central pit and a row of other cremation burials/small pits. These included a few other deposits associated with urns, while unurned ones were concentrated at the eastern side of the interior. Some cremation burials were close to the inner edge of the ditch, and three more were found cut into the upper filling of the primary ditch on its outer edge, so probably still inside the presumed position of the external bank. Typically for the period the burials were either small (1-31 g) or larger (111-299 g) and, where there were traces of urns, they were mainly just fragments of bucket urn. Externally there were five cremation burials, three token deposits (2-30 g) and two full remains (451g and 487 g), together with two inhumation burials. One of these was of a 14 to 15 year old youth in a very tightly crouched or bound position, radiocarbon dated to 1412-1265 cal BC. The other a tightly crouched adult dated to 1505-1395 or 1335-1325 cal BC, cut by one of cremation deposits. Seven other cremation deposits were found in the general vicinity of the cemetery in trial trenching.

On the floodplain at Yarnton middle Bronze Age domestic debris in the upper filling of a rectangular Neolithic long enclosure ditch showed it was still a visible earthwork when a pit containing cremated human bone and charcoal dated to 1520-1320 and 1490-1260 cal BC was dug in its north-east corner. Another pit to the north dated to 1290-920 and 1390-1040 cal BC produced a sequence of fills containing cremated human skull and long bone fragments amongst burnt stone and animal bones, some also burnt, including a significant proportion of pig and some young sheep as well as cattle and deer. A few other middle Bronze Age pits with domestic debris, including misfired pottery, were found nearby (Hey *et al.* forthcoming b).

Other examples of Neolithic and early Bronze Age monuments being reused for middle Bronze Age burials include a Bronze Age cremation dated to 1700 to 1440 cal BC inserted in the terminal of one of the ditch sections of a Neolithic segmented ring ditch at Reading Business Park/Green Park (Brossler *et al.* 2004, 7). In an initial discussion of the discoveries at Perry Oaks/T5 it was suggested that a somewhat comparable segmented oval Neolithic enclosure had been partly remodelled, with the entrance narrowed in the middle Bronze Age, but it does not appear to have been reused for burials. Although it was thought that this might have been the intention (Barrett *et al.* 2001, 223) this was not discussed further in the full report (Framework Archaeology 2006). Not far away at Prospect Park a small oval ring ditch of probable earlier Bronze Age date had an undated deposit of burnt material within it (though not central) and two middle Bronze Age urned cremations outside it nearby, possibly not associated (Crockett 2001). At the Eton

Rowing Course a probable Beaker barrow had two cremations buried just outside the ditch, one dated to 1320 to 990 cal. BC (Allen *et al.* 2000, 71-6). This may have been an outlier of a more substantial cemetery associated with another ring ditch not far away (see below).

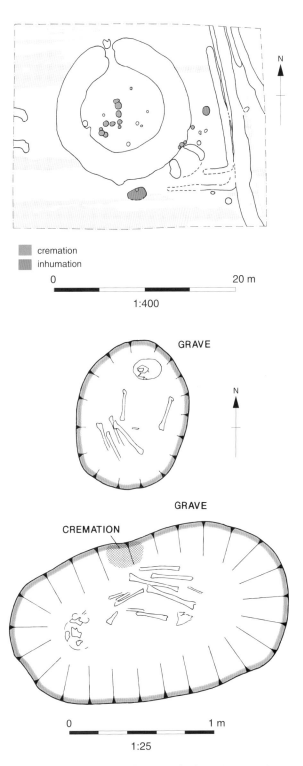

Fig 8.4 Formal burial places in the later Bronze Age: reuse of a Neolithic ring ditch as a Bronze Age urnfield and inhumation burial ground, Shorncote

Detailed analysis of the sequence at Imperial Sports Ground is still in progress, but the interim report (Crockett 2001) indicates that a middle Bronze Age cremation cemetery lay a short way to the west of a Neolithic mortuary enclosure which enhanced magnetic susceptibility highlighted as a possible pyre site. There was also an east facing penannular enclosure containing cremation burials due north of a double ring ditch, again possibly suggesting respect for the general area of Neolithic ritual activity. The double ring ditch and penannular cemetery were in the centre of a double width field which was part of a coaxial field system aligned on various earlier prehistoric monuments.

Amongst the major ceremonial and funerary complexes of the Upper Thames Valley there are only a few cases indicating continuing use or reuse of monuments for burial in the middle to late Bronze Age, but this may partly be due to limitations of investigation. Large areas of the complexes at Standlake, Stanton Harcourt, Cassington and Dorchester-on-Thames were destroyed before the 1970s with only limited salvage investigation of the more obvious ring ditches. Given the character and location of many later Bronze Age burial deposits – often small, usually off-centre, in secondary ditch fills or in spaces between barrows – it is likely that the small number of cases where middle Bronze Age or later funerary deposits are recorded do not show the full picture. The recorded examples include inhumation and cremation burials inserted singly into barrows but also 'urnfields', where a significant number of cremation burials, often contained within or accompanied by urns, were concentrated in a particular area, sometimes extending into partly silted up ditches. In some cases solitary burials also occur further away from pre-existing monuments.

At Stanton Harcourt Barrow XV 4/4a was a pear-shaped ring ditch that formed the south-eastern end of a conjoined group of three ring ditches of varying sizes (Hamlin 1963; Barclay *et al.* 1995, 93-5, fig. 49). None had central burials but a small middle Bronze Age cremation cemetery of five burials was found in the upper fill of the ditch. Two of the burials were of children unaccompanied by vessels, a third deposit contained the remains of three adults accompanied by a large cinerary urn, with a fourth contained a small bucket urn with no bones acting as an accessory deposit. The fifth deposit incorporated the remains of another individual with fragments of an unclassifiable urn. A further deposit in a comparable stratigraphic position on the opposite side of the ring ditch was of an adult accompanied by sherds of an unclassified urn. About 9 m outside the ring ditch group another cremation burial contained remains of at least one adult and parts of a bucket urn. Unlike a similar group of conjoined ring ditches on the other side of the barrow cemetery at Gravelly Guy (Lambrick and Allen 2004, 51-61; Barclay *et al.* 1995, 89-93) no earlier burials were found in this complex and the

sequence of construction was not clear. The possibility that part or all of the ring ditch complex originated in the middle Bronze Age cannot be ruled out, though on balance this seems less likely than the broadly similar circumstances of a barrow at Standlake, where a simpler small ring ditch was associated with a much larger urnfield (see below).

At the Neolithic and early Bronze Age linear barrow cemetery at Barrow Hills, Radley two barrows, one at each end of an intermittent southern row of barrows, contained middle and late Bronze Age burials. Barrow 16, excavated in the 1930s at the north-east end of the cemetery, contained eight secondary cremation burials with Deverel-Rimbury pottery in a tight cluster in the south-east quadrant of the interior of the ring ditch. A notable feature of these was that several were inserted into surviving traces of original topsoil without penetrating the gravel, implying that comparable burials would have been destroyed by ploughing and/or topsoil stripping (Barclay and Halpin 1999, 162-6, fig 5.11). At the south-west end of the barrow cemetery two middle to late Bronze Age inhumation burials had been inserted into the backfill of an infilled pond barrow. The earlier of these, dated 1310-1000 cal BC, was of a man aged 40 to 50. He was buried in a tightly crouched position with his head to the west but was incomplete and semi-articulated, as if buried as a partly decayed bound or bagged corpse. The feet and limbs were well preserved but little of the torso survived, and they appeared too tightly packed to have been disturbed later. The other burial, dated to 1020-810 cal BC, was inserted into the backfill of this barrow, probably somewhat later. It consisted of the complete body of a 14 to 16 year old buried in a crouched position, on the right side, head to the north-east (Barclay and Halpin 1999, 53, fig 4.12). About 40 m away, the almost complete carcass of an unbutchered calf dated to 1190-890 cal BC was buried in the backfill of another small pond barrow (Barclay and Halpin 1999, 42-4, fig 4.5).

Another example of such an association is at Berinsfield Wally Corner, where a solitary cremation of an infant accompanied by sherds of bucket urn lay immediately adjacent to an undated pond barrow (Boyle *et al.* 1995 11, 13-4, fig 7).

At Mount Farm near Dorchester-on-Thames (Lambrick 1979; forthcoming) a broken collared urn and cremations and inhumations dating to the latter part of the early Bronze Age were found in a band *c* 3-5 m wide round much of the inside of a flat-bottomed ring ditch with an internal diameter of 21 m (Fig. 8.5). The latest burial was the inhumation of a young woman of 17-20 dated to 1680-1220 cal BC, who was buried in a grave dug through one of the postholes of an earlier timber ring. There was no dating evidence from primary fills of the ditch, nor any central burial, but the dating and distribution of the funerary deposits, the size of the ditch and its relationship with two double-ditched field boundaries that respected it, suggest that the monument

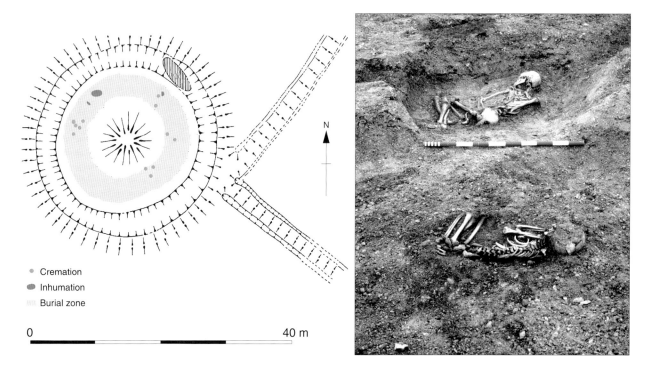

Fig. 8.5   Continued use of formal burial places in the middle Bronze Age: (left) *interpretative plan of early Bronze Age ring ditch at Mount Farm indicating burial zone;* (right) *middle Bronze Age inhumation burials within the Mount Farm ring ditch*

originated as a disc barrow with a small central mound and an outer bank. The secondary fills of the ring ditch, particularly in its southern extent, contained a moderate scatter of Deverel-Rimbury pottery (mostly coarse bucket urns) and animal bone (mostly cattle) radiocarbon dated to 1520-1090 cal BC, which may or may not have been associated with funerary activity. These fills were cut by a large waterhole with an access ramp making use of the hollow of the partly silted ring ditch which produced radiocarbon dates of 1508-931 cal BC and 1310-820 cal BC, and by an oval pit packed with charcoal and burnt quartzite, and a few sherds of middle Bronze Age globular urn. About 20 m north-west of the barrow was an isolated, unaccompanied cremation burial.

A similar sequence was found in the Middle Thames Valley at Field Farm, Burghfield (Butterworth and Lobb 1992, 7-17) where a ring ditch with an internal diameter of 41.5 m and a narrow ESE entrance was found beneath a ploughed round barrow 0.4 m high. There was a central spread of charcoal around a hearth at the centre of the ring ditch accompanied by the collapsed remains of a Neolithic Mortlake ware pot and a semicircular or D-shaped setting of small postholes *c* 2.5-3 m across open to the east-north-east. The ring ditch may have been later – a burnt layer in secondary fill of the ditch produced a radio-carbon date of 2130-1710 cal BC and there was a central pit with fragments of early Bronze Age pottery, cremated bone and flints dated on associated charcoal to 2280-1780 BC. A small number of

cremation burials and accessory deposits occurred in a band 7.5 m to 9.5 m inside the inner edge of ditch. Three of these were associated with earlier Bronze Age collared urns and two with Deverel-Rimbury style pots, but one of the collared urn deposits produced a remarkably late radiocarbon date of 1310-910 cal BC. A burnt posthole in the same ring of features provided an archaeomagnetic date of 1860-1650 BC. A shallow V-shaped cut in the terminal on the south side of the 'entrance' to the ring ditch contained burnt stone, charcoal and late Bronze Age pottery. Environmental evidence from the main barrow ditch suggests that in the Neolithic and early Bronze Age the area was mature oak woodland with grassy clearings which became more open in the later Bronze Age. Other smaller ring ditches associated with middle Bronze Age burials were constructed nearby suggesting continued creation of funerary monuments into the middle Bronze Age (see below).

Not far from Field Farm, at Herons House, Burghfield a middle Bronze Age bucket urn and charcoal radiocarbon dated to 1550-1000 cal BC were recovered from a circular scoop cut into the upper fill of a ring ditch. Charcoal from the ring ditch thought to be derived from scrub clearance produced a comparable radiocarbon determination of 1500-1010 cal BC, suggesting that the burial had been inserted into an earlier overgrown earthwork (Bradley and Richards 1980). Middle Bronze Age pottery was also found in the upper fills of two other small ring ditches near Burghfield, which might have been recut at this period, though in this case there were no definite middle Bronze Age cremation or inhumation burials (Lobb 1983-5 13-5, fig. 2).

New barrows in the middle Bronze Age

In addition to the evidence of the continued use or reuse of pre-existing monuments and barrows, there is increasing, though often inconclusive evidence that some ring ditches and barrows were built as new monuments in the middle Bronze Age. Close to the main barrow at Field Farm were other ring ditches (Butterworth and Lobb 1992, 7-17), of which one contained later Bronze Age material, but not in a primary position. Another produced two cremation burials associated with Deverel-Rimbury urns, one with a surprisingly early radiocarbon date of 2460-1740 cal BC. A fourth irregularly shaped, segmental ring ditch had a near-central pit with an almost complete barrel urn inverted over dense charcoal and cremated human bone. As at Mount Farm, there was also a single outlying middle Bronze Age cremation burial not marked by a barrow or ring ditch.

In the barrow cluster at the Eton Rowing Course (Allen *et al.* 2000, 76-7) a ring ditch 21.5 m in diameter with a narrow gap in the ditch on the south side had two middle Bronze Age cremation burials, though not in the central area which had been disturbed (Fig. 8.6). One was accompanied by a inverted decorated globular urn dated to 1530-1410 cal. BC. A line of three cremation pits lay just outside the ditch on the north-east, one containing the base of a middle Bronze Age vessel, another dated to 1390-1100 cal. BC. No pottery was recovered from the primary fills of the ditch but several other middle Bronze Age cremation deposits were found in the secondary fills, as well as a spread of pottery and unburnt animal bones. Alongside the ring ditch there was a segmental ditch of which two segments contained large deposits of later Bronze Age flint knapping debris. Although not conclusive evidence, the extensive use of this monument for burial and other rituals over a few centuries after 1500 cal BC, its small size, the gap in the ditch and absence of earlier finds are all consistent with an origin in the middle Bronze Age rather than earlier.

At Cippenham a ring ditch of similar form and history, with a narrow southern entrance gap and secondary cremation burials and dumping of middle Bronze Age pottery and other finds in the ditch, may be another middle Bronze Age ring ditch (Ford *et al.* 2003, 96-9, figs 4.2-4.6). An external 'cremation cluster' of five small pits was found about 60 m to the SSW of the ring ditch. These included a pit with a collared urn and burnt flint but no burnt bone, a second with a complete inverted bucket urn, globular urn sherds, flint flakes and burnt flint but only 8 g of cremated bone. A third produced 110 g of the cremated remains of a young adult and an infant with a small quantity of burnt flint and the fourth another token cremation and some burnt flint. The fifth pit contained only charcoal and burnt flint.

The east-facing penannular enclosure containing cremation burials in the centre of a double width field at Imperial Sports Ground may be another example of a new middle Bronze Age funerary monument, added to a pre-existing group of burial and ceremonial earthworks (Crockett 2001).

At Wey Manor Farm, Addlestone a small pit contained a probable cremation deposit of charcoal and fragments of burnt bone with one undiagnostic

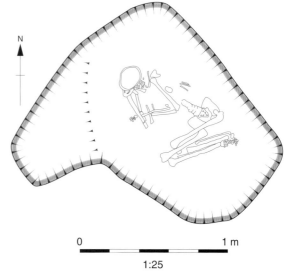

Fig. 8.6 Formal burial places in the later Bronze Age: Middle Bronze Age ring ditch with cremation burials and possibly contemporary inhumation burial at Eton Rowing Course

piece of pottery. A second, similar pit produced fragments of a ceramic cup but no human remains. Both were located within a small complete sub-circular ring gully (Hayman 1999; forthcoming f). This produced four sherds of pottery, three probably middle Bronze Age, together with small quantities of struck flint, burnt flint and a piece of fired clay. An adjacent partial ring gully of probable middle Bronze Age origin might have been another barrow or burial enclosure, but did not produce human remains and might be domestic. In the surrounding area a concentration of 26 cremation or related deposits, some of them demonstrably pre-dating a middle to late Iron Age ring gully, may represent a broadly contemporary cemetery, though they were not radiocarbon dated and there were no associated finds apart from a few struck flints and pot sherds. Despite their concentration in a small area these deposits did not intercut, suggesting that they were marked to deter disturbance by later additions. Three other isolated cremation burials may have been unconnected with the cemetery group, perhaps not contemporary or excluded from burial in the main cemetery. They may have belonged to a different social group.

It should be no surprise that some small barrows and ring ditches on the gravels originated as middle Bronze Age cemeteries. Looking slightly further afield to the sands of the Surrey Heaths (Barrett 1973, 127), a 1.8 m high bowl barrow at Sunningdale contained 25 cremation burials (Fig. 8.9). They were concentrated off-centre in the south-west sector of the barrow, two in cists without urns and about equal numbers of the rest with either upright or inverted Deverel-Rimbury urns. They were found at various levels within the barrow, including at the base, suggesting that the barrow was added to as more burials were inserted into it. At Whitmore Common, Worplesdon two small bowl barrows were excavated by Pitt-Rivers in the 1870s, both of which produced primary Deverel-Rimbury cremation deposits. One produced three urns and two fragments as primary deposits. The other, with a causewayed ditch, covered two urns, an unaccompanied cremation burial and some burnt deposits.

One of the largest of all middle Bronze Age cremation cemeteries in the Thames Valley was found in the middle of the 19th century at Standlake, associated with a small ring ditch which had no earlier datable burials and might be an example of a late burial monument. A pioneering excavation by Stephen Stone (1857; 1858) showed that the urnfield occupied the south-west half of a small circular ring ditch with an internal diameter of 17 m. The site was briefly re-excavated by Derrick Riley against severe time constraints during its destruction in 1943 for accelerated wartime production of gravel (Riley 1946/7, 30-34). In all, a concentration of 88 small pits were found, 78 containing cremation burials, of which 71 were accompanied by complete or fragmentary urns. By the 1940s only

six survived and were described by R J C Atkinson (Riley1946/7, 42 and Pl III). No central burial or distinctively earlier pottery from the site was identified. A burnt and broken barbed-and-tanged arrowhead from one cremation burial associated with pottery of unknown character might have been either redeposited or a curated object. Riley (1946/7, 31-2) argued that the ring ditch probably pre-dated the middle Bronze Age urnfield.

Other ring ditches with no central burials (or any burials at all) are quite common in the Upper Thames Valley (eg Williams 1946/7, 59-64, fig. 18; Case 1963; Barclay *et al.* 1995, 78-105) and just over half the cremation burials at Standlake were inserted high in the secondary fill of the ditch. There was a large area of burning, termed by Stone the '*ustrinum*', in the top of the ditch, which may have marked the position of a pyre or pyre rake-out. Its exact character is unclear and similar examples of burning at Field Farm and Mount Farm offer a variety of other explanations. It may be that the urnfield was a secondary addition to an earlier barrow but in the light of more recent discoveries, the possibility that the ring ditch and urnfield both represent a middle Bronze Age burial ground added to the larger barrow cemetery is also plausible if allowance is made for how the urnfield cemetery developed. As we have seen, an off-centre distribution is a common characteristic of middle Bronze Age burials associated with barrows and if the cemetery represents several generations of burials, as seems likely from its size, it would not be surprising if the primary and much secondary silting of the ditch had already taken place by the time the latest burials were inserted.

Viewed as a group, these small, unobtrusive ring ditches and barrows of possible middle Bronze Age origin effectively mark the last hints of the social and religious impetus that had created the much commoner, more conspicuous funerary monuments of the late Neolithic and earlier Bronze Age barrow-building tradition. Other than any symbolism implicit in the accompaniment by urns, there is little sign of distinct social hierarchy or ranking in the off-centre and ditch-fill locations of the middle Bronze Age burials. They also lack obvious patterns of deposition, except that the absence of intercuts suggests that burials were marked to avoid disturbance. They seem to reflect, along with the reuse and minor remodelling of earlier monuments, a low level continuation of the traditions of earlier times, as if the need for an earthwork had come to be seen more as the traditional means of marking the location of burial grounds rather than signifying the importance of their occupants. Possibly relevant to this is the common, though not universal pattern of choosing or creating ring ditches and hengiform enclosures that had small entrance gaps, and in some cases segmented ditches, as though there was some concern that the dead should not be entirely enclosed.

The final use of barrows for funerary purposes seems to have been at the turn of the first millennium BC or soon after, as indicated by the late Bronze Age inhumation burial of 1020-810 cal BC and the roughly contemporary nearby calf burial, dated to 1100-890 cal BC already noted at Barrow Hills, Radley (Barclay and Halpin 1999). Otherwise there is no clear evidence of significant remodelling or reuse of earlier funerary monuments for multiple burials or the creation of new barrows in the late Bronze Age.

'Flat' urnfield cemeteries (Figs. 8.7-8.10)

Parallel to the declining tradition of burying the dead in and around visible earthwork monuments, middle Bronze Age burials also took the form of 'flat' urnfield cemeteries and isolated burials unassociated with earlier barrows. In many respects the evidence of these unenclosed urnfields resembles concentrations of cremation burials which reflect ongoing use, reuse or remodelling of earlier monuments described above, except that the decision to use a funerary monument or not must have been deliberate. As we have seen, cremation urnfields can be associated with pre-existing or newly built barrows, and one difference that may distinguish these cemeteries is not so much whether or not they are associated with barrows, as the absence of inhumations. These do occur as insertions in pre-existing monuments like that at Mount Farm and as isolated burials (see below), but seem to be unknown in flat urnfield cemeteries.

Choices of burial rite and location may have reflected community, family or personal preferences, perhaps either seeking to retain a connection with traditional burial practice or move on from them. Reverence for long-defunct as well as active burial traditions and new places for the deposition of the departed is an enduring characteristic of human society. Such preferences are common in our own society, including use of ancient burial grounds with family connections or newer cemeteries, or the scattering of cremated remains at places of special spiritual significance, including ancient megalithic and other monuments.

The clearest examples of non-monumental cemeteries in later prehistory are a number of major middle Bronze Age urnfields, some of which, like that at Standlake, were found in the last century. At

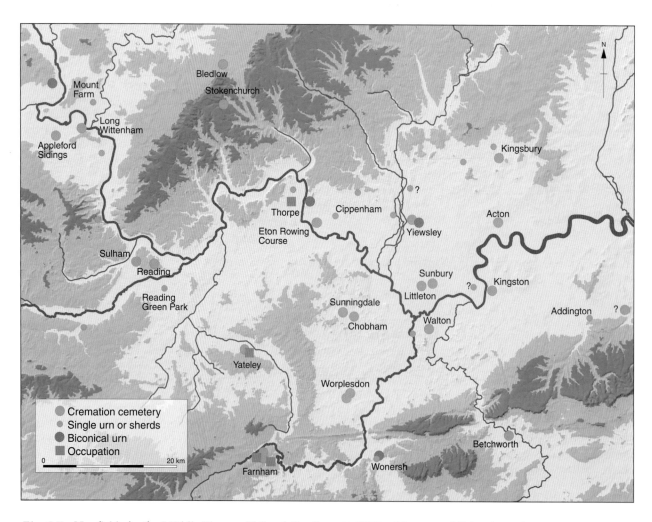

Fig. 8.7   Urnfields in the Middle Thames Valley (after Barrett 1973 with some additions). IPR/117-40C British Geological Survey. © NERC 2009. NEXTMap Britain Elevation Data from Intermap Technologies. All rights reserved

300

Fig. 8.8 Middle Bronze Age cremation urn, Green Park, Reading

Ashford Common an urnfield of at least 71 urned cremation burials or other deposits, including possible pyre sites, was discovered in 1870, though only fully reported a century later (Fig. 8.7; Barrett 1973). Many of the urns were inverted, as was the case with all 15 urned cremations found during gravel digging in the 1900s at Sulham near Reading where two unurned cremations had also been found (Barrett 1973). Further afield, Barrett reported a cemetery with 18 pots from Yiewsley, just off the gravels east of the Colne, and other cemeteries are known at Yately in the Blackwater Valley, Chobham, and gravel pits at Farnham. A number of other moderate to large collections of urns, such as those from Oaklands Park, Walton-on-Thames, and Tilehurst Road Reading are from sites of uncertain character (Barret 1973).

At the small end of the size range of such urnfields, Barrett also reported groups of three urns from Littleton Reservoir and six from Acton. Another very small group is reflected in a cluster of at least five urned burials within a 3 m by 2 m area at Shortheath Lane (Fig. 8.10), Abbots Farm

Sulhamstead (Lobb 1992). These urns represent three styles, cordoned bucket urns, sub-biconical cordoned urns and a perforated urn of uncertain type (Ellison 1975; Ellison 1980).

The origins of urnfield cemeteries in the Thames Valley are not altogether clear. Those associated with older monuments or ring ditches like Shorncote may simply have reused a traditional sacred place as a suitable location with no implication of continuity of use or of funerary tradition. This could also apply to Stanton Harcourt and possibly Standlake. However, the development of such cemeteries from a continuing tradition of earlier Bronze Age cremation, either continuing the use of burial monuments or conversion to flat cemeteries is also plausible, though this whole issue is greatly complicated by both the dating and possible cultural use of relevant types of urn.

Collared urns normally associated with the earlier Bronze Age are recorded for some urnfield collections in west London, including Kingston and Oaklands, but these are old finds with little detailed record, so it is not clear that they were actually from the same areas as the main assemblages of urns (Barrett 1983). More recent finds include Foxley Fields Farm, Finmere north of Bicester where a scattered group of five cremation burials, apparently not associated with any barrow or ring ditch, included two with inverted collared urns, but apparently no Deverel-Rimbury pottery (Hancock *et al.* 2003). Due to the restricted size of the excavation it is not clear if these were part of a larger scattered urnfield, and detailed analysis and radiocarbon dating are still awaited. The small 'cremation cluster' at Brook Farm, Cippenham appears to represent an isolated group of features, albeit not far from a ring ditch, some with cremated bone and with both collared and globular urns present (Ford *et al.* 2003).

Even where collared urns were used for burials in urnfields, attributing their origin to the early Bronze

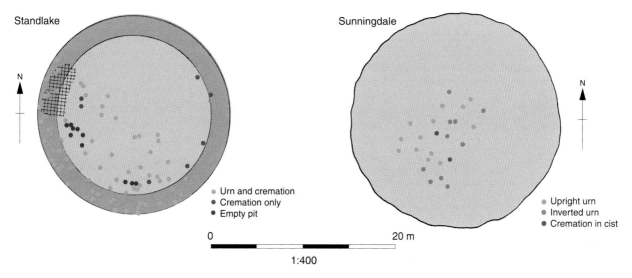

Fig. 8.9   Urnfields associated with funerary monuments: (left) *ring ditch at Standlake;* (right) *barrow at Sunningdale*

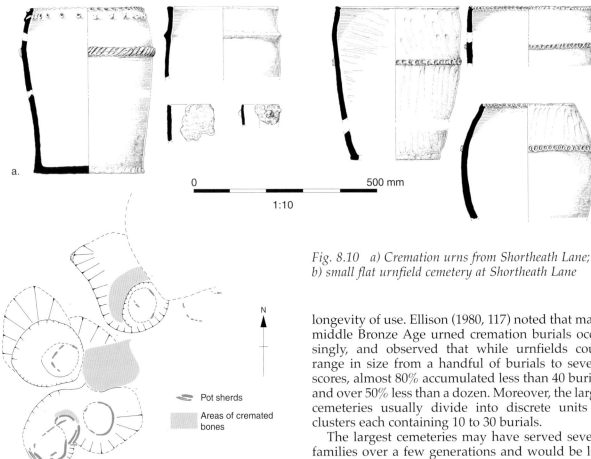

Fig. 8.10   a) Cremation urns from Shortheath Lane;
b) small flat urnfield cemetery at Shortheath Lane

longevity of use. Ellison (1980, 117) noted that many middle Bronze Age urned cremation burials occur singly, and observed that while urnfields could range in size from a handful of burials to several scores, almost 80% accumulated less than 40 burials and over 50% less than a dozen. Moreover, the larger cemeteries usually divide into discrete units or clusters each containing 10 to 30 burials.

The largest cemeteries may have served several families over a few generations and would be less likely to fall into disuse when one family moved on. However, the majority of urnfields might have been the burial grounds of a single family, perhaps used only for a couple of generations. On this basis any distinction between 'dispersed' burials occurring in ones and twos and small 'cemeteries' of several cremations becomes indistinct. Dispersed burials might reflect only local social or economic circumstances precluding further burials at that location, not that these burials were deliberately made 'outside' formal cemeteries. Similarly, it is questionable whether the use of urns to contain or accompany cremations is a necessary feature for a small group of cremations to qualify as a 'cemetery'. For example a small cemetery of at least six cremation burials at Appleford Sidings were unaccompanied and produced only one flint for dating evidence (Booth and Simmonds forthcoming).

It may be that overt marking of the burials was what defined a cemetery. It seems clear from the fairly regular spacing and lack of intercutting cremation burials, even in the largest cemeteries, that the burials must have been individually marked by some visible memorial, perhaps posts or stakes as present at some earlier Bronze Age cremation burials, including two at Rollright (Lambrick 1988, 72, 79).

Resolution of these issues is greatly hampered by the dearth of Bronze Age urnfields excavated to modern standards using current techniques of

Age is not entirely reliable, both because this style of pottery continued to be made into the middle Bronze Age when Deverel-Rimbury styles took over, and because some urns used for burial might have been heirloom objects used for burials broadly contemporary with those accompanied by typical Deverel-Rimbury urns. Although there are thus indications that some formal urnfields had earlier Bronze Age origins, this is not clear on current evidence in the absence of thorough programmes of precision radiocarbon dating.

A further issue concerns the origins of middle Bronze Age urnfields in terms of their size and the dynamics of their development. They were not created in their final form, but grew incrementally, perhaps from a single initial burial, and the eventual number of deposits may reflect nothing more than the dynamics of family and community life. Some very small urnfields must reflect deaths within a family that moved away after a single generation, but the larger ones could represent burials over several generations. The 'size' of such urnfields may thus reflect a combination of factors, such as the number of families, size of the community or extent of geographical area they served, as well as their scientific analysis. The limited number of discoveries of substantial urnfields since the advent of mechanised quarrying early in the 20th century, despite the increase both in gravel production and rescue archaeology is striking and suggests that current approaches have not yet re-established an effective means of identifying such cemeteries in the modern world of machine excavation. It is very unlikely that this is because 20th century intensification of cultivation has destroyed many urnfields, since it would be more likely simply to have truncated them. In any case many isolated cremations have been turning up, as described below. It is more likely that inadequate attention is being paid to investigating areas where such cemeteries were located – presumably beyond the limits of settlements and fields that archaeologists now investigate on an increasingly large scale. Until this is resolved it is likely that little progress will be made in advancing understanding urnfields in the Thames Valley. Although there seems to be growing evidence that major urnfields were not located within or very close to fields and settlements, it is still worth noting that small clusters of unurned cremation burials, like that at Appleford (see above) or Home Farm Laleham (see below) did occur within field systems, and some isolated burials did have urns (see below).

Middle to late Iron Age cemeteries and burials within structures

Middle Iron Age cemeteries

Until relatively recently it was thought that, in keeping with most of central southern England, formal burial grounds did not exist in the early or middle Iron Age of the Thames Valley (Whimster 1981). No early Iron Age cemeteries have yet been identified but the discovery of a cemetery of 35 individuals adjacent to the settlement at Yarnton (Hey *et al.* 1999; Hey *et al.* forthcoming a) highlights the possibility that such burials may have been more common than hitherto appreciated. This is illustrated by burials of three individuals at Gallows Leaze (Wilson and Cater 2005), which show certain similarities to the Yarnton cemetery.

The burials at Yarnton were located in three separate groups, a northern group of 15 graves and a southern group of 10 about 20 m apart, with a further 10 'outliers' scattered along the edge of (and in one case within) the adjacent middle Iron Age settlement (Fig. 8.11). With the possible but doubtful exception of three extended bodies recovered in salvage work, all the burials were in crouched positions, some lying on their left side, others on the right, but the vast majority aligned with the head to the north in shallow deliberately dug graves. There was no sign of binding or constriction and there were no grave goods.

Of the 35 individuals, 3 were neonates, 3 infants, 6 juveniles, 2 young adults, 9 prime adults, 1 ageing

adult and 10 other adults. The neonates were all located in the 'outlying' group within or close to the main settlement area, but otherwise the cemetery groups are a representative cross section of the community. Amongst 18 of the adults there were 8 males, 4 possible males, 3 females and 3 possible females. The heights of six men averaged 1.68 m and five women 1.58 m.

High precision radiocarbon dating of five samples from the northern group and two each from the southern group and outliers suggests that burial started around 420-230 cal BC and lasted till 290-150 cal BC, possibly spanning as much as 220 years, but more likely a much shorter period, perhaps only a couple of generations. At Owslebury a total of 70 burials, some inhumations but mainly cremations, partly within the settlements and partly in a cemetery were thought to span 150 years and may represent only two nuclear families (Collis 1994, 108).

Although rare, a number of other well-attested or suspected middle Iron Age cemeteries have been identified in southern Britain, including 28 burials in an Iron Age quarry at Suddern Farm, Hampshire (Cunliffe and Poole 2000, vol 2, pt 3, 153-74), 18 mostly infants and children at Winnall Down (Fasham 1985), at least 41 in two groups at Mill Hill, Deal in Kent (Parfitt 1995, table 46) and possibly 8 at Cockey Down, Salisbury (Trust for Wessex Archaeology 1996). It is likely, as Gill Hey and others have suggested, that other Iron Age cemeteries may have been missed amongst the many records of undated burials, such as the 50-odd reports of such remains for Oxfordshire (Blair 1994, 72). Other possible candidates in the Thames Valley are more doubtful.

An example that illustrates the point is a group of three deliberately dug graves only 5 m to 10 m apart found in a pipeline excavation at Gallows Leaze north of Berwick Salome (Wilson and Cater 2005). One grave contained a man in his 40s, buried in a crouched position oriented NW-SE with his head to the north-west on the base of a circular pit. The bones were dated to 410-60 cal BC and the grave fill contained four abraded sherds of late Iron Age pottery. A second adult had been tightly buried in a small grave oriented NW-SE, head to the south-east with two possible stakeholes in the base of the grave at the head and the foot of the body. The bones were radiocarbon dated to 350-310 or 210-40 cal BC and four sherds from the same pot datable to 50-100 AD were found in the grave close to a suspected root hole are thought to be intrusive. The third grave contained the body of a 15 to 17 year old in a crouched position in an oval grave oriented NW-SE, head to the north-west, radiocarbon dated to 40 cal BC to 130 cal AD, with two pieces of pottery datable only to between the middle Iron Age and the early Roman period in the fill.

Although the number of burials is small and the full layout of the settlement activity unclear beyond the limits of the 15 m wide pipeline easement, the spatial pattern seems comparable to that at Yarnton,

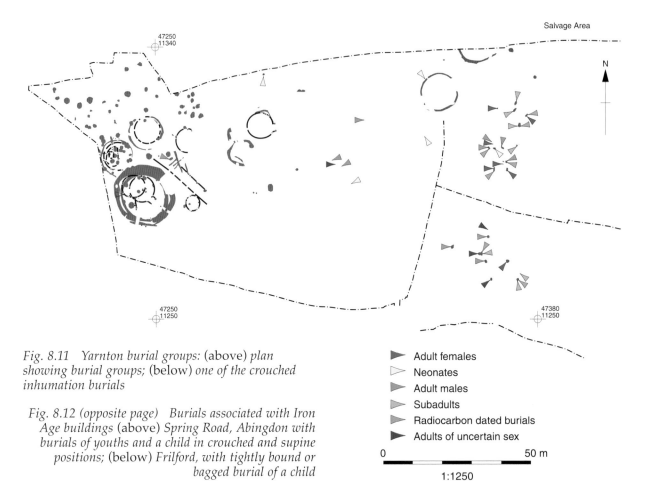

Salvage Area

47250
11340

N

47250
11250

47380
11250

Fig. 8.11 Yarnton burial groups: (above) *plan showing burial groups;* (below) *one of the crouched inhumation burials*

Fig. 8.12 (opposite page) Burials associated with Iron Age buildings (above) *Spring Road, Abingdon with burials of youths and a child in crouched and supine positions;* (below) *Frilford, with tightly bound or bagged burial of a child*

► Adult females
▷ Neonates
► Adult males
▷ Subadults
► Radiocarbon dated burials
► Adults of uncertain sex

0   50 m

1:1250

with the burial cluster of two adults and a youth peripheral to a settlement area in which there were infant burials. Unlike the close dating of the large group at Yarnton, however, only two of the Gallows Leaze radiocarbon dates overlap (spanning a much wider 4th to 1st century BC range) with the third for the youth significantly later, not quite overlapping the other two at the 95% confidence level.

The burials at Yarnton and Gallows Leaze were discovered by means of a watching brief on topsoil stripping of an area adjacent to a settlement and pipeline monitoring and excavation. Such work has been carried out often enough and on a sufficient scale since the 1960s at quarries and other extensive development sites to make it unlikely that such cemeteries are anything other than exceptional. The short chronological span of the Yarnton cemetery in the context of the much longer-lived domestic settlement that was continuously occupied long before and long after its use, reinforces the impression that this was an exception rather than the norm. The Gallows Leaze burials suggest that the Yarnton cemetery reflects certain practices that may have been more common but seldom developed into the chronologically and spatially distinct clusters of interments that we regard as a cemetery. With such cemeteries being so rare it is impossible to know why they were established. There need not have been a single reason. In the case of the short-

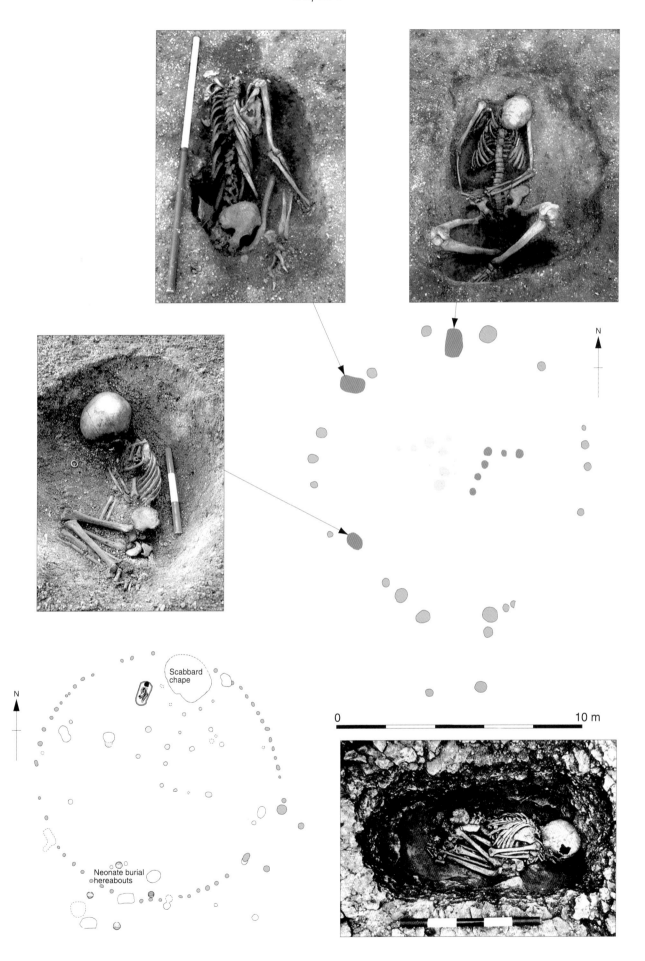

Scabbard
chape

Neonate burial
hereabouts

0   10 m

lived, apparently broadly representative cemetery at Yarnton the possibility that it reflects a sudden outbreak of infectious disease has been suggested (Hey *et al.* 1999; Hey *et al.* forthcoming).

Buildings as formal burial places in the middle Iron Age

While human burials in and around settlements and buildings are not uncommon, it is rare to find evidence of buildings used as burial places. At Spring Road, Abingdon, a cluster of three burials in purpose-cut graves seem to have been placed close to the wall inside a post-built roundhouse (Fig. 8.12; Allen and Kamash 2008). Radiocarbon determinations suggest they all date to the 4th-3rd century cal BC. A young man of 20-24 was buried in a half-sitting position, lying supine with his back raised against the northern edge of the grave. A fragmentary spindle whorl recovered from the fill may not have been directly associated with the burial. Another young man of 19-21 had been laid out crouched and prone, on a north-south alignment. A later circular feature may have removed most of the skull and upper vertebrae, or it might have been made to accommodate the head which was removed in some other way (Fig. 8.12). The third burial was a child of four or five buried in a crouched position on its right side, head to the south-east and legs tightly flexed. A bone ring was found near the skull (Fig. 8.19). Disarticulated bones of a three month old infant were also discovered in the backfill of the child's grave.

Another crouched burial possibly of Iron Age date, laid on its left side and facing west, was disturbed by modern grave digging. Two sherds of early Iron Age pottery were recovered from the fill, while a piece of Roman pottery may have come from topsoil overlying the grave. In 1999 grave diggers found another crouched inhumation which might have been of similar date.

The association of the Spring Road burials with the post-ring of a roundhouse is intriguing in the context of the child burial and infant opposite each other close to the northern and southern walls of the stake-built roundhouse at Frilford (Fig. 8.12; Harding 1987, 7, fig. 3). In both cases the burials were young, including children, were similarly spread out, positioned close to the main structural ring of the buildings, and in both cases the buildings may have had internal partitions of somewhat unusual form. Both sites have other sacred possible structures – at Spring Road a pre-existing post ring, at Frilford a later Romano-celtic shrine and possibly another Iron Age and later shrine adjacent (see below, Chapter 9).

Late Iron Age cemeteries

In the late Iron Age cremation re-emerged as a standard burial rite and the inclusion of grave goods in addition to pottery urns containing cremated remains became much commoner. The occurrence of high status inhumation and cremation burials defined by particularly rich grave goods

was also a new feature for the region in this period, characteristic of the so-called Aylesford Swarling culture which extended from Kent and Essex into the north-east part of the Thames basin in Hertfordshire. Cremation cemeteries, some very extensive, are a particular feature of the heart of Catuvellaunian territory around Verlamion (Verulamium) and Welwyn in the middle and upper reaches of tributary valleys draining the Chiltern dip slope.

The major cemetery at King Harry's Lane just outside the oppidum of Verulamium contained 463 cremations, most placed in urns and buried in a small pit, often accompanied by other vessels and grave goods, typically personal objects like bracelets and personal ornaments, mirrors and toiletry equipment, spoons, small tools and gaming pieces, likely to reflect both male and female burials. Some of the richest burials were placed in large grave pits surrounded by clusters of satellite burials, in some cases in the middle of rectangular ditched enclosures which presumably served to demarcate social or familial groups (Stead and Rigby 1989).

In the heart of the Thames Valley, although many of the new features of late Iron Age practice were adopted for individual interments, they did not occur in cemeteries but simply became an additional new style of burial alongside continuing older traditions. A key feature of this was disposal of the dead in a wide range of locations not recognisable as places set aside for formal burial. In the next section we will examine the tradition of burials that were not placed in formal monuments and cemeteries.

Burial practices away from formal burial grounds

Middle to late Bronze Age cremation burials in fields and by boundaries

In contrast to the lack of large urnfields discovered in recent years, large-scale excavation prior to gravel extraction or other development has led to the frequent discovery of cremation and token deposits occurring in isolation or widely dispersed around fields or settlements. Many such cremation deposits are now known, mostly from the Middle Thames Valley but increasingly in the Upper Thames as well. Some are associated with urns, more often they are unaccompanied. A few are associated with the odd sherd of pottery, flintwork or other objects but these seldom amount to what might be termed 'grave goods', and the vast majority are not well dated. So far there has been little or no systematic radiocarbon dating of such cremation burials, especially unaccompanied ones. As a result, their attribution to the middle or late Bronze Age is often largely supposition based on spatial associations with fields or domestic activity of this date. In a few cases, where deposits of this type are recurrently found in the vicinity of field boundaries and other datable features, such associations are quite strong. In other cases this is less clear. Lacking any actual dating evidence, assigning such deposits to the later Bronze Age relies on an assumption that in the absence of datable activity of later periods, they are unlikely to be late Iron Age, Roman or Saxon.

The practice of placing burials in 'boundary' contexts can be traced back to the early Neolithic, often in connection with ditches of causewayed enclosures or associated with some cursus monuments and, most obviously, in the ditches of barrows or just outside them. The appearance of fields and other land divisions from the middle to late Bronze Age onwards was accompanied with a practice of burying people in or close to boundaries unassociated with ceremonial or funerary monuments – a practice that is evident archaeologically only because it was then that the boundaries were given physical expression. The extent to which this was common practice seems variable and may be subject to vagaries of preservation.

It is not uncommon to find apparently isolated middle Bronze Age cremation deposits, though increasingly extensive excavations show they are often less isolated than might appear. In the Upper Thames Valley a number of cremation burials have been found on the floodplain at Yarnton. Apart from those already noted as possibly associated with a Neolithic long enclosure, a small pit containing part of a cremated adult human body dated to 1440-1310 cal BC was found on the north bank of a palaeochannel close to another small pit. On the south side of the channel was another undated small pit containing the cremated remains of a young adult (possibly female) and a further pit some distance away contained a well-made bone pin and a sherd of middle Bronze Age pottery. Other remains of middle Bronze Age activity were dispersed across the floodplain (see Chapter 4).

Discoveries of later Bronze Age cremation and, more rarely, inhumation burials in and around fields are increasingly common. In a few cases, as at Imperial Sports Ground, some of the cremation burials were associated with pre-existing monuments respected by the fields (Crockett 2001). Some such deposits occur in small groups, mostly unaccompanied by vessels, blurring any clear distinction between these burials and what might be regarded as small urnfield 'cemeteries' of more formal character. But while it appears that most were not associated with overt funerary monuments or cemeteries, it does not necessarily mean they were unmarked.

At Home Farm, Laleham nine cremation burials and 23 cremation-like deposits, the majority believed to be Bronze Age, were dispersed around a middle Bronze Age field system (Hayman 2002b; forthcoming c). Prior to the discovery of the first of these burials at Home Farm, unurned cremations were largely unrecognised in Surrey (none were

recorded in the Sites and Monuments Record for Surrey in 1991). Since then similar features have been discovered at a number of locations, four at Church Lammas (Hayman 1991d; forthcoming b) and several at Hengrove Farm near Staines (Hayman forthcoming d). The Home Farm deposits were found in different parts of an extensive field system, generally away from the main areas of domestic activity. None were urned burials and most were only token deposits of bone, and there seems to be some variation in detailed location. In one place five cremation burials and a couple of other charcoal-rich deposits lay within 5 m of two boundary gullies aligned as a T-junction though not meeting. Two others lay about 5 m from another boundary gully and in another location a row of four cremation burials with significant quantities of bone lay in a rough line orientated parallel to a boundary about 25 m away, as if they respected some above-ground boundary feature with no other subsoil manifestation. Two others close to boundaries contained material suggesting an earlier origin than the field system, while another two were not obviously close to boundaries. None of these was closely dated by finds and have not been radiocarbon dated so their full significance is not clear. However, they do seem to indicate the recurrent deposition, at least on this site, of human cremations within fields, often respecting their boundaries. Given their distance from the boundary gullies and the apparent absence of a gully in one case, it is reasonable to suggest that they may have been placed alongside well grown hedges.

At Perry Oaks/T5, the most extensive area of field systems and boundaries investigated in the Thames Valley, cremation burials were rare, but this may not be a reliable indication since much of the area was truncated by a sewage works. A small cemetery lay close to the Colne floodplain but otherwise two small cremation deposits, one associated with a middle Bronze Age globular urn, were identified (Barrett *et al.* 2001, 223; Framework Archaeology 2006, 151-2).

At the Eton Rowing Course, a number of burials were found within one of the extensive middle Bronze Age field systems about 40 m from an earlier prehistoric barrow. Four cremation burials, three in inverted barrel urns, were found within the larger of the southern pair of enclosures and a crouched inhumation burial lay in the smaller primary enclosure adjacent. A number of other middle and late Bronze Age cremation burials, most of them individual, have been found at locations along the Maidenhead to Windsor Flood Alleviation Scheme. Some were associated with ditches or in occupation areas (Allen *et al.* forthcoming b). The most notable cluster was at Marsh Lane East where they were associated with parallel boundary ditches and possibly a post-built roundhouse (see Chapter 9). On the other side of the river at Weir Bank Stud, Bray a single cremation burial of an unaccompanied adult was found probably within a field about 9 m away from a middle Bronze Age boundary ditch (Barnes and Cleal 1995).

At Reading Business Park/Green Park the cremated bones of a youth and an adult dated to 1220-890 cal BC were found in an inverted Deverel-Rimbury bucket buried in a small pit immediately next to a boundary ditch of a field system, also thought to be of middle to late Bronze Age origin. Two late Bronze Age cremation burials lay in the corner of a field in another part of the Reading Business Park/Green Park complex with a third less evidently close to a boundary (Jennings and Moore 1992, 11, figs 4 and 8), while two or possibly four more came from pits within the late Bronze Age settlement (Brossler 2004, 110).

In the Upper Thames Valley at Appleford Sidings, the small cremation cemetery noted above was close to or within a middle Bronze Age field system, and an isolated cremation and single inhumation burial of similar date were also found (Booth and Simmonds forthcoming).

Hayman (2002b) has argued that it is common for prehistoric cremation burials in barrows to be associated with 'accessory' deposits containing little if any burnt bone, either representing a token offering from the pyre or accompanying other material for the afterlife, and that there is no obvious reason why this point may not be extended to include more scattered cremations not associated with formal burial places or containers. Unfortunately there is little hard evidence available to demonstrate the validity of this idea, particularly as many of the cremation burials and associated deposits of burnt material at Home Farm and elsewhere are not accompanied by urns and produced no other direct dating evidence. It is still possible that these deposits do not relate to the

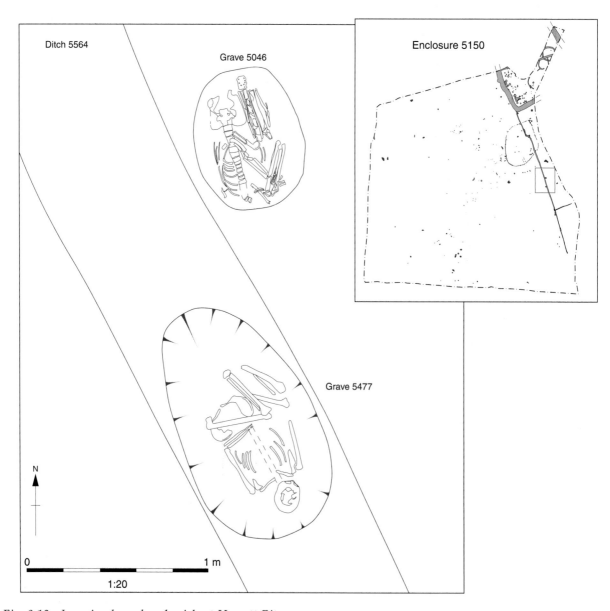

Fig. 8.13   Iron Age boundary burials at Horcott Pit

period of occupation and fields represented, that the deposits without bone relate to other activities associated with burning or that the variable bone content relates to different periods, traditions or techniques of cremation and recovery of pyre material for burial. Nevertheless, the theory is worth testing through more systematic radiocarbon dating of such deposits, despite their unprepossessing character.

Overall, the common occurrence of cremation burials and associated deposits in and around fields suggests that as the practice of burial in formal monuments declined in later prehistory a strong tradition of disposing of the dead within the wider environment developed.

Late Bronze Age and Iron Age inhumation burials associated with boundaries

During this period the practice of burying the dead in or alongside boundaries seems to have become firmly established. At Roughground Farm, Lechlade the skeleton of a young man of 18 to 23,

dated to 350-40 cal BC (one sigma) lay on his left side, head to the south-west in a shallow oval deepening at the base of an early Iron Age ditch, some distance from other evidence of early Iron Age settlement. A second burial of a man of 30-35 was found placed in a crouched but prone position head to the NNE in a small grave *c* 2 m south of the same ditch about 20 m away, thought to be of a similar date (Allen *et al.* 1993, 45).

At Watchfield three pits or graves containing human remains were found in the vicinity of a funnel-shaped entrance to part of an early or middle Iron Age field system. In the centre of the entrance track was the double inhumation burial of a woman and a juvenile male. The other (undated) double inhumation of a woman with fragmentary remains of an infant lay about 15 m away to the south on the other side of the boundary where it had turned a right-angle corner. Also on that side of the boundary about 5 m to the north was the pit containing a cattle skull, a trepanned skull and human femur (Birbeck 2001, 229-31, figs 3, 5).

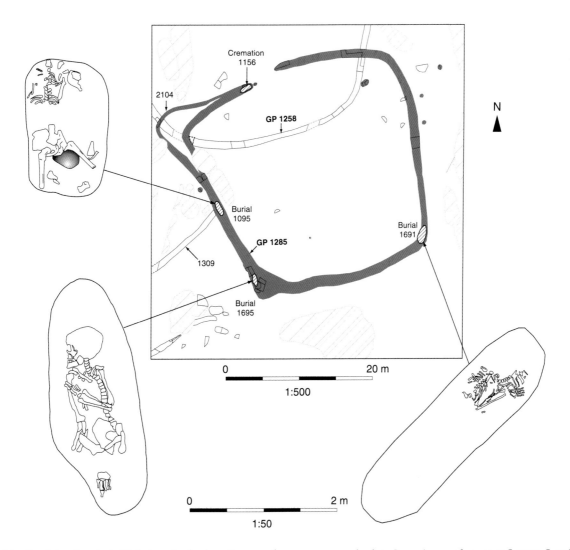

Fig. 8.14 Burials placed at ditch terminals, junctions and corners around a late Iron Age enclosure at Latton Lands

309

At Horcott Pit the tightly bound crouched skeleton of an adult dated 380-160 cal BC was crammed into a small pit immediately next to a boundary ditch only a metre from another grave containing a less tightly crouched skeleton of a 15 to 17 year-old boy, dated to 370-110 cal BC, which had been dug into the upper ditch fill (Fig. 8.13). The graves were close to a former gap and kink in the boundary ditch, and the very shallow smaller grave may have been cut through a bank bordering the ditch (Lamdin-Whymark *et al.* forthcoming).

At Gallows Leaze, Berwick Salome north of Benson the group of three burials discussed above was adjacent to a trackway or boundary halfway between two areas of middle Iron Age settlement about 100 m apart. A fourth inhumation burial of a neonate radiocarbon dated to 370-100 cal BC was found in a small grave within one of the occupation areas, and parts of three others were found in various ditches (Wilson and Cater 2005).

At Latton Lands human burials were inserted into the upper ditch fills of a late Iron Age enclosure (Fig. 8.14). Two were buried in the corners of the enclosure ditch and another at a junction with a separate ditch midway along its western side. A cremation burial was inserted in the ditch terminal on the west side of the only entrance to the enclosure (Powell *et al.* forthcoming). Two late Iron Age or early Roman crouched inhumation burials, one with a brooch of *c* 0-60 AD, the other possibly later, and overlain by a deliberate deposit of sheep mandibles, pottery and burnt stone, were cut into enclosure ditches at Gravelly Guy (Lambrick and Allen 2004, 251, Pl. 6.2, fig. 6.3). Two much later Roman burials sited adjacent to the long-lived boundary that divided the arable land from pasture are amongst many that demonstrate the continuing connection of burials and boundaries that persisted through the Roman period (Lambrick and Allen, 2004, 229, fig. 6.6, Pl. 6.3) and beyond.

Bound and bagged burials

A common characteristic of several of these and some other later Bronze Age and Iron Age inhumation burials is that the bodies were tightly bound, possibly bagged or even mummified before burial. Often the graves were only just large enough to accommodate the body after it had been constrained, suggesting that the burial was crammed into the grave rather than carefully arranged.

An unusual middle Bronze Age example has been excavated at Appleford Sidings where a young woman of 18 to 25 was buried in a small, roughly oval grave pit, 0.95 m long, 0.6 m wide and 0.14 m deep below gravel surface. She was in a tightly crouched position, on her back with arms folded across her stomach, head to the east and her legs turned to the north with the knees drawn up to her chest. Most unusually for such inhumations, which usually lack grave goods, a globular urn had been placed at the left side of her body.

At Sutton Courtenay the skeleton of an adult female dated to 1200-990 cal BC lay in a small, deep oval pit in a tightly bound crouched position, again unusually placed on her back rather than on one side, with her head below her thighs. She had suffered from debilitating brucellosis (Fig. 8.15; Hey forthcoming). The burial seems to have been isolated, predating the establishment of an Iron Age settlement on the site by at least 200 years.

In addition to the early and middle Iron Age bound or bagged burials associated with boundary contexts at Roughground Farm and Horcott, a tightly crouched skeleton at Roughground Farm of a 30-35 year old adult male dated to 1310-820 cal BC was crammed into an isolated small oval pit, apparently some distance from other contemporary features (Allen *et al.* 1993, 45, 57, figs 7 and 32).

One of the burials close to a field boundary at Reading Business Park/Green Park was a similarly tightly bound crouched skeleton, probably of a woman over 30, placed on her left side, head to the north-west in a small, shallow pit

Fig. 8.15 Bound/bagged burial at (above) *Sutton Courtenay;* (below) *Mount Farm*

cut by a group of other pits (Moore and Jennings 1992, 11). Another crouched inhumation burial of a woman of over 30, in this case placed on her right side head to the south-west, was found in a small oval pit between two houses of the late Bronze Age settlement. The burial was undated and there was no evidence to indicate whether it was contemporary either with the settlement or with the earlier fields.

Tightly bound or bagged bodies are not such an obvious feature of the commoner inhumations of Iron Age date but examples include the Lynches Trackway, north-east of Cirencester where an apparently isolated middle Iron Age burial of a young man of 17-25 dated to 355-289 or more likely 235-33 cal BC, had been placed on his left side, head to the north in a small oval pit (Mudd *et al.* 1999, 76). Others include one at Mount Farm (Fig. 8.15) and the 15-17 year old adolescent, lying on his/her left side, head to the north in a small oval grave within the penannular stake walled structure at Frilford (Fig. 8.12; Harding 1987, 7, 17). Amongst several burials within an early to middle Iron Age settlement at Bourton-on-the-Water (see below) one was the tightly bound or bagged body of an elderly woman lying in a pit along with other disarticulated human bones (Nichols 2006, 60).

Disposal of human remains in watery places

Human remains in later prehistory were often disposed of in various bodies of water (Fig. 8.3). The role of rivers and streams as boundaries and the frequent association of waterholes and wells close to field boundaries may indicate a further connection between burials and boundaries. Watery places may have been regarded as suitable locations for the disposal of human remains for other reasons. They may have been regarded as liminal zones between different worlds and a reliable water supply was likely seen as a necessity of life for a successful farming community, and so a suitable place for deposits that would find favour with the gods.

Most human remains from watery places are fragmentary, disarticulated bones and cannot always be assumed to be deliberate. The occurrence of human remains in waterlogged deposits at the bottom of waterholes is rare. In particular there is little evidence that recently dead bodies or body parts were thrown into waterholes and wells when they were in use, which would contaminate the water supply, but this is not so obviously true of river channels. However, the detailed depositional circumstances are complicated in the case of river finds by potential effects of the river itself and in the case of waterholes by the possibility that some remains may reflect deposition (whether deliberate or not) with settlement debris rather than a direct association with water.

River channels

The nature of the discovery, and retrieval of skulls, usually through observations of spoil by workmen during dredging, means that details of context and association with other bones, including mandibles, are usually lacking.

Bradley and Gordon (1988) reviewed the evidence of human skulls recovered from the Thames, of which nearly 300 survive and several more were reported with original finds of metalwork. It is noticeable that while animal bones had been retained there were very few other human bones, including mandibles or cervical vertebrae, suggesting that the skulls had been selected already in a defleshed, disarticulated condition for deposition in the river. There was a bias towards prime adult males aged between 25 and 35. Four out of six skulls that were radiocarbon dated produced dates within the late Bronze Age (with others into the first millennium AD) and there is a spatial correlation with the main areas where weapons (also mainly but not exclusively late Bronze Age) were deposited (Bradley and Gordon 1988, 505, fig. 1). Other rivers in Britain and Europe do not display as clear a correlation of human skulls and weaponry and the Thames evidence is only suggestive rather than proven (Bradley 1990, 108-9). Some recent investigations in more controlled conditions have provided greater understanding of the character of human remains in the river, including the discovery of non-cranial material.

The skull of a mature, perhaps male human recovered from a small palaeochannel at Abbey Meads is unusual in its association with five of the neck vertebrae, including the atlas and axis bones, but no other body parts. There was no direct evidence of decapitation, whether after death or as the cause of it, but it cannot be ruled out. It is also possible that these remains were detached from the remainder of the body during recent quarrying rather than in antiquity. Unfortunately the date of deposition is also uncertain since it might either be contemporary with a Bronze Age occupation layer observed in the side of the excavations or with the muds of later, possibly Roman, date that overlay it. A human femur is also unprovenanced.

Two undated human skull fragments were amongst a range of votive objects of Bronze Age, Iron Age, Roman and Saxon date deposited in the river channel at Shepperton (see above), but it is not clear whether they are late prehistoric.

At the Eton Rowing Course two deliberately placed late Bronze Age pots were found on a sandbank in the river demarcated by three wooden posts (Fig. 8.3). The sandbank also produced several human bones, a mandible dated to 1370-1020 cal BC, a male skull 1130-890 cal BC, a tibia 1000-820 cal BC, a female skull 970-800 cal BC, another skull vault and an ulna (Allen *et al.* 2000, 90). The group strongly suggests that the sandbank was a place of special significance, perhaps over a long period, though at least one bone seems to have been redeposited. It is much less clear whether the remains represent a particular funerary practice rather than some other ritualistic behaviour.

One of the more remarkable older finds of human remains, and the clearest evidence for deliberately inflicted serious injury or death, is the fragment of human pelvis with a late Bronze Age spearhead embedded in it, recovered with part of a skull from Dorchester (Ehrenberg 1977, 37, fig. 15, Pl. 1). This was a chance recovery and there is no reliable indication whether other parts of the body were present. On the basis of other finds from the river it seems on the whole unlikely, and a variety of scenarios might be envisaged for the events behind this trauma and the circumstances of deposition. Perhaps the simplest is that whatever the circumstances of the attack, the broken-off spearhead was irrecoverable from the body (maybe ethically as much as physically), and so was deposited in the river in the same way as other body parts found in rivers.

Burials and disarticulated remains in waterholes

Some bones and bodies were deposited in waterholes, though their position within primary silts or later deposits seems to have varied considerably. Often the human bones occur relatively low down, though not necessarily in silts that accumulated while the waterhole was in use. There is a possibility that the association with water was a factor in these deposits, echoing the disposal of human remains in the river. However, it is also usually the case that whatever the state of infilling of waterholes, human remains are found in association with domestic rubbish, which was often taken outside the settlement and deposited in abandoned waterholes (see above, Chapter 7).

At Latton Lands in the Upper Thames Valley two femur fragments and part of a cranial vault were found in a small waterlogged undated pit of probable middle or late Bronze Age date (Stansbie and Laws 2004). At Shorncote Quarry a skull fragment was found in primary silts of a waterhole (Brossler *et al.* 2002, 44-5) and at Watkins Farm a complete body was laid out in an extended position around the lower side of a ramped well which contained wood radiocarbon dated to 1400-1250 cal BC. This date, from the only feature indicating any significant pre-Iron Age activity on the site, was regarded as anomalous in the original report, partly on environmental grounds (Allen 1990, 10). In the light of clearer understanding both of the character of late Bronze Age occupation and the chronology of environmental change in the Upper Thames Valley based on results from Yarnton, the dating of the waterhole and associated inhumation is now regarded as genuine (T Allen and M Robinson pers. comms.). At Mount Farm a skull fragment and two other human bones came from the upper fills of a middle to late Bronze Age ramped well, though this

was cut through an earlier Bronze Age ring ditch that continued to be used for burials into the middle Bronze Age (Myres 1937, 16; Lambrick forthcoming).

A trepanning disc was found close to the bottom of a waterhole at Green Park at a similar level to some wooden objects including an oak disc (Brossler *et al.* 2004, 30, fig. 3.13 and 99-103, figs 4.23 and 4.24). In another more recently excavated area (Webley *et al.* forthcoming) a tibia shaft came from the primary fill of a Bronze Age waterhole and small deposits of cremated human bone came from the upper fills of two other Bronze Age waterholes, one associated with a scatter of middle Bronze Age potsherds, suggesting either that the burial was disturbed or that the material had been thrown into the backfilled waterhole.

In much of the Middle Thames Valley, however, human bone is absent from waterholes although animal bone does survive (though often not well). Given the number of Bronze Age waterholes that have now been investigated on the west London and Surrey gravels the absence of human bone may be a genuine feature, which, as we shall see, may have continued through the Iron Age.

Burials in and around middle to late Bronze Age settlements

The relative dearth of substantial middle Bronze Age settlement evidence other than waterholes in most of the Thames Valley makes it difficult to tell how far disposal of the dead, or of body parts, formed part of domestic life. However, several examples already cited for the Upper Thames, including Yarnton, suggest that various practices that characterise late Bronze Age and more particularly Iron Age settlements had ancient origins.

At Corporation Farm, Abingdon an undated double inhumation burial was exposed on the periphery of the middle Bronze Age settlement enclosures (see above). They were not radiocarbon dated and had no associated pottery, so they may have instead been associated with Neolithic and Bronze Age ring ditches nearby. A fragment of human cranium found with pig mandibles and remains of a dog in the terminal of a middle Bronze Age enclosure ditch has a much clearer context and date, comparable in character to Iron Age deposits of animal parts and human bones placed in ditch terminals and pits (see below).

Another group of late Bronze Age cremation burials associated with a settlement was found on a limestone spur east of the Bayswater Brook northeast of Oxford, where evaluation revealed three unurned cremations, one identifiable as adult and one juvenile amongst a scatter of small pits and postholes accompanied by shell and quartz-tempered pottery (Allen 1995, 55-6).

The late Bronze Age settlement at Cassington West Extension produced 28 cremation-like deposits, of which five contained more than 200 g of cremated bone and another five between 20 and 100 g. Only one of the group was accompanied by pottery, but many were associated with probable buildings of the late Bronze Age settlement (C Hayden pers. comm.). Early Iron Age cremation burials have been noted in postholes of roundhouses at both Horcott and Yarnton (Lamdin-Whymark forthcoming; Hey *et al.* forthcoming).

Late Bronze Age cremation and pit burials were found in and around the settlement at Reading Business Park/Green Park, though it was difficult to demonstrate contemporaneity (Moore and Jennings 1992). Late Bronze Age cremation burials are also recorded on the Maidenhead to Windsor Flood Channel in areas with evidence of domestic occupation (Allen *et al.* forthcoming b).

Human remains in late Bronze Age and early Iron Age midden settlements

A notable feature of late Bronze Age and early Iron Age midden settlements (see Chapters 7 and 9) is the presence of human skull fragments and other bones. At Runnymede 61 contexts contained human bone, of which 28 were skull fragments and one a neonatal bone. All lay within the midden deposits (Longley 1976; Needham 1992) apart for one near complete skull from a pit (Needham 1992, 61). Skull fragments were present in other midden settlements – four from Whitecross Farm (Cromarty *et al.* 2006), one from Bray (Anon 1960, 58; Anon 1963/4, 102-3) and three from Castle Hill (Hingley 1980c), though none (nor any other bones) are reported from Woodeaton (Harding 1987). Further afield, 32 skull fragments, some worked, were found at All Cannings Cross, and several at Potterne (Cunnington 1923; Lawson 2000). Although not necessarily a midden site as such, it is also worth noting another nine, including a perforated trepanning disc, from occupation layers and a posthole at Ivinghoe Beacon (Cotton and Frere 1968). Although the variation in the number of fragments found must reflect the extent of excavations, human skull fragments seem to be disproportionately common in midden deposits and river or waterhole deposits compared with the wider range of human bones from pits and ditches. What is less certain is whether this is a particular feature of specialist midden sites or of midden-like deposits generally. A more detailed volumetric and depositional characterisation of relevant contexts is needed to investigate these issues fully.

Human remains at Iron Age settlements in the Upper Thames Valley

Occurrence of human remains

Human bones and burials are frequent finds in most Iron Age settlements in the Upper Thames Valley. Complete burials account for about 25% of human bone deposits in settlements but this is

variable, as is the extent to which they represent adults, youths or infants. Amongst stray bones and partial burials, stillborn or neonates represent an approximately equal proportion to those of children and adults, but this is variable from site to site. The proportion of contexts containing human remains is also variable.

Amongst the pit cluster and other settlements on the higher gravel terraces at Yarnton/Cresswell Field, City Farm, Ashville/Wyndyke Furlong, and Coxwell Road the number of deposits of human remains range from one to eight, which, allowing for differences in sampling equates to human remains of some sort occurring in about 0.8% to 3% of pits, though the figure was higher for one of the areas at Coxwell Road (Hey *et al.* forthcoming; Case *et al.* 1963/4; Parrington 1978; Muir and Roberts 1999). Other settlements seem to have had denser concentrations of human remains. For example, in the early to middle Iron Age settlement at Gravelly Guy 59 deposits of human remains were found amongst over 800 pits and ditches, equating to *c* 6.4% of pits containing some human remains, with complete or partial burials of both neonates and adults present in up to 2.4% of them (Fig. 8.16). At Bourton-on-the-Water seven deposits of human bone (four more or less complete bodies) were found amongst only 61 pits excavated in 2003, equating to 11.5% of pits containing some bones and 6.5% with complete or partial burials. At Mount Farm there were 24 deposits on a site with only 50-odd pits. Amongst other settlements with relatively high occurrences of human remains, the early to middle Iron Age ditched enclosures on the Corallian ridge at Watchfield had two double inhumation burials and two stray bones (Birbeck *et al.* 2001), while excavation of a possible enclosed settlement on much the same geology at Barton on the north-eastern side of Oxford produced two Iron Age crouched inhumation burials and an early Roman one in a cluster of only eight pits (Moore 2005).

At first sight, finds of human remains seem less common on low-lying pastoral sites than on longer-lived mixed farming settlements on the higher gravel terraces. Despite fairly extensive excavation no early to middle Iron Age human remains were found at Latton Lands, Shorncote/Cotswold Community, Claydon Pike, Slade Farm Bicester, Ireland's Land and Whitehouse Road (Powell *et al.* forthcoming b; Ellis *et al.* 2000; Norton 2006; Mudd 1993). At Farmoor, Mingies Ditch, Watkins Farm, and Thornhill Farm the few human remains consisted of only a few skull fragments and longbones (Lambrick and Robinson 1979; Allen and Robinson 1993; Allen 1990; Jennings *et al.* 2004). At Thrupp near Abingdon, a complete inhumation burial was found and a few fragments of human bone occurred amongst possible domestic debris incorporated into the Iron Age causeway not far away (Everett and Eeles 1999, 128, 145; Ainslie 2002, 38).

At Fields Farm, Bicester a single inhumation of a young woman was found in a grave pit 25 m outside the middle to late Iron Age enclosed settlement but no human bones were found within the settlement (Cromarty *et al.* 1999, 201, figs 6 and 18).

The relative dearth of human burials and bones in these settlements may reflect only the short duration of occupation, perhaps as little as a third or less compared with some sites established in the earlier Iron Age, so the *rate* of occurrence was actually probably similar. This is not easy to assess, however, both because the longevity of sites can be estimated in only very broad terms, and because where burials or stray bones occur in relatively small numbers their presence or absence is particularly dependent the chances of discovery by excavation.

Iron Age forts are different again, and highly variable. At Castle Hill, Little Wittenham, human remains were found in nine of the 16 excavated middle Iron Age pits, including one in which the remains of a man, deliberately dismembered parts of a woman and a child had been buried one after another (Fig. 8.16; see below). At Segsbury 15 features contained human remains but only three were pits (a complete burial of a child of two, and a cremation); the others (including a torso) were from postholes, ditches and the fort ramparts. At Blewburton excavation of a trench across the main ditch of the fort in 1948-9 produced a remarkable burial of a horse with the partly dismembered remains of a man, while at Aylesbury there were further instances of unusual human burials associated with animal remains. At Salmonsbury there were five pit burials and two graves while at Cassington Big Ring a double burial of a woman and child lay on the base of the ditch (see below for further discussion of these remains).

This variation in the rate of occurrence of human remains within settlements does not seem to be due to the vagaries of which parts of settlements and what proportion of features have been sampled. At the completely excavated settlement of Gravelly Guy the distribution of such remains was fairly evenly spread but the City Farm and Yarnton settlements had many fewer burials despite thorough sampling. The reasons for the presence of more human burials and other special deposits at some settlements are uncertain and may vary. At Castle Hill the hillfort was not the main focus of settlement but may have had other special functions (also evident from unusual evidence of feasting) and might even have been a place where bodies were excarnated. This may also apply to Segsbury (see Chapter 9). Of the apparently 'ordinary' farming settlements, both Gravelly Guy and Mount Farm were on sites close to pre-

Fig. 8.16 Pit burials in the Upper Thames Valley: (above) Gravelly Guy; *(centre and below)* Little Wittenham

existing Neolithic and Bronze Age funerary complexes and it is conceivable that there was some lingering tradition or superstition about occupying an ancient burial ground or finding human bones. The unusual concentration of burials along with various unusual finds at Bourton-on-the-Water may reflect some particular status as a settlement preceding the nearby fort at Salmonsbury (Nichols 2006, 74).

Burial practices

Many early to middle Iron Age inhumation burials within settlements in the Upper Thames Valley were placed in ordinary looking circular pits, sometimes on the base like a grave but often within the fill or even in a scoop in the top of the backfilled pit, clearly not deliberately dug as graves. Where burials lie on pit bases these might be assumed to have been dug as graves. This is more clearly the case with some bound burials and inhumations associated with boundaries, which were usually in roughly oval graves. Burial in a crouched position, on either the right or left side was preferred, occasionally prone or in other non-standard positions, usually with the head to the north, but again with considerable variation within these broad trends.

Although small numbers of inhumation burials are common at Iron Age settlements, they are far too few to account for the total population. It is reasonable to assume that the more frequent occurrence of stray bones and occasionally partial bodies is the result of excarnation – the exposure of the dead, perhaps at some distance from settlements. If this practice had been carried out within or directly adjacent to settlements significantly more finds of human bones might be expected.

The predominance of skull fragments and longbones (more rarely semi-articulated body parts) suggests that bones were sometimes brought back to the settlement, perhaps as tokens of remembrance. Few show obvious signs of curation but it is possible that remains were sometimes kept for some time before deliberate burial or accidental deposition through natural processes of settlement decay. Although bones from excarnated bodies could also have been collected and deposited accidentally by scavenging dogs or birds, very few show signs of gnawing.

There is some evidence from Iron Age pits and ditches to suggest that bodies or body parts were sometimes deposited in an incomplete state. At Beard Mill, Stanton Harcourt a pit contained human bones described as 'dismembered and heaped haphazard in the partly filled pit; the foot bones were found articulated but placed on top of a couple of rib bones; arm and leg bones lay above a badly damaged cranium. Parts of the body were missing and no determination of age or sex was possible' (Williams 1951, 14). An incomplete late Iron Age torso was found in a ditch at Mount Farm (Lambrick forthcoming) and an incomplete torso

was also found in a posthole at Segsbury (Lock *et al.* 2005). At Bourton-on-the-Water one pit contained the lower limbs and pelvic girdle of an elderly woman and another contained a left foot (Nichols 2006, 60). In most cases there is no sign of cuts on the bones of dismembered body parts and it seems reasonable to suppose that they are remains collected from incompletely decomposed bodies that had been excarnated.

In some cases disarticulated human bones, especially skull fragments, are found in association with animal offerings, suggesting they were deliberately buried, as are some human remains occurring in separate layers in pits or ditches that have other 'special deposits'. Several examples of such associations were identified at Gravelly Guy, including an early Iron Age human mandible placed on a setting of stones and bones, and a similar deposit with a middle Iron Age skull fragment and a trepanning disc pendant found in a pit with an unusual collection of clay plates, loomweights, oven daub and an articulated front leg of a dog. At Bourton-on-the-Water a human jaw had been placed next to a horse jaw (Nichols 2006, 61) and at Watchfield the skull of a man who had survived an extensive trepanning operation lay in an irregular pit with an inverted cattle skull placed next to it, along with a human femur (Birbeck *et al.* 2001, 229, 272-4). At Aylesbury disarticulated human remains were associated with unusual burials and concentrations of goat and lamb bones (Farley 1986 a, b).

Disarticulated human bones and partial bodies occur both in pits and ditches, both at the bottom and within their fills, in most cases suggesting little care in deposition; however a comparable pattern of occurrence also applies to inhumations, and there are some convincing cases of skull fragments or other bones having been deliberately placed. Skulls were found on the base of storage pits at Hill Farm, Little Wittenham (Allen *et al.* forthcoming a) and at Abingdon Vineyard (Allen pers. comm.). At Barton, Oxford a humerus was found on the base of a storage pit (Moore 2005) and at Steeple Aston a group of longbones was found in a pit at the terminal of an enclosure ditch (Hacking in Cook and Hayden 2000, 192-3 and fig. 6). At Watkins Farm several fragments of the skull and other bones of a man who had met a violent death were found in one of the recuts of the ditch surrounding the central roundhouse (Allen 1990, 14).

Human remains and Iron Age settlements in the Middle Thames Valley

Bone does not survive on the most acidic soils in the Middle Thames Valley and no human remains or other bones were present, for example, at the Brooklands sites. As has already been noted in relation to later Bronze Age waterholes uncremated human remains are also notably scarce or absent on the less acidic gravels, and this is also the case for Iron Age pits, waterholes and penannular gullies associated with houses and animal pens. None were found at Ashford Prison, Lower Mill Farm, Hengrove, Cippenham, or in the numerous pits and other features at Thorpe Lea Nurseries. At Dorney there is evidence of middle to late Bronze Age burials in and around burial ring ditches and early to middle Iron Age human bones were recovered from the old river channel, but the human remains from the area of the middle to late Iron Age enclosure were all from Roman contexts, though it is possible that some might be redeposited (Allen *et al.* 2000, 96-9).

Although bone preservation is less reliable than on the more calcareous gravels of the Upper Thames, animal bones are present on the same sites and human remains of other periods are quite well-represented. Likewise, while it is true that apart from Taplow pipeline there are no extensive pit scatter settlements (or certainly none excavated) on the Middle Thames gravels, the scale of excavation at several middle Iron Age settlements is comparable to that of similar sites in the Upper Thames area.

The absence of uncremated human bone from later Bronze Age and Iron Age settlements on the Surrey and west London gravels – and possibly other parts of the Middle Thames – increasingly appears to be a genuine regional difference, despite the problem of soil conditions. Although more detailed analysis of relative survival conditions is needed to confirm the pattern, Rob Poulton (pers. comm.) suggests that it might correlate to the especially rich deposits of later prehistoric metalwork in the adjacent reaches of the Thames. This would reinforce the notion that such offerings were connected with funerary rites (see above), and certainly the pattern at Dorney seems broadly consistent with this.

Although more evidence is needed to test this idea fully, the pattern might indicate that the particular social mores and traditions which led to burials and other human remains occurring in the pits and ditches of settlements in the Upper Thames Valley (see below) did not apply in the lower reaches of the Middle Thames Valley, or were expressed in archaeologically less visible ways. One possibility is that the tradition of cremation burial may have continued into the middle Iron Age. At Isleworth an early or middle Iron Age 'cremation' consisting of only 9 g of bone and the base of an associated pot was found next to a ditch (Bell 1996) and at Perry Oaks/T5 a group of undated cremation burials close to an Iron Age waterhole and other burning is another intriguing although as yet unconfirmed possibility (Ken Welsh pers. comm.). Even so, this evidence is unlikely to account for the 'missing' human remains that might otherwise be expected in and around Iron Age settlements, but it might be a positive indication that other funerary practices were in use at this time.

Late Iron Age cremation burials and high status burials

Although pit burials within and around settlements characteristic of the early to middle Iron Age continued into the late Iron Age and probably even the Roman period, other burial practices emerged anew. This mainly focussed north of London, the general absence of richly furnished late Iron Age burials in west London and Surrey apparently continuing on from the absence of early and middle Iron Age burials noted above. This seems to include the absence of urned cremation burials, although it should be noted that many undated cremation or cremation-like deposits assumed to be middle or late Bronze Age are seldom demonstrably not late Iron Age.

In addition to cemeteries noted earlier in this chapter, more isolated cremation burials are quite common in the broad 'core' area of Catuvellaunian territory around Verlamion and Welwyn but are rarer elsewhere in the Thames Valley away from the main Aylesford Swarling cultural zone (Cunliffe 1991). Further upstream, south of Reading and in the lower Kennet Valley, a number of late Iron Age burials have been found in the general area north and northwest of the oppidum of Calleva Atrebatum (Silchester).

Particularly notable is an isolated cremation burial dated to the 1st century BC, possibly before 50 BC, found at Latchmere Green not far from Silchester in 1994 (Fulford and Creighton 1998). It consisted of the cremated remains of an adult of about 30 together with a child under five years, whose ashes had been placed with cremated pig bones in a pottery jar of local type familiar from Calleva. The burial was accompanied by fragments of at least two fibulae and a very finely decorated bronze mirror for which no close parallels are known, but perhaps suggesting that these were the remains of a woman of some status.

In the lower Kennet Valley at Burghfield a bead rim bowl containing cremated human bones was accompanied by several high quality pottery vessels datable to 25-50 AD, including a butt-beaker, a *terra nigra* plate, an imitation *terra nigra* dish and a saucepan pot (Whimster 1981, Vol. ii, 357). Nearby at Pingewood was a cluster of five token cremation burials, two associated with bases of late Iron Age pots and a sixth outlier of uncertain date (Johnston 1985, 23). A cremation burial at Beenham was accompanied by a coarse ware urn and other sherds (Whimster 1981, Vol. ii, 357), as was another at Green Park 2 (Brossler *et al.* forthcoming).

North-west of the main Chiltern escarpment a number of late Iron Age cremation burials are known, including three chance finds at the foot of the Chilterns in southern Oxfordshire. At Pyrton near Watlington a pit contained the calcined bones of a woman accompanied by two butt-beakers, a necked foot-ring bowl and a flat dish together with a Colchester brooch and a smooth perforated flint

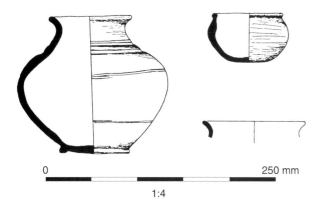

Fig. 8.17   Late Iron Age cremation burial group from Kingston Blount, Oxon.

pebble that may have been used as a bead, amulet or charm (Case 1958). Two cremation burials of an adult in a necked jar and an infant or child in a bead-rim bowl are known from Aston Rowant (Whimster 1981 Vol. ii, 357), and another urned cremation was found nearby at Kingston Blount (Fig. 8.17; Chambers 1976).

Further north, on the Corallian ridge north of Thame another high status mirror burial was found in a shallow oval grave during excavation for a pipeline at Dorton, west Buckinghamshire (Farley 1983). The cremated remains of a person of uncertain age and sex, together with the mirror, were contained in a wooden box accompanied by three amphorae and two flagons. On the central axis of the grave was a ceramic cup close to a thin wooden plank that might have been a gaming board and a metal hoop of uncertain function, perhaps part of a bucket, wheel or bier. The burial is broadly similar to the richer well known grave at Welwyn (Stead 1967) and is the most westerly occurrence of a distinct cluster of such burials centred in the Chilterns and spreading into East Anglia, while also being part of a wider distribution of mirror burials (Farley 1983, 288-9, 295-6; Whimster 1981; Fulford and Creighton 1998).

Until relatively recently few late Iron Age cremation burials were known from the core area of the Upper Thames Valley and they remain scarce, though the very extensive excavations on the gravels have revealed several examples. Few have been exposed in recent excavations around Dorchester-on-Thames or Abingdon, despite extensive investigations on several sites. A possible exception is an unurned and undated cremation burial found just inside the entrance of the inner rectangular enclosure at Barton Court Farm (Miles 1984, 6, fig. 5; fiche 3:C3-4, 4:E2 fig. 76). There were also two undated crouched inhumation burials on the site, one of a man of 35-40 lying just inside a possibly contemporary circular post-built structure, the other a woman of uncertain age, also undated. Several infants were found in the ditches of the late Iron Age enclosure. Another is the burial of a

warrior with accompanying shield and weapons at Sutton Courtenay, discovered in the early 19th century, which may have been contemporary with reported late Iron Age cremation burials nearby (Whimster 1979). However, the dating of the burial and character of the supposed cremations is uncertain, and they may in fact be Saxon.

Further upstream three late Iron Age or early Roman cremation burials were found at Yarnton, one in a broken pottery urn with a well-preserved Aucissa brooch with extremely fine repoussé La Tène ornament. Although probably of post-conquest date, it is a fine example of the continued survival of celtic art styles (Hey et al. forthcoming). At Gravelly Guy, where there is stronger evidence of the continuation of crouched inhumation burial into the late Iron Age or early Roman period, there was also a cremation burial of an adult with at least one bone of a baby in a small necked bowl accompanied by the cremated remains of a sheep's leg, possibly a joint of meat, and bird bone fragments. A number of nails lying amongst the charcoal suggested that a wooden box was used as a container.

At Langford Downs near Lechlade a late Iron Age urned cremation burial was found in a pit dug into an earlier barrow (Williams 1946-7, 63), a relatively unusual context compared with the commoner reuse of such monuments in middle Bronze Age and Saxon times. At Thornhill Farm four poorly dated cremation and three inhumation burials, probably of post-conquest date, were found amongst a complex sequence of enclosures that displayed continuous development from the middle Iron Age onwards (Jennings et al. 2004, 65).

A remarkable group of late Iron Age burials from the Thames Valley was found at Latton Lands, where three inhumations and one cremation burial associated with late Iron Age or early Roman pottery were cut into the natural fill of a rectangular enclosure ditch at critical points round its perimeter (Fig. 8.14; Powell et al. forthcoming). One of the graves cut the western ditch of the enclosure at its junction with another ditch and contained the partially cremated remains of a man dated by three radiocarbon determinations to 160 cal BC-cal AD 70. His body was in a prone position against the western side of the grave with the legs flexed upwards and crossed, the spine arched and the hands over the back of the pelvis, suggesting they had been tied. The corpse had been burnt in situ. The skeleton lay between burnt timber planks and some bones were scorched and burnt. The sides of the grave had also been scorched and the soil surrounding the skeleton contained fragments of cremated bone, including teeth and vertebrae, and charcoal of a variety of species. The burning was very intense on the front of the skeleton, suggesting that a fire was lit in the base of the grave and the body then placed on top of it. A broken knife of late Iron Age type that continued in use into the early Roman period was found directly below the burial and a late Iron Age/early Roman pottery vessel was inserted between the legs. The body of another man was buried with no grave goods in a crouched position in a grave cut into the south-western corner of the enclosure ditch, and a third man was similarly buried at the south-eastern corner, with an Aucissa type brooch, dated to AD 43-70, in the grave fill. A small pit cut into the western ditch terminal at the entrance of the enclosure contained a large quantity of oak and fruitwood charcoal, together with cremated human and animal bone. The quantity of bone was not sufficient to represent an entire body and it may have been a deposit of pyre debris.

Finally, it is worth noting a high status mirror burial from a small group of inhumation burials found in 1879 by quarry workmen at Birdlip, high on the edge of the Gloucestershire Cotswolds at the northwest extremity of the Thames catchment (Green 1949). This remarkable group consisted of a small cemetery of three, possibly four late Iron Age burials. Three were in stone-lined cist graves laid out side by side each with the corpse buried in an extended position with the head to the north. The central burial was accompanied by a remarkably rich collection of grave goods (Fig. 8.18), consisting of a range of jewellery (a substantial bead necklace and a bronze armlet or anklet) probable toiletry equipment (an elaborately decorated mirror and

tweezers), dress accoutrements (a fine silver-gilt La Tène III brooch) and a number of items of less certain function (four other large, crude bronze rings, two bronze bowls, a decorated cast bronze tool handle, a possible bronze wire handle perhaps from a casket, and another bronze looped handle or terminal). There may have been a fourth interment nearby that contained a bronze bucket and sheet bronze ring, and a gold torque may also be from the area. The local doctor who excavated the skeletons identified the central one as that of a woman and the two either side as men, but only one skull survives. The physiology of the surviving skull, thought to be from the central grave, is not definitely female and although it is said to be 'the Birdlip Lady' there is no sign of staining on it from the large bronze bowl that was recorded as covering the head when it was excavated. Equally uncertain is the tantalising reference to a fourth grave and other high status objects (Green 1949; see also www.glos-city.gov.uk/Content.aspx?cindex =155&citem=6786&urn=1404 accessed 13/07/2006).

Taking the evidence of late Iron Age burial in the Upper Thames as a whole, it seems evident that new practices were introduced alongside older traditions. Although the dating evidence is not generally good enough to prove whether they are pre- or post-conquest, a perpetuation or adaptation

Fig. 8.18 The Birdlip mirror burial

of pre-existing practices seems evident at Gravelly Guy, Yarnton, Latton Lands and probably Barton Court, both from the continuation of inhumation rites alongside cremation burial and the location of burials in pits and ditches or alongside boundaries, sometimes with human and animal bones combined. Over most of the Thames Valley the relatively limited occurrence of late Iron Age cremation burials in and around settlements or in more isolated locations can also be seen as a continuation of traditional practices. Such sporadic occurrence was only superseded by formal cemeteries in quite a restricted area and/or for particular people until cemeteries became common in the Roman period. Cremation and disposal of the dead as isolated burials in and around settlements continued well into the first century AD, even as more formal cemeteries became gradually established across the Thames Valley (Henig and Booth 2000).

Apart from cremation burial recurring as a cultural norm, late Iron Age burials tend to reflect a more overt expression of status reflected in the character of grave goods, especially clear in the isolated high status mirror burials. However, caution is needed in assessing how far this was a new phenomenon. Although such overt expression of status is not apparent in equivalent isolated burials of earlier times, it may have been a feature of other rites such as disposal of remains in the river, which may have been accompanied by high status weaponry and other objects.

The social and spiritual status of people

'Normative' rites and disposal of the majority

The overall pattern of late prehistoric burial practices tells us something of spiritual and social attitudes towards certain groups or classes of people. The broad trend is the well-established pattern of earlier prehistoric traditions of formal cemeteries and monuments becoming less common and an increasing trend towards disposal of bodies in the wider environment, including water, boundaries and settlements. This may also be reflected in trends away from formal burial rites of inhumation or cremation in the early to middle Bronze Age towards excarnation, dispersing bodies naturally into the environment in the Iron Age, before more formal disposal rites re-emerged in the Roman period. This accords with the importance played by the natural world in Iron Age religion (Green 1996a). It might also reflect an increasing interest in land and water as vital personal and communal resources bound up with spiritual, social and economic values.

Throughout later prehistory it is clear that the human remains recovered by excavation represent only a small fraction of the population as a whole. The relatively few who were given formal burials in special burial places and monuments seem to have been accorded special respect. However, other practices visible in the archaeological record seem to represent exceptional treatment of individuals who may not have been regarded as fully fledged members of society or were the subject of dishonour or disapprobation, possibly condemning them to sacrifice for some greater good. The divergences of such practices could be linked with formal social hierarchies of kinship, class, initiation or social caste and with informal perceptions of social status connected to economic or physical disadvantage or social ostracism.

Between these extremes were the vast majority of people not afforded the sort of burial easily detected archaeologically. For them little more can be said except to observe that the paucity of formal burials may indicate that excarnation was the normative rite for most people. This could explain the occurrence of stray human bones in various contexts throughout prehistory which become more 'visible' in the later Bronze Age and Iron Age because by then there were more below ground features in the landscape to capture stray body parts or to serve as deposition sites for human remains. Within the disposal options for this largely invisible majority of dead people may be many diverse practices that reflected social class or status. For example, if the deposition of human remains in the river was associated with high status objects (Bradley and Gordon 1988) it could include individuals of high social rank or status.

Fitzpatrick (1997) argued that burials in pits within Iron Age settlements are so common that it should, in the absence of alternatives, be regarded as the 'normative' rite. This appears to disregard the options of disposal by excarnation and the occurrence of burials and stray remains outside settlements. More importantly, if the longevity of settlements and relatively short life expectancy are taken into account, it is clear that the deliberate burial of human bodies and disposal of stray bones or body parts occurred very rarely, whether within or outside settlements in the Thames Valley. This suggests that the people whose remains are found were not buried in what would have been regarded as the 'normal' manner and despite the lack of hard evidence it is possible to propose reasons why they may have been treated differently.

Grave goods

Grave goods can provide clues as to the status of people at the time of their death but they are not a major element of late prehistoric burial rites in the Thames Valley. Although middle Bronze Age cremations were often in or accompanied by pottery urns they were seldom accompanied by any other surviving grave goods. These are even less common in the late Bronze Age.

Grave goods are rare in the early to middle Iron Age of southern England but they do occur, and the numbers are increasing for Thames Valley sites. At

Gravelly Guy two of the four adult burials had grave goods – a woman with a shale spindle whorl (Fig. 8.19), a man with two bone toggles – and two deposits of disarticulated remains of children were accompanied respectively by a spearhead and dog tooth pendant (Lambrick and Allen 2004, 248-9). At Bourton-on-the-Water a miniature axe amulet was found with the remains of three individuals (Nichols 2006, 26). At Cassington a probable pre-Roman bracelet was found on a bronze-stained human tibia which may derive from an Iron Age burial disturbed during mechanical excavation (Kirk and Case 1950, 106). A child burial at Spring Road, Abingdon was accompanied by a bone ring possibly deliberately placed near the head (Fig. 8.19; Allen and Kamash 2008).

As we have seen, it is also possible that 'grave goods' were an important element of the deposition of human remains in the river, though as the excavations at the Eton Rowing Course and observations at Abbey Meads, Chertsey have shown, the association between human remains and deliberately deposited objects is difficult to demonstrate even when recovered under controlled conditions.

Grave goods were a much more significant feature of late Iron Age cremation burials, and were clearly signs of social status. In some respects this was a departure, emphasising the role of high status individuals in society. Amongst late Iron Age

Fig. 8.19 Iron Age grave goods: child burial with bone ring, Abingdon Spring Road; Gravelly Guy burial with spindle whorl

burials which continue the early to middle Iron Age tradition of inhumation burials in pits and ditches, grave goods remain rare. This uncommon practice would have underlined the social and cultural distinctions that the new burial rites sought to reinforce.

Evidence of the status of people buried in funerary monuments and cemeteries

Those accorded 'special' rites of cremation or inhumation burial and burial in barrows or other cemeteries in the middle to late Bronze Age apparently included males and females, children and adults. Because cremation was common and many deposits are token ('cenotaph' deposits) it is difficult to identify precise patterns, but apparently gender and age were not qualifying factors for such rites, perhaps because kinship or social status were more important. Ellison (1980) suggested that groups of cremation burials within some of the larger urnfields may reflect social or family groups. Whether cremations were placed in or buried with urns may be a further indication of social standing. Perhaps distinctions of social rank or class were principally expressed by the qualification for burial in a formal cemetery.

There is no evidence from grave goods or manner of burial of social distinctions amongst those buried in the middle Iron Age cemetery at Yarnton. If it was in use for only one or two generations, as suggested by the radiocarbon dates, the 25 individuals in the two main clusters could represent all adult members of the community and some children who died in that period. The presence of infant burials in the nearby settlement but not the main cemetery clusters suggests that they were disposed of separately within the settlement (Hey *et al*. 1999; Hey *et al*. forthcoming a). However, if the cemetery reflects only burials over a generation or two, the apparent absence of perinatal infants need not be surprising and there is not much better evidence for disposal of infants within settlements being 'normal' than there is for adults.

So far as can be established from cremated remains, late Iron Age cemeteries in the area around Verlamion and Welwyn also reflect a cross-section of society, but what becomes more evident at this time than in earlier cemeteries is the identity of family or individual burial plots and a relatively elaborate ranking of status and wealth (Stead and Rigby 1989). These might reflect notions of class or other social hierarchy. Significant social distinctions also seem clear from the wide range of grave goods and burial rites of greater or lesser elaboration amongst the isolated late Iron Age burials more widely scattered across the Thames Valley (see above).

It is likely that while such distinctions may have become more marked in the late Iron Age, earlier examples may be masked by the absence of a normative burial rite that expressed such characteristics for the whole social spectrum in an archaeologically visible way. Burial in urnfields and barrows may have been reserved for leading members of society, and while grave goods and other signs of social prestige are largely absent from the Yarnton cemetery and burials in and around settlements, disposal of bodies in the river may well have been accompanied by deposition of weapons and ornaments that reflected status.

Young children

The available evidence suggests that the treatment of neonates and children in the middle to late Bronze Age was little different to adults, but there are hints, as in the ring ditch at Mount Farm, that children and young people were sometimes buried in specific locations. However, neonate and child burials are common within Iron Age settlements, although their rate of occurrence compared with adults is highly variable. At Gravelly Guy an unusually high proportion of deposits contained human remains, of which neonates accounted for 72% of total deposits and 75% of complete burials. Mount Farm also produced a large number of human remains and a high proportion of neonates (58% of all remains and 50% of complete burials). Most sites have far fewer remains, some only adults, others equal numbers. Even where their occurrence is frequent, the number of neonates found on settlement sites is insufficient to account fully for the likely rate of perinatal death. It is thus not clear, contrary to some assumptions, that there was a general practice of burying infants in settlements that did not apply to adults. The occurrence of both is highly variable and cannot account for all deaths. There are likely to have been other reasons why some people were selected for burial within and around settlements.

One widely canvassed idea is that infants were not regarded as fully fledged members of society or that infanticide was practised. If so it is not possible to tell whether there was an element of sex discrimination as known in other cultures. While uninitiated infants and children may not have been regarded as fully fledged members of society, that in itself need not mean that they would automatically be deprived of normative burial. It is perhaps more likely that some fell within a wider spectrum of people whose social status made them more suitable than others for burial within and around settlements (Scott 1999).

People buried in and around settlements compared with the Yarnton Cemetery

Wait (1985, 83-121, 233-45) argued that people buried within Iron Age settlements were in a minority and, using ethnographic parallels, suggested that they were either liminal people (eg the very young or very old) or outcasts ostracised as social or religious minorities or for some social or religious infraction of accepted norms. He noted that the general character of pit burials is consistent with ethnographic evidence that outcasts 'usually receive a non-normative treatment of the body, a different mode of disposal, a different place of disposal, frequently associated with social rubbish and dirt, and rarely have a normal age/sex distribution' (Wait 1996, 494-5).

However, as Wait noted for Gravelly Guy (Lambrick and Allen 2004, 248-9), such explanations should not be treated too simplistically. Not all infant or elderly dead were treated in this way. Moreover the presence of grave goods with some individuals seems inconsistent with status as outcasts. It has also been argued that such burials represent sacrifices, which is less inconsistent with the presence of personal objects. There is a further possibility that single bones or partial body parts represent votive deposits of curated remains. This complicates the issue of the extent to which the minority buried within settlements reflect distinctions of social class or caste, socio-economic status, or social ostracism.

To put this issue into some perspective comparisons can be drawn between the Yarnton burials and inhumation burials from pits and graves in and around settlements (Fig. 8.20). The former apparently represent a 'normal' cross section of people (albeit buried in an unusual way for the period) and the latter people specifically selected for non-normative treatment. The comparison is extremely tentative due to the limitations of sample numbers and the incompleteness of identifiable characteristics on many bodies (about 50 pit/ditch burials and 25 in the cemetery). There are also fundamental differences in the grouping, chronological and geographical spread of the two datasets. Nevertheless, it reveals some differences which, even if not statistically reliable, raise interesting questions about the status of people buried within settlements.

The exercise demonstrates that most complete burials in and around settlements in the Thames Valley are of women, whereas the two main clusters in the Yarnton cemetery were equally balanced. If the outliers are added, the group as a whole was if anything dominated by men. This diverges from the national picture, which suggests the ratios were roughly equal (Wait 1985, 92-3; 1996, 492). The conclusion may be either that there are regional variations or that the proportions vary with different kinds of site, hillforts being relatively under-represented in this sample.

There is also some divergence in age ranges between the settlement burials and the Yarnton cemetery. Apart from the absence of neonates, the cemetery reflects a reasonably natural pattern of mortality, lowest among small children and young adults. The burials in and around settlements are different. Apart from the presence, and sometimes high proportion, of neonates, the incidence of deaths of young people of 17-25 is equal highest (with old people) amongst the burials in settle-

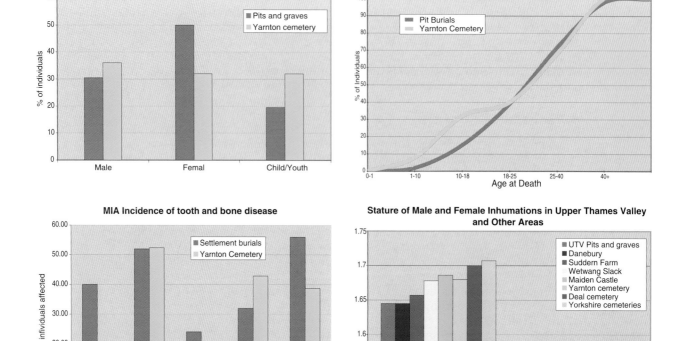

Fig. 8.20 Comparison of burials in the middle Iron Age Yarnton cemetery and burials in and around settlements

ments, whereas it is equal lowest (with small children) at Yarnton. The settlement burials also show a high incidence of older women, though comparisons with the cemetery are complicated by methods of reporting estimated age. These trends apply both to settlement burials as a whole and a subset of only middle Iron Age ones.

The occurrence of common chronic health problems, including bad teeth (caries, abscesses, tooth loss) and degenerative joint disease seems to have been much the same across both the cemetery group and settlement burials, although at Bourton-on-the-Water there was a particularly high incidence of health problems, including a child who died of a brain infection and a woman who was partly paralysed. However, there does seem to be some difference in nutritional status. A higher incidence of hypoplasia (cracking or ridging in tooth enamel possibly signifying poor nutrition) seems more evident amongst individuals buried in settlements (25% generally, 40% for the middle Iron Age) compared with the cemetery group (affecting only 5%).

Furthermore, both men and women in these contexts appear to have been on average about 30-50 mm shorter than those in the cemetery, again evident both in general and for just middle Iron Age settlement burials. While this may not be statisti-

cally significant with such small samples, it is consistent with the sharp difference in hypoplasia, both independently potentially indicating that people buried in pits and ditches may have come from a relatively impoverished background with poorer nutrition early in life.

The age profile, sex ratios and nutritional background of burials in and around settlements thus diverge both from the expected profile of a normal population and from the people buried in the Yarnton cemetery. This evidence suggests that such burials might represent relatively disadvantaged people, especially the very young, young adults, elderly women and the relatively malnourished. The combination of the higher occurrence of hypoplasia and lower stature, but not other health issues as compared with the Yarnton group, may indicate that relatively socially disadvantaged people were singled out, but not the decrepit as such. This is consistent with the high occurrence of young adults amongst the settlement burials. The biases in sex and age reinforce the impression that social and cultural factors were important in determining who was buried in and around settlements.

The combined evidence is consistent with those buried in pits and ditches being social or socio-economic outcasts. While small infants may never have gained status as full members of society, some children and adults who were socially and physically disadvantaged may have been regarded as a burden. Other people might have lost their social status through infractions of socially accepted behavior and become outcasts not accorded normal funerary rites. Burial in a pit or latrine, or in or alongside a boundary ditch might have been a mark of such disregard.

This does not, however, conversely imply that the Yarnton group reflect the missing 'normative' burial rite. Wait notes that ethnographically disease can be a reason for deviation from normal burial practice. This accords with the possibility raised by Hey *et al.* (1999) that the cemetery reflects an outbreak of contagious disease. The relatively normal age and sex profile of the group and typical occurrence of other chronic disease, while remaining exceptional in terms of the place and mode of disposing of the bodies, is consistent with this theory.

While most individuals buried within or around settlements might be of lower status, caste or class, it does not mean that everyone of comparable status was treated in this way. There must have been more symbolic meaning to the practice.

If the normative rite was excarnation and scattering of bones into the environment – including the river and curation of body parts – it is possible that the key distinction for normative or non-normative disposal was burial. If it was believed that the soul became part of an 'otherworld' related to liberation into the wider environment, the non-normative contrast may have been to dispose of and bury the remains of social outcasts, criminals and victims of disease in ways that precluded release of the soul of unclean or outcast individuals.

Dismemberment, decapitation, disapprobation, sacrifice and cannibalism

If people buried in and around settlements can be supposed to have been disadvantaged, it raises questions about whether the manner of disposing of these bodies reflects social attitudes to people who had lost the respect of their peers as outcasts or criminals. Sacrificial rituals, which are well attested in the celtic world, may be evident in such burials (Wait 1985, 118-120, 235-45; 1996, 495; Ross 1967). Dismemberment or other mutilation of corpses, whether or not in the context of sacrifice, may have been a means of controlling the soul of the dead to prevent the passage to the 'otherworld'.

In many cases burials were placed in open pits rather than being buried in deliberately cut graves. This raises questions about the circumstances of burial. Was it coincidental that the pits were open and available for use when someone happened to die or was this form of burial used only when there happened to be a pit available? Were pits deliberately dug or emptied to form a grave when somebody died? Were the bodies of new born babies and even adults mummified and curated before burial?

Some burials may represent deliberate killings. Social outcasts and criminals may have been selected for ritual killing as a form of punishment when norms of behaviour had been violated. Disadvantaged infants and young adults, especially women, could have been preferentially selected as innocent victims of sacrifice to appease the gods or the forces of nature when the need arose. Sacrifice in the context of crop failure and the need to bring good fortune for the next crop has been advanced as a possible explanation for burials in storage pits and graves within and around settlements (Cunliffe 1983, 166; 1992, 77; Wait 1985, 120; Walker 1984, 461-2). Alternatively if pits were used as latrines, the disposal of bodies in them may have been a particular mark of disapprobation. In the case of hillforts, sacrifices may have been made to give thanks for a major communal undertaking or to help resolve conflict.

Ritualised killing, whether execution as punishment of the guilty or sacrifice of the innocent, is well attested for the Iron Age in Scandinavia and Britain from bog bodies of people killed with cutting weapons or garroted or strangled (Glob 1969). There is little evidence from the Thames Valley of violent death from swords, axes, spears or other weapons – the broken skull in the central house enclosure at Watkins Farm being one exception – but garroting is a form of violent killing that would leave little trace on skeletal remains.

Since ritual killing need leave little or no archaeological trace it is usually difficult to prove, but there is sufficient circumstantial evidence to suggest that deliberate killing and/or mutilation of corpses was relatively common. The most persuasive evidence takes the form of double burials. A number of explanations for double burials can be proposed, including deaths in childbirth, disease, accidents and curation of bodies through mummification prior to burial, but deliberate killing is another.

Some later Bronze Age cremation burials contain the remains of more than one person, including a young adult and infant at Wood Farm, Cippenham (Ford *et al.* 2003) and two examples of an adult and sub-adult in ditches at Green Park (Brossler *et al.* 2004, 107). Late Iron Age double cremations include the mirror burial at Latchmere Green of an adult of about 30 years, probably female from the character of the grave goods, together with a child of under five years (Fulford and Creighton 1998) and the Aston Rowant burial of an adult and child (Whimster 1981 vol. ii, 357).

Double inhumation burials are even more likely to represent simultaneous deaths. In the Thames Valley most of these were burials of women with children, possibly mothers and sons or daughters. The undated double inhumation burial just outside the middle Bronze Age settlement at Corporation Farm, Abingdon was of a 30 year-old woman crammed into a small pit with a nine year-old child placed immediately above her (Barclay *et al.* 2003, 37-9). At Watchfield two double burials, one at least datable to the Iron Age, were found. One (undated) was of a woman of 18-30, buried in a crouched position on her right side head to north, face to face with a child, possibly a boy, of seven to nine years, also crouched but on his left side (Fig. 8.21). Her left arm was beneath him and right leg between his legs, clearly showing they had been buried together, indicating what the excavator referred to as 'some form of ritual activity beyond normal funerary practices' (Birkbeck *et al.* 2001, 230-2 and 267-9). The other double burial at Watchfield was less obviously abnormal. A young woman of 18-25 was buried in a crouched position on her right side, head to the east with the fragmentary remains of a newborn infant apparently 'in' her left hand by her head. It may be that the infant represents bones accidentally found and placed in the grave, or that the burial is of a mother and baby who both died of complications in childbirth, but it is also possible that both were sacrificed.

At Cassington Big Ring a 22-28 year old female was laid in a crouched position on her right side, head to the southeast, with a child of two-and-a-half in a flexed position, also on his/her right side with head to the north-west. They were buried in the bottom of a recut or cleared out entrance terminal of the Big Rings late Iron Age fort (Case 1982 131 and 148). The skull of the woman was described as 'slewed backwards out of articulation to face south,' which could suggest decapitation.

The burials at Castle Hill included a pit containing the crouched burial of a man at the base, articulated parts of a woman with leg tendons severed at the knee halfway up, and an infant in the top (Fig. 8.21). Apart from a possible deliberate deposit of charred material, the fill around the man and woman was sterile, suggesting that the pit may have been dug (or emptied to be reused) for these burials. This group demonstrates the parallel rites of immediate burial of complete bodies and the dismemberment and partial burial of bodies, possibly after excarnation.

Another case of two inhumation burials in a single pit was recorded at Purwell Farm, Cassington where two adult males, both apparently incomplete, were found at different levels, one above the other. The lower body was a notably robust individual but complete only down to the waist and unusually positioned on his back with arms to the sides (Dawson 1961). Whether the degree of incompleteness of the bodies represents the condition in which they were buried or later disturbance is not clear.

Although it is unlikely to be entirely coincidental, there is also no direct evidence that the two bodies

Fig. 8.21 Double burials, mutilations and anomalous burials: (above) Watchfield double burial; (centre) burial of a mutilated woman, Castle Hill, Little Wittenham; (below) partially cremated burial with burnt timbers at Latton Lands

were buried on the same occasion. If one or both were incomplete when buried it may indicate pre-burial dismemberment of the corpses or partial decay and disarticulation through exposure, but not necessarily ritual killing (see below).

Dismemberment may also have been a feature of the burial of the man and horse in the hillfort ditch at Blewburton (Collins 1952-3). The man's legs lay partly over and partly beneath the horse's hind quarters. His skull lay where the horse's forelegs should have been and was detached from his backbone, which lay inside the horse's ribcage with the lower jaw 0.75 m away. The arms were placed next to the horse's forelegs. Beneath the horse was the base of a pot, the top of which lay above the man's legs. There was also a fine adze hammer, and the complete skeleton of a dog lay on the base of the ditch beneath the horse's hooves and the man's skull. It seems clear that these remains represent one episode of ritual burial but it is not clear how far the configuration of the bodies resulted from burial of dismembered body parts or differential settling as the corpses decayed.

At Aylesbury a severed skull with three cervical vertebrae packed around with limestone blocks lay on the base of the hillfort ditch. It is not clear if the separation of the head and neck was due to partial decomposition through excarnation, mutilation of the body, or was the cause of death. Other human bones were also found in the ditch. Within the area of the fort parts of four or five bodies lay in extended positions in various orientations. Two, accompanied by a complete goat carcass, were placed around the western edge of a hollow in which other human bones were found associated with parts (including articulated limbs) of at least 30 beasts, mostly young lambs (Farley 1986a, b). One of the human burials was of a young person positioned face up, legs widely spread, accompanied by a goat on one side and the torso of a goat or sheep on the other. Detailed analysis of the remains has not yet been published but the preliminary accounts indicate that these burials might represent some sort of ritual killing, possibly associated with feasting, while the severed head from the ditch might be a foundation deposit or evidence of a punishment killing.

At Abbey Meads a skull with an attached vertebra might be another example of dismemberment or decapitation, although it is possible that other parts of the body were lost in quarrying (Jones in prep). At the West Settlement at City Farm Hanborough a pit contained a crouched human skeleton complete except for the skull, which was found 'more or less vertically a few inches from the vertebrae'. It is not entirely clear that this was how the body had been buried rather than the result of subsequent decay or disturbance by burrowing animals (Case *et al.* 1964/5 47-8).

At Latton Lands the partially cremated skeleton of an adult associated with burnt timbers and accompanied by a large pottery vessel and an iron knife of late Iron Age or early Roman type was radiocarbon dated to the pre-conquest period (Fig. 8.21; Powell *et al.* forthcoming). This combination of burial and burning in the late Iron Age is extremely rare and may represent a failed cremation or some sort of purification ritual.

The possibility that cannibalism was practised in later prehistoric Britain has been widely debated. The evidence is ambiguous but a growing number of cases make a strong case for it (Taylor 2001). The most convincing evidence from the Thames Valley takes the form of human long bones of probable late Bronze Age date recovered from the river channel at Eton Rowing Course. These exhibit knife marks and the smashing of the ends in a manner typical of extracting bone marrow for consumption. This suggests both deliberate dismemberment and possible cannibalism (Allen *et al.* 2000, 90-1). The presence of these bones in the river, putatively a place of normative disposal of bodies, is significant in terms of the cultural role of cannibalism and of the river as a place for the dead.

It does seem likely that human sacrifice was practised in the Thames Valley, and if the instances of double burials noted above are indicative of the practice, it was probably not confined to these cases. The presence of grave goods or personal objects with some pit burials suggests that such burials were not just confined to social outcasts. It has long been recognised that the Danish and other bog bodies included well-groomed people, some in the prime of life, who were not much involved in heavy manual labour (Glob 1969).

However, it would probably be a mistake to suppose that all burials in and around settlements were the result of sacrifice. It is more likely that a range of different social and cultural factors were at play in the burial of some individuals in these non-normative rites. Burial instead of excarnation of the victims of disease, ostracism for social infractions, sacrifice and cannibalism could all be reflected in the varied practices evident in late prehistoric burial in the Thames Valley.

Overview of changing burial customs

Some broad trends in later prehistoric burial rites in the region are consistent with general practice in southern Britain (Ellison 1980; McKinley 1997; Brück 1995; Whimster 1981; Wilson 1981; Wait 1985). Throughout later prehistory only a small proportion of the population was buried in ways that are archaeologically detectable. This suggests that many remains were scattered after cremation or excarnation, in effect allowing corporeal remains to be dispersed into the environment, including deliberate deposition in rivers and other wet places.

The frequent occurrence of token cremation deposits and stray human bones, especially skull fragments and longbones, in and around settlements suggests that people retained or collected token remains which they may have curated before disposal. Considerable variation is discernible in the occurrence of stray bones, but skulls, or more often skull fragments, and longbones are most common, suggesting that these were selected for curation or deposition.

For deliberate burials, cremation was predominant in the early Bronze Age, continued as the principal rite into the middle Bronze Age and was still commonly practised into the late Bronze Age. Early Iron Age examples come from postholes at Horcott (Lamdin-Whymark *et al.* forthcoming) and Cresswell Field, Yarnton (Hey *et al.* forthcoming b). Thereafter they became extremely rare till the late Iron Age, with no definite middle Iron Age examples. Cremation re-emerged in the late Iron Age, but with significant regional variation in occurrence.

Inhumation burial had become rare by the early Bronze Age and only gradually re-emerged as a common rite in the middle to late Bronze Age. By the early to middle Iron Age it was predominant and continued into the late Iron Age. Burial in monuments and reuse or refurbishment of older monuments was common in the middle Bronze Age but, compared with earlier times, few new earthwork monuments were built.

'Flat' cemeteries in the form of urnfields became a feature of the middle Bronze Age. Some of these may have originated around earlier cremation burials, and some continued into the late Bronze Age. Otherwise burial in cemeteries was rare apart from an important regional cluster of late Iron Age cemeteries in Catuvellaunian heartlands and a few very unusual middle Iron Age inhumation cemeteries. Isolated burials away from settlements, particularly those in or associated with boundaries, seem to have been a regular feature of burial practices throughout later prehistory.

Disposal of human remains within settlements occurred throughout later prehistory, but was more common in the late Bronze Age and Iron Age, especially the middle Iron Age. The apparent increase may, however, partly reflect increases in the longevity and intensity of settlement. Although human remains are often present within Iron Age settlements, numbers vary considerably. The rate of occurrence is generally low, indicating that this was not the normal means of disposing of the dead.

Where complete bodies were buried and orientations recorded, virtually all adults were buried in crouched positions with only a few babies and rare adults buried in an extended position. Through the late Bronze and Iron Age most bodies were oriented with the head roughly to the north. Practice varied whether they were placed on their left or right sides and their vertical position within pit fills and ditches varied, only some being buried in demonstrably deliberately dug graves.

The practice of binding bodies tightly or burying them in bags in small graves seems to have been a regular feature of some burials. Although particularly noted for the late Bronze Age and early Iron Age, the practice was not restricted to these periods.

Apart from cremation urns and, occasionally, flints with middle Bronze Age cremations, few burials were accompanied by (surviving) grave goods until the late Iron Age, when it became more common for high status burials and cremations, but seldom for continuing practices of burial in and around settlements. Occasionally inhumation burials were part of or accompanied by other 'special' deposits (eg of animal bone, pottery etc), which may reflect funerary rituals and/or feasting.

Differences in the sex and age ratios and nutritional status of the burials from the Yarnton cemetery as compared with inhumations in and around settlements suggest that settlement burials may be of relatively disadvantaged members of society, outcasts or people not regarded as full members of society. On some sites where human remains are relatively common many are of neonates or small infants.

There is some evidence to indicate the practice of ritual killing, dismemberment and/or decapitation of corpses and cannibalism, but it is difficult to tell how prevalent this was.

Burial Practice	EBA	MBA	LBA	EIA	MIA	LIA	RB
New barrows	X	x					
Reuse of earlier monuments	X	X	x				
Cremation burials	X	X	X	x	?	X	X
Crouched inhumation burials		x	X	X	X	X	x
'Flat' cemeteries	?	x			(x)	x	X
Bound inhumation burials	?	x	x	x	(x)		
Human remains in waterholes	?	x	x	?	?	?	?
Burials in and near boundaries	?	x	x	x	x	x	x
Excarnation	?	?	??	??	??	?	?
Human remains from river	?	?	x	?	(x)	?	?
Burials within settlements	?	(x)	x	x	x	x	x
Disarticulated remains in 'special' deposits		x	x	x	x	x	x
Dismemberment possible ritual killing *etc*		?	(x)	(x)	x	(x)	?

X = recurrent probably normative rite; x = recurrent/occasional but probably not normative rite; (x) = rare occurrences; ?? = not well attested but possibly normative rite; ? = not well attested but possible

In reviewing changes in burial practice through prehistoric times, archaeologists have tended to emphasise the importance of changes in practice rather than examining common factors or the demise and revival of particular traditions. Many of these traditions can be traced to periods long before and long after those in which they predominated. The features outlined above suggest no particularly sudden radical changes in practice but a series of overlapping gradual trends showing how some practices became less common as others became more so. Changing preferences for cremation and inhumation burial were quite fluid, both practised in the later Bronze Age and late Iron Age. Underlying this may be common threads in terms of the locations of burial or disposal in cemeteries or in and around settlements and boundaries. The location may have been more important than the particular rite used to 'process' the body. Likewise, both cremation and excarnation may have been viewed in a similar way, as means of removing the corruptible flesh to allow the soul to escape to an afterworld, leaving behind purified whitened bones.

As in earlier times, and throughout later prehistory, the majority of people were not buried in formal burial places such as barrows and cemeteries. However, the idea that most dead people must have been treated in what are so far archaeologically unrecognisable ways is increasingly questionable. It may be difficult to establish *where* all the bodies are – and hence very difficult to establish any picture of particular populations – but we now have a good deal of evidence for the wide variety of places and means of *how* the dead were disposed of.

What we now know about late prehistoric disposal of the dead in the Thames Valley to some extent reinforces traditional views and assumptions, but it also provides a different and much less simplistic picture of how traditions overlapped, grew and waned, lasted for longer or shorter periods, disappeared and re-emerged. This summary may not apply to all parts of the Thames Valley and the lower reaches of the Middle Thames is so lacking in Iron Age burials that several of these observations may not apply. This may indicate a significant difference in practice, perhaps with more emphasis on excarnation away from sites and deposition in the river.

Chapter 9 – Communal interrelationships: sacred places, defence and politics

In Chapter 8 we explored the links between disposal of the dead and deposition of domestic debris and valued objects and ordinary domestic and farming life. In Chapter 5 we saw how symbolic aspects of the design of houses and other structures may have incorporated personal and family shrines or other expressions of spiritual connections. These features of ordinary homes and farms were rooted not only in tradition and superstition, but also widely shared religious and social beliefs that helped bind communities together (eg Ross 1967; Wait 1985; Green 1986; 1995a). These beliefs are also reflected in deposits of objects in bodies of water in the Thames Valley (Wait 1985; 1995).

While social, cosmological and practical influences may have been deeply interwoven in the design and daily use of houses, the evidence from Gravelly Guy and elsewhere suggests that recognisable 'special deposits' may only have been made a few times every generation for any given family, and the disposal of dead bodies within and around settlements would have been rarer still. Such deposits were probably made to mark special events or crises that affected personal and family life, or even the entire community. These events may have resembled those of our own lives, even if the beliefs and rituals reflected in the deposits do not.

Social, religious and political interaction, however, was certainly not confined to the home and farm, and in this chapter we will consider how particular places reflect communal interaction and political leadership on a wider scale.

Ceremonial structures, shrines and other sacred places

Early historical literary and artistic sources make it clear that particular places in the natural environment would have been regarded as sacred groves and water bodies, and it is possible that structures and shafts or wells were symbolic representations of such places which served as shrines for worship and making offerings to the gods (Ross 1967; Wait 1985; Webster 1995). However, it is often difficult to clearly identify such places, and even more so to trace the transition from the earlier prehistoric ceremonial and funerary monuments to the shrines of much later celtic tradition.

The building of ceremonial monuments largely ceased by the end of the early Bronze Age. Although some henge monuments and other structures continued to be respected and used in the later Bronze Age, it is difficult to identify many examples of the construction of new structures. A number of well-attested major ceremonial structures, including substantial buildings and timber rings associated with major late Bronze Age enclosures have been discovered elsewhere in Britain and Ireland, as at Navan and Mucking (Waterman 1997; Bond 1988). None has yet been found in the Upper or Middle Thames Valley and it is not clear how far the creation of structures associated with ceremonial or religious activities persisted at a more modest local scale.

Compared to earlier periods, the more abundant evidence of domestic structures, fields etc. may obscure the existence of such structures, especially if they were integrated into living areas with other activities reflecting the spiritual and ritual side of life. The following sections explore three possible lines of evidence for later prehistoric ceremonial and religious structures in the Thames Valley, all of which entail problems of interpretation.

Post-rings

Four examples of possible later prehistoric timber rings have been identified in the Upper Thames Valley, though none is very securely dated (Fig. 9.1). At Spring Road, Abingdon a double arc of postholes made up 60-80° of a timber post circle with a diameter of about 18-20 m (Allen and Kamash 2008). The postholes were sealed by a layer of ploughsoil which contained five sherds of middle Iron Age pottery. Seventeen postholes assigned to the outer arc were closely and fairly evenly spaced, the gaps between them being 0.2 m to 0.4 m apart, allowing the posts to have been placed not more than 0.5 m apart, possibly with an even spacing of 0.3-0.4 m. The postholes were 0.36-0.52 m wide and 0.45-0.66 m deep, some oval and aligned radially. Where post-pipes were discernible they were on the inner side of the arc, indicating how the posts were slid into position from the outside before standing them upright on the inner edge of the circle. An inner arc of posts is represented by seven mainly circular postholes, spaced at *c* 1 m intervals, one with a post-pipe 0.15 m wide. Although limited dating evidence was consistent with that from the outer arc the distribution of these postholes was not as regular, none was sealed by ploughsoil and two might be associated with a Saxon sunken-featured building. Radiocarbon dates on animal bone from the primary fill of a posthole in the inner arc and from the post-pipe in the outer arc produced dates of 1690-1510 cal BC and 1520-1310 cal BC respectively.

At Gravelly Guy a penannular ring of 23 postholes formed a setting 19 m in diameter with an

8 m wide entrance to the east (Lambrick and Allen 2004, 61-3, figs 2.13, 2.14, Pl. 2.6). The postholes were generally about 1.0 m in diameter, several with post-pipes which were D-shaped or segmental in plan, suggesting that the ring was built of large split timbers *c* 0.6 m in diameter. The setting was discovered amongst early to middle Iron Age and later settlement features, but the soil filling all the postholes was reddish brown characteristic of features predating the darker soils typical of the later prehistoric settlement. Wherever there were relationships with other features the postholes were earlier. They produced no dating evidence so it is not clear how much earlier than the early Iron Age the timber ring might have been. A possible clue is that its axis, determined by a diameter passing through the centre of the entrance gap, was quite accurately oriented towards the Stanton Harcourt

barrow, a large and originally quite prominent Wessex II bell barrow dated to the end of the early Bronze Age (Barclay *et al.*. 1995, 97-9). The preferred interpretation is, therefore, that it was probably built towards the end of the early Bronze Age or in the middle Bronze Age.

At Standlake 19 postholes measuring up to 0.35 m across were fairly regularly spaced 1.5 m to 2.0 m apart, forming an approximate 13 m diameter ring around the outside of a small annular ditch (Catling 1982 97-9, figs 49, 56, 57). The ditch produced about 85 pieces of late Bronze Age to early Iron Age pottery, most from the south-east quadrant. The postholes contained no pottery but they were so closely concentric with the ring ditch that it is likely they were broadly contemporary. This highly unusual arrangement has no close comparisons elsewhere in the Thames Valley, but resembles one

Gravelly Guy

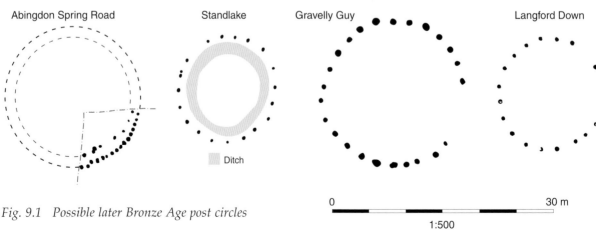

Fig. 9.1 Possible later Bronze Age post circles

at Down Farm, Dorset with radiocarbon dates in the late Bronze Age (Barrett *et al.* 1991).

An undated 15.2 m diameter post-ring found at Langford Downs, east of Lechlade is another possible example. A ring of 18, possibly originally 20 postholes up to 0.5 m across, spaced 1.25 m to 2.5 m apart, formed a circle (Williams 1946-7) cut by a late Iron Age settlement enclosure ditch. There was some trace of earlier Iron Age activity from the site and the post-ring was attributed to that period of occupation, though no pottery was found in the postholes. The diameter of the post-ring is outside the range normal for an ordinary roundhouse of simple construction, and this may have been another middle to late Bronze Age (or early Iron Age) ring. Like those at Standlake and Gravelly Guy and perhaps Spring Road it was located on the periphery of an earlier Bronze Age barrow cemetery.

These timber rings share several characteristics. They are circular, broadly similar in diameter with small to medium-sized posts and related to nearby barrow clusters. Although not part of a well-defined barrow complex such as Stanton Harcourt, the Spring Road example is about the same distance from the nearest barrow as Gravelly Guy, and a Beaker burial was found very close by. They are also very enigmatic, each quite different in detailed form, the dating evidence mostly poor and, in the absence of human bone, votive deposits or much other material, there is no obvious explanation for how they were used. If they do represent small ceremonial enclosures or free-standing rings it suggests that in parts of the Upper Thames Valley a tradition of monument building lingered or was revived at a low level into the later Bronze Age or even the early Iron Age. Until more examples are found with better evidence to put these sites into context, they will remain something of a mystery.

Sacred enclosures and shrines

There is tantalisingly little convincing evidence of sacred enclosures, shrines or other structures in the later Bronze Age of the Upper and Middle Thames Valley, though this is partly due to the character of late prehistoric religion, which was seldom expressed through impressive architecture. So far as sacred places were marked by structures they might have various roles related to death, commemoration of ancestors or communication with the gods (Webster 1995).

It has been suggested that a middle Bronze Age rectangular enclosure at Church Lammas, Staines is an example (Fig. 9.2). The enclosure was 40 m long by 25 m wide, defined by modest ditches with two entrance gaps about 2-3 m wide placed asymmetrically along the north-east and south-east sides (Hayman 1991; forthcoming b). The ditch on the south-west side extended beyond the corners of the enclosure which, together with a pair of ditches parallel to the enclosure, indicates that it might have been part of a rectilinear field system. Off-centre

within the enclosure was a much smaller enclosed space approximately 8 m square defined by smaller flat-bottomed gullies under 1 m wide, with a single 1.5 m wide entrance facing towards the south-east. A steep-sided pit *c* 1.7 m wide by 0.7 m deep was the only feature within the inner enclosure. It produced a modest number of Bronze Age calcined flints, worked flints, pottery and bone of no special note. The sharp angles at the corners of the enclosing gullies suggest that they held split trunk sleeper beams for a timber structure, or might have been simple earthwork features associated with a low bank or hedge intended to enclose the pit. A number of other pits and postholes lay within and outside of the outer enclosure, all significantly smaller than the one in the inner enclosure. They produced modest amounts of domestic debris. Four possible cremation burials, small features with high densities of pottery, some charcoal and fragments of burnt bone were also found, though such deposits

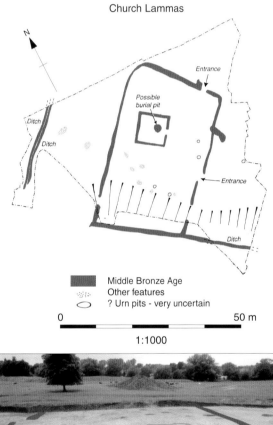

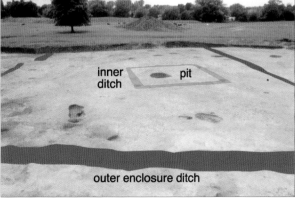

Fig.9.2   *Sacred enclosures and shrines: middle Bronze Age domestic or ceremonial site at Church Lammas*

usually occur away from the focus of domestic activity.

Pending full publication of the Church Lammas enclosure it is not clear how to interpret it because of its unusual form and relatively early date compared with later Iron Age shrines, which it resembles. The paucity of finds indicates minor if any domestic use, but also provides no direct evidence for use as a sacred enclosure or shrine. The excavations at Cassington West and elsewhere have indicated that cremation or cremation-like deposits are a feature of some late Bronze Age settlements, so it is principally the unusual square structure within the larger rectangular enclosure reminiscent of later celtic shrines (cf Webster 1995) that suggests a ceremonial or religious use. The contemporaneity of the inner square structure with the deep pit is unproven but on domestic sites of this period it is unusual for such pits to be enclosed.

The late Iron Age so-called 'temple' or shrine excavated by W.F. Grimes at Heathrow, one of the first prehistoric structures in Britain to be inter-preted as a religious building (Fig. 9.3; Grimes and Close-Brooks 1993), is a more convincing example of a sacred enclosure, but not without comparable problems of interpretation. The concentric rectangular post-built structures pointing almost due east were located within a large sub-rectangular enclosure known as Caesar's Camp. The site had a long history of activity evidenced by Neolithic pits, a moderate amount of late Bronze Age domestic debris from small pits, postholes and 'occupation hollows' and a middle Iron Age settlement consisting of non-overlapping penannular house enclosures, some of which must have extended substantially beneath the bank of the enclosure. There were also other small pens and a somewhat larger sub-rectangular enclosure that was late in the sequence, and various other intersecting gullies.

The 'shrine' stood roughly in the middle of the western side of the enclosure, facing inwards. It consisted of a central rectangular slot 5.3 m long and 4.4 m wide with a 0.6 m gap in its eastern side and deepenings indicating the position of larger

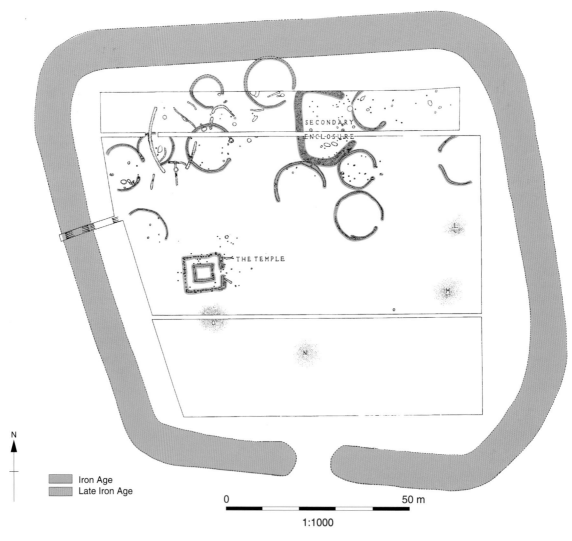

Fig. 9.3   Sacred enclosures and shrines: Heathrow

posts at the corners and terminals of the slot. The outer rectangle measured 9.15 by 10.7 m, set concentrically 2.3 to 2.45 m from the inner one with a matching entrance. It consisted of postholes forming an irregular palisade. In places, especially the east-facing façade, there was evidence of double posts. Finds were limited to a few sherds indicating a middle to late Iron Age date, though in the absence of anything more substantial, it is possible that the shrine was later and the finds derived from the middle to late Iron Age settlement.

Cutting across the middle of the 'shrine' was a linear gully that formed one side of an apparently unfinished, slightly off-square enclosure *c* 35 m across, the western side of which followed the line of the outer structure. The structure might have been the *temenos* enclosure of a Roman temple that was never built (Grimes and Close Brooks, 1993, 338).

The relationship of the structure to the large enclosing earthwork is somewhat uncertain (Fig. 9.3). Drawings of the then substantially preserved earthwork by William Stukeley show a southern entrance. This was still just visible in 1944, despite years of ploughing, and was confirmed by excavation (Grimes and Close-Brooks 1993, 310-1, fig. 2). The northern half of the enclosure effectively enclosed the site of the middle Iron Age settlement, with the shrine centrally placed on the west side, leaving the southern part of the interior apparently devoid of structures. It is not clear where the enclosure fits within the sequence relative to the Iron Age settlement and 'shrine' structure. It is possible that the houses under the bank had been superseded and that the enclosure, remaining settlement and shrine were all extant together. Alternatively, the shrine and enclosure might have been contemporary, post-dating the settlement. It is less likely, given the position of the shrine central to one side of the enclosure, that the enclosure post-dates both the settlement and the shrine structure, but the shrine could have post-dated the enclosure. As Grimes and Close-Brooks (1993) noted, Heathrow would not be the only late Iron Age shrine to occupy the site of an abandoned settlement. This is also evident with the latest structure at Danebury and in the first millennium AD at Gallows Hill, Thetford.

Grimes believed that the concentric structure represented an inner cella with an outer colonnade, a kind of timber prototype for later Romano-Celtic temples. However, aspects of its layout, reconstruction, date and possible cult associations all bring this interpretation into question. Derks (1998, 179) has argued that, whatever its origins, it should not be interpreted as a precursor to masonry Romano-Celtic temples. If it was a shrine there are no other known examples in Britain of this type of concentric layout but both the inner and outer settings resemble structures found at Danebury and other sites, all datable to the middle to late Iron Age. It is possible that the concentric post-built walls were successive structures rather contemporary (Grimes & Close-Brooks 1993, 338), but the problem of lack

of evidence and suitable parallels for such a sequence persist. Black (1986, 203) suggested that the inner structure was a free-standing funerary structure with the outer posts representing a palisade fence, not a roofed ambulatory.

There are a number of Belgic sanctuaries in the Somme-Oise area of northern France with comparable layouts, emphasising the significance of enclosure (Webster 1996, 455-9). Unlike Heathrow (or Church Lammas, which is also comparable in plan) they have produced much more significant evidence of ritualistic behaviour, including funerary activity, probably involving animal and human sacrifice, and deposition of weapons, jewellery and other valuable objects. However, a lack of votive objects or buried materials indicating a specifically religious or spiritual status was also noted at Danebury. If these places were shrines, sanctuaries or temples as their layout suggests, it is possible that they were concerned with veneration of natural phenomena or other beliefs that would have left little material trace.

In the Upper Thames Valley a possible shrine of somewhat different character has been identified at Smith's Field, where a 20 m diameter penannular gully enclosed a shallow square gully *c* 10 m across with a cow burial at one corner (Fig. 9.4). This gully enclosed a setting of posts 4 m square with a small pit or scoop off-centre (Allen, 2000, 20, fig. 1.11). A comparable four-post structure at Roughground Farm, Lechlade dated to the 2nd century AD enclosed a cremation burial in an urn and was surrounded by a horseshoe-shaped fence (or building) within a square gully, in this case set diagonally to the four-poster (Allen *et al.* 1993). Both features are comparable to burial enclosures in the Champagne region of northern Gaul believed to be mortuary houses or shrines. The layout also resembles some Romano-Celtic temples or shrines.

Celtic temples or shrines

The existence of Romano-Celtic temples in Britain and Gaul which reflect the continued survival of celtic religious ideas has prompted the persistent question of continuity of location on the sites of pre-existing temples. Derks suggested that a process of *Romanitas* led to the development of a distinctive architectural form that emerged as part of 'an articulation between the cultural codes of the local communities and those of the Roman state' (Derks 1998, 183-4, 241). However, while some Romano-Celtic temples such as those at Uley and Hayling Island do seem to have had Iron Age origins (Woodward and Leach 1993; King and Soffe 1994) this need not have been the case elsewhere and the evidence is often ambiguous. In the Thames Valley the issue of whether Iron Age temples or shrines pre-dated Roman ones has arisen at various sites, notably at Frilford and Woodeaton in Oxfordshire and Farley Heath in Surrey.

At Frilford part of a stake-built circular structure

underlying a rectangular Romano-British masonry temple and a broad penannular ditch beneath a circular stone-built Roman possible shrine nearby were thought to be Iron Age precursors to a Roman-Celtic temple complex (Fig. 9.4; Bradford and Goodchild 1939; Harding 1972, 61-4). Harding re-excavated the stake circle in 1964, demonstrating its full character. In reporting these results 15 years after his 1972 review he reappraised both structures, concluding that in neither case was there sufficient evidence to demonstrate the previously claimed continuity of religious function (Harding 1987, 16). From these excavations it is clear that the Iron Age structures were located amongst numerous pits, gullies and postholes, including a four-poster crossed by the stake wall, which

suggest the existence of an extensive early to middle Iron Age settlement. This has been confirmed by recent investigations *c* 50 m to the east (Lock *et al.* 2003, 86).

Harding (1987, 7-8) argued that the stake-walled structure beneath the rectangular temple building could not have supported a roof and was an open enclosure, though he cited parallels with other stake-walled houses. However, as discussed in Chapter 5 the reasons for rejecting this as a circular building are questionable and it would be unique for the area as a pen, especially with its 'porched' entrance. The 'stake' wall was actually constructed of small posts set in holes 'cut not driven 8-10 cms into the limestone capping' (Harding 1987, 7) and is unlike any other post-built roundhouse in the immediate region, though arguably similar to the early Iron Age house at Dunston Park and possibly those at Groundwell Farm, if the wall trenches there were created in the course of removing posts (see Chapter 5).

Apart from its structural design, the stake-walled Frilford structure is unusual in terms of the contents of three internal features – the grave of a tightly bound adolescent on the north side, a hollow on the south side (roughly if not exactly opposite) containing the near complete remains of a small

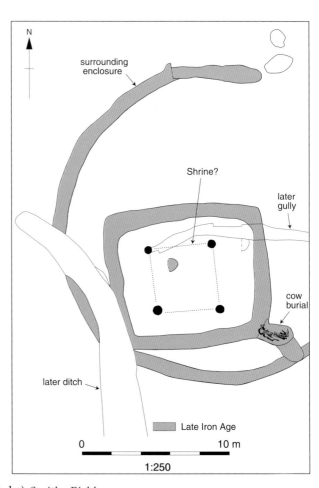

Fig. 9.4 *Sacred enclosures and shrines:* (left) *Frilford;* (right) *Smiths Field*

infant and a substantial pit immediately inside the wall line which contained an unusual sword chape. Neither the position of the latter in the fill of the pit nor its other contents were unusual and indeed all the features and finds from the site are broadly typical of ordinary early to middle Iron Age domestic settlements. It is not unreasonable, therefore, to conclude as Harding did in 1987, that there is no real connection or demonstrable physical continuity between this structure and the later temple. Nevertheless, that does not entirely eclipse the manifold unusual elements of the structure if these features were contemporary, as seems likely from their positions. As discussed above (Chapter 8) burials are not normally found inside Iron Age houses in the region but there is an interesting parallel with three purpose-dug graves at Spring Road, Abingdon is only *c* 5 km to the east.

The penannular ditch underlying the circular Roman building at Frilford is also unusual in that it is west-facing, very broad (probably the result of multiple recutting) and produced both early and middle Iron Age pottery in some quantity (Bradford and Goodchild 1939, 13-14, fig. 5, 10). A comparable, though south-east facing, site with a similarly diverse date range of pottery has since been excavated at Thrupp, near Abingdon (Everett and Eeles 1999, 128, fig. 12). But with no suggestion of a religious connection, the Frilford example remains odd. Apart from facing west, the ditch surrounded an unusual setting of six double postholes clearly respecting the inner edge of the ditch opposite the entrance, with an iron ploughshare placed on the base of the front central one. These postholes were originally interpreted as the position of a structure to support votive objects. The ditch produced no obvious special deposits or unusual artefacts, but the complex is also unusual compared with other domestic Iron Age sites succeeded by Roman ones in that it was levelled with sterile clay when the post structure was removed and the ditch infilled prior to the construction of the Roman circular shrine. Reversing his previous (1972) opinion that this was an Iron Age shrine preceding a Roman one, Harding (1987, 10-12) again suggested that this was all fortuitous.

The principal objection to any direct Iron Age to Roman continuity in use of either site as a shrine is the dating evidence, which has no obviously late Iron Age pottery. Harding found evidence to suggest that the rectangular temple structure was not built before the second century AD and there was no clear evidence of an early date for the circular shrine. But while it is thus clear that at Frilford there was no direct continuity of use with Roman buildings directly replacing Iron Age ones, such as can be seen at Hayling Island (King and Soffe 1994), this does not automatically invalidate the interpretation of the Iron Age structures as a religious site.

The dating evidence and stratigraphy are not sufficiently clear to demonstrate relationships conclusively but the combination of unusual structures, burials and votive objects, together with the sequence of structures pre-dating a Roman shrine, is too much of a coincidence to be dismissed entirely. Given that flatter locations were available nearby the levelling of the penannular gully and the posthole setting with the plough share, coupled with new votive offerings in a square pit within the new circular shrine look like deliberate acts. A site with strong folk traditions or continued low level use as a special religious place could have been selected for a new shrine to give it legitimacy so, although there was no direct structural rebuild, Harding's original view that 'the case for the continuity of sanctity of Site C from Iron Age to Roman times therefore seems comparatively watertight' (Harding 1972, 62) could be correct.

If the Frilford structures were shrines it is intriguing to note that contrary to what might be expected from assumed cosmological associations (Parker Pearson 1996; 1999), the burials (clearly related to death) are associated with the east-facing structure and the ploughshare (possibly symbolic of life) is from within a west-facing one. Does this invalidate the interpretation, or just add to doubts such as those Pope (2007) has raised about putting too much weight on cosmological interpretations?

Excavation of a Romano-Celtic temple complex at Woodeaton in the 1940s and 1960s (Kirk 1949; Harding 1987, 27-59) exposed several pre-Roman deposits, but no evidence of a pre-existing late prehistoric shrine or temple. A relatively well-stratified sequence of deposits yielded an unusually rich range of finds that suggest the site was an important place for many centuries before it became a Roman religious centre (Bagnell Smith 1995, 1998). However, they are not well understood. It may have originated as a late Bronze Age or early Iron Age midden site (Fig. 7.13 and see below). There was a distinct middle to late Iron Age horizon with indications of metalworking and other activity (Harding 1987, 31-3). The unusually large quantities of pre-Roman artefacts include brooches and pins, a sword scabbard and chape, a tin sheet impression of a rare coin of Cunobelin, several other Belgic coins, six miniature bronze spears and four miniature bronze axes. These would not be expected on an ordinary Iron Age settlement, but they could be explained convincingly as later votive deposition of antique items as evidence of a pre-Roman shrine (Smith A 2001, 156). On the other hand, the long history as a special place in terms of artefact presence reaches back at least to the 6th or 7th century BC, so the continuity of similar activity on the site is highly plausible.

Aerial photography recently revealed two circular masonry shrine structures within the temple *temenos* either side of the rectangular temple (Henig and Booth 2000, 89, fig. 4.7). These are doubtless Roman but the photographs and an extensive unpublished geophysical survey (Johnson 2003, Oxfordshire SMR PRN 2379) show several penannular and circular gullies and ditches which may be Iron Age. It is unclear whether these represented domestic activity or religious structures. The clear evidence of an extensive and important late Bronze Age or early Iron Age and later settlement is not dissimilar to Frilford but only further investigation can resolve the possibility of an Iron Age religious centre at Woodeaton.

At Farley Heath, Surrey excavations in 1995 produced, apart from a curving gully of uncertain character, no obvious evidence of pre-Roman structures (Poulton in prep). There was no indication that the Roman temple was preceded by an Iron Age shrine in this location, although Iron Age pottery was recovered, together with an incomplete 4th century BC La Tène 1 brooch (Cotton 1982), a ladle, horse fitting and two weapons, all of Iron Age or immediately post-conquest date. These could represent curated antiques deposited after the conquest.

Overall the evidence for Iron Age shrines preceding Romano-Celtic ones in the Thames Valley is ambiguous, although rather more convincing evidence has been found on the edge of the Thames catchment on the top of the Cotswold scarp at Uley and at other sites further afield (Woodward and Leach 1993). The number of Iron Age shrines identified is very small, and almost all present significant interpretative problems (Smith, A 2001, 15-16). This is not particularly surprising if, as the classical authors indicated, attention was focussed on natural features and 'sacred groves'.

Other sacred or symbolic structures

The White Horse at Uffington

Prominently sited on the scarp of the Berkshire Downs, the famous Uffington White Horse is one of the most remarkable prehistoric sites in the Thames Valley. Indeed, it was already recognised as one of the 'Wonders of Britain' in the Middle Ages (Miles *et al.* 2003, 61-78). For centuries its date and original purpose was uncertain, varying from Saxon, based on documentary evidence of its existence and legendary associations with King Alfred, to prehistoric, based on similarities with the form of horses depicted on late Iron Age coins.

Investigations in the 1990s showed that although the White Horse may originally have been formed by exposing the underlying chalk, it was not purely a chalk-cut figure, but artificially constructed of clean packed chalk. This gives it a much whiter, longer-lasting finish than would be the case if it was just left as the exposed decayed surface of the natural chalk. Using optical dating of underlying hillwash it has been possible to demonstrate that it was probably later Bronze Age or early Iron Age (1380-550 BC at 68% confidence). Although not at all precise, this also makes it clear that it has only a 2.5% chance of being later than *c* 210 BC (Miles *et al.* 2003, 75-7).

Through centuries of maintenance by which the surface was scoured and fresh layers of chalk added, its shape has been modified, creating distinct negative and positive lynchets on the steep slope that it occupies. Nevertheless, the Horse still retains its original highly stylised form. Although its visibility from close at hand may have had some significance, its position immediately below the top of the scarp crest suggests that the Horse was not designed to be viewed either from the top of the hill or immediately below, but was a symbolic image intended to be seen from a distance, as befits its size and design. It still performs this role.

By the time the Uffington hill figure was constructed, horses were becoming culturally important animals and it is significant that in this case a horse was chosen as a highly visible and important symbol in the landscape. With the associated modified conical Dragon Hill just below it and a series of Neolithic and Bronze Age monuments overlooking the dramatic natural bowl known as the Manger, White Horse Hill was a place of special importance – 'a possible cult centre or sacred landscape that evolved from the Neolithic through to the historic period' (Miles *et al.* 2003, 246). If not designed as a territorial symbol, it may well have become one, and certainly seems to have been associated with the nearby hillfort where people would have gathered from the surrounding area. The Vale over which the Horse presides is named after it, as is the modern administrative district of the Vale of White Horse.

Linear structures

At Yarnton (Hey *et al.* forthcoming b) several late Bronze Age or early Iron Age rows of parallel slots and holes represented by shallow, elongated and circular pits were found in an area of late Neolithic and early to middle Bronze Age activity (Fig. 9.5). They were sited either side of and partly within a former palaeochannel which was later crossed by a middle Iron Age raised path. The holes ranged from elongated slots *c* 2-2.5 m by 0.45 m to small circular holes 0.4-0.5 m diameter. Most were set about 0.5 m apart, in over 30 rows varying from 1 m to over 40 m in length, consisting of up to over 40 individual features. Some of the rows were close set, others further apart, some parallel, others set at a slight angle to each other, but none clearly intersected. Two of the longer rows were cut into the tops of two partly filled middle Bronze Age ditches dated to *c* 1500-1200 BC. These had been dug parallel to each other, 60 m apart, across the palaeochannel. They ran between a higher area with a concentration of Neolithic and Bronze Age activity on the south side of the channel and the northern bank, where the eastern ditch was aligned on a ring ditch and penannular enclosure surrounding an oak tree.

The slots and holes might represent the positions of timber corduroy trackways or wooden stepping stones. The longer slots were placed close to and across the half-filled middle Bronze Age ditches

(see Chapter 3)

(especially the eastern one), as though they needed longer timbers to bridge them. The rows located in drier places between the ditches were formed of shorter slots and shallow circular holes, possibly for short log ends placed vertically. The possibility that these were successive pathways would conform to other evidence of increasing water levels on the site shortly before the onset of alluviation. This is also attested by the raised sand and gravel middle Iron Age causeway which succeeded them on a similar alignment.

But if the slots and holes did hold timbers, none of them contained organic material and they must have remained open after the timbers had rotted or been removed before being filled with alluvium. Moreover, the circular holes in particular do not fit this interpretation well, and an alternative explanation for these features is that they were cut and left open as suggested for more conventional pit alignments in other parts of the Upper Thames Valley (see Chapter 3). However this is also problematical as they are unlike any other such alignments, both in form and the number of parallel rows of slots and holes.

While all the rows broadly belong to the same period, this could have spanned several hundred years, so they may well not have all been open or in use exactly simultaneously. Whether or not these features represent a series of open 'pit' alignments or wooden pathways (or something else entirely), it is relevant to note their close spatial relationship to the middle Bronze Age linear ditches aligned in one direction on a penannular enclosure and ring ditch (both with ceremonial connotations), and in the other on an area of earlier prehistoric activity that lay on the axis of an earlier Neolithic enclosure which continued to be respected into the middle Bronze Age. This complex web of seemingly long-lasting relationships suggests that the slot and hole alignments may also have had a ceremonial rather than a practical purpose.

Linear structures of a quite different form have been identified at Hartshill Copse, where the 10th century cal BC ironworking site was associated with two long post alignments or palisade fences, traced for over 80 and 60 m respectively (Fig. 9.6; Collard *et al.* 2006). The alignments were constructed of posts about 0.2 m diameter set about 0.2 m apart, which met or crossed each other at a sharply oblique angle. The two main roundhouses were built along a central axis symmetrically bisecting the oblique angles formed by the close-set fences. The only broadly similar structure of the same period is at Barleycroft, Cambridgeshire, where Evans and Knight (2001, 85, 91) suggest that the alignments acted as visually impressive symbolic screens enclosing or dividing large areas of land within an extensive ceremonial space, in which the

Palaeochannel

Neolithic
Late Neolithic/ Early Bronze Age
Middle Bronze Age
Bronze Age
Late Bronze Age/ Early Iron Age
Iron Age Causeway

0   50 m

1:1000

Fig. 9.5 Ditches, causeways and slot alignments at Yarnton

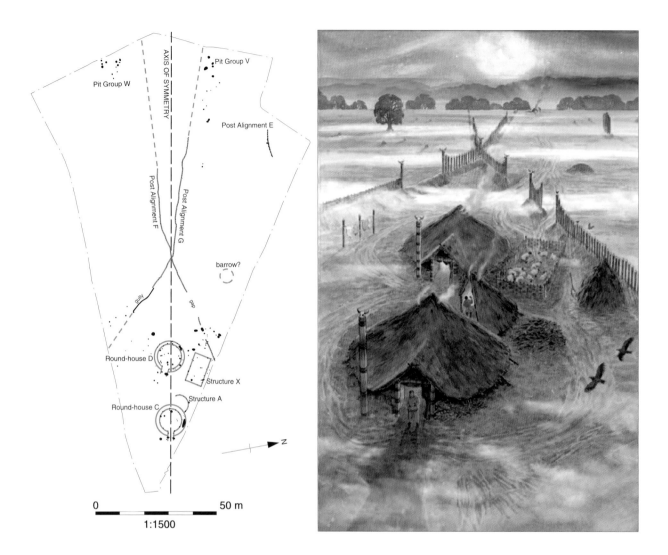

Fig. 9.6   Timber post alignments at Hartshill Copse

ritual and domestic or agricultural domains were closely interrelated. This would broadly fit with the Hartshill Copse arrangement, which the excavators argue would have been seen as a very special place because of its role in early iron working.

Although unusual structures of the kind recorded at Yarnton and Hartshill Copse present challenges of interpretation, which have tradition-ally attracted the default explanation as being evidence of 'ritual' activities (ie they cannot be explained in obvious functionalist or utilitarian terms), they nevertheless offer some insight into how places and activities may have been valued in special ways that are far from obvious today. Hartshill Copse is perhaps clearest in showing how the practical world of craft production could be deeply imbued with symbolic and social impor-tance in the adoption of new technology.

Pits

There is some evidence that the Neolithic and early Bronze Age tradition of ritual shafts continued into later prehistory (Wait 1985), though the distinction

between ritual pits, wells and shafts is unclear. Wait (1985, 320-36) listed three possible examples for the Thames Valley, all on chalk hills overlooking the valley, at Ibsden (with three upright logs), Rotherfield Peppard (15.5 m deep with deer skulls, pots and a complete oak tree trunk) and Ashtead (6 m deep, probably 6th century BC, with ashes, pottery and animal bone). The 2.4 m shaft with deer bones, querns and other finds at Carshalton is probably another (Proctor 2002). More generally we have already seen that pits and waterholes were used as repositories for special deposits that may well have had connections (among other things) with notions of the underworld and the different associations of air, earth and water. We have also seen that pits and graves were deliberately dug for the deposition of the dead or of votive offerings.

A much more doubtful possibility is that rings of pits, such as one at Frilford and another at Thrupp are other examples of unusual, though not neces-sarily ritualistic features. Although orderly group-ings of pits in rows and even pairs are quite a common feature of settlements, isolated regular rings of pits partly or fully linked by gullies are more unusual. The earlier of these two sites was at Frilford, where a series of at least six pits were cut by a very variable sub-rectangular ditch forming a small, squarish enclosure about 8.5 m across in each direction (Lock *et al.* 2002, 76-8). The pits were round or oval between *c* 0.8 and 1.5 m across and much the same depth as the ditch (*c* 0.8 m). Little of their fills had survived the ditch digging, but pottery suggested they were early Iron Age – as were the much more prolific finds from the ditch. There was a small amorphous cluster of postholes and one other small pit within the enclosure. No particularly notable finds, animal or human bones were reported in the preliminary summary, but detailed analysis of the whole site is awaited. It is possible that this site was just an unusual form of domestic or agricultural enclosure. A number of similar small square enclosures have been recorded by geophysics at Hill Farm and Castle Hill Little Wittenham, but they have not yet been investigated.

At Thrupp a broadly oval or D-shaped ring about 9 m across was formed by a circular arc of five regularly spaced 1.1 m diameter pits, three linked by a broad shallow gully on the south side, an amorphous scatter of six or seven pits of more variable shape and size and further gullies to the north (Everett and Eeles 1999, 120-1, fig. 3). Within the ring of pits there was a very small rectangular pit at the centre and a number of pits of various shapes and sizes mostly around the periphery, one with a layer of clean soil containing two whole pots overlying dark soil with concentrations of bone and stone at one end. Other finds included a perforated stone, a loomweight, a bone weaving comb and a worn piece of bone (conceivably once a weaving comb that had lost both its teeth and head).

In the absence of other examples it is difficult to say whether these pit rings are of more than purely domestic significance – it is possible for example that the pits and gullies respected a house or other structure, though they are not closely similar to instances of this at other sites like Ashville and Gravelly Guy.

Riverside and terrestrial middens

The creation of large surface middens through the dumping and reworking of discarded objects and rubbish-rich soil seems to have been a particular phenomenon of the late Bronze Age and earliest Iron Age (Fig. 7.18). As extensive undisturbed layers of artefact rich soil these sites are far from common, with only four or five examples known in the Thames Valley. Two were on islands in the river at Runnymede (Longley 1980; Needham 1991; Needham and Spence 1996) and Whitecross Farm (Cromarty *et al.* 2006), and a possible third site is suspected close to or on an island within the Thames at Bray (Anon 1960, 58; Anon 1963/4, 102-3). The other examples were on higher ground, Castle Hill, Little Wittenham in a saddle between

two chalk hills (Hingley 1980c; Allen *et al.* forthcoming b), Woodeaton on the top of a low hill (Harding 1987) and perhaps Ivinghoe Beacon on a chalk promontory of the Chiltern escarpment (Cotton and Frere 1968; Brown 2001; Barker *et al.* 2003). Apart from Bray, which is only evident from salvage observations, these sites have all been sampled and Runnymede, which is by far the largest, has been subject to detailed investigation. Further afield a number of very large middens, some up to 300 m across and up to 2 m thick, are known on the chalk hills south of the Thames Valley around the Vale of Pewsey, notably at All Cannings Cross (Cunnington 1923), Potterne (Lawson 1994; 2000) and East Chisenbury (Brown *et al.* 1994; McOmish 1996). A few other possibilities have been suggested elsewhere (Needham 2000, 241).

Some of these sites began to accumulate material in the middle Bronze Age but most date to the late Bronze Age, some continuing well into the early Iron Age (Needham 2007). Sample excavations have shown that these middens contain a wider variety and number of artefacts and high status items than contemporary settlements, suggesting that the deposition of materials was not haphazard discard of ordinary domestic refuse. It apparently derived either from high status settlement or from gatherings of people from a wide area bringing items of particular value. Chalk platforms and other structural evidence from within middens also suggest that they were not simply rubbish heaps. The riverside situations of Runnymede and Whitecross Farm (and perhaps Bray) may indicate that they functioned as trading entrepôts utilising riverine transport.

At Runnymede a highly complex sequence of shifting channels and sedimentation, including a sequence of Neolithic deposits predated the late Bronze Age midden. The midden itself covered an area of about 1.5 ha and was generally about 0.2-0.45 m thick, with thicker deposits in some areas, on what by then was an island in the Thames (Needham 1991, 66-8, figs 20-25; Needham and Spence 1996, 41-6, figs 5-7; Needham 2000, 232-4 figs 11.9-11.10). It was at least partly enclosed by timber palisades or waterfront structures. They may have combined different roles as revetment, landing stages or defensive and symbolic enclosures reflecting the importance of the site. The area of the midden also contained rectangular posthole structures which perhaps defined platforms or buildings of some kind.

Needham suggests that the large amounts of refuse found at Runnymede would have derived not just from a resident population but also materials brought by visitors, and that very little was removed from the site (Needham and Spence 1996, 242-8). According to this interpretation, both the occupants and frequenters of the site were engaged in refuse generating activities, notably food consumption, pottery breakage and craft production. This could have been in the context of large gatherings of visitors (perhaps vassals or subjects), expert craftsmen, traders and others bringing significant quantities of food, raw materials and reusable refuse as the basis for such activity. There is actually little evidence for river-borne trade and exchange and Needham questions the idea that sites like Runnymede were entrepôts – or at least whether this was their main role. They may primarily have been communal gathering and production centres at which settlement and exchange were also important, but perhaps not their most distinctive function.

The Whitecross Farm site at Wallingford was sampled twice in the 1950s (Anon. 1952-3, 125; Anon.1960, 55-8) and trial trenched and test pitted in 1985-6 and 1991 (Cromarty *et al.* 2006), when it was shown to occupy a cigar-shaped eyot 20-25 m wide and at least 150 m long (*c* 0.23 ha), the northern end eroded by later channel migration. The undisturbed midden deposits and occupation soil on the surface of the island were only about 0.2 m thick but including a disturbed horizon may have been at least half as much again. The site resembles Runnymede in its river island location, revetment and timber river channel structures, along with midden deposition and an unusually rich range of artefacts, albeit not apparently as dense or diverse. A number of postholes suggest the presence of structures on the island, though excavations were not sufficiently extensive to define them. The charred remains of a timber structure found in the adjacent channel may represent the superstructure of the jetty or bridge identified there, or the discarded remains of a burnt building. The density of finds and their character, including the use to which flint tools had been put, suggested that the main concentration of midden material was towards the southern downstream end of the eyot. Perhaps the inhabitants lived in the cleaner north end of the island. The jetty or bridge found in the adjacent silted up channel was roughly halfway along the western side of the eyot.

Given the relative thinness and paucity of finds in the upstream part of the Whitecross Farm site it is worth noting the possibility of an important riverside settlement downstream of Runnymede at Syon Park, a major area of later Bronze Age and Iron Age river deposition. At Snowy Fielder Way, Isleworth just south of the park, a middle Iron Age ditch running parallel to a palaeochannel may have marked the southern (upstream) tip of a large former island now occupied by Syon Park (Bell 1996). The ditch was on the line of a smaller earlier one and a number of gullies, small pits and postholes suggest an occupation site at this location. A substantial quantity of late Bronze Age and early Iron Age pottery was recovered from midden-like deposits in a large shallow pit, but a buried soil horizon dipping towards the palaeochannel was sealed by upcast from the later ditch and contained few finds. While there is thus no indication of a midden resembling those at Runnymede or Whitecross Farm, the results are consistent with being at the upstream end of another major late prehistoric island settlement.

One of two terrestrial midden sites in the Upper Thames Valley, Castle Hill lies on a fairly flat plateau area in the saddle between the twin Sinodun Hills just outside the hillfort on the eastern hill (Rhodes 1948; Allen *et al.* forthcoming a). Augering and small scale excavation show that it is at least 60 m wide, over 100 m across and up to 0.5 m thick. The main period of accumulation was the early Iron Age, continuing only partially into the middle Iron Age. What seemed to be the corner of an unusual rectangular chalk floored 'building' found within the midden deposit (Harding 1972, 33-4, fig. 6) has been re-examined. In the light of the identification of similar structures in other middens it is now better seen as a specialised platform, though it is also worth noting the possible rectangular building at Runnymede. So far the finds contained within the deposit at Castle Hill have not proved as rich as some other sites. What is interesting is its association with an extensive contemporary settlement immediately outside a late Bronze Age hilltop enclosure and Iron Age hillfort, which appears to have functioned principally as a communal gathering place and centre of ritual activity (see below).

The Woodeaton site has not previously been recognised as a midden of comparable form, but seems to fulfil most of the criteria. The excavations of the 1950s and 1960s aimed to investigate the well known Roman temple and look for a possible Iron Age predecessor (Goodchild and Kirk 1954; Harding 1987, 27-59). The exceptional richness of the early and later Iron Age finds from Woodeaton has long been recognised (Harding 1972; 1987, 35-41) but the possible significance of the thick, finds-rich stratified soil deposits in which the objects were found seems to have been overlooked as a possible midden, and there has never been a consideration of animal bones or other environmental material. In the 15 m by 15 m area excavated by Harding the thickness of deposit varied from about 0.15 to 0.4 m, mostly around 0.25 m to 0.35 m. It thinned out significantly away from the main area of the later Romano-Celtic temple, possibly as a result of being less well protected from ploughing. A similar deposit and concentration of small pits and postholes was found recently in trial trenching about 120 m to the south-east. It is not known how far in other directions the midden deposit spread, but fieldwalking in the 1990s revealed a very extensive area of Iron Age activity about 300 to 400 m across (Fig. 1.10). An unpublished geophysical survey by A E Johnson for Mrs J Bagnall Smith (Johnson 2003, Oxfordshire SMR PRN 2379) revealed several circular or penannular enclosures and linear ditches, one of which appears to correspond approximately with the edge of the Iron Age pottery scatter.

Harding found that the middle to late Iron Age material was clearly stratified in the upper parts of the deposit and that in places there was an intervening layer of cobbling. Apart from a possible beam slot it was difficult to discern features in the dark midden material but some, including a small pit with metalworking debris, had been dug through the cobble layer. Other pits and postholes were only seen at the level of the subsoil. No clear buildings were identified, but some of the posthole arrangements suggested a rectangular structure (Harding 1987 31-3, fig. 10, 11).

Some of the metalwork may be late Bronze Age, possibly curated items deposited at the same time as the early Iron Age pottery. The upper level of midden material contained globular bowls and saucepan pots indicating use (or reactivation) well into the middle Iron Age. But despite several significant middle to late Iron Age metalwork finds from the site, it seems that the midden ceased to accumulate in the late Iron Age. There is also some doubt as to whether the early to middle Iron Age accumulation was continuous. The finds suggest that it was active in the 7th to 5th centuries and in the 3rd to 2nd or early 1st centuries BC, but not necessarily in between. The distinct separation of layers and cobbled surface also point to a period when the midden was not being enhanced. It is thus possible that the midden reflects two short-lived periods of accumulation in the early and middle Iron Age. Some of the late Iron Age metal-work and coins could be curated objects brought as votive offerings to the Romano-Celtic shrine. Whether or not there was an Iron Age shrine as such, Woodeaton was clearly an exceptional place in the Iron Age and this may well have influenced the siting of the Roman temple.

A possible midden site at Ivinghoe is suspected from an extensive dark soil horizon containing 27 scattered bronzes dated to c 1100-750 cal BC, found during the 1960s excavation, and more recently a complete Wilburton sword and large quantities of other finds – pottery, spindle whorls and loomweights, bone implements and several human skull fragments (Cotton and Frere 1968; Marshall and Northover 2003). While this may be merely well-preserved domestic occupation, the presence of so many bronzes suggests otherwise.

Weaponry and human remains in the river

As we have seen in Chapter 8 (Fig. 8.2) riverine deposition of weapons and human remains is evidence for a wide range of funerary rites and water-related cults that reflect a view of the river as a sacred place for votive offering and perhaps a resting place for the dead. While important items of personal and domestic metalwork have been recovered from some parts of the Thames, notably around Brentford and Syon Reach, the vast bulk of the material is weaponry of one sort or another – swords, spears, daggers and occasionally shields (Fig. 9.7). While this might reflect biased recovery, it seems evident that mostly weaponry rather than tools was deposited in watery places. Conversely, it is tools and ornaments, not weapons, that make

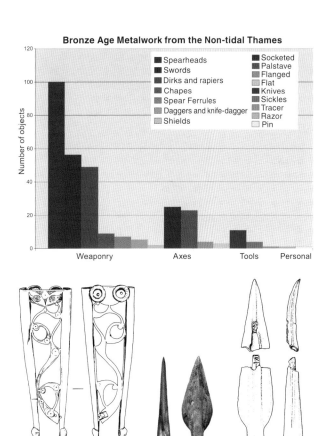

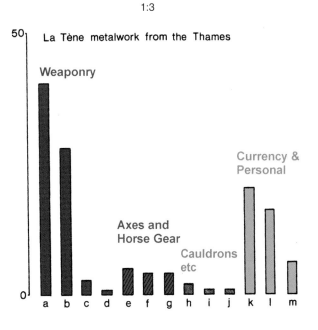

Fig. 9.7 Later prehistoric weaponry and river deposition from the Thames: bronze chape from Little Wittenham and spearheads from Henley and Taplow

up the bulk of lost terrestrial metalwork hoards (Bradley 1990), despite some finds of weapon fragments in founders' hoards. There is little doubt that there was a special association between the river and weaponry, and the incidence of human bones, especially skulls, in the Thames has led to much speculation about the origin of this material. This phenomenon is common to some other British rivers, notably the Witham in Lincolnshire, and several in north-west Europe (Bradley 1998).

Such behaviour may have been related to a warrior cult involving the deposition of excarnated remains of men along with their weapons in the river (Bradley and Gordon 1988; Bradley 1998). Some weapons, especially late Iron Age shields, were relatively flimsy parade pieces rather than functional weapons, suggesting that the deposition of weaponry in the river had an element of symbolic political power and ostentation of wealth or status. This may have included deliberate and irrecoverable disposal of valuables as votive offerings. Jill York (2002) found that through the Bronze Age an increasing proportion of weapons were bent or broken prior to deposition, rendering them unusable or symbolically 'killing' them, perhaps removing their power to kill as a symbol of the death of their owner or of political or military defeat.

If it is correct to see concepts of warriorship, status, wealth and power symbolically represented in the deposition of weaponry in the river, should this be seen as reflecting personal or communal conflict? Despite Caesar's account of the battle he fought to cross the Thames somewhere in the vicinity of Brentford, it is doubtful whether even a small part of the weaponry recovered was lost in riverside battles. Another possibility, suggested by archaeological and historical sources on the continent, is that the weapons of a defeated war band were sacrificed after a battle (Richard Bradley pers. comm.). There also may have been a general symbolic connection between the disposal of weaponry in the river as an act bound up with inter-community or personal relations and potential for conflict. Destroying weapons by rendering them physically useless or consigning them to an inaccessible and/or sacred place could have been a powerful symbol of political or military defeat. It might also have been a way of renouncing the means of conflict as has the IRA in modern times, or perhaps the votive offering of surplus armaments was an expression of overwhelming power. Whether made at a personal or community level, such actions could have had great significance in conveying messages about political status and power.

The means of conflict

Deposits of weaponry in the Thames are a major source of evidence for the range of late prehistoric weaponry available for personal combat. In the earlier Bronze Age archery equipment and daggers were the chief weapons, whereas in later prehistory longer thrusting swords were developed as the principal weapons for hand-to-hand fighting. Daggers did continue to develop, however, and re-emerged in the Iron Age as a standard part of the arsenal of weaponry. The late Bronze Age technical advance of casting sockets meant that more effective spears were developed both as thrusting weapons and projectiles. Other improvements enabled effective forging of larger billets of metal into swords. As swords and spears increased in importance as weapons, shields became more important for defence.

Production of flint arrowheads ceased and no true metal equivalents were developed, but sling shots made of stone or fired clay, which become common in the Iron Age, indicate that the sling largely replaced archery as the main form of projectile weaponry, along with thrown spears. Ceramic or stone slingshots in small numbers are relatively common finds in Iron Age settlements. They may have been used for hunting, though the relative paucity of deer or other wild animal bones suggests this was not a common activity. They might also have been useful against cattle rustlers and the like. They tend to be much more common at defensive sites. At the hillfort at Segsbury a large number of flint pebble slingstones was found, over 544 in an early Iron Age pit in the middle of the fort, 20 in a ditch terminal by its eastern entrance and another 64 in other contexts (Lock *et al.* 2005, 122-3). A group of 148 flint pebble slingshots were found at Uffington (Miles *et al.* 2003, 185-6). Although no definite collections were found in the hillfort excavations at Castle Hill, numerous suitably sized flint pebbles are found in patches of glacial drift there, and a heap of such pebbles were found on top of a pot in an early Iron Age pit outside the hillfort (Allen *et al.* forthcoming b).

During the late Bronze Age and Iron Age warfare became more mobile as horse-riding and in due course lightweight chariots were developed, offering greater speed and manoeuvrability. The picture painted by the classical authors of the warlike tribes of Britain and Gaul make clear reference to their skill in mounting high speed attacks using chariots. Few of the chariot burials of East Yorkshire were, however, accompanied by weaponry (Stead 1991). In the Thames Valley there is some evidence of horse harness and wheeled vehicles, including wheel ruts in the entrance to the fort at Cherbury, which may have included chariots, but there is little physical indication of provision for chariot warfare. Harding (1972 58-9) noted that the palisade trenches associated with sections of the North Oxfordshire Grims Ditch at Model Farm, Blenheim and Callow Hill might have been designed as a defence against chariots, and that causewayed gaps were incorporated in the circuit designed to allow counterattacks. Thomas (1957) thought the 'palisade' features were for stock control and Copeland (1988, 284) suggested more plausibly that these incomplete earthworks were marking out ditches and was sceptical of military, as opposed to political or economic interpretations of these earthworks.

Wounds or evidence of causes of violent death are sometimes found on human bones, such as lethal slashing wounds to a male skull at Watkins Farm (Allen 1990, 57), but on the whole these are rare. Parry fractures, such as a well-healed example on the arm of an old woman at Bourton-on-the-Water (Nichols 2006), are also classic signs of inter-personal violence, but can also result from shielding against a falling object or other accidents. These types of fracture are rarely identified on later prehistoric human bones in the Thames Valley and, bearing in mind their provenance, they are probably better interpreted in the context of social and ritual behaviour actions rather than fighting.

The condition of weapons used in conflict recovered from the Thames also provides evidence of combat. Jill York (2002) showed that an increasing proportion of the Bronze Age weapons found in the Thames had been used in combat at some stage before they were deposited. A fine middle to late Bronze Age shield dredged from the river at Clifton Hampden has perforations corresponding to the cross-section of a typical spearhead of the period, suggesting that the shield was successfully used for defence, given that only the tip of the spear had penetrated the metal. An unusual example is a male human pelvis found at Queensford Mill near Dorchester-on-Thames which had the tip of a spearhead embedded in it (Ehrenberg 1977, 37, fig. 15, pl 1). This provides more direct evidence of human violence but the context is unclear. It could be the excarnated remains of a man killed in a fight, the rest of the body, perhaps unburdened by metal, having washed further away.

Defensive enclosures and forts

In the previous section we have looked at weapons and their use, considering their symbolic, precautionary and possible actual role in inter-personal or communal conflict. We now turn to the defensive and territorial earthworks of the late Bronze Age and Iron Age and consider similar issues in terms of their social, economic and religious uses along with their symbolic, precautionary and actual role in political conflict.

It is currently fashionable to downplay the formerly popular vision of late prehistoric society as riven by warfare and defence and in many practical respects this is probably correct. The vast majority of people in the Thames Valley probably led peaceful lives in harmony with their neighbours and within a relatively secure economic and social system. Life on the surrounding hills may have been much the same. However, even if life was largely peaceful, there were undoubtedly substantial political tensions against which precautions had to be taken. Nonetheless, defensive enclosures and forts were not just military installations. Quite apart from the ceremonial, social and economic roles that they were designed to fulfil, the construction and maintenance of such works clearly reflected a significant degree of social and political control and co-operation, symbolising and cementing communal identity, meeting the need for defence and making an overt statement of political authority.

Middle to late Bronze Age valley floor enclosures

As we have seen, the midden site at Runnymede was at least partly surrounded by a substantial timber revetment formed of small diameter piles, which could have formed a defensive enclosure with a palisaded structure (Needham 1991, 114-5 fig. 47). A similar structure may have existed at Whitecross Farm where a palisade trench constructed along the river bank seems rather elaborate for a mere revetment, which could have been made using driven stakes (Cromarty *et al.* 2006, 23-5, 31). Whether these can be described as defensive structures is debatable as in neither case is there evidence of their form above ground. A simple revetment structure at Anslows Cottages was composed of driven stakes of similar dimensions and spacing to the Whitecross Farm structure. The timber palisades at Rams Hill had larger post-pipes (Bradley and Ellison 1975, 20-3) while those in the palisades at Hartshill Copse were of similar size.

Only 300 m south of Runnymede on the dry gravel terrace overlooking the floodplain, Petters Sports Field, Egham is another possible later Bronze Age high status enclosure, suggested by the terminal of a large north-south ditch heading roughly towards the Runnymede site (O'Connor 1986). A hoard of late Bronze Age metalwork was deposited after the ditch had largely silted up, and 89% of the late Bronze Age pottery from the site came from the top fill of the ditch overlying the hoard, probably derived from settlement activity immediately to the east (Fig. 6.11). These were contemporary with the final stages of the Runnymede settlement. Although the quantity of pottery from the upper levels of the ditch was substantial, it is not otherwise distinct from other dumps of domestic debris in the top of infilled waterholes on ordinary settlements, and finds from the small patches of settlement features investigated were sparse and unremarkable. The Petters ditch may represent part of an important enclosure, but it is unclear whether it was significant as a settlement before the ditch silted up and became a dump. Indeed, the ditch may not have belonged to an enclosed site at all and could have been a major linear boundary resembling the deep ditch at Stanwell (O'Connell 1990).

Immediately to the south of Heathrow Airport at Mayfield Farm a large double-ditched concentric enclosure 200 m in diameter enclosing an area of 3.14 ha was identified from cropmarks (Cotton 1991,

153; Merriman 1990). Trial trenching produced apparently late Bronze Age pottery, although this material is not easily distinguished from late Neolithic material. It has also been suggested that the enclosure was a major henge monument (Lewis and Cotton 2000). If it is late Bronze Age, it would be the largest such enclosure in the Thames Valley.

Other suggested examples of late Bronze Age enclosures or other major settlements on the gravel terraces and floodplain of the Thames valley are even more doubtful. Champion (1980, 238) speculated that a large enclosure containing a middle Iron Age settlement and 'shrine' at Caesar's Camp, Heathrow was a major late Bronze Age enclosure re-used in a later period. This interpretation has been superseded by the full publication of the site (Grimes and Close-Brooks 1993). While there were finds of pottery, perforated clay slabs and other objects that reflect late Bronze Age activity, the ploughed out bank of the enclosure clearly overlay parts of the middle Iron Age settlement. In the Upper Thames Valley there is no evidence to support David Yates's supposition (1999; 2001) that the fort at Burroway is of middle or late Bronze Age origin (see below). This claim appears to be based on a particular theory of the organisation of middle to late Bronze Age society derived partly from the only marginally less speculative site at Marshall's Hill (see below).

In common with other middle to late Bronze Age enclosures around the Thames estuary and in Kent, Carshalton and the related sites at Runnymede and Petters Sportsfield did not develop into Iron Age forts. However, arcs of gullies and pits within the enclosure at Mayfield suggest that at least part of it was occupied in the Iron Age, though not necessarily as a defensive enclosure.

Late Bronze Age hilltop enclosures (Fig. 9.8)

Location and interior usage

The best known and most thoroughly investigated example of a middle to late Bronze Age hilltop enclosure in the Thames basin is Rams Hill on the Berkshire Downs (Fig. 9.9; Bradley and Ellison 1975; Needham and Ambers 1994). The oval enclosure occupied an area of about a hectare, entirely within what was to become a much larger Iron Age fort. Its defences went through three stages of development from the last quarter of the second millennium cal BC to the turn of the first millennium cal BC (Needham and Ambers 1994). The first enclosure, constructed in the last quarter of the second millennium BC, was formed by a ditch and dump rampart faced with chalk blocks and sarsens, with two main entrances to the south and northeast, of which the southern one was investigated. This primary dump rampart was replaced late in the second millennium cal BC by a palisade of large posts fronting a timber-framed or timber-laced rampart. The site may have been abandoned or the

ramparts neglected for a period as the ditch fills showed evidence of partial scrub regeneration and erosion and levelling of the rampart. Subsequently, a double palisade was constructed in the hollow of the partly infilled ditch, with animal burials at the south entrance dated to the late 11th to 10th century cal BC.

Initially the southern entrance was little more than a gap in the enclosure with a dog burial marking the terminal of the palisade on the western side. Subsequently, the entrance was developed as a palisaded entrance passage with large postholes at the inner end suggesting a gate. Allowing for various post replacements due to decay, the basic form of the entrance passage seems to have remained much the same throughout most of the lifetime of the enclosure. At some stage further large postholes were added halfway along the passage, creating a double-gated arrangement. This would have been useful for controlling stock as well as for defence. At the southern entrance a palisaded passage with substantial postholes for a gate was exposed. In the final rebuilding this second gate was rebuilt with a slot to hold a horizontal timber, perhaps a gate stop. A third narrow postern entrance to the west was burnt down and subsequently blocked.

In the 20-25% of the interior excavated domestic occupation was sparse, with only four post-built structures or buildings, eight or nine four-posters, four suggested pairs of postholes and a thin scatter of small pits, tree throw holes and hollows. The chronological relationship of the interior occupation to the timber-built ramparts is not entirely clear, but a D-shaped structure and a porched roundhouse may have predated its later phases (Needham and Ambers 1994). Apart from the ditch and palisade trenches, finds were sparse and mostly unexceptional with only three unstratified metal objects – the butt of palstave, an awl and a possible razor. Overall the character of the settlement at Rams Hill is comparable with other low-density middle to late Bronze Age settlements described in Chapter 4. If the sample of the interior excavated is reasonably representative and occupation was continuous, the number of post-built buildings and other structures would equate to only a couple per half-century of the life of the enclosure. Indeed, as Bradley and Ellison surmised (1975, 216), it is far from clear that Rams Hill was occupied on a long term basis, and its importance was not its role as a settlement.

Within the Iron Age hillfort on Castle Hill, Little Wittenham, immediately overlooking the Thames at Dorchester-upon-Thames, a sub-circular enclosure of similar size, measuring about 100 m across and covering an area of roughly 0.8 ha, has recently been identified through geophysics and trial trenching (Figs. 1.8 and 9.8). Surprisingly, mollusc evidence from the lower ditch fills is indicative of tree cover and phytolith evidence from the ditch and late Bronze Age buried soil layers beneath the ramparts

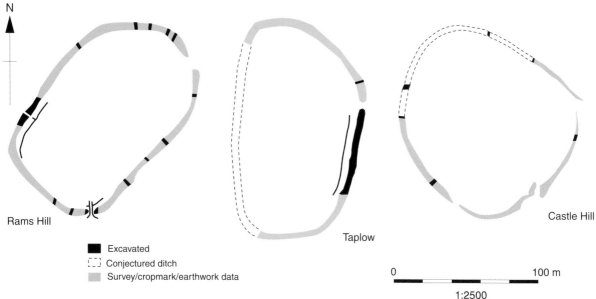

N

Rams Hill

■ Excavated
⌐ ⌐ Conjectured ditch
▓ Survey/cropmark/earthwork data

Taplow

Castle Hill

0   100 m

1:2500

Fig. 9.8   Late Bronze Age hilltop enclosures: (above) *artist's impression of Carshalton;* (below) *plans of Rams Hill, Taplow, and Castle Hill*

of the later hillfort is also consistent with wooded conditions. This suggests that woodland regeneration occurred soon after construction of the enclosure or that the hilltop was only partially cleared in the first place. Significant amounts of pottery, animal bone and worked flint were recovered from the lower ditch fills. The faunal remains included a notably high proportion of pig, with cattle and

sheep/goat also represented, while charred plant remains were sparse, although some wheat grain was present. Part of the interior is now covered by plantation and could not be surveyed using geophysics, and although the interior of the enclosure outside the plantation appears to have been relatively barren, this could be the result of plough truncation. However, a significant area of late

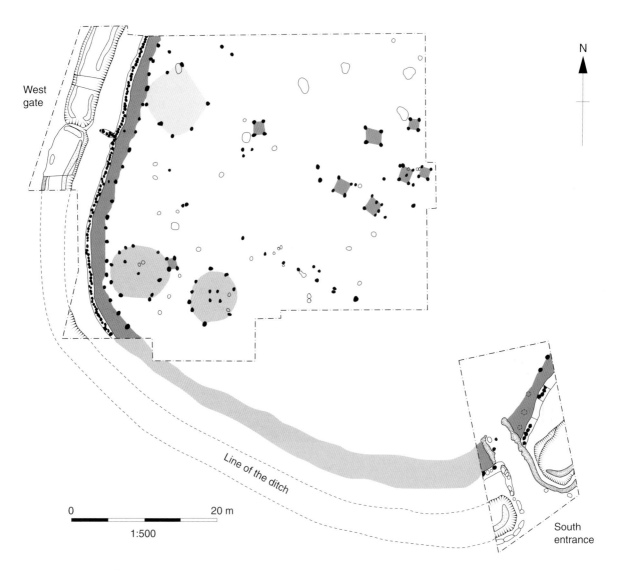

N

Fig. 9.9 Interior of Ram's Hill late Bronze Age hilltop enclosure

Bronze Age settlement was identified outside the enclosure and hillfort (Hingley 1978; Allen and Lamdin-Whymark 2005), so the sparseness of internal features may be genuine.

The enclosure was apparently defined by a simple flat-bottomed ditch with a simple internal dump rampart, possibly no more than a moderately substantial bank, like the initial phase of Rams Hill. The full character of this enclosure is not clear. Its entrances, where one might expect more detailed evidence of its development, have not been investigated and evidence for woodland regeneration following construction raises questions about its role. Compared with Rams Hill it is thus less clear that this enclosure was overtly defensive in character, or rather, in the absence of a palisade or timber framed rampart, it is less clear that it became so.

Another late Bronze Age hilltop enclosure was recently discovered at Taplow Court, Buckinghamshire, once again within a later hillfort, high on an elongated gravel bluff immediately overlooking the Thames only 100-150 m from the river (Fig. 9.8; Allen

and Lamdin-Whymark 2000; Allen *et al.* forthcoming d). The defences, which saw several phases of development, consisted of timber palisades and a ditch. One of the innermost lines of postholes contained charcoal dated to the middle Bronze Age, suggesting that the site was initially enclosed by a simple palisade before more elaborate ditched defences were constructed. The first enclosure ditch contained late Bronze Age 'plain ware' pottery. The lower silts were dated to 1070-790 BC using optically stimulated luminescence (OSL). A palisade trench parallel to the inner edge of the ditch also produced 'plain ware', and further palisade or fence lines ran along the outside edge of the ditch. The late Bronze Age ditch had largely silted up by the time much of a 9th-8th century BC bipartite bowl resembling those at Petters Sports Field, was deposited.

The enclosure had an eastern entrance respected by several rebuildings of its defences, but only a limited part of the entrance was investigated and there may have been other entrances (Allen and Lamdin-Whymark 2000; Allen *et al.* forthcoming d).

Little of the interior was excavated but one or two possible post-built structures and a few small pits were exposed. Rather like Castle Hill, a significant area of late Bronze Age settlement has been located (in a pipeline excavation) only 0.6 km east of the enclosure (Collard 2004).

Further from the river up the Wey valley at Carshalton a large late Bronze Age circular enclosure *c* 150 m diameter has been sampled on various occasions (Fig. 9.8; Adkins and Needham 1985). Recent small-scale excavation has produced evidence for pits both inside and outside the enclosure (Groves and Lovell 2002).

Other possible late Bronze Age hilltop enclosures

Apart from Rams Hill, Castle Hill, Taplow and Carshalton there are a number of other possible candidates for late Bronze Age hilltop enclosures, some located close to the river. Bradley (1984, 122-2, fig. 5.4) has suggested that a poorly understood subcircular former earthwork at Marshall's Hill, Reading might have been a late Bronze Age hilltop enclosure on the basis of finds of pottery from the interior and a general concentration of metalwork in the river nearby. However, there was no direct dating evidence from the enclosure circuit itself, and its form and size are unclear.

Windsor Castle is obviously persuasive topographically and has a concentration of metalwork in the river nearby. Later Bronze Age and early Iron Age pottery was recovered and a few features identified in work connected with the medieval castle (B Kerr and R Brown pers. comm.) but any evidence of prehistoric defences may have been destroyed or masked by the later castle.

At Bozedown Camp, Whitchurch, another known defensive site overlooking the Thames, a fairly substantial ditch containing typical middle to late Bronze Age flint-tempered pottery ran parallel to and just outside the main hillfort ditch (Wood 1954; Howel 1996). Within the hillfort overlooking the Thames at St Anne's Hill, Chertsey (Fig. 9.10) there is good evidence of late Bronze Age occupation contemporary with the Petters Sports Field settlement a few kilometres to the north. This, however, is largely based on typical 9th to 8th century BC pottery redeposited in features that also contained sherds more characteristic of the early Iron Age a century or two later (Jones forthcoming).

Early origins are also proposed for various small, circular univallate hilltop forts in relatively non-defensive locations on the Cotswolds, such as Chastelton Ring (Leeds 1931a), and Lyneham (Bayne 1957). This has been only recently demonstrated for a long-suspected defensive site at Camp Gardens on the rounded hill occupied by the town of Stow-on-the-Wold. Two radiocarbon dates of 1400-990 cal BC and 1390-1005 cal BC were obtained from a section of ditch suspected to form part of a hilltop enclosure preceding an Iron Age

Fig. 9.10   Middle Thames Valley hillfort at St Anne's Hill, Chertsey on the far hill overlooking gravel terraces, now characterised by flooded quarries

hillfort on the site (Parry 1999). Closer to the Thames Valley small-scale excavation in the 1980s at the small univallate enclosure on the low hill at Round Hill Bladon, just south of Woodstock produced a small collection of probable late Bronze Age pottery and evidence that the ramparts were burnt (Ainslie 1988).

Investigations in the 1940s and 1960s at Blewburton Hill on the chalk on the north-eastern fringes of the Berkshire Downs revealed a palisaded enclosure and possible traces of a medium-sized external ditch, now thought to date from the 8th century BC or earlier (Collins 1947; 1949; Collins and Collins 1953; Harding 1976). There was little evidence of occupation in the interior but only a small area was investigated and it has not been subjected to geophysical survey.

On the Chiltern escarpment the well-known promontory fort at Ivinghoe Beacon has produced many late Bronze Age objects, several house plans, small pits and geophysical evidence of palisades (Cotton and Frere 1968; Barker *et al.* 2003, 121-4). However, it is not clear if a separate hilltop enclosure or an open settlement pre-dated the hillfort. A wide range of late Bronze Age to middle Iron Age radiocarbon dates have been obtained on animal bones from beneath collapsed material, possibly from the rampart (Green 1981). Also on the Chilterns, flint-tempered pottery has been recovered from the small but impressive hillfort at Pulpit Hill (Barker *et al.* 2003, 121-4).

Iron Age forts

On the Cotswolds the development of forts with drystone wall ramparts is evident from numerous sites, perhaps most impressively at the early Iron Age Crickley Hill (Dixon 1976; 1994). Rainsborough, another drystone walled fort just east of the upper reaches of the Cherwell Valley, is unusual in being multivallate from the early Iron Age (Avery *et al.* 1967). Madmarston in north Oxfordshire was also multivallate but more typically of middle Iron Age origin (Fowler 1960). These latter two sites were notable for the pioneering use of geophysics to explore their interiors and, although primitive at the time, this seemed to confirm the sparse internal occupation features, especially pits, which is a feature of other Cotswold forts, including Crickley Hill. Apart from Crickley there has been little extensive excavation of hillfort interiors in the Cotswolds but recent geophysical surveys at Chastleton and Lyneham have indicated a similar dearth of internal occupation evidence (Alex Lang pers. comm.). At Madmarston it is now clear from aerial photography that there was a significant Iron Age settlement outside the fort (Fig. 9.17 and below).

Amongst the rolling hills of mid-Buckinghamshire, excavations in the centre of Aylesbury have revealed remains of a hillfort which, though not extensively explored (see Chapter 8), is remarkable for a large pit or hollow associated with bones of kids and lambs and numerous human remains, some suggesting mutilation or sacrifice (Farley 1987). Pending full publication the sequence is not fully clear, though Kidd (2007) has speculated that the remarkable sacrificial deposits might be associated with a shrine predating the fort.

The later Bronze Age hilltop enclosures at Rams Hill, Castle Hill, and Taplow developed into fully-fledged forts in the early and middle Iron Age. The new enclosures were on a greatly enlarged scale, not only in terms of the areas enclosed, but also the size of their earthworks. At Rams Hill and Castle Hill there is some evidence that the sites were abandoned and wooded over prior to refortification (Bradley and Ellison 1975, 217; Allen *et al.* forthcoming a). None of the excavations combine detailed dating of the rampart sequences with large samples of both their late Bronze Age and the Iron Age interiors.

The rampart of the large outer circuit of Rams Hill was constructed in the 7th century cal BC, but the fort may have been unfinished (Bradley and Ellison 1975 67-9) and there is little evidence that it developed far into the Iron Age. Although the 1972-3 excavations focused on the interior of the Bronze Age enclosure rather than the enlarged hillfort, the results are nonetheless notable for the absence of any Iron Age occupation evidence. It is possible that the site was abandoned in favour of nearby Uffington where the first phase of construction was roughly contemporary with the last at Rams Hill (Miles *et al.* 2003, 119-20, 249-50).

At Taplow the upper levels of the silted up Bronze Age enclosure ditch included upcast gravel from a new U-profile ditch about 8 m wide and 2.8 m deep. This was part of a timber-framed rampart built on a corduroy of timbers lying at right-angles to the line of the ditch, of which charred remains were preserved due to the subsequent firing of the rampart. Extensive reddening of the gravel fill implied the presence of enough timber in the rampart to cause a substantial conflagration. At the entrance, the curving rampart facing and one of the large gate postholes were also burnt. Charcoal from this gatepost was dated to 710-520 cal BC. Middle Iron Age potsherds were found in the backfill of the gate posthole, indicating that the firing of the rampart did not take place until after 400 BC. A V-profile ditch aligned parallel to the early Iron Age ditch and 30 m beyond it was over 3 m deep and at least 9 m wide. It is undated, and too little of the adjacent area was excavated to expose any postholes alongside it, but the wide gap between this and the U-profile ditch may represent the position of a substantial dump rampart. It seems clear that both the inner U-profile ditch and V-profile outer ditch were open at the same time since Saxon pottery dumps were found halfway up the fills of both. This indicates that Taplow may have become a multivallate fort, though none of the ditches has been traced along their whole length. Only a very small and largely uninformative

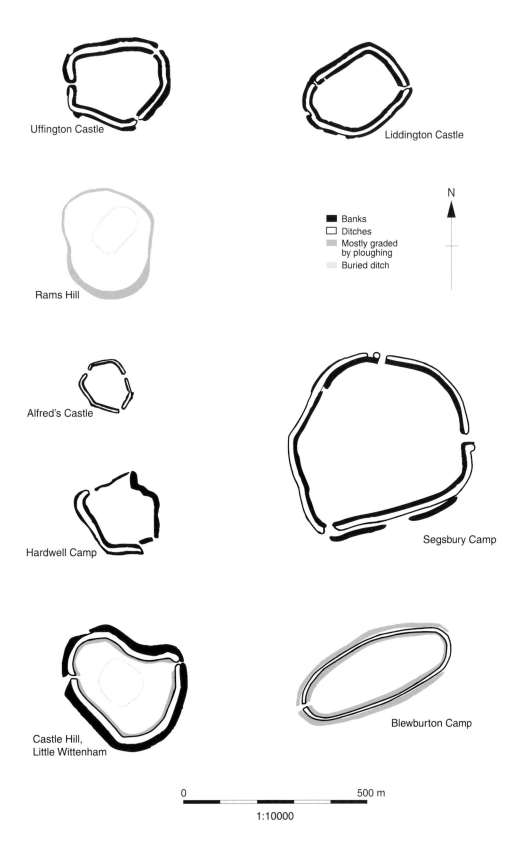

Fig. 9.11 Iron Age hillforts on the scarp of the Berkshire Ridgeway and outlying chalk hills

Fig. 9.12 (overleaf) Hilltop enclosures: Castle Hill

The late Bronze Age enclosure at Castle Hill, Little Wittenham was defined by a flat-bottomed ditch and simple dump rampart. The full character of this enclosure remains uncertain since its entrances have not been investigated for evidence of development. The absence of a palisade or timber framed rampart and evidence for woodland regeneration following construction of the earthworks raise doubts as to an overtly defensive role.

During the early and middle Iron Age Castle Hill developed into a fully-fledged fort on an enlarged scale but the construction date of the enhanced earthworks is uncertain. The Iron Age ditch was 17 m wide and at least 7.5 m deep. The counterscarp bank was composed of alternate layers of chalk and fine loam, probably the product of successive scourings of the ditch followed by periods of stabilisation and turf formation. Relatively large amounts of early Iron Age pottery and bone had accumulated in the top of the Bronze Age ditch, evidence of some level of domestic activity. However, the contents of an early Iron Age pit hint at specialised feasting activity rather than ordinary domestic occupation. It contained large numbers of bones of young sheep and piglets, fine red-finished pottery and a decorated lid with central European parallels.

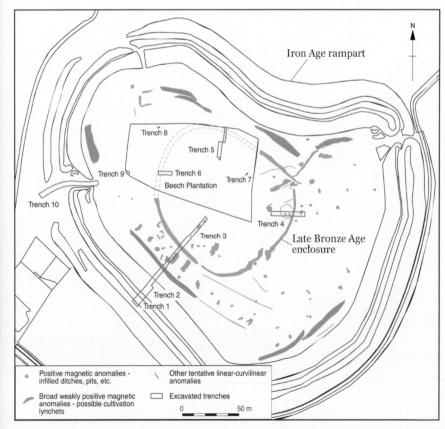

Iron Age rampart

N

Trench 8

Trench 5

Trench 9

Trench 6

Trench 7

Beech Plantation

Trench 10

Trench 4

Trench 3

Late Bronze Age enclosure

Trench 2

Trench 1

Positive magnetic anomalies - infilled ditches, pits, etc.

Other tentative linear-curvilinear anomalies

Broad weakly positive magnetic anomalies - possible cultivation lynchets

Excavated trenches

0   50 m

Left page clockwise from top left:
* *Castle Hill from the air (Time Team 2003)*
* *Aerial photograph of Castle Hill and surroundings (RAF vertical series 1396, 106G/UK Apr.46/541)*
* *early Iron Age pot*
* *Interpretation of the geophysical survey of the hillfort*
Right page
(above) View of the excavated Iron Age ditch and rampart
(centre) Section across the fort (Trenches 1,2,3) showing different elements of its development
(below left)
* *Late Bronze Age enclosure ditch*
* *Pit burial*

CASTLE HILL

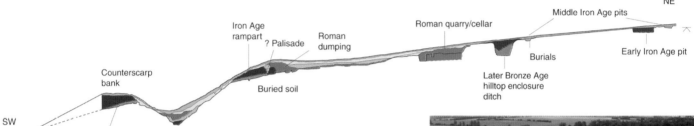

SW

NE

Counterscarp bank

Preserved buried soil

Iron Age hillfort ditch

Iron Age rampart

? Palisade

Roman dumping

Buried soil

Roman quarry/cellar

Middle Iron Age pits

Early Iron Age pit

Burials

Later Bronze Age hilltop enclosure ditch

bout half of the middle Iron Age pits at Castle Hill produced human burials or bones. One contained three successive burials including evidence of defleshing and possibly sacrifice. As if to emphasise the point, the ramparts, the interior and the immediate surroundings of the hillfort remained a burial place throughout the Roman period.

UFFINGTON CASTLE

U ffington Castle lies on the scarp of the Berkshire Downs overlooking the Vale of the White Horse. It has extensive counterscarp banks showing evidence of a strong tradition of maintenance, possibly associated with rescouring of the adjacent White Horse (Miles et al. 2003). The sequence of development of the defences began with an early Iron Age timber-framed box rampart with entrances to the east and west. The eastern entrance probably consisted of a timber-lined passage with massive gates and guard rooms either side of the inner end.

A fter a period of decay and possibly abandonment, the fort was remodelled in the middle Iron Age. An enlarged, V-shaped ditch was dug and large dumped bank built, initially revetted with chalk and sarsen walls. These eventually eroded out, leaving

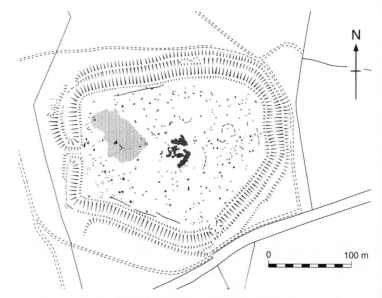

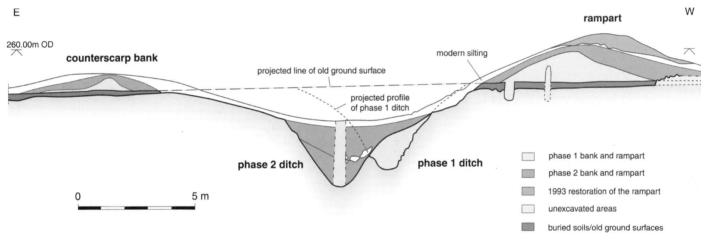

E W

260.00m OD

counterscarp bank

rampart

projected line of old ground surface

modern silting

projected profile
of phase 1 ditch

phase 2 ditch

phase 1 ditch

0   5 m

☐ phase 1 bank and rampart

☐ phase 2 bank and rampart

☐ 1993 restoration of the rampart

☐ unexcavated areas

☐ buried soils/old ground surfaces

the bank rising almost straight out of the ditch, as is typical of hillforts in southern Britain (Avery, 1993, 106). One of the changes resulting from this remodelling was the demolition and blocking of the original east entrance of the fort. This would have altered the dynamics of its use, possibly re-routing the roadway which formerly passed directly through the fort to follow the top of the ridge instead.

Detailed geophysical survey and limited sample excavation of the interior has emphasised a relative dearth of internal occupation, prompting the suggestion that its use was largely concerned with reinforcing communal and territorial identities associated with the White Horse.

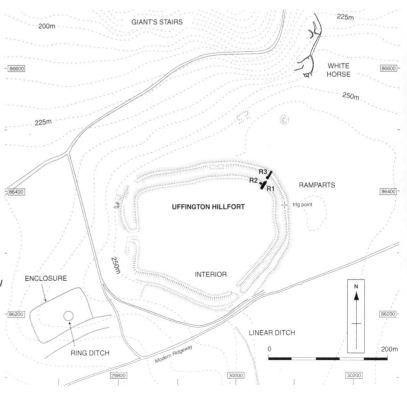

Left page:
(above) The White Horse
(centre) Plan of the hillfort , interpretation of 1989 magnetometry survey
(below) The ditch and ramparts
Right page:
(above left) Aerial view of the middle Iron Age hillfort
(above right) Excavating the timber-framed box rampart
(centre) Section across the ditch and ramparts
(below) Plan showing excavated trenches and the surrounding archaeological landscape

sample of the interior was exposed and the character of the remainder was not much clarified by geophysics hampered by modern services and other features. It is thus impossible to judge fully the extent of interior occupation.

The date of construction of the Iron Age hillfort defences at Castle Hill is not clear as the entrance areas, where the full sequence might most clearly have been revealed, were not investigated (Fig. 9.12). Although traces of a vertical revetment were found at the back of the rampart, there is little evidence for the method of construction of the defences. The large size of the ditch and the elongated slope on the inner side indicate that a combination of remodelling and erosion may have destroyed the front of the original rampart. Continual maintenance of the ditch over a long period is demonstrated by the limited depth of silt (0.8 m) that accumulated during the Iron Age and the unusually large counterscarp bank (up to 5 m high).

Uffington Castle (Fig. 9.13) also showed evidence

of a strong tradition of maintenance and remodelling, probably associated with the adjacent White Horse (Miles *et al.* 2003, 249-51). These changes may have resulted in the diversion to the top of the ridge of the routeway which once passed through the fort. A similar sequence to that at Uffington is apparent at Liddington, *c* 12 km to the west, where the original western entrance was blocked (Hirst and Rahtz 1996). Geophysical survey and small-scale excavation at Uffington failed to reveal much evidence of internal occupation, despite the almost obsessive degree of maintenance of the defences. The hillfort may have been a focus of gatherings which reinforced communal and territorial identities through maintenance of the earthworks. This may have been linked to the adjacent White Horse, perhaps also relating to major ditched land divisions (Miles *et al.* 2003, 123-4, 250). If this is correct, it raises intriguing questions about how far the nearby Hardwell Camp, only 2.5 km to the north-west, may have overlapped chronologically

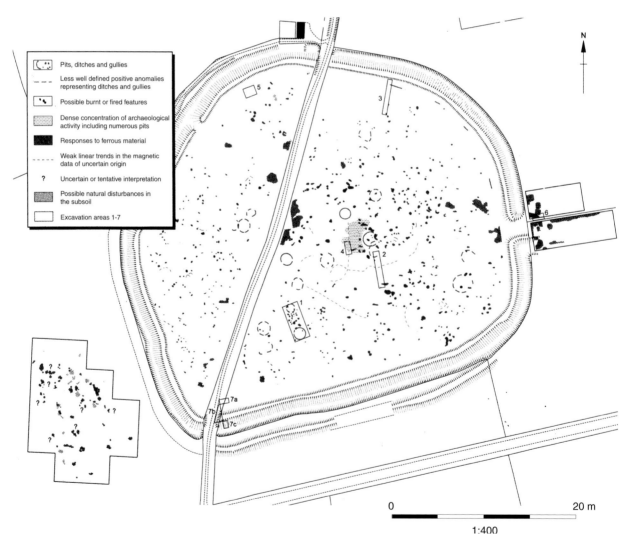

Fig. 9.14   *Interpretative plan of geophysical survey of Segsbury hillfort*

Fig. 9.13 *(previous spread)   Hilltop enclosures : Uffington Castle*

with Uffington and whether it performed a complementary role.

At the 11 ha univallate fort at Segsbury *c* 9 km to the east of Uffington the sequence is somewhat different (Fig. 9.14; Lock *et al.* 2005). A fence with posts spaced *c* 1.5 m apart was replaced by a similar structure with a chalk bank. This was subsequently encased in a much larger bank 7 m wide, revetted at the rear by a palisade of posts set roughly 0.5 m apart in a trench. It appears to reflect a massive enlargement of the main ditch to 10 m wide and 4 m deep. The wooden front of the bank was initially maintained, making an unusually wide box rampart, but it evolved into a continuous 'glacis' style slope with the inner face of the ditch. The rear revetment was reinforced or replaced by rough drystone walling of chalk and sarsen blocks.

There is more evidence of internal occupation in the interior of Segsbury, but the geophysics and small-scale sampling suggest that, although present across most of the 11 ha interior of this large fort, pits and other features are few. Clusters of pits seem to be associated with circular or penannular ditched enclosures, perhaps suggesting individual domestic units rather than the highly differentiated and much denser layout of roadways, storage pits and houses evident in some 'developed' hillforts in Wessex, including Danebury (Cunliffe and Poole 1991a). The density of settlement features was nothing like as great as some contemporary open settlements in the Thames Valley. Postholes representing houses were not identified, suggesting that occupation was probably not permanent. Carbonised remains of crop-processing were notably scarce compared with sites on the floor of the Thames Valley, and the domestic animals eaten included a high proportion of sheep and lambs, especially in the middle Iron Age. Occupation may have been largely seasonal, connected with large-scale gatherings for seasonal sheep fairs that involved a wide range of communal activities, including exchange and feasting (Lock *et al.* 2006, 144-9).

Further east the scarp of the Berkshire Downs becomes less prominent, but on an outlying hill at Blewburton the palisaded enclosure was replaced by a timber-framed box rampart. The entrance passage, the main focus of excavations in the 1940s and 1960s, was remodelled at least three times. Harding's (1976) interpretation of the sequence suggests that the initial palisaded enclosure had a double passage entrance 8 m wide and at least as long, with a quartzite and chalk cobbled surface. This was then substantially narrowed to 4 m wide and lengthened to 10 m with much more substantial gateposts when the box rampart was constructed. When the defences were changed to a dump rampart the entrance was realigned, widened and lengthened, creating a passage lined with drystone wall revetments built of imported stone. The cobbled street surface was up to 1 ft thick in hollows with an accumulation of mud but no wheel ruts. The drystone walling revetment survived *in situ* up

to 10-11 courses, the bottom course being chalk blocks up to 1 ft long with Corallian limestone above. Its upper courses had tumbled across most of the width of the entranceway, covering a remarkable series of apparently deliberate sacrificial animal offerings that perhaps marked the closure or abandonment of the fort (see Chapter 8). Excavations in the interior have been limited and, although they revealed little sign of intensive occupation, this has not been confirmed by detailed geophysical survey.

In recent years there have been a number of new geophysical and earthwork surveys of hillforts along the Chilterns. At Ivinghoe Beacon, still the most thoroughly excavated of the Chiltern forts, new work has clarified the character of occupation revealed by the excavations of Frere and Cotton (1968). The excavations exposed houses and other features comparable to Rams Hill but with much better stratigraphic survival, including midden-like deposits (see above). Ivinghoe is often seen as an early example of the use of a late Bronze Age/early Iron Age timber box rampart (Cunliffe, 1991, 316), but there have always been some doubts as to whether the rampart was a later addition to an unenclosed late Bronze Age settlement. Unfortunately this was not resolved by an attempt to radiocarbon date the sequence (Green 1981). The more recent evidence of house platforms and possible midden deposits outside the enclosure perhaps supports the argument that the ramparts were added to a pre-existing settlement (Brown, 2001; Barker *et al.* 2003).

Only limited evidence is available for other Chiltern hillforts. New survey work has been undertaken at Pulpit Hill, a small 1 ha hillfort of comparable scale to the Alfred's Castle enclosure but with larger earthworks and a more conventional scarp-edge setting for a fort (Barker *et al.* 2003). A single trench has been dug across the ramparts at Bozedown Camp overlooking the river at the southern end of the Goring Gap, suggesting it is early Iron Age (Wood 1954). Further east, also overlooking the river, fieldwork at Danesfield, Medmenham has shown it was in use during the middle Iron Age (Keevil and Campbell, 1991).

In the Surrey section of the valley there are two hillforts relatively close to the river. St George's Hill is a univallate fort on plateau gravel overlooking the confluence of the River Wey and the Thames. Several Iron Age settlements are known along the valley of the Wey (Hanworth and Tomalin 1977; Hayman 1991) but so far the hillfort has produced very little evidence of occupation (Stevenson 1999). However, it is very close to the Brooklands complex and may be complementary. At the hillfort on St Anne's Hill, Chertsey small-scale excavation has revealed an area of dense pits and postholes datable to the early Iron Age and including some late Bronze Age elements (Jones, P forthcoming). It may have replaced Petters Sports Field and Runnymede as the main communal focus during the early Iron

Age, but the full character and extent of the settlement are unclear.

There are fewer defended enclosures in the Middle Thames Valley. Excavations of both ramparts and interiors have been less extensive, so much less is known of their chronological development and the nature of interior use than in the Upper Thames. It is also less clear how their occupation and use may have differed from undefended settlements.

Early to middle Iron Age valley forts

Of all Iron Age forts in the Thames Valley that at Burroway is one of the least well-known, but in terms of survival this almost flat site has arguably the highest potential of all (Fig. 9.16). It is a univallate fort occupying a flat island within the floodplain of the Thames south-east of Clanfield in what today seems one of the more remote parts of the valley, despite being central to the Upper Thames Valley north of the Corallian Ridge. The site is known only from aerial photography and two very limited excavations (Sturdy and Case 1961-2; Lambrick 1984b). A small trench in the interior revealed an undisturbed occupation layer with a posthole and a stakehole sealed beneath a layer of undisturbed alluvium under the modern ploughed horizon, but the extent of the settlement is entirely unclear.

The enclosure is oval, apparently with a single entrance to the north-east associated with a possible annexe or large hornwork. Excavations by David Sturdy and the Clanfield Archaeological Society in 1962 investigated the main enclosing ditch, which produced a few rather indeterminate sherds of possibly middle Iron Age pottery. One of two tiny trenches excavated in 1983 (Lambrick 1984b) showed that the burnt rampart encased a timber structure and was constructed on an *in situ* corduroy of timbers laid on the pre-alluvial ground surface. A vertical posthole found in the burnt clayey soil forming the body of the rampart had filled with more burnt rampart material, while the underlying corduroy of timbers resting on the old ground surface was charred by the intense burning of the rampart above. The timber construction suggests that the fort may have been early Iron Age in origin and, like other forts, could have been remodelled later, but its full character and dating have yet to be established. Although the banks are almost ploughed flat the state of preservation is in other respects exceptional, and indeed far better than most hillforts on dry sites that have impressive banks but ploughed out interiors and no waterlogged material.

The much better known low-lying valley fort at Cherbury is unusual in the region both for its topographical siting on a flat spur of Corallian sand and stone surrounded by alluvial deposits (Bradford 1940; Arkle 1942) and for its relatively large size (c 8 ha) with multiple ramparts (Fig. 9.15). Although the defences were explored in the 1930s,

Fig. 9.15 The valley fort at Cherbury: (above) *aerial view of the hillfort* (photo GWG Allen*);* (below) *the defences*

no excavations have been carried out in the interior, though faint crop marks and a recent geophysical survey suggest some occupation. More generally, scattered sherds of pottery suggest middle Iron Age and possibly some earlier Iron Age occupation, but the date and sequence of the fort's development and any pre-existing use of the site remain obscure.

The defensive works at Cherbury were quite complex, though not especially substantial. Triple banks and ditches still survive on the western side of the fort next to an area of wet peaty woodland, Turf Pits Covert. On the eastern side the outer banks have long since been ploughed flat, probably pushed into the ditches. In normal winters there is standing water in all the ditches on the western side despite local drainage. Excavations by J S P Bradford in 1939 showed that the ditches were broad and fairly shallow, the inner one on the south side with 1.2-1.5 m of silt, and at the eastern entrance reaching a maximum 1.8 m deep. A 24 m length of the inner rampart was investigated exposing a drystone wall revetment that probably ran all the way around the fort, most likely built using limestone from the ditches. In places it was still standing about 1.5 m high, and with fallen material would originally have stood to over 2 m

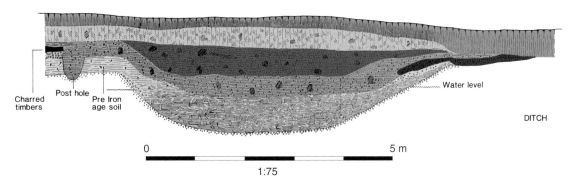

Charred timbers

Post hole

Pre Iron age soil

Water level

DITCH

0   5 m

1:75

305/007

Sharney Brook

310/007

N

Burroway Brook

R. Thames

1962 Section hereabouts

305/000   310/000

0   500 m

1:10000

Fig. 9.16 The valley fort at Burroway:
(above) *general view;* (centre) *the defensive ditch;*
(below left) *location plan;* (below right) *burnt*
rampart with in situ timbers

(Bradford 1940, 17, Pl V). It appears that the banks revetted by this walling were partly formed using sand scooped from behind the rampart tail and dumped along the fringe of the geological peninsula. There was no revetment nor any evidence of timber reinforcement of the outer defences, so far as could be established from the limited investigation, but it is not clear whether the outer defences represent one or more later additions. The unusual form of the defences at Cherbury may be due to its low-lying location and geology, with the number and wetness of the ditches making up for their relative shallowness, exploiting the then very marshy surroundings.

The original entrance was to the east, though it is not now very clear. The natural dry ground approach would have been from the north, making it necessary to skirt the ramparts to reach the entrance, where the causeway between the ditches was metalled with small stones in which wheel ruts were visible. At least one remetalling was necessitated by the accumulation of thick mud. The upper surface had some Roman pottery embedded in the surface. A much more solid cobbled street was found in the entrance passage through the inner rampart which was flanked by dry-stone walling still surviving up to 12 courses high, with massive postholes for the timber gateway. A sherd of a Frilford/Cassington bowl with characteristic swag and impressed circlet decoration was found in fallen debris from walls close to the right hand gateway posthole. This suggests middle to late Iron Age occupation but the origins and overall sequence of development of Cherbury is far from clear.

There are a number of other places within the Thames floodplain or other low-lying valley locations with the place-name element 'bury'. This could mean either 'barrow' or 'fortified enclosure', but as yet only Cherbury, Burroway and the larger and later Salmonsbury (see below) clearly relate to Iron Age forts.

Extra-mural settlement

At Cherbury, as at Castle Hill and Taplow, there is a large unenclosed settlement known from cropmarks and fieldwalking, in this case less than 1 km to the west of the hillfort (Hingley and Miles 1984; Miles and Lewis 1985). Another recently discovered extra-mural settlement away from the Thames is an extensive settlement known from cropmarks at the foot of Madmarston Camp in north Oxfordshire (Fig. 9.17; Allen 2000). As noted above the relationship between St Georges Hill and the Brooklands complex might be similar (R Poulton pers. comm.).

Castle Hill is the largest and most fully mapped and sampled extramural settlement (Allen *et al.* forthcoming a). The extent of occupation, covering an area about 700 m long and 200-300 m wide is one of the largest settlements known in the Thames Valley. It appears to have spanned much the same period from the late Bronze Age to middle Iron Age as the adjacent sequence of defensive enclosures. There is good evidence of late Bronze Age occupation from work by Rutland in the small car park below the hillfort (Hingley 1980c) and extensive indications of early Iron Age settlement spreading further west. In the middle Iron Age settlement appears to have concentrated slightly further from the fort, extending into the area now occupied by Hill Farm (Fig. 9.17). Here sample trenches exposed evidence of a fairly typical settlement of penannular gullies, four-posters and pits. In the area investigated there was little evidence for late Iron Age activity, though if the settlement continued to shift location round the south-east side of the hill this might be the origin of an area of Roman settlement known from fieldwalking and geophysics southeast of Hill Farm.

The extramural settlements serve to reinforce the impression that many, if not most, middle to late Bronze Age hilltop or riverside enclosures and Iron Age forts in the Thames Valley were not primarily intended to enclose or defend important settlements. Indeed, unlike the 'developed' hillforts of Wessex such as Danebury, it would be very difficult in most cases to distinguish the extent and density of settlement found within them from their non-defensive counterparts, which often display a much greater density of settlement features and domestic debris. It is evident that some late Bronze Age unenclosed settlements were considerably more extensive (eg Shorncote/Cotswold Community) and in some cases more intensive (eg Reading Business Park/Green Park) than what we know of Rams Hill. Likewise, early to middle Iron Age sites such as Gravelly Guy, Yarnton or the Ashville complex were as extensive and certainly more densely occupied than hillforts in use over similar periods.

The role of hilltop enclosures and forts as communal sites of special status

It has thus become clear in the last fifteen years that late prehistoric defensive sites in and around the Thames Valley were seldom important as permanent settlements, but they are likely to have fulfilled a range of other communal roles in relation to economic, religious and political interaction.

The effort involved in constructing places used for communal purposes such as shrines, middens and fields clearly varied. From the later Bronze Age onwards the construction of major enclosures, defensive forts, oppida and territorial boundaries would have been on a very different scale of undertaking in social and political terms, involving major civil engineering works on an increasingly large scale. Their architectural appearance and visual presence in the landscape were doubtless powerful symbolic statements of political control which had strong militaristic overtones.

In all cases their creation and maintenance is likely to have been significant as a means of

Castle Hill

Madmarston

Fig. 9.17   Settlements outside hillforts: (above) Castle Hill, Little Wittenham; (below) cropmarks (centre of photo) showing extra-mural settlement at Madmarston

exercising, imposing and displaying political power, both within communities and in relation to others. This is suggested by a number of character-istics. Their design, variously involving continuous walls of timber, gleaming chalk and tunnel-like entrances, sometimes flanked by stone brought from miles away and guarded by massive gates hung on huge posts, must have been intended to impress. The creation of the massive counterscarp bank at Castle Hill by regular scouring of the chalk may be parallelled at some other chalkland forts. Several of these have lesser external banks, including Uffington where it is suggested that such scouring would have been associated with ongoing maintenance of the White Horse.

The design, construction and maintenance of defensive enclosures such as earthworks would have played an important role in symbolising and demonstrating the power of communities to mobilise a population and hence their control over territory. Leaders would have used this both to establish political authority over a population and demonstrate it to potential rivals. For the most part the result was peaceful co-existence and inter-change, a characteristic of the region borne out by the broader pattern of settlements which, at least on the valley floor, were largely unenclosed or had only minor protection against raiding or unrest.

The bizarre funerary and feasting deposits, especially at Castle Hill and Aylesbury, suggest an association with religious and ritual gatherings. Animal burials that seem to mark the foundation and decommissioning of the entrances at Rams Hill and Blewbury reinforce this strong ritualistic element. At Segsbury there are a number of human burials, including a dismembered torso, but the size of the enclosed area and the character of its sparse but extensive internal settlement suggest that again it had a different role. The excavators believe it had a connection with sheep farming, possibly related to an unusual cluster of banjo enclosures within its immediate downland hinterland.

Where in all this ritual symbolism and political, economic and social roles did defence fit in? The scale and character of the ramparts and entrance structures of late prehistoric forts were clearly designed to be defensible as well as impressive. Apart from serving as a symbolic representation of power, most forts would have been designed as refuges or stock-holding areas in time of trouble. The stockpiles of sling shots found at several forts (see above) suggests that the need for such defence and protection was sufficiently real for preparations to be made.

Whether actual conflict took place is debatable. In the Thames Valley at Burroway, Taplow and Bladon

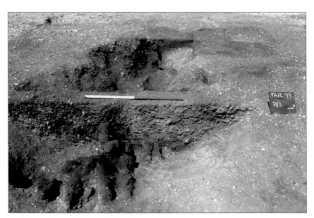

Fig 9.18 The burnt fort at Taplow: (left) *Iron Age hillfort ditch during excavation;* (above right) *reddened, burnt gravel;* (below right) *charred timber-framing of the Iron Age rampart*

Round Hill there is evidence for the burning of fort ramparts, and at Rams Hill the minor western gate was burnt down. At Burroway fired clay is visible around the entire circuit and, where the surviving bank was tested, the full thickness of it was reddened, with a charred corduroy of timbers beneath (Fig. 9.16). Similar evidence was associated with the probable box rampart phase of the fort at Taplow, where at least the eastern sector of the ramparts was burnt, leaving extensive areas of scorching and charred timbers (Fig. 9.18). The extent of the burning at Round Hill is not known but was certainly distinct in the small area excavated (Ainslie 1988). Several forts on the Cotswolds have evidence of burning, including Crickley Hill (Dixon 1976), Leckhampton (Champion 1976) and Rainsborough (Avery *et al.* 1967). In some cases evidence of burning is visible from surface indications, including personal observation by the author of abundant burnt stones in the rampart materials of a small fort at Bibury.

The incidence of burnt ramparts may be under-recorded since they do not seem to have been systematically observed like vitrified forts in Scotland. As with vitrified forts, the cause of such conflagrations is difficult to demonstrate with certainty (Ralston 1995, 66-8) and it is possible that some occurred as a result of accidents rather than attack. Once a fire got going within the interstices of a timber-framed rampart it would be extremely difficult to put it out short of creating a breech either side of the burning area, which may not have been possible to achieve in a short time. The incidence of burnt forts is an interesting phenomenon but not proof of conflict.

A theory invoked to explain the synchronous change in the design of hillfort ramparts in the middle Iron Age is that it reflects a period of unrest in which fortifications had to be refurbished, often after a period of abandonment. This does not mean that the need arose in the context of actual conflict or even any real threat if it was more to do with political rivalry and one-upmanship. Whether fires occurred accidentally or in the course of conflict, it is possible that the ease with which a timber-laced rampart could be burnt down once a conflagration got going was a powerful stimulus to change the design of ramparts to less combustible dump construction with stone revetments or glacis form.

Late forts and enclosed oppida

Late Iron Age use of hillforts

On current evidence there seems to have been no significant late Iron Age activity at Alfred's Castle, Uffington, Segsbury, Rams Hill, Castle Hill or Taplow at this period (Gosden and Lock 2003, 75; Miles *et al.* 119-24; Lock and Gosden 2006; Bradley and Ellison 1975; Allen *et al.* forthcoming a; Allen *et al.* forthcoming d), nor is late Iron Age occupation a

feature of forts in the Middle Thames Valley (eg Stevenson 1999; Jones forthcoming). This does not mean that all these forts were totally abandoned or that there are not exceptions. For example, at Castle Hill there are a few sherds of late Iron Age pottery from the ditch and, in the light of the earlier Iron Age burials, it is interesting that a significant number of Roman cremation and inhumation burials have been found around the hillfort, suggesting that it remained an important focus of burial throughout the Roman period, even when it ceased to be defensive. The sequence of middle to late Iron Age and Roman shrines at Uley high on the Cotswolds is also striking in this respect (Woodward and leach 1993). The small fort at The Ditches, North Cerney became a settlement of some status (Trow 1998) and other sites like Blewburton may have been re-occupied and refortified some time after 100 BC, even if not for very long (Harding 1972, 50). However, while there are some exceptions it seems clear in general terms that hillforts in the Thames Valley ceased to be of much importance in the late Iron Age after about 100 BC.

Enclosed oppida

A more distinct feature of the later middle and late Iron Age is the fortification of a number of large valley floor settlements as 'enclosed oppida' (Figs 9.19 & 9.20). These are striking both because the density of settlement features was apparently much greater than that of the earlier forts and also because some were on a significantly larger scale, and many sited on the valley floor.

At Salmonsbury a more or less square area of land occupying about 22.5 ha at the confluence of the Dickler and Windrush was enclosed by a double ditch and banks (Dunning 1976). A stream now crosses the northern side of the enclosed area, and the low-lying position of the site makes it possible that the ditches acted as moats. The limited excavation of the interior produced some evidence of earlier Iron Age occupation and good evidence, supported by recent geophysical survey, that there was an intensive middle to late Iron Age settlement with numerous houses, pits and other features, including several human burials. The defences may have been created to enclose a pre-existing extensive middle Iron Age settlement or, alternatively, the settlement could have grown from smaller scale origins within them, but they probably date to the later middle to late Iron Age.

On the other side of the Thames from Castle Hill the well known fortified site at Dyke Hills at Dorchester-on-Thames was defined by a single very large ditch between two banks, almost certainly dug as an artificial river channel cutting off an area of about 44 ha bounded on the other three sides by the rivers Thames and Thame (Fig. 9.21). About a quarter of the interior was dry gravel terrace surrounded by lower-lying floodplain land. The drier area is known from aerial photography to include extensive settlement traces but they have never been excavated. They may have originated from a period before the massive defensive ditch was dug, probably some time in the late Iron Age.

At the confluence of the Thames and the Ock at Abingdon a dense settlement of uncertain extent was enclosed in the late Iron Age in a similar way to Dyke Hills (Fig. 9.22). Three curving ditches to the north and west enclosed an area of about 33 ha, bounded on the other sides by the Rivers Thames and Ock (Allen 1989; 1990b; 1991; 1993; 1994; 2000; Allen *et al.* forthcoming a). The two main inner and outer ditches were 10-12 m wide and 2.6 m deep and originally flowed with water, probably capturing the river Stert and diverting it along the ditches. Radiocarbon dates from the lower fills provide a probable construction date somewhere between 200 cal BC and 55 cal AD. The third, much smaller ditch lay between the others and may not have been a continuous part of the defences or contemporary with the other ditches. A strip 10 m wide inside the inner ditch devoid of late Iron Age and early Roman features suggests the position of a major bank that was levelled and thrown back into the ditch to allow redevelopment in the 2nd century AD.

Excavations covering about 1 ha of the interior revealed a dense sequence of intercutting pits, ditches and gullies. The settlement originated in the early Iron Age and had an important middle to late Iron Age component, followed by further dense early Roman activity. The distribution of finds from numerous small-scale excavations in Abingdon (eg Parrington and Balkwill 1975; Parrington 1979) suggests that most late Iron Age and early Roman finds come from an area of at least 15 ha within the defences, and that it was not until the later Roman period that occupation spread beyond them as Abingdon developed as a small Roman town.

Cassington Big Ring, on a spur of gravel overlooking the river Evenlode and the floodplain of the Thames, is a 5.2 ha site defined by a single large oval ditch. Much of the interior was destroyed by gravel digging in the 1950s with only limited investigation, though the aerial photographic evidence is fairly clear, showing numerous Bronze Age ring ditches. Whether due to the presence of these ancient burial places or for other reasons, the site was not a focus of earlier Iron Age settlement, although a number of settlements existed nearby.

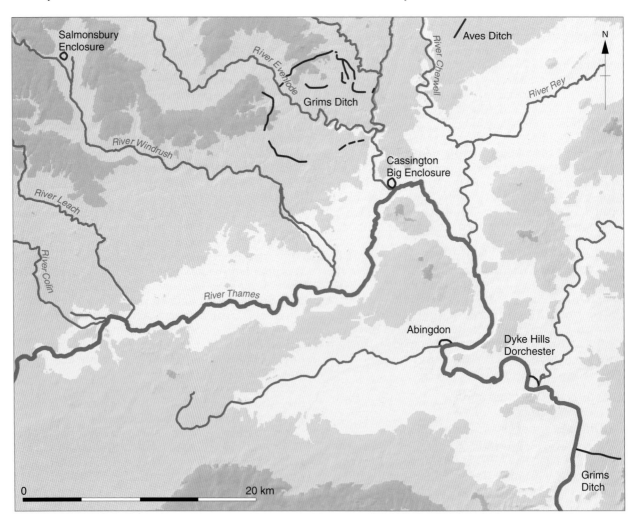

Fig. 9.19   Major later Iron Age earthworks in the Upper Thames Valley (see Fig. 9.28 for wider territorial context)

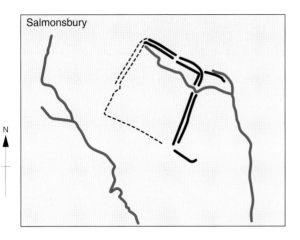

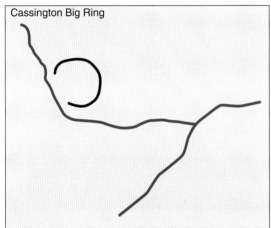

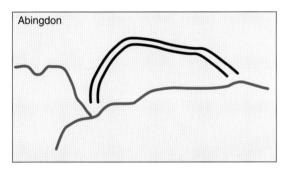

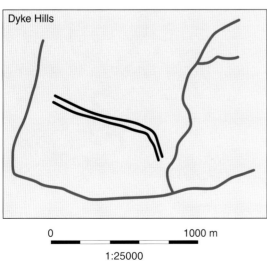

There is evidence of late Iron Age occupation from domestic debris from the unfinished ditch of the Big Ring, but there were few pits and only four early kilns in the interior and no imported pottery or other high status objects. Despite the defensive ditch there is nothing to suggest that it developed into a densely occupied high status settlement site on a par with Salmonsbury, Abingdon or Dyke Hills, or for that matter the smaller high status site at The Ditches. It appears that after the initial construction around the beginning of the 1st century AD, its substantial ditch was allowed to silt up and become overgrown for half a century. It may have been the threat of Roman invasion that triggered the redigging of the partly silted ditch, but in the event nothing much transpired and the site sank back into the obscurity of an ordinary farm. The Roman military strategy was to bypass all these major late Iron Age defensive settlements and establish a fortress at Alchester (Sauer 2000).

No equivalent settlements have been defined within the Middle Thames Valley, possibly reflecting a different geo-political background arising from the more limited pattern of Iron Age settlement in this part of the valley. Some way further down the tidal Thames a major late Iron Age settlement overlooking the river at Woolwich might be comparable.

Territorial oppida and proto-towns

The term 'territorial oppidum' is applied to major tribal centres of the late Iron Age which are often characterised by extensive dyke systems, though in practice the extent of these differs substantially, as does their proposed role as centres of settlement. The main places considered here are Calleva, Verlamion, Bagendon and the North Oxfordshire Grims Ditch (Figs. 9.23-4).

The Atrebatic centre at Calleva (Silchester) and the Catuvellaunian one at Verlamion (later Verulamium, now St Albans) are in the Middle Thames Valley south and north of the Thames, and both became Roman cities. In the Upper Thames Valley a major Dobunnic centre was established at Bagendon which was succeeded by the separate Corinium (Cirencester) as a major Roman city. With uncertain tribal associations, the sheer physical extent of the North Oxfordshire Grims Ditch poses numerous challenges to coherent investigation and its character remains especially enigmatic. Further from the floor of the valley, high on the Cotswolds at Minchinhampton Common the irregular series of dykes known as the Bulwarks are equally enigmatic.

The site with the least extensive dykes and the clearest enclosed settlement area is Calleva (Silchester) where the main Iron Age inner earthwork defences enclosed 32 ha (Fig. 9.25). The 'inner earthwork', which was subsumed into the later

Fig. 9.20 Late Iron Age valley forts or enclosed oppida of the Upper Thames Valley

town, may or may not have been pre-conquest (Fulford and Corney 1984, 287-8) though the character of the very orderly, seemingly well planned internal settlement (see below) probably makes this likely (Fulford and Timby 2000). Of the other possible pre-Roman earthworks there the most impressive are west of the Roman town wall, with the section in Rampier Copse still surviving almost 5 m above the ditch.

In the area later to be occupied by the basilica there is evidence of dense occupation developing from about 0-25 BC onwards. It housed a popula-

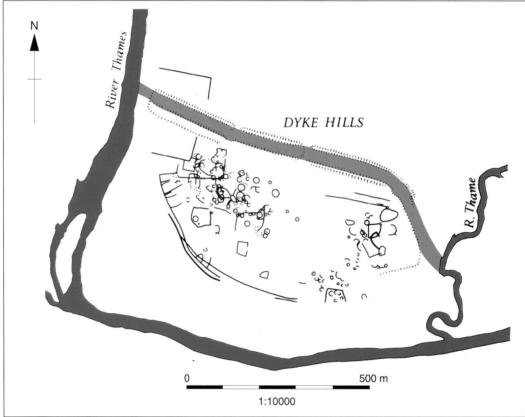

Fig. 9.21   Dyke Hills, Dorchester-on-Thames

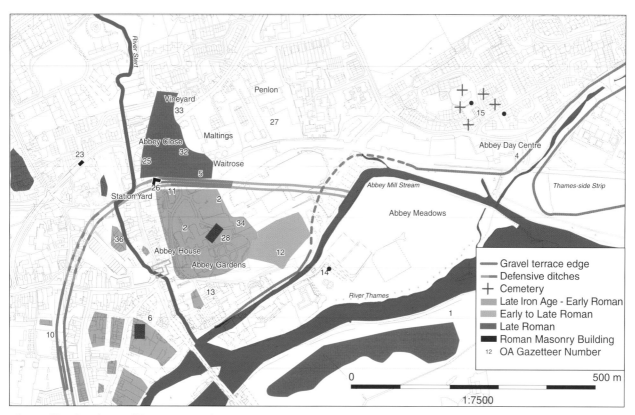

Areas of late Iron Age and Roman occupation

The late Iron Age inner defensive ditch at Station Yard

Fig. 9.22 Late Iron Age and Romano-British enclosed site at Abingdon

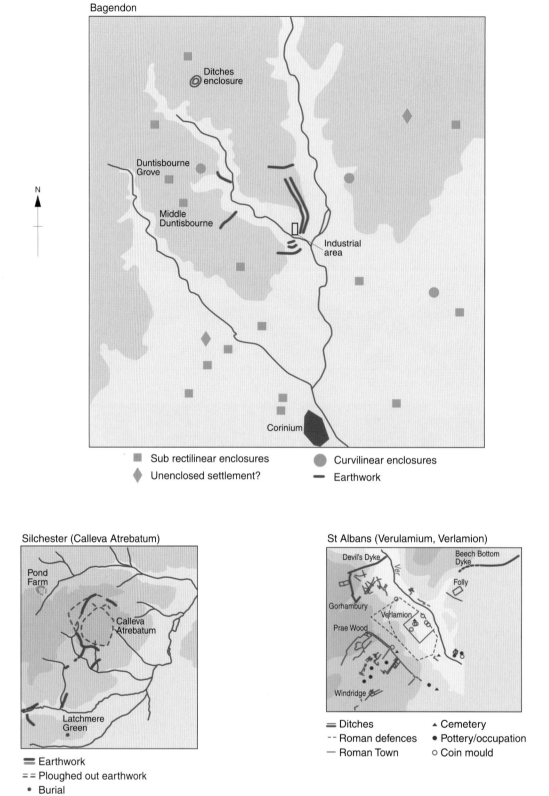

Fig. 9.23   *Territorial oppida:* (above) Bagendon; (below left) Silchester (Calleva Atrebatum) *and* (below right) St Albans (Verulamium, *Verlamion)*

tion that had adopted a significant degree of Roman acculturation, including Roman forms of styli and graffiti in Latin, imports of pottery, oil, wines and other preserved food from France and the Mediterranean, together with other indications of a Romanised diet. The remains of a rectilinear street-pattern, rectangular plots and timber-framed buildings with orderly rows of pits and wells indicate organised regular planning of the settlement. This is comparable to contemporary urban centres in northern France (Haselgrove 2007, 509), but not well-paralleled in Britain. It is not clear whether the whole was laid out in this way by the early 1st century AD but, if so, Calleva would have had the appearance of a Roman town with a regular street grid and town blocks (*insulae*). Indeed, in some senses the town plan represents as much an import as the traded goods that the settlement consumed.

Bryant (2007) has suggested that north of the Thames there were six major Catuvellaunian social, religious and economic foci in the eastern Chilterns, at Verlamion, Braughing, Baldock, Welwyn, Wheathampstead and Ashridge. He has challenged traditional ideas of what constituted oppida in late Iron Age Britain, concluding that while all of them reflect some aspects of a 'central place' as defined in economic, political or religious terms, the differences between them are too great to assume they all had similar origins and roles.

Several wealthy late Iron Age burials, including three in the Welwyn area and two near Baldock, demonstrate the existence of a powerful ruling aristocracy in the surrounding area. Most impressive of all is the Catuvellaunian 'royal' burial housed in what must have been a very impressive tomb and shrine just outside Verlamion (St Albans)

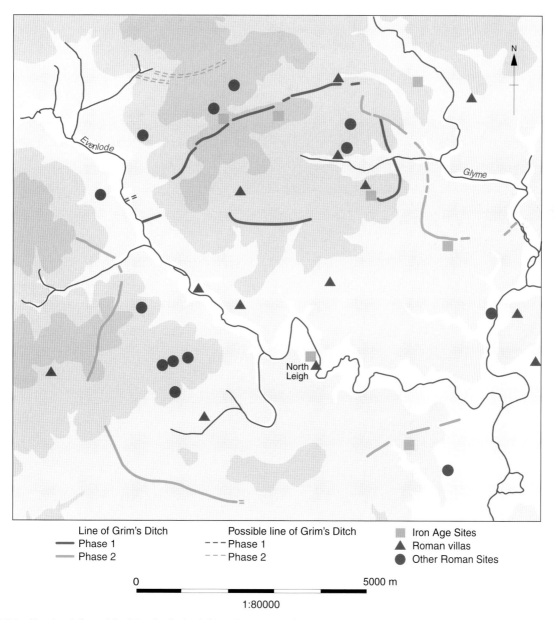

Line of Grim's Ditch   Possible line of Grim's Ditch   ▨ Iron Age Sites
— Phase 1   - - - Phase 1   ▲ Roman villas
— Phase 2   - - - Phase 2   ● Other Roman Sites

0   5000 m

1:80000

Fig. 9.24   Territorial oppida: North Oxfordshire Grims Ditch

at Folly Lane (Niblett 1999). Verlamion is broadly defined by an impressive network of major dykes, including the curious Beech Bottom Dyke linking the heads of two dry valleys. Bryant (2007, 71-2) believes this might have been a ceremonial routeway into the religious complex rather than a dyke in the more conventional sense of a large ditch and bank. There is no clear single focus of occupation within the complex, nor is there a definitive early defensive enclosure. Although dykes, cemeteries and high status burials and clusters of settlement are known at the other sites, any of which could have been sub-regional centres of power, it is Verlamion that appears to represent 'the civitas cult centre of the Catuvellaunii' (Bryant 2007, 78). Recent discussions by Haselgrove and Millett (1997, 285-6), Niblett (1992; 1999) and Bryant (2007) have stressed its role as a major ceremonial centre and religious complex, coupled with having a royal mint. By about AD 10 Verlamion had emerged as an important political centre, and was probably the royal residence, cult centre and burial place of the Catuvellaunian kings. It would naturally have attracted intensive social and economic interchange and domestic settlement, but it does not seem to have developed as a significant late Iron Age urban centre like Calleva.

At the western end of the Thames Valley in Dobunnic territory, Bagendon was another network of dykes with some evidence of high status imported and exchanged pottery and other objects, and of iron smelting and a mint. These indicate a place of some political and economic importance as a source of materials for exchange and trade. It is widely seen as the key centre of Dobunnic aristocracy but only a small area has been excavated. While it was prolific in terms of finds of highly significant character, very little is understood of the form or extent of contemporary settlement (Clifford 1961; Moore 2006).

At about 9 km across, the North Oxfordshire Grims Ditch is by far the largest of these late Iron Age territorial oppida, and the most enigmatic (Fig. 9.24). If it was intended to define an area within which settlement and political centres could be developed for economic, political and social activity like the other three sites, no distinct centre of importance has been found. There is a possibility that it never developed as such a centre, although after the Roman conquest Akeman Street was aligned to pass through it and it was the focus for a number of early Roman villas. Although there is ambiguous evidence of direct development of these villas from pre-conquest farms they may, nevertheless, indicate that special settlement rights might have been established. The possible political context of this is discussed further below.

Territorial linear ditches

As we have seen in Chapter 3, the major linear dyke systems on the Berkshire Downs and the Chilterns,

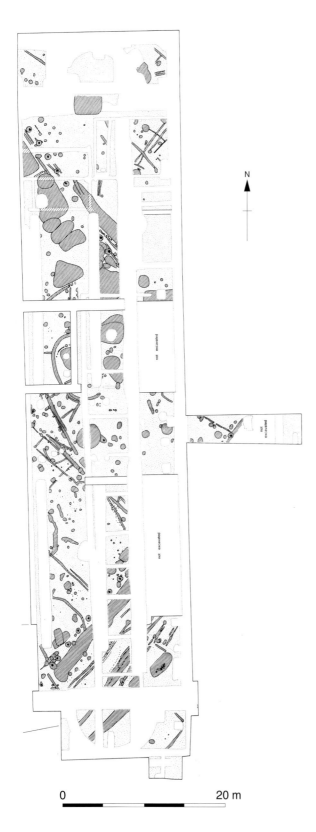

Fig. 9.25 Late Iron Age Calleva: the rectilinear layout of ditches, fencelines and beam slots of buildings fronting onto probable streets suggests highly organised urban planning early in the 1st century AD

known as the Grims Ditch, are thought to be of late Bronze Age or early Iron Age origin, though Lock *et al.* (2005, 136) refer to the Berkshire Downs ditch as late Iron Age. They are likely to have been significant land divisions, perhaps related to other ditches and dykes defining large-scale landuse units. Whether they also defined larger scale political entities is less clear but possible.

The construction of major earthworks in connection with territorial politics became much more common during the late Iron Age around the turn of the first millennia BC/AD. Recent work on Aves Ditch (Sauer 2005) and the South Oxfordshire Grims Ditch (Cromarty *et al.* 2006) has indicated that these are likely to be late Iron Age earthworks. Together with the enclosed oppida and the North Oxfordshire Grims Ditch they represent a group of major civil engineering works of about the same period, all on or close to tribal territorial bound-

aries. Simply in terms of the logistics and visibility of their construction they would have been major statements of political control – a massive coercion of labour but on an essentially peaceful basis.

The South Oxfordshire Grims Ditch, consisted of a ditch 4 to 8 m wide and 2 to 3 m deep with a substantial bank on its north side (Fig. 9.26). It was built to demarcate or cut off a very large area of territory within a great loop of the Thames from a point just south of modern day Wallingford across the south end of the Chilterns to a point just north of Henley, though the eastern end of its course is still somewhat speculative (Bradley 1968, 2; Hinchliffe 1975).

Previously there was much debate as to whether it was likely to be late prehistoric or Saxon, but excavations of the western end where it was crossed by the Wallingford bypass (Cromarty *et al.* 2006, 157-200) produced a small amount of late Iron Age material in and beneath the bank and early Roman

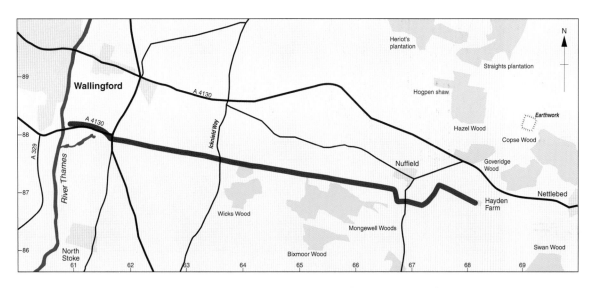

Fig. 9.26   Late Iron Age territorial linear dykes: South Oxfordshire Grims Ditch

Fig. 9.27   Artist's impression of the Grims Ditch at Aldermarston, Berks. This linear earthwork is still undated but is not dissimilar in scale from Aves Ditch

material in deposits reflecting initial erosion of the bank. This reinforced Hinchliffe's previous conclusions (1975) that the boundary is most likely to be of late Iron Age origin. An intriguing but unexplained element of the west end of the Ditch at Mongewell (Fig. 9.26) is how its line deviates slightly where a short stream rises from a spring (now an ornamental lake) to create a triangular area with the Thames forming the third side. It is not clear if this was intended to create an area of settlement or perhaps some form of control point for passage along the river.

Further north, in the Cherwell Valley, Aves Ditch is a broadly comparable linear dyke traceable over at least 4.2 km, and probably significantly longer, running in a straight line at an angle to the river

Cherwell (Fig. 9.27). Its northward extent beyond Fritwell is not known, while its southern end heads for the Cherwell at a point where Akeman Street would later cross it. Small scale excavations have recently shown the ditch to be 3-4 m wide and 1.5 m deep (Sauer 2005). It cut a pre-existing Iron Age settlement enclosure and a small amount of pottery, probably of late Iron Age origin, is the main indication of its date. A broad archaeomagnetic date of *c* 250 BC-AD 150 provides very broad agreement. At 5.8 m^3 per metre length, it is reckoned that construction of the identifiable length would have taken 170,000-290,000 man-hours – 100 people for 215-360 eight hour days. Sauer suggests that the dyke represents a territiorial boundary at the western limit of Catuvellaunian influence.

Political geography: political centres, tribal areas, rivers as boundaries, hillforts and central places

The notion of certain places being 'central' to a large geographical and social territory, functioning as intensive settlements, hubs of exchange and redistribution and the seat of social, religious or political authority has become almost synonymous with hillforts, especially in relation to the so-called 'developed' hillforts of the middle to late Iron Age in Wessex, such as Danebury (Cunliffe 1983; 1984). This concept has been challenged (eg by Hill 1996), both because as settlements many hillforts are not very different from other settlements or were not much occupied, and because the idea makes various assumptions about the character of Iron Age society, such as hierarchies of settlement and social status, that do not necessarily apply everywhere. Some regions do not have hillforts, or if they do they display rather different characteristics (Collis 1996; Hill 1996).

In the Thames Valley there is little evidence that hilltop and valley floor enclosures or later forts ever developed or fulfilled all the roles associated with 'central places.' Nevertheless, the construction, maintenance, and use of hillforts in a variety of roles as gathering places would have made them important as social and political focal points and potential refuges.

However, if forts were not functioning as 'central places' it raises the question of whether any other places can be seen as acting as socio-economic and political hubs. The most obvious candidates would be either especially large settlements like Bourton-on-the-Water and Ashville/Wyndyke Furlong, which have been seen as precursors of the enclosed oppida of Salmonsbury and Abingdon, or the special midden sites like Runnymede and Whitecross Farm, which also appear to have been special gathering places. But it is doubtful how far these can be regarded as centres of political and economic power, especially in the case of Ashville and Whitecross Farm.

At Castle Hill the combination of major settlement, midden and defensive enclosure and fort associated with ritualistic activities could be seen as a kind of disaggregated 'central place', where several elements came together at one location but were not confined within the defensive element. There are other defensive enclosures with external settlements of which we know even less, and it is possible that these too were places of importance for a combination of economic, social, religious and political reasons. An intriguing feature of the Castle Hill complex is how the relationship between the defensive enclosure and the external settlement was established at an early stage and continued to develop through the early and middle Iron Age.

For most of the late Bronze Age to middle Iron Age awareness of politics would have been at local level through communities negotiating their rights and responsibilities in the sharing and management of land resources and, on a less local scale, through occasional contribution to the construction and maintenance of local defensive enclosures and more regular engagement in communal gatherings for religious, social and economic purposes.

Heads of families, clan leaders and tribal councils probably existed as a hierarchy of authority through which laws, rights and customs were agreed. In practical terms it may have been local clan chiefs or warlords who exercised most political power. Compared with earlier periods, the means of commanding loyalty and exerting authority in the late Bronze Age and earlier Iron Age would have been different in its physical expression: hillforts instead of henges, more sedentary settlement and physical division and enclosure of land and, especially in the centuries up to *c* 800 BC, a strong emphasis on weaponry and other metalwork as the currency of prestige. Underlying this, the social hierarchy of different layers of kinship, tribal or economic allegiances might not have changed much over several centuries.

But by the end of the later prehistoric period a different picture emerges. Control of territory had become increasingly important as communities became more settled, while at the same time existing family, clan and tribal hierarchies had allowed the emergence of an aristocracy whose status may have been based at least in part on their control of land and economic resources. From this it was a relatively short step, under the influence of overseas models of power, personal ambition and increasing practical economic and political interchange, to establish territorially defined kingdoms led by identifiable individuals. The recognition of named leaders, some styling themselves king on their coinage, the hints of Dobunnic aristocrats competing for control, and the political intrigues with Rome that established client kings sympathetic to the Empire in the south-east, all suggest that what may have started as a social hierarchy was politically rationalised into a much clearer tribal structure in the later Iron Age.

This change was associated with a clearer focus of political and economic power in specific locations and with particular people in the late Iron Age. It was probably driven by a mixture of economic factors and local, regional and external political relations that we can only surmise. Nevertheless, it may not be unrealistic to see this as the emergence of a form of politics that we recognise today – remote authority seeking to impose centralised control, with power vested in a few individuals concerned with being identifiable leaders and much concerned with geo-political issues that seemed to have little bearing on people's ordinary lives.

The existence of tribal territories with aristocratic and kingly leaders, some of whose identities we know, is clear from historical sources. Furthermore, a reasonably good idea of the geographical extent of these three major territories can be deduced from the distribution of tribal coinage (Fig. 9.28), although this is not without some problems of circular argument (Haselgrove 1996; Creighton 2000). The general impression is that the emergence of these stronger tribal entities represented a fairly major shift or coalescing of some smaller, less well defined geo-political entities. In most cases the earlier defensive sites ceased to be maintained and refurbished and there is little evidence of occupation. The people of the Thames

Valley would have been encouraged, through means such as the circulation of coinage and the construction of major public works, to appreciate that they were now the subjects of self-styled kingly rulers seeking to exert real political power over tribal territories that may have been familiar in terms of social and cultural identity, but not the real seat of political power.

It is likely that the Thames and some of its tributaries like the Cherwell emerged as natural political

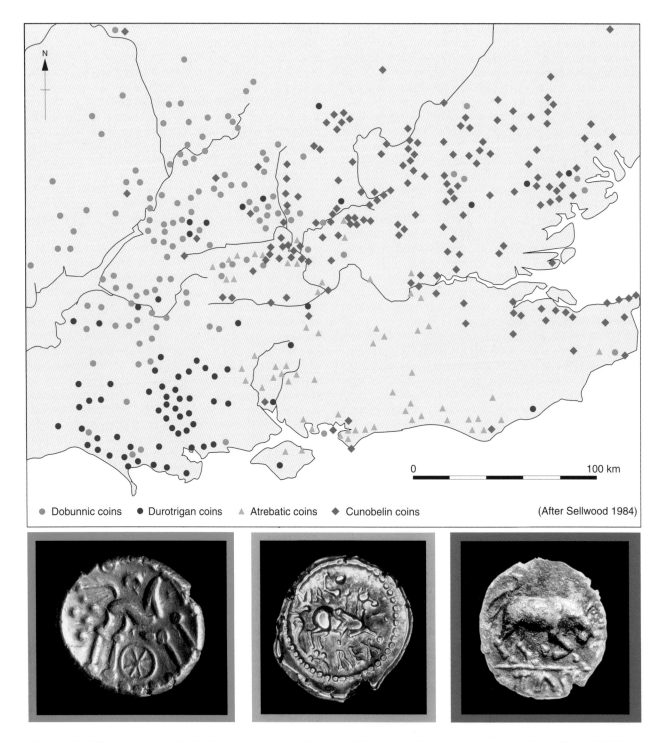

● Dobunnic coins   ● Durotrigan coins   ▲ Atrebatic coins   ◆ Cunobelin coins   (After Sellwood 1984)

Fig. 9. 28   The emergence of tribal territories in the Thames Valley as evidenced by coinage (after Sellwood 1984a)

boundaries at the same time as remaining favoured areas for essentially peaceful settlement. This dual role of the river as boundary as well as a thread of prosperous settlement and communication almost certainly had deep cultural and economic origins. We have already seen that distributions of various objects reflecting local and regional and wider exchange networks, such as briquetage, querns, pottery as well as later coinage, appear to respect the river. For a long time the Thames had been an important symbolic repository for weaponry, possibly reflecting a highly complex set of 'liminal' attributes of life and death, overworld and under-world, into which a distinction of cultural or tribal 'belonging' would naturally fit. The possibility that the deposition of weaponry somehow symbolised peaceful co-existence between potentially warring neighbours concurs with the ambiguity of a warrior cult and the apparent peace and prosperity of ordinary existence.

Late Iron Age power politics

The history of political relationships between would-be tribal kings and powerful local leaders is patchy but at least some bare bones are known. Even if we have little clear idea of exactly who built what or precisely when and why they did so, the outcomes of large-scale construction works are evident archaeologically.

Continental trade was already well established long before the mid 1st century BC, but Caesar's campaigns and eventual annexation of Gaul in 58-51 BC and expeditions to Britain in 55 and 54 BC, brought Rome into close political contact with Britain for the first time. There is still much debate about what Caesar achieved by his military incursions into Britain. Some argue that they had sufficient political impact to be seen as a virtual conquest of south-eastern Britain at this time (Creighton 2000, 216), but others believe that the invasions were militarily unimportant, though with deeper significance in ideological terms. Either way, Britain now lay on the immediate frontier of the Roman Empire, with all the increased economic and political contact that this would bring.

Even before Caesar's expeditions large tribal entities existed in Britain, probably developing in the later 2nd/early 1st century BC with the increasing concentration of power within elite groups (Creighton 2000, 216). For those in positions of leadership, and particularly those with political and economic ambitions to develop their power bases, the growing contact with the expanding Roman Empire, particularly after Caesar's expeditions of 55 and 54 BC, offered important opportunities for advancement. Caesar's *Gallic Wars* provides a brief and highly polemical account of British society at the time, mentioning a number of kingly leaders. References are gleaned from other classical texts which, together with the increasing occurrence of inscribed coins, provide an indication of how the dynastic politics of southern Britain emerged and developed in the late Iron Age.

Over much of southern England between the English Channel and the Thames the Atrebates held sway with important centres at Chichester and Winchester. They established another major centre at Calleva (Silchester) in the northern part of their territory (Fulford and Corney 1984; Fulford and Timby 2000). The earliest inscribed coins from this southern region are of Commios, who may have had influence over large areas of central southern England, possibly including parts of the Thames Valley. He seems to have been succeeded by Tincomarus and Epillus in the later 1st century BC. Pre-Roman coins of Epillus self-styled 'REX', which carry the marks of CALLE or CALLEV are generally believed to have been produced at Calleva about 0 BC to AD 10. Reading University's long-running Silchester project provides the following glimpse of late Iron Age politics:

> *'Eppillus described himself as son of Commius, a claim he shared with two other leaders, Tincomarus and Verica. While Tincomarus, fleeing to Rome by AD 7, was probably ousted by Eppillus, Eppillus himself appears to have been ejected by his brother Verica who ruled until the beginning of the 40s, when he was forced out of Britain, probably by the Catuvellaunian prince, Epatticus or Caratacus. It is reasonable to presume that all three ruled from Silchester for some or all of their respective reigns. The fact that they all claimed to be descendants of a certain Commius, who is usually identified as the Gallic leader of the Atrebates who escaped to Britain from Julius Caesar about 50 BC, adds weight to the hypothesis that Commius was the original founder of Calleva.'*

North of the Thames the dip slope of the Chilterns was rapidly transformed from a relative backwater into one of the most politically and economically important parts of Britain, with Verlamion emerging as its royal centre (Nibblett 1992; 1999; Bryant 2007). Cassivellaunus, who apparently led a larger conglomeration of lesser tribal rulers of the Catuvellauni and Trinovantes north of the Thames, was the first named leader of stature. Inscribed coins of Tasciovanus dating to the later 1st century BC are amongst the earliest of this dynasty, but those bearing the name of his son, Cunobelin (c AD 10-40), many in silver and bronze imitating classical prototypes, are much more widespread. They are distributed across much of eastern England, with some south of the Thames and west of the Cherwell, indicating the height of the political and economic influence of this tribal grouping. It seems that Cunobelin's brother Epaticcus took control of the Calleva region from the Atrebates in the late 30s to 40s AD, to be succeeded by Caratacus just prior to the Claudian invasion.

To the west and north-west the Dobunni also seem to have been subject to political rivalries with competing aristocrats vying for control, though the dynastic links between rulers named on Dobunnic coinage are far less evident. The earliest seem to have been those of Bodvoc and/or Corio, perhaps ruling different parts of Dobunnic territory simultaneously in the later 1st century BC. Other named rulers include Anted, Comux, Eisu, Catti and Inam (Van Arsdell 1989, 272-83), but it is unclear if there was ever a large unified and distinct 'Dobunnic territory.' One literary source from the time of the invasion suggests some degree of Catuvellaunian hegemony over them (Dio Cassius 60.20.2).

The Dobunni had a major pre-Roman centre at Bagendon, which like Verlamion and Calleva has produced evidence of being a mint though the nature of the settlement there is uncertain and it seems clear that there was far less development of external relations with Rome. The North Oxfordshire Grims Ditch also falls within presumed Dobunnic territory west of the Cherwell but close to the probable tribal boundary with the Catuvellauni.

Within this context of the emergence of self-styled kingdoms and dynastic struggles, the major territorial oppida can be seen as having a special role as centres or expressions of power. While the enclosed oppida bear some resemblance to earlier hillforts, albeit on a larger scale and with different status as settlements, the extensive linear dyke systems associated with territorial oppida were not defensive, but seem to have been intended to demarcate areas of special political, religious and economic importance. They were massive undertakings, and their construction would have required significant numbers of people living in the area for some time. Like the earlier hillforts, it may be that it was the mobilisation of the resources needed to construct them and their visible presence as a major civil engineering achievement that initially fulfilled their main political purpose.

In some respects the current absence of a focus of late Iron Age settlement within the North Oxfordshire Grims Ditch and, more particularly, the absence of a major Roman town within or near the complex compared with the more developed nature of the other examples, raises some interesting questions about the how the territorial oppida related to their political opportunities and local patterns of settlement.

At Verlamion and Calleva political relations with Roman interests ensured favourable conditions for growth and more or less direct transition into fully fledged Roman cities established as administrative centres for the tribal areas, with no sign of a major early Roman fortress nearby. Bagendon did not follow quite the same route. It seems likely that it reflects the initial establishment of pre-Roman aristocratic or kingly control and associated exchange and a possible focus of settlement of uncertain extent. Historical sources and archaeology indicate that, compared with the Atrebates and Catuvellaunian/Trinovantian tribes, there may not have been the same degree of established political contact and economic relations with Rome to allow direct transition towards development as a

Roman city after the conquest. Instead, Cirencester was founded from Roman military origins at the initial frontier of control, though likely through peaceful means.

The North Oxfordshire Grims Ditch is different again. It could be seen to reflect the same sort of expression of power, but not developing beyond an initial stage of ability to amass and mobilise a major workforce, possibly in two or more stages as suggested by Copeland (1988). On present evidence the area never developed as a major tribal or sub-tribal seat of power or economic exchange. It certainly did not become an urban centre under the Roman regime and was perhaps never intended to. A recognised feature of the North Oxfordshire Grims Ditch is the significant cluster of early Roman villas within its circuit. It is generally assumed that these must reflect an early development of substantial farming estates in the area, though only some of the villas were built on the site of pre-conquest farms. It might be that the huge area covered by the Grims Ditch defined an area of special land rights or estates intended to form the foundations of a cluster of settlements from which a more significant political and economic centre might have developed. Alternatively such estates might have been carved out after it was realised that the enclave created within the Grims Ditch was never going to work as a major centre. If some special form of landholding did apply within the area defined by Grims Ditch, such estates could have been valued assets by the 1st century AD and perhaps could more easily be developed as villas than in areas where land was under more communal control.

Another enigma about the North Oxfordshire Grims Ditch is the power responsible for such a massive undertaking. It might be seen as a Dobunnic attempt to establish another power centre at the eastern end of their territory (Copeland 1988, 287) but, more speculatively, Sauer (2005, 30-6) suggests that it could be seen as a Catuvellaunian attempt to expand into Dobunnic territory at the western extremity of their area of control. Allen (2000, 28-9) has argued against this.

Much of this is speculative, but the general thrust of Copeland's argument, seeing the North Oxfordshire Grims Ditch as an expression of political control over territory that was only ever half completed, is probably the best explanation for something that otherwise makes little sense. Furthermore, we cannot say that it was a 'failure'. The very act of mobilising the labour force to construct such massive earthworks might have been a sufficient expression of control to represent the stamp of political authority on a large surrounding area.

What is perhaps most noticeable about the four territorial oppida in the Thames basin is their different character and different trajectories of development. The two easterly centres at Verlamion and Calleva were the least extensive in terms of earthwork dykes. They seem to have been within the tribal control of client kings closely connected to the Roman empire and developed more or less directly into Roman cities. They lie within what Haselgrove (1982) has characterised as a 'core zone' of economic and political influence.

In the 'peripheral zone' outside this core area Bagendon was in the territory of the Dobunni, who were not in close alliance with Rome and seem to have been led by competing aristocrats. Unlike Calleva and Verlamion, Bagendon did not develop into a major Roman town, but was replaced by the *civitas* capital that developed out of the nearby Roman fort at Cirencester. The North Oxfordshire Grims Ditch, also on the boundary between 'core' and 'periphery' and between Dobunnic and Catuvellaunian territory, lacks clear evidence of high status pre-conquest settlement, and it never became a Roman urban centre. This conforms to the idea of developments in the 'core' zone being driven by external economic and political influences.

Hill (2007) challenges the idea of the 'core and periphery' as taking insufficient account of other longer term economic and social development of previous centuries both within and beyond the core zone, noting that major changes, some of similar character, were also happening elsewhere. One of those was the emergence of individual aristocratic or kingly leaders, as evident in Ireland.

It seems nonetheless likely that both the zone of contact and history of established settlement patterns and land holding were important considerations. The way that late Iron Age dynastic politics emerged would have been dictated by available opportunities and this would have varied regionally, related to long term settlements and established land rights. An intriguing point is that Calleva and most of the Catuvellaunian centres reviewed by Bryant (2007) seem to have developed in areas that were not important in the middle Iron Age, but may have been relative backwaters. These areas may have offered relatively unconstrained opportunities

for building new power bases exploiting under-used but basically fertile land, with the advantage of relatively close continental contacts that provided both political and economic advantages.

Further up the Thames Valley life could have been a great deal more difficult for aspiring political leaders, with the valley bottom already fully exploited and embedded in ancient rights, with the surrounding hills already having undergone two or three centuries of development with the proliferation of enclosed farming settlements. Bagendon and the Ditches site were established between the densely settled Severn and Upper Thames Valleys (Moore 2006), in an area where a number of enclosed settlements have been shown to be relatively devoid of settlement and possibly set in a wooded environment (Mudd 1999, 521-3). This suggests a relative backwater, but with less good continental contacts than those further east and south. The North Oxfordshire Grims Ditch also avoided the most densely settled part of the Upper Thames, but it was close to the tribal boundaries which may have made it less likely to succeed, even though it was possible to mobilise resources to construct the earthworks.

The politics of the late Iron Age in the Upper Thames Valley is thus an intriguing picture of frontier rivalry and power struggles expressed through the ability to coerce massive labour forces, but probably involving little or no actual conflict. The real centres of power were far to the east, west or south of the Upper Thames frontier zone and, except when increasingly powerful and far-off tribal leaders decided to expand or consolidate their control over the further reaches of their or their neighbours' territory, ordinary people were quite happy to get on peaceably together, possibly paying little regard to political territory except in so far as it may have determined where they had to send tribute and whose earthworks they had to help construct.

Chapter 10 – Conclusions: the impact of change and legacies of late prehistoric society

Looking back at what we have now reviewed, we can draw together some strands of evidence for how people understood their surroundings – what they saw as their ordinary living space, their contacts with a wider world and their personal and communal horizons. These outlooks and relationships changed over 15 centuries, and it is worth considering what factors shaped the main changes that successive generations saw. In Chapter 1 a number of possible 'drivers of change' were suggested as a framework for reviewing broad patterns of social and economic development, and we can now briefly consider how some of these factors helped shape human society and the environment of the Thames Valley in late prehistory, and what sort of legacy they left.

Population dynamics

In the past archaeologists tended to be assertive in their assumptions about the interactions of population and cultural, social and economic development. From the 1930s to the 1960s the ruling theory of late prehistoric Britain was that change resulted from an influx of continental invaders, resulting in both population and social change through a process of cultural diffusion, both from overseas and within Britain. In the 1970s and 1980s such theories were largely dismissed and models based more on population dynamics, socio-economic pressures and technological or social 'breakthroughs' were developed (Cunliffe 1978). These ideas started with an assumption of population growth and then sought evidence for how such growth would have been limited by the carrying capacity of land, resulting in tensions (assumed to be evident from the construction of hillforts etc). These were seen as being released by breakthroughs in agricultural technology (new crops and better ploughs) and enhanced economic conditions (overseas trade, creation of oppida as centres of political and economic exchange) and social frameworks (the emergence of chiefdoms and kingship from more basic tribal networks).

The effects of population change have not figured much in recent approaches to later prehistory, perhaps partly because picking out, and arguably over-emphasising a few particular 'indicators' in this way is liable to over-simplify the general picture. Is this neglect justified? Clearly we cannot directly measure population change, but nor can we directly read the cosmological minds of prehistoric communities or measure their agricultural output. Yet that does not prevent us from developing

models to help us understand what influenced the evolving interaction between prehistoric people and the world. It is widely accepted that later prehistory was generally a period of substantial growth in population, albeit not evenly across the country. Although we have no direct archaeological evidence of rates of birth and death or of actual population levels, we cannot ignore the effects of population change as a major underlying factor influencing how life in late prehistoric Britain changed (Cunliffe 2005, 583-4).

Developing a model of population change

The general character of some key social developments in late prehistory, from mobile herding and horticultural communities to permanent sedentary farming settlements and the first hints of urbanism, makes it instructive to examine the role that population change may have played, both in influencing and being influenced by the changes that took place.

By 'guesstimating' possible population levels and rates of change over the duration of our period and adding some assumptions about the intensity of landuse in terms of arable and pastoral production, we can obtain some idea of whether population growth is likely to have led to significant pressure on resources.

This approach might seem speculative but the two principal parameters of the model – assumptions about the rate of population growth and relative productivity of arable or pastoral landuse – involve strong multiplier effects which mean that small adjustments to the variables make a big difference to the resulting pattern of hypothetical landuse. This is because on top of the typically exponential pattern of even modest population growth, there is a substantial (approximately five-fold) difference in the amount of land needed to raise animals for meat and dairy products as compared with growing crops to provide a roughly equivalent level of subsistence.

The series of graphs shown in Figure 10.1 represent a hypothetical calculation of how population growth might have affected landuse demand in the Upper Thames basin in late prehistory. This is based on a number of fairly arbitrary assumptions. For example, in *The Farming of Prehistoric Britain* Peter Fowler adopted the approach of considering how large the population of Britain might have been at the height of the Roman period and how fast it might have grown to get there from what was assumed to be a much lower base point in earlier prehistory (Fowler 1983, 32-6). Using pre-industrial census data we might reasonably guess that the Upper Thames area equated to roughly 2.5% of British population, giving a starting population of about 2,200 which, for the sake of this exercise we will assume is spread over an area equivalent to modern Oxfordshire (*c* 260 km²). Fowler's estimate of the average rate of growth in later prehistory was just over 0.22% per annum. This is modest compared with the fastest growth in Britain recorded since censuses began, of 1.67% per annum in the early years of industrialisation (Wrigley 1969, 54) or high rates of growth of between 0.7% and 3% per annum for forager communities (Shennan 2002, 118). Although there would have been fluctuations between much higher and much lower rates of growth, all we need for this exercise is a hypothetical long-term trend.

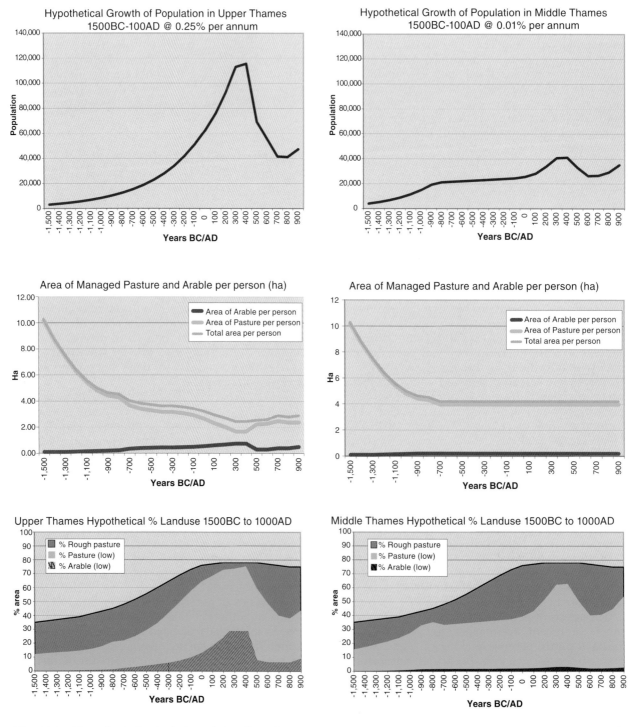

Fig. 10.1   *Hypothetical calculation of the effect of population growth on landuse in the Upper Thames Valley* (left) *and Middle Thames Valley* (right)

To examine the possible implications of the projected population growth for pressure on landuse some further assumptions need to be made about the amount of productive arable and pasture-land required per head of population. We cannot assume modern yields or production methods but a few authors (eg Gregg 1998) have examined the basis for making these types of calculation. They can to some extent be verified (and modified) by reference to experimental data from long term trials (Reynolds 1979; 1987-9; 1995) and by modern indicators of conservation stocking rates on unimproved pastures. At Gravelly Guy this approach was used to examine landuse requirements and the potential for generating surpluses for a group of settlements at Stanton Harcourt (Lambrick and Allen 2004, 484-7). Allowing for sufficient production to provide reserves for poor harvests, animal disease etc. and for generation of surplus for exchange, it can be calculated that a typical late prehistoric settled farming community would need about 0.45 ha of arable land per person and 2.45 ha of pasture. This involves a stocking rate of about two beasts per hectare, which compares with a recommended two and a half beasts (grazing units) for the intensively grazed ancient common pasture at Port Meadow, Oxford, though actual stocking levels have been much higher, leading to problems of deterioration in pasture (Camilla Lambrick pers. comm.).

However, figures that seem appropriate for developed Iron Age farming settlements like Gravelly Guy need not apply to earlier or later eras. For the purposes of this exercise we might envisage that at the end of the early Bronze Age at around 1500 BC, arable may have been at little more than a horticultural scale and grazing was at a much lower density. However, by the height of the Roman period the balance of landuse may have reached something more like Domesday. By then the estimated proportion of land devoted to arable for most of the Upper Thames area was between 50% and 75%. For the Middle Thames the figure was between 25% and 50%, but with significant areas thought to have been less than 25% (Darby 1977, 129-34, fig. 43).

Throughout the earlier part of the period it seems likely that there would have been extensive areas of semi-cleared rough grazing and scrub that would not have been used regularly as more trees were cleared, with new areas only gradually brought into fully managed condition. By the Roman period it is assumed that little unmanaged rough grazing was left. This appears to be the pattern at Sidlings Copse, where rough bracken and scrub were apparently persistent for much of later prehistory following initial clearance in the Bronze Age and prior to significantly increased grassland in the Roman period (Day 1991).

Discussion

The model for the Upper Thames suggests that by *c* 1500 BC a small population of a couple of thousand

mobile pastoralists with access to large areas of grazing land at the rate of 10 ha per person could easily be accommodated within the area. With exponential population growth at 0.2% per annum, if usage remained at that level it would have been necessary to clear the whole area for low intensity grazing by about 700 BC. This seems unlikely and in practice there may be many cultural and social reasons why ever-increasing forest clearance on a large scale became less satisfactory than managing cleared land in ways that gradually reduced the hectarage per head. So, for example, if intensity of grazing were lowered to about 4 ha per person not much more land need have been cleared until the late Bronze Age. However, by that time the need for more land would be escalating rapidly, with ongoing population growth, while the scope for reducing the grazing land per head would have started to be more problematic. Another strategy to get more from the existing land would be to shift the balance of landuse towards more arable combined with renewed clearance, as perhaps reflected in increased run-off detectable on the Thames floodplain (see Chapter 2). Only a modest increase in arable per head would have been needed for more intensive clearance and improved pastoral management to be kept in check for a few centuries.

But by the middle Iron Age the exponential growth in population would once again have put pressure on existing pastoral resources, perhaps resulting in the establishment of more permanent farmsteads and settlements. This would have allowed more intensive management of grazing in areas not previously densely settled, perhaps reflected in the proliferation of pastoral farmsteads on the lower lying terraces and floodplain of the Thames and the gradual proliferation of enclosed settlements on parts of the Cotswolds and Berkshire Downs. The model suggests that the balance of pastoral and arable landuse per head through the Iron Age could have been maintained at about the same level through more clearance and gradually taking in hand more rough pasture.

By the late Iron Age and into the Roman period it may again have ceased to be possible to produce enough food maintaining the same arable to pastoral landuse ratio, triggering the need for a major expansion of arable. This seems evident on the gravels and perhaps the extensive field systems on the Berkshire Downs. There may also have been further expansion of arable into claylands and parts of the Cotswolds. Although there have been few excavations of any scale in these areas to substantiate this, a large expansion of arable at this period seems evident from the acceleration of alluviation on the Thames floodplain (Robinson and Lambrick 1984; Robinson 1992b; Lambrick 1992b and see Chapter 2).

Although it is based on some arbitrary assumptions and should not be taken as more than illustrative, the model provides a reasonably plausible scenario for how population increase might have resulted in increased pressure on landuse, leading to the emergence of sedentary farming eclipsing the residential mobility of earlier practices.

While this scenario may work in crude terms for the Upper Thames region, a similar rate of population growth need not apply to the rest of the valley. The pattern of settlement development in the Middle Thames Valley was different, with more evidence of middle to late Bronze Age fields, domestic activity and exchange of prestige goods, but relatively little sign of more intensive Iron Age settlement of the kind seen in the Upper Thames. David Yates (1999, 2001) postulated a major disruption and possible a shift in population in the late Bronze Age and early Iron Age associated with a supposed abandonment of field systems. However, this is predicated on assumptions of abandonment of fields that may be highly misleading. Other evidence, as that noted at Perry Oaks/T5 and elsewhere suggests continued low level use and occupation.

Using the same underlying parameters, the second set of graphs in Figure 10.1 assumes a faster rate of population growth for the middle to late Bronze Age at c 0.3% per year, but thereafter a significant slow down to a very modest rate of population growth of 0.02% per year after the late Bronze Age, picking up to 0.05% to 0.1% in the late Iron Age and back to 2% in the Roman period. If population growth was low in the Iron Age there may have been some need to take more land into productive use, but little need to adjust intensity of landuse. This may have lasted even into the Roman period, though the growth of towns would have altered the picture.

Although this scenario is again hypothetical, it is reasonably plausible. The key point is that we need only envisage a much slower rate of population growth (not even stagnation or decline) to create very different conditions. The different trajectory of change that seems to characterise the Middle Thames compared with the Upper Thames could thus simply be due to a slowing in population growth. This might have been triggered by a major social or economic disruption, disease, famine or warfare. Needham's (2007) 'Great Divide' of 800 BC involving a collapse in the over-inflated social and economic importance of prestige goods provides one scenario. This would have had substantial consequential effects and if the quantity of metalwork in the Thames is an indicator, these would have been much greater in the Middle Thames Valley than the Upper Thames. But it may be that the 'Great Divide' scenario tries too hard to see everything in terms of universal sudden change. Economic and land management issues may have contributed to a slowing of population growth over a couple of centuries, with wider effects that need not have been especially catastrophic. Economic growth and social influence may have shifted elsewhere over a longer period, the apparent collapse of the prestige goods economy possibly more a symptom than a cause. We do not need to invoke soil exhaustion, migration or widespread abandonment of land to explain what happened, though any of these could have been contributory factors.

Taking a wider view of the influence of population dynamics, we can thus plausibly suggest that this was an important underlying factor influencing the dissimilar trajectories of change that seem apparent in the different parts of the Thames Valley in later prehistory – the Upper Thames characterised by sustained moderately fast growth, the Middle Thames by rapid initial growth and then only very slow growth through the Iron Age. Within these broad trends changes in growth are likely to have been much more variable, not only through time but also geographically. For example, population pressure in the higher reaches of the Upper Thames may not have had much effect on the intensity of landuse until the middle Iron Age.

While population dynamics in relation to available resources can have important influences on the pattern of change, this is not an independent variable. It involves highly complex feedback loops of social and economic factors that either accelerate or slow down growth. In the end population is only one element and needs to be considered within a much broader context of environmental, economic and social conditions. Even if we recognise that population pressure helped to induce changes in land management practices and other aspects of society, there are still major questions as to why adaptations happened in one way and not others. Some important changes will have had nothing to do with population issues.

The emergence of fields and farms

Organising the land

A central question for this review of late prehistory in the Thames Valley has been why and how did people start to organise their use of land more systematically and settle in permanent settlements? There has been a general, often tacit assumption that permanent settlement goes with the division and enclosure of land to facilitate greater control and more intensive agricultural use. Standard interpretations also usually envisage the emergence of fields and permanent settlement as a fairly radical shift in social and economic organisation in the middle Bronze Age (Yates 1999; 2001), though some have questioned whether the break from the earlier Bronze Age was really as marked as many claim (Brück 2000).

Enclosure of land into networks of fields does not automatically require permanent settlement. Likewise, as Richard Bradley (pers. comm.) has observed in relation to present day coaxial field systems in Spain, the existence of fields does not need imply that they were all in constant use, either seasonally or from one year to the next. The tacit assumption that a similar establishment of fields would have happened at the same time across large geographical areas is also highly questionable. Archaeologists tend to seek the origins of permanent settlement and fields by back-projecting their vision of a fully developed late prehistoric farming system to see when it began, and are then liable to compound this by drawing sweeping conclusions from a few examples that fit the earliest origins. There is a more powerful logic in investigating how, why and when earlier practices of mobile living in apparently unenclosed landscapes declined or ceased. On this basis we need to consider why field systems might have emerged in a mainly seasonal pastoral economy. Instead of assuming that such changes must have been organised and co-ordinated everywhere at the same time, we should look for evidence of whether or not this was the case.

Why fields were created and how they evolved

Like a number of other parts of Britain, the earliest fields that we know of in the Thames Valley are networks of highly regular rectilinear paddocks and fields, sometimes covering tens of hectares, often with many standard distances or proportions evident between parallel boundaries. Yates has been so struck by such characteristics that he sees the emergence of fields as an 'agricultural revolution' in which,

> *'The shock of a new managed and controlled landscape represents a momentous period of change in the lives of individuals and the priorities of communities. It is this lifestyle change and the intensification of agriculture that characterises the Later Bronze Age. However, the pace of change was not confined solely to an agricultural revolution for at the same time there was a fundamental shift in regional power and wealth toward the lowlands of eastern England'* (Yates 2001, 65).

In asserting this claim, Yates has noted an apparent correlation between the main areas of fields and the incidence of metalwork and high status enclosures, suggesting that these reflect regional enclaves of socio-economic power. It is certainly the case that the vast bulk of middle Bronze Age metalwork comes from the area in west London and Surrey where the coaxial fields are most extensive, while further upstream, where fields were not coaxial or were generally not as common, there is very much less metalwork and more is later Bronze Age (York 2002, 80-1, figs 2, 3). As Needham (2007, 59) has pointed out, however, the high status enclosures and most of the metalwork in the Middle Thames post-date the main period when the field systems were laid out, indicating that if there is a connection, the enclosed settlements and main period of metalwork deposition grew out of the socio-economic system that created the fields, rather than being associated with their establishment.

These sites are also very variable in character. Some field 'systems' and high status enclosures that

Yates includes are very dubious and it is far from clear why the creation of field systems need represent the emergence of sub-regional centres of power involved in intensifying landuse. The relationship, if it exists, looks subtler than Yates's model of an 'agricultural revolution' might suggest. A much more gradual evolution of farming over several centuries underpinning the social and economic system that led to the construction of enclosures and ostentatious accumulation of metalwork deposited as hoards or votive offerings is more realistic.

According to Yates, the demise of such field systems was no less dramatic than their creation: 'Social dislocation appears to have affected many farming communities at the end of the Bronze Age. The extent of collapse is so widespread that it suggests a general crisis' (Yates 2001, 78). This would correspond to Needham's (2007) 'Great Divide' of *c* 800 BC but, like Brück's challenge to whether the early to middle Bronze Age transition has been seen aright, this idea is also open to question, not least because change is seldom so one-dimensional.

Andrew Fleming and Joanna Brück are more circumspect about the possible origins of such fields. Fleming (1985; 1987; 1994) observed that the Dartmoor reaves were clearly related to pre-existing markers in the landscape, were not entirely uniform in detailed character, were not necessarily merely functional constructs, and may have reflected embedded notions of how land should be divided. Noting the wide disparity in the dates of coaxial field systems, he speculated about how the concept might have been transmitted down the ages through oral tradition but concluded 'although it may be useful to think of coaxial field systems in functional terms, as responses to the management of communally owned land, the detailed working out of such a scheme remains to be done' (Fleming 1987, 201). The key issue is whether or not such a systematic layout need reflect the exercise of some sort of high level economic and social 'control' and 'decision' making (Fleming 1994, 73).

Brück (2000) has challenged the idea that the early to middle Bronze Age transition was a period of agricultural 'intensification', suggesting that a different, non-capitalist model of the relationship between people and the natural resources around them needs to be developed that takes more account of contemporary attitudes so far as we can discern them.

In looking at how land was divided, enclosed and settled we have seen in Chapter 3 that some characteristics that seem very distinctive archaeologically, such as the varied subsoil manifestation of boundaries and settlement components, can be misleading or risk being misread. To arrive at a clearer understanding of the dynamics of the emergence and development of settled farming communities in the Thames Valley in later prehistory we need to consider the evidence in fresh ways. The categories of 'forms' and 'types' of fields and settlements used to describe the evidence and impart order to it do not explain how people interacted and worked together as family or community groups in adapting to changing balances of different farming activities and developments in social organisation and landuse.

As Brück (2000, 281) emphasises, it is generally accepted that in the earlier Bronze Age there is no clear evidence of permanent farmsteads and a high degree of residential mobility can be assumed, in which 'people appear to have incorporated a range of subsistence resources into an annual cycle which involved movement between a series of different locales.' Groups may have changed in composition for different tasks during the year, with larger gatherings at ceremonial and funerary complexes at particular times. People probably lived mainly as mobile pastoralists moving from one favoured grazing ground to another, with temporary horticultural plots for growing their crops, which they may have fenced off for the summer.

It is also clear that people acted communally, sometimes in significant numbers, to build ceremonial and funerary monuments. This seems to have been a key means of cementing society, through reference to common ancestry and shared spiritual beliefs. It is also reasonable to assume, though difficult to demonstrate, that day-to-day living and rights of ownership in animals and agricultural produce was essentially family-based; that is to say it would have been vested in small, though not necessarily fixed family groups.

Larger, perhaps kin-related communities of several families or larger groups of multiple communities may have held general rights to broad territories and land was shared in common (Brück 1999), perhaps based on long-fallow agriculture (Barrett 1994, 136-46). Within these communal rights each family might have been responsible for looking after its own animals and crops, or its share of such resources held in common. As Johnston (2001) points out using ethnographic parallels, such rights might have been highly complex and multifaceted. Far from being a simple one-to one relationship of each group of people having access to a particular area of land, such rights could have involved many different types of access over different areas to different resources for different kinds of usage, possibly with complicated rules of inter-commoning.

But as the population grew this kind of family-based, communally-negotiated use of land from which everyone sought to make their living relatively independently and yet within a communally agreed set of rights, may have started to cause tensions over how much good grazing was available. This difficulty could have started to become a critical issue where people had problems finding good pasture for a decent period of grazing within a day or two's walk for their animals.

Coping with this pressure may not have been simple. As Johnston noted in relation to field clearance in the north-west and the establishment of the Dartmoor reaves in the south-west (Johnston 2001; 2005), we should not assume that rights to the use of land only became established when people started to lay out fields. It is very possible that social and traditional rights of neighbouring kinship or tribal groups restricted expansion of settlement into neighbouring areas, even if there was much more space. Furthermore, it is important to recognise that, while systems of tenure and landuse rights develop from practical arrangements for the use and allocation of land and resources, they then begin to shape and constrain how landuse is managed and settled (Johnson 2001, 103). Early Bronze Age clearance cairnfields tend to be earlier than the main period when fields were demarcated by visible boundaries. Johnson argues that they may have been a means of symbolically marking the breaking of new ground, reflecting both the labour involved and staking a claim with structures which were like miniature burial mounds with possible symbolic offerings, small pits and other elements that suggest they were not just heaps of fieldstone cleared to make way for cultivation. They may have symbolised both the labour of breaking ground and asserting ancestral rights to it. Indeed, while it is clear that they were associated with clearance, it is not at all apparent whether this was in the context of permanent settlement or arable agriculture, and such cairnfields could have been the accumulated result of many different episodes of clearance activity over a significant period.

In a predominantly pastoral economy increasing production to meet a growing population would mean over-wintering more animals on a recurrent basis to provide a larger breeding stock each year, in effect mirroring human population growth, but with more than one animal per person. When land was shared with other free-ranging pastoralists there may have been both practical and socio-political or cultural reasons why competition for space could not simply be resolved by going further afield to provide additional grazing. Within existing tracts of available land a growing population would tend to increase competition for grazing, resulting in less security for each family's livestock property and possibly a greater need to split or amalgamate herds and flocks to make best use of scarce grazing. Where expansion could no longer conveniently be achieved through more clearance in favoured areas, the key would have been to find ways of increasing production from existing areas.

A critical issue would have been the need to sustain livestock through the winter, when grass and other vegetation hardly grows and much larger areas are required for grazing than in the eight-month growing season when pastures continually grow well. As we have seen in Chapter 7, autumn culling was practised. There is currently insufficient evidence to tell whether kill-off patterns changed in the course of the Bronze Age, but it is noticeable that by the Iron Age more animals were kept longer for secondary products. As this trend indicates, increased culling to ease pressure on winter pastures is not a long term solution in a scenario of population growth since it cumulatively restricts overall reproductive capacity year-on-year and hence may limit the number of people a given area can support.

Collection of leaf fodder may have figured as a means of increasing pastoral production to allow more animals to over-winter, but this is labour intensive and has limited potential as a way of increasing the capacity of a given area. Where population growth was greatest there would have been growing pressure for families to find other ways to secure sufficient winter feed for their animals from communally shared grazing lands. Obtaining more productivity from grassland management is likely to have been an effective means of management that did not involve major recurrent annual labour inputs.

Initially this could have included groups trying to protect their interests as a community by establishing stronger rights to particular areas of land, thereby limiting competition on grazing and providing a clearer basis for increasing its productive capacity. Establishing stronger rights on a reasonably amicable basis would have meant establishing agreed demarcations of rights to land. This may be the basis of the form that later field systems adopted, reflecting some generally established norms for the allocation and sharing of land (Johnston 2005, 17).

Coaxial patterns may be only the most strikingly regular means of doing this, and it is possible to envisage how this might have started as simple agreement by reference to visible features in the landscape such as barrow mounds, topographical features, distinctive trees and large posts, which could be coupled with a few paced-out measurements to define strips of land over which families had particular rights. Visually linking relatively few landmarks in this way could have resulted in the establishment of long straight coaxial land divisions within which animals could be tethered or shepherded long before any physical boundaries or barriers were marked out on the ground. Giving physical expression to such boundaries as stock-proof fences or hedges would then have been a further step of reinforcing such demarcation. We should not assume that this always entailed the creation of archaeologically visible ditches. As Johnston (2005) observes in relation to Dartmoor, and as we have seen in relation to Perry Oaks/T5, there is considerable scope for how such land divisions can be subdivided and modified in piecemeal ways without disturbing the basic orderliness of the overall pattern. Physical enclosure is perhaps best seen as the physical manifestation of a widely accepted social means of sharing land, rather than a grand plan imposed by some higher authority.

Increasing productive capacity of grazing could have begun by temporarily demarcating areas and then permanently enclosing sufficient land for more controlled use. The need to create physical barriers to enclose smaller areas to control livestock, either within a coaxial system or more agglomerative patterns of small fields, may have been motivated by two considerations: first, in summer to keep animals off cereals, flax and other crops; and second, and perhaps more importantly, in late summer and autumn to allow enough growth of 'fog' (long grass kept for winter grazing) to last the whole winter and early spring. This would have meant keeping animals out of enclosed areas in late summer to allow the grass to grow and then letting them in, field-by-field, to eat off the tall thick grass over the winter in a controlled manner. There were medieval rights of 'foggage', and foggage farming systems not only have long historical roots but are also currently seeing a revival in Britain as a form of low-cost, low-input agricultural extensification (Hollins 1990).

The enclosure (or tethering) of animals to control grazing would help explain (especially with dry winters) the characteristic proliferation of wells and waterholes amongst Bronze Age field systems. As we have seen in Chapter 7 there is consistent evidence from most waterlogged deposits in wells and waterholes to indicate that most enclosure was primarily concerned with management of grassland. Moreover, the evidence of meadow-like conditions with late summer flowering plants would often be consistent with management of some grassland as foggage to provide winter grazing. It is worth noting that very much larger areas of enclosed land would be needed to provide a family's animals with foggage for grazing through the winter than would be needed to grow their cereals in the summer.

The high frequency of waterholes and extensive scattered evidence of domestic occupation within coaxial and other early field systems would accommodate the notion of organisation at the level of the family unit – ie each family looking after its own animals and doing its own horticultural work rather than sharing these tasks between the community. This is also consistent with the amorphous, widely scattered patterns of domestic occupation associated with such field systems, which may reflect continuity of 'residential mobility', with fields representing one of the 'favoured locales' without implying a switch from long- to short-fallow agriculture, as Barrett suggests (1994, 147-9).

How far it is possible to associate blocks of fields or particular strips within coaxial field systems with individual families is far from clear, but there may be some hints from similarities and differences in the layout of strips, and more evidence may emerge from more detailed artefactual analysis of scattered domestic occupation debris than has yet been undertaken for some of the larger sites. If such field systems did develop over generations, the apparently regular linear halving and quartering of strips within the Perry Oaks/T5 coaxial fields might reflect a process of subdivision through inheritance. Although this is also a feature of a few parts of the Dartmoor reaves, it is not especially common, leading Fleming (1988, 64-5, figs 34, 37) to suggest that such inheritance was not an established norm. It may well be that inheritance of land, rather than of broader land rights plus ownership of animals and crops, might have been a relatively late development.

If we are correct about the continued family-based management of animals and crops and ongoing semi-mobile pattern of living in the later Bronze Age, we need to consider how and why this changed. We should not assume either that the same changes happened everywhere at the same time, or that a mixture of life styles might not have existed in some places. Instead of seeing this in terms of Yates's 'general crisis' at the time of Needham's 'great divide,' there is evidence, mainly from waterholes and other domestic debris, that in the early Iron Age some field systems continued in use as hedged enclosures, long after the ditches ceased to be cleared out and recut. In some places fields might have been adapted to fit new ways of organising land management, with settlements based in new locations. Although in some cases fields were probably abandoned, this is difficult to prove and appearances may be misleading. The evidence in the Thames Valley can be seen to fit several scenarios and the idea that there was a collapse of society with widespread abandonment of fields and a movement of settlement from the Middle to the Upper Thames (Barret and Bradley 1980; Yates 1999; 2001) may have been greatly exaggerated.

One of the more intriguing questions relating to the early field systems of the Thames Valley is why new ones of similar character ceased to be created by the end of the Bronze Age (or perhaps the early Iron Age in the case of Lady Lamb Farm), and why existing fields were not subject to more redesign and modification. Iron Age fields are of different character. To understand what was behind these changes we need to consider how they related to the emergence of permanent farming settlements and the changes in social and economic relationships that this brought.

How permanent farming settlements became established

The evidence suggests that the establishment of permanent year-round farms was not automatically part of the development of early field systems, and that settled farms did not always have extensive ditched field systems. Nevertheless, there are links between the character of fields and settlements that seem to reflect changes in the social and economic relationships that were an important part of the emergence of a settled farming society. However this was not a simple shift from one form of living to another. There are gradations in the range of lifestyles between highly dispersed patterns of settlement, recurrently used areas of occupation and more permanent settlements better integrated with topography and landuse. Moreover, it is clear that the transition from residential mobility and seasonal occupation to permanently settled farms took place at very different times in different parts of the Thames Valley, and may well have continued as complementary styles of living. Within the range of different kinds of settlement reviewed in Chapter 4, the key 'signature' of the emergence of permanent farming settlements seems to be the establishment of compact, relatively intensely occupied open settlements integrated with topography and landuse boundaries, and the establishment of enclosed farming settlements.

There is evidence from Perry Oaks/T5, Ashford Prison and Hengrove, that at least within areas of middle Bronze Age field systems this focussing of settlement did not take place until the middle or even later Iron Age, though it may have been earlier at Thorpe Lea Nurseries. In the Maidenhead-Slough area and the Kennet valley some sites like Taplow pipeline, Aldermaston Wharf and Reading Business Park/Green Park suggest that some degree of intensification of settlement was beginning to happen both within field systems and beyond them at different stages in the late Bronze Age and earliest Iron Age. But this is not common, and unlike the Upper Thames, where such intensification, once established, often continued well into the Roman period, these settlements do not seem to have lasted – or if they did it was not within the same location. In most of the Middle Thames Valley settlement seems to have remained very dispersed in and around field systems or in the wider countryside until the middle to late Iron Age when small open and enclosed settlements start to appear in a more tangible form.

Where later Bronze Age field systems have been found in the Upper Thames Valley, on the gravels area round Dorchester, Appleford and Didcot and better drained parts of the broad vale between the Chalk and the Corallian Ridge, there is mixed evidence of how settlement patterns developed. The indications of relatively intensive later Bronze Age settlement outside the hilltop enclosure at Castle Hill appears to have continued to develop through the Iron Age, but otherwise the evidence so far is for more intensively occupied areas to have emerged in the early Iron Age (and certainly seem to have been established by the middle Iron Age).

In the Yarnton and Cassington area above Oxford, where no field systems have been found, there is growing evidence of a marked change from very dispersed occupation on the floodplain in the middle to late Bronze Age to more nucleated settlements from the late Bronze Age onwards. The late Bronze Age settlement at Cassington West is the first manifestation of a more intensive form of relatively compact, ordered settlement focussed in one place, but it had shifted again by the early Iron Age. Only a kilometre or so away at Yarnton, the same sort of change in settlement character occurred, but not until the early Iron Age when there was a more marked shift from very scattered occupation activity on the floodplain to an even more organised form of settlement on the adjacent gravel terrace. This settlement then continued to evolve, gradually migrating along the terrace edge until after many further changes it became the modern village of Yarnton.

In the Stanton Harcourt area the absence of clear evidence of later Bronze Age settlement preceding the ring of early Iron Age settlements that grew up round the earlier prehistoric ceremonial complex is striking, but it can nevertheless be argued that the pattern of compact, ordered settlements here grew directly out of a much more amorphous pre-existing pattern of occupation and landuse.

In the higher reaches of the Upper Thames around Lechlade, there is some evidence of large scale land division in the early Iron Age and a few indications of enclosure of land into extensive fields, but again the patterns of late Bronze Age and early Iron Age settlement at Latton, Shorncote/ Cotswold Community and Horcott was highly dispersed. In these areas the emergence of more compact intensive forms of settlement (eg at Latton, Horcott and Cotswold Community) are broadly middle to late Iron Age, though at Bourton-on-the-Water and a number of other sites on the dip slope of the Cotswolds it may well have been earlier.

As we have seen in Chapter 4 and Chapter 9, enclosed settlements were established at a wide range of dates in different parts of the valley, but apart from defensive sites were often middle to late Iron Age in origin. How this related to the character of pre-existing settlement within the general area is very seldom evident, though sometimes, as with middle Iron Age enclosed settlements on the Upper Thames gravels, it can be seen as a filling up of an already settled landscape. Elsewhere such settlements were established in apparently previously unoccupied – though not necessarily unused – places with little evidence of pre-existing forms of occupation.

The combined evidence indicates that the emergence of permanent settled farming as indicated by the establishment of more compact, intensively occupied settlements integrated into landuse patterns took place in different parts of the valley over a period of about 500 to 700 years. This long emergence of fully settled farming and the lack of a close connection with the establishment of field systems suggests that there was no great universal cultural, social or economic crisis, nor any ideological or political impetus. It is more the case that relatively mobile and more settled styles of living co-existed for a very long period and indeed, bearing in mind the traces of ephemeral occupation for most of later prehistory as well as deliberate seasonal settlements like Farmoor, there is no good evidence that this stopped. It may be that this mixture of lifestyles was an effective way of managing land and working with different communities.

A common factor in the coalescence of ephemeral occupation into more compact settlements may have been that people started to switch from an essentially family-based management of animals and crops in a mobile or only semi-settled mode of existence to a more settled, communal approach. This may in some cases simply have meant better organisation or integration of landuse for settlement and production. In others it may have involved a switch towards more arable production. Essentially, it would have involved a change in the dynamics of relationships between people with regards to the management of land and food production. This may have seen a redistribution of tasks previously confined within the capabilities of a family to a broader sharing amongst the community, allowing better division of effort between more and less labour-intensive activities. As people became more reliant on each other and hence less free to move independently, it is easy to see how this could have become a self-reinforcing stimulus for creating larger, more permanent settlements.

This would have entailed a significant change in life style. In terms of more recent history it might have been equivalent to people shifting from countryside to town during the industrial revolution in the 19th century. Ways of working would have changed, as would social interaction and the physical form of settlement. Yet most of the customs of everyday life would have remained much the same.

The way that settlements and landuse division developed in relation to food production is another relevant consideration. A good way of increasing food production from a given area of land would have been to increase crop production, thereby benefiting from the four- or five-fold increase in nutritional value per hectare that can be achieved with cereals compared with animal husbandry. Doing this on a significant scale has other implications. In particular, crop-growing, especially on an agricultural rather than horticultural scale, is significantly more labour intensive so there is a limit to the expansion that can be achieved by a single family trying to be entirely self-sufficient within its own resources. Beyond that limit it becomes sensible to divide up arable and pasture areas on a larger scale and work together in larger groups, not single families, so that a few people can look after everyone's herds while more people can be involved with ploughing, sowing, weeding and harvesting crops. This also dispenses with the need to manage everything in small fields, and the need for innumerable separate water supplies largely disappears. Large herds can less readily be watered in this way and it becomes more sensible for herders to take animals to the local spring, stream or river. Enclosure of land into extensive field systems and provision of water supplies would thus have become a far less pressing need as settlement and landuse became more communally organised and better integrated with natural resources.

Beyond what could be achieved at a horticultural scale, a switch to more crop growing could thus have been a stimulus to changing the social basis of farming and the organisation of landuse. This need not have happened simultaneously in all parts of the Thames Valley. However, as explained above (cf Lambrick 1992), if the population was continuing to increase exponentially, the requirements to maintain and expand pastoral production would soon have kicked in, albeit at different times in different places. It is noticeable that the relatively few signs of early Iron Age land division and enclosure and much more extensive middle Iron Age evidence is again associated with settlements that seem to have been predominantly engaged in pastoralism. But these land boundaries, trackways, fields and paddocks display different characteristics from their Bronze Age predecessors.

While it is easy to see how the highly regular Bronze Age patterns might reflect preconceived principles and patterns of land sharing (Johnston 2005), Iron Age landuse boundaries and fields seem to be much more pragmatic. They largely reflect practical considerations of topography and pre-existing landuse, with settlement patterns organised to make best use of different resources. There is also more evidence of layouts that allow funnelling of animals in large herds, as at Watchfield and Cleveland Farm. Whereas settlement tended to retreat from rising water tables on low-lying ground in the early Iron Age, such areas were seen to have added value for more intensive specialist pastoral settlement, with renewed enclosure of land for control of pasture in the middle Iron Age. This is particularly evident in the Upper Thames Valley and seems to have included specialised summer grazing camps, of which the well known, but in some respects still unique site at Farmoor, may only be the most extreme example. A similar pattern, again apparently reflecting an emphasis on pastoralism, also seems apparent in the resurgence of middle Iron Age settlement in the Surrey-Middlesex part of the Middle Thames Valley.

If this idea is correct it appears that this shift from family-based mobile pastoralism that typified earlier agricultural communities to the more communally based arrangements of mixed farming in later prehistory was not the synchronous, culturally inspired explosion of fields and permanent settlement that is sometimes portrayed as an 'agricultural revolution.' It is much more likely to have been a recurrent evolution of lifestyles following different trajectories in different areas according to local circumstances. In some cases it may not have been complete even into the late Iron Age and Roman period. Even where the evidence superficially indicates that the change was general and quite sudden at a local level, as at Stanton Harcourt, more detailed consideration suggests that it could have been much more gradual (Lambrick and Allen 2004, 483). It was an adaptation that would often have had to be shoehorned into older traditions or developed alongside them in different ways (see below).

Social and farming developments were inextricably intertwined as people worked together, increasing production both for subsistence and exchange in relation to varying levels of population growth. At the end of the Iron Age and into the Roman period, with population still rising in the Upper Thames Valley and probably reasserting itself in the Middle Thames, a new impetus to enclose land seems to have emerged, involving a major investment of effort to establish new field systems and enclosures, perhaps both stimulated by and encouraging the emergence of a new political climate (cf Chapter 9).

Although in many cases these late developments resulted in the obliteration of the remnants of thousand year-old fields which had long since ceased to have their ditches maintained, in other cases they built on and elaborated Iron Age and earlier boundaries and enclosures. This may often have made sense pragmatically. In some places, including Stanton Harcourt, arrangements based on ancient landuse rights seem to have been so embedded in local society that they did not finally outlive their practical use until well into the Roman period. If such rights had already lasted 1,500 years or more it is not entirely far-fetched that just occasionally parts of them survived in adapted form much longer, even up to the present day. There is possible evidence for this at Port Meadow, Oxford and other comparable areas of floodplain common grazing pastures, and perhaps for more field and estate boundaries than we might suspect.

What happened to residential mobility

We have focussed on how and why fields and permanent year-round farms and villages emerged as key features of later prehistory society in the Thames Valley. We also need to consider what happened to earlier ways of living and whether mobile, seasonal farming was completely replaced by more permanent farming. As discussed in Chapter 4, there is some evidence that this remained part of the pattern of how people lived. But how genuine is this pattern? To what extent did partially transhumant ways of life persist into the Iron Age and might this kind of lifestyle have been a feature of how land was gradually cleared and converted to additional grazing land? There are difficulties in addressing these questions because of the lack of solid evidence. Nevertheless, it is something that warrants more attention than it has so far been given. In particular we may need to be more assiduous in looking for later Bronze Age and Iron Age sites that are as ephemeral and odd in terms of domestic occupation as Neolithic and early Bronze Age ones. Instead of dismissing sites with very slight traces of occupation as somehow being 'insignificant' because they do not conform to the model of settled farms, we need to be more open to the possibility that mobile seasonal living continued to be an important component of later prehistoric society.

The short-lived summer 'shielings' on the Thames floodplain at Farmoor, in a location that was positively unsuited to year-round occupation, have been seen as exemplifying a relatively extreme response of a permanently settled society to maximise pastoral production (Lambrick and Robinson 1979; Lambrick 1992). This may be correct, but transhumant grazing is a well-recognised element of developed farming systems and might have resembled the sometimes long distant pannage (and sometimes grazing and/or mowing) rights which are well documented in medieval landuse rights up and down the Thames Valley. Within the overall picture of maximising pastoral production in a range of different ways, it is reasonable to envisage that a wider pattern of mobile seasonal occupation of grazing lands and woodland may always have been part of the pastoral economy (cf Hill 2007; Blair 1991, 17-22, 50-5).

Community and family interaction

Family and community involvement in crafts and exchange

The emergence of settled farming communities and more intensive land management would have entailed an adjustment of social and communal relationships, both amongst families and at wider levels of community interaction and support as well-ordered settlements became the hub of landuse management. The analysis at Gravelly Guy indicated how responsibility for different elements of social and economic activity may have been shared between people interacting at different levels of family and communal grouping (Lambrick and Allen 2004, 488). Food preparation and many domestic crafts were undertaken within the family household, arable production was probably carried out by multiple households acting together as settlement groups, and animals owned by individual households may have been managed partly by the individual families but also on a wider communal basis of several settlements sharing common grazing lands. Smithing, potting and other specialist crafts may also have been carried out at different levels of social interaction and, depending on the skills involved and status attached to the products, would have involved a wider network of interchange (Chapter 6).

This range of social and economic interaction would have varied considerably with the character of settlements. For mobile pastoralists or isolated farms it would have been different from places like Stanton Harcourt where multiple household communities emerged. A broad model has our period beginning with a family-based economy working within a framework of shared rights established through kinship and wider exchange

networks, gradually changing (at different times up and down the valley) to a more complex, but still quite fluid mixture of communal management of resources and continued relative independence, still within a system based more on traditional rights and negotiated co-operation than economic or political control.

Social relations and the bounding space

There has been much debate over the last two decades about the significance of settlement enclosure. Hingley (1984; 1999) has highlighted how the densely settled valley floor in the Upper Thames Valley is characterised by closely distributed open settlements, whereas the less densely occupied Cotswolds are characterised by more isolated enclosed ones, a pattern modified, but not fundamentally altered by more recent work (Moore 2006; Alex Lang pers. comm.). Hingley (1984, 85) proposed that enclosed settlements represented individual groups who had appropriated territory to themselves, whereas on the valley floor the clusters of open settlements represented the management of resources at a communal scale, reflecting a much longer history of intensive use. He suggested that this represented 'two distinct forms of society' with 'contrasting topologies of space' reflecting differences in the 'organisation of corporate social groups and the structure of social relations of production.' He saw the communal organisation of the valley floor in terms of a more tribally based 'Germanic' mode of production (Bonte 1981) in which 'domestic' property (eg cattle) is owned and managed by individual groups, while 'wild' resources held in common (eg pasture) are managed communally.

Since then it has become clearer how the pattern of landuse and settlement at Stanton Harcourt may have been influenced by a pre-existing ceremonial complex (Lambrick (1992b; Lambrick and Allen 2004). Hingley (1999, 242-5) has subsequently suggested that this inheritance reinforced his idea that settlement patterns reflected the Germanic mode of production, with the large pastoral core representing the 'wild' rather than 'domesticated' space. As discussed above, more detailed consideration of the Gravelly Guy evidence suggests that a wide gradation of different levels of individual and social interaction can be inferred (Lambrick and Allen 2004, 488). Hey (2007, 160) has pointed out that the pastoral area at Stanton Harcourt would have been at the heart of communal interaction, and that Iron Age communities in open settlements on the valley floor probably had access to less intensively managed grasslands as well as immediate grazing grounds. In this case other 'wild' areas would have been the lower terraces and floodplain which, by the middle Iron Age, were beginning to attract small pastoral farms, several of which appear to have been single or double household units of both enclosed and unenclosed form.

An alternative perspective would suggest that both on the Cotswolds and on the lower terraces and floodplain new settlements, mostly of small scale, were being established from the middle Iron Age onwards in areas without much evidence of earlier Iron Age farms. In this sense both areas could be seen to have been subject to a similar process of filling out the landscape with new farms in areas that were previously only lightly managed grassland. Bonte's model of 'domesticated' property and 'wild' resources is derived from nomadic pastoralist tribes rather than the establishment of settled farms, so the strength of Hingley's observations may have most relevance in considering how pre-existing rights based on residentially mobile pastoralists might have already established different kinds of communal or individual rights and access to land. This may have become much more constrained in heavily used areas on the higher gravel terraces and less so on the lower-lying valley floor and less densely used surrounding hills. This would adequately explain the observed differences without needing to propose a fundamentally different form of tenure or social interaction in the management of land. The enclosure of relatively isolated settlements on the hills around the Thames Valley may have been as much a practical measure as a symbol of social or economic independence.

The extent to which the boundedness of settlements defined social and economic inter-relationships is debatable. The recurrent appearance of enclosures in the middle Iron Age has also been thought to reflect an increasing desire to emphasise distinctions of community or family space. Enclosure ditches are often seen as liminal features that not only physically constrained the use of space but also symbolically demarcated it (Taylor 1997, 196; Hill 1996, 102-3; 2007). Tom Moore (2007, 273) has suggested that the appearance of ditches defining individual houses on unenclosed settlements in the middle Iron Age is another expression of the bounding of space that blurs the distinction between 'enclosed' and 'unenclosed settlement.' He raises the rhetorical question of why earlier houses and other boundaries were not marked by gullies, but this might be a matter of survival as clearly some were. Gullies might have been dug deeper to improve surface drainage as silty soils became more compacted by intensified use.

A problem with the debate about how physical boundaries might reflect Iron Age social relations and cosmological concepts is that it is too firmly rooted in their physical manifestation as ditches (ie what survives best archaeologically) rather than starting from a more basic question of how boundaries may have been perceived. As we have seen, 'open' settlements can exhibit very clear internal and external boundaries and divisions, evident from the disposition of other features that had social and practical meaning, and may well have been more evident above ground than the absence of a ditch might suggest. At Gravelly Guy many boundaries and divisions came to be defined by ditches and gullies in the middle Iron Age but it is striking that almost all of them were already defined by the distribution of earlier Iron Age features. They simply emphasised some existing boundaries and divisions while others continued to be unmarked by any ditch.

The current recognition of a supposed 'increasing desire by communities to identify themselves through boundaries' in the middle to late Iron Age is thus strongly biased to what survives below ground for archaeologists to investigate. There is no corresponding theorising about the social or cosmological significance of the broadly corresponding middle Iron Age decline of post-built roundhouses or the relative lack of late Iron Age storage pits just because they become *less* visible. It is too simplistic to infer a sudden interest in the bounding of space just because it becomes more visible archaeologically.

The question is thus not so much why an interest in defining boundaries developed in the middle to late Iron Age, as why it became more fashionable to use ditches to do so, and why, in open settlements like Gravelly Guy as much as enclosed ones, these features were sometimes unduly deep. Clearly ditches were used for a range of special deposits, but this is no different from earlier periods. They may have been more obvious and more effective physical barriers, but how far was this practical and how far embued with cosmological meaning? As Pope (2007) has argued for roundhouses, interpreting enclosed settlements only in terms of their symbolic meanings is as restrictive as only seeing their functional value.

Producers and consumers?

Another aspect of social and economic interrelationships that has been the subject of some debate is whether it is possible to distinguish differences in the role of settlements as predominantly producers or consumers of arable produce, and in what sense some settlements can be seen as 'specialist' pastoral farms. In Chapter 7 we reviewed the evidence for agricultural specialisation and some of the implications that this has in terms of the possible economic, and by inference social, interdependence between settlements.

The idea of 'specialisation' and distinctions between 'producers' and 'consumers' which emanated from pioneering studies in the Upper Thames Valley in the 1970s and 1980s have been criticised from two points of view. One has been to highlight the problems of finding evidence for such roles amongst the charred remains of crop processing and bones of animals consumed for meat, both of which are riven with taphonomic complexities that inhibit easy interpretation. The other has been to challenge the use of modern economic terms such as 'specialisation' and 'intensification,' with their overtones of capitalist economics that does not provide close parallels for the kinds of interaction that would have occurred in the Thames Valley over 2000 years ago (Brück 2000).

So what should we make of this in the broader context of how communities interacted? The apparent difficulty of finding detailed and reliable biological evidence to support the idea of speciali-sation or different emphasis in arable production is unfortunate. Its absence, however, is only a lack of support, not a positive indication that such distinc-tions did not exist. Moreover, if we are correct in supposing that full-blown arable farming devel-oped from a more horticultural mode of crop growing, it is reasonable to see low-level growing of crops alongside animal husbandry as the default basis from which differences should be judged. From this perspective it is not unreasonable that some settlements would have become involved in larger-scale arable production while others did not, and that there remained a role for predominantly pastoral farms in which arable agriculture played little part, though its products, whether home grown or not, became an increasingly important part of the general diet.

Similarly, although it is difficult to find evidence in the animal bones for 'specialist' pastoral produc-tion, the differences in the form and character of settlements, their possible social interrelationships and the agricultural produce that they generated, still indicate that there were real differences of emphasis in animal husbandry.

Both with charred crop remains and animal bones there are more general indications of genuine differences in the emphasis of agriculture which broadly correlate with what might be expected from communities intimately familiar with the natural environment and its varied poten-tial for different aspects of animal and crop husbandry. The overall picture is one of mixed farms with a balance of arable and pastoralism and others where pastoralism was clearly dominant. Both may have been self-sufficient, or some pastoral farms may have been reliant on provision of cereals from elsewhere. Perhaps the main distinction was that mixed farms were often capable of producing a surplus of both animals and their byproducts and crops, whereas those primarily concerned with animal husbandry would have only generated surpluses in that area. In many cases both would have contributed to the local economy and its interaction with wider exchange networks. The demand for agricultural produce, both for subsistence and exchange for other goods, was almost certainly an important driver of change, as was the success or failure of the system in providing what was needed. We have already looked at this in terms of changing population levels, but there were other social, cultural and economic factors that both encour-aged and inhibited change.

Social and political hierarchies

Sites like Allen's Pit and Alfred's Castle and perhaps some of the smallest hillforts might have been the residences of local chiefs, and clearly a degree of political authority was required to mobilise the resources needed to build major enclosures and hillforts. However, there is little indication that the interrelationships between communities can be interpreted in terms of a settlement hierarchy. So far as early defensive enclosures and hillforts were special places, this was more in the context of various communal functions than as seats of power. It may be that Allen's Pit and Alfred's Castle indicate that there are other settlements where particularly important families or individuals resided, and these may not yet have been identified, but if so the evidence is far from clear. For example, it is not the case that enclosed farming settlements were of a socially different status from open settlements in hierarchical terms, even if there were differences in relative isolation. Comparison of the quality of finds assemblages and houses both within settlements and between them may reflect some distinctions in status and involvement in different exchange networks, but this is not tied to particular types of settlement or discernible patterns of social or economic independence or interdependence. Likewise, although some issues of personal status and family fortunes may be reflected in the incidence of burials and 'special' deposits, these do not seem to be related more generally to the social status of communities, except insofar as some of the more striking examples seem to occur in the context of hillforts acting as communal gathering places.

Although based mainly on the absence of positive evidence of a settlement hierarchy, the general impression is that the personal status and wealth of families or individuals and the influence they carried in society was expressed in other terms, such as lineage, possessions, animal herds or prestige objects. In effect, this would have been the legacy of the residential mobility from which later prehistoric farming developed and, as discussed below, it may have been a long time before that embedded system of communal ownership and management of land broke down sufficiently to allow the development of individually owned estates through which social and political prestige was expressed in the form of settlements. Nonetheless there may have been exceptions. Too little is known of the dispersed enclosed settlements of the surrounding hills, but even if enclosure was not intrinsically a sign of status, it may be amongst the banjo enclosures and other elaborate settlements that the personal prestige of individual or family land ownership first became manifest in the outward form of settlements. The enclosed settle-ments at Groundwell Farm on the Corallian ridge near Swindon and at Tongham Nurseries at the head of the Blackwater Valley are among a few excavated on a sufficient scale that have produced some hints of some social status. Watkins Farm, which after a period of late Iron Age abandonment was refurbished as a Roman settlement with pottery suggesting relatively high status, may be another albeit exceptional example within the Thames Valley.

The development of a clearer political and territorial framework of authority at tribal level in the late Iron Age must have emerged from traditional tribal and cultural loyalties and interactions. In physical terms it appears to have been expressed mainly at a fairly high level, notably in the abandonment of older defensive enclosures and the construction of new centres of different character with all the trappings or aspirations of kingly power. While this new form of personal political power might have emerged from a competing aristocratic elite at a regional tribal level to be expressed through massive civil engineering works, there is little evidence that a similar process worked through at lower levels, at least not on the Thames gravels. Again, too few enclosed sites off the gravels have been excavated to know whether they would tell a story of emerging individual estates.

Within the valley, embedded communal rights and relationships may have been too complicated for individual control of land to be carved out, but there may nevertheless have been a subtle yet profound change in how such relationships worked at local level. Existing social and political structures would provide authority for exerting more control over land and production without relying on a looser pattern of relatively independent interactions. Symptoms of such control filtering down to local level may be evident in a number of recurrent patterns of change. The evidence of a hiatus in the settlement record in the late Iron Age noted 15 years ago (Lambrick 1992b) has, on the whole, been reinforced by recent work. This is evident through recurrent abandonment or shifts of settlement and changes in the normal components of settlements, the most interesting of which is the widespread decline (though not abandonment) in the use of storage pits. Tim Allen and Gill Hey have suggested that this is highly unlikely to be due to technical innovation, as underground grain storage is highly effective and it also has the benefit to the producer or consumer of the grain of being a good way to hide a key economic asset. However, from the point of view of an authority seeking to levy tribute based on a proportion of measurable (ie visible) production there are obviously disadvantages. The relatively sudden reduction in the number of classic storage pits towards the end of the Iron Age could be explained by the imposition of a centrally driven form of taxation (Allen 2000, 32), which would have been especially sensitive at a time when the arable component of production was becoming a more important part of the economy. If this was the case, it is also easy to see how such ideas may have been imported through the growing political and economic influence of Rome.

Inertia versus innovation: the effect of belief systems, rights, traditions and new ideas

A recurrent theme of this account of late prehistory in the Thames Valley, and one which in many ways embues all the other themes discussed here, is the tension between pressures for change and the established rights and traditions that framed people's lives and shaped the trajectory of change – and occasionally held it back.

Tenure as a possible influence on trajectories of settlement and landuse change

We have seen above how pre-existing rights and traditions may have shaped the way that communities interacted, and how social and political power was expressed and exercised. We can detect a probable shift from family- to community-based patterns of settlement and landuse occurring at different times up and down the Thames Valley. It also seems clear that the trajectories of change and adaptation that individual communities experienced were by no means uniform. Lambrick (1992b) described how the establishment of new compact and intensive settlements around Stanton Harcourt can be seen to reflect a strong respect for long established traditions and rights of land management around an earlier prehistoric funerary and ceremonial complex, which continued to act as the broad framework for settlement in the area until the middle of the Roman period. This is only one example and it is worth considering how patterns of adaptation and restraint might have shaped other trajectories of settlement development in various parts of the Thames Valley, and whether they might have been influenced by the opportunities and restraints of different forms of inherited tenure.

At first sight the different trajectories of settlement and landuse change seem baffling, but they may be at least partly explicable if we take the view, as suggested above, that the physical manifestation of land organisation, either as land division and field enclosure or as landuse divisions, reflects rights that long pre-dated definition by ditched boundaries. Although we should be aware of the potential complexity of rights to shared resources (Johnston 2001, 99-103), for the purpose of this discussion we can tentatively suggest four types of tenure that might have shaped the development of these areas.

The first is the 'coaxial field' type – presumptively the rigorous communal division of a large block of land into regimented strips that were held in common though perhaps not rotated like medieval fields. They were sometimes subject to subdivision, either to add more members to the community or in some kind of partible inheritance. This could have been a highly restrictive form of tenure allowing little leeway for development without the consensus of growing numbers of descendants (a notorious problem of systems based on partible inheritance).

Secondly, we can suggest a looser 'aggregate field' model in which individual families had control over loosely defined blocks of land within the wider landscape, enabling them to carve out individual-istic blocks of fields on different orientations. This may be discerned at Reading Business Park/Green Park or from cropmarks at Northfield Farm. Here we might envisage more individual family control, and hence more opportunity to redefine, abandon or relocate in a much less restrictive way. This might explain why the fields at Mount Farm and probably Northfield Farm were readily superseded by new arrangements, whereas the coaxial fields not far away at Appleford Sidings remained largely unchanged into the Roman period.

A third form might be called the 'ancestral landuse' model, based on spatial zoning of rights (traditional grazing lands, ancestral sacred places etc). This would perhaps have provided a general communal framework within which some areas could be strictly controlled and held in common while others would be allocated for freer use by individual families or groups. This kind of model envisaged for the Stanton Harcourt complex might also apply to other major funerary and ceremonial complexes in the Upper Thames Valley like Abingdon, Cassington and Standlake.

The fourth model, which we might refer to as 'open' or 'unencumbered land,' would have been the least restrictive, being tied neither to pre-existing land division or very specific restrictions on particular areas. Instead, families with a very general right to use the land would have relative freedom to occupy it as best befitted their interests without there being any particular pressure on resources. This is the kind of arrangement that might be reflected in the reorganisation of the highly dispersed areas of domestic occupation at Yarnton, Cotswold Community and Latton Lands into more compact settlements integrated into landuse. It might also apply to what could be termed pioneering settlements in areas with little pre-existing restraint on settlement. This would include middle Iron Age pastoral settlements on low-lying terraces and floodplain sites or new settlements on the surrounding hills.

In very broad terms the potential restrictiveness of the 'coaxial' model of tenure envisaged here might have contributed to restricting development on the West London and Surrey gravels, whereas the looser arrangements of some of the Upper Thames areas may have facilitated much freer adaptation to landuse pressures. The relative influence of this in relation to basic population pressure and environmental change is impossible to tell. The point is that potentially complex and varied arrangements of tenure and rights to use land could have been another important factor in restricting or facilitating change.

Technology and exchange

In the past technology has been evoked as a key factor in driving change, or at least enabling people to meet pressures to develop new ways of increasing production, developing new forms of conflict or other strands of social life. But as explored above and in many other studies, technology seldom explains change. In only a few areas is it possible to identify technological changes that may have had profound social and economic implications.

There was a whole series of major technical innovations in metallurgy, allowing the forging of larger, more impressive objects and decorative techniques (Northover 1995). The combination of technical innovation, the status of the craftsmen who worked metal, the symbolic value of metal objects (especially weaponry) probably was important in underpinning a prime economic commodity of exchange (Rowlands 1980; Needham 1990; 2001; 2007; Bradley 1990). The recent discoveries at Hartshill Copse (Collard *et al.* 2006) have confirmed that the basic technical innovation of iron production long preceded the demise of bronze as the metal of status. The elaborate ceremonial structures associated with a site involved with this innovative new technology show how important – perhaps magical – it must have seemed. It is still far from clear, however, how far adoption of iron as the preferred metal for tools and weapons was due to difficulties in forging large enough pieces to make equivalent objects, and how far, as seems likely, it was bound up with established customs and concepts of value and status attached to the possession and display of bronze metalwork (Thomas 1999; Needham 2007).

An example of a technology available long before it was generally taken up is evident in how improved rotary querns made from new, sometimes more distant, sources of stone were available from the middle Iron Age onwards, but not much used for many decades. Most people continued with saddle querns from established sources until a quite sudden switch in the later Iron Age or Roman period to sources which previously only occasionally supplied querns. The explanation for this is far from clear. One possibility might be that other changes in storage and processing of grain (eg more being stored, traded or paid in taxes as bags of processed flour instead of grain) induced a demand for more efficient means of milling flour in larger quantities than those required for purely domestic use. It is also possible that querns were part of a very ancient attachment to stones from other places as prestige items, like bronze and other objects made of exotic stone. Querns were not just acquired from the nearest convenient source and were almost certainly seen as objects that had status as well as practical value embedded in complex social and trading networks, perhaps including how agricultural produce was traded out from the valley to other areas.

An interesting example of how the uptake and maintenance of technical 'improvements' were dependent on wider cultural fashions seems evident in the innovations in ceramic crafts. This included greater use of slip and inlay and improved control of firing conditions in the late Bronze Age and early Iron Age. However, in the middle Iron Age the decorative schemes reliant on these techniques were superseded by other tastes involving less sophisticated or different technologies, which may have been part of wider changes in broad fashion that changed the general shape of vessels. Likewise, changes in pottery fabrics seem to have been as much a matter of fashion as technology.

Another important innovation of the period was the breeding of horses and the development of harness, initially with antler cheek pieces, later with more sophisticated metal bridles of a basic design that has lasted until the present day. There is little doubt that innovations of horse breeding, harness and wheels had profound effects for the speed and effectiveness of communication and exchange networks and in relation to warfare. The high craftsmanship and artistic skill that went into making items of harness highlight the significance of these innovations, reflecting the cult status of horses and horsemanship and the associated importance of wheeled vehicles. Votive deposition of horse skulls, legs, long bones and occasionally whole carcasses in 'special deposits,' sometimes particularly associated with entrances, is significant in that it is much commoner than the relative proportion of horse bones to other animals in domestic waste. As noted in Chapter 7, horses may have been especially significant for farming, at least in parts of the Upper Thames Valley, where horse breeding became a distinctive part of the local economy for a few hundred years.

It used to be suggested that innovations in crops and cultivation were fundamental to the development of an agrarian Iron Age society, but the patterns of landuse, cropping and crop-processing suggested here reflect a picture in which broad patterns of landuse were heavily influenced by differences in population pressure and embedded landuse rights. Despite its rise to dominance, the introduction of spelt wheat was probably not fundamental to the development of the agricultural economy, nor were other crops.

It is sometimes suggested that storage of grain in large pits was a profoundly significant technical innovation of the period, but this is still uncertain because there has been too little experimental work with small pits. Furthermore, while pit storage may have been highly advantageous, as Reynolds' experiments proved, the apparent decline in the use of pits in the late Iron Age and early Roman period suggests that it was not fundamental to a productive arable economy.

Taking these trends overall, it seems clear that technological innovation and exchange could be powerful facilitators of important cultural, social and economic trends, in some cases intimately bound up with an added value as cult objects or symbols of social status that could have major economic implications. In some cases, especially with metalwork, the changes that such innovations underpinned would otherwise not have happened. However, the importance of the 'Bronze Age' to 'Iron Age' transition was not technological in the sense of the practical implications of having iron instead of bronze tools and weapons, but in the socio-economic and cultural implications of the prestige attached to such objects. It is also clear that many technological innovations were not so influential, and their adoption or decline was as much or more reliant on changes in fashion and social value as any practical need.

Belief systems and religion

As we have seen in relation to houses, waterholes, boundaries, enclosures, defensive sites, middens, the river and a range of mundane contexts such as pits, cosmological outlook, beliefs and superstitions imbued almost every aspect of life. As Pope (2007) has observed, the narrow functionalist approach to Iron Age studies that typified the 1970s and 1980s is at risk of being replaced by an equally narrow emphasis on cosmological explanations that are often hard to demonstrate. They also risk missing the very essence of the inextricable intertwining of beliefs, superstitions and practical concerns that seem to have been so prevalent in late prehistoric society.

In many respects, the evidence for how belief systems permeated so many aspects of ordinary life is remarkably consistent throughout later prehistory in the Thames Valley. Indeed, the sheer variety of placement modes and character of burials and specialist deposits suggests a significant degree of continuity in beliefs and abstract ideas about the world.

The great diversity and relatively small number of ceremonial structures and shrines and the sheer oddness of some largely unexplained structures is not conducive to revealing much about religious beliefs. On the contrary, in keeping with the evidence of the importance of the natural world in celtic religion, beliefs appear not to have been generally expressed through the design and use of sacred structures or, if they were, such buildings were not common. Recurrence of expression seems more evident in where and how people, animals and objects were deposited, suggesting connections with the natural world, particularly related to earth and water and to some extent animals. Many of the similarities of deposition between humans and animals in settlement sites suggest that animals were in some sense treated as equivalent to people, but the meaning behind this might be double-edged where sacrifices are concerned.

Superficially the main changes in belief systems apparent from later Bronze Age and Iron Age burial practices are first, a relative decline in overt display of status and wealth and of disposal in formal burials within mounds or cemeteries during the middle Bronze Age and second, the re-emergence of overt displays of status and use of cemeteries on the periphery of the study area in the late Iron Age.

Trends in the ways that human bodies were disposed of (by cremation or inhumation burial in whole or part) seem to have been more superficial than the consistency of where they were put. Carr (2007) has drawn attention to the possible similarities in relation to cremation and excarnation, suggesting that both could have embodied similar underlying attitudes to life and death. Although inhumation may have been regarded in a different light, it nevertheless paralleled in many ways the places where cremations were interred. In many respects there is thus a remarkable degree of consistency in the ideas that lay behind the manner and place of deposition of the dead. The gradual shift from cremation to inhumation burial in the later Bronze Age to Iron Age should not be seen as part of the so-called 'Great Divide,' but more symptomatic of the continuity of some deeply held beliefs.

Survivals and legacies

The inheritance from earlier prehistory

Brück (2000) has questioned whether the early to middle Bronze Age transition was as revolutionary as is sometimes claimed and, as we have seen, much the same sort of questioning might be directed at Needham's 'Great Divide' and the growing fashion to detect another major general change in the 4th century BC. The difficulty seems to be the desire of archaeologists to pigeonhole their observations into chronological packages with common boundaries. But as a means of detecting wider patterns of change this is based on a flawed conception of how change actually happens at different rates and trajectories in different places and times and at different scales. Consideration of issues of 'continuity' and 'discontinuity' (eg Needham 2007, 55) likewise tend to oversimplify the ways that change happens, disguising rather than illuminating the dynamic complexity of drivers of change.

We have already seen how late prehistoric communities inherited many patterns of life and death from previous generations that continued and were adapted over several centuries. In some ways it is still not entirely clear how persistent some of these were. For example, while we can plausibly suggest that the rights and constraints on land that shaped Iron Age settlement in the Stanton Harcourt area lasted well into the Roman period, the varied sequence of development at Yarnton appears to have been more fluid. Perhaps most under-explored is the possibility that earlier prehistoric mobile pastoral life-styles persisted alongside the emergence of settled farming in some parts of the Thames Valley. Likewise in funerary traditions many practices endured while others changed and, even in terms of exchange, basic sources of sought-after commodities like querns persisted well into the later Iron Age and were only superseded by new technology and sources long after their initial introduction.

We can also see recurrent patterns of change, like the emergence of nucleated intensive long-lived settlement of various forms, not all synchronous at the beginning of the middle Bronze Age or at the 'Great Divide,' nor the 4th century enclosure revolution or the late Iron Age emergence of dynastic politics – but spread through much of our period, reflecting the varied fortunes of different communities.

Legacies to Roman administered Thames Valley

Amongst the legacies that persisted into the Roman period are several broad trends with a momentum that was to last well beyond the conquest, just as much of what was new in terms of Roman culture, trade, and politics had already started to become established in the century before the arrival of Roman rule. The broad patterns of population growth and environmental change were already well-established and continued to be a major influence. For the first time, human society in the Thames Valley had had a sufficient impact on the environment to have induced significant changes in the hydrology of the river itself as the impact of humans on the vegetation cover of the catchment rapidly accelerated. Already old habitats were being transformed and new ones created, though further new habitats and changes in the balance of landuse would emerge from the need to feed an army and growing urban population.

More generally the pattern of settlement and landuse along the valley floor established through later prehistory, with modifications in the late Iron Age, persisted largely unchanged until the 2nd century AD (see Booth *et al.* 2007). The extent to which the valley floor then became a relative backwater compared with the surrounding hills is an issue that needs much more investigation off the gravels than has yet been attempted. It may reflect very deep-seated patterns of communal rights over land that were variable in the constraints and opportunities available under the new regime. It is quite possible that the recurrent disruption of settlement pattern in the 2nd century AD (Lambrick 1992b; Booth *et al.* 2007) reflected an eventual breaking or modification of those shackles, only when Roman rule was fully established and secure. Likewise, although new Roman religions made their appearance, many Iron Age practices persisted on ordinary rural sites, suggesting that entrenched traditions lasted a long time alongside new cultural practices.

Fig. 10.2 *Floodplain common land at Port Meadow, Oxford:* (above) *surviving earthworks of Iron Age houses picked out by recent flooding;* (below left and right) *animals have been grazing Port Meadow for millennia and botanical survey has shown a remarkable similarity of modern plants to samples from waterlogged Iron Age penannular ditches*

Living legacies today

In examining the trajectories of change in later prehistory, it is important to recognise how different aspects of environment and society change in different ways and at different rates. Some of the inheritances and legacies that were left have proved remarkably long-lived and, despite the separation of two millennia from the end of our period, it is worth considering whether there are aspects of today's environment and society that we can see as originating in late prehistory – what we might call 'living legacies.' So much has changed in the last two millennia that we might expect both that the links are either only general or highly individualistic. Moreover, where such legacies exist not all the detail can be shown to have a continuous thread of survival over the last 2000 years.

Social and political relationships

Amongst the more intangible general legacies, we can see the later prehistoric period as a time when the physical expression of basic foundations of social cohesion changed from ancestry and social links expressed through ritual monuments to the clearer definition of society's economic and territorial resource base familiar to us today. It was also a period which, at its latter end, saw the first emergence in the Thames Valley of a kind of politics based on kingship and large geographical territories that has a ring of familiarity with our own more recent history (and some contemporary non-democratic societies). Even though we may have only hazy ideas of what this was like, it seems easier to imagine this kind of politics than that of earlier prehistory.

Landuse

This change in the economic and geographical foundations of social relationships was accompanied by an intensification and consolidation of the impact of human society on the environment and of broad patterns of landuse and settlement that are still recognisable today, albeit in an even more intensified form. The character of the settled farming landscape that had emerged by 50 AD would have been far more familiar to us today than its early beginnings in 1500 BC. More specifically and locally, the relics of later prehistory in terms of earthworks and ancient monuments continue to have a role in present-day society. Although very different from how they originally functioned, they continue to draw people to such places for the impressiveness of the original engineering achievement and wider intangible meanings.

Port Meadow and other common grazing land

There are some legacies that are much more dynamic. Perhaps the most 'living' legacy in a literal sense is Port Meadow, which as far as we can tell from the close similarity of its ancient and present day botanical composition, is still being grazed in much the same manner as it was at least 2,200 years ago, and perhaps much longer (Fig. 10.2). Down the ages the way that common rights are exercised there have changed, but if it were possible to trace their history, it would not be surprising if they had some sort of origin in much older, prehistoric landuse rights.

Technology

Technologically it might initially appear that we have long since moved on from the developments of later prehistory. While it is interesting that the earliest evidence of ironworking in Britain comes from the Thames Valley, a more specific living legacy is the basic design of some woodworking and other tools, especially later Bronze Age chisels and gouges and Iron Age axe- and adze-hammers. In basic form these are still replicated in modern equivalents.

Boundaries

A different 'living' legacy has been the persistence of the Thames as a political boundary, from tribal areas to kingdoms that became tribally oriented administrative arrangements of Roman Britain, and later persisted from shires, hundreds and parishes to counties and districts. It may not be possible to demonstrate this as a continuous thread of development, but it is certainly a recurrent pattern, with the river remaining an important political and administrative boundary until recent times, though since 1974 there has been steady erosion of this role.

Another legacy of prehistory in terms of boundaries was only appreciated with the discovery of the defences of the Abingdon oppidum. These subsequently dictated the layout of properties in medieval and post-medieval Abingdon and, despite encroachment, can still be traced in parts of the modern urban layout.

Much more speculatively, it would not be surprising if it were found that in many parts of the Thames catchment major land divisions and boundaries – and perhaps remnants of fields – can be traced back to the later prehistoric period. Although it is perhaps unlikely that this will be as marked as in West Penwith, Dartmoor or Essex, the exploration of this issue in the Chilterns and elsewhere has only recently begun. It may not be entirely fanciful to suggest that the origins of some Cotswold estates might be traced back this far.

The White Horse

There can be little doubt that the most iconic living legacy of the period, both as a direct survival and in symbolic terms, is the Uffington White Horse (Fig. 10.3). Created as a symbol of identity, it has probably maintained that role in various guises and through several different social, political and economic conditions to continue to provide not only the identity of the Vale over which it presides, but also a much-used icon of modern social institutions and businesses (Miles *et al*. 2003, 15-24, 267-8, 299-300).

Fig. 10.3   *The iconic White Horse at Uffington: (above) visitors enjoying the view over the Vale of the White Horse during excavation; (centre left) excavation of colluvium and earlier layers of the Horse's 'beak' from which it was dated to c 1380-550 BC; (below) aerial view; the Vale of the White Horse District Council's logo with the Horse perpetuating the enduring identity of the area*

Prehistoric foundations of the modern world?

It may be an exaggeration to see late prehistory as having laid the foundations of modern characteristics of the Thames Valley but, apart from particular living legacies such as the White Horse or Port Meadow, the more fundamental point is that in numerous ways it would certainly seem an infinitely more familiar world to us if we could go back to the end of the Iron Age than it would be to return to the end of earlier prehistory.

The state of research

In compiling this review a number of significant issues that are highly encouraging for future progress have emerged, but also others that threaten to hold back progress.

Amongst the most encouraging trends has been the recovery of the much more complete plans of settlements and fields that have been emerging from large-scale gravel extraction and other major development. Time and again it has been possible to achieve a much better grasp of the overall picture than has been possible from small, partial views.

Conversely, it remains problematical that some investigations are still too often focussed on investigating what is supposed to be the most significant parts of sites without appreciating how this risks failure to reveal enough to appreciate their real significance and may merely reinforce, rather than test or challenge existing ideas.

Over-reliance on cropmarks to target areas of investigation without the benefit of detailed geophysics to provide context is a further issue in development-led archaeology, especially given how many recent research projects have demonstrated the value of detailed geophysics coupled with sample excavation – not a new approach but of added value with modern geophysics.

If getting a broad enough picture is one challenge for investigation and sampling of large areas, ensuring that adequate finds and environmental samples are recovered to allow interpretation is another, as is the use of carefully targeted radiocarbon and other scientific dating methods.

The principles behind the Perry Oaks/T5 approach, which in some ways reflects practices of the 1970s and 1980s (and earlier) of seeking to recover enough material to develop and modify hypotheses in the field, has a great deal more merit than arbitrary percentage rate basis of sampling. It is now widely recognised that arbitrarily low levels of sampling to find and characterise sites through evaluation have been too crude to be effective for identifying many types of site. The same problem applies to sampling strategies in excavation if routine sampling suppresses a more intelligent question-led approach. Part of the problem is that the reporting of results has often become standardised in ways that are not necessarily conducive to forward-thinking analysis. For example, understanding the dynamics of change and making inter-site comparisons would benefit from more analysis of the character and quantity of material per volume of material excavated, or rates of occurrence over time. The reporting of results in ways that allow new kinds of comparison to be made is as much a key to enabling the generation and exploration of fresh ideas as ensuring that sufficient data is recovered to address pertinent questions.

In several of the projects referred to in this book, these issues have clearly been considered, but there is plenty of scope for generating new insights into late prehistory from the opportunities provided by the aggregates and other industries operating in the Thames Valley.

Bibliography

Abbreviations

AM	Ashmolean Museum
Antiq J	*Antiquaries Journal*
Archaeol J	*The Archaeological Journal*
BAJ	*Berkshire Archaeological Journal*
BBOAJ	*Berks Bucks and Oxon Archaeological Journal*
BL	British Library
Bodl. Lib.	Bodleian Library, University of Oxford
CBA	Council for British Archaeology
CBA9	*Council for British Archaeology Group 9 Newsletter*
CUCAP	Cambridge University Collection of Aerial Photographs
NMR	National Monuments Record
OA	Oxford Archaeology
OUCA	Oxford University Committee for Archaeology
PCRG	Prehistoric Ceramics Research Group
PPS	*Proceedings of the Prehistoric Society*
RCHME	Royal Commission on the Historical Monuments of England
RIB	*Roman Inscriptions of Britain*
SyAC	*Surrey Archaeological Collections*
SMA	*South Midlands Archaeology*
SMR	Sites and Monuments Record
TBGAS	*Transactions of the Bristol and Gloucestershire Archaeological Society*
TVAS	Thames Valley Archaeological Services
VCH	Victoria County History (the Victoria History of the Counties of England)
WAM	*Wiltshire Archaeological and Natural History Magazine*

Bibliography

Adkins, L and Needham, S P, 1985 New research on a Late Bronze Age enclosure at Queen Mary's Hospital, Carshalton, *SyAC*, **76**, 11-50

Ainslie, R, 1988 Bladon Round Castle, *SMA* **18**, 94

Ainslie, R, 1992 Excavations at Thrupp near Radley, Oxon, *SMA* **22**, 63-6

Ainslie, R, 1999 Thrupp near Radley, *SMA* **29**, 30-31

Ainslie, R, 2002 Abingdon, Barton Lane, *SMA* **32**, 36-8

Allason-Jones, L, 1996 *Roman jet in the Yorkshire Museum*, The Yorkshire Museum, York

Allason-Jones, L, and Jones, JM, 1994 Jet and other materials in Roman artefact studies, *Archaeologia Aeliana*, 5th Series, **XXII**, 265-72

Allen, D, 1986 Excavations in Bierton, 1979 *Records of Bucks* **28**,1-120

Allen, D F, 1960 The origins of coinage in Britain: a reappraisal, in S S Frere (ed.), *Problems of the Iron Age in southern Britain*, Institute of Archaeol Occ Pap **11**, London, 97-308

Allen, G W G, 1984 Discovery from the air, *Aerial Archaeology* **10**, 37-89

Allen, S, Allen, J R L and Fulford, M G, 1991-3 A late Iron Age-early Roman site at Streatley, *BAJ* **74**, 145-6

Allen, T G, 1981 Hardwick-with-Yelford: Smithsfield, *CBA Group 9 Newsletter* **11**, 124-7

Allen, T G, 1989 Abingdon, Vineyard development, *SMA* **19**, 44-7

Allen, T G, 1990a *An Iron Age and Romano-British enclosed settlement at Watkins Farm, Northmoor, Oxon.*, Oxford Archaeol Unit Thames Valley Landscapes Mono: the Windrush Valley, Vol **1**, Oxford

Allen, T G, 1990b Notes on Abingdon Vineyard, *SMA* **20**, 73-8

Allen, T G, 1991 An 'oppidum' at Abingdon, Oxfordshire, *SMA* **21**, 97-9

Allen, T G, 1993 Abingdon, Abingdon Vineyard 1992: Areas 2 and 3, the early defences, *SMA* **23**, 64-6

Allen, T G, 1994 Abingdon, Abingdon Vineyard, Area 3, *SMA* **24**, 33

Allen, T G, 2000 The Iron Age background, in Henig, M and Booth, P *Roman Oxfordshire*, Sutton, Stroud, 1-33

Allen, T G, 2007 Oxfordshire Later Bronze Age and Iron Age Historic Environment Resource Assessment (Draft) http://www.buckscc.gov.uk/bcc/get/assets/docs/archaeology/Later%20Prehistory%20Oxfordshire%20nature%20of%20evidence.pdf

Allen, T G, Darvill, T C, Green, L S and Jones, M U, 1993 *Excavations at Roughground Farm, Lechlade, Gloucestershire: a prehistoric and Roman landscape*, Oxford Archaeol Unit Thames Valley Landscapes: the Cotswold Water Park **1**, Oxford

Allen, T G, Hacking, P and Boyle, A, 2000 Eton Rowing Course at Dorney Lake. The Burial Traditions, *Tarmac Papers* **4**, 65-106

Allen, T G, Hey, G and Miles, D, 1997 A line of time: approaches to archaeology in the upper and middle Thames valley, England, *World Archaeology* **29(1)**, 114-29.

Allen, T G, and Kamash, Z, 2008 *Saved from the grave: Neolithic to Saxon discoveries at Spring Road Municipal Cemetery, Abingdon, Oxfordshire, 1990-2000*, Oxford Archaeol Thames Valley Landscapes Mono **28**, Oxford

Allen, T G and Lamdin-Whymark H, 2000 The Rediscovery of Taplow Hillfort, *SMA* **30,** 22-8

Allen T, Lamdin-Whymark H, and Maricevic, D, 2006 Taplow, Taplow Court (Phase 2), Cliveden Road. *SMA* **36,** 19-21

Allen, T G, Miles, D and Palmer, S, 1984 Iron Age buildings in the Upper Thames region, in Cunliffe and Miles (eds) 1984, 89-101

Allen, T G and Mitchell, N, 2001 Dorney, Eton Rowing Lake, *SMA* **31,** 26-30

Allen, T G and Moore, J, 1987 Standlake: Eagle Farm, *SMA* **17,** 96-7

Allen, T G and Robinson, M A, 1993 *The prehistoric landscape and Iron Age enclosed settlement at Mingies Ditch, Hardwick-with-Yelford, Oxon,* Thames Valley Landscapes Mono: the Windrush Valley **2,** Oxford

Allen, T G and Welsh, K, 1996 Eton Rowing Lake, Dorney, Buckinghamshire, *SMA* **26,** 23-30

Allen, T G and Welsh, K, 1997 Eton Rowing Lake, Dorney, Buckinghamshire. Second Interim Report, *SMA* **27,** 25-34

Allen, T G and Welsh, K, 1998 Eton Rowing Lake, Dorney, Buckinghamshire, *SMA* **28,** 75-84

Allen, T G, Cramp, K, Lamdin-Whymark, H and Heatley, L forthcoming a Castle Hill and the Surrounding Landscape,Little Wittenham, Oxfordshire, 2002-2006, Oxford Archaeol Thames Valley Landscapes Mono, Oxford

Allen, T G, Barclay A, and Bradley, P forthcoming b Bridging the River, Dividing the Land The Archaeology of a Middle Thames landscape Vol 2: Middle Bronze Age to Roman, Oxford Archaeol Thames Valley Landscapes Mono, Oxford

Allen, T G, Hayden, C and Lamdin-Whymark, H, forthcoming d Excavations at Taplow Court, Buckinghamshire: a late Bronze Age and Iron Age hillfort, Oxford Archaeol Thames Valley Landscapes Mono, Oxford

Andrews, P, 1996a Prospect Park, Harmondsworth, London Borough of Hillingdon: settlement and burial from the Neolithic to the Early Saxon Periods, in Andrews and Crockett 1996, 16-50

Andrews, P, 1996b Hurst Park, East Molesey, Surrey: riverside settlement and burial from the Neolithic to the Early Saxon periods, in Andrews and Crockett 1996, 51-104

Andrews, P, 1996c Prospect Park and Hurst Park: the settlements and the landscape, in Andrews and Crockett 1996, 108-11

Andrews, P and Crockett, A, 1996 *Three excavations along the Thames and its tributaries, 1994,* Wessex Archaeol Rep **10,** Salisbury

Anon, 1946-7 Notes and News *Oxoniensia* 11-12 162-3

Anon, 1960 Archaeological Notes from Reading Museum *BAJ* **58** 52-65

Anon, 1963/4 Archaeological Notes from Reading Museum *BAJ* **61** 96-109

Anon, 2003 *An Investigation into Iron Age Diet at Yarnton, using Stable Carbon and Nitrogen Isotopes,*

unpublished Univ of Oxford BA dissertation (Candidate Number 21101)

Arkle, W J, 1942 Place-names and topography in the Upper Thames country, a regional essay, *Oxoniensia* 7 1-23

Armstrong, L, 1979 Standlake, Oxfordshire, CBA Group 9 *Newsletter* **9,** 31-7

Arnold, D E, 1985 *Ceramic Theory and Cultural Process,* Cambridge

Astill, G G and Lobb, S J, 1989 Excavation of prehistoric, Roman and Saxon deposits at Wraysbury, Berkshire, *Archaeol J* **146,** 68-134

Atkinson, R J C, 1942 Archaeological sites in Port Meadow, Oxford, *Oxoniensia* 7, 24-35

Avery, M, 1993 *Hillforts in Southern England,* Brit Arch Rep (Brit Ser) **231** Oxford

Avery, M, Sutton, J E and Banks, J W, 1967 Rainsborough, Northants, England: excavations 1961-5, *PPS* **33,** 207-95

Bagnall-Smith, J, 1995 Interim report on the votive material from the Romano-Celtic temple sites in Oxfordshire, *Oxonensia* **60,** 177-203

Bagnall-Smith, J, 1998 More votive finds from Woodeaton, Oxfordshire, *Oxoniensia* **63,** 147-85

Baker, S, 2002 Prehistoric and Romano-British landscapes at Little Wittenham and Long Wittenham, Oxfordshire, *Oxoniensia* **67,** 1-28

Bannister, N R, 2004 The Surrey Historic Landscape Characterisation project, in Cotton *et al.* (eds) 2004, 119-32

Barclay, A 1999 Earlier prehistoric pottery, in Mudd *et al.* 1999, 315-20

Barclay, A, Boyle, A, Bradley, P and Roberts, M R, 1997 Excavations at the former Jewson's Yard, Harefield Road, Uxbridge, Middlesex, *Trans Lond Middlesex Arch Soc* **46** 1-25

Barclay, A, Boyle A and Keevil G D, 2001 A Prehistoric enclosure at Eynsham Abbey, Oxfordshire, *Oxoniensia* **66,** 105-62

Barclay, A, Bradley, R, Hey, G and Lambrick G, 1996 The earlier prehistory of the Oxford region in the light of recent research, *Oxoniensia* **61,** 1–20.

Barclay, A, Fell, V and Wallis, J, 1995 An iron socketed axe from the River Thames, Buscot, Oxfordshire, *Oxoniensia* **60,** 417-19

Barclay, A, and Glass, H, with Parry, C, 1995 Excavations of Neolithic and Bronze Age ring ditches, Shorncote Quarry, Somerford Keynes, Gloucestershire, *TBGAS* 113, 21-60

Barclay, A, Gray, M and Lambrick, G, 1995 *Excavations at the Devil's Quoits, Stanton Harcourt, Oxfordshire 1972-3 and 1988,* Oxford Archaeol Thames Valley Landscapes Mono: The Windrush Valley Vol **3,** Oxford

Barclay, A and Halpin, C, 1999 *Excavations at Barrow Hills, Radley, Oxfordshire. I: the Neolithic and Bronze Age monument complex,* Oxford Archaeol Thames Valley Landscapes Mono **11,** Oxford

Barclay, A, Lambrick, G, Moore, J and Robinson, M, 2003 *Lines in the landscape, cursus monuments* in the Upper Thames Valley, Oxford Archaeol Thames Valley Landscapes Mono **15**, Oxford

Barker, L, Brown, M and McOmish, D, 2003 Analytical Earthwork Survey at Three Chilterns Hillforts in Solik, M, (ed.), *New Perspectives on Chiltern Landscapes. Papers presented at the Chiltern Historic Environment Conference 2003*

Barnes, I, Boisnier, W A, Cleal, R M J, Fitzpatrick, A P and Roberts, M R, 1995 *Early Settlement in Berkshire: Mesolithic-Roman Occupation Sites in the Thames and Kennet Valleys*, Wessex Archaeol Report **6**

Barnes, I, Butterworth, C A, Hawkes, J W and Smith, L, 1997 *Excavation at Thames Valley Park, Reading, 1986-88*, Wessex Archaeol Report No **14**, Salisbury

Barnes, I and Cleal, R M J, 1995 Neolithic and Bronze Age settlement at Weir Bank Stud Farm, Bray, in Barnes *et al.* 1995

Barnes, I and Hawkes, J W, 1991-3 Archaeological Excavations at Broadwater, Hurst *BAJ* **74**, 95-107

Barrett, J C, 1973 Four Bronze Age cremation cemeteries from Middlesex, *Trans London Middlesex Archaeol Soc.* **24**, 111-34

Barrett, J C, 1980 The pottery of the later Bronze Age in lowland England, *PPS* **46**, 297–320

Barrett, J C, 1994 *Fragments of Antiquity: an archaeology of social life in Britain 2900-1200 BC*, Blackwell, Oxford

Barrett, J C and Bradley, R (eds), 1980a Settlement and society in the British Later Bronze Age, BAR Brit Ser **83**

Barrett, J C, and Bradley, R, 1980b The Later Bronze Age in the Thames Valley, in Barrett and Bradley, 1980a

Barrett, J C, Bradley, R and Green, M, 1991 *Landscape, Monuments and Society. The Prehistory of Cranbourne Chase,* Cambridge, Cambridge University Press

Barrett, J C, Lewis, J S C, and Welsh, K, 1999 Perry Oaks - a history of inhabitation, part 1, *London Archaeol*, **9 (7)**, 195-9

Barrett, J C, Lewis, J S C, and Welsh, K, 2001 Perry Oaks – a history of inhabitation, part 2, *London Archaeol*, **9 (8)**, 221-7

Bateman, C, Enright, D and Oaky, N, 2003 Prehistoric to Anglo-Saxon settlements to the rear of Sherborne House, Lechlade: excavations in 1997, *Trans Bristol Gloucestershire Archaeol Soc* **121**, 23-96

Bayne, N, 1957 Excavations at Lyneham Camp, Lyneham, Oxon, *Oxoniensia* **22**, 1-10

Bean, S C, 2000 *The coinage of the Atrebates and Regni,* Oxford University School of Archaeology Mono **50**, Oxford

Bell, C, 1996 An Archaeological Excavation on Land Adjacent to Snowy Fielder Waye, Isleworth London Borough of Hounslow Middlesex, *Trans London and Middlsex Arch Soc* **47**, 35-60

Bender Jørgensen, L, 1990 Stone-Age Textiles in North Europe in *Textiles in Northern Archaeology,*

Textile Symposium in York North European Symposium for Archaeological Textiles Mono **3**, London Archetype Publications, 1-10

Benson, D and Miles, D, 1974 *The Upper Thames Valley, an Archaeological Survey of the River Gravels*, Oxford Archaeol Unit Survey no. **2**, Oxford

Bersu, G, 1940 Excavations at Little Woodbury: part 1, *PPS* **6**, 30-111

Biddulph, E, 2003 Appleford Sidings, Oxfordshire, 1993-2000 Post Excavation Assessment and Research Design Oxford Archaeology unpubl. client report

Birbeck, V, 2001 Excavations at Watchfield, Shrivenham, Oxfordshire, 1998, *Oxoniensia* **66**, 221-88

Bird, D, 2004 Roman religious sites in the landscape, in Cotton *et al.* (eds) 2004, 77-90

Bird, J and Bird, D G (eds), 1987 *The Archaeology of Surrey to 1540*, Surrey Archaeol Soc, Guildford

Black, E W, 1986 Romano-British Burial Customs and religious Beliefs in South East England, *Archaeol J* **143**, 201-39

Blair, W J, 1991 *Early Medieval Surrey*, Alan Sutton, Stroud

Blair, W J, 1994 *Anglo-Saxon Oxfordshire,* Alan Sutton, Stroud

Bond, D, 1988 *Excavation at the North Ring, Mucking, Essex: A Late Bronze Age Enclosure,* East Anglian Archaeol **43**

Bonner, D. and Parkhouse, J., 1997 Investigations at the Prehistoric Site at Coldharbour Farm, Aylesbury in 1996, *Records of Bucks* **39**,73-139

Bonte, P, 1981 Marxist theory and anthropological analysis: the study of nomadic pastoralist societies, in Kahn and Llobera (eds), *The Anthropology of Pre-Capitalist Societies*, 22–56, Macmillan, London

Booth, P M, 1993 Archaeological evaluation at Appleford Sidings, near Didcot, Oxfordshire 1993, Oxford Archaeol Unit internal report

Booth, P M, 1997 A Prehistoric-Early Roman site near Lock Crescent, Kidlington, *Oxoniensia* **62**, 21-49

Booth, P, Boyle, A, and Keevill, G D, 1993 A Romano-British Kiln Site at Lower Farm, Nuneham Courtenay, and Other Sites on the Didcot to Oxford and Wootton to Abingdon Water Mains, Oxfordshire, *Oxoniensia* **58**

Booth, P, Dodd, A, Robinson, M and Smith, A, 2007 *The Thames through Time. The Archaeology of the Gravel Terraces of the Upper and Middle Thames. The early historical period: AD 1-1000* Oxford Archaeol Thames Valley Landscapes Mono No. **27**, Oxford

Booth, P M and Edgeley-Long, G, 2003 Prehistoric settlement and Roman pottery production at Blackbird Leys, Oxford, *Oxoniensia* **68**, 201-62

Booth, P M and Simmonds, A, 2004 An Iron Age and early Romano-British site at Hatford Quarry, Sandy Lane, Hatford, Oxfordshire, *Oxoniensia* **69**, 319-354

Booth, P M and Simmonds, A, forthcoming *Appleford's Earliest Farmers: Archaeological Work at Appleford Sidings, Oxfordshire, 1993-2000*, Oxford Archaeol Thames Valley Landscapes Mono, Oxford

Bourn, R, 2000 Manorhouse Farm Hatford, Oxfordshire: An Iron Age and early Romano-British settlement, in R J Zeepvat (ed.) *Three Iron Age and Romano-British settlements on English gravels*, Brit Arch Rep (Brit Ser) **312**, Oxford, 5-74

Bowden, M, Ford, S and Gaffney, V, 1991-3 The Excavation of a late Bronze Age artifact scatter on Weathercock Hill, *BAJ* **74**, 69-83

Bowden, M, Ford, S and Mees, G, 1991-3 The Date of the Ancient Fields on the Berkshire Downs, *BAJ* **74**, 109-33

Bowler, D and Robinson, M, 1980 Three round barrows at King's Weir, Wytham, Oxon., *Oxoniensia* **45**, 1-8

Boyle, A, Dodd, A, Miles, D and Mudd, A, 1995 *Two Oxfordshire Anglo-Saxon cemeteries: Berinsfield and Didcot*, Oxford Archaeol Thames Valley Landscapes Mono **8**, Oxford

Boyle, A, Jennings, D, Miles, D and Palmer, S, 1998 *The Anglo-Saxon cemetery at Butler's Field, Lechlade, Gloucestershire Volume 1: Prehistoric and Roman activity and Anglo-Saxon grave catalogue*, Oxford Archaeol Thames Valley Landscapes Mono **10**, Oxford

Boyle, A, Keevill, G D, and Parsons, M, 1993 The assessment and excavation at Fullamoor Farm, Clifton Hampden, in Booth *et al.*1993, 106-115

Bradford, J S P, 1940 The Excavation of Cherbury Camp 1939 an Interim Report, *Oxoniensia* **5** 13-20

Bradford, J S P, 1942a An early Iron Age settlement at Standlake, Oxon., *Oxoniensia* **22**, 202-214

Bradford, J S P, 1942b An Early Iron Age site at Allen's Pit, Dorchester, *Oxoniensia* **7**, 36-60

Bradford, J S P and Goodchild, R G, 1939 Excavations at Frilford, Berks. 1937-8, *Oxoniensia* **4**, 1-70

Bradley, P, Charles, B, Hardy, A and Poore, D, 1995 Prehistoric and Roman activity and a Civil War Ditch: excavations at the Chemistry Research Laboratory, 2-4 South Parks Road, Oxford, *Oxoniensia* 70, 142-202

Bradley, R, 1968 The South Oxfordshire Grims Ditch and its significance, *Oxoniensia* **33**, 1-13

Bradley, R, 1978 *The Prehistoric Settlement of Britain*, Routledge, London

Bradley, R, 1985 Exchange and social distances: the structure of bronze artefact distributions, *Man* **20**, 692-704

Bradley, R, 1990 *An archaeological analysis of prehistoric hoards and votive deposits*, Cambridge University Press, Cambridge

Bradley, R, 1998 *The passage of arms: an archaeological analysis of prehistoric hoards and votive deposits*, Cambridge University Press, Cambridge

Bradley, R and Ellison, A, 1975 *Rams Hill: a Bronze Age defended enclosure and its landscape*, Brit Arch Rep (Brit Ser) **19**, Oxford

Bradley, R, Entwistle, R and Raymond, F, 1994 *Prehistoric land divisions on Salisbury Plain: the work of the Wessex Linear Ditches Project*. English Heritage Archaeol Rep **2**, 122-36

Bradley, R and Gordon, K, 1988 Human skulls from the River Thames, their dating and significance, *Antiquity*, **62**, 503-509

Bradley, R, Lobb, S, Richards, J and Robinson, M, 1980 Two late Bronze Age settlements on the Kennet Gravels: excavations at Aldermaston Wharf and Knight's Farm, Burghfield, Berkshire, *PPS* **46**, 217-95

Bradley, R and Yates, D, 2007 After 'Celtic' fields: the social organisation of Iron Age agriculture, in Haselgrove and Pope 2007, 94-102

Brady, K, Smith A and Laws, G, forthcoming 2007 Excavations at Abingdon West Central Redevelopment: Iron Age, Roman, medieval and post-medieval activity in Abingdon, *Oxoniensia* **72**

Bramwell, D, Cowles, G S and Wilson, R, 1986 Bird bones, in Miles (ed.) 1986

Branch, N P and Green, C P, 2004 The environmental history of Surrey, in Cotton *et al.* (eds) 2004

Branigan, K, 1973 *Town and country: the archaeology of Verulamium and the Chilterns*, Spurbooks, Bourne End

Branigan, K, 1985 *The Catuvellauni*, Gloucester

Brennand, M, and Taylor, M, 2003 The survey and excavation of a Bronze Age timber circle at Holme-next-the-Sea, Norfolk, 1998-9, *PPS* **69**, 1-84

Briggs, G, Cook, J and Rowley, T (eds), 1986 *The Archaeology of the Oxford Region*, Oxford Univ Dept of External Studies

Britnell, W J, 1976 Antler cheekpieces of the British Late Bronze Age, *Antiq J* **56**, 24-34.

Brossler A, Early, R and Allen, C, 2004 *Green Park (Reading Business Park): Phase 2 Excavations 1995: Neolithic and Bronze Age sites*, Oxford Archaeol and OUCA Thames Valley Landscapes Mono **19**, Oxford

Brossler, A, Gocher, M, Laws, G and Roberts, M, 2002 Shorncote Quarry excavations of a late prehistoric landscape in the Upper Thames 1997 and 1998, *TBGAS* 120 37-87

Brossler, A, Brown, F, Guttman, E and Webley, L, forthcoming Prehistoric Settlement in the lower Kennet Valley: Excavations at Green Park (Reading Buisness Park) Phase 3 and Moores Farm, Berkshire, Oxford Archaeol Thames Valley Landscapes Mono, Oxford

Brothwell, D, 1972 Paleodemography and early Britsh populations *World Archaeology*, **4(1)**, 1972, 75-87

Brown, A, 1977 Plant remains, in Durham, B, 1977

Brown, A G, 1991 The Changing Role of Flint in Later British Prehistory Unpubl doctoral thesis, University of Reading

Brown, A G and Bradley, P, 2006 Worked Flint, in Cromarty *et al.* 2006, 58-67

Brown, G, Field, D and McOmish, D, 1994 East Chisenbury Midden complex, in Fitzpatrick and Morris 1994, 46-9

Brown, M, 2001 *Ivinghoe Beacon, Ivinghoe, Buckinghamshire,* English Heritage Survey Report AI/17/2001

Brown, N and Cotton, J, 2000 The Bronze Age, in *Museum of London Archaeological Service 2000*

Brück, J, 1995 A place for the dead: the role of human remains in Late Bronze Age Britain, *PPS* **61**, 245-277

Brück, J, 1999a Houses, Lifestyles and Deposition on Middle Bronze Age Settlements in Southern England, *PPS* **65**, 145-166

Brück, J, 1999b What's in a settlement? Domestic practice and residential mobility in Early Bronze Age southern England, in Brück, J and Goodman, M (eds), *Making Places in the Prehistoric World: themes in settlement archaeology,* University College London University Press, London, 52-74

Brück, J, 2000 Settlement, landscape and social identity: the early middle Bronze Age transition in Wessex, Sussex and the Thames Valley, *Oxford Journal of Archaeology* **19(3)**, 273-300

Brück, J, (ed), 2001 *Bronze Age landscapes: tradition and transformation,* Oxbow, Oxford

Brück, J and Goodman, M (eds), 1999 *Making Places in the Prehistoric World: themes in settlement archaeology,* University College London University Press, London

Bryant, S R, 2007 Central places or special places? The origins and development of oppida in Hertfordshire, in Haselgrove and Moore 2007, 62-80

Bryant, S R and Burleigh, G, 1995 The later prehistoric dykes of the eastern Chilterns, in Holgate 1995, 17-27

Bryant, S R and Niblett, R, 1997 The Late Iron Age in Hertfordshire and the Northern Chilterns, in Gwilt and Haselgrove (eds) 1997, 270-81

Buck, C E, Kenworthy, J B, Litton, C D, and Smith, A F M, 1991 Combining archaeological and radiocarbon information: a Bayesian approach to calibration, *Antiquity,* **65**, 808–21

Bull, E J, 1993 The Bi-Axial Landscape of Prehistoric Buckinghamshire, *Records of Bucks* **35**, 11-18

Butterworth, C A and Hawkes, J W, 1997 Floodplain excavations and observations (W244), 1988, in Barnes *et al*. 1997, 78-110

Butterworth, C A and Lobb, S J, 1992 *Excavations in the Burghfield Area, Berkshire,* Wessex Archaeol Rep **1**, Salisbury

Calkin, J B 1953 Kimmeridge coal money and the Romano-British shale armlet industry, *Proc. Dorset Nat Hist and Archaeol Soc* **75**, 45-71

Campbell, G E, 1992 Excavations at Lower Bolney, Harpsden, South Oxfordshire, 1991, *Oxoniensia* **57**, 29-42

Campbell, G, 1992 Bronze Age Plant Remains, in Moore and Jennings 1992, 103-12

Campbell, G, 2000 Plant utilisation: the evidence from charred plant remains, in Cunliffe, B W, *The Danebury Environs Programme The prehistory of a Wessex Landscape Volume 1: Introduction* English Heritage and OUCA Mono **48** Institute of Archaeology, Oxford, 45-59

Campbell, G and Hamilton, J, 2000 Danebury Environs: agricultural change in the Iron Age, in Bailey, G, Charles R and Winder, N, *Human Ecodyamics* Symposia of the Association for Environmental Archaeology **19**, Oxbow Books Oxford, 114-22

Campbell, G and Straker, V, 2003 Prehistoric crop husbandry and plant use in Southern England: development and regionality, in K Robson Brown (ed.) *Archaeological Sciences* **99**, Brit Arch Rep (Int Ser) **111**, Oxford, 14-30

Canham, R, 1979 Excavations at Shepperton Green, 1967 and 1973, *Trans London Middlesex Archaeol Soc* **30**, 97-124

Carew, T, Bishop, B, Meddens, F, Ridgeway, V, 2006 *Unlocking the Landscape: Archaeological Excavations at Ashford Prison, Middlesex,* Pre-Construct Archaeology

Carr, G, 2005 Woad, tattooing and identity in Later Iron Age and early Roman Britain *Oxford Journal of Archaeology* **24(3)**, 273-92

Carr, G, 2007 Excarnation to cremation: continuity or change? In Haselgrove and Moore 2007, 444-53

Carr, G and Knussel, C, 1995 The ritual framework of excarnation by exposure as the mortuary practice of the early and middle Iron Ages of central southern Britain, in Gwilt and Haselgrove 1997, 167-73

Carruthers, W J, 1992 Plant remains, in Butterworth and Lobb 1992, 149-58

Carruthers, W J, 1997 Carbonised plant remains, in Barnes *et al*, 1997, 72-7

Case, H J, 1958 A late Belgic burial at Watlington, *Oxoniensia* **23**, 139-41

Case, H J, 1963 Notes on the finds and on ring ditches in the Oxford region, *Oxoniensia* **28**, 19-52

Case, H. J, 1982a The Vicarage Field, Stanton Harcourt, in Case and Whittle 1982, 103–117

Case, H J, 1982b Cassington, 1950-2: late Neolithic pits and the big enclosure, in Case and Whittle 1982, 118-51

Case, H, Bayne, N, Steele, S, Avery, G and Sutermeister, H, 1964-5 Excavations at City Farm, Hanborough, Oxon, *Oxoniensia* **29-30**, 1-98

Case, H J and Whittle, A W R, 1982 *Settlement Patterns in the Oxford Region: Excavations at the Abingdon Causewayed Enclosure and Other Sites,* CBA Res Rep **44**, London

Cassius Dio, u.d. *Roman History Books 56-60,* Harvard University Press

Catherall, P D, Barnett, M and McClean, H, 1984 *The Southern Feeder, the Archaeology of a Gas Pipeline,* British Gas Corporation, London

Catling, H W, 1982 Six ring-ditches at Standlake, in Case and Whittle 1982, 88-102

Challinor, D, 2006 The Wood Charcoal and Charred Plant Remains from Perry Oaks, in Framework Archaeology 2006, CD Section 10

Chambers, F, 2004 Pollen from Blackditch, in Lambrick and Allen 2004, 420

Chambers, F and Botterill, E W, 2006 Pollen Analysis, in Cromarty *et al.* 2006, 142-4

Chambers, R A, 1973 A cemetery site at Beacon Hill, Lewknor, Oxfordshire, in D A Hinton and T Rowley (eds), Excavations on the route of the M40, *Oxoniensia* **38**, 138-45

Chambers, R A, 1976a Two Belgic cremations from Kingston Blount, Oxon, 1975, *Oxoniensia* **41**, 354-5

Chambers, R A, 1976b Late Iron Age material from Ducklington, *Oxoniensia* **41**, 36-7

Chambers, R A 1977 A crouched pit burial at Cassington Mill, Oxon., 1976, *Oxoniensia* **42**, 256-7

Chambers, R A and Williams, G, 1976 A Late Iron Age and Romano-British settlement at Hardwick, *Oxoniensia* **41**, 21-35

Champion, T C, 1980 Settlement and environment in later Bronze Age Kent, in Barrett and Bradley 1980, 223-43

Champion, T C and Collis, J C, 1996 *The Iron Age in Britain and Ireland: Recent Trends,* J R Collis Publications, Dept Arch and Prehistory, University of Sheffield

Charles, B, 2004 The faunal remains, in Jennings *et al.* 2004, 132-3

Clapham, A, 1995 The plant remains, in Barnes and Cleal 1995

Clifford, E M, 1961 *Bagendon, a Belgic oppidum: a record of the excavations, 1954-56,* Cambridge

Clinch, G ,1905 Early Man, in Page, W (ed.), The Victoria County History of the County of Buckingham 1, 177-94 (reprinted London 1969)

Coe, D, Jenkins, V and Richards, J, 1991 Cleveland Farm, Ashton Keynes: Second Interim Report: Investigations May-August 1989, *WAM* **84**, 40-50

Coleman, L, and Collard, M, 2005 Taplow to Dorney Pipeline, Taplow, Buckinghamshire, Unpubl post-excavation assessment and updated project design, Cotswold Archaeology

Coleman, L, and Hancock, A, 2004 Iron Age and Romano-British remains at Filkins and Carterton, *Oxoniensia* **69**, 355-383.

Coleman, L, Havard, T, Collard, M, Cox, S, and McSloy, E, 2004 Denham, The Lea, Interim Report, *SMA* **34**, 14-17

Collard M, Darvill, T and Watts, M, 2006 Ironworking in the Bronze Age? Evidence from a 10th Century BC Settlement at Hartshill Copse, Upper Bucklebury, West Berkshire *PPS* **72**, 367-422

Collins, A E P, 1947 Excavations on Blewburton Hill, 1947, *BAJ* **50**, 4-29

Collins, A E P, 1949 Excavations on Blewburton Hill, 1948 and 1949, *BAJ* **53**, 21-64

Collins, A, and Collins, F, 1952-3 Excavations at Blewburton Hill, 1953, *BAJ* **57**, 52-73

Collins, J R, 1977 The proper study of mankind is pots, in Collis 1977, 29-31

Collis, J R (ed), 1977 *The Iron Age in Britain - a Review,* Sheffield

Collis, J R, 1994 An Iron Age and Roman Cemetery at Owslebury Hampshire, in Fitzpatrick and Morris 1994, 106-8

Collis, J R, 1996 Hillforts, enclosures and boundaries, in Champion and Collis 1996, 87-94

Cook, J and Rowley, T 1985 *Dorchester Through the Ages,* Oxford University Department for External Studies.

Cook, J, Guttmann, E B A, and Mudd, A, 2004 Excavations of an Iron Age site at Coxwell Road, Faringdon, *Oxoniensia* **69**, 181-285

Cook, S and Hayden, C, 2000 Prehistoric and Roman settlement near Heyford Road, Steeple Aston, Oxfordshire, *Oxoniensia* **65**, 161-210

Cool, H, 2006 Shale and Metal Objects, and Worked Bone in Nichols 2006, 38-43

Coombs, D, Northover, P and Maskall, J, 2003 The Tower Hill Axe Hoard, in Miles *et al.* 2003

Cooper, N (ed.), 2006 *The Archaeology of the East Midlands: An Archaeological Resource Assessment and Research Agenda,* University of Leicester Archaeological Services, Leicester

Copeland, T, 1988 The north Oxfordshire Grim's Ditch: a fieldwork survey, *Oxoniensia* **53**, 277-92

Copley, M S, Berstan, R, Dudd, S N and Evershed, R P, forthcoming Organic residue analysis of potsherds from Yarnton Cresswell Field, in Hey (ed.) forthcoming

Corcoran, J, 1952 Tankards and tankard handles of the early British Iron Age, *PPS* **18**, 85-102

Costwold Archaeology 2003 Land at Foxley Fields Farm (Finmere Quarry) Finmere, Oxfordshire: Post-Excavation Assessment and Updated Project Design, unpublished client report 01012 prepared on behalf of Premier Aggregates Ltd.

Cotswold Archaeology 2004 Abingdon Pipeline, Oxfordshire. Archaeological Evaluation and Programme of Archaeological Recording, unpublished client report 04010 produced for RSK ENSR Environment on behalf of Transco.

Cotton, J, 1982 An Iron Age brooch from Seymour's Nursery, Ewell, *SyAC*, **73**, 169-71

Cotton, J, 1991 Prehistory in Greater London, *Current Archaeology* **11(4)** 151-4

Cotton, J, 2000 Foragers & Farmers: Towards the development of a settled landscape in London, *c* 4000-1200BC, in Haynes, Sheldon and Hannigan 2000, 9-35

Cotton, J, Crocker, G and Graham, A (eds), 2004 *Aspects of Archaeology and History in Surrey: Towards a Research Framework for the County,* Surrey Archaeol Soc, Guildford

Cotton, J, Mills, J and Clegg, G, 1986 *Archaeology in West Middlesex: the London Borough of Hillingdon from the Earliest Hunters to the Late Medieval Period,* London Hillingdon Borough Libraries

Cotton, J and Needham, S P, 1999 A Late Bronze Age Metalwork Hoard from Little Woodcote, *Surrey Arch Soc Bull* **329**, 4-6

Cotton, M A, 1956-7 Weycock Hill, 1953, *BAJ* **55**, 48-68

Cotton, M and Frere, S, 1968 Ivinghoe Beacon excavations 1963-65, *Records of Bucks* **18**, 187-260

Cowell, R, Fulford, M and Lobb, S, 1977-8 Excavations of Prehistoric and Roman Settlement at Aldermaston Wharf 1976-7 *BAJ* **69**, 1-35.

Coy, J, 1982 The animal bones, in Gingell 1982, 69-73

Creighton, J, 2000 *Coins and Power in Late Iron Age Britain*, Cambridge University Press, Cambridge

Crockett, A, 1996 Iron Age to Saxon Settlement at Wickhams Field, near Reading. Berkshire: Excavations on the site of the M4 Granada Reading Motorway Service Area, in Andrews and Crockett 1996, 113-70

Crockett A, 2001 The archaeological landscape of Imperial College Sports Ground. Part 1, Prehistoric, *London Archaeologist* **9**, 295-299

Cromarty, A M, Barclay, A, Lambrick, G and Robinson, M, 2006 *Late Bronze Age ritual and habitation on a Thames eyot at Whitecross Farm, Wallingford: The archaeology of the Wallingford By-pass, 1986-92*, Oxford Archaeol Thames Valley Landscapes Mono **22**, Oxford

Cromarty, A.M, Foreman, S and Murray, P, 1999 The excavation of a late Iron Age enclosed settlement at Bicester Fields Farm, Bicester, Oxon., *Oxoniensia* **64**, 153-233.

Cropper, C, and Hardy, A, 1997 The excavation of Iron Age and Medieval features at Glympton Park, Oxfordshire, *Oxoniensia* **62**, 101-7

Cunliffe, B W, 1978 Settlement and Population in the British Iron Age, in Cunliffe and Rowley 1978, 3-24

Cunliffe, B W, 1983 *Danebury: Anatomy of an Iron Age Hillfort* Batsford, London

Cunliffe, B W, 1984 *Danebury: an Iron Age hillfort in Hampshire*, 2 vols., CBA Res Rep **52**, London

Cunliffe, B W, 1992 Preface, in Fulford and Nichols (eds) 1992, ix-x

Cunliffe, B W, 1993 *Wessex to AD 1000*, Longman, Harlow

Cunliffe, B W, 2005 *Iron Age Communities in Britain*, (4th ed.), Routledge, London

Cunliffe, B W and Miles, D (eds), 1984 *Aspects of the Iron Age in central southern Britain*, OUCA Mono **2**, Oxford

Cunliffe, B W and Poole, C, 1991a *Danebury: an Iron Age Hillfort in Hampshire* **4**, *the Excavations, 1979-1988: the site*, CBA Res Rep **73**, London

Cunliffe, B W and Poole, C, 1991b *Danebury: an Iron Age Hillfort in Hampshire* **5**, *the Excavations, 1979-1988: the finds*, CBA Res Rep **73**, London

Cunliffe, B W and Poole, C, 2000 *Suddern Farm, Middle Wallop, Hants, 1991 and 1996. The Danebury Environs Programme. The Prehistory of a Wessex Landscape*, English Heritage and OUCA Mono **49**, Institute of Archaeology, Oxford

Cunliffe, B W and Rowley, T (eds) 1978 *Iron Age Communities in Europe* Brit Arch Rep (Int Ser) **S-48**, Oxford

Cunnington, M E, 1923 *The Early Iron Age Inhabited Site at All Cannings Cross Farm, Wiltshire*, Devizes

Dalwood, H, Dillon, J, Evans, J, and Hawkins, A, 1989 Excavations in Walton, Aylesbury, 1985-1986, *Records of Bucks* **31**, 137-225

Dalwood, H, and Platell, A, 1988 Aylesbury Past Project 1987-88, *SMA* **18**, 35-39

Darby, H C, 1977 *Domesday England*, Cambridge

Darby, H C and Campbell E M J (eds), 1971 *The Domesday Geography of south-east England*, Cambridge

Darvill, T, Hingley, R, Jones, M and Timby, J, 1986 A Neolithic and Iron Age site at the Loders, Lechlade, Gloucestershire, *TBGAS* **104**, 27-48

Davis, J, 1981 Grim's Ditch in Buckinghamshire and Hertfordshire, *Records of Bucks* **23**, 23-31

Davis, J, and Evans, J G, 1984 Grim's Ditch, Ivinghoe, *Records of Bucks* **26**, 1-10

Dawkins, W B, 1862 Traces of the early Britons, *The Gentleman's Magazine and Scientific Review*, London, August 1862, 144-9

Dawkins, W B, 1864 On the traces of the early Britons in the neighbourhood of Oxford, *Proc Oxford Archit Hist Soc* NS Vol **1**, 1860-1864

Dawson, G J, 1963 Excavations at Purwell Farm, Cassington, *Oxoniensia* **26**, 1-6

Day, C, 1998-2003 Valley Sediments and prehistoric impact on the chalkland of southern Britain a method for locating archae-colluvium, *BAJ* **76**, 1-13

Day, S P, 1991 Post-glacial vegetational history of the Oxford region, *New Phytologist* **119**, 445-70

Day, S P, 1993 Woodland origin and 'ancient woodland indicators': a case-study from Sidlings Copse, Oxfordshire, UK, *The Holocene* **3(1)**, 45-53

De Jersey, P, The Celtic Coin Index (http://athens.arch.ox.ac.uk/coins/)

De Roche, C D, 1977 An analysis of selected groups of early Iron Age pottery from the Oxford region, BLitt thesis, Univ. Oxford

De Roche, C D, 1978 The Iron Age pottery, in Parrington 1978, 40-74

Denvir, A-M, undated *Fulachta Fiadh – An Irish Mystery* http://www.angelfire.com/fl/burnt-mounds

Derks, T, 1998 *Gods, Temples and ritual practices: the transformation of religious ideas and values in Roman Gaul*, University Press, Amsterdam

Dixon, P, 1976 Crickley Hill, 1969-1972, in Harding 1976a 162-175.

Dixon, P, 1994 *The Hillfort Defences Crickley Hill Vol. 1*, University of Nottingham, Nottingham

Dobney, K, and Ervynck, A, 2007 To fish or not to fish? The exploitation of aquatic animal resources during the Late Iron Age around the North Sea, in Haselgrove and Moore 2007

Done, G, 1991 The animal bone, in Needham 1991, 327-342

Drewett, P, 1980 Black Patch and the later Bronze Age in Sussex, in Barrett and Bradley 1980, 377-96

Drewett, P, 1982 Later Bronze Age downland economy and excavations at Black Patch, East Sussex, *PPS* **48**, 321-400

Duncan, D, Lambrick, G, and Barclay, A, 2004 Final Bronze Age to Middle Iron Age pottery, in Lambrick and Allen 2004, 259-303

Dunning, G C, 1976 Salmonsbury, Bourton-on-the-Water, Gloucestershire, in Harding (ed.) 1976, 75-118

Durham, B 1977 Archaeological investigations in St Aldates, Oxford, *Oxoniensia* **42**, 169-72

Edgeworth, M, 2006 Changes in the Landscape: Archaeological Investigation of an Iron Age Enclosure on the Stoke Hammond Bypass, *Records of Bucks* **46**, 119-148

Edwards, E, 1978 The human remains, in Parrington 1978, 90-2

Ehrenberg, M R, 1977 *Bronze Age Spearheads from Berkshire, Buckinghamshire and Oxfordshire*, Brit Arch Rep (Brit Ser **34** Oxford

Ehrenreich, R E, 1985 *Trade, Technology and the Ironworking Community in the Iron Age of Southern Britain*, Brit Arch Rep (Brit Ser) **144**, Oxford

Ellis, P, Hughes, G and Jones, L, 2000 An Iron Age boundary and settlement features at Slade Farm, Bicester, Oxfordshire: a report on excavations, 1996, *Oxoniensia* **65**, 211-265.

Ellison, A B, 1980 Deverel Rimbury urn cemeteries: the evidence for social organisation, in Barrett and Bradley 1980, 115-26

Elsden, N, 1996 Cranford Lane Harlington, London Borough of Hillingdon, Post excavation Assessment report, Museum of London Archaeological Servoce, unpubl. rep.

Elsden, N, 1997 Excavations at Nobel Drive Harlington and six sites to the north of Heathrow airport, *London and Middlesex Archaeol Coll* **48**, 1-13

Enright, D, 1999 A Bronze Age Pin from Siddington Glos, *TBGAS* **117**, 151-3

Entwhistle, R, 1994 Settlements, territories and 'Celtic' fields: the changing role of boundary earthworks, in Bradley *et al.* 1994, 122-36

Evans, C and Knight, M, 2001 The 'community of builders': the Barleycroft post alignments, in Brück 2001, 83-98

Evans, M, 1995 The mollusca from the henge ditch, in Barclay, A, Gray, M, and Lambrick, G, 1995, 62-67

Evans, J G, 1992 Mollusca, in Butterworth and Lobb 1992, 130-43

Evans, J G, Davies, P, Mount, R and Williams, D, 1992 Molluscan taxocenes from Holocene overbank alluvium in Central Southern England, in Needham and Macklin 1992, 65-74

Everett, R N and Eeles, B M G, 1999 Investigations at Thrupp House Farm, Radley, near Abingdon, *Oxoniensia* **64**, 118-152

Farley, M E, 1983 Mirror Burial at Dorton, Buckinghamshire, *PPS* **49**, 269-302

Farley, M E, 1986a Excavations at the Prebendal Court Aylesbury 1985, *SMA* **16**, 37-38

Farley, M E, 1986b Aylesbury *Current Archaeology* **101**, 187-9

Farley, M E, 1995 The Buckinghamshire Chilterns in Later Prehistory in Holgate, 1995, 28-30

Farley, M E, Shackley, M L and Cundill, P R, 1984 A Middle Iron Age Site in the Vale of Aylesbury, Buckinghamshire in Catherall *et al.* 1984, 28-35

Fauduet, I, 1993 *Les Temples de Tradition Celtique en Gaule Romaine*, Paris

Featherstone, R and Bewley, R, 2000 Recent aerial reconnaissance in north Oxfordshire, *Oxoniensia* **65**, 13-26

Fell, V, 1997 Iron Age iron files from England *Oxford Journal of Archaeology* **16(1)**, 79-98

Fenton, A, 1983 Grain Storage in Pits: Experiment and Fact, in O'Conner, A and Clarke, D V (eds), *From the Stone Age to the 'Forty Five*, John Donald Edinburgh, 567-588

Fitzpatrick, A P, 1984 The deposition of La Tène Iron Age metalwork in watery contexts in southern England, in Cunliffe and Miles 1984,178-88

Fitzpatrick, A P, 1997 Everyday life in Iron Age Wessex, in Gwilt and Haselgrove 1997, 73-86

Fitzpatrick, A P, 1998-2003 A Late la Tene Dagger from the Thames at Windsor Berks, *BAJ* 76 14-6

Fitzpatrick, A P, Barnes, I, and Cleal, R M J, 1995 An Early Iron Age settlement at Dunston Park, Thatcham, in Barnes *et al.* 1995, 65-92.

Fitzpatrick, A P and Morris, E L, (eds) 1994 *The Iron Age in Wessex: Recent work*, Association Française D'Etude de L'Age du Fer, Trust for Wessex Archaeology, Salisbury

Fleming, A, 1978 The prehistoric landscape of Dartmoor, part 1, south Dartmoor, *PPS* **44**, 97-124

Fleming, A, 1983 The prehistoric landscape of Dartmoor, part 2, north and east Dartmoor, *PPS* **49**, 195-241

Fleming, A, 1985 Land tenure, productivity and field systems, in Barker, G and Gamble, C (eds) *Beyond domestication in prehistoric Europe,* London, 129-46

Fleming, A, 1987 Coaxial field systems some questions of time and space, *Antiquity* **61**, 188-202

Fleming, A, 1994 The reaves reviewed, in Griffiths, F M (ed), *The archaeology of Dartmoor: perspectives from the 1990s*, Devon Archaeol Soc, Exeter, 63-74

Forcey, C, Hawthorne, J and Witcher, R (eds), 1998 *TRAC 97 Proceedings of the seventh annual Theoretical Roman Archaeology Conference, Nottingham*, Oxbow Books, Oxford

Ford, S, 1982 Fieldwork and excavation on the Berkshire Grims Ditch, *Oxoniensia* **47**, 13-36

Ford, S, 1982-3 Linear Earthworks on the Berkshire Downs, *BAJ* **71**, 1-20

Ford, S, 1987 *East Berkshire Archaeological Survey*, Dept of Highways and Planning, Berkshire

County Council Occ Pap **1**

Ford, S, 1991 The archaeology of the Cleeve-Didcot pipeline in South Oxfordshire 1989, *Oxoniensia* **55** (1990), 1-40

Ford, S, 1994-7 Loddon Valley (Berkshire) Fieldwalking Survey, *BAJ* **75**, 11-33

Ford, S, Bradley, R, Hawkes, J, and Fisher, P, 1984 Flint-working in the metal age, *Oxford Journal of Archaeology* **3(2)**, 158-173

Ford, S, Entwistle, R and Taylor, K, 2003 *Excavations at Cippenham, Slough, Berkshire, 1995-7*, TVAS Mono **3**, Reading

Ford, S and Hazell, A, 1989 Prehistoric, Roman and Anglo-Saxon settlement patterns at North Stoke, Oxfordshire, *Oxoniensia* **54**, 7-23

Ford, S, Howell, I, and Taylor, K, 2004 *The Archaeology of the Aylesbury-Chalgrove Gas Pipeline, and the Orchard, Walton Road Aylesbury*, TVAS Mono **5**, Reading

Ford, S, Lowe, J and Pine, J, 2006 Early Bronze Age, Roman and medieval boundaries and trackways at Howbery Park, Crowmarsh Gifford, Oxfordshire, *Oxoniensia* **71**, 197-210

Foreman, S, 1998 Excavations in Advance of the Environment Agency Maidenhead, Windsor and Eton Flood Alleviation Scheme, *SMA* 28, 26-31

Foreman, S, Hiller, J, and Pitts, Q, 2002 *Gathering the People, Settling the Land: The Archaeology of a Middle Thames Landscape Vol 3: Anglo Saxon to Post medieval*, Oxford Archaeol Thames Valley Landscapes Mono **14**, Oxford

Fowler, P J, 1960 Excavations at Madmarston Camp, Swalcliffe, 1957-8, *Oxoniensia* **25**, 3-48

Fowler, P J, 1978 The Abingdon ard-share, in Parrington 1978, 83-8

Fowler, P J, 1983 *The Farming of Prehistoric Britain*, Cambridge University Press, Cambridge

Fox, C, 1939 The socketed bronze sickles of the British Isles: with special reference to an unpublished specimen from Norwich, *PPS* **5**, 222-248

Framework Archaeology, 2005 PSH02 T5 Fieldwork 2002-2005 Project Design Update Note 2, unpubl. client rep., Oxford Archaeology and Wessex Archaeology

Framework Archaeology, 2006 *Landscape Evolution in the Middle Thames Valley: Heathrow Terminal 5 Excavations Volume 1, Perry Oaks*, Framework Archaeol Mono **1**, Oxford and Salisbury

Fulford, M, 1992 Iron Age to Roman: A period of radical change on the gravels, in Fulford and Nichols 1992, 23-38

Fulford, M and Corney M, 1984 *Silchester: excavations on the defences 1974-80, with a field survey of the extra-mural territory*, Britannia Mono **5**, London

Fulford, M and Creighton, J, 1998 A Late Iron Age Mirror Burial from Latchmere Green, near Silchester, Hampshire, *PPS* **64**, 331-342

Fulford, M and Nichols, E (eds), 1992 *Developing landscapes of lowland Britain. The archaeology of the British gravels: a review*, Soc of Antiqs Occ Pap **14**, London

Fulford, M and Timby, J, 2000 *Late Iron Age and Roman Silchester: excavations on the site of the forum-basilica 1977, 1980-86*, Britannia Mono **15,** London

Gardner, E, 1912 Some prehistoric and Saxon antiquities found in the neighbourhood of Weybridge, *SyAC* **25**, 129-35

Gates, T, 1975 *The middle Thames valley: an archaeological survey of the river gravels*, Berkshire Archaeol Comm Pub **1**, Reading

Gent, H, 1983 Centralized storage in late prehistoric Britain, *PPS* **49**, 243-68

Gerloff, S, 1975 *The Early Bronze Age Daggers in Great Britain and a Reconsideration of the Wessex Culture*, Prähistorische Bronzefunde, **6 (2)**, Munich

Gibbard, P L, 1985 *The Pleistocene History of the Middle Thames Valley*, Cambridge University Press, Cambridge

Gibson, A, 1998 *Stonehenge and Timber Circles*, Tempus, Stroud

Gibson, A 2002 *Prehistoric Pottery in Britain and Ireland*, Tempus, Stroud

Gibson A and Woods A, 1990 *Prehistoric Pottery for the Archaeologist*, Leicester University Press, Leicester

Giorgi, J A and Robinson, M A, 1984 The environment, in M Foreman and S Rahtz, Excavations at Faccenda Chicken Farm, near Alchester, 1983, *Oxoniensia* **49**, 38-45

Gingell, C, 1982 Excavation of an Iron Age enclosure at Groundwell Farm, Blunsdon St Andrew, 1976-7, *WAM* **76**, 33-75

Glob, P V, 1969 *The Bog People*, Faber and Faber, London

Gloucester City Council n.d *The Birdlip Grave Group* http://www.glos-city.gov.uk/Content.aspx?URN=1279 accessed 18 June 2007

Godwin, H, 1975 *The History of the British Flora*, 2nd edn, Cambridge

Goodburn, D, 1984 Recent Finds of Ancient Boats from the London Area, *London Archaeol*, **5**, 423-8

Goodchild, R and Kirk, J R, 1954 The Romano-Celtic Temple at Woodeaton, *Oxoniensia* **19**, 15-37

Gosden, C and Lock, G, 1998 The Hillforts of the Ridgeway Project Excavations at Segsbury Camp 1997, *SMA* **28** 54-63

Gosden, C and Lock, G, 1999 The Hillforts of the Ridgeway Project: excavations at Alfred's Castle 1998, *SMA* **29**, 44-53

Gosden, C and Lock, G, 2000 The Hillforts of the Ridgeway Project: excavations at Alfred's Castle 1999, *SMA* **30**, 82-90

Gosden, C and Lock, G, 2001 The Hillforts of the Ridgeway Project Excavations at Alfred's Castle 2000 *SMA* **31** 80-9

Gosden, C and Lock, G, 2007 The aesthetics of landscape on the Berkshire Downs, in Haselgrove and Pope 2007, 279-292

Graham, D and Graham, A, 2002 Investigation of a

Bronze Age mound on Frensham Common, *SyAC*, **89**, 105-118

Grahame, M, 1998 Redefining Romanization: material culture and the question of social continuity in Roman Britain, in Forcey *et al.* 1998, 1-10

Grant, A, 1984 Animal husbandry in Wessex and the Thames Valley, in Cunliffe and Miles 1984, 102-19

Gray, M, 1970 Excavations at Northfield Farm, Long Wittenham, Berkshire, *Oxoniensia* 35, 107-9

Gray, M, 1977 Excavations at Northfield Farm, Long Wittenham, *Oxoniensia* **42**, 1-29.

Grayson, A J, 2004 Bradford's Brook, Wallingford, *Oxoniensia* **69**, 29-44

Green, C, 1949 The Birdlip Early Iron Age Burials, a Review, *PPS* **15**, 188-90

Green, H S, 1981 The Dating of Ivinghoe Beacon, *Records of Bucks* **23**,1-3

Green, M J, 1986 *Gods of the Celts,* Alan Sutton, Stroud

Green, M J, 1995a The gods and the supernatural, in Green 1995b, 465-89

Green, M J (ed), 1995b *The Celtic World*, Routledge, London

Gregg, S A, 1988 *Foragers and farmers: population interaction and agricultural expansion in prehistoric Europe*, Chicago and London

Greig, J R A, 1991 The botanical remains, in Needham 1991, 234-6

Greig, J, 2004 Pollen from Yarnton floodplain, in Hey 2004, 369-79

Grimes, W F, 1943-4 Excavations at Stanton Harcourt, Oxon., 1940, *Oxoniensia* **8-9**, 19-63

Grimes, W F, 1960 *Excavations on defence sites 1939-45. I. Mainly Neolithic and Bronze Age,* Ministry of Works Archaeol Rep **3**, London

Grimes, W F and Close-Brooks, J, 1993 The excavation of Caesar's Camp, Heathrow, Harmondsworth, Middlesex, 1944, *PPS* **59**, 303-60

Groves, J and Lovell, J, 2002 Excavations within and close to the Late Bronze Age enclosure at the former Queen Mary's Hospital Carshalton 1999, *London Archaeologist* **10**, 13-19

Guilbert, G C, 1975 Planned hillfort interiors, *PPS* **41** 203-21

Guilbert, G C, 1982 Post-ring symmetry in round-houses at Moel-y-Gaer and some other sites in prehistoric Britain in Drury, P J, (ed), *Structural reconstruction: approaches to the interpretation of the excavated remains of buildings* Brit Arch Rep (Brit Ser) **110**, Oxford, 67-86

Gwilt, A and Haselgrove, C (eds), 1997 *Reconstructing Iron Age Societies*, Oxbow Mono **71**, Oxford

Hald, M, 1980 *Ancient Danish Textiles from Bogs And Burials: A Comparative Study of Costume and Iron Age Textiles* Publications of The National Museums Stiftsbogtrykkeri,Copenhagen

Hall, M, 1998 The archaeology of the Ashbury to Bishopstone pipeline, South Oxfordshire/

Wiltshire, 1993, *Oxoniensia* **63**, 199-220

Halpin, C, 1983 Abingdon: ex-MG car factory site, *SMA* **13**, 113-4

Hambleton, E, 1999 *Animal Husbandry Regimes in Iron Age Britain. A Comparative Study of Faunal Assemblages from British Iron Age Sites,* Brit Arch Rep (Brit Ser) **282**, Oxford

Hamilton, J, 2004 The animal bones, in Stansbie and Laws 2004

Hamlin, A, 1963 Excavations of ring ditches and other sites at Stanton Harcourt, *Oxonienia* **28**, 1-19

Hamlin, A, 1966 Early Iron Age sites at Stanton Harcourt, *Oxoniensia* **31**, 1-24

Hamlin, A and Case, H J, 1963 Excavations of ring-ditches and other sites at Stanton Harcourt and notes on the finds and on ring ditches in the Oxford region, *Oxoniensia* **28**, 1-52

Hancock, A, Harrison, E and Kenyon, D, 2003 Land at Foxley Fields Farm, (Finmere Quarry), Finmere, Oxfordshire Post-excavation Assessment and Updated Reasearch Design, Cotswold Archaeology, Unpubl.client rep.

Hanworth, R, 1987 The Iron Age in Surrey, in Bird and Bird 1987, 139-64

Hanworth, R, and Tomalin, D J, 1977 *Brooklands, Weybridge: the excavation of an Iron Age and medieval site,* Surrey Arch Soc Res Vol **4**.

Harcourt, R A, 1974 The dog in prehistoric and early historic Britain, *J Archaeol Science* **1**, 151-75

Harden, D B and Treweeks, R C, 1945 Excavations at Stanton Harcourt, Oxon., 1940, *Oxoniensia* **10**, 16-42

Harding, A F, 2000 *European Societies in the Bronze Age,* Cambridge University Press, Cambridge

Harding, D W, 1966 The pottery from Kirtlington, and its implications for the chronology of the earliest Iron Age in the Upper Thames region, *Oxoniensia* **31**, 158-161

Harding, D W, 1972 *The Iron Age in the Upper Thames Basin,* Clarendon Press, Oxford

Harding, D W, 1974 *The Iron Age in Lowland Britain,* Routeledge and Keegan Paul, London

Harding, D W, 1976a (ed) *Hillforts: Later Prehistoric Earthworks in Britain and Ireland,* Academic Press, London

Harding, D W, 1976b Blewburton Hill, Berkshire: Re-excavation and Reappraisal, in Harding, 1976a, 133-46

Harding, D W, 1987 *Excavations in Oxfordshire, 1964-66,* University of Edinburgh Department of Archaeology Occ Pap **15**, Edinburgh

Harding, D W, Blake, I M and Reynolds, P J, 1993 *An Iron Age Settlement in Dorset: Excavation and Reconstruction,* University of Edinburgh Department of Archaeol Mono **1**, Edinburgh

Hardy, A and Cropper, C, 1999 *Excavations at Larkwhistle Farm, Brimpton, Berkshire,* OAU Occ Pap **2**, Oxford

Harman, M, 1987 The human remains excavated in 1981, in Chambers , RA, The Late- and Sub-Roman Cemetery at Queenford Farm, Dorchester-on-Thames, Oxon., *Oxoniensa* **52**, 60-1

Harman, M, 1990 The human remains, in Allen 1990a

Harman, M, 1995 The human remains, in Boyle *et al*. 1995, 106-8

Harman, M, 1998 The human remains, in Boyle *et al*.. 1998, 43-52

Harman, M and Miles, D, 1986 The human burials, in Miles, 1986, fiche 4:C1-D6

Harris, S A, Robinson, J P and Juniper, B E, 2002 Genetic clues to the origin of the apple, *Trends in Genetics* **18**, 426-30

Harrison, S, 2003 The Icknield Way: Some Queries, *Archaeol J* **160**, 1-22

Haselgrove, C, 1984a Comment on Hingley *Scottish Archaeol Rev*, **3**, 27-31

Haselgrove, C, 1984b "Romanisation" before the conquest: Gaulish precedents and British consequences, in T F C Blagg and A C King (eds), *Military and civilian in Roman Britain. Cultural relationships in a frontier province*, Brit Arch Rep (Brit Ser) **136**, Oxford, 5-63

Haselgrove, C, 1996 Iron Age coinage: recent work, in Champion and Collis, 1996, 67-86

Haselgrove, C, 1997 Iron Age brooch deposition and chronology, in Gwilt and Haselgrove 1997, 51-72

Haselgrove, C and Millett, M, 1997 Verlamion reconsidered, in Gwilt and Haselgrove 1997, 282-96

Haselgrove, C and Moore, T, (eds), 2007 *The Later Iron Age in Britain and Beyond*, Oxbow, Oxford

Haselgrove, C and Pope, R, (eds), 2007 *The Earlier Iron Age in Britain and the Near Continent*, Oxbow, Oxford

Hawkins, D, and Leaver, S, 1999 An Iron Age settlement at Alpine Avenue, Tolworth, *SyAC* **86**, 141-9

Hayman, G N, 1991a A later Neolithic to early Bronze Age farmstead at Lower Mill Farm, Stanwell, *Surrey Arch Soc Bull* **261**

Hayman, G N, 1991b Bronze Age settlement evidence at Home Farm, Laleham, *Surrey Arch Soc Bull* **262**

Hayman, G N, 1991c Recent excavations at the former Brooklands race-track, *Surrey Arch Soc Bull* **258**

Hayman, G N, 1991d Bronze Age enclosure at Church Lammas near Staines *SyAC* **82**, 207

Hayman, G N, 1998 Archaeological excavation of Bronze Age, Iron Age and Roman settlements, enclosures and boundary features at Thorpe Lea Nurseries, Egham, Surrey, Client Report prepared by Surrey County Archaeol Unit

Hayman, G N, 1999 A Bronze Age enclosure and round-house at Wey Manor Farm, Addlestone (TQ 058 634), *Surrey Arch Soc Bull* **326,** 10

Hayman, G N, 2002a Archaeological work at Runfold Farm (Farnham Quarry), Client Report prepared by Surrey County Archaeol Unit

Hayman, G N, 2002b Archaeological Discoveries, principally of Neolithic and Bronze Age date, within the Home Farm, Laleham, Mineral Extraction Site, 1991-1999 Surrey County Archaeol Unit client rep.

Hayman, G N, forthcoming a Thorpe Lea Nurseries: The Excavation of Bronze Age, Iron Age and Roman Remains near Egham, Surrey, between 1989 and 1994

Hayman, G N, forthcoming b The Excavation of a Bronze Age Enclosure at Church Lammas, near Staines, Surrey in 1991

Hayman, G N, forthcoming c Excavations at Home Farm Laleham

Hayman, G N, forthcoming d Excavations at Hengrove

Hayman, G N, forthcoming e The Discovery of Bronze Age Features at Vicarage Road, Sunbury, Unpubl. draft report Surrey County Council

Hayman, G N, forthcoming f Archaeological Evaluation and Excavation Work within the Phase 1-3 Mineral Extraction Areas at Wey Manor Farm, Nr. Addlestone, Surrey

Haynes, I, Sheldon, H and Hannigan, L, (eds), 2000 *London Under Ground: The Archaeology of a City*, Oxbow, Oxford

Hearne, C M, 2000 Archaeological evaluation in the Vale of the White Horse, near Abingdon, 1992-99, *Oxoniensia* **65**, 7–12.

Hearne, C M and Adam, N, 1999 Excavation of an extensive Late Bronze Age settlement at Shorncote Quarry, near Cirencester, 1995–6, *TBGAS* **117**, 35-73.

Hearne, C M and Heaton, M J, 1994 Excavations at a late Bronze Age Settlement in the Upper Thames Valley at Shorncote Quarry near Cirencester 1992, *TBGAS* **112**, 17-57

Henderson, J, 1989 The Earliest Glass Beads in Britain and Ireland, in M Feugère (ed) *La Verre Preromaine en Europe Occidentale* Montagnac, 19-28

Hedges, J, 1975 Excavations on two Orcadian Burnt Mounds at Liddle and Beaquoy *Proc Soc Antiq Scot* **106**, 38-98

Henig, M and Booth, P, 2000 *Roman Oxfordshire*, Sutton, Stroud

Hey, G, 1995 Iron Age and Roman settlement at Old Shifford Farm, *Oxoniensia* **60**, 93-176

Hey, G, 2004 *Yarnton: Saxon and medieval settlement and landscape*, Oxford Archaeol. Thames Valley Landscapes Mono **20**

Hey, G, 2007 Unravelling the Iron Age landscape of the Upper Thames Valley, in Haselgrove and Moore 2007, 156-72

Hey, G, Bayliss, A, and Boyle, A, 1999 Iron Age inhumation burials at Yarnton, Oxfordshire, *Antiquity* **73**, 551-62

Hey, G, and Bell, C, 1999 Yarnton, Floodplain 1998, *SMA* **29**, 85-88

Hey, G and Lacey, M, with Linford, N, David, A and Shepherd, N 2001 *Evaluation of Archaeological Decision-making Processes and Sampling Strategies*, Oxford

Hey, G, (ed.), forthcoming a Yarnton: Iron Age and Roman Settlement and Landscape, Oxford

Archaeol Thames Valley Landscapes Mono, Oxford

Hey, G, Dennis, C and Bell, C forthcoming b *Yarnton: Neolithic and Bronze Age Settlement and Landscape*, Oxford Archaeol Thames Valley Landscapes Mono, Oxford

Hey, G, Garwood, P. Barclay, A, Bradley P and Robinson, M, forthcoming Thames Through Time. The Archaeology of the Upper and Middle Thames: landscape and habitation through the Mesolithic, Neolithic and early Bronze Age, Oxford Archaeol Thames Valley Landscapes Mono, Oxford

Hill, J D, 1995 *Ritual to Rubbish in the Iron Age of Wessex: A Study on the Formation of a SpecificArchaeological Record*, Brit Arch Rep (Brit Ser) **242**, Oxford

Hill, J D, 1996 Hillforts and the Iron Age of Wessex, in Champion and Collis 1996, 95-116

Hill, J D, 1997 The end of one kind of body and the beginning of another kind of body? Toilet instruments and Romanization in southern Britain during the first century, in Gwilt and Haselgrove (eds) 1997, 96-107

Hill, J D, 2007 The dynamics of social change in later Iron Age eastern and south-eastern England *c.* 300 BC-AD 43, in Haselgrove and Moore 2007, 16-40

Hinchliffe, J, 1975 Excavations at Grim's Ditch, Mongewell 1974, *Oxoniensia* **40**, 122-35

Hinchliffe, J and Thomas, R, 1980 Archaeological investigations at Appleford, *Oxoniensia* **45**, 9-111

Hingley, R, 1980a The Upper Thames Valley Survey, *CBA9* **10**, 141-3

Hingley, R, 1980b The Frilford/Garford/Marcham survey, *CBA9* **10**, 143-4

Hingley, R, 1980c Excavations by R A Rutland on an Iron Age site at Wittenham Clumps, *BAJ* **70**, 21–55.

Hingley, R, 1984a Towards social analysis in archaeology: celtic society in the Iron Age of the Upper Thames Valley, in Cunliffe and Miles 1984, 72-88

Hingley, R, 1984b The Archaeology of settlement and the social significance of space, *Scottish Archaeol Rev* **3**, 22-27

Hingley, R, 1990a Iron Age currency bars: the archaeological and social context, *The Archaeol J* **147**, 91-117

Hingley, R, 1990b Domestic organisation and gender relations in Iron Age and Romano-British households, in Samson, R (ed.) *The Social Archaeology of the House*, Edinburgh University Press, 125-48

Hingley, R, 1996 Prehistoric Warwickshire: a review of the evidence, *Trans Birm and Warwicks Arch Soc* **100**, 1-24

Hingley, R, 1997 Iron, iron working and regeneration: a study of the symbolic meaning of metalwork, in Gwilt and Haselgrove (eds) 1997, 9-18

Hingley, R, 1999 The creation of later prehistoric landscapes and the context of the reuse of

Neolithic and earlier Bronze Age monuments in Britain and Ireland, in B Bevan (ed.), *Northern Exposure: Interpretative Devolution and the Iron Age in Britain*, Leicester Archaeol Mono **4**, Leicester, 233-251

Hingley, R and Miles, D, 1984 Aspects of Iron Age settlement in the Upper Thames Valley, in Cunliffe and Miles 1984, 52-71

Hinton, D A, 1997 The 'Sole-Dickleburgh field system' examined, *Landscape History* **19**, 5-12

Hirst, S and Rahtz, P, 1996 Liddington Castle and the Battle of Badon: excavations and research 1976, *Archaeol J* **153**, 1-59

Hodder, I and Hedges, J W, 1977 Weaving Combs - their typology and distribution with some introductory remarks on date and function, in Collis 1977, 17-28

Hodder, M, and Barfield, L H, 1991 *Burnt mounds and hot stone technology*, Papers for the Second International Burnt Mound Conference, West Bromwich

Holgate, R, (ed) 1995 *Chiltern Archaeology, Recent Work: A Handbook for the Next Decade*, Dunstable

Hollins, A, 1990 Fordhall Farm Our Organic Farming System, http://www.fordhallfarm.com/Fordhall%27s%20Organic%20Farming%20System.rtf

Howell, L, 1996 The excavation of a Bronze Age Ditch at the Field Test Centre at Castrol Technology Centre, Pangbourne, Berkshire, *Oxoniensia* **61**, 35-8

Howes, L and Skelton, A, 1992 Excavations at Carshalton House, 1992, *London Archaeologist*, **7 (1)**, 14-18

Huckerby, E, forthcoming Pollen, in Brossler *et al.* forthcoming

Hull, G, 1998 A Middle Bronze Age field ditch? Excavations at Bankside Close, Isleworth *Trans London and Middlesex Arch Soc* **49**, 1-14

Humphrey, J, 2005 The Flint, in Lock *et al.* 2005, http://www.arch.ox.ac.uk/__data/assets/pdf_file/1528/flintreport.pdf accessed 30/11/06

Hurcombe, L, 2000 Plants as raw materials for crafts, in A S Fairburn (ed.), *Plants in Neolithic Britain and beyond*, Neolithic Studies Group Seminar Papers **5**, Oxbow Oxford, 155-173

Jarrett, M G and Wrathmell, S, 1981 *Whitten: an Iron Age and Roman Farmstead in South Glamorgan*, Cardiff

Jarvis, M G, 1973 *Soils of the Wantage and Abingdon district*, Memoir of the Soil Survey of Great Britain: England and Wales, Harpenden

Jeffery, P, 1991 Burnt Mounds, Fulling and Early Textiles, in Hodder and Barfield 1991, 97-107

Jennings, D, 1998 Prehistoric and Roman activity, in Boyle *et al.* 1998, 9-34

Jennings, D, Muir, J, Palmer, S and Smith, A, 2004 *Thornhill Farm, Fairford, Gloucestershire: an Iron Age and Roman Pastoral Site in the Upper Thames Valley*, Oxford Archaeol Thames Valley Landscapes Mono **23**, Oxford

Johnson, A E, 2003 Woodeaton Romano-Celtic temple, Oxfordshire, Topsoil magnetic suscepti-bility and magnetometer (gradiometer) survey, Oxford Archaeotechnics survey 2190600/WOO/JBS, unpublished survey carried out for Mrs J Bagnall Smith

Johnstone, J and Bowden, M, 1985 Excavations at Pingewood, *BAJ* **72**, 17-52

Johnston, R, 2001 'Breaking new ground': land tenure and stone clearance during the Bronze Age, in Brück 2001, 99-109.

Johnston, R, 2005 Pattern Without a Plan: Rethinking the Bronze Age Coaxial Field Systems on Dartmoor, Southwest England *Oxford Jn Archaeol* **24(1)** 1-21

Jones, G, 2007 The Iron Age pottery, in Miles *et al.* 2007, 43-51

Jones, M K, 1978 The plant remains, in Parrington 1978, 93-110

Jones, M K, 1981 The development of crop husbandry, in Jones and Dimbleby 1981, 95-127

Jones, M K, 1984a The Ecological and Cultural Implications of Carbonised Seed Assemblages from Selected Archaeological Contexts in Southern Britain, Unpubl. D.Phil. Thesis, University of Oxford

Jones, M K, 1984b Regional patterns in crop production, in Cunliffe and Miles 1984, 120-5

Jones, M K, 1985 Archaeobotany beyond subsis-tence reconstruction, in Barker, G and Gamble, C (eds) *Beyond Domestication in Prehistoric Europe: Investigations on Subsistence Archaeology and Social Complexity*, London, 107-28

Jones, M K, 1986 The carbonised plant remains, in Miles 1986, Fiche 9:A1-9:B5

Jones, M K (ed.), 1988a *Archaeology and the Flora of the British Isles*, OUCA Oxford, 86-91

Jones, M K, 1988b The arable field: a botanical battleground, in Jones 1988a, 86-91

Jones, M K, 1993 The carbonised plant remains, in Allen and Robinson 1993, 120-3

Jones, M K and Dimbleby, G (eds), 1981 *The Environment of Man, the Iron Age to the Anglo-Saxon Period, Oxford*, Brit Arch Rep (Brit Ser) **87**, Oxford

Jones, M K, with Robinson, M, 1993 The carbonised plant remains, in Allen and Robinson 1993, 120-123.

Jones, P, forthcoming Archaeological Fieldwork at Abbey Meads, Chertsey Unpubl draft report, Surrey County Council Archaeol Field Unit

Jones, P and Poulton, R, 1987 Iron Age hut circles discovered near Lower Mill Farm, Stanwell (T003577418), *Trans London Middlesex Archaeol Soc*, **38**, 1-10

Kahn, P and Llobera, P (eds), 1981 *The Anthropology of Pre-Capitalist Societies*, Macmillan, London

Keevill, G D, and Campbell, G E, 1991 Investigations at Danesfield Camp, Medmenham, Buckinghamshire, *Records of Bucks* **33**, 87-99

Keevill, G D, and Durden, T, 1998 Archaeological work at the Rover Plant site, Cowley, Oxford, *Oxoniensia* **62**, 87-99

Keith-Lucas, D M, 1997 Pollen, in Barnes *et al.* 1997, 99-106

Keith-Lucas, D M, 2000 Pollen analysis of sediments from Moor Farm, Staines Moor, Surrey, *SyAC* **87**, 85-93

Kenward, H K and Williams, D, 1979 *Biological evidence from the Roman warehouses in Coney Street,* Archaeology of York **14/2** CBA, London

Kidd, A M, 2004 Hillforts and Churches: a coincidence of locations?, *Records of Bucks* **44**, 105-110

Kidd, A M, 2006 An archaeological resource assess-ment of the later Bronze and Iron Ages (the First Millennium BC) in Northamptonshire, http://www.le.ac.uk/archaeology/research/projects/eastmidsfw/pdfs/19nh1stmill.pdf

Kidd, A M, 2007 Buckinghamshire Later Bronze Age and Iron Age Historic Environment Resource Assessment (2nd draft) Solent Thames Archaeological Research Framework, http://www.buckscc.gov.uk/bcc/get/assets/docs/Bucks_Iron_Age.pdf

King, A and Soffe, G, 1994 The Iron Age and Roman Temple on Hayling Island, in Fitzpatrick and Morris 1994, 114-6

King R, 1998 Excavations at Gassons Road, Lechlade 1993, in Boyle *et al.* 1998, 269-81

King, R, Barber A and Timby, J, 1996 Excavations at West Lane, Kemble: An Iron Age, Roman and Saxon burial site and Medieval building, *TBGAS* **114**, 15-54

Kirk, J, 1949 Bronzes from Woodeaton, Oxon., *Oxoniensia* **14**, 1-45

Kirk, J and Case, H, 1950 Notes and news, *Oxoniensia* **15**, 104-09

Knight, D, 1984 *Late Bronze Age and Iron Age settle-ment in the Nene and Great Ouse basins*, Brit Arch Rep (Brit Ser) **130**, Oxford

Knight, D, 2002 A Regional Ceramic Sequence: Pottery of the First Millennium BC between the Humber and the Nene in J D Hill and A E Woodward (eds), 2002 *Prehistoric Britain: the Ceramic Basis,* Oxbow Mono, Oxford

Lambrick, G H, 1978 Iron Age Settlements in the Upper Thames Valley, in Cunliffe and Rowley 1978, 103-19

Lambrick, G H, 1979 Mount Farm, Berinsfield, *CBA Group 9 Newsletter* **9**, 113-5

Lambrick, G H, 1984a Pitfalls and possibilities in Iron Age pottery studies: experiences in the Upper Thames Valley, in Cunliffe and Miles 1984, 162-77

Lambrick, G H, 1984b Clanfield Burroway, *CBA Group 9 Newsletter* **14**, 104-5

Lambrick, G H (ed.), 1985 *Archaeology and Nature Conservation* Oxford University Department for External Studies, Oxford

Lambrick, G H, 1988 *The Rollright Stones: megaliths,*

monuments and settlement in the prehistoric landscape, English Heritage Archaeol Rep **6**, London

Lambrick, G H, 1992a Alluvial archaeology of the Holocene in the Upper Thames Basin 1971-1991: a review, in Needham and Macklin 1992, 209-26

Lambrick, G H, 1992b The development of late prehistoric and Roman farming on the Thames gravels, in Fulford and Nichols 1992, 78-105

Lambrick, G H, 1996 Gill Mill, *SMA* **26**, 56

Lambrick, G H, 1999 *Community and Change in the Iron Age of the Upper Thames,* Paper presented to the Prehistoric Society Conference, May 1999

Lambrick, G H and Allen, T G, 2004 *Gravelly Guy, Stanton Harcourt, Oxfordshire: the Development of a Prehistoric and Romano-British Community,* Oxford Archaeol Thames Valley Landscapes Mono **21**, Oxford

Lambrick, G H and De Roche, C D, 1980 The Iron Age pottery, in Hinchliffe and Thomas 1980, 45-59

Lambrick, G H and McDonald, A, 1985 The archaeology and ecology of Port Meadow and Wolvercote Common, Oxford, in Lambrick 1985, 95-109

Lambrick, G H and Robinson, M A, 1979 *Iron Age and Roman riverside settlements at Farmoor, Oxfordshire,* CBA Res Rep **32**, Oxford Archaeological Unit Report 2, London

Lambrick, G H and Robinson, M A, 1988 The development of floodplain grassland in the Upper Thames Valley, in Jones 1988a, 55-75

Lambrick, G H and Wallis, J, 1989 Ducklington, Gill Mill, *SMA* **19**, 49-50

Lambrick, G H, forthcoming Excavations as at Mount Farm, Dorchester

Lamdin-Whymark, H, Brady, K and Smith, A, 2007 Excavation of a Neolithic to Roman Landscape at Horcott Pit, near Fairford, Gloucestershire 2002-3, *TBGAS*

Lane Fox, A, 1870 On the threatened destruction of the British earthworks near Dorchester, Oxfordshire. *J of the Ethnological Society of London* Vol 2 (4), 412-16

Lawrence, G F, 1930 canoes http://ads.ahds.ac.uk/catalogue/adsdata/cbaresrep/pdf/020/02001051.pdf

Lawson, A 1976 Shale and jet objects from Silchester, *Archaeologia* **105**, 241-75

Lawson, A J, 1994 Potterne, in Fitzpatrick and Morris 1994, 42-6

Lawson, A J, 2000 *Potterne 1982-5: Animal Husbandry in Later Prehistoric Wiltshire,* Wessex Archaeology Report **17**, Salisbury

Leech, R, 1977 *The Upper Thames Valley in Gloucestershire and Wiltshire: an archaeological survey of the river gravels,* Committee for Rescue Archaeology in Avon, Gloucestershire and Somerset, Survey No. **4**

Leeds, E T, 1931a Chastleton Camp, Oxfordshire, a hill-fort of the early Iron Age, *Antiq.J.,* **11 (4)**, 382-398.

Leeds, E T, 1931b An Iron-Age site near Radley, Berks, *Oxoniensia* **11**, 399-404

Lewis, J and Cotton J, 2000 The Neolithic Period, in Museum of London 2000

Lewis M J T, 1966 *Temples in Roman Britain,* Cambridge

Lloyd Morgan, G, 1995 Appearance, life and leisure, in Green 1995b, 95-120

Lobb, S J, 1977-8 Brimpton - excavation and watching brief *BAJ* **69**, 37-44

Lobb, S J, 1979-80 The excavation of a late Bronze Age settlement at Furze Platt Berkshire *BAJ* **70**, 9-17

Lobb, S J, 1983-5 Excavation of two ring ditches at Burghfield by RA Rutland 1969 *BAJ* **72**, 9-16

Lobb, S J, 1992 Excavation at Shortheath lane, Abbotts Farm Sulhamstead, in Butterworth and Lobb 1992, 73-8

Lobb, S J and Morris, E L, 1991-3 Investigation of Bronze Age and Iron Age features at Riseley Farm Swallowfield, *BAJ* **74**, 37-68

Lobb, S J and Rose, P G, 1996 *Archaeological Survey of the Lower Kennet Valley,* Wessex Archaeology Report **9**, Salisbury

Lock, G, Gosden, C, Griffiths, D, Daly, P, Trifkovic, V, and Marston, T, 2002 The Hillforts of the Ridgeway Project: Excavations at Marcham/Frilford 2001, *SMA* **32**, 69-83.

Lock, G, Gosden, C, Griffiths, D, and Daly, P, 2003 The Ridgeway and Vale Project: Excavations at Marcham/Frilford 2002, *SMA* **33**, 84-91.

Lock, G, Gosden, C and Daly, P, 2005 *Segsbury Camp: Excavations in 1996 and 1997 at an Iron Age Hillfort on the Oxfordshire Ridgeway,* OUCA Mono **61**, Oxford

Longley, D, 1976 The archaeological implications of gravel extraction in north-west Surrey, *SAS Research Volume,* **3**, 1-35

Longley, D, 1980 *Runnymede Bridge 1976: Excavations on the Site of a Late Bronze Age Settlement,* Surrey Arch Soc Res Vol, 6

Lovell, J and Mepham L, 1998-2003 Excavations at East Park Farm Charvil Berkshire Evidence for prehistoric and Roman Activity on the Thames Floodplain, *BAJ* **76**, 17-36

MacDonald, P, 2007 Perspectives on insular La Tène art, in Haselgrove and Moore 2007, 329-38

Major H, 2005 Metalwork Report, in Wilson and Cater 2005, 212-6

Manning, W H, 1972 Ironwork hoards in Iron Age and Roman Britain *Britannia* **3**, 224-250

Marchant, T, 1989 The evidence for textile production in the Iron Age, *Scot Archaeol Rev* **6**, 5-12

Marshall, A, 1990 *A pit based enclosure of mid Iron Age date at the Park, Guiting Power,* Cotswold Archaeol Res Group, Res Rep **5**.

Marshall, A, 1991 *A defensively ditched, trapezoidal enclosure of later Iron Age date and Roman farmsteading area at The Bowsings, Guiting Power, Glos,* Cotswold Archaeol Res Group, Res Rep 6

Marshall, A, 1995 From Iron Age to Roman: The Park and Bowsings sites at Guiting Power, *Glevensis* **28**, 13-19

Marshall, G and Northover, P 2003 The excavation and metallographic analysis of a Bronze Age sword recovered from Ivinghoe Beacon, *Records of Bucks* **43,** 27-38

Masefield, R, 2003 An archaeological evaluation at Didcot West, Fields 21-23, unpubl client report, Cotswold Archaeology

Masefield, R, Glover, G and Pearson, M 2003 A41 Aston Clinton bypass, Site D, Trig Hill: an archaeological assessment, unpubl. client rep., Cotswold Archaeology

Mayes, A, Hardy, A and Blair, J 2000 The excavation of early Iron Age and medieval remains on land to the west of Church View, Bampton Oxon., *Oxoniensia* 65, 267-90

McGrail, S, 1995 Celtic Seafaring and Transport, in Green 1995b, 254-81

McKinley, J, 2001 Human Bone, in Birbeck 2001, 266-74

McOmish, D, 1996 East Chisenbury: ritual and rubbish at the British Bronze Age-Iron Age transition, *Antiquity* **70**, 68–76

McOmish, D S and Field D J, 1994 A survey of the earthworks at St Ann's Hill, Chertsey, *SyAC* **82**, 223-225

Mepham, L, 1992 Pottery, in Butterworth and Lobb 1992, 40-8

Merriman, N, 1990 *Prehistoric London,* HMSO

Merriman, N, 2000 Changing approaches to the first millennium BC, in Haynes *et al.* 2000, 35-51

Miles, D, 1986 *Archaeology at Barton Court Farm, Abingdon, Oxon.* Oxford Archaeol Unit Rep **3**, CBA Res Rep **50**, Oxford and London

Miles, D, 1997 Conflict and complexity: the later prehistory of the Oxford region, *Oxoniensia* **62**, 1-19

Miles, D and Lewis, N A, 1985 Archaeology and Nature Conservation: Problems and Potential at Cherbury Camp, Oxfordshire, in Lambrick 1985, 111-9

Miles, D, Palmer, S, Lock, G, Gosden, C and Cromarty, A.M, 2003 *Uffington White Horse and its Landscape. Investigations at White Horse Hill, Uffington, 1989–95 and Tower Hill Ashbury, 1993-4,* Oxford Archaeol Thames Valley Landscapes Mono **18**, Oxford

Miles, D, Palmer, S, Smith, A and Edgeley Long G, 2007 *Iron Age and Roman Settlement in the Upper Thames Valley: Excavations at Claydon Pike and Other Sites within the Cotswold Water Park,* Oxford Archaeol Thames Valley Landscapes Mono **26**, Oxford

Moffett, L, 1988 Charred seeds and crop remains from the Iron Age enclosure, in Lambrick 1988, 103-5

Moffett, L, 1999 The prehistoric use of plant resources, in Barclay and Halpin 1999, 243-7

Moffett, L, 2004 The evidence for crop-processing products from the Iron Age and Romano-British periods and some earlier prehistoric plant remains, in Lambrick and Allen 2004, 421-445

Moore, J, 2005 An Archaeological Excavation at Bernwood First School, North Way, Barton, Oxford, unpubl. client rep. prepared by John Moore Heritage Services on behalf of Barratt Mercia

Moore, J and Jennings, D, 1992 *Reading Business Park: a Bronze Age Landscape* Oxford Archaeol Unit Thames Valley Landscapes: the Kennet Valley 1, Oxford

Moore, T, 2003 Rectangular Houses in the British Iron Age: Squaring the Circle, in Humphrey, J (ed.) *Re-searching the Iron Age,* Leicester University Mono **11**, Leicester, 47-58.

Moore, T, 2006 *Iron Age Societies in the Severn-Cotswolds: Developing narratives of social and landscape change,* Brit Arch Rep (Brit Ser) **421**, Oxford

Moore, T, 2007a The Early to Later Iron Age transition in the Severn-Cotswolds: enclosing the household? in Haselgrove and Pope 2007, 259-78

Moore, T, 2007b Life on the edge? Exchange, community and identity of the Severn-Cotswolds, in Haselgrove and Moore 2007, 41-61

Morris, E L, 1981 Ceramic exchange in western Britain: a preliminary view, in H. Howard and E. L. Morris (eds) *Production and distribution: a ceramic viewpoint,* Brit Arch Rep (Int Ser) **120**, 67-81, Oxford

Morris, E L, 1985 Prehistoric salt distributions: two case studies from western Britain, *Bull Board Celtic Studies* **32**, 336-79

Morris, E L, 2004 Prehistoric pottery in Brossler *et al.* 2004

Morris, E L, forthcoming Prehistoric pottery in Brossler *et al.* forthcoming

Mould, C, 1996 An archaeological excavation at Oxford Road, Bicester, Oxfordshire, *Oxoniensia* **61**, 65-108

Mudd, A, 1993 Excavations at Whitehouse Road, Oxford, 1992, *Oxoniensia* **58**, 33-85

Mudd, A, 1995 The excavation of a late Bronze Age/early Iron Age site at Eight Acre Field, Radley, *Oxoniensia* **60**, 21-65

Mudd, A, Williams, R J and Lupton, A, 1999 *Excavations alongside Roman Ermin Street, Gloucestershire and Wiltshire. The archaeology of the A419/A417 Swindon to Gloucester Road Scheme,* 2 Vols, Oxford Archaeol Unit

Muir, J and Roberts, M K, 1999 *Excavations at Wyndyke Furlong, Abingdon, Oxfordshire, 1994,* Oxford Archaeol Thames Valley Landscapes Mono No. **12**, Oxford

Mulville, J and Levitan, B, 2004 The animal bone, in Lambrick and Allen 2004, 463-78

Museum of London Archaeological Service, 2000 *The Archaeology of Greater London: an Assessment of Archaeological Evidence for Human Presence in the Area now Covered by Greater London,* London

Musson, C, 1970 House plans and prehistory, *Current Archaeology* **21**, 267-75

Myres, J N L, 1937 A prehistoric and Roman site on Mount Farm, Dorchester, *Oxoniensia* **2**, 12-40

Mytum, H, 1986 An early Iron Age site at Wytham Hill, near Cumnor, Oxford, *Oxoniensia* **51**, 15-24

Mytum, H and Taylor, J W 1981 Stanton Harcourt: Linch Hill Corner, *CBA 9* **11**, 139-41

Neal, D S, Hunn, J R and Wardle, A, 1990 *Excavation of the Iron Age, Roman and Medieval Settlement at Gorhambury, St. Albans*, Historic Buildings and Monuments Commission for England, London

Needham, S, 1987 The Bronze Age, in Bird and Bird 1987, 97-138

Needham, S, 1990 *The Petters Field Late Bronze Age Metalwork: An Analytical Study of the Thames Valley Metalworking in its Settlement Context*, British Museum Occ Pap **70**

Needham, S P, 1991 *Excavation and salvage at Runnymede Bridge 1978, The Late Bronze Age Waterfront Site*, British Museum, London

Needham, S P, 1992 Holocene alluviation and interstratified settlement evidence in the Thames valley at Runnymede Bridge, in Needham and Macklin 1992, 249-260

Needham, S P, 1993 The structure of settlement and ritual in the late Bronze Age of south-east Britain, in Mordant, C and Richard, A (eds), *L'habitat et l'occupation du sol à l'Age du Bronze en Europe*, Actes du Colloque International de Lons-le-Saunier, 49-69

Needham, S P, 2000 *The Passage of the Thames: Holocene Environment and Settlement at Runnymede*, Runnymede Bridge Research Excavations **1**, British Museum Press, London

Needham, S P, 2001 When expediency broaches ritual intention: the flow of metal between systemic and buried domains, *Journal of the Royal Anthropological Institute* **7(2)** 275–98

Needham, S P, 2007 800 BC, The Great Divide, in Haselgrove and Pope 2007, 39-63

Needham, S P, and Ambers, J, 1994 Redating Rams Hill and reconsidering Bronze Age enclosure, *PPS* **60**, 225-243.

Needham, S P and Burgess, C B, 1980 The later Bronze Age in the lower Thames valley: the metalwork evidence, in Barrett and Bradley 1980, 437-469

Needham, S P and Macklin, M G (eds), 1992 *Alluvial Archaeology in Britain*, Oxbow Mono **27**, Oxford

Needham, S P, Ramsey, C B, Coombs, D, Cartwright, C and Pettitt, P, 1997 An independent chronology for British Bronze Age metalwork: the results of the Oxford radiocarbon accelerator programme, *Archaeol J*, **154**, 55-107

Needham, S P and Sørensen, M L S, 1988 Runnymede Refuse Tip: a consideration of midden deposits and their formation, in Barrett, J C and Kinnes, I A (eds) *The Archaeology of Context in the Neolithic and Bronze Age: Recent Trends*, Sheffield, 113-26,

Needham, S P and Spence, T, 1996 *Refuse and Disposal at Area 16 East Runnymede*, Runnymede Bridge Research Excavations **2**, British Museum Press, London

Niblett, R, 1995 A new site at Verulamium, in Holgate 1995, 96-102

Niblett, R, 1999 *The excavation of a ceremonial site at Folly Lane, Verulamium*, Britannia Mono **14**, London

Nichols, P W, 2006 An archaeological Excavation at Bourton on the Water Primary School Gloucestershire, 2003 Unpubl. Client rep., Gloucestershire County Council Archaeol Services

Northover, J P, 1984 Iron Age bronze metallurgy in central southern England, in Cunliffe and Miles 1984, 126-45

Northover, J P, 1995 The technology of metalwork, in Green 1995b, 285-309

Northover, J P, 2006 Copper-alloy metalwork, in Cromarty *et al.* 2006, 47-57

Norton, A, 2006 Excavations at Ireland's Land, Northmoor, Oxfordshire, *Oxoniensia* **71**, 175-96

OA, 2004 Cotswold Community, Wiltshire and Gloucestershire 2003-4, Archaeological Excavation Interim Report, unpubl. MSS, Oxford Archaeology

OAU, 1989a Bowmoor, Kempsford, Gloucestershire: archaeological assessment, September 1989, unpubl report, Oxford Archaeol Unit

OAU, 1989b Churchberry Manor, Fairford, Gloucestershire. Archaeological Assessment, unpubl report, Oxford Archaeol Unit

OAU 1998 Wallingford Rowing Club, Mongewell, Oxfordshire, unpubl evaluation report, Oxford Archaeol Unit

OAU, 2001 Allcourt Farm, Little London, Lechlade, Glos, unpubl post-excavation assessment report, Oxford Archaeol Unit

O'Connell, M, 1986 Petters Sports Field : Excavations of a Late Bronze Age/Early Iron Age Site, *SyAS Research Volume*, **10**

O'Connell, M, 1990 Excavations During 1979-1985 of a Multi-period site at Stanwell, *SyAC*, **80**, 1-62

O'Kelly, M J, 1954 Excavations and experiments in ancient Irish cooking places *Jn Royal Soc Antiq Ireland* **84**, 105-55

Osborne, P J, 1969 An insect fauna of Late Bronze Age date from Wilsford, Wiltshire. *Journal of Animal Ecology* **38**, 555-566

Osborne, P J, 1989 Insects, in Ashbee, P, Bell, M and Proudfoot, E, *Wilsford Shaft: excavations 1960-62*, 96-99 and fiche C1-7, London, English Heritage Archaeol Report **11**

Oswald, A, 1997 A doorway on the past: practical and mystic concerns in the orientation of roundhouse doorways, in Gwilt and Haselgrove 1997, 87-95

Parfitt, K, 1995 *Iron Age burials from Mill Hill, Deal*, British Museum Press, London

Parker, A G 1995a Late Quaternary Environmental Change in the Upper Thames Basin, Central-Southern England, unpubl D.Phil. thesis, University of Oxford.

Parker, A G, 1995b Pollen analysis, in Mudd 1995, 50-53

Parker, A G, 1999 The pollen and sediments of Daisy Banks Fen, in Barclay and Halpin 1999, 254-67

Parker, A G and Robinson, M A, 2003 Palaeoenvironmental investigations on the middle Thames at Dorney, UK, in Howard, A J, Macklin, M and Passmore D G (eds), *Alluvial Archaeology in Europe*, Lisse, Rotterdam, 43-60

Parker Pearson, M, 1993 *Bronze Age Britain*, Batsford and English Heritage, London

Parker Pearson, M, 1996 Food, fertility and front doors in the first millennium BC, in Champion and Collis 1996, 117-32

Parker Pearson, M, 1999 *The Archaeology of Death and Burial*, Sutton, Stroud

Parker-Pearson, M and Richards, C (eds), 1994 *Architecture and Order: Approaches to Social Space*, Routeledge, London

Parkhouse, J and Bonner, D, 1997 Investigations at the Prehistoric Site at Coldharbour Farm Aylesbury in 1996, *Records of Bucks* **39**, 73-139

Parrington, M, 1978 *The Excavation of an Iron Age Settlement, Bronze Age Ring-Ditches and Roman Features at Ashville Trading Estate, Abingdon (Oxfordshire) 1974-76*, Oxford Archaeol Unit Report **1**, CBA Res Rep **28**, London

Parrington, M, 1979 Excavations at Stert Street, Abingdon, Oxon, *Oxoniensia*, **44**, 1-25

Parrington, M and Balkwill, C, 1975 Excavations at Broad Street, Abingdon, *Oxoniensia* **40**, 5-58

Parry, C, 1998 Excavations near Birdlip, Cowley, Gloucestershire, 1987-8, *TBGAS*, **116**, 25-92

Parry, C, 1999 Excavations at Camp Gardens, Stow-on-the-Wold, Gloucestershire, *TBGAS*, **117**, 75-87

PCRG, 1991 *The Study of Later Prehistoric Pottery: General Policies*, Prehistoric Ceramics Research Group, Occas Pap **1**, Oxford

PCRG, 1992 *The Study of Later Prehistoric Pottery: Guidelines for Analysis and Publication*, Prehistoric Ceramics Research Group, Occas Pap **2**, Oxford

Peacock, D P S, 1968 A petrological study of certain Iron Age pottery from western England, *PPS* **34**, 414-27

Peacock, D P S, 1987 Iron Age and Roman quern production at Lodsworth, West Sussex, *Antiq J* **67**, 61-85

Pelling, R, 2000a Charred plant remains, in Booth, P and Hayden, C A, Roman settlement at Mansfield College, Oxford, *Oxoniensia* **65**, 324-8

Pelling, R, 2001a Charred plant remains, in PM Booth, J Evans and J Hiller *Excavations in the extramural settlement of Roman Alchester, Oxfordshire, 1991*, Oxford Archaeol Mono **1**, 418-22

Pelling, R, 2001b Charred plant remains, in J Moore, Excavations at Oxford Science Park, Littlemore, Oxford, *Oxoniensa* **66**, 212-3

Pelling, R, 2002 The charred plant remains, in Foreman *et al.* 2002, 49-55

Percival, J, 1921 *The Wheat Plant*, Duckworth, London

Piggott, C M, 1946 The late Bronze Age razors of the British Isles, *PPS* **12**, 121-41

Pine, J, 2003 Late Bronze Age occupation, Roman enclosure and early Saxon Occupation at Waylands Nursery, Welley Road, Wraysbury, Berkshire, 1997, in Preston 2003, 118-37

Pine, J and Ford, S, 2003 Excavation of Neolithic, late Bronze Age, early Iron Age and early Saxon features at St Helen's Avenue, Benson, Oxfordshire, *Oxoniensia* **68**, 131-78

Pine, J and Preston, S, 2004 *Iron Age and Roman settlement and landscape at Totterdown Lane, Horcott near Fairford, Gloucestershire*, TVAS Mono **6**, Reading

Poole, C, 1984 Objects of fired clay, in Cunliffe 1984, 398-407

Poole, C, 1991 The loomweights, in Cunliffe and Poole 1991b

Poole, C, 1995 Pits and propition, in B Cunliffe, *Danebury Vol 6: A hillfort community in perspective*, CBA Res Rep **102**, London

Pope, R, 2007 Ritual and the Roundhouse: a critique of recent ideas on the use of domestic space in later British Prehistory, in Haselgrove and Pope 2007, 204-228

Poulton, R, 2004 Iron Age Surrey, in Cotton *et al.* 2004, 51-64

Poulton, R, forthcoming a Archaeological discoveries made in a gravel pit near Shepperton, Surrey

Poulton, R, forthcoming b Excavations at Shepperton Ranges

Poulton, R, in prep. Excavations at Farley Heath Roman temple in 1995, and a review of earlier work on the site

Powell, A, 2002 The animal bone, in Foreman *et al.* 2002, 44-9

Powell, A and Clark, K, 2006 The Animal Bone, in Cromarty *et al.* 2006, 105-10

Powell, K, Laws, G and Brown, L, forthcoming A late Neolithic early Bronze Age enclosure and Iron Age and Romano-British settlement at Latton Lands, Wiltshire, *WAM*

Preston, S (ed.), 2003 *Prehistoric, Roman and Saxon Sites in Eastern Berkshire. Excavations 1989-1997*, TVAS Mono **2**, Reading

Proctor, J, 2002 Late Bronze Age/Early Iron Age placed deposits from Westcroft Road, Carshalton: their meaning and interpretation, *SyAC* **89**, 65-103

Pryor, F M M, 1996 Sheep, stockyards and field systems: Bronze Age livestock populations in the Fenlands of eastern England, *Antiquity*, **70**, 313-324

Pryor, F M M, 2001 *The Flag Fen Basin: archaeology and environment of a Fenland landscape*, English Heritage Archaeol Rep, Swindon, , 255-98

Pryor, F M M, 2006 *Farmers in Prehistoric Britain*, NPI Media Group

Rahtz, P, 1962 Excavations at Shearplace Hill, Sydlings St Nicholas, Dorset, *PPS* **28**, 289-337

Ralston, I, 1995 Fortifications and defence, in Green 1995b, 59-81

Rankin, D, 1996 *Celts and the Classical World*,

Thames and Hudson, London

Ray, K, 1990 Science and anomaly: burnt mounds in British prehistory *Scottish Archaeol Review* **7**, 7-14

RCHME, 1976 *Iron Age and Romano-British monuments in the Gloucestershire Cotswolds, County of Gloucester* **1** HMSO, London.

RCHME, 1995 *Thames Valley Aerial Photographic Transcriptions*, Royal Commission on the Historical Monuments of England

Read, C H, 1909 A bronze torc and spear-head from the Thames, and a dagger-blade of the Bronze Age from Sproughton, Suffolk. *Proc Soc Antiq* **22**, 86-88

Reynolds, P J, 1974 Experimental Iron Age storage pits: an interim report, *PPS* **40**, 118-31

Reynolds, P J, 1979 *Iron-Age farm: the Butser experiment*, British Museum Publications, London

Reynolds, P J, 1981a Deadstock and Livestock, in Mercer, R (ed.) *Farming Practise in British Prehistory*, Edinburgh University Press, 97-122

Reynolds, P J, 1981b New approaches to familiar problems, in Jones and Dimbleby 1981, 19-49

Reynolds, P J, 1987-9 *Butser Ancient Farm Yearbooks 1986-8*

Reynolds, P J, 1995 Rural life and farming, in Green 1995b, 176-209

Rhodes, P P, 1948 A prehistoric and Roman site at Wittenham Clumps, Berkshire, *Oxoniensia* **13**, 18-31

Richardson, K M and Young, A, 1951 An Iron Age A site on the Chilterns, *Antiq J* **31**, 132-48

Richmond, A, Rackham, J and Scaife, R, 2006 Excavations of a prehistoric stream-side site at Little Marlow, Buckinghamshire, *Records of Bucks* **46**, 65-102

Riley, D N, 1946/7 A Late Bronze-Age and Iron-Age Site on Standlake Downs, *Oxoniensia* **11/12**, 27-43

Roberts, J, 1998 A contextual approach to the interpretation of the early Bronze Age skeletons in the East Anglian Fens, *Antiquity* **72**, 188-197

Roberts, M R, 1993 Lady Lamb Farm, Fairford Oxford Archaeol Unit,unpubl. client rep.

Roberts, M R, 1995 Excavations at Park Farm, Binfield, 1990: an Iron Age and Romano-British settlement and Mesolithic flint scatters, in Barnes *et al.* 1995, 93-132

Robinson, M A, 1981a Investigations of Palaeoenvironment in the Upper Thames Valley, unpubl.PhD diss., University of London

Robinson, M, 1981b The Iron Age to Early Saxon environment of the Upper Thames terraces, in Jones and Dimbleby 1981, 251-286

Robinson, M A, 1983 Arable/pastoral ratios from insects, in Jones, M K (ed.), *Integrating the Subsistence Economy*, Brit Arch Rep (Int Ser) **181**, Oxford, 19-55

Robinson, M A, 1984 Landscape and environment of Central Southern England in the Iron Age, in Cunliffe and Miles 1984, 1-11

Robinson, M A, 1986 Waterlogged plant and inver-

tebrate evidence, in Miles 1986, microfiche chapters VIII, IX and XI

Robinson, M A, 1988a Molluscan evidence for pasture and meadowland on the floodplain of the Upper Thames Basin, in Murphy, P and French, C (eds), *The exploitation of wetlands*, Brit Arch Rep (Brit Ser) **186**, Oxford, 101-112

Robinson, MA, 1988b The significance of tubers of *Arrhenatherum elatius* (L.) Beauv. from Site 4, excavation 15/11, in Lambrick 1988, 102

Robinson, M A, 1990 The waterlogged seeds, insects and other biological evidence, in Allen 1990, 64-72

Robinson, M A, 1991 The Neolithic and late Bronze Age insect assemblages, in Needham 1991, 277-326

Robinson, M A, 1992a Environmental archaeology of the river gravels : past achievements and future directions, in Fulford and Nichols (eds) 1992, 47-62

Robinson, M A, 1992b Environment, archaeology and alluvium on the river gravels of the South Midlands, in Needham and Macklin 1992, 197-208

Robinson, M A, 1992c Insect assemblages, in Butterworth and Lobb 1992, 143-149

Robinson, M A, 1992d Insect remains from two late Bronze Age waterlogged features, in Moore and Jennings 1992, 112-16

Robinson, M A, 1995a Plant and invertebrate remains, in Hey 1995, 158-167

Robinson, M A, 1995b Plant and invertebrate remains, in Mudd 1995, 41-50.

Robinson, M A, 1999a Land and freshwater Mollusca, in Mudd *et al.* 1999, 494-500

Robinson, M A, 1999b Charred plant remains, in Hardy and Cropper 1999, 11-12

Robinson, M A, 2000a Middle Mesolithic to late Bronze Age insect assemblages and an early Neolithic assemblage of waterlogged macroscopic plant remains, in Needham 2000, 146-67

Robinson, M A, 2000b A preliminary investigation of waterlogged sediments from the early fort ditches at Alchester for environmental evidence, in Sauer 2000, 64-5.

Robinson, M A, 2002 Waterlogged macroscopic plant and insect remains, in Brossler *et al.* 2002, 74-78

Robinson, M A, 2003a The palaeohydrology of the St Aldates area of Oxford in relation to archaeology and the Thames crossing *and* Environmental reports, in A Dodd (ed.) *Oxford before the University*, OUCA Oxford, 68-64 and 365-390

Robinson, M A, 2003b Carbonised plant remains, in Pine and Ford 2003, 170

Robinson, M A, 2004a The plant and invertebrate remains, in Jennings *et al.* 2004, 133-145

Robinson, M A, 2004b Waterlogged plant and invertebrate remains and mollusca, in Hey 2004, 379-409

Robinson, M A, 2004c Invertebrate and water-logged macroscopic plant remains from Gravelly

Guy and Blackditch in Lambrick and Allen 2004, 405-17

Robinson, M A, 2006a Macroscopic plant and invertebrate remains, in Cromarty *et al.* 2006, 110-141

Robinson, M A, 2006b The macroscopic plant remains, in Fulford *et al.* 2006

Robinson, M A, 2007 The environmental archaeology of the Cotswold Water Park, in Miles *et al.* 2007, 355-64

Robinson, M A, 2008 Charred plant remains, in Allen and Kamash 2008

Robinson, M A, forthcoming a The developing environment (by A Parker and M Robinson), Eton Rowing Course excavations, OA in prep

Robinson, M A, forthcoming b Macroscopic plant and invertebrate remains, in Hayman 1998 (currently unpubl.)

Robinson, M A, forthcoming d Charred plant remains, in Hamerow, H, Hey, G and Hayden, C, Anglo-Saxon and earlier settlement at Drayton Road, Sutton Courtenay, Oxfordshire, *Archaeol. J.*

Robinson, M A, forthcoming e Waterlogged plant remains, invertebrates and molusca, in Lambrick forthcoming

Robinson, M A and Hubbard, R N L B, 1977 The transport of pollen in the bracts of hulled cereals, *Journal of Archaeol Science* **4**, 197-9

Robinson, M A and Lambrick, G H, 1984 Holocene alluviation and hydrology in the Upper Thames Basin, *Nature* **308**, 809-814.

Robinson, M A, and Straker, V, 1991 Silica skeletons of macroscopic plant remains from ash, in Renfrew, J M (ed.), *New Light on Early Farming,* Proceedings of the 7th Symposium of the International Work Group of Palaeoethnobotanists, 3-13

Robinson, M A and Wilson, B, 1987 A Survey of environmental archaeology in the South Midlands, in Keeley, H C M (ed.), *Environmental Archaeology: a Regional Review* Vol 2, Historic Buildings and Monuments Commission for England Occ Pap **1**, London, 16-100

Robinson, M and Hey, G, forthcoming Settlement and landscape, in Hey *et al.* forthcoming b

Rodwell, J S (ed.), 1992 *British plant communities 3. Grasslands and montane communities,* Cambridge University Press, Cambridge

Rodwell, W, 1978 Relict landscapes in Essex, in H C Bowen and P Fowler (eds), *Early Land Allotment,* Brit Archaeol Rep (Brit Ser) **48**, Oxford, 89-98

Roe, F E S, 2002 The worked stone, in Foreman *et al.* 2002, 37-9

Roe, F E S, 2003 Whetstones, querns and other non-structural worked stone, in A Hardy, A Dodd, G D Keevill, 2003, *Aelfric's Abbey: Excavations at Eynsham Abbey, Oxfordshire, 1989-92,* OA Thames Valley Landscapes Mono **16**, 290-6

Roe, F E S, 2004 Worked stone, in Hey 2004, 304-5

Roe, F E S, in prep The worked stone, in Hey *et al.* forthcoming a

Rohl, B and Needham, S, 1998 *The Circulation of Metal in the British Bronze Age.* British Museum Occas Pap No **102**, British Museum Press, London

Rolleston, G, 1869 Researches and excavations carried on in an ancient cemetery at Frilford, Abingdon, Berks, in the years 1867-1868, *Archaeologia* **42**, 417-85

Rolleston, G, 1884 *Scientific Papers and Addresses* vol 2, Oxford

Rook, T, Lowery, P R, Savage, R D A and Wilkins, R L, 1982 An Iron Age mirror from Aston, *Hertfordshire Antiq J* **62**, 18-34

Ross, A, 1967 *Pagan Celtic Britain,* Columbia University Press, New York

Rowlands, M J, 1980 Kinship alliance and exchange in the European Bronze Age, in Barrett and Bradley 1980, 15-57

Rowley, T, 1973 An Iron Age settlement site at Heath Farm, Milton Common, *Oxoniensia* **38**, 23-40

Rowley, T, 1985 Roman Dorchester, in Cook and Rowley 1985, 21-8

RPS, 2001 Didcot West: an Initial Archaeological Evaluation, Vols 1-2, RPS Consultants, unpubl client rep, Oxford

RPS, 2005 Archaeological Investigations for the A41 Aston Clinton Bypass, Buckinghamshire, unpubl rep

Ruben, I, and Ford, S, 1992 Archaeological Excavations at Wallingford Road, Didcot, South Oxfordshire, 1991, *Oxoniensia* **57**, 1-28

Russell, M J G, 1989 Excavation of a multi-period site in Weston Wood, Albury: the pottery, *SyAC* **79**, 3-51

Sahlins, M, 1976 *Culture and practical reason,* University of Chicago Press, Chicago

Salisbury, C R, 1992 The archaeological evidence for palaeochannels in the Trent valley, in Needham and Macklin 1992, 155-62

Saller, R, 2002 Framing the debate over growth in the ancient economy, in W Scheidel and S von Reden (eds), *The ancient economy,* Edinburgh Univ Press, Edinburgh, 251-69

Salter, C, 2004 Ferrous metalworking debris, in Hey 2004, 307-11

Salter, C and Ehrenreich, R, 1984 Iron Age iron metallurgy in central southern Britain, in Cunliffe and Miles 1984, 146-61

Salway, P, 1981 *Roman Britain,* Oxford

Salway, P, 1993 *The Oxford Illustrated History of Roman Britain,* Oxford

Salway, P, 1999 Roman Oxfordshire, *Oxoniensia* **64**, 1-22

Sandford, K. S, 1924 The river gravels of the Oxford district, Quaternary, *J Geological Society,* **80**, 113

Sauer, E W, 1999 Aves Ditch: an Iron Age tribal boundary?, *Current Archaeol* **163**, 268-9

Sauer, E W, 2000 Alchester, a Claudian 'vexillation

fortress' near the western boundary of the Catuvellauni: new light on the Roman invasion of Britain, *Archaeol J* **157**, 1-78

Sauer, E W, 2005 *Linear Earthwork, Tribal Boundary and Ritual Beheading: Aves Ditch from the Iron Age to the Early Middle Ages,* Brit Archaeol Rep (Brit Ser) **402**, Oxford

Saville, A, 1979 *Excavations at Guiting Power Iron Age Site, Gloucestershire 1974,* Committee for Rescue Archaeology in Avon Gloucestershire and Somerset Occ Pap **7**

Savory, H N, 1937 An early Iron Age site at Long Wittenham, Berks, *Oxoniensia* **2**, 1-11

Scaife, R, 1999 Pollen from 'Latton Roman Pond', in Mudd *et al.* 1999, 510-12

Scaife, R, 2000 Palynology and palaeoenvironment, in Needham 2000, 168-187

Scaife, R, 2004a Pollen from waterlogged samples in the floodplain sequence, in Lambrick and Allen 2004, 417-20

Scaife, R, 2004b Pollen analysis of a Bronze Age Waterhole in Brossler *et al.* 2004, 111-3

Scaife, R, forthcoming Pollen analysis, in Brossler *et al.* forthcoming

Scheidel, W and von Reden, S, (eds), 2002 *The ancient economy,* Edinburgh Univ Press, Edinburgh

Scott, E, 1991 Animal and infant burials in Romano-British villas: a revitalization movement, in Garwood, P, Jennings, D, Skeates, R and Toms, J (eds), *Sacred and Profane, Proceedings of a Conference on Archaeology, Ritual and Religion Oxford, 1989,* Oxford Univ Comm Archaeol Mono **32**, 115-21

Scott, E, 1999 *The Archaeology of Infancy and Infant death,* Brit Archaeol Rep (Int Ser) **819**, Oxford

Seager Smith, R 2000 Worked Bone and Antler, in Lawson 2000

Selkirk, A, 1998 Bound and trussed woman from Brackmills, *Current Archaeology* **158**

Sellwood, L, 1984a Tribal boundaries viewed from the perspective of numismatic evidence, in Cunliffe and Miles 1984, 191-204

Sellwood, L, 1984b Textile manufacture *and* Objects of bone and antler, in Cunliffe 1984, 438-9; 375-8

Serjeantson, D, 1996 The animal bones, in Needham and Spence 1996, 194-223

Serjeantson, D, Field, D, Penn, J and Shipley, M, 1991-2 Excavations at Eden Walk Kingston: environmental reconstruction and prehistoric finds, *SyAC* **81**, 71-90

Serjeantson, D, Wales, S, *et al.* 1994 Fish in later prehistoric Britain, in Heinrich, D (ed.), *Archaeo-ichthyological studies: papers presented at the 6th Meeting of the I.C.A.Z. Fish Remains Working Group, Offa,* Wachholz, Neumunster, 332-39

Shand, P, Henderson, E, Henderson, R, and Barclay, A, 2003 Corporation Farm, Wilsham Road, Abingdon: a summary of the Neolithic and Bronze Age excavations, 1971-4, in Barclay *et al.* 2003, 31-40.

Shennan, S, 2002 *Genes, Memes and Human History,* Thames and Hudson, London

Smith, A T, 2001 *The differential use of constructed sacred space in southern Britain from the late Iron Age to the 4th century AD,* Brit Archaeol Rep (Brit Ser) **318**, Oxford

Smith, A, 2007 Excavations at Abingdon West Central redevelopment, Oxfordshire, *Oxoniensia* **71**

Smith, A, Powell, K, Hey, G and Laws, G, forthcoming Excavations of a prehistoric, Roman and medieval landscape at Cotswold Community, Gloucestershire and Wiltshire, Oxford Archaeol Thames Valley Mono, Oxford

Smith, R A, 1908 The Weybridge bucket and prehistoric trade with Italy, *SyAC* **21** 165-9

Smith, W, 2001 When method meets theory: the use and misuse of cereal producer/consumer models in archaeobotany, in U Albarella (ed.), *Environmental archaeology, meaning and purpose,* Kluwer Academic, Netherlands, 283-98

Smith, W, 2002 *A Review of Archaeological Wood Analyses in Southern England,* Centre for Archaeol Rep **75/2002**, English Heritage

Sommerfeld, C, 1994 *Gerätegeld Sichel: Studien zur Monetären Struktur Bronzezeitlichen Horte im Nordlichen Mitteleurope,* Reike, Vorgeschichtliche Forschungen **19**

Stace, C, 1997 *New flora of the British Isles* (2nd ed.), Cambridge University Press, Cambridge

Stansbie, D and Laws, G, 2004 Prehistoric settlement and medieval to post-medieval field systems at Latton Lands, *WAM* **97**, 106-43

Stead, I M, 1967 A La Tène III burial at Welwyn Garden City, *Archaeologia* **101**, 1-62

Stead, I M, 1987 The Chertsey Shield, *SyAC* **77**, 181-3

Stead, I M, 1991 *Iron Age Cemeteries in East Yorkshire,* English Heritage, London

Stead, I M, Bourke, J B and Brothwell, D (eds.), 1986 *Lindow Man: The Body in the Bog,* British Museum Press, London

Stead, I M and Rigby, V, 1986 *Baldock: the excavation of a Roman and pre-Roman settlement, 1968-72,* Britannia Mono **7**, London

Stead, I M and Rigby, V, 1989 *Verulamium: the King Harry Lane Site,* English Heritage Archaeol Rep **12**, London

Stevens, C, 2004 Iron Age and Saxon settlement at Jugglers Close, Banbury, Oxfordshire, *Oxoniensia* **69**, 385-416

Stevens, C J, 1996 *Iron Age and Roman Agriculture in the Upper Thames Valley: Archaeobotanical and Social Perspectives,* unpubl Ph.D Thesis, University of Cambridge.

Stevens, C J, 2003a An investigation of agricultural consumption and production models for Prehistoric and Roman Britain, *Environmental Archaeology* **8.1**, 61-76

Stevens C J, 2003b The arable economy, in Bateman *et al.* 2003, 76-81

Stevens, C J, 2004 Charred plant remains, in Hey 2004, 351-64

Stevens, C J, forthcoming The charred plant remains, in Hey *et al.* forthcoming a

Stevens, C J and Wilkinson, K, 2001 Economy and environment, in Walker *et al.* 2001

Stevenson, J, 1999 An Archaeological Watching Brief at St George's Hill, Weybridge, Surrey, Client report prepared by Surrey County Archaeol Unit

Stone, J F S, 1941 The Deverel- Rimbury settlement on Thorny Down, Winterbourne Gunner, South Wilts., *PPS* **7**, 114-33

Stone, S, 1856–9 Account of certain (supposed) British and Saxon remains, *Proceedings of the Society of Antiquaries of London* (Ser. 1) **4**, 92–100.

Straker, V, Robinson, M and Robinson, E, 1984 Biological investigations of waterlogged deposits in the Roman fortress ditch at Exeter, *Devon Archaeol Soc Proc* **42**, 59-69

Sturdy, D, 1963 Traces of Saxon Nomadic life near Oxford, *Oxoniensia* **28**, 95-8

Sturdy, D and Case, H J, 1961-2 Archaeological Notes, *Oxoniensia* **26-7**, 336-9

Sumbler, M G (ed.), 1996 *British Regional Geology: London and the Thames Valley*, 4th edition, British Geological Survey, HMSO, London

Sutton, J E G, 1966 Iron Age hill-forts and some other earthworks in Oxfordshire, *Oxoniensia* **31**, 28-42.

Taylor, J, 1997 Space and place: some thoughts on Iron Age and Romano-British landscapes, in Gwilt and Haselgrove 1997, 192-203.

Taylor, K, 2002 Abingdon, Morlands Brewery, Ock Street, *SMA* **32**, 66-7

Taylor, M, 2001 The wood, in Pryor, FMM, *The Flag Fen Basin: archaeology and environment of the Fenland Basin*, English Heritage Archaeol Rep, London

Taylor, M, 2004a Wooden object, in Hey 2004, 295-7

Taylor, M, 2004b Worked Wood in Brossler *et al.* 2004, 100-3

Taylor, M, 2004c The Wooden Bowl in Stansbie and Laws 2004, 126

Taylor, M, Gale, R and Lambrick, G, 2006 Waterlogged Wood in Cromarty *et al.* 2006, 142-54

Taylor, M, forthcoming Waterlogged Wood, in Brossler *et al.* forthcoming

Taylor, T, 1996 *The Prehistory of Sex*, Fourth Estate, London

Thacker, F S, 1914 *The Thames Highway, i, General History* (reprinted 1968)

Thacker, F S, 1920 *The Thames Highway, ii, Locks and Weirs* (reprinted 1968)

Thomas, N, 1955 Excavations at Vicarage Field, Stanton Harcourt, 1951, *Oxoniensia* **20**, 1-28

Thomas, N, 1957 Excavations at Callow Hill, *Oxoniensia* **22**, 11-53

Thomas, R, 1980 A Bronze Age field system at Northfield Farm? *Oxoniensia* **45**, 310-311

Thomas, R, 1984 Bronze Age metalwork from the Thames at Wallingford, *Oxoniensia* **49**, 9-18.

Thomas, R, 1999 Rise and fall: the deposition of Bronze Age weapons in the Thames Valley and the Fenland, in A F Harding (ed), *Experiment and Design: Archaeological Studies in Honour of John Coles*, Oxbow, Oxford, 116-122

Thomas, R, Robinson, M A, Barret, J C and Wilson, R, 1986 A late Bronze Age riverside settlement site at Wallingford, Oxon, *Archaeol J* **143**, 174-200

Thompson, B and Allen, M J, 1992 Pollen, in Butterfield and Lobb 1992, 159-65

Thompson, I, 1982 *Grog-tempered 'Belgic' pottery of south-eastern England*, Brit Archaeol Rep (Brit Ser) **108**, Oxford

Timby, J, 2003a Pottery, in Bateman *et al.* 2003, 47-63

Timby, J, 2003b The pottery, in Pine and Ford 2003, 144-57

Timby, J, 2004a The Pottery in Stansbie *et al.* 2004, 106–143

Timby, J, 2004b The Pottery in Jennings *et al.* 2004, 90-108

Timby, J and Harrison, E, 2004 Pottery, in Pine and Preston 2004, 55-68

Tinsley, H M and Grigson, C, 1981 The Bronze Age, in Simmons, I and Tooley, M J, *The Environment in British Prehistory*, Duckworth, London

Topping, P, 1989 Early Cultivation in Northumberland, *PPS* **55**, 161-80

Trow, S D, 1988 Excavations at Ditches hillfort, North Cerney, Gloucestershire, 1982-3, *TBGAS* **106**, 19-85

Trow, S D and James, S, 1989 Ditches villa, North Cerney, an example of locational conservatism in the early Roman Cotswolds, in K Branigan and D Miles (eds) 1989 *The economies of Romano-British villas*, Sheffield, 83-6

Trust for Wessex Archaeology, 1996 Clarendon to Cockey Down Water Main, Salisbury, Wiltshire, Unpubl. client rep. for Wessex water

Turnbull, P, 1984 Stanwick in the Northern Iron Age, *Durham Archaeol Journal* **1**, 41-9

Van Arsdell, R D, 1989 *Celtic Coinage of Britain*, Spink, London

Van Arsdell, R D, 1994 *The Coinage of the Dobunni: Money Supply and Coin Circulation in Dobunnic territory*, OUCA, Oxford

Van der veen, M, 1987 The plant remains, in Heslop, D H, *The Excavation of an Iron Age Settlement at Thorpe Thewles, Cleveland, 1980-1982*, CBA Res Rep **65**, London, 93-61

Van der Veen, M, 1992 *Crop Husbandry Regimes: an Archaeobotanical Study of Farming in Northern England 1000 BC–AD 500*, Sheffield Archaeol Mono **3**, Collis Publications, University of Sheffield, Sheffield

Van der Veen, M, 1999 The economic value of chaff and straw in arid and temperate zones, *Vegetation History and Archaeobotany* **8**, 211-24

Van der Veen, M H, Mattousch, T and Boersma, J G, 2007 Longitudinal development of caries lesions after orthodontic treatment evaluated by quantitative light-induced fluorescence, *American Jnl Orthod Dentofacial Orthop* vol **131** **(2)**, 223-8

Varndell, G, Coe, D, Hey, G and Canti, M 2007 The Crow Down hoard, Lambourn, West Berkshire, *Oxford J Archaeol* **26 (3)**, 275-301

VCH, 1990 Wolvercote: Economic History in *A History of the County of Oxford: Volume 12: Wootton Hundred (South) including Woodstock* 314-20. URL: http://www.british-history.ac.uk/report.asp?compid=5563. Date accessed: 31 July 2007.

Wait, G A, 1985 *Ritual and Religion in Iron Age Britain*, Brit Arch Rep (Brit Ser) **149**, Oxford

Wait, G A and Cotton, J, 2000 The Iron Age, in Museum of London 2000, 101-17

Walker, G, 1995 A middle Iron Age settlement at Deer Park Road, Witney. Excavations in 1992, *Oxoniensia* **60**, 67-92

Walker, G, Langton, B and Oakey, N, 2001 *An Iron Age Site at Groundwell West, Wiltshire: Excavations in 1996*, Cotswold Archaeol Trust, Cirencester

Wallis, J, 1981 Radley: Abingdon peripheral road, *CBA9* **11**, 132-4

Wallis, J and Lambrick, G H, 1989 Ducklington: Gill Mill Farm, *SMA* **19**, 49-50

Warrington, K, 1924 The influence of manuring on the weed flora of arable land, *Journal of Ecology* **12**, 111-126

Waterman, D, 1997 *Excavations at Navan Fort 1961-71*, The Stationery Office, Belfast

Watts, D J, 1989 Infant burials and Romano-British christianity, *Archaeol J* **146**, 372-83

Watts, D, 1991 *Christians and Pagans in Roman Britain*, London

Weaver, S D G and Ford, S, 2004 An early Iron Age occupation site, a Roman shrine and other prehistoric activity at Coxwell Road, Faringdon, *Oxoniensia* **69**, 119-80

Webster, G, and Hobley, B, 1964 Aerial reconnaissance over the Warwickshire Avon, *Archaeol J* **71**, 1-22.

Webster, J, 1995 Sanctuaries and Natural Places, in Green 1995b, 445-64

Webster, J and Cooper, N (eds), 1996 *Roman Imperialism: post-colonial perspectives*, Leicester Archaeol Mono **3**, Leicester

Wheeler, R E M and Wheeler, T V, 1936 *Verulamium: A Belgic and two Roman cities*, Rep Res Comm Soc Antiqs London **11**, Oxford

Whimster, R, 1979 A possible La Tène III inhumation from Sutton Courtenay, Oxfordshire, *Oxoniensia* **44**, 93-6

Whimster, R, 1981 *Burial practices in Iron Age Britain*, Brit Arch Rep (Brit Ser) **90**, Oxford

Whimster, R, 1992 Aerial photography and the British gravels: an agenda for the 1990s, in Fulford and Nichols (eds) 1992, 1-14

Whittle, A, 1991 Wayland's Smithy, Oxfordshire: excavations at the Neolithic tomb in 1962-3 by R J C Atkinson and S Piggott, *PPS* **57 (2)**, 61-101

Whittle, A, Atkinson, R J C, Chambers, R and Thomas, N, 1992 Excavations in the Neolithic and Bronze Age complex at Dorchester-on-Thames, Oxfordshire, 1947–1952 and 1981, *PPS* **58**, 143–201.

Wigley, A, 2007 Pitted histories: early first millennium BC pit alignments in the central Welsh Marches, in Haselgrove and Pope 2007, 119-34

Williams, A, 1946-7 Excavations at Langford Downs, Oxon (near Lechlade) in 1943, *Oxoniensia* **11-12**, 44-64

Williams, A, 1951 Excavations at Beard Mill, Stanton Harcourt, Oxon, 1944, *Oxoniensia* **16**, 5-22

Williams, R J, and Zeepvat, R J, 1994 *Bancroft. The Late Bronze Age and Iron Age settlements and Roman Temple-Mausoleum and the Roman Villa, Vol. 1: Excavations and Building Materials*, Bucks Archaeol Soc Mono **7**

Williamson, T, 1987 Early co-axial field sytems on the the East Anglian boulder clays, *PPS* **53**, 419-31

Williamson, T, 1998 The 'Sole-Dickleburgh field system' revisited, *Landscape History* **20**, 19-28

Wilson, C E, 1981 Burials within settlements in southern Britain during the pre-Roman Iron Age, *Bull Inst Archaeol Univ London* **18**, 127-70

Wilson, D, 1993 Iron Age pottery, in Allen and Robinson 1993, 70-5

Wilson, R, 1978 The animal bones, in Parrington 1978, 110-39

Wilson, R, 1979 The vertebrates, in Lambrick and Robinson 1979, 128-33

Wilson, R, 1980 Bone and shell report, in Hinchliffe and Thomas 1980, 84-90

Wilson, R, 1986 Faunal remains: animal bones and marine shells, in Miles 1986, microfiche 8: A1-G10

Wilson, R, 1990 The animal bones from Watkins Farm, Northmoor, Oxon, in Allen 1990a, 94-8

Wilson, R, 1992 Considerations for the identification of ritual deposits of animal bones in Iron Age pits, *Int J Osteoarchaeol* **2**, 341-9

Wilson, R, 1993 Reports on the bones and oyster shell, in Allen and Robinson 1993, 123-45

Wilson, R, 1996 *Spatial patterning among animal bones in settlement archaeology: An English regional exploration*, Brit Arch Rep (Brit Ser) **251**, Oxford

Wilson, R, forthcoming Animal Bones in Lambrick forthcoming

Wilson, T and Cater, D 2005 Chalgrove to East Ilsley Gas Pipeline Archaeological Watching Brief and Excavations Draft Report, Network Archaeology unpubl client rep

Winton, H, 2003 Possible Iron Age 'Banjo' enclosures on the Lambourn Downs, *Oxoniensia* **68**, 15-26

Wise, J, 1991 A survey of prehistoric and later earthworks on Whiteleaf Hill, *Records of Bucks* **33**, 108-113

Wood, P, 1954 The early Iron Age camp on Bozedown, Whitchurch, Oxon, *Oxoniensia* **19**, 8-14

Woodward, A and Leach, P, 1993 *The Uley Shrines: excavation of a ritual complex on West Hill, Uley,*

Gloucestershire 1977-9, English Heritage Archael Rep **17**

Woodward, P J, 1987 The excavation of a late Iron Age Trading Settlement and Romano-British BB1 Pottery Production Site at Ower, Dorset, in N Sunter and P J Woodward, *Romano-British Industries in Purbeck*, Dorset Nat Hist Archaeol Soc Mono, Dorchester, 44-124

Wymer, J J, 1961 The discovery of a gold torc at Moulsford, *BAJ*, **59**, 1-35

Yates, D T, 1997 Bronze Age Field Systems in Lowland Britain: the Thames Valley, unpubl. MA diss., Reading University.

Yates, D, 1999 Bronze Age field systems in the Thames Valley, *Oxford J Archaeol* **18(2)**, 157-170

Yates, D, 2001 Bronze Age agricultural intensification in the Thames Valley and estuary, in Brück 2001, 65-82

York, J, 2002 The life cycle of Bronze Age metalwork from the Thames, *Oxford J Archaeol* **21 (1)**, 77-92.

Young, R and Humphrey, J, 1999 Flint use in England after the Bronze Age: time for a re-evaluation? *PPS* **65**, 231-242

Zeepvat, R J (ed.) 2000 *Three Iron Age and Romano-British settlements on English gravels*, Brit Arch Rep (Brit Ser) **312**, Oxford

Index

by Paul Backhouse and Lisa Brown

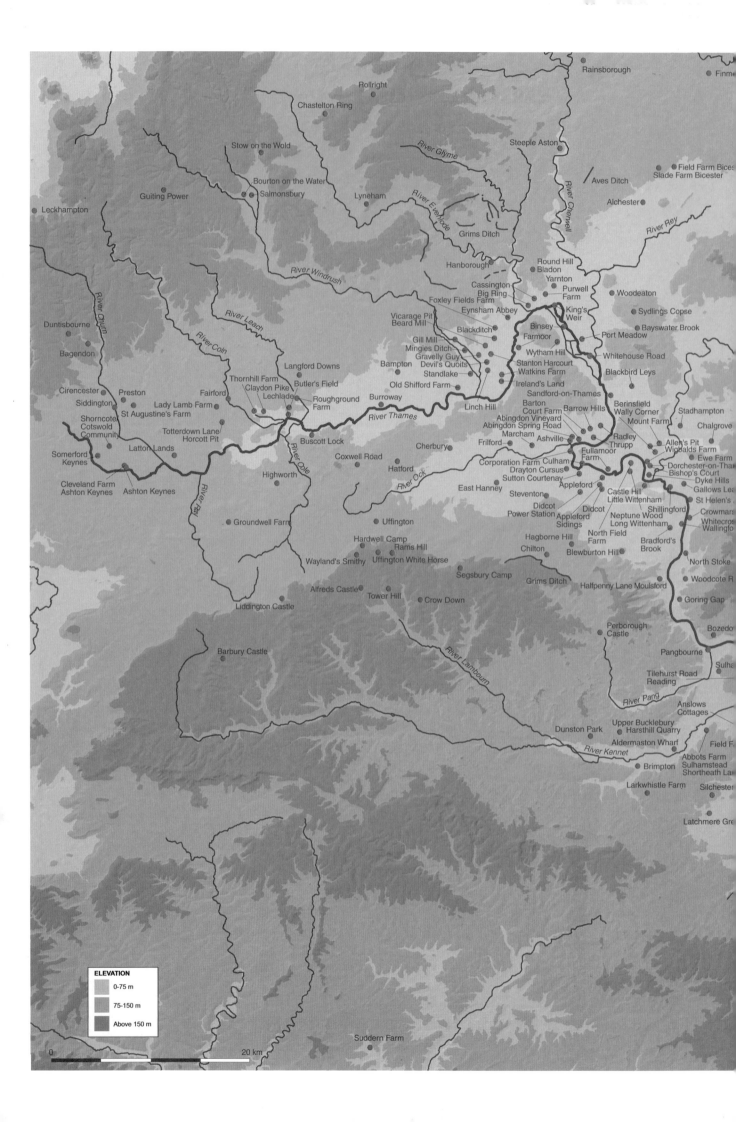